Guitars, Gavels & GOLD

CONTEMPORARY LEGAL ISSUES IN THE ARTS, ENTERTAINMENT, AND MUSIC BUSINESS

Barry Neil Shrum, Esq.

Kendall Hunt
publishing company

Kendall Hunt
publishing company

www.kendallhunt.com
Send all inquiries to:
4050 Westmark Drive
Dubuque, IA 52004-1840

ISBN: 979-8-7657-4845-9

Published in the United States of America

My thanks, first and foremost, to my wonderful wife and son who give me so much support. Many additional thanks to all of those at my firm, Shrum Hicks & Associates, PC who contributed ideas and thoughts to the creation of this work, particularly Abbey, Tess and Victoria who contributed to its organization, grammar, and typographical correctness! Thank you.

Contents

Introduction

When it comes to making it big in the music industry, there is one bit of advice almost every insider will offer the up-and-coming would-be music star—*get a good entertainment attorney*. There is a very good reason this type of advice persists: there are few other areas of specialized legal practice that are more fluid, more wrought with peril, or more downright confusing than the entertainment industry broadly and more specifically, the music sector. Understanding current legal trends and cases are essential for the entertainment attorney, but the would-be star can also benefit from some of the principles that can be gleaned from the legal issues that arise in the music industry every day. The goal of this work is to shine a light on some of the current cases, both ongoing and decided, that directly impact the music and entertainment industries.

© DW labs Incorporated/Shutterstock.com

The enterprise of music started humbly in the early nineteenth century in approximately five buildings on 28th Street between Fifth and Sixth Avenues in the Manhattan "Flower District" of New York City, growing up alongside the other sectors of the entertainment industry that flourished in the city that never sleeps. The area in New York where music begins its evolution was called *Tin Pan Alley*, ostensibly because when pedestrians walked by the buildings where the bright sounds of clanging cymbals and pinging pianos were lofting from the open windows, the sound echoed through the alleyway like a cacophony of tin pans being banged together![1]

© lynea/Shutterstock.com

[1] According to the Online Etymology Dictionary, "tin pan" was slang for "a decrepit piano" *circa.* 1882 and the term came to mean a "hit song writing business" by 1907.

In the Tin Pan Alley days, the commodity of the music business revolved around “sheet music,” a 16 × 11 sheet of approximately 80 lb paper folded in the middle to form an 8.5 × 11 pamphlet, on the front of which was printed a colorful cover, and inside of which on either side was printed the musical transcriptions, or scores, of current songs written by popular composers such as John Philip Sousa, Irving Berlin, Victor Herbert, and George Gershwin, among many others. This pantheon of writers cranked out reams of sheet music for the publishers in Tin Pan Alley, with names such as Shapiro Bernstein and Leslie Mohr, who then “published” the sheets. To exploit the sheet music, the publishers would hire traveling “song pluggers”[2] to load up their suitcases with reams of music and travel to music stores in big cities across the country, stocking the proprietors’ shelves with the sheet music. To market the music, the plugger would then perform the sheet music on the store’s rickety piano singing along with any accompanying lyrics. Sometimes, the plugger would roll the piano out on the sidewalk to make a broader impact. Customers wandering into and around the story would hear the plugger’s rendition, purchase the associated sheet music, take it home, invite their friends over, and play it on their nice pianos in their “parlor,” with their friends singing along. This was the way music was consumed in the days of Tin Pan Alley. At that time, the primary U.S. copyright law, the first Copyright Act of 1790, was almost 100 years old. As technology evolves, however, laws are forced to change with them.

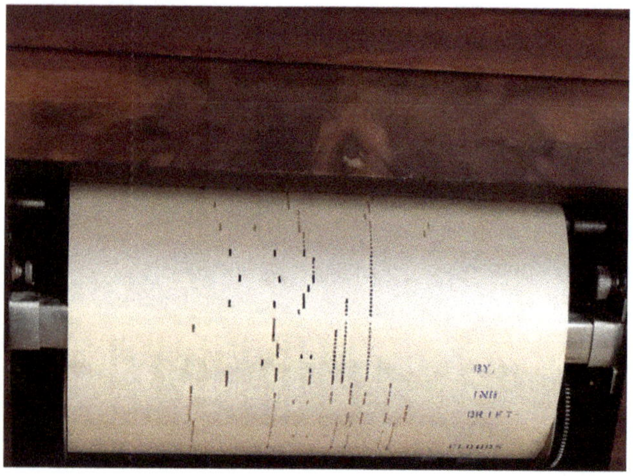

In 1896, Edwin S. Votey invented the first practical pneumatic piano player, called the Pianola, which kicked off the business of manufacturing and selling the “player piano.” The player piano was self-playing.” It contained a pneumatic (later electro-mechanical) mechanism that operated the action of the hammers using perforated paper or metallic rolls into which holes were punched in order to program the keys that played the music. By 1903, the Aeolian Company had more than 9,000 roll titles in their catalog and was adding approximately 200 titles per month, including many of the musical compositions owned by the Tin Pan Alley publishing companies. Slowly, the consumers’ parlor pianos, requiring a human component, were replaced by these new, fandangled Pianola, churning through the music without mistake. The problem, of course, is that Tin Pan Alley’s publishers, and therefore the composers, were not being compensated for the performance of their music by these mechanical maestros, as when a consumer purchased sheet music to play along with.

In his 1906 essay, entitled *The Menace of Mechanical Music*, none other than John Philip Sousa warns society of this dastardly mechanical music that is “sweeping across the country with the speed of a transient

[2] The monikers of “publisher” and “song plugger” have endured over the years, although the tasks performed by each have evolved over the years to include additional functions.

fashion in slang or Panama hats, political war cries or popular novels" and was becoming a "substitute for human skill, intelligence, and soul." He described the device as "mathematical system[s] of megaphones, wheels, cogs, disks, cylinders, and all manner of revolving things." Sousa, and others like him, was concerned that mechanical music would cause "social decline" as people stopped making music together.[3] He realized, to his dismay, that the "automatic music" was usurping the role of sheet music. In the article, Sousa argued against the prevailing view at the time that a player piano roll was not a "copy" of the sheet music as defined by the archaic 1790 Copyright Act. He supports his argument with an appeal to Article I, Section 8, Clause 8 of the Constitution:[4]

> [M]y claim is, that the words "exclusive" and "writings," particularly the latter, are so broad in their meaning that they cover every point raised by existing copyright laws, even to the unauthorized use of musical compositions by mechanical-reproducing apparatuses, and all this because these two words deal, not alone with the letter, but with the spirit as well.

© Everett Collection/Shutterstock.com

To reverse the perceived effects of this new and evolving technology of the player piano as well as other threats to their livelihood, Sousa, Herbert, and other Tin Pan Alley composers fought to force the current perception of copyright to evolve by attacking the issue on several legal fronts: first, they threw their support behind a "new copyright bill" that was being circulated in a congressional committee, a bill that would ultimately lead to the passage of the 1909 Copyright Act, that included, among other things, the provision that reproduction of musical composition in a mechanical player roll should generate a royalty to the songwriters and publishers. This royalty ultimately garnered the name "mechanical royalty" because of the origins of its implementation; second, after the passage of the 1909 Copyright Act, which granted an exclusive right to *performance*, Victor Herbert realized that some of his musical compositions were being played, without payment of royalties to him, at such prominent locations as the famous Shanley's restaurant and the Vanderbilt Hotel in NYC, he initiated legal proceedings to enforce his rights to receive *performance royalties* when his music was played as dinner music and in the lobby of the hotel. The restaurant and hotel proprietors objected to paying the composers, arguing that they had paid the performers, the performance was not "for profit," and that "[t]he music was not a necessary incident to the service of food [or a renting a room]. . . ."

[3] Sousa's article was originally published in *Appleton's Magazine*, Vol. 8 (1906), pp. 278–84. See, John Philip Sousa and "The Menace of Mechanical Music," *Journal of the Society for American Music* 3, no. 4 (November 2009): 431–63.

[4] This clause, sometimes referred to as either the "Progress Clause" or, less accurate, the "Copyright Clause," states: *Congress shall have . . . [the] power to secure for limited time to authors and inventors the exclusive right to their respective writings and discoveries.*

Shanley argued that, in fact, "[the performance] may have driven more patrons from the dining room than it lured in."[5] Chief Justice Oliver Wendell Holmes soundly rejected these arguments, holding that:

> *[Music is] part of the total for which the public pays* and the fact that the price of the whole is attributable to a particular item which those present are expected to order is not important. It is true that music is not the sole object, but neither is the food, which probably could be got cheaper elsewhere.[6]

© Everett Collection/Shutterstock.com

Justice Holmes made it clear that if a restaurant owner believes that music does not contribute to its profitability, it is free to let its customers eat in silence. His ruling firmly established a songwriter's exclusive right to receive performance royalties and as a result of the ruling, ASCAP, SESAC and later, BMI[7] evolved as mechanisms of collection to funnel the collection of performance royalties to songwriters and their publishers.[8]

The story of how the music and entertainment industries evolved from their fairly humble roots in a small segment of New York to the world emphasizes the necessity for *those who create the music* to stay informed, not only with regard to rapidly changing technologies but especially with regard to the necessary reactions of the laws and the legal system. New laws are passed with each session of Congress, many of which implicate the rights of copyright owners. New cases are being litigated every year in courts across the country, many of which implicate the rights exploited in the music industry.

The purpose of this book, then, is generally to educate and inform anyone who wants to become a professional in the music industry, whether your desire is to write songs and/or create music or be a music mogul who manages or represents the talent. But more specifically, it is aimed toward the rising law student who thinks that music law might be his or her career path of choice.

---

[5] *Herbert v. Shanley Co.*, 242 U.S. 591, at 592–593 (1917).

[6] *Ibid.*, at 594–595.

[7] These are acronyms for the performance rights organizations, originally as follows: American Society of Composers, Authors and Publishers; Broadcast Musicians Incorporated; and Society of European Stage Authors and Composers.

[8] Sousa continuously fought for the rights of composers, for example, he testified in front of Congress in 1927 and 1928 for the specific purpose of encouraging legislation regarding the commissioning of military bandmasters.

© Gorodenkoff/Shutterstock.com

Before explaining the structure of the book, it is also helpful to illuminate the reader as to what, exactly, an "entertainment attorney" does. The phrase is used first and foremost by a myriad of practitioners who have a wide variety of legal specializations and focus, and second by people who may have graduated from law school but do not practice law, rather serving in some managerial or agency capacity. Universally, lawyers can be categorized as either *litigators or barristers*, on the one hand, and/or *transactional* or *solicitor* on the other.[9] Most people who graduate from law school are simply not cut out for the rigors of the first category involving stepping into a courtroom and litigating a case in front of either a jury or a judge, or both, and so they gravitate to positions that allow them to review *various business transactions* that may be presented by clients or their employers for consultation on an ad hoc and as needed basis. Thus, the true litigator in the entertainment industry is rare. This dichotomy of practice areas is even more pronounced in the narrower focus of music law where many young law students envision themselves more as deal makers than barristers.

Most entertainment attorneys rarely move to the far side of the "bar" that is found in most courtrooms[10] if they ever see the inside of a courtroom at all! They review and revise transactions, like other lawyers, except that these transactions center around the music industry: recording agreements, producer agreements, exclusive songwriter agreements, catalog sales, life rights agreements, etc. Others focus primarily on defending the rights of the creators exclusively and concentrate their practice on filing and/or defending lawsuits. Then there are those of us who try to balance the two sides of the equation by focusing the bulk of our practice on the drafting side of the deal, whilst in the remainder, prosecuting on behalf of or defending our clients against infringement or breach of contract actions. The advantages of the dual approach are numerous: (a) it allows the lawyer to keep abreast of current trends in music law; (b) it provides a great depth of understanding as to what language needs to be used for contract clauses to be effective; and (c) it makes life more interesting.

Throughout this volume, I will be drawing on my dual expertise as both a litigator and transactional attorney who has focused his career on the entertainment industry and practices in Music City, the

[9] The terms "barrister" and "solicitor" are traditional British descriptors, used more infrequently in the United States, where a barrister defends people in court as an advocate, whereas a solicitor prepares legal documents and does legal work outside court on behalf of clients.

[10] Yes, that is the traditional "bar" of which a *barrister* is a member, referring to a physical railing or barrier, or in some instances pieces of furniture, that segregates the courtroom participants—the judge, parties, attorneys, and jury members—from the area where the "commoners" would gather to witness the proceedings. The common area is usually populated, ironically perhaps, with church pews! We are called barristers because we are summoned to the "bar" to advocate for the interests of clients during legal proceedings.

hotbed of music activities in the United States, to share with you my experiences and knowledge in order to give you a solid foundation on which to build your music law career. Thus, many of the sections in this textbook are focused primarily on a single case involving two or more parties who have been to court, litigated their issue, and had it resolved by a trier of fact, thus rendering an opinion. In those chapters, you will be asked to read the abridged text of the opinion contained in the Appendix, then answer a debate question, preparing to argue both the affirmative and negative arguments presented at the beginning of each chapter. A good lawyer can argue both sides of the position.[11] This will train you to think critically about both sides of the issue and develop stronger arguments for your clients. Some chapters are presented in more of an informational format, explaining various aspects of a matter or process, thus providing fodder for further exploration. Finally, there will be sections involving contractual issues in which I will illustrate how case precedent often defines the parameters of contractual language.

Through this process, I hope to share with you the joy I have found in my practice of entertainment law over the past 30 years. Indeed, the labyrinths of music law can be an exciting journey, one which I hope we can enjoy together.

BNSesq
Music Row, October 2022

[11] Note that this is a skill best confined to the rigors of legal practice and not with your spouse at home, where it can lead to the antidote to *happy wife, happy life*.

1 Life Cycle of a Copyright Infringement Action

© Olivier Le Moal/Shutterstock.com

Most of the case decisions in this book involve issues of copyright infringement. Since the Copyright Act of 1976 is a federal law, the federal court system, which includes the Supreme Court, has sole and exclusive jurisdiction over copyright law pursuant to the United States Constitution which, in Article III, Section II, states that "[t]he judicial power shall extend to all cases, in law and equity, *arising under . . . the laws of the United States. . . .*" This means that when a songwriter believes that her copyright has been copied by a third party without her permission, she can only file the copyright infringement action in a federal court. In fact, any litigation regarding federal laws or a federal issue, including those related to patent and trademark, as well as copyright, must originate in a federal court.

Although the Constitution authorized the establishment of a Supreme Court, it gave Congress the authority to decide how it is organized. Congress first exercised this power in the Judiciary Act of 1789, which, at the time, created a Supreme Court with six justices and established the lower federal court system consisting of district and circuit courts. Since this book explains several Supreme Court cases, it is important to understand the structure of the federal court system in order to understand the circuitous route that a case can sometimes transverse before it ever arrives at 1st Street NE in Washington.

So, a copyright infringement action begins life in a United States district court, which is the trial court, otherwise known as a *court of first impression*. Each state and territory in the United States have *at least one* district court, with many larger states having as many as three or four. For example, in Tennessee, there is an Eastern, Middle, and Western District Court. In total, there are 94 district courts in the United States.

Federal judges are nominated by the President and confirmed "with the advice and consent" of the Senate. They may "hold their Offices during good Behavior," that is, a district judge may only be removed by the impeachment process with which, unfortunately, everyone in America is very familiar.

A *court of first impression* is the court in which the pleadings and motions get filed and, if it goes to trial, in which the trial takes place. The trial court usually consists of the judge, a bailiff, a clerk, a court reporter, and a jury six or twelve. At this stage in the life of a copyright infringement lawsuit, the party who brings the action is referred to as a "plaintiff," and the party who responds is referred to as the "defendant." Here, the plaintiff files a pleading, referred to specifically as a "complaint," against the defendant. The complaint usually contains a description of the parties, a set of facts describing the conflict, a series of "counts" that enumerate the legal theories upon which the plaintiff believes relief should be granted, and finally a "prayer" to the court asking for that relief; each paragraph in this succession is numbered seriatim. Once the complaint is accepted by the court, the plaintiff receives "filed-stamped service copies" of the complaint that get personally "served" on the defendant. The case has not officially begun until the complaint is served and the plaintiff returns the "service of process." Once served, then the defendant has a narrow window of days in which to file a response, referred to as the "answer" to the complaint, in which defense counsel responds to each numbered paragraph in the complaint in order. In addition, the defendant can identify affirmative defenses to which it is entitled, as well as draft "counterclaims" to the complaint, something that is sometimes described as "countersuing" in common parlance, although in the context of an infringement action that term is less than precise. This initial pleading stage is frequently dotted with motions to dismiss the complaint on its face, although judges are reluctant to prevent a plaintiff's day in court at this early stage.

Once this initial phase has run its course, the assigned judge will establish a date for what is referred to as a case management conference (CMO). This conference is required to all parties, and counsel for both sides is required to collaboratively draft an order for the conference agreeing on certain "deadlines" for such things as written discovery, depositions, disclosures, dispositive motions, and even a proposed length of trial as well as an appropriate date for that trial. Once that order is approved and filed by the court, the parties are bound to that schedule unless they obtain judicial fiat to change the deadlines.

Once the CMO is solidified, the parties enter into the discovery phase of the litigation. Each party will produce interrogatories (questions) and document requests to which the other party must deliver sworn answers and produce documents and evidentiary materials. Later, the parties begin to issue requests for depositions of potential witnesses who might possess information about the matters outlined in the complaint. In the deposition, the attorney will pose a series of questions to the witness, who answers them under oath in the presence of a court-certified court reporter who records with precision the questions and the answers. Because of the fluidity of the discovery process, under the federal rules, the opposing attorney cannot raise the normal objections you often hear on court-related television shows and in the movies, but rather is confined to objecting to the form of the question and preserving objections for trial. In a copyright infringement action, this deposition phase is where the parties' respective experts are disclosed and, subsequently, deposed as well.

When adequate discovery has been produced and all witnesses deposed, the parties enter into one of the final phases of the litigation prior to trial, called the dispositive motion phase. Here, either party may file what is known as a motion for summary judgment, in which that party basically makes the argument that even if the judge takes every bit of evidence the parties have produced into consideration in the light most favorable to the moving party, there is no *genuine issue of fact* that should be decided by a jury. If the judge believes that to be true, the case will be dismissed on the summary judgment motion.

If not, the case will proceed to trial. At the trial in the court of first impression, the jury is empaneled through the attorneys' *voir dire*, the opening arguments made, the witnesses called, and the evidence presented, all precisely recorded in the court record by the reporter. The trial transcripts, as it is called, are very important if the case moves up the ladder of the federal court system to the circuit level.

© Gorodenkoff/Shutterstock.com

Once the federal district court, the *court of first impression*, has decided the case, either party has an absolute right to appeal to a United States Circuit Court of Appeal. Therefore, the circuit courts are strictly *appellate* courts that hear appeals from courts of first impression. There are 12 federal circuits that divide the country into different regions, starting with the First Circuit in the upper northeast corner and working their way up and down and across the country. Each United States. Circuit Court has *jurisdiction* over cases that are tried in the district courts sitting in the states they oversee. The Fifth Circuit, for example, includes the states of Texas, Louisiana, and Mississippi. Cases from the district courts *of those states are* appealed to the United States Court of Appeals for the Fifth Circuit, which is headquartered in New Orleans, Louisiana. As a side note, the Federal Circuit Court of Appeals has nationwide jurisdiction over very specific issues such as patents. The number of judges assigned to a circuit court varies, ranging from six justices in the First Circuit to twenty-nine in the Ninth Circuit.

An appeal to a circuit court is initiated by filing an appellate brief with the circuit court having jurisdiction over your "circuit." The person filing the appeal is called the "appellant." The brief is filed either at the end of the trial when a decision has become final or, if the appellant believes the matter requires it, filed during the trial (the latter appeal is known as "interlocutory"). The appellant brief will make arguments urging the court to either "affirm" (uphold) the opinion of the district court or reverse it. In certain circumstances, the circuit court also has the option of "remanding" the case back down to the trial court for further proceedings to clarify certain issues. Once the appellant has filed for an appeal, the *appellee*, or the party responding, will have an opportunity to weigh in on the issues in the form of a brief as well. When all briefing has concluded, the circuit panel will assign a date for an oral argument where the parties' attorneys appear before the panel and make arguments, responding to concerns and questions from the justices. In most circumstances, an appeal is heard by a panel of three of the judges appointed to that circuit, although if the issues in the matter rise to a certain level of perceived importance, the circuit court may sit *en banc*, or in other words, all of the justices will hear the oral arguments and decide the case. These *en banc* opinions carry more weight and are usually decided only after the three-judge panel has first heard the case in order to clarify the issue. When an *en banc* panel has ruled and "published" the opinion, future panels may not overrule the previous decision unless the original panel can take up the case again *en banc* to reconsider the first panel's decision. As you might imagine, the *en banc* process usually involves matters that involve a controversial or highly politicized issue.

The circuit court of appeals is an *appellate* court, as opposed to a *court of first impression* like the district courts. The primary significance of that distinction is that the appellate court **does not** hear any new evidence—no new witness, no new testimony, and no new documentary submissions. The appellate court only makes determinations as to any *errors of law* or *justice* that may have occurred in the underlying trial. If you recall from the earlier note, the court reporter records everything that happens in the district court during the trial in order to produce what is called the trial transcript. That transcript is the only material the circuit court will consider, other than the briefs and the oral arguments from the appellate counsel. That is because, as noted, the court of appeals does make rulings as to fact but rather only considers whether the underlying trial was conducted in accordance with the law.

The Supreme Court of the United States is the highest court in American jurisprudence. As noted at the beginning of this chapter, the Supreme Court was established by the Constitution and organized by Congress. Congress has actually varied the number of justices on the Supreme Court several times, ranging from five to ten. Shortly after the Civil War, the number of seats on the bench was fixed at nine justices, but there is no Constitutional provision that prevents them from changing it again. Currently, one of those nine is appointed as a "Chief Justice," and there are eight "Associate" justices. All are appointed for lifetime terms by the president and confirmed by the senate.

The Supreme Court has "original jurisdiction," or exclusive right to hear, certain cases: (a) suits between two or more states and/or cases involving ambassadors and other public ministers, and (b) any case involving a point of constitutional and/or federal law (this is referred to as its appellate jurisdiction). In addition to the aforementioned copyright issues, other examples of cases the Supreme Court might hear include cases to which the United States is a party, cases involving treaties, and cases involving ships on the high seas and navigable waterways (admiralty cases).

Another area of exclusive jurisdiction the Supreme Court possesses relates to the checks and balances our founders wanted to create, but it is not technically found in the Constitution, and that is the power of "judicial review," or the ability of the Court to declare a legislative or executive act in violation of the Constitution. The Court itself established this doctrine in the case of *Marbury v. Madison*, decided in 1803. In *Marbury*, the Court had to decide whether an Act of Congress or the Constitution was the supreme law of the land. The Judiciary Act of 1789 gave the Supreme Court original jurisdiction to issue writs of mandamus (legal orders compelling government officials to act in accordance with the law). A suit was brought under this Act, but the Supreme Court noted that the Constitution did not permit the Court to have original jurisdiction in this matter. Since Article VI of the Constitution establishes the Constitution as the Supreme Law of the Land, the Court held that an Act of Congress that is contrary to the Constitution could not stand. In subsequent cases, the Court also established its authority to strike down state laws found to be in violation of the Constitution.

When exercising its *appellate jurisdiction*, the Supreme Court is neither required to take the appeal, nor does a party have an absolute right of appeal, as they do when appealing an opinion of the district court to the circuit. Instead, The Certiorari Act of 1925 gives the Supreme Court discretion to decide whether or not to hear an appeal. In order to access this power, a party must file a petition for a *writ of certiorari*, in order to have the matter reviewed. The party filing this petition is known, no surprise, as the "petitioner," and consequently the party responding to the petition is referred to as the "respondent." The Supreme Court agrees to hear about 100–150 of the more than 7,000 cases that it is asked to review each year.

As conceived by the Founders of this country, the Supreme Court plays a vital role in the "checks and balances" of our constitutional system of government. Because of the aforementioned power of judicial review, the Supreme Court plays a critical role in ensuring that each branch of government recognizes the limits of its own power. Additionally, as the highest court in the land, it is the court of last resort for those seeking justice and protects constitutional rights and liberties by striking down federal or state laws that violate the United States Constitution. Finally, the Supreme Court balances the rights of society against those individuals who make up our democratic government by ensuring that popular majorities cannot pass laws that harm and/or take undue advantage of unpopular minorities. In short, the Supreme Court serves as a bulwark to ensure that the changing views of a majority do not undermine the fundamental values common to all Americans, that is, life, liberty, the pursuit of happiness, the right to own our intellectual creations, freedom of speech, freedom of religion, and due process of law.

2 The Contours of Copyright

CASE NO. 1	CHAPTER CASE STUDY	**Debate Question**	
		Are the names, addresses, and phone numbers contained in a copyrighted telephone directory entitled to protection as an expression?	
	Feist v. Rural, 499 U.S. 340 (1991)	**Affirmative**	**Negative**
		Yes, the person who solicits and assembles the information is entitled to the fruits of their labor.	No, no one person can possess a monopoly in mere facts such as a person's name, address, and phone number.

A. Ideas and Expression

Learned Hand was one of the greatest jurists of all time, even though he never sat on the Supreme Court. The quote below is from his Second Circuit opinion in *Nichols v. Universal Pictures Corporation.*[1] In *Nichols*, the plaintiff argued that the defendants infringed her play, *Abie's Irish Rose*, about a young Jewish man who marries an Irish Catholic girl against the wishes of both of their fathers. Defendants' *The Cohens and Kellys* was a movie that was based on a play about an Irish boy who marries a Jewish girl from a feuding family. Both works were comedic in nature. In his opinion, Judge Hand noted that the protection of a literary text generally cannot be limited to the exact text, or else an infringer could make trivial changes to avoid infringement. He observed, however, that if the copied text involves universally accepted concepts and "stock characters," as was the case here, there can be no infringement since these elements are "to some extent in . . . the public domain." In other words, these are archetypal ideas. Judge Hand further outlined what we have come to know as the idea/expression dichotomy, an imaginary divide between an

[1] 45 F.2d 119 (2d Cir. 1930).

idea, which is not entitled to copyright protection, and the expression of that idea, which is entitled to protection. He describes it thusly:

> Upon any work, and especially upon a play, a great number of patterns of increasing generality will fit equally well, as more and more of the incident is left out . . . ; but there is a point in this series of abstractions where they are no longer protected, since otherwise, the playwright could prevent the use of his "ideas," to which, apart from their expression, his property is never extended.
>
> Nobody has ever been able to fix that boundary, and nobody ever can. . . . [just as] the skeleton is a part of the body, [yet] it pervades and supports the whole. In such cases, we are rather concerned with the line between expression and what is expressed.

Using the metaphor of the skeleton supporting the whole of the body, Judge Hand points out that the dividing line between idea and expression cannot be fixed, but rather it is mutable depending on the facts. "[T]he skeleton is a part of the body, [yet] it pervades and supports the whole. In such cases we are . . . concerned with the line between expression and what is expressed." This special legal principle is so longstanding, and critical to an understanding of intellectual property, that it was codified in Section 102 of the 1976 Copyright Act when it defines the subject matter of copyright in general:

> (a) Copyright protection subsists, in accordance with this title, in *original works of authorship fixed* in any tangible medium of expression . . . [but] (b) *In no case does [it] extend to any idea* . . . embodied in such work. (Emphasis Added)

If you research the holdings of the Supreme Court regarding the concept of intellectual property, particularly copyright, you will find that the mutability of the idea/expression dichotomy is what places it in the realm of the metaphysical. In fact, the dichotomy is one of the underlying "traditional contours" of copyright law, as discussed later in the chapter. For our purposes, we can expand the principle to help us identify the ideas and concepts that can be protected by intellectual property laws. As one English court phrased it, the owner of an intellectual property can be identified as "the person who clothes an idea in form. . . ." *Donoghue v. Allied Newspapers Limited* (1938). If we use the metaphor of a seamstress' dummy, as he pins different cuts of fabric on the tool to begin to form the clothing, first the front panels, then the lapels, and finally the pockets, the "idea" of a jacket begins to take on the personality of the seamstress and the "expression" of a men's sports jacket.

This dichotomy between idea and expression has been called copyright's "built-in First Amendment accommodation" by the Supreme Court.[2] One of the Court's seminal cases that elaborated on the role of

---

[2] *Eldred v. Ashcroft*, 537 U.S. 186, 219 (2003) (*citing Harper & Row*, 471 U.S., at 560).

the idea/expression dichotomy in protecting free speech was *Feist Publications, Inc. v. Rural Telephone Services, Co.*,[3] in which the justices give us a means of divining when an "idea" has moved far enough along the mutable spectrum of originality to be considered a protectable expression under copyright law. In the underlying case, Rural Telephone Services produced a local directory to comply with a state statute that lists all of their subscribers. Feist published a regional telephone directory consisting of an entire region of the state. Feist asked Rural for a license to include their listing in the regional directory, but Rural refused. Rural brought an infringement action against Feist for copying the names, addresses, and telephone numbers from its local directory for use in Feist's own regional directory that covered more territories. Rural placed red herrings, *i.e.*, fake names and numbers, among their listings so they could easily identify if someone had copied their listings. Justice Sandra O'Connor ruled that Rural's directory was nothing more than an alphabetic list of subscribers, which it was required to compile under law, containing no creative expression, and that a compilation of facts is not protectable. In her ruling, O'Connor discusses the importance of "thought" and "conception" in proving original expression. She relies on Section 102 of the Copyright Act and provides some structure for the application of the idea/expression dichotomy to cases involving copyright: somewhere along its continuum, the idea is clothed in a form that becomes protectable. Her construct of the idea/expression dichotomy appears below:

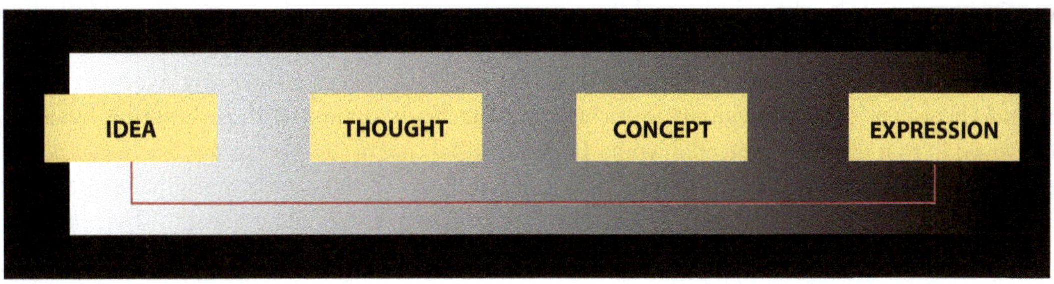

Source: Barry Neil Shrum

On the idea side of the spectrum resides the archetypal ideas (*i.e.*, notes, chords, sounds, colors, words, and other building blocks of nature that are in the continuum of thought and are not protected). Justice O'Connor indicates that copyright protection is unavailable for this "narrow category of works in which the creative spark is utterly lacking or so trivial as to be virtually non-existent." Consider as a good example the 1913 painting on the left in the illustration below, entitled *Black Circle*, created by Kazimir Malevich, founder of the Russian Supremacism movement. Does this work contain a creative spark that

---

[3] 499 U.S. 340 (1991), see Appendix, Case Study No. 1.

would move it further along the spectrum toward expression, or is it "utterly lacking" or "so trivial as to be non-existent"? Malevich himself described his artwork as a "desperate struggle to free art from the ballast of the objective world" which he accomplished by focusing on what he described as pure form. In so doing, Malevich's expression of the circle may have merged with the idea of a circle since there is only one way of expressing the "pure form" of a circle. The merger doctrine is a corollary of the idea/expression dichotomy that the Supreme Court has articulated in several cases involving copyright infringement; when there are no or few other ways of expressing a particular idea, it can be said that the expression and the idea have merged, and copyright protection is unavailable when that occurs. Compare Malevich to the example of Piet Mondrian to the right. Can it also be said that Mondrian's expression of squares, lines, and colors has "merged" with the idea of squares, lines, and colors? In the Mondrian example, in contrast to that of Malevich, it can effectively be argued that there are other significant ways of expressing the same ideas contained in Mondrian, and thus his work contains more of a "creative spark" than does Malevich's. The principles of idea/expression and merger exist in copyright law to enable its purpose of granting an individual the exclusive ownership in an expressed idea so that their original expression will inspire and encourage other individuals in society to build freely upon the ideas, building blocks, and facts conveyed in that original, protected work. In the seminal case of *Harper v. Row*, the Supreme Court confirmed this when it stated that "copyright law assures authors the right to their original expression but encourages others to build freely upon the ideas and information conveyed by a work." That being true, which of the following examples might be more likely to infringe on Mondrian's work?

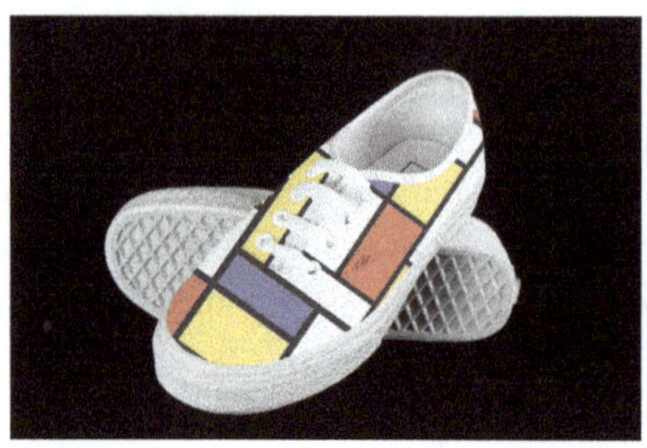

The use of thick lines and blocks of color in the shoe on the left is simply a use of pure ideas, even if it was directly inspired by Mondrian, whereas the shoe on the right more clearly borrows Mondrian's original expression of those ideas or at the very least was directly inspired by him. As a creative work moves along this spectrum between idea and expression, it begins to take on the "stamp of the author's originality" which Justice O'Connor described in Feist as an indicator of when copyright protection becomes available. Originality, therefore, is the gray matter through which the synaptic spark of an original expression flows and is what permeates the middle segments of the spectrum between idea and expression. In other words, the more an author clothes the form of an idea in originality, the more protection the resulting creative work will possess. Placement of other works by Mondrian positioned along the idea/expression dichotomy below serves to illustrate how the use of merged ideas can become increasingly clothed in originality so that works with more creativity will be easier to protect under copyright law and principles. The first work positioned over the idea segment is close to the situation described in regard to Malevich, where the idea is merging with the expression, whereas the work positioned above the expression segment uses variations of size, shape, primary colors, and arrangement that tend to show more of the author's "stamp" of originality.

© Kendall Hunt Publishing Company

Having defined the starting point of the spectrum as works that are utterly lacking creativity and the middle sections as increasingly complex levels of originality, Feist also defines the final terminus of the idea/dichotomy spectrum as works that contain "original intellectual conceptions" (*i.e.,* that are uniquely original, novel, and innovative). If we assume Malevich to be the example of a merged idea, then perhaps the work of Dutch artist M. C. Escher would be the perfect example of a more novel use of ideas. Although, like Malevich, he uses simple ideas like walls, doors, and stairs in the creation of his art, the expression of those ideas goes far beyond merger. Think about Escher's work entitled *Drawing Hands,* which also contains the use of certain simple ideas, just as Malevich uses the idea of circle: the human hand, pen and pencil, cuffs and cuff links, corkboard, thumb tacks, and parchment. Even though both artists' works contain archetypal ideas, Escher's use is more innovative and novel in that, it paradoxically depicts two hands in the act of drawing one another into existence in a two-dimensional world, creating what some critics have described as a "strange loop" where the viewers' eyes keep

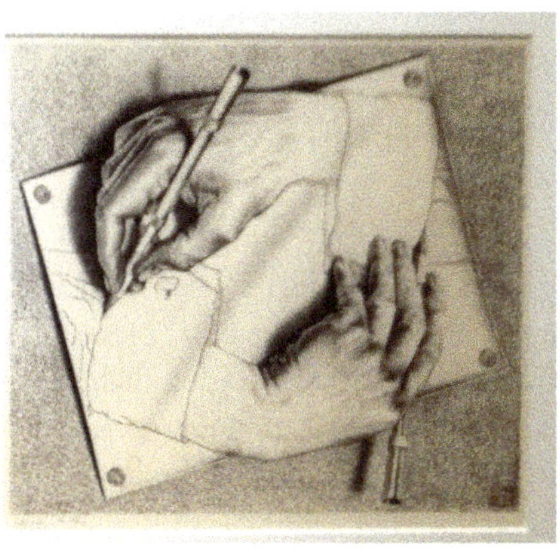

© Vyychan/Dreamstime

circling back to the same place as if looking at a mobius. Escher's expressions instantly draw the viewer into a logical conundrum of space and movement. Although Escher used building blocks and pure forms drawn from the continuum of thought, his originality clothed them in a very novel and unique expression. Legally, the same cannot be said of Malevich's *Black Circle*, where there is only one way to express the pure idea of a circle conveyed therein. Using the idea/expression dichotomy, the Supreme Court in Feist reestablished originality as a Constitutional requirement for copyright protection, and firmly establishes it as the *sine qua non* (*i.e.*, an essential element of intellectual property ownership). Using principles derived from Feist and the idea/expression dichotomy, we can develop a framework to approach all forms of entertainment properties and their protection, properties such as movie treatments, idea pitches, and components of a celebrity's rights of publicity as just a few examples. This technique will assist in determining when these creative thoughts are just archetypal ideas and when they have moved far enough along the spectrum to be owned and protected.

Although on the topic of *Feist* regarding when an idea is just an idea and when can it be protected, it is important to draw attention to several other legal principles the Supreme Court has described as additional contours to make this distinction, that of simultaneous use of ideas and/or independent creation and fair use. These traditional contours—the idea/expression dichotomy, fair use, and independent creation—serve as a counterbalance against the dramatic effect that copyright's exclusive monopoly in expressed original ideas has on free speech. In other words, they serve to protect our First Amendment rights against an unreasonable abuse of the monopoly of copyright.

© Pung/Shutterstock.com

Simultaneous use of ideas. Imagine that a photographer and an oil painter set out to Baker Beach on the bank of the San Francisco Bay in order to capture their vision of the Golden Gate Bridge at sunrise, each arriving at 5:00 a.m. The oil painter sets up an easel at almost the exact spot as the photographer, each having a stunning view at almost the exact same angle. If their creative expressions end up looking almost identical, has one artist infringed the copyright of the other? The answer to that question, of course, is a resounding no, because, as we know from our application of the idea/expression dichotomy, each artist is entitled to capture their unique expression, the photograph, and the painting, of the same idea (*i.e.*, the Golden Gate Bridge at sunrise). This answer is supported by the legal concept of simultaneous creation or, to be more precise, the *simultaneous use of ideas*. Overlaying this concept onto the spectrum of the idea/expression dichotomy, it is easy to see how the "pure" idea of capturing the Golden Gate Bridge at the "golden hour" is not protectable by either the artist or the photographer, since they may both use the same idea in its pure form, as it is part of the public domain. But when they filter their individual expressions of that idea through their sieve of experience and their unique minds, the painting and the photograph, respectively and separately, are protected as expression. Justice Oliver Wendell Holmes eloquently describes this creative expression as a creator's "personal reaction" to nature:

> . . . [Original expression] is the personal reaction of an individual upon nature. Personality always contains something unique. It expresses its singularity even in handwriting, and a very modest grade of art has in it something irreducible, which is one man's alone.

That "irreducible something" is the person's unique application of personality and experience to the archetypal idea embedded in their expression. That is what makes their expression what Locke described as the fruit of their intellectual labor.

Independent creation. The legal principle of independent creation is likewise related to the ideas of simultaneous use of ideas and the idea/expression dichotomy. One of the hypotheticals frequently proposed in a copyright law class is that of two different people at two different places during two different times independently creating two works of art that are substantially the same. Since §102(a) of the Copyright Act states that copyright protection exists for "original works of authorship fixed in a tangible medium of expression," each of these independent authors would each own the copyright to what essentially is the same creative work. This apparent enigma is created by the fact that the term "original" is purposely left undefined in the Copyright Act. This is because Congress intended to let the courts establish standards of originality and to allow the categories of copyrightable works to expand in response to technological advances. As that interpretation has evolved over the years, the concept of originality means simply that a work was independently created by its author as opposed to being copied from another work. The Second Circuit succinctly summed it up in *Batlin & Son v. Snyder* (1976), "[o]riginality means that the work owes its creation to the author and this, in turn, means that the work must not consist of actual copying."[4] Returning to the scenario of the photographer and painter underneath the Golden Gate Bridge, if the photographer brought an infringement action against the painter because the painting was so substantially similar to the photograph that it must mean the artist copied their work, these legal principles can be joined to illustrate the appropriate defense: the photographer and the painter simultaneously used the same idea in the creation of their tangible expression, and each independently created their works of art without copying each other; therefore, there is no infringement. The flexibility that these principles give to the monopolies of intellectual properties serves to fulfill their purpose by allowing the dissemination of expressive arts based on universal ideas and concepts, thereby fueling what the Supreme Court referred to as the "engine of free expression." In *Harper & Row v. Nation Enterprises*,[5] the Court said:

> It should not be forgotten that the Framers intended copyright itself to be the engine of free expression, and only if that engine is adequately fueled will public access to literary, musical and artistic creations be ensured.

The idea/expression dichotomy, the simultaneous use of ideas, and independent creation combine to make the fuel that drives the engine.

---

[4] 536 F.2d 486 (2nd Cir. 1976).

[5] 471 U.S. 539 (1985).

Fair use. Another significant contour of copyright addressed in §107 of the Copyright Act is the principle of fair use of a copyrighted expression. Fair use serves as an additional safeguard that is embedded into the concept of intellectual property and serves to balance the interest of the creator in owning their expressed works against the interest of society in allowing its citizens the right to freedom of speech. In certain circumstances where the interests of society outweigh the exclusive right of a creator to control their work, fair use says that the otherwise protected expression can be used. This additional wrinkle in the contours allows the public to use not only the archetypal ideas and facts contained in a protected expression but also the actual expression itself when it is used for purposes of criticism, comment, news reporting, teaching, scholarship, or research. These various legal doctrines drawn from copyright law precedents provide creators of entertainment properties with the fluidity to use any idea they can derive from what has been described herein as the continuum of thought, which can be thought of as a river that runs from the beginning of time until now through which flows nonprotected facts, ideas, themes, thoughts, building blocks of art, music, and literature, original creations that have lost copyright protection, and everything else that is often referred to as the public domain. But incorporating the legal concepts discussed in this chapter, the continuum of thought includes not only all such archetypal ideas but also those archetypal ideas that are embedded in copyrighted works. These archetypal ideas embedded in a copyright are also available for use by the public from the moment they are created. Finally, also running through the river of thought is the expressed creation itself to the extent it is used for certain carefully defined societal purposes intended to support our First Amendment rights. This broader understanding of the public domain (*i.e.,* the continuum of thought) may be used for inspiration, giving the artist, entertainer, filmmaker, songwriter, and anyone who creates a fluid palette of tools which can be used to create new intellectual properties.

3 The Progress Clause

CASE NO. 2	CHAPTER CASE STUDY	**Debate Question**	
		Are the purposes of the Progress Clause frustrated by the retroactive extension of the length of protection?	
	Eldred v. Ashcroft 537 U.S. 186 (2003)	**Affirmative**	**Negative**
		Yes, extending the length of protection for copyrighted works violates the "limited times" language of the Progress Clause and thereby frustrates the purpose.	No, providing an extension of time for the protection of copyrighted works allows for additional incentives for creators to create.

A. The Progress Clause

When the thirteen colonies delivered their Declaration of Independence, drafted by Thomas Jefferson, to King George, they realized that it would be necessary to form an alliance against the impending battle for that independence that would inevitably occur. In order to coordinate their efforts, the colonies created a permanent alliance, called the "United States," which was to be governed by the Article of Confederation. These articles were essentially a treaty between what was, at the time, a very loosely aligned group of independent and self-sovereign entities, governed by the Continental Congress in which each colony had a controlling vote.

During the American Revolution, the colonies begin to replace their colonial governments with republican constitutions based on the principle of separation of powers, organizing government into legislative, executive, and judicial branches. It soon became obvious to many of those involved that it would be necessary to construct a similarly-structured counterpart at a "federal" level having ultimate overriding authority over the states. So, this league of states convened a "Constitutional Convention" which would take place at the Pennsylvania State House in Philadelphia from May 25 to September 17, 1787.

© Wangkun Jia/Shutterstock.com

Each state sent a delegate to the convention with instructions to revise the league of states and construct the first system of government under the Articles of Confederation. However, several of these delegates—primarily James Madison, representing Virginia and Alexander Hamilton, representing New York—realized that the Articles of Convention could not be transformed and that it would actually be necessary to create an entirely new framework for the federal government, one that more closely represents the republican form already assumed by most of the colonies. For this, it would be necessary to draft an entirely new governing document in the form of a constitution.

As compared to Jefferson's emotional and persuasive writing expressed in the Declaration of Independence, the U.S. Constitution is benign and sometimes downright boring. It is structured very formally, outlining in each article the requirements, formalities, and operative procedures for the congressional, presidential, and judicial branches of the new government, respectively. It is more precisely described as an "owner's manual" rather than the Declaration's "dear john" approach. In its original form, before the amendments were added to gain support for its passage, the U.S. Constitution did not guarantee the citizens of these United States with a single personal right, save for one: the Progress Clause.

© Mike Flippo/Shutterstock.com

In the first article of the Constitution, where the authority of Congress is established, Article 1, Section 8, Clause 8 provides the one and only ultimately "personal" right, giving the legislative branch the power:

> To promote the Progress of Science and useful Arts, by securing for limited Times to Authors and Inventors the exclusive Right to their respective Writings and Discoveries.

Granting to authors and inventors the *exclusive right* to their respective writings and discoveries, this clause is also the only enumerated rights of Congress in which the *means* of establishing personal rights is specified, that is, *by securing for "limited times."* As you might expect, this mechanism has drawn criticism over the years and has been the subject of much debate as to what is meant by the somewhat phrase "limited times."

One of the more notable debates about this issue occurs between the architect of the Constitution, Madison, and his longtime political ally and good friend, Thomas Jefferson. At the time of the convention, Jefferson was serving as George Washington's ambassador to France, but that did not impede his involvement in the thought process and structuring of the new framework. He and Madison exchanged almost 2,000 pieces of correspondence concerning the matters. In one such exchange, Jefferson mused to Madison that the "limited times" should be based on the average life of a person, which at that time was around 20 years. Thus, a direct link between life expectancy and the length of time a copyright is protected was engrained into our country's *zeitgeist* and has continued to persist.

© ilikeyellow/Shutterstock.com

In 1998, at the request of several copyright holders, including Disney on behalf of some of its primary revenue generators, including Mickey Mouse, Congress exercised its authority under Article 1, Section 8, Clause 8 to pass an extension of the term of copyright protection. Called the Sonny Bono Copyright Term Extension Act (CTEA), after its primary sponsor of Sonny & Cher, the act essentially extended the term of protection for copyright works, retroactively and prospectively, for an additional 20 years, from life plus 50 years to life plus 70 years. The CTEA brought U.S. copyright law in compliance with most other civilized countries who had already established life plus 70 years as the standard of protection. The circumstances surrounding the passage of the CTEA, specifically that the Disney Corporation was publicly vocal about its support of the bill, reignited the debate as to the interpretation of the Progress Clause's "limited times" language.

Chief among the CTEA's antagonists was Lawrence Lessig and his team at the Berkman Center for Internet and Society, who sought out exemplary plaintiffs in order to get the issue in front of the Supreme Court. Lessig found Eric Eldred, who was an Internet publisher whose specialty was republishing legacy works that had lost their copyright protection and fallen into what is known as the public domain. Eldred maintained that the pragmatic result of the CTEA was to prevent a large number of works from entering the public domain in 1998 and the following 20 years, as would have occurred under existing law if the 20-year extension had not been granted by Congress. The plaintiffs in *Eldred v. Ashcroft* argued that materials with which they had worked, and which were ready to republish were now unavailable due to copyright restrictions.

Writing for the 7-2 majority in the case, Justice Ruth Bader Ginsberg reminded us that the Progress Clause provides for a fluid system of protection that does not specify a specific term so long as it promotes the progress of arts and science. Because of the focus on corporate support for the CTEA, emphasized by Lessig, the Court reminded us that the Progress Clause is agnostic to this issue, and that even a profit-making motive to exploit the copyright within its term is perfectly compatible with the system. Finally, the Court also noted that the copyright system as it evolves from the Progress Clause does not give the creator a monopoly in the forms or building blocks contained in the copyrighted works, and therefore, if Eldred so desired, he was free to publish his own creations as well as the wealth of material that remained in the public domain. She noted:

> Copyright gives the holder no monopoly on any knowledge. A reader of an author's writing may make full use of any fact or idea she acquires from her reading.

The voices in society that decry the demise of the "public domain" as a result of the copyright term extension should reread Justice Ginsberg's opinion and understand how it relates thereto. In the next chapter, we will examine a second case spearheaded by Dr. Lessig with specific regard to the public domain, and in his arguments therein illustrated well the general misunderstanding about what is in the public domain and what purpose it serves. We will explore that misunderstanding later, but for now understand that the public domain is comprised of not only creative works that, for whatever reason, are no longer protected by copyright laws, but also of all ideas and "knowledge" contained in every copyrighted work available. After all, the purpose of offering the monopoly to the individual was for the "progress of arts and sciences." So, those ideas contained in the copyrighted works are also part of the "public domain."

4 The Public Domain

CASE NO. 3		Debate Question	
	CHAPTER CASE STUDY	Do the contours of copyright, as recognized by the Supreme Court, adequately protect freedom of speech and the First Amendment?	
		Affirmative	**Negative**
	Golan v. Holder 565 U.S. 302 (2011)	Yes, because the public domain is more than just "expired" works and is rather defined by the contours, which provide more room for creativity based on not only expired works but also copyright works.	No, you can only utilize works prior to 1923 that have fallen into the public domain to create derivative works, frustrating the Progress Clause.

The Uruguay Round was the eighth round of multilateral trade negotiations conducted within the framework of the General Agreement on Tariffs and Trade (GATT), spanning from 1986 to 1993 and embracing 123 countries as "contracting parties." Among other things, the Round led to the creation of the World Trade Organization. During the Round, with specific regard to copyright, certain contracting parties to the treaty expressed distraught with the United States because the works of their citizens that were protected in their home country had fallen into the public domain in the United States for failure to honor its commitments and obligations under the treaties. The contracting

© Bernsten/Shutterstock.com

parties called attention to the Trade-Related Aspects of Intellectual Property Rights (TRIPS) portion of the multilateral GATT treaties, requiring conformity to the Berne Treaty, specifically including Article 18, which called for recognition (or, in the case of the United States, restored recognition) of the copyrights of certain foreign works that had previously fallen into the public domain. The United States agreed to fulfill its obligation so, in 1994, Congress passed legislation to implement the resulting Uruguay Round Agreement, which included TRIPS. This implementing legislation was called the Uruguay Round Agreements Act (URAA). Specifically, the §514 of the URAA extended copyright protection to all foreign works that were in public domain in the United States if the term of protection had not expired in the source country, or work had fallen into public domain through noncompliance with formalities. Section 514 was codified at 17 U.S.C. §104A.

© Bilk Sergey/Shutterstock.com

This action did not sit well for Dr. Lawrence Lessig and his selected group of artists, including musician Lawrence Golan, the conductor for the Denver Philharmonic, who had made prior use of certain works, such as *Stavinsky* while they were in the public domain. In 2004, on their behalf, Lessig filed a lawsuit in the United States District Court for the District of Colorado[1] to challenge the restoration of copyright, arguing, *inter alia*, that doing so (a) violated the "limited times" language of the Progress Clause by taking works out of the public domain and (b) violated their First Amendment rights by depriving them of their right to use public domain works. The case also included a claim that the Copyright Term Extension Act, discussed in *Eldred*, *infra.*, violated the "limited times" language as well, using similar arguments as those made in *Eldred.* This additional claim was dismissed from the *Golan* lawsuit as a result of the Supreme Court's ruling in *Eldred.* The remaining constitutional challenge to the 1994 URAA remained.

In 2005, the District Court dismissed the remaining claim as to the URAA, holding that §514 of the URAA does not violate the Progress Clause or the First Amendment.[2] The District Court also handily rejected Golan's First Amendment challenge, seeing "no need to expand upon the settled rule that private censorship via copyright enforcement does not implicate First Amendment concerns."

[1] *Golan v. Ashcroft.* When a party litigates the constitutionality of an issue, the U.S. Attorney General, at that time John Ashcroft, is named as the defendant.

[2] By this time, the style of case had amended to *Golan v. Gonzales* to recognize the new attorney general, as it did again later in 2009 when it became *Golan v. Holder.*

The U.S. Court of Appeals for the Tenth Circuit *affirmed in part* and *reversed in part*. The Court agreed that §514 of the URAA does not exceed Congress' authority under the Progress Clause, but it vacated the district court's First Amendment ruling stating the following:

> Based on the Eldred Court's analysis, we examine the bedrock principle of copyright law that works in the public domain remain there and conclude that §514 alters the traditional contours of copyright protection by deviating from this principle. . . . [S]ince §514 has altered the traditional contours of copyright protection in a manner that implicates plaintiffs' right to free expression, it must be subject to First Amendment review.

The Tenth Circuit thus remanded it back to the court of first impression for further proceedings in accordance with its rulings. On remand in 2009, Judge Babcock reversed his earlier holding that the First Amendment was not violated by resurrecting foreign copyright claims. Babcock instead found that aspects of the URAA violated First Amendment rights of the "reliance parties," that is, defined in the URAA as parties who had been using a work formerly in the public domain before the URAA became effective. The reliance parties, he said, relied on the public domain status of these works to create derivate works and would now no longer be able to do so but instead would have to negotiate "reasonable compensation" to the owners whose works had been restored. He ruled as follows:

> In the United States, that body of [copyright] law includes the bedrock principle that works in the public domain remain in the public domain. Removing works from the public domain violated Plaintiffs' vested First Amendment interests. [. . .] Accordingly—to the extent Section 514 suppresses the right of reliance parties to use works they exploited while the works were in the public domain—Section 514 is substantially broader than necessary to achieve the Government's interest.

This time, the government appealed Babcock's decision. This time, the Tenth Circuit changed direction and, on June 21, 2010, reversed the judgment of the district court, remanding the case again, this time with instructions to the District Court to grant summary judgment *in favor of the government*, thus upholding the constitutionality of the URAA copyright restoration. The procedural history of this case illustrates that the life of a constitutional case can take years to grow and, often, courts change course in their attempt to wrestle with difficult issues. After the loss, Golan filed a *writ of certiorari* with the Supreme Court of the United States in an appeal for them to hear the case and, on March 7, 2011, the Court granted the writ. Oral arguments were subsequently heard on October 5, 2011.

Just as was the case in *Eldred*, Justice Ruth Bader Ginsberg wrote the opinion for the six-member majority, consisting of Chief Justice John Roberts and justices Kennedy, Scalia, Thomas, and Sotomayor. Justice Kagan abstained and Justices Breyer and Alito dissented. While recognizing the fact that the URAA did, in point of fact, end the free and unrestricted use of certain works previously in the public domain. There is a great deal of conflict in our current *zeitgeist* as to what constitutes the public domain and who owns it. For example, in a post on Stanford Libraries' website regarding Copyright & Fair Use, Rich Stim writes:

> The term "public domain" refers to creative materials that are not protected by intellectual property laws such as copyright, trademark, or patent laws. The public owns these works, not an individual author or artist. Anyone can use a public domain work without obtaining permission, but no one can ever own it.[3]

While some of what Stim states here is true, there are obvious errors in his portrayal of the public domain that reflect a more widespread opinion. First, while is certainly true that "creative materials that are not protected" by copyright are found in the public domain, that is *not* the definition of the public domain. The public domain also contains, for example, the ideas, concepts, and themes that are found in *every copyrighted work* ever written and published. As Ginsberg points out in *Golan*, those ideas, concepts, and themes become "instantly available for public exploitation at the moment of publication." There is no need for an author to wait for the life plus 70 years to create a protectable expression based on an idea he/she reads in a copyright work that inspires him/her. Second, Grim incorrectly believes that the "public owns these works" that are in the public domain. That statement is false, *no one owns the public domain.*

© Sven Hansche/Shutterstock.com

History is almost always the best reference when it comes to defining a term whose misuse had led to misunderstanding. The most appropriate reference with regard to the meaning of the "public domain" may be the public spaces of ancient Athens. The Greeks referred to an area situated beneath the northern slope of the Acropolis as the "ἀγορά," translated as "marketplace." At the apex of the slope stood the famous Parthenon. The Greek word ἀγορά had several connotations—"gathering place," "assembly," and "forum"—and so it in this area, along the sacred Panathenaic Way, that members of the πόλις, or body politic, congregated to conduct affairs of the state, commerce and business was conducted, or simply to hang out and discuss the important ideas of the day or watch performers play in the street, or listen to famous philosophers, such as Aristotle, Socrates, or Plato. Though they were maintained and regulated by the state, much as they are today, no one person or entity really owned the public spaces and all free citizens were able to make use of them. In many ways, the agora was akin to a river teaming with the life of free-flowing thought. The concept

[3] Rich Stim. *Copyright Overview: Welcome to the Public Domain.* https://fairuse.stanford.edu/overview/public-domain/welcome/.

of a *public domain* evolved from the ancient Greeks concept of the ἀγορά, so it is a grave disservice to narrow its meaning down to include only creative works that are no longer protected. The public domain is much more than that.

A correct reading of Ginsberg's opinion helps to clarify what the extent and true meaning of the public domain. The *Golan* Court ultimately upheld the constitutionality of the URAA, and Ginsberg explained the Court's rationale in by making two points relevant to the copyright contours. First, with regard to whether the URAA violated the Progress Clause, the Ginsberg explored and explained the breadth of the copyright construct as envisioned by the founders. The Court stated that the purpose of the Progress Clause is benefit society by *not only* encouraging the creation of new works but also the publication and dissemination of *existing* works. Justice Ginsberg masterfully traces the historical precedent of prior times when the government has taken works out of the public domain and granted copyright protection, including when the very first copyright act of 1790 was passed by the First Congress. She noted that the publication and dissemination of existing works are important and essential steps toward granting access to and spreading knowledge and learning, which fulfils the progress of arts. This accommodation to existing works makes more ideas accessible for the creation of new works. The Court rejected this argument.

Next, the Court addressed the alleged violation of the First Amendment by concisely summarizing the speech protective contours of copyright, including originality, fair use, and idea/expression, to "safeguard" free speech and properly balance the Progress Clause against the First Amendment. As the Supreme Court has asserted on several occasions, not only copyright is an acceptable *limitation* on speech, but it is also an "engine of free expression," and "supplies the economic incentive to create and disseminate ideas." For these reasons, the Court held that the Progress Clause does not exclude application of copyright protection to works in the public domain and, thus, the URAA did not violate the First Amendment. As Ginsberg said in the course of her opinion, "the Copyright Clause is meant to benefit and enrich the public with knowledge, culture, and all that can be gained from expressive works."

We explored the traditional contours of copyright in Chapter 2, but because they play such a crucial role in the thought process of both the *Eldred* and *Golan* opinions, it is important to revisit Justice Ginsberg's recitation of the "traditional contours of copyright" that have guided the Supreme Court for many decades as they applied to the issues in those cases. She described this speech-protective contours as the Copyright Construct's "built-in First Amendment Accommodations."

Source: Barry Neil Shrum

The first and most basic contour of copyright, as noted earlier, is the requirement, found at 17 U.S.C. §102(a), that a creative work must contain a "modicum of originality" in order to be protectable. Protection and encouragement of new expression ensures the insertion of "fresh" works of authorship into the marketplace, thus benefiting society as required by the Progress Clause. In other places, *Feist* for example, the Supreme Court uses the phrase "stamp of fresh authorship" to describe originality and confirms that only elements that are "original" can be protected through copyright. It can be correctly stated that the more original a work is, the greater the degree of a protection. New—*not copied*—ideas, expression, information, arts, and creations all benefit the public by ensuring the free exchange of ideas. Arguing against the application of this contour to the restoration of copyright to foreign works via the URAA, Justice Breyer, writing for the dissent in *Golan*, states that:

> [The URAA] does not encourage anyone to produce a single new work. By definition, it bestows monetary rewards only on owners of old works—works that have already been created and already are in the American public domain.

As noted above, however, and as Ginsberg pointed out, encouraging owners to disseminate existing works is *just as important* to infusing the marketplace of ideas as is the creation of new works, rendering Breyer's first premise invalid.

Einstein once said "I very rarely think in words at all. A thought comes and I . . . try to express [it] in words. . . ." In his attempt to explain his creative process, Einstein, perhaps unwittingly, is describing the second tradition contour of copyright, that is, the distinction that is drawn between expression and ideas[4], the contour of the idea/expression dichotomy. As Ginsberg notes, "every idea, theory, and fact in a copyrighted work becomes instantly available for public exploitation at the moment of publication."[5] It is the author's expression *alone* that gains copyright protection. The idea/expression dichotomy thus protects an author's rights to expression while allowing for the free communication of ideas.

Finally, the final speech-protective contour is perhaps the most powerful, and that is the concept of "fair use" found at 17 U.S.C §107, which specifically provides latitude for use of a copyright works itself in case involving bastions of free speech: commentary, criticism, scholarship, and research. The principle of fair use is a limitation on an author's exclusive rights to reproduction and distribution that "allows the public to use not only facts and ideas contained in a copyrighted work, but also [the author's] expression itself in certain circumstances."[6]

Taking into consideration the traditional contours of copyright as Ginsberg summarized in the context of the general misunderstanding as to the meaning of the phrase, it is perhaps better to understand the *public domain* as "continuum" of thought: returning to the concept of the teaming river that begins from the earliest moment of human history and continues until this very moment. The river is not owned by anyone person or entity, but rather every free citizen can "fish" in the river. We draw from the river the building blocks of creative thought and action. These building blocks of creation—musical notes and chords, words, colors, shapes, etc.—exist in nature separate from our use of them. No one person owns them.

---

[4] 17 U.S.C. 102(a) and (b), respectively.

[5] *Eldred*, 537 U.S., at 219.

[6] *Ibid.*

When we apply our creative efforts to those primordial forms, we can express them in an original way that can be protected by current copyright laws. As Ginsberg pointed out on several occasions, when those expression become part of the agora, or public spaces, every thought, idea, and nonoriginal expression that has merged into this river of thought becomes *instantly* available for use by any other free citizen, who can use the primordial forms used in the expression to an original expression of their own, thus perpetuating the cycle. In fact, Ginsberg clearly understood that similarities between these concepts when she stated that the Progress Clause is intended "to benefit and enrich the public with knowledge, culture, and all that can be gained from expressive works." The public domain is thus intended to be the "marketplace" of free expression for the body politic of our modern era.[7]

[7] The Supreme Court, in fact, often refers to the copyright construct as the "marketplace of free expression."

5 Fair Use and Parody

CASE NO. 4	CHAPTER CASE STUDY	**Debate Question**	
		Does a commercial use automatically disqualify a secondary work as a fair use?	
		Affirmative	**Negative**
	Campbell v. Acuff-Rose Music, Inc., 510 U.S. 569 (1994)	Yes, whether a secondary use is commercial is the most important consideration under the purpose and character analysis.	No, if a secondary work transforms the original into something having a new purpose and character, the commerciality of a work is not as relevant.

In Chapter 4, we discussed that the contour of fair use found in 17 U.S.C §107 allows not only the subsequent use of the ideas and facts contained in a copyrighted work but also the use of the expression itself when necessary to balance the substantial societal interest in the protection of free speech against the individual's monopoly in a copyright. Examples of the types of speech-protective purposes allowed under the fair use doctrine include, *inter alia* commentary, education, research, and criticism. In this chapter and the next two chapters, we examine how parody, pop art, and appropriation push the fair use allowance to a breaking point and perhaps even shatter it altogether.

© Yury Zap/Shutterstock.com

As the Supreme Court has repeatedly reaffirmed, the fair use principle is one of the most critical of the speech-protective contours.

Justice Sandra Day O'Connor, writing the majority opinion in *Steward v. Abend,*[1] calls fair use an "equitable rule of reason" that:

> . . . permits courts to avoid the rigid application of the copyright statute when, on occasion, it would stifle the very creativity which that law is designed to foster.

Historically, *equitable rules of reason* were applied by a "court of equity" to balance the respective conflicting rights of two parties. So, as applied to copyright, O'Connor is referring to the application of the fair use analysis codified at 17 U.S.C. §107 to balance the exclusive rights of the author, guaranteed by the Progress Clause, against the rights of all citizens to free speech, guaranteed by the First Amendment, when the latter right would otherwise be stifled by the exclusive nature of the author's copyright. Fair use thus serves as the primary safeguard of our free speech rights, which might otherwise be constrained if the monopoly rights given to copyright owners were absolute. Since the application of fair use is court-driven and somewhat open-ended in its application, it functions as a flexible component of the copyright construct, responding to changes in technology or institutional and creative norms. That flexibility makes it nearly impossible to predict how a court will apply the fair use doctrine in any particular set of facts. We see this flexibility and unpredictability play out in several of the Supreme Court cases examined in the next few chapters as well as in *Campbell.*

© Becca Eley/Shutterstock.com

Before the fair use doctrine was codified in the 1976 Copyright Act, it developed as a precedent in early case law. The first case to apply the fair use doctrine was *Folsom v. Marsh,*[2] which involved an infringement action brought in 1841 by the owner of a copyright in a 12-volume historical biography of George Washington. The defendant created a condensed version, which utilized verbatim copies of a total of 353 pages of the twelve volumes. In finding infringement, Justice Joseph Story wrote:

> [The] nature and objects of the selections made, the quantity and value of the materials used, and the degree in which the use may prejudice the sale, or diminish the profits, or supersede the objects, of the original work.

Justice Story's opinion became the major tenets of the "fair use doctrine" later incorporated into Section 107, which identifies four factors used in evaluating whether a "use made of a work in any particular case is a fair use":

1. the ***purpose and character*** of the use, including whether such use is of a commercial nature or is for nonprofit educational purposes;
2. the ***nature*** of the copyrighted work;

---

[1] 495 U.S. 207, at 236 (1990), *citing Sony Corp. of America v. Universal City Studios, Inc.,* 464 U.S. 448 and *Iowa State University Research Foundation, Inc. v. American Broadcasting Cos.,* 621 F.2d 57, 60 (CA2 1980).

[2] 9. F.Cas. 342 (C.C.D. Mass. 1841).

3. the ***amount and substantiality*** of the portion used in relation to the copyrighted work as a whole;
4. the ***effect of the use upon the potential market*** for or value of the copyrighted work.

The statute gives examples of the types of works that would most probably fall under the fair use exception, including criticism, commentary, news reporting, teaching, scholarship, and research; all bastions of free speech. It is important to notice several things here: (a) this list is intended to be illustrative and not exhaustive; (b) the fair use doctrine is a legal defense which, if found, means that the secondary work *is not an infringement*; (c) since it is a defense, it is not technically a personal right;[3] (d) just because a work falls into one of the specified categories does not *guarantee* that it is a fair use; and (e) just because a type of use is not identified does not mean that it is *not* a fair use.

© Stefano Chiacchiarini '74/Shutterstock.com

In 1994, the Supreme Court clarified some uncertainties of the fair use doctrine in the decision for *Campbell v. Acuff-Rose Music, Inc*, affectionately referred to in some circles as the "Pretty Woman case." As the story goes, 2 Live Crew approached the publisher of the Roy Orbison classic *Pretty Woman*, Acuff-Rose, requesting a license to use a sample of the song and the recording in their song of the same title, to be featured on their 1989 album *As Nasty as They Want to Be*. Acuff-Rose denied their request, but 2 Live Crew decided to use it over their objections and without their permission. Luke Skyywalker Records, 2 Live's record label, released the album and sold 250,000 copies before Acuff-Rose discovered the impermissible use. Acuff-Rose filed a complaint for infringement, naming the members of 2 Live Crew, Luther R. Campbell, Christopher Wong Won, Mark Ross, and David Hobbs, as well as their record company, for infringement of both the recording and the musical composition. In their answer to the complaint, 2 Live Crew asserted that their song was a *parody* of the original that should be protected under the fair use doctrine. Parody is not one of the exemplary uses identified in Section 107; however, the U.S. Middle District court in Nashville, Tennessee, agreed with the defendants that their song was a parody and was thus not an infringement, but rather a "fair use" of the original. On appeal, the Sixth Circuit Court of Appeals focused on the first factor, the purpose and character of the use, and reversed the decision based on the fact that the 2 Live's parody was "blatantly commercial." The Supreme Court granted certiorari on behalf of 2 Live Crew.

Justice David Souter, writing the majority opinion, compared the character of the two songs. The Orbison song, a 1960s romance diddy, involves a man seeing a woman walking down the street, and he asks her

[3] It is most accurately described as an "exemption" or a "defense," not as a "right" or "privilege." Because of its speech-protective qualities, however, some scholars and courts have ascribed to fair use the status of a *quasi-right*.

to spend the night with him. She rejects his advances and walks away, but ultimately walks back to him. In contrast, Souter observed, the 2 Live Crew version is set in the 1990s, and their derivative of the song "derisively demonstrates how bland and banal the Orbison song seems to them by degenerat(ing) into a play on words, substituting predictable lyrics with shocking ones." Their words, according to Souter, "can be taken as a comment on the naivete of the original of an earlier day, as a rejection of its sentiment that ignores the ugliness of street life and the debasement that it signifies."[4] As such, Souter opined, the Sixth Circuit erred in its overemphasis on the commercial nature of the secondary work and rejected its notion that commerciality automatically prevents a work from claiming a fair use exception, stating:

> If, indeed commerciality carried presumptive force against a finding of fairness, the presumption would swallow nearly all of the illustrative uses listed in the preamble of paragraph (§)107, including news reporting, comment, criticism, teaching, scholarship, and research, because these activities are generally conducted for profit in this country.

Souter thus deemphasized the effect that a commercial purpose previously held over whether a use is fair. Instead, the focus on the first factor should be on whether the secondary work *transforms* the original into something that serves a different purpose. Some degree of "mimicking" is necessary, according to Souter, to achieve a parodic effect:

> Parody needs to mimic an original to make its point, and so has some claim to use the creation of its victim's (or collective victims') imagination, whereas satire can stand on its own two feet and so requires justification for the very act of borrowing.

In other words, Justice Souter ruled that parody serves, by its very nature, a transformative purpose, and that is more important than whether the use is commercial.

In examining the second factor, the *nature* of the copyrighted work, the creative nature of the Orbison song weighed against a finding of fair use, however, the fact that the vast majority of parodies are based on creative works reduces the impact of this factor, according to Souter. In point of fact, the second factor almost always weighs in favor of the original work in the analysis and, to such a degree, is almost always a non-factor in fair use analysis.

Under the third factor, the *amount and substantiality* of the portion used in relation to the copyrighted work as a whole, Justice Souter expanded the degree to which a parodist may copy from an existing work, arguing that the amount of the original creative work that was copied must be balanced against the amount of original material contributed by the parodist in order to serve its purposes. The Court found that 2 Live Crew had contributed substantial new material, new lyrics, and certainly new musical effects, but questioned whether there was enough in the record to ascertain whether 2 Live Crew's use of the iconic Orbison baseline, used through the parody, was *excessive*. The Supreme Court thus remanded the case back down to the district court for a trial to determine if this use was too much to achieve its purpose. The case was settled in 1996, and Acuff-Rose reluctantly issued a mechanical license for the 2 Live Crew Song and Orbison was identified as a co-writer.

---

[4] *Campbell*, at 583.

© Juli Hansen/Shutterstock.com

So, while parody is not one of the exemplary uses identified in the front matter of 17 U.S.C. §107, the *Campbell* case clearly establishes it as a necessary literary component of free speech and therefore a parodic work may well qualify as fair use if it transforms the original. One recent example helps to illustrate this conclusion in tangible terms. During the 2008 presidential election, Barrack Obama's campaign gained steam through a combination of what I will describe as "guerilla" marketing techniques, primarily social media marketing and good old-fashioned street marketing. Wrapped up in the street side of the campaign, street artist Frank Shepard Fairey designed a stylized stencil portrait of Obama in shades of red, white, and blue that prominently featured the word "Hope," among other things, across the bottom of the poster. The iconic image appeared on posters and vinyl stickers and quickly became a prominent feature defining the Obama campaign.

In February 2009, the Associated Press announced that the Hope Poster was based on a photograph taken by one of its freelance photographers, Manie Garcia. Shortly following the announcement, Fairey destroyed all copies of photographs he had referenced when he created the poster. The AP subsequently entered into discussion with Fairey's attorney, Antony Falzone of the Fair Use Project, regarding the use of its copyrighted photograph to create a derivative work. Shortly thereafter, Fairey filed suit against the AP asking for a declaratory judgment in his favor based on a finding of fair use. During the course of the trial, Fairey's lawyers convinced him to come clean and admit that he had, in fact, relied on the Garcia copyright in the creation of the Hope Poster.

Part of the evidence presented during the litigation included the comparative analysis seen here. Using the four-factor analysis outlined in Section 107 of the Copyright Act, compare the original photograph, taken at a press conference where soon-to-be President Obama was joined by actor George Clooney, to the derivative work created by Fairey. The first factor compares the purpose and character of each work. The Garcia photograph is commercial in purpose and, as a photograph, might be protected as to some original composition and framing elements, but as a "news" photograph will incur some obstacles as to protecting the fairly standardized flash lighting as well as the selection of shutter speed, aperture, focus and depth of field. Fairey, on the other hand, could argue that the Hope Poster was created for a socially beneficial purpose and that he therefore "transformed"

Source: stevesimula. https://creativcommons.org/licenses/by-sa/2.0/

the mundane news photograph into an icon for productive social change. Fairey might even be said to have exercised his free speech rights in this context. That being the case, a transformative work is more likely to be treated as a fair use under the *Campbell* court's reasoning. The second factor of the analysis, the comparative *nature* of the original versus the secondary work, is normally of very little value in making a fair use analysis. Since almost all works are generally *creative* in nature and created as such, this factor is rarely used by any court to draw significant conclusions.

When considering the third factor of the fair use analysis, the *amount and substantiality* of the original used by the secondary work, it might be said here that Fairey used all of the original's elements in the creation of his derivative. Notice that the light reflection and shadowing on the original photograph are identical to the light and shadowing on the Hope Poster, and Fairey utilized the red, white, and blue thematic colors of the photograph expressed by Garcia through depth of field. The Supreme Court has stated that if the heart of the work is taken, even if it is a small amount, the use is unlikely to be fair.[5] So, in addition to the *quantity* of the original used, the *quality* of what was used must be examined as well. Thus, in evaluating the third factor, it is equally, if not more, important to consider not only the amount of copyrightable material that has been copied but also the *quality* of what is copied, *i.e.*, whether any uncopyrightable ideas are contained in the copyrighted work. As the Supreme Court pointed out in *Harper & Row*, even "appropriation of the 'heart' of the manuscript in this sense is irrelevant to copyright analysis because copyright does not preclude a second author's use of information and ideas." In applying these thoughts to the Hope Poster, the colors of red, white, and blue are primary colors that are to be expected of any work that is focused on a U.S. presidential election; the shadows and highlights that are cast on Obama's face and color are functions of physics affected mostly by the direction of the light coming into the space. Those elements are the ideas and forms that are excluded from copyright protection by §102(b) of the idea/expression dichotomy and as such are not protected elements of Garcia's copyright.

The fourth factor in our fair use analysis should consider the effect of the Hope Poster upon the potential market for, or value of, the Garcia photograph. Stated another way, does the derivative work, the Hope Poster, serve as a *substitute* for the original work, the Garcia photograph, from the standpoints of both marketplace and value? Here, the courts generally allow for not only *actual harm* but consider any harm to *potential* markets for the original. Consideration must be given for future uses of the original. It is conceivable, for example, that Garcia had the intention to create a campaign poster for the Obama campaign and his bubble burst upon the discovery of the Hope Poster, thus losing the huge financial windfall Fairey instead achieved as a result of the derivative. It is important here, as well, to acknowledge that courts will generally permit *some degree of harm* to the owner of the copyright *if* there is a significant public benefit that was achieved as a result of the derivative. So, on balance, in this case, while the Hope Poster did, in fact, supplant the opportunity Garcia may have had to create his own derivative poster, the benefit to society may, in fact, have outweighed the harm.

Unfortunately, like most copyright infringement actions, this case was settled on the courthouse steps, so we will never know how the analysis would have actually played out in court.

---

[5] *Harper & Row v. Nation Enterprises*, 471 U.S. 539 (1985).

6 Fair Use and Pop Art

CASE NO. 5	CHAPTER CASE STUDY	**Debate Question**	
		Is it necessary for a secondary work to "comment" on the original in order to qualify as a fair use?	
	Campbell v. Acuff-Rose Music, Inc., 510 U.S. 569 (1994)	**Affirmative**	**Negative**
		Yes, in order to be "transformative," the secondary work must comment on the original.	No, as long as the secondary work produces a new message, it is not necessary that it comment on the original work used.

In the previous chapter, the Supreme Court evolved a new definition of "transformative" in the *Campbell* opinion, expanding it to include parodies. In that case, the Supreme Court established that the 2 Live Crew song, incorporating the hook and base melody of Roy Orbison's *Pretty Woman*, was a parody that likely transformed Orbison's song by commenting on the urbanity of the original by adding a new meaning and a new material. In that case, the Supreme Court pointed out that it was necessary for the secondary work to directly "comment on" the original in some way in order to prove transformative. In the case study of Chapter 6, we examine a Second Circuit case, *Cariou v. Prince*, in which this court seems to diverge from the apparent instructions in *Campbell* and held that a secondary use *does not* need to comment on or critique the original in order to be transformative as long as it produces a new message. This intermediary opinion is relevant to the study of fair use because the subsequent opinion of the Second Circuit in *Warhol v. Goldsmith*, discussed in the next chapter, incorporates much of its reasoning, and the case is now before the Supreme Court.

In 2000, Patrick Cariou published a book of portraiture and landscape photography entitled *Yes Rasta*. The photographer, Cariou, spent 6 years living among Rastafarians in Jamaica and developing friendships with many. These intimate relationships allowed Cariou to serenely capture poignant photographic imagery of the culture, the people, and their environment. In his deposition in the underlying case, Cariou testified that he wanted the resulting book to be "extreme classical photography [and] portraiture," but definitely did not "want that book to look pop culture at all."[1]

© Todamo/Shutterstock.com

Richard Prince is an appropriation artist *ala* Warhol, whose pop art involves taking photographs and other images from a variety of sources, in other words, copying works that others have produced, and incorporating them into paintings and collages that he then presents as his own work. In most other art forms, including music, for example, this would be considered blatant copyright infringement, but in appropriation art is hailed as a badge of honor.[2] Prince discovered and bought Cariou's book *Yes Rasta* in a bookstore in St. Barths in 2005. Without permission from, nor even communication with, Cariou, the owner of the copyright, Prince copied approximately 30 photographs from Cariou's book, and enlarged them in their entirety, using them to create a series of what he calls "paintings" and "collages" for an upcoming exhibition at the Eden Rock hosted in Saint Barthélemy. He then painted blotches, stripes, and tattoos on the Rastafarians captured in the photographs and added objects such as guitars, masks, and even works to create a derivative series of "creative" works. He called the series *Canal Zone*, and, in 2007 and 2008, he exhibited them first at the Eden Rock, then later at New York's Gagosian Gallery. When the series was on display at the Gagosian, the museum published the series and sold an exhibition catalog that contained the reproductions of the Prince adaptations featuring Cariou's photographs.

On December 30, 2008, Cariou sued both Prince and the Gagosian, alleging that *Canal Zone* and the exhibition catalog infringed his copyrights in the photographs used by Prince. The defendants raised the fair use defense. Judge Batts of the Southern District Court of New York found that Prince's adaptation did not constitute fair use because it did not "comment on Cariou, on Cariou's Photos, or on aspects of popular culture closely associated with Cariou or the Photos"[3] and was thus not transformative. The district court based this decision in large part on Prince's deposition testimony that he "do[es]n't really have a message," that he was not "trying to create anything with a new meaning or a new message," and that he "do[es]n't have any . . . interest in [Cariou's] original intent."[4] Thus, Batts entered an order

---

[1] Cariou Dep. 187:8–15, Jan. 12, 2010.

[2] In the genre of sound recordings, for example, if a person takes a sample, uses it to create another sound recordings incorporating that sample, that *generally* requires a sample license, the lack of which is considered infringement. However, note that this is the exact scenario as found in *Campbell*, where the Supreme Court found that the secondary "parody" was transformative.

[3] *Cariou v. Prince*, 784 F. Supp. 2d 337, 349.

[4] Prince Dep. 338:4-339:3, Oct. 6, 2009.

granting the plaintiff's motion, entering a permanent injunction, and compelling the defendants to deliver to Cariou all infringing works that had not yet been sold, or for him to destroy, sell, or otherwise dispose of them.

Prince and Gagosian appealed the district court's decision, again contending that the work was transformative and therefore constituted fair use. The appellants argued to the Second Circuit that the district court committed reversible error in requiring that a secondary use "comment on" the original in order to qualify as fair use. The Second Circuit agreed with the Appellants that the fair use analysis does not require that a secondary use comment on the original artist or work. The Court ruled that 25 of the 30 works in Prince's series were, in fact, fair use, and remanded the case back down to the district court for a determination in accordance with that holding as to whether the remaining five qualified.

© New Africa/Shutterstock.com

It is important to consider this ruling regarding criticism and commentary in the context of other holdings. Notice that the fair use exception, 17 U.S.C. §107 actually lists "criticism" and "commentary" as among the several illustrative examples of fair use. The Second Circuit uses this to state, correctly, that the list is not exhaustive, and that secondary works may qualify for fair use even if it falls outside the scope of criticism, comment, news reporting, teaching, scholarship, and research. Traditionally, however, particularly as it regards a parody, courts have held that to qualify as fair use, the secondary work must "comment on or criticize" the original work. In fact, *Campbell*, where the focus is on the *transformative* nature of the secondary work, can easily be read to specifically require it, particularly in cases involving a parodic fair use.[5]

The Second Circuit, at least to some degree, concedes this point with regard to some of Prince's works when, with regard to its opinion, it cautions:

> Our conclusion should not be taken to suggest, however, that any cosmetic changes to the photographs would necessarily constitute fair use. A secondary work may modify the original without being transformative. For instance, a derivative work that merely presents the same material but in a new form, such as a book of synopses of television shows, is not transformative.

It is difficult to reconcile this portion of the Second Circuit's opinion with the outcome in this case where, in fact, most of the Prince series *does*, in fact, merely add "cosmetic changes" to the enlargements of the

---

[5] See 510 U.S. 569 at 583 (1994).

photographs: blue and white blotches of color over the eyes of the Rastafarians; collages of the Rastafarians holding different objects; and distortions of the original images. The cautionary caveat is given because such cosmetic changes could be considered as neither criticism nor transformation. The Second Circuit acknowledges this when it says "[i]n . . . works, such as [Prince's] *Graduation*, Cariou's original work *is readily apparent*: Prince *did little more than paint blue lozenges over the subject's eyes and mouth, and paste a picture of a guitar over the subject's body*."[6] Nonetheless, the Second Circuit found it dispositive that:

> Prince has created collages on canvas that incorporate color, feature distorted human and other forms and settings, and measure between ten and nearly a hundred times the size of the photographs. Prince's composition, presentation, scale, color palette, and media are fundamentally different and new compared to the photographs, as is the expressive nature of Prince's work.[7]

Instead, the Second Circuit concludes that "to qualify as a fair use, a new work generally must alter the original with 'new expression, meaning, or message,'"[8] that is, the secondary work must be transformative. With regard to the analysis of whether a work is transformative, the Second Circuit states that:

> What is critical is how the work in question appears to the reasonable observer, not simply what an artist might say about a particular piece or body of work. *Prince's work could be transformative even without commenting on Cariou's work or on culture, and even without Prince's stated intention to do so.* Rather than confining our inquiry to Prince's explanations of his artworks, we instead examine how the artworks may "reasonably be perceived" in order to assess their transformative nature.[9]

Although the Second Circuit relies on *Campbell* for its most critical question as to whether a secondary work appears to the "reasonable" observer to perceive transformation, it is important not to take *Campbell*'s point here to the extreme. To wit, Justice Souter placed the element of reasonable observation in the *context* of both commentary and criticism:

> While we might not assign a high rank to the parodic element here, we think it fair to say that 2 Live Crew's song reasonably could be perceived as commenting on the original or criticizing it, to some degree.[10]

Taking Souter at face value in *Campbell,* then, it is not entirely clear whether divorcing the reliance on the public's reasonable perception of transformation in a secondary work from the element of commentary and

© Luke W. Choi/Shutterstock.com

[6] *Cariou v. Prince,* 714 F.3d 694 at 701 (2d Cir. 2013), *cert. denied* 134 S. Ct. 618 (2013).

[7] *Ibid,* at 706.

[8] *Ibid, citing, Campbell,* 510 U.S. at 579.

[9] *Cariou,* 714 F.3d at 707, *citing Campbell,* 510 U.S. at 582. Emphasis added.

[10] *Campbell* at 583.

criticism on the original is defensible, even where the secondary work may not be based on parody. Are not the two concepts so entwined that to separate them renders both essentially "dead," that is, ineffective guidance as the inquiry of a transformative fair use? Are both elements necessary, at least according to Justice Souter in *Campbell*?

The Second Circuit actually waffles in the dissonance created by this bifurcation when it acknowledges that "[t]he focus of our infringement analysis is primarily on the Prince artworks themselves, and we see twenty-five of them as transformative *as a matter of law*"[11] but, as seen below, later acknowledges to comparing the original to the secondary work. The Court revealingly points to the case of *Brownmark Films, LLC v. Comedy Partner*[12] as instructive on its point that it can determine as a matter of law that the Prince works are transformative. The *Brownmark* court considered whether an episode of the animated television show *South Park* was a parody of a viral Internet video titled "*What What (In The Butt).*" That court decided on a motion to dismiss that "[w]hen the two works . . . are viewed side-by-side, the South Park episode is clearly a parody of the original . . . video." Note two things, however, about the supporting citation: (a) the case involved a work of *parody* like the works in *Campbell*; and (b) the court specifically stated that it viewed the two works "side-by-side," not just the secondary work in isolation. The Second Circuit's opinion in *Cariou* fails to consider either of these components because it was focused only on how the transformation in Prince works might be perceived by a reasonable observer. To do this, there is no need for a comparison with the original to make a judgment that the original has been transformed. That simply cannot be the intent of *Campbell.*

In fairness to the Circuit Court, it must be admitted that in subsequent language it backs off its "primary focus" on the Prince work and notes that it did conduct a side-by-side comparison of the works at issue, concluding that:

> Here, looking at the artworks and the photographs side-by-side, we conclude that Prince's images, except for those [5 works] we discuss separately below, have a different character, give Cariou's photographs a new expression, and employ new aesthetics with creative and communicative results distinct from Cariou's.[13]

The Second Circuit's circumlocution might be ascribed to what seems to be their enamor for Prince and other appropriation artists like him, such as Warhol. The stark difference in the way the court describes Prince and the way it references Cariou is palpable, particularly when the Court analyses the four fair use factors regarding the impact of the secondary work on the market and value of the original. In each reference to Cariou in this regard, the Court points out several times that he has not "aggressively" or "actively" marketed the book and that it has only generated $8,000 in royalties. In sharp contrast, the Court's description of Prince speaks in terms of him being "established" in the art and celebrity communities, referencing collective sales in excess of $10,000,000. The Court almost becomes a fanboy when it references Prince's client list which "included a number of the wealthy and famous such as the musicians,

---

[11] *Cariou*, at 707. Emphasis added.

[12] 682 F.3d 687 (7th Cir.2012).

[13] *Cariou*, at 707–708.

Jay–Z and Beyonce Knowles, artists, Damien Hirst and Jeff Koons, professional football player, Tom Brady, model, Gisele Bundchen, Vanity Fair editor, Graydon Carter, Vogue editor, Anna Wintour, authors, Jonathan Franzen and Candace Bushnell, and actors, Robert DeNiro, Angelina Jolie, and Brad Pitt."[14] The Second Circuit's focus on Prince's fame and fortune is misplaced in an analysis of whether Cariou's potential market for derivative works has been usurped by Prince's secondary work. But not for Prince, Cariou could have commissioned either Warhol or Koons, similar appropriation artists, to create works similar to those created by Prince, and the fortune might have been Cariou's. As Souter confirmed in *Campbell*:

> The market for potential derivative uses includes only those that creators of original works would in general develop or license others to develop.[15]

It was erroneous of the Second Circuit to assume that because he had not sought development of these avenues of exploitation, Cariou would not have eventually done so absent Prince copying his creations and doing so without his permission.

While the Supreme Court denied certiorari to hear this case on appeal, the case examined in the next chapter, *Warhol v. Goldsmith*, also originates in the Second Circuit and is being considered by the Supreme Court right now. The Supreme Court will most likely find it necessary to address the *Cariou* case when forming an opinion as to *Warhol*. The writ of certiorari in that case incorporates much of the same logic use here, and the *Warhol* ruling will ultimately affect the precedent set here by the Second Circuit.

---

[14] *Ibid* at 709.

[15] *Campbell*, 510 U.S. at 592. The Second Circuit used this exact same citation, but draws an entirely different conclusion from it.

7 Fair Use and Appropriation Art

CASE NO. 6			
	CHAPTER CASE STUDY	**Debate Question**	
		In order to find a secondary work transformative, may a court consider the intended meaning of a work in order to determine whether the conveyed meaning differs from the original?	
		Affirmative	**Negative**
	Warhol v. Goldsmith, 499 U.S. 340 (1991)	Yes, because a work of art that is "transformative" and conveys a different meaning or message from its source material is fair use, not an infringement.	No, when it is apparent that the allegedly infringing work is derived from the original work it is irrelevant whether the intended meaning differs.

In Chapters 5 and 6, we examined how the Supreme Court's interpretation of the four-factor test in 17 U.S.C. §107 has evolved, and in many ways expanded, since it was codified in 1976. In this chapter's case study, *Warhol v. Goldsmith*, the courts rely extensively on the *Campbell* and *Cariou* cases in order to apply the principles to appropriation art.

The genesis of this chapter's case study occurred in 1981, when Lynn Goldsmith, on assignment for *Newsweek* magazine, took a hauntingly striking portrait of the artist, Prince. Goldsmith is well-known for, among other things, her portraiture of famous musicians and celebrities. To create the right mood, Goldsmith spent hours in conversations with Prince and applied makeup, eyeshadow, and lipstick in order to capture Prince's mysticism and the intensity in his eyes. The photograph became an instant classic. Three years later, *Vanity Fair* licensed the photograph to be used in an article entitled "Purple Fame" and, unbeknownst to Goldsmith and in breach of the license, commissioned the pop artist Andy Warhol to create one of his iconic silkscreens of Prince for publication with the article. Warhol cropped the photograph and screen printed it, and his edited version of the Goldsmith appeared in the magazine.

© nefali/Shutterstock.com

Warhol is well-known as an "appropriation" artist, that is, for "borrowing" the creations of other people and entities and incorporating them into his own creations. For example, Warhol similarly "borrowed" Otto Bettman's famous photograph of Marilyn Monroe to create a well-known silkscreen of the superstar in 1962 ("Marilyn Diptych") and borrowed the design and trademark of the Campbell's soup can, with which he had an obsession, for other cultural pop art pieces. At first glance, one might get the impression that Warhol is simply drawing inspiration from the ideas contained in the original works, as the Progress Clause intends, but a closer examination of the silk screening process leads to the conclusion that Warhol is actually *copying* the original works in order to create his pop art. There is no doubt that Warhol's silkscreen prints are perceived as culturally valuable, as one of the Monroe prints sold just recently for $195,000,000. Of course, the question, in this case, is not as to the value of the creation, or its aesthetic value, but whether it constitutes legal and fair use of the original Goldsmith.

Serigraphy, or screen printing, is not a new process: it is said to have originated in China during the Song Dynasty (960–1279 AD). In the early 1900s, as technology evolved and photosensitive materials were created, the process was modernized to more closely resemble the process used now. The process is quite simple, but what is important to understand for the purpose here is that when a person wishes to silkscreen a photographic image, the actual image is used in its entirety to begin the process. In other words, the silkscreener must actually copy the original photographic image, as Warhol did in the case of both Marilyn and Prince.

This issue came to a head when Prince died in 2016. Before his death in 1987 and, again, without the consent of Goldsmith, Warhol created 15 different versions of the edited silkscreen he had created for *Vanity Fair* in 1984. Upon Prince's death, *Vanity Fair* printed one of the versions in a memorial. With all of the press surrounding his death, Goldsmith became aware of the various derivatives and filed a lawsuit against the magazine's publisher together with The Andy Warhol Foundation for the Visual Arts, Inc. for, *inter alia*, copyright infringement.

The Foundation argued that its namesake transformed Goldsmith's photograph and gave it new meaning, a necessary prerequisite to their primary argument that Warhol's design is not infringement pursuant to the fair use doctrine. In 2019, the issue went before Judge John G. Koeltl of the U.S. District Court in Manhattan, where he agreed with the Foundation, finding that Warhol had sufficiently "transformed" Goldsmith's photograph "from a vulnerable, uncomfortable person to an iconic, larger-than-life figure." Realistically, however, in comparing the two works, it is extremely difficult to maintain that the mere addition of primary and secondary colors through the silk screening process makes the image of Prince "larger-than-life." In fact, it can be argued that the Warhol print does transform the image in the least, but rather crops and copies it in its entirety and then adds the colors through the process. It would seem that here, as in *Cariou*, the justices were a bit enamored by the celebrity of Warhol which may have been affecting their objectivity.

On appeal, the Second Circuit reversed Judge Koeltl, finding that the district court erred in its assessment and application of the four fair-use factors found in 17 U.S.C. §107, and the works in question do not qualify as fair use as a matter of law because the Warhol screen prints are virtually identical to the Goldsmith photograph. Judge Gerard Lynch, writing for the court, points out that the Circuit's opinion relied on the Supreme Court's guidance in the *Campbell* case concerning the application of the first of the four factors, that is, *the purpose and character of the work* as to when a work is considered "transformative" in nature. The *Campbell* court noted that in order to evaluate whether a new work is transformative, the new work must at least "mimic an original to make its point"[1]; thus, the court must examine how it "may reasonably be perceived" by the "reasonable person."[2] Such a subjective evaluation must gauge "whether the new work merely supersedes the objects of the original creation, or instead adds something new, with a further purpose or different character, altering the first with new expression, meaning, or message."[3]

As the Second Circuit itself has recognized, this emphasis on perception essentially blurs the line between a work that may be perceived as "altering the first with new expression" and one that uses "the same material but in a new form . . . without adding something new," which, of course, is a *derivative* work requiring a license from the owner of the original copyright. The Court recognized this conundrum when it states:

> While that description may be a useful shorthand, it is likewise susceptible to misapplication if interpreted too broadly. Indeed, many derivative works "add something new" to their source material.

The problem, of course, is that if a court is considering whether an *adaptation* is infringing, an entirely different analysis should be conducted more in line with Justice Learned Hand's abstraction test, extracting the ideas from their protectable expressions. For this reason, in distinguishing a *transformative* work from a *derivative* work, the Second Circuit considered the *purpose* of both the primary and secondary works. If the purposes align, the secondary work is derivative, if not then the secondary work is transformative. It would be curious if this distinction can be drawn without being purely subjective, as the Second Circuit itself recognizes in *Warhol*:

> But purpose is perhaps a less useful metric where, as here, our task is to assess the transformative nature of works of visual art that, at least at a high level of generality, share the same overarching purpose (*i.e.*, to serve as works of visual art).

It would seem that a flawed metric is not a metric at all and will lead to widely divergent results. For example, in the 2006 case of *Blanch v. Koons*, 467 F.3d 244 (2d Cir. 2006), the Second Circuit found Koons' use of Blanch's original photograph *Silk Sandals by Gucci* to create a painting was *transformative*

---

[1] *Campbell,* 510 U.S. at 580–81.

[2] *Cariou*, 714 F.3d at 707, *quoting ibid*, 510 U.S. at 582.

[3] *Campbell,* 510 U.S. at 579.

where he allegedly used the original image as "fodder for his commentary on the social and aesthetic consequences of mass media," while in the earlier case of *Rogers v. Koons,* where Koons recreated Roger's original photograph as a three-dimensional statute intended "as a commentary of society," they adjudged the sculpture be an infringing *adaptation*, even though the Koons' stated purpose in both cases were very similar, if not identical. Further, using the same metrics, the Second Circuit found transformation for the majority of Prince's pop art copies of Cariou's photograph, where the purpose of Cariou's original photograph was to create "deliberately composed portraits and landscape photographs depict the natural beauty of Rastafarians and their surrounding environs," while the majority of the adaptations by Prince were "crude and jarring works" that were "hectic and provocative."[4] In *Warhol,* the Court attempts to explain these apparent inconsistencies as follows:

> The sculpture at issue in Rogers was a three-dimensional colorized version of the photograph on which it was based. See 960 F.2d at 305. In Blanch, however, Koons used Blanch's photograph, depicting a woman's legs in high-heeled shoes, as part of a larger work in which he set it alongside several other similar photographs with "changes of its colors, the background against which it is portrayed, the medium, the size of the objects pictured, [and] the objects' details." 467 F.3d at 253. In so doing, Koons used Blanch's photograph "as raw material for an entirely different type of art . . . that comment[ed] on existing images by juxtaposing them against others." Id. at 262 (Katzmann, J., concurring). And in Cariou, the copyrighted works found to have been fairly used were, in most cases, juxtaposed with other photographs and "obscured and altered to the point that Cariou's original [was]barely recognizable." 714 F.3d at 710. The works that were found potentially infringing in Cariou, however, were ones in which the original was altered in ways that did not incorporate other images and that superimposed other elements that did not obscure the original image and in which the original image remained, as in the Koons sculpture at issue in Rogers, a major, if not dominant component of the impression created by the allegedly infringing work. See id. at 710-11.

Thus, a restatement of the Second Circuit's perception test to determine when a secondary work is transformative is as follows: *the secondary work itself must reasonably be perceived as embodying an entirely distinct artistic purpose, one that conveys a "new meaning or message" entirely separate from its source material.*

Unfortunately, when the lower court in *Warhol v. Goldsmith* attempted to apply this test, the Second Circuit found that they did it wrong and committed a reversible error. After examining Warhol's "Prince" series of screen prints, the district court found that the Warhol series "*can reasonably be perceived to have transformed* Prince from a vulnerable, uncomfortable person to an iconic, larger-than-life figure."[5] The Second Circuit described this as an erroneous application of its precedent because, it said, "whether a work is transformative cannot turn merely on the stated or perceived intent of the artist or the meaning or impression that a critic . . . draws from the work." In other words, the Circuit cautioned the district court not to position itself as an "art critic" because "such perceptions are inherently subjective," and the result is that any adaptation could thus be treated as transformative.

---

[4] 467 F.3d at 25.

[5] *Warhol,* 382 F. Supp. 3d at 326.

© photo_gonzo/Shutterstock.com

In *Warhol*, the Second Circuit attempts to hone the perception test down to a finer point. The test should be objectively applied by examining "whether the secondary work's use of its source material is in service of a 'fundamentally different and new' artistic purpose and character, such that the secondary work stands apart from the 'raw material' used to create it," that is, "something more than the imposition of another artist's style on the primary work. . . ." With this sharply hewn explanation, the Second Circuit deems that the perceived purpose of Warhol's work is not different than that of the Goldsmith photograph and, as such, is not *transformative* with the meaning of the first factor of the fair use analysis. The Court objectively determined that the Prince Series of silkscreens retained the "essential elements" of the Goldsmith photograph, modifying it only to "magnify some elements of th[e original] material and minimize others." The Court held that because the Prince Series remained "recognizably derived" from the original it failed to transform and was thus, not fair use. In doing so, the Second Circuit specifically rejected what it considered the *subjective* evaluation of the Prince silkscreens as "immediately recognizable Warhols" because doing so would create a "celebrity-plagiarist bias" toward more well-known artists. It is important to note that the Second Circuit's reasonable perception test differs significantly from the opinion of the Ninth Circuit, which considers a work "transformative" when it conveys a different meaning or message from its source material.

The Foundation filed a writ of certiorari with the Supreme Court for review of the Second Circuit opinion, which was granted on March 28, 2022. Amici briefs and other proponents on the side of the Foundation argue that copying is essential to "creativity" in art and argue that appropriation artists must have some room to build on, allude to, and transform works that came before them. They argue that fair use embodies not only notions central to copyright law itself, but with regard to creativity, which invokes consideration of the First Amendment. Of course, opposing amici briefs argue that the concept of copyright *already* possesses "speech-protective" contours that ensure an artist's ability to create. This is not an issue of free speech, but rather, whether Warhol's usage of Goldsmith's copyright is permissible as a fair use. The oral arguments are scheduled to be heard on October 12, 2022.

8 Fair Use and Technology

CASE NO. 7		Debate Question	
	CHAPTER CASE STUDY	Does the use of a software interface (e.g., an "API") in the context of creating a new computer program constitute fair use?	
	Google, LLC v. Oracle America Inc., 593 US _ (2021)	**Affirmative**	**Negative**
		Yes, if the API serves a transformative purpose it qualifies as a fair use.	No, if the "heart" of the API is copied, it fails the amount and substantiality prong of the fair use analysis.

In prior chapters, we witnessed how courts applied the malleable concept of fair use to the world of music and arts to allow those forms of creation to accommodate the First Amendment. In this chapter, we will examine how the Supreme Court applied the concept of fair use to software design, specifically Application Programming Interfaces (APIs) used extensively in the technology industries.

The world of computers and technology evolved over the years. At first, it generated a lot of excitement when IBM introduced the world's first "personal computer" in the fall of 1981, but over the years as "micro" technologies allowed the computer to become handheld devices and cellular phones, computerization is so common as to be almost passé. *Google, LLC v. Oracle America Inc.* involves the application of copyright law to the rather complex interaction of APIs; therefore, a little remedial knowledge about how the computer interface and APIs work may be useful.

A person using a computer, types on a keyboard in their native language, but that is a language that the computer's hardware does not comprehend primarily because it only "speaks" in binary code, that is "on" and "off" or, more precisely zeros and ones. This obstacle is overcome by using two different interfaces: (1) a "user interface" allows the user to interact with the hardware and make it perform certain functions that are directed using hardware input such as a keyboard, mouse, and monitor; and (2) various software

or "programs" known as "operating systems," and "programming language" translates the user's input on the hardware into machine readable code to perform certain functions.

In contrast to this model of facilitating communications between a user and their computer, but in a similar sort of translation activity or mediatory function, an API is a type of "software interface" that allows two or more computer *programs* to communicate with each other. One of the courts in this line of cases described it as a tool that "allow[s] programmers to use . . . prewritten code to build certain functions into their own."[1] For example, the software used by your local bank has an API that can be accessed by Quickbooks, for example, to allow you to download all of your transactions into your online accounting software. Furthermore, if you have software used to track your invoices that software may have an API that allows it to communicate with the same Quickbooks account online. This API process allows a programmer to draw upon a vast library of prewritten, generally open-source, code to incorporate their own software coding in order to carry out repetitive and common software functions and tasks.

A document or standard that describes how to build or use such connections or interfaces is called an API specification. An API is often made up of different components, which act as tools or services available to programmers. A program or a programmer who uses one of these component parts is said to "call" that particular component of the API into action. The calls are used by a programmer through such programming technics as subroutines, methods, requests, or endpoints. An API specification defines how to make these calls, that is, it explains how to use or implement them.

One purpose of such APIs is to keep the internal details of how a system works known only to the programming, exposing only those segments that programmers of the other software will find useful. In this way, the interface created by the API remains consistent even if the internal details of the original programmer later change or are revised. An API may be custom-built for a particular pair of systems, or it may be a "shared standard" allowing interoperability among many systems. These shared standards very frequently consisted of what is known as "open-source" such that anyone can have access to the APIs that allow bilateral communications. APIs have been developed for programming languages, software libraries, computer operating systems, and computer hardware, among other things.

Java is a trademark for a programming language developed by one of the legacy companies of Silicon Valley, Sun Microsystems, in late 1990. Java included a programming language, a virtual machine, and a set of libraries, all of which used a set of APIs to communicate. These various libraries provide instructions

[1] *Oracle America, Inc. v. Google, Inc.*, 750 F.3d 1339, 1349 (2014).

for programmers telling them how to call certain library functions and what results to expect back when they did. When the programmer utilized Java calls in their programs, it allowed the programs to run on any computer that supported Java, leading to Sun's marketing slogan "write once, run anywhere." The Java language was released in 1995 under the Sun Community Source License, which made the source code readily available for free, but required that products using the code be maintained according to Java standards. It also required that any commercial *derivative* works be licensed by Sun. Programmers complained that the Sun licensing was too restrictive so, bowing to the pressure, Sun developed OpenJDK, a development kit, in 2007 and revised the license of the various Java packages using what is known as the GNU General Public License, which allows developers the rights necessary to make derivative works, including the ability to release applications under a new open-source licensing structure.

Just a few years prior to the release of OpenJDK, Android, Inc. began the development of its now ubiquitous Android operating system as a mobile platform. Like many tech startups, Android, Inc., along with its new operating system, was swallowed up by the much larger Google, led by executive chairman Eric Schmidt. Google envisioned the Android operating system as being free and open, allowing software developers to use their tools free of charge, thus making Google's hardware more attractive to the end user. For this purpose, Schmidt wanted to incorporate the Java SE libraries into their newly acquired operating system, so he approached Sun's president Jonathan I. Schwartz about licensing the Java libraries for use in Android. Schmidt reportedly offered between $30 and $50 million for the acquisition, but Schwartz refused the straight licensing deal and wanted a financial stake in Google instead.

© Sundry Photography/Shutterstock.com

When negotiations stalled, the rebuffed Schmidt instructed his team to develop a cleanroom version of the Java SE Libraries for use in the Android platform. A cleanroom design[2] is the method of copying a design by reverse engineering the software and then recreating it without reference to the original, hence the "cleanroom" moniker. As the name implies, the design team works in an environment that is "clean" or free, that is, demonstrably uncontaminated by knowledge of the proprietary techniques used by the competitor. Experienced lawyers are usually involved in the process, reviewing the programming along the way to ensure that no copyrighted material is included. This process is a proactive method of defending against a copyright infringement action because it relies on independent and simultaneous creation, and on the idea/expression dichotomy.

Google's cleanroom libraries became the engine behind Android's "Dalvik virtual machine," a core part of the new system. In order to hasten the process of completing Android and prevent the

[2] Also known as the "Chinese wall" technique.

"drudgery" of recreating what it considered open-source code, Google included 37 API calls and around 11,500 lines of code which were taken from Apache Harmony, a separate open-source clean-room Java implementation developed by the Apache Software Foundation (ASF). Unfortunately, Apache had its own failed licensing issues with Sun and the lines of code taken from Apache by Google were central to Java. Google released a beta version of the Android platform on November 5, 2007, and later that month released the software development kit (SDK) in which they noted that the beta version included some Java technologies. To further complicate this increasingly complicated situation, ASF ceased maintaining the Apache Harmony in 2011, and Google took over the maintenance of its libraries.

In 2009, Oracle Corporation announced that it was acquiring Sun Microsystems for $9.50, or a total of $7.4 billion gross, an acquisition that would take nearly a year to complete. In an interview with *PC World*, Oracle's CEO, Larry Ellison, commenting on the acquisition, noted that the Java language was one of the primary reasons the company was interested in the purchase, calling it "the single most important software component we have ever acquired."[3] Acquisition of the Java technologies would allow Oracle to more easily integrate it into their own cloud-based, enterprise-level applications known as Oracle Fusion, which already used Java-based APIs.

Shortly following the acquisition, on August 13, 2010, Oracle filed a lawsuit against Google in the District Court for the Northern District of California for, among other things, copyright infringement for its use of Java technologies without a license. They alleged that Google had copied, without their permission, a nine-line range check function, several test files, the structure, sequence and organization (SSO) of the Java (API), and the API documentation.[4] In all, Oracle alleged that there were thirty-seven separate APIs, which Google had derived from the Apache Harmony project.

The copyright phase of the litigation began on April 16, 2012. After a two-day trial, the jury determined that Google infringed the copyright related to the code, SSO, and documentation of the APIs as well as the range check function, but they deadlocked on whether these uses fell within the fair use exception. In response to the deadlock, Oracle asked the district judge for, and received, a directed verdict that the fair use defense be dismissed since the jury was split. After the patent phase of the trial, Judge William Alsup issued a final verdict that the APIs were not entitled to copyright protection and that the remaining infringements constituted one infringement and were therefore subject to the maximum statutory limit for damages of $150,000 for willful infringement.

In 2013, Google removed the problematic Dalvik virtual machine that incorporated some Java technologies and replaced it with the Android Runtime, which had been built within Google without using any of the Java source code but continued using the JavaSE APIs up until the release of the Android Nougat version in 2016, when it was fully replaced by OpenJDK.

---

[3] Elizabeth Montalbano (April 20, 2009). "Oracle, Entering Hardware Arena, Agrees to Buy Sun for $7.4 Billion." PC World. Retrieved October 1, 2022.

[4] The complaint also alleged violations of seven prior patents related to the Java technology, but these allegations were ultimately rejected.

Oracle filed an appeal with the U.S. Court of Appeals for the Federal Circuit, asking it to reverse Judge Alsup's ruling regarding the lack of copyright protection for the APIs. The Court of Appeals found that the Oracle's API packages were, in fact, both "creative" and "original" and so ruled that the "structure, sequence and organization" of an API is copyrightable. The District Court reversed and remanded the case for a second trial to consider whether Google's use of the APIs is non-infringement under the doctrine of fair use. The Circuit Court found the transcript insufficient lacking in facts related to fair use and thus insufficient for its rule on that point. In October 2014, Google filed a writ of certiorari with the Supreme Court asking for a review of the circuit's ruling, which was denied.

The second trial, ordered by the Circuit Court, began on May 9, 2016, specifically on the issue of whether Google's copying of 37 Java APIs was a use protected by §107. This time, the jury decided in favor of Google, finding that Oracle's copyrights were not infringed by Google because its reimplementation of the Java APIs was protected by fair use. Oracle appealed this decision to the Federal Circuit on October 26, 2016.

© Michael Vi/Shutterstock.com

As it had the first time, the Federal Circuit ruled in favor of Oracle's finding, through a rather elaborate analysis on the basis of a "mixed" case of fact and law, that Google's use could not be fair because it did not satisfy the four fair use factors as a matter of law and that it was not *transformative* in nature. The court stated that, "[i]t is undisputed that Google copied verbatim the declaring code of the 37 Java API packages 11,500 lines of Oracle's copyrighted code. It also copied the SSO of the Java API packages." The Circuit pointed out that Google's purpose for using the Java APIs was simply to "reuse" the technology for the purpose of enhancing its nascent Android platform and making it more attractive to developers who were already familiar with the Java open-source. The Circuit once again remanded the case back to the California district court to determine damages.

In January 2019, Google once again petitioned the Supreme Court for a writ of certiorari for review of the Federal Circuit's holding. This time the writ was granted. In its petition, Google again focused on whether copyright extends to a software interface like an API, and, even if it does, whether the use of the Java API by Google falls under the fair use exception, as both juries had determined.

In writing for the majority, it was clear from the recitation of facts that Justice Stephen Breyer was leaning in favor of the fair use defense.[5] Justice Breyer initially elaborated in great detail how an API functions in the context of Java's API:

---

[5] The reader might recall that Breyer was one of the two dissenting justices in both *Eldred* and *Golan* and would have sided with the petitioners in those cases, thus making a 20-year extension to the copyright term unconstitutional and prohibiting Congress from removing items in the public domain and granting them copyright protection.

> An API divides and organizes the world of computing tasks in a particular way. Programmers can then use the API to select the particular task that they need for their programs. In Sun's API (which we refer to as the Sun Java API), each individual task is known as a "method." The API groups somewhat similar methods into larger "classes," and groups somewhat similar classes into larger "packages." This method-class-package organizational structure is referred to as the Sun Java API's "structure, sequence, and organization," or SSO.

Breyer continues his explanation by explaining that these APIs are accessed *via* something programmers refer to as *implementing code*, which is used to tell the hardware which method in the API to call up to perform the desired task. He acknowledge that Google's implementing code was developed independently of Oracle's and, therefore, was not an issue in the case. Rather, the issue concerns what is referred to as the *declaring code*, which a method call uses to actually locate and invoke a particular implementing code that is needed to instruct a computer on how to carry out a particular task. In some ways, this declaring code performs an organizational function that divides the tasks into various groups and arrangements. Simple keyboard shortcuts are assigned to initiate each declaring code for specific tasks such that programmers do not necessarily need to write code to perform complex functions, rather they simply type in the shortcut.

For the majority of its programming in the Android language, Google did not copy the Sun Java APIs, rather it created its own task-implementing programs, implementing code, and declaring code. For 37 of the packages, however, Google did, in fact, copy the declaring code from the Java APIs. By so doing, Google allowed Android programmers familiar with Java's shortcuts with which they were already familiar. But for copying, the programmers would be required to learn an entirely new system to call up the common tasks. According to Oracle, three of the 37 packages copied by Google are "fundamental to being able to use the Java language at all."[6]

As do many of the Supreme Court justices when deciding issues of copyright, Breyer gives a nod to what he calls the "practical objective" of the Constitution's Progress Clause, that is, to "promote the progress of science and useful arts. . ."[7] and recognizes that Congress exercises this power to create copyright statutes. He identified four specific provisions of the current Copyright Act (of 1976) that are particularly relevant for his ruling in the instant matter:

1. **17 U.S.C. §102(a)** requires that for a work to be protected under copyright law, it must be a work of "'authorship,' that work must be 'original,' and the work must be 'fixed in any tangible medium of expression'."[8]
2. **§102(a)** as amended also identifies certain kinds of exemplary works that include *computer programs,* which the Act defined in §101 as "a set of instructions to be used directly or indirectly in a computer in order to bring about a certain result."

---

[6] *Oracle*, 872 F. Supp. 2d, at 982.

[7] Art. I, Sec. 8, Cl. 8.

[8] Breyer references the *Feist* case here implying consideration of the idea/expression dichotomy discussed in the third referenced statute.

3. **§102(b)** limits the breadth of §102(a) by limiting application of the Act to any "idea, procedure, process, system, [or] method of operation. . . ." This, in conjunction with §102(a)'s requirement of fixation in a tangible medium of expression, according to Breyer, combines to create the idea/expression dichotomy which protects *expression* of an idea, but not the *idea* itself.
4. **§107** imposes a limitation on a copyright owner's rights such that the owner cannot prevent another person from making a "fair use" of her copyrighted material.

While cordoning off these four provisions of the Copyright Act for application to the instant matter, in truth Breyer spends most of the majority opinion in the "equitable rule of reason" area of the fair use doctrine and its four-factor analysis. According to Justice Breyer, these "general principles" of §107 allow the "judicial balancing, depending upon relevant circumstances, including 'significant changes in technology.'"[9] New technologies, such as computer software, challenge the traditional paradigms of copyright protection, such as books, movies, and musical compositions in that their purposes are more functional in nature. As noted by the Rehnquist court in a case decided in the era when the nascent computer industry was just beginning to evolve, "[w]hen technological change has rendered its literal terms ambiguous, the Copyright Act must be construed in light of its basic purpose."[10] In other words, according to Breyer, fair use can "distinguish between *expressive* and *functional* features of computer code where those features are mixed."[11]

Google's petition raises two alternative issues: (1) whether the Java APIs constitute a process, system, and/or method of operation that is not protectable under §102(a), and (2) whether Google's use of the Java API constitutes a fair use. If either of these issues is answered in the affirmative, it would dispense with Oracle's claim of copyright.

In answering the first question as to whether an API is entitled to copyright protection, Breyer essentially sidesteps the issue by pointing out that the nature of computer programs, that is, that they are primarily functional, "makes it difficult to apply traditional copyright concepts" to them. For that reason, he dismissed the analysis by indicating that the Court would not overturn or modify earlier case law interpreting the issue. Thus, the focus of most of Breyer's opinion is the application of the fair use doctrine to Java's APIs.

The nature of the copyrighted work. With regard to the first factor identified in §107, the nature of the copyrighted work, Breyer focuses on the originality, or the creative nature, of the *declaring code.* While the declaring code falls into Congress' definitional example of what a computer program is, the court notes that it differs from copyrightable computer code in that it is:

> inextricably bound together with a general system, the division of computing tasks, that no one claims is a proper subject of copyright. It is inextricably bound up with the idea of organizing tasks into what we have called cabinets, drawers, and files, an idea that is also not copyrightable.[12]

---

[9] *Google*______; *citing Sony Corp. of America v. Universal City Studios, Inc.*, 464 U.S. 417, 430 (1984).

[10] *Twentieth Century Music Corp. v. Aiken*, 422 U.S. 151, 156 (1975).

[11] *Google*______, *emphasis added.*

[12] *Ibid.*

In that context, the declaring code serves an "organization function" similar to the Dewey Decimal System, which means the first factor favors fair use, benefiting Google.

The Purpose and Character of the Use. Of all the factors, the second factor most often has the most positive influence on the Supreme Court's finding of fair use, and this case is no different. When determining this factor, the Supreme Court, since *Campbell*, has asked whether the secondary use "adds something new, with a further purpose or different character, altering" the copyrighted work "with new expression, meaning or message," that is, is it *transformative* in character.[13] One commentator, attempting to broaden the application of fair use, opined that the focus should be on whether it "fulfill[s] the objective of copyright law to stimulate creativity for public illumination."[14] Breyer found that public illumination, or more precisely the necessary transformation, is the fact that Google's purpose in using the Java APIs was to create a new product, that is, Android, that would expand the usefulness of smartphones, offering programmers a "highly creative an innovative tool for the software environment."[15] In this sense, Breyer concludes, Google's use was "consistent with that creative 'progress' that is the basic constitutional objective of copyright itself."[16] Thus, he said, the purpose and character of Google's use of the Java API were transformative, and the second factor favored fair use, tilting the scales almost inextricably toward Google.

Amount & Substantiality. The third §107 factor examines not only the *quantitative* amount of the original work that is copied in the secondary work but also the *qualitative* value of what is copied, that is, did the secondary work copy the "heart" of the original work's creative expression?[17] With reference to the qualitative nature of Google's copying, Breyer noted that what Google copied, that is, the declaring code, is "virtually all" that is needed to implement hundreds of different tasks, and thus could be viewed as the "heart" of Java, as Oracle argued. Breyer posited, however, that a better way to view this case was to take into account the approximately 12,000 lines of declaring code copied in the context of the several *millions* of lines of surround code that Google *did not copy.* This leads to the conclusion that the comparatively *de minimis* amount of declaring code copied—approximately 0.04%—code whose function is to call up generic tasks, was copied not because of its originality or uniqueness, but because it would encourage programmers to make use of the new creation, Android, in their creative endeavors, because they were already familiar with Java's—that is the declaring code's—functionality. As Breyer himself concluded, "[t]he "substantiality" factor will generally weigh in favor of fair use where, as here, the amount of copying was tethered to a valid, and transformative, purpose."[18]

Market effects. The fourth statutory factor focuses upon the "effect" of the copying in the "market for or value of the copyrighted work."[19] In evaluating this factor, potential profit, or for that matter even actual

---

[13] *Campbell*, at 579.

[14] Leval, *Toward a Fair Use Standard*, 103 Harv. L. Rev 1105, 1111 (1990).

[15] *Google.*

[16] *Ibid.*

[17] *Harper & Row*, 471 U. S., at 564–65.

[18] *Google.*

[19] 17 U. S. C. §107(4).

© LDprod/Shutterstock.com

profit, is not dispositive. Breyer noted that the benefit to the public created by a transformative technology has to be weighed against financial loss, real or potential. It is undeniable, of course, that Google has had billions of dollars in profit from its Android operating system, which has ultimately been licensed by more than 70% of the world's smartphones.[20] What is not as clear is whether Sun/Oracle could have entered the smartphone market and, if so, how successful it would have been. But what is even more undeniable is that Google's Android technology, borrowing it is 0.04% of Java's API, has led to many more "creative productions of new expressions" that have transformed the world as we know it—something that Java script, even as popular as it was, would never have been able to achieve.

The Supreme Court acknowledged this last point, finding support in the underlying transcript of testimony from the trial court pointing to the very different markets between Google and Java, whereas Oracle's primary focus was desktop and laptop computers, and Google's focus was on smartphones. Even when Oracle attempted to enter the mobile marketplace, its focus was more on "feature" phones, lacking a touchscreen, than on emerging smartphone technology. Oracle had failed in its attempts to enter the mobile phone marketplace by licensing its Java script technologies and its corporate documentation even indicated that it had projected declines in the revenues for the mobile phone market. This leads to the inevitable conclusion that Google's Android operating system did not affect the market.

In addition, the court examined the testimony of one economist who told the jury that Android and Java were "two products . . . on very different devices" and, thus, Android was not a market substitute for Java. If the petitioner's market is distinct from the respondent's, a reasonable conclusion can be drawn that a programmer who learned the Java declaring code could easily make the transition from the laptop market for their talents to the smartphone market, and *vice versa*, thereby not diminishing the need and/or value of Java programming at all.

Ultimately, with regard to the fourth factor, Breyer concluded that:

> The uncertain nature of Sun's ability to compete in Android's market place, the sources of its lost revenue, and the risk of creativity-related harms to the public, when taken together, convince that this fourth factor—market effects—also weighs in favor of fair use.

---

[20] The dominance of Apple's iOS is strictly a U.S. phenomenon; as of 2022 Android phone users are approximately 70% of the world market (a decline from 77% from 2021) and Apple has about 25%, mostly in the United States.

Based on its analysis of the fair use factors, the majority determined that Google took "only what was needed to allow users to put their accrued talents to work in a new and transformative program, Google's copying of the Sun Java API was a fair use of that material as a matter of law." It reversed the Federal Circuit's contrary judgment and remanded the case for a decision in conformity with its ruling.

Given the current proliferation of APIs in the technology industry, not only in hardware and software applications but also in cloud computing, this opinion will have a tremendously positive impact on the development, interoperability, and innovation of computer technologies for generations to come.

9 Choreography, Pantomime and Ideas

<table>
<tr><td rowspan="4">CASE NO. 8</td><td rowspan="2">CHAPTER CASE STUDY</td><td colspan="2">Debate Question</td></tr>
<tr><td colspan="2">Whether choreography or pantomime can be effectively copyrighted under the Copyright Act of 1976?</td></tr>
<tr><td rowspan="2">Kyle Hanagami v. Epic Games Inc. 22-CV-2063-SVW-MRW (2022)</td><td>Affirmative</td><td>Negative</td></tr>
<tr><td>Yes. 17 U.S.C. §102(a)(4) specifically identified both as copyrightable categories, and combinations of otherwise unprotectable elements that convey a modicum of originality can be protected.</td><td>No, while the Act might specify choreography and pantomime as protectable categories, if the intrinsic test eliminates forms are based on the "building blocks" of movement from the copyrighted work, it is not entitled to protection.</td></tr>
</table>

The Supreme Court cases examined thus far have dealt with several sections of the Copyright Act, including §§101, 102(a-b), and 107. These opinions dealt with everything from telephone directories, musical parodies, and appropriation art to application programming interfaces, exploring issues ranging from whether the names and addresses in a phone book can be protected by copyright, to whether a foreign work whose term of protection has expired in the United States can be withdrawn from the public domain. In this chapter, the goal is to apply the nuanced precedents that were developed in those cases to two areas of copyright protection designated by §102(a), choreography and pantomime, particularly in connection with a recent California case dealing with a series of dance steps that were incorporated into an "emote" in a video game. Are the various basic dance steps in choreography more similar to the names and numbers in *Feist,* or do they contain enough originality such that they more closely resemble the potentially protectable declaring code found in an API?

At 17 U.S.C. §102(a)(4), the Copyright Act of 1976 identifies choreography and pantomimes as exemplary categories of "works of authorship," thus giving them copyright protection. Details of the Copyright Office's policies, procedures, and registration issues are outlined in Circular 52 titled, "Copyright Registration of Choreography and Pantomime." The Copyright Office defines *choreography* as:

> The composition and arrangement of related series of dance movements and patterns organized into a coherent whole.

The common elements identified in these types of works are listed as, "rhythmic movements of dancers' bodies in a defined sequence and a defined spatial environment, a series of dance movements or patterns organized into an integrated, coherent, and expressive compositional whole, a story, theme, or abstract composition conveyed through movement, a presentation before an audience, a performance by skilled individuals, [and] musical or textual accompaniment."

Additionally, *pantomimes* are defined as:

> The art of imitating, presenting, or acting out situations, characters, or events using physical gestures and bodily movements.

© Lucky Business/Shutterstock.com

Similarly, these works include elements of presenting before an audience, including a defined sequence and defined spatial environment, a story or theme conveyed through movement and musical accompaniment. Pantomimes have increased emphasis on silent movement with the absence of dialogue, as well as gestures and facial expressions.

These categories are some of the most elusive works of authorship when it comes to identifying the amount of *originality* necessary in their expressed forms. Like stand-up comedy and other performance arts, the line between what can be protected and what is not is what the Supreme Court has described as *evanescent*, that is, just when you think you have a handle on the concept, it disappears like vapor.

As with all copyrighted works, pantomimes and choreography must be *original* and *fixed in a tangible medium of expression* in order to be granted copyright protection. The tangible format used to record these mediums include dance notation formats (e.g., labanotation), video recordings of a performance, textual or literary descriptions, photographs, and drawings.

This principle of 17 U.S.C. §102(b) that restricts the application of copyright to facts and ideas is particularly stringent on choreography; in that, not all categories of choreography can be copyrighted due to their subject matter. Circular 52 identifies four main categories of dance that are ineligible for copyright protection: (1) common movements or gestures, (2) social dances, (3) ordinary motor activities and athletic movements, and (4) routines not performed by humans.

As it often does, technological advances pushed these dusty old legal principles to the breaking point. In 2019, a new platform for sharing videos, TikTok, was developed that transformed the social media landscape. TikTok became the optimal method to create an audience for your video content and connect with fans; the dream was now to get your TikTok to "go viral," that is, be shared and liked by millions of social media and Internet users. Part of TikTok's sudden rise in popularity can be ascribed to the fact that many of its users created "viral dance challenges." These challenges consist of users imitating original dance routines created by other users in hopes of creating a viral "hit." Due to the significant rise of these challenges, many choreographers of these original dance routines were not given credit and, in some instances, did not give their permission for these dances to be reproduced. The situation was very akin to when YouTube first became available, and users of that platform were sharing videos using copyrighted sound recordings without permission. Likewise, there has been an increase in these choreographers' works being utilized in video games without authorization by the game developers. Some examples include Ana Coto's viral roller-skating TikTok, 2 Milly's "Dance Step," BlocBoy JB's "Shoot," etc. As a result, frustrated choreographers have been increasingly filing for copyright protection of their original works in accordance with §102(a)(4) and some of them are resorting to protecting their work from such exploitation through the aid of litigation.

© Pryimak Anastasiia/Shutterstock.com

For example, in early 2022, the complaint of *Kyle Hanagami v. Epic Games Inc.* was filed in the United States District Court for the Central District of California claiming direct infringement, contributory infringement, and unfair competition against Epic Games Inc. ("Epic"). Kyle Hanagami ("Hanagami"), the plaintiff in that action, is a professional choreographer and dance instructor in Los Angeles, California and the defendant Epic is a computer software manufacturer that creates and distributes video game software. Hanagami filed the complaint against Epic for using and selling a section of his copyrighted choreography as an "emote," that is, programming slang for emotions for character conveyed through dance steps or movements—for their video game, Fortnite Battle Royale ("Fortnite"), neither seeking permission, compensating, nor crediting Hanagami. In August 2020, Fortnite sold an emote entitled, "It's Complicated" for 500 V-Bucks on their electronic marketplace (1,000 V-Bucks cost $9.99). Although Fortnite can be played for free, it also contains an in-game marketplace where players can purchase virtual add-on elements with which to customize the game's characters, including such items as new clothes, weapons, or the aforementioned "emotes" that make the virtual character perform certain actions or emotions. The emote at issue in the instant case, titled *It's Complicated* by Epic, contained a portion of the choreography Hanagami registered in 2017, a video of a dance performance posted on his YouTube page. The copied section is comprised of two seconds, four counts of music, and eight poses.

On May 27, 2022, Epic filed a motion to dismiss on the grounds that the steps in question were mere ideas or common dance steps that constitute "building blocks for a choreographer's expression." As such, they argued, the copied dance was unprotectable; therefore, they did not misappropriate it. In response to Epic's motion to dismiss, Hanagami argued that the portion copied was the heart of his copyright in that it contained "the most recognizable portion of [his] Registered Choreography, [including] the portion for the hook at the beginning of the chorus of the song[.]"

© Aris-Tect Group/Shutterstock.com

The District Court ruled in favor of the defendant on August 24, 2022. Justice Stephen V. Wilson started his analysis by focusing on the elements of copyright infringement set forth in *Feist*, particularly the second element that requires both actual copying and, more significantly, "unlawful appropriation." Recall that in *Feist*, the Supreme Court was examining whether a telephone directory publisher was infringing the copyright when it appropriated the alphabetized names, numbers, and addresses of Rural Telephone Company's subscribers in its copyrighted telephone directory. The Supreme Court found that those facts could not be misappropriated. To evaluate the element in this case, Justice Wilson cited *Rentmeester v. Nike, Inc.*,[1] which stated:

> Photos can be broken down into objective elements that reflect the various creative choices the photographer made in composing the image—choices related to subject matter, pose, lighting, camera angle, depth of field, and the like, none of those elements is subject to copyright protection when viewed in isolation.

To evaluate what elements could be *unlawfully misappropriated*, the *Rentmeester* Court eliminated the "objective" elements of composing a photograph by ostensibly applying an analysis developed in the Ninth Circuit's described as using a combination of the extrinsic and intrinsic tests:

> The test for substantial similarity in the Ninth Circuit contains both an "extrinsic" and an "intrinsic" component. The extrinsic component compares "specific criteria which can be listed and analyzed" to determination whether the works are substantially similar. *Funky Films, Inc. v. Time Warner Entm 't Co., L.P.*, 462 F.3d 1072, 1077 (9th Cir. 2006). The intrinsic component examines an ordinary person's subjective impressions of the similarities between the two works. *Id.*

However, in the case of a motion to dismiss, as here, which is decided on issues of law, not equity, the most relevant is the extrinsic test, known in other circuits as the *abstraction* test. In respect to that, the court opined that, just as the Ninth Circuit had done with the photograph in *Rentmeester*, all of the *unprotectable elements* in Hanagami's dance program, the common "steps," should be "filtered out" by the court to

[1] 883 F.3d 1111, 1117 (9th Cir. 2018).

determine when the remaining *protectable* elements shared by the works are substantially similar. Comparing the copyright in the dance to that of the photograph, the District Court noted that one of the photographs "highly original elements" was a particular pose but nonetheless found that the pose alone was not copyrightable.

Based on defendant's references to the Compendium of the United States Copyright Office concerning choreography, Justice Wilson surmised that "choreographic works are composed of a number of individual poses that, when 'viewed in isolation,' would not be protectable."[2] Using this reasoning, Justice Wilson found that the steps copied from Hanagami's video were unprotectable when extracted from the context of the work.

© ArtFamily/Shutterstock.com

Considering the intrinsic, or totality test, the court determined that Hanagami's choreography consisted of 480 steps, whereas only a small component, 40 counts (or 8%), were used by Epic. In addition, the identical steps were performed in different settings (physical vs virtual world), by different performers (human vs animated character), and for a different audience (YouTube/dance studio vs video game). Using these comparisons, the court determined that, other than the steps which are not protectable in isolation, there were no other similarities in the creative elements of the works, and thus the works were not substantially similar.

For the reasons stated above, District Court granted the motion to dismiss in favor of the Epic. The District Circuit's opinion, in this case, appears to run contrary to 17 U.S.C. §102(a)(4) as well as the Copyright Office's interpretative comment in Circular 52 that "rhythmic movements of dancers' bodies in a defined sequence and a defined spatial environment is entitled to protection." As will be argued below, breaking the fluid art of interpretive dance down to isolated images of the "steps" does not account for the stamp of the author's fresh authorship. In dance, just as in pantomime, part of the "artist's" creativity is *their body,* and their stamp of fresh authorship is their precise mastery over the fluid and exquisite movement of each limb in motion. The apparent doltish incomprehension of the art of dance by the District Court is further revealed by its comparison to a Ninth Circuit opinion in which a three-note sample was deemed to be a *de minimis* use and therefore not protectable, where the court viewed *Newton v. Diamond*[3] to be conceptually similar to Hanagami. In *Newton,* the Ninth Circuit considered

---

[2] *Kyle Hanagami v. Epic Games Inc., slip. op.* at p. 15.

[3] *Newton,* 204 F. Supp. 2d 1244, 1254 (C.D. Cal. 2002).

whether three notes in the underlying music composition sampled from an original sound recording were protectable, and erroneously decided that while the original composition was sufficiently original to be protected, the order granting dismissal would be upheld where the three-note use was not significant enough (*de minimis*) to be protected.

The Ninth Circuit, in this author's humble opinion, is replete with inconsistencies and erroneous rulings with regard to the copyright protection of the arts. Dance is one of those art forms that elude most legal scholars whose appreciation of the finer nuances thereof is minimal and observational at best, creating a recipe for misapplication of the Copyright Act's clear language. As noted earlier, Circular 52, although not binding precedent, is certainly clear in its interpretation that "*rhythmic movements of dancers' bodies* in a defined sequence and a defined spatial environment" are elements protectable elements. As such, it is difficult to justify the court's extraction of a handful (40) of *static images* from the video recording of those rhythmic movements (480) to determine whether the "defined sequence" is protectable, any more than lifting three basic notes from a musical composition and analyzing them out of their context of their melody provides a suitable approach. Metaphorically, the District Court's approach in *Hanagami* is similar to taking x-rays of a set of maternal twins, examining the similar skeleton, and claiming that it somehow speaks to the unique personality traits of each individual twin. The abstraction test, or what the Ninth Circuit calls the intrinsic test, is pushed to its limits in cases such as this involving an original combination of admittedly unprotectable elements if considered in isolation from the creative whole. Ironically, the Ninth Circuit recognizes that in such cases, *substantial similarity* can be found in a combination of such elements.[4] Inconsistent application of its own legal precedent is just a small part of the fallout that can occur when the bright lights of the entertainment industry are introduced to the dusty halls of justice.

Hanagami was appealed to the Ninth Circuit on September 23, 2022.

[4] See *Satava v. Lowry*, 323 F.3d 805, 811 (9th Cir.2003).

10 Natural Law's Influence on the Fair Use Doctrine

CASE NO. 9	CHAPTER CASE STUDY	**Debate Question**	
		Whether the current fair use doctrine, codified at 17 U.S.C. §107, is based on common law and arises out of natural law principles, and whether that should be considered when applying the doctrine?	
		Affirmative	**Negative**
	Folsom v. Marsh, 9 F Cas 342 (CCD Mass 1841)	Yes. The natural law basis of the common law copyright is the source of the fair use doctrine.	No, U.S. laws are notoriously based on utilitarian principles, and thus any vestige of natural law in the fair use doctrine has long been eliminated.

During the last two centuries, the Supreme Court has molded and shaped the contours of copyright, particularly the doctrine of fair use, to devise what it calls an *equitable rule of reason* for the purposes of protecting society's First Amendment right of free speech against the harshness that a pure monopoly would create without any such exception. In the modern era, since 1991, the Supreme Court began laying a foundation for the speech-protective contours in *Feist v. Rural* by elucidating the idea/expression dichotomy of 17 U.S.C. §102(a) and (b). They have since expanded on *Feist's* principles and applied the traditional contours to parody in *Campbell* and to modern arts and technology in *Warhol* and *Google*. Both *Eldred* and *Golan* helped refine the outer limits by exploring the meaning of the "limited times" language and "public domain" as applied to copyright and, by extension, to fair use. But in order to have a complete and well-rounded view of the doctrine of fair use, the question still remains as to its origins. To explore the dark corners of where it all began, it is necessary to ask the right question; in a chapter entitled *Understanding Fair Use*, L. Ray Patterson proposed that the precise question is not *what is fair use?;* but rather, *what is copyright.* To explain, Patterson points out that the concept of fair use is "a **derivative** concept, not an original one, and the nature of its host [*i.e., copyright*], so to speak, should determine its content."[1] To answer the question, the informative article maintains that copyright is originally based on the *concept of natural law.*

Ayn Rand espoused a similar basis for intellectual properties in her 1964 essay entitled *Patents & Copyrights* where she points out that, "[t]he government does not 'grant' a patent or copyright in the sense of a gift, privilege, or favor, it simply recognizes these are *pre-political* rights, *morally* belonging to the creator of the work."[2] Rand's conclusion here that a copyright "morally" belongs to the "creator of the work" takes a few pages out of John Locke's works. Locke, the progenitor of the natural law theory, specifically developed what is known as the labor theory of property ownership, that all natural resources are given to us by a personal, benevolent God and that, when one of his subjects applies labor to one of those natural resources and converts it into something that benefits society, the "fruits" of that person's labor belonged to his or her. This acquisition theory of ownership persisted in the early American colonies and even into modern jurisprudence. In the terms that Patterson developed regarding copyright, Locke's theory describes a *common law* copyright, whereas actual codification of the concept, such as the 1976 Copyright Act, is described as a *positive law* copyright. Patterson's basic premise is that the fair use doctrine derives from the common law copyright, not the positive law, even though it may ultimately be codified there, and that to fully understand the derivative fair use concept one must return to the common law. He further noted that our modern conception of fair use, based on positive law (*i.e.,* 17 U.S.C. §107), creates significant misperceptions and misunderstandings of the fair use doctrine. Understanding the fair use doctrine this way, based on common law and therefore natural rights, will not only help broaden our understanding of its importance but give us pragmatic depth in our application of it to current issues.

Benjamin John/Alamy Stock Photo

Most of the American colonies took their cues from England when it came to issues such as copyright. In the City of London, daily life generally centered around something known as "livery companies," which consisted of trade associations and guilds, of which most of the 110 livery companies were styled the "Worshipful Company of ________" filling in the blank with their respective craft, trade or profession. These livery companies, or more

[1] *Emphasis added.* L. Ray Patterson, "Understanding Fair Use, in *Law and Contemporary Problems*, vol. 55, no. 2, Copyright and Legislation: The Kastenmeier Years (Spring, 1992), pp. 249–66 (18 pages).

[2] The essay was originally published in the May 1964 issue of *The Objectivist Newsletter*, then later included in an anthology of her works titled *Capitalism: The Unknown Ideal*, 1967.

precisely the liverymen who controlled them, had a great deal of control over the civic structure, generally retaining voting rights to select mayors and officers and granting others corporate entities. This association of liverymen was known as the Corporation of London. In 1403, the Corporation of London approved the formation of a guild of stationers, holding the monopoly on publishing that was known as the Worshipful Company of Stationers and Newspaper Makers. The Stationers' Company was housed in "Stationer's Hall" in London. Once a member of the Stationer's guild laid claim to the "copyright" of a text, it was recorded on a "register" in Stationer's Hall, and that member owned the copyright *in perpetuity,* that is forever. No person nor Stationers' Company member, other than the registered owner of the "copy," had the "right" to copy the registered work. This was known as "the stationer's copyright," and is the derivation of our modern term "copyright." The guild received a royal charter of incorporation from Queen Mary I[3] on May 4, 1557.

Walter Thornbury, "Old and new London: a narrative of its history, its people, and its places" (1873)

If an independent third party infringed the copyright, that is, decided to publish a text that was identified on the register as belonging to one of the Stationers, that person was referred to as a "pirate," an ancient term for an infringer and was subject to severe penalties. The Stationers' Company was legally empowered to seize "offending books," together with the presses on which they were printed, that violated the standards of content set down by the Church of England, and of course Bloody Mary in her reign of terror against Protestant teachings. Depending on the severity of the transgression, the pirates could either be brought before ecclesiastical authorities, usually the Bishop of London or the Archbishop of Canterbury, or perhaps in later years, before an English court that sat at the royal Palace of Westminster known as the "Star Chamber," which consisted of privy counselors and common-law judges. The Star Chamber acted like a *court of equity*, imposing punishment for actions that were deemed to be *morally reprehensible* but were not in violation of the letter of the law. This gave the Star Chamber great flexibility in applying punishment for actions the court felt *should be unlawful*, even when in fact it was *technically not.* The invention of printing marks the beginning of Crown censorship, strengthened by a skillful alliance with private privilege made possible with royal charters, all driven by the exploitation of political, religious, and economic exigencies made possible by the printing press. Thus, the censorship of the press played a central role through the intensely turbulent decades of the Protestant Reformation and toward the English Civil War, generally oppressing citizens and subjects who had different philosophical and religious beliefs than that expressed by the Crown.

In many ways, society's response to the bloody tyranny of Queen Mary ultimately led to the formation of the United States and, more indirectly, to the formation of common law copyright. The English subjects

[3] Also known as "Bloody Mary" because of her tyranny against Protestants in the mid-1500s in England.

were generally divided in their response to this tyranny, but for purposes of this discussion, it was the separatists,[4] that is, the English Separatist Church, who felt that the church/state was so corrupt that the only feasible course of action was to leave England and form their own church. Some separatists migrated to the Netherlands in a largely unsuccessful attempt, but by 1620, several members of the English Separatist Church set sail aboard the Mayflower for New England and eventually landed near Plymouth, Massachusetts, which would, in time, become known as the Pilgrims.

These early North American colonists shared a dissatisfaction with the church and had a definite mindset that everyone was free to establish a church that was more aligned with their spiritual views. This freedom to practice religion according to one's beliefs led to the creation of countless different churches, denominations, and doctrines in the colonies, but more importantly, became a core part of the identity of the United States and the mindset that every citizen has personal empowerment and independence. As this religious and political growth and freedom grew and evolved, the power of the Stationers' Company devolved over the years and began to wane, culminating in the passage of an empowering act known as the Licensing Act of 1692, which lapsed two years later. When the Licensing Act lapsed in 1694, the stationers' copyright, as well as the monopoly of the Stationers' Company created by its royal grant, was effectively gutted and other third-party stationers and booksellers began to publish the texts and works on the register without impunity. The stationer's lobbied Parliament for 16 years to return to them their copyright, an effort which ended with the passage of England's Copyright Act of 1710, which finally removed the ownership of the right to copy from the hands of the "booksellers" of the Stationers' Company and returned it to its owner according to natural law, its creator. The 1710 Copyright Act, thus, eliminated those features of the stationers' copyright that had made it such an effective instrument of monopoly and censorship, that is, its perpetual nature and its limitation to members of the Stationers' Company. As a nod to the Stationers' Company, however, the new act continued the stationers' old copyrights for a period of 21 years from the statute's effective date of April 1710.

When a centuries-old industry, especially a monopoly backed by the government, is threatened with the loss of livelihood, as was about to happen in the year 1731 when the stationers' copyrights expired, the industry tends to fight back and fight back hard. The Stationers' Company was no exception and so, in 1731, the booksellers settled in for a 40-year "Battle of the Booksellers," a political tug of war that lasted until 1774 when the House of Lords decided *Donaldson v. Becket*.[5] Sun Tzu once said that "to know your enemy, you must become your enemy," and so in the turbulent throws of the war, the Stationers' Company did indeed step into the shoes of the authors they had oppressed for all of those years and adapted their arguments. The Statute of Anne replaced the stationers' copyright, which had been perpetual, with a limited duration of ownership for an initial period of 14 years and one renewal of the same length.

So, in numerous trials, lasting numerous decades, both the book industry and the judges fought over the question of whether the Statute of Anne really abolished a common law perpetual copyright. The booksellers

---

[4] The other group, called the *non-separatists*, believed Queen Mary had not done enough to eliminate the Catholicism in the Church of England, and wanted to reform it. They became known as the "Puritan's" and, in modern theological terms, were Calvinists.

[5] 1 Eng Rep 837 (1774).

were seeking to override the Statute of Anne, what Patterson called *positive law*, with the judicial recognition of an author's perpetual *common law* copyright based on *natural law*. They argued that as the creator of a work, the author should have a common law copyright by virtue of the Lockean natural law construct, the labor acquisition theory. As such, this common law copyright existed *in perpetuity*. Of course, the booksellers were interested in protecting their livelihood, so the lynchpin in their argument was that the author should be forced to assign this perpetual copyright to the booksellers, as it had always been the custom.

(261)

Anno Octavo

Annæ Reginæ.

An Act for the Encouragement of Learning, by Veſting the Copies of Printed Books in the Authors or Purchaſers of ſuch Copies, during the Times therein mentioned.

Whereas Printers, Bookſellers, and other Perſons have of late frequently taken the Liberty of Printing, Reprinting, and Publiſhing, or cauſing to be Printed, Reprinted, and Publiſhed Books, and other Writings, without the Conſent of the Authors or Proprietors of ſuch Books and Writings, to their very great Detriment, and too often to the Ruin of them and their Families: For Preventing therefore ſuch Practices for the future, and for the Encouragement of Learned Men to Compoſe and Write uſeful Books; May it pleaſe Your Majeſty, that it may be Enacted, and be it Enacted by the Queens moſt Excellent Majeſty, by and with the Advice and Conſent of the Lords Spiritual and Temporal, and Commons in this preſent Parliament Aſſembled, and by the Authority of the ſame, That from and after the Tenth Day of April, One thouſand ſeven hundred and ten, the Author of any Book or Books already Printed, who hath not Transferred to any other the Copy or Copies of ſuch Book or Books, Share or Shares thereof, or the Bookſeller or Bookſellers, Printer or Printers, or other Perſon or Perſons, who hath or have Purchaſed or Acquired the Copy or Copies of any Book or Books, in order to Print or Reprint the ſame, ſhall have the ſole Right and Liberty of Printing ſuch Book and Books for the Term of One and twenty Years, to Commence from the ſaid Tenth Day of April, and no longer; and that the Author of any Book or Books already Compoſed and not Printed and Publiſhed, or that ſhall hereafter be Compoſed, and his Aſſignee, or Aſſigns, ſhall have the ſole Liberty of Printing and Reprinting ſuch Book and Books for the Term of Fourteen

6 Ttt 2

British Government, Statue of Anne (1709)

The Stationers' Company made this argument in *Millar v Taylor.*[6] Andrew Millar was a bookseller who, in 1729, purchased the publishing rights to James Thomson's poem *The Seasons*. After the term of the exclusive rights granted under the Statute of Anne expired, a third party, Robert Taylor, began publishing a competing publication that contained Thomson's poem. The Court of the King's Bench, led by Lord Mansfield,[7] sided with Millar, finding that common law rights were not extinguished by the Statute of Anne. It was a major victory for the bookseller monopolies because it meant that their copyright, as now interpreted under common law, was perpetual, and no works ever entered the public domain. Once a bookseller acquired a copyright, it was his forever. Millar died shortly after the case was decided and, as a result, the decision was never appealed and therefore was not a decision of a court of last resort. The importance of *Millar* is that it legitimized the natural law theory of copyright which is still a residual component of modern copyright theory.

The final authoritative decision, the final blow as it were in the Battle of the Booksellers, was made in the House of Lords' 1774 decision of *Donaldson v. Becket*,[8] which effectively overruled *Millar*. The *Donaldson* case involved the same poem as *Millar*, that is, *The Seasons*, by James Thomson, except that in this case, the competing publisher was Andrew Donaldson, the appellant in this case, who sought to publish the poem, ostensibly owned by London bookseller, Mr. Becket.[9] The Lords held that when an author

[6] 98 Eng Rep 201 (1769); Lord Mansfield, the chief judge on this case, had previously represented the copyright-holding booksellers in various suits filed in the Court of Chancery in the 1730s. Justice Yates, the dissenting judge, had previously represented the challengers of common-law copyright in a similar case, *Tonson v. Collins*.

[7] Justices Aston and Willes concurred in the judgment, with Sir Joseph Yates dissenting.

[8] 1 Eng. Rep. 837 (1774).

[9] It is uncertain how and when Becket obtained the rights to the Millar estate and/or the copyright in the poem.

published a work, the only protection available to him or her was the statutory copyright pursuant to the Statute of Anne, which, of course, was a matter of Patterson's *positive law,* that is, statute.[10] The general principle established in *Donaldson* is that *before publication* an author owns his or her creation on the basis of common law or, in other words, the natural law, but *following publication* the positive law attaches. In effect, *Donaldson* creates the *common law* copyright granting the author the *right of first publication.* Because an author by reason of creation owns the common law copyright of a work before publication, and because creation is also a condition for statutory copyright after publication, it follows that the source of the author's right to a statutory copyright is the act of creation. As colonies of England, the American states were equally concerned with the concept of copyright and, 15 years after *Donaldson* created the English common law copyright, the Constitutional Congress inserted Article I, Section 8, Clause 8 into the Constitution of the United States, granting Congress the explicit power to enact copyright statutes as a matter of *positive law.*[11]

The Founders of the United States would have understood "copyright" in the same sense as their British counterparts. The 1790 Copyright Act, passed by the first United States Congress, was a direct copy of the Statute of Anne. The history of copyright in the United States emphasizes the statutory nature of the right and, in fact, when passing the 1790 Act, the congressional record specifically disclaims any foundation on a *natural* right.

In addition, the Supreme Court later used the House of Lords' decision in *Donaldson* as governing precedent for its first copyright case, *Wheaton v. Peters,*[12] decided in 1834. Ironically, the case arose because Richard Peters abridged Henry Wheaton's publication of Supreme Court's opinions, thereby creating less expensive Supreme Court reporters, which devastated Wheaton's market for the more expensive ones. As in England, the issue arose as to whether the United States copyright statutes had replaced the common law as the exclusive mechanism for copyright protection. Wheaton originally sued in Pennsylvania, where the court found that some of the formal requirements of copyright had not been met by Wheaton; therefore, there was no statutory protection for his works. He further noted that when there is no federal protection under statute, the creator must look to the states for common law, assuming that such existed.

In his writ of certiorari, Wheaton argued that requiring registration and the deposit of a copy of the copyrighted work with the Department of State were improper prerequisites to copyright protection and that, even assuming such failure, his work was protected by common law. Writing for the majority, Justice John McLean held that because Congress was granting authors the protection of copyright, it could require them to observe the statutory formalities. With regard to the common law argument, McLean wrote that "Congress, then, by this act.[13]"[14]

---

[10] As support for this proposition, the Lords also examined the Star Chamber's ruling respecting books and observed these as "heinous exertions of unconstitutional power," yet even the Star Chamber never recognized a perpetual right to copyright.

[11] See, *Patterson*, p. 253.

[12] 33 U.S. (8 Pet.) 591 (1834).

[14] 33 U.S. at 660–661.

Although the Supreme Court found, as it had the House of Lords in construing the Statute of Anne, that the 1790 Act provided the *exclusive mechanism* for the protection of *published works*, it did so not on the ground that the Act had "preempted" existing common law rights, but rather on the ground that there was no federal common law and that, therefore, such rights "originated, if at all, under the acts of Congress." Thus, *Wheaton* "finally anointed the positive law theory of copyright as official United States doctrine."[15] The two dissenting justices in *Wheaton*, however, "urging acceptance of the natural law theory that had been advocated vigorously by Wheaton's lawyers."[16] In addition to these dissents in *Wheaton*, its dictum may be more informative: "[i]t may be proper to remark that the Court is unanimously of opinion that no reporter has or can have any copyright in the written opinions delivered by this Court, and that the judges thereof cannot confer on any reporter any such right."[17] In other words, while an author may claim statutory protection for summaries and ancillary materials, no one may lay claim to the judicially authored texts of the opinions themselves.

Two relevant points can be derived from the Supreme Court's holdings in *Wheaton*: (1) when a creative work is unpublished, state and common law will be invoked for its protection;[18] and (2) the origins of the fair use doctrine can be derived from its disclaimer about court opinions as belonging to the public. The common law, therefore, is more relevant when one turns to the *origins* of the fair use doctrine. Furthermore, as fate would sometimes have it, sitting on the Supreme Court bench at the time of *Wheaton* was Associate Justice Joseph Story, nominated by James Madison, who 7 years later decided the seminal case that established the doctrine of fair use, *Folsom v. Marsh.*[19]

In the days when Story was a Justice, following the passage of the Judicial Act of 1789 that created the federal circuit court system, the judicial districts, that is, the "circuit" did not have dedicated justices. As a result, two of the Supreme Court justices were appointed as "circuit riders" to travel the sometimes-long distances between circuits on horseback or in carriages to hear cases together with the state circuit judges. It was during one of these circuits that Story traveled from Washington to the state of Massachusetts where he heard arguments on behalf of the United States District Court for the District of Massachusetts in the case of *Folsom v. Marsh.*

When the first president of the United States, George Washington, died in 1799, he left behind a voluminous collection of correspondence. He bequeathed the collection to his nephew, Supreme Court Justice Bushrod Washington, who subsequently gave it over to the Harvard University historian, Jared Sparks. From 1834 to 1838, Sparks published *The Writings of President Washington*, a 12-volume work of

---

[15] *Patterson*, p 255.

[16] *Ibid.*

[17] 33 U.S. at 668.

[18] *Cf., International Copyright: Report of the Honorable W.E. Simonds, of Connecticut*, from the House Committee on Patents Accompanying H.R. 10881, June 10, 1890, which strongly criticized *Wheaton* and clearly asserted that copyright is premised on authors' natural rights.

[19] 9. F.Cas. at 342.

© Everett Collection/Shutterstock.com

nearly 7,000 pages, the vast majority of which were individual letters written by Washington. The series was subsequently printed by Harvard's official printer, Charles Folsom.[20]

In 1840, Boston publisher Bela Marsh announced a new two-volume Life of Washington by the Reverend Charles Wentworth Upham, a writer and anthologist, and U.S. Representative from Massachusetts. Upham was another Harvard historian who had graduated about 10 years after Sparks and traveled in the same circles. Upham copied a total of 353 pages from the 12-volume biography verbatim, which consisted primarily of Washington's letter. Folsom sued for "piracy of copyright."

What Upham created was an abridgment which, in modern parlance, is a derivative work based on the original. Around this time, the derivative right in a copyrighted work was not firmly established and, in fact, many publishers and authors used other creations freely with an understanding that they were creating a new work. Particularly in the United States, which was the anti-monopolistic land of freedom, copyright was a device to promote learning, and creating a derivative work promoted progress. For them, preventing the creation of a derivative work was a form of censorship, restricting their newfound freedom of speech. The Copyright Act very narrowly granted the author the right to print, reprint, publish, and vend and only applied, as we have seen, to a book that had been printed or published. Many American courts leading up to the *Folsom* opinion, and even after, held that it was not an infringement of the copyright for another author to abridge a copyrighted book because in doing so the second author produced a new book.

On appeal, Upham argued that the doctrine of "fair abridgment," prevalent in both England and the colonies, gave an author the "right to abridge and select" parts of another work if what was taken, qualitatively or quantitatively, was necessary for a justified purpose, in this case, historical scholarship, and did not supersede the original. Story, as will be seen, did not agree with this very British *fair abridgment* doctrine. Patterson summarizes it as such:

> Although well established in American law, the abridgment doctrine was based on the positive law theory of copyright and was a product of English precedent that American judges did not like. Whether intuitively or otherwise, the judges must have been influenced by the notion that it was unfair for a later author or publisher to take a free ride on the original author's back. *Such a result was inconsistent with the universal notions of justice that comprise natural law.*[21]

---

[20] David A. Kluft, "George Washington and the American Birth of Fair Use," *Massachusetts Lawyers Weekly*, Feb. 14, 2014. A revised version of the article is available at *A Presidents Day Copyright Story: George Washington and the "First" Fair Use Case*, Foley Hoag Trademark & Copyright Law Blog, Feb. 21, 2014.

[21] *Patterson*, at 255.

Patterson points out that this conflict between the abridgment doctrine and natural law motivated Story to use natural law theories in *Folsom* in an effort to supplant the English-inspired doctrine and create the first iteration of the four-factor fair use analysis. As will be seen, Justice Story held that whether a usage is "fair" is a very fact-specific inquiry that must examine "the nature and objects of the selections made, the quantity and value of the materials used, and the degree in which the use may prejudice the sale . . . of the original work."[22]

In his opinion, Justice Story begins by acknowledging that the concept of intellectual property belongs to a very elevated plane in his oft-quoted description:

> Patents and copyrights approach, nearer than any other class of cases belonging to forensic discussions, to what may be called the *metaphysics of law*, where the distinctions are, or at least may be, very subtle and refined, and, sometimes, almost *evanescent.*

This description has been referred to time and again by the Supreme Court when discussing copyright. The idea that copyright is *metaphysical* and *like a vapor* speaks to the fact that it is so easily misunderstood. Even from the beginning, for example, the First Congress misunderstood the underlying principles of natural law, that is, even though the Progress Clause has the utilitarian purpose of benefiting the whole of society, it achieves its goals by granting to the individual his or her rights in the fruits of his or her intellectual labor and, therefore, is based on the Lockean principle of first acquisition, or in other words, *natural law.* Story used this basis to *expand* the scope of the copyright owners' rights by giving them the ability to control, for the first time, the creation of adaptations and derivative works from their original creations.

At the time Upham created the abridged version of Folsom's published work, the colonies had come to accept the English abridgment doctrine as law. Story rejected that premise and effectively expanded copyrightable subject matter significantly by permitting derivative works to be considered one of the rights of the copyright holder and thus eviscerated the abridgment doctrine once and for all.

The appellee also argued that even if the abridgment doctrine did not apply, an original work could be used for "fair and reasonable criticism." He based this argument, in part, on the fact that the bulk of the 12-volume George Washington biography, as well as the 353 pages he copied, consisted of letters written by Washington, who was now dead and, regardless, were in actuality the public property because they became property of the United States government and, as such, not entitled to copyright protection. Story dismissed the government property argument by pointing to the fact that just because a property belongs to the government does not mean that a private citizen has any right to possess that property or make use of it for personal purposes.

In addressing the fair criticism component, while Justice Story accepted the premise that, under certain circumstances, a derivative work *may* be used fairly, he firmly disagreed with the appellee's assertion that his abridgment was such a use, when he stated that "[t]he entirety of the copyright is the property of the author; and it is no defense, that another person has appropriated a part, and not the whole, of any property."

[22] 9 F.Cas. at 349.

On this point, Justice Story issued the following ruling, cited above, that is attributed as the genesis of the fair use doctrine:

> [A] reviewer may fairly cite largely from the original work if his design be really and truly to use the passages for the purposes of fair and reasonable criticism. On the other hand, it is as clear, that if he thus cites the most important parts of the work, with a view, not to criticize, but to supersede the use of the original work, and substitute the review for it, such a use will be deemed in law a piracy. . . .
>
> In short, we must often . . . look to the *nature and objects* of the selections made, *the quantity and value of the materials used*, and the degree in which the use may *prejudice the sale, or diminish the profits*, or *supersede the objects*, of the original work.[23]

Story's ruling effectively supplanted the *fair abridgment* doctrine of our merry old ancestors in England and replaced with what has evolved into the *fair use* doctrine. In the end, Story's theory for proposing this fair use concept was that the statutory monopoly allowed by the Progress Clause did not *create*, but rather *secured*, the author's *natural law property right*.[24] In his mind, the fair use doctrine remained a natural law doctrine attached to copyright and remained in all respects a statutory, or positive law, concept. Despite the *Folsom* opinion, it would be many decades before this fair use concept would be widely accepted. Several later decisions were decided contrary to Story's fair use doctrine and consistent with the abridgment doctrine. Congress itself ignored fair use in both the 1870 and 1909 revisions of the Copyright Act.

When Senator John Little McClellan (D–AR) of the 94th Senate proposed S. 22 to amend the 1909 Act on January 15, 1975, the bill had been almost 20 years in the making, the arduous result of numerous reports, white papers, and committees, arising from the persistent efforts of then-Registrar of Copyright Barbara Ringer and her staff, who had spent countless hours drafting and redrafting. What would ultimately be the 1976 Copyright Act passed the senate the following month, and then made its way through the house to pass in September of that same year. The 1976 Act brought U.S. copyright law out of the nineteenth century and brought it into alliance with the rest of the world in most ways. Consequently, the 1976 Copyright Act gave the owners of a copyright, for the first time, the right to do more than merely make copies of a book: among other things, it added, notably, a bundle of five[25] exclusive rights to be possessed by the copyright owner: *reproduction, distribution, public performance, and display and adaptation or creation of derivative works.* It also, of course, codified the fair use doctrine.

---

[23] *Op. cited. Emphasis Added.*

[24] As a member of the Supreme Court when Wheaton was decided, Story would have been familiar with the idea that a natural right underlies the Progress Clause, being present when Paine, counsel for Wheaton, argued "had the convention designed to take away, or to authorize Congress to take away the common law property, they would have used the words *vest*, or *grant*; and would have carefully avoided the word *secure*." 33 US (8 Pet) at 602–3. *Emphasis in original.*

[25] The 106 "bundle of rights" initially consisted of five rights until the sound recording gained digital performance rights in 1996.

These rights are exclusive and divisible, yet they are limited by certain exceptions laid out in Section 107–122 of the U.S. Copyright Act. The exception that most concerns this treatment is, of course, §107. The codification of Story's fair use doctrine, based on natural law, together with its juxtaposition in the sections dealing with the caveats to the exclusive rights, seemingly at least places it squarely in the context of statutory or "positive" law. So, with Story's emphasis on the natural law and the statute's emphasis on positive law, how are we then to understand fair use in the modern world? Do we interpret it to be devoid of its origins and only treat it as a set of rules to be followed, or do we understand it in the context of its evolution from Lockean theory?

The Congressional Report that accompanied the S.22 contains a very lengthy description of the fair use doctrine and explains why it was decided to codify the doctrine and make it statutory. One of the most important notations in the Record is found as the general background of the problem is discussed:

> Indeed, since the doctrine is an equitable rule of reason, no generally applicable definition is possible, and each case raising the question must be decided on its own facts.[26]

Acknowledging the fact that the fair use doctrine is undefined in existing case law, Congress nonetheless draws attention to the evolution of four factors that directly resulted from Story's decision in *Marsh*, the four factors of §107 previously identified. In his article on the subject, Patterson concludes that as a result of the codification of the fair use doctrine "it follows that fair use, being derivative of copyright, should also be a positive law concept correlated to the uses of copyright."[27] For him, the issue is settled, and we should "jettison" the "dated fair use baggage [of natural law]" in order to gain "a better understanding of the concept."[28] He further explains that since Congress was granting an "enhanced copyright" in terms of scope and length, the purpose of the "codified fair use [was] to counterbalance" the enhancement. The Congressional Report, however, seems to contradict his conclusions, however, when it notes that "[t]he bill endorses the purpose and general scope of the *judicial doctrine* of fair use, *but there is no disposition to freeze the doctrine in the statute. . . .*"[29] In fact, in this section from whence this quote derives, dealing with Congress' "general intention behind the statute," it states:

> The statement of the fair use doctrine in section 107 offers some guidance to users in determining when the principles of the doctrine apply. However, the endless variety of situations and combinations of circumstances that can rise in particular cases precludes the formulation of exact rules in the statute. . . . Beyond a very broad statutory explanation of what fair use is and some of the criteria applicable to it, the courts must be free to adapt the doctrine to particular situations on a case-by-case basis. *Section 107 is intended to restate the present judicial doctrine of fair use, not to change, narrow, or enlarge it in any way.*[30]

Thus, their intent was not to change or narrow the doctrine of fair use, let alone "jettison" the natural law roots of the "judicial doctrine," but rather to offer guidance to users in determining where its principles apply.

---

[26] HR Rep No 94-1476, 94th Cong, 2d Sess 65 (1976), p. 63.

[27] Patterson, p. 264.

[28] *Ibid.*

[29] *Emphasis added.* HR Rep No 94-1476, p. 264.

[30] *Ibid.*

11 Anatomy of the Astroworld Negligence Complaint

CASE NO. 10		Debate Question	
	CHAPTER CASE STUDY	Is a performer liable for personal injuries and death resulting to concertgoers who are crushed by a crowd in a mosh pit?	
		Affirmative	**Negative**
	Acosta, et al. v. Apple, Inc., et al. Complaint	Yes, particularly if he encourages the crowd to act violently and does not proactively curtail the harmful activity.	No, the performer is not responsible for injuries and death caused by third parties.

What kind of concert must it be if, after the show, some of the attendees suffer from post-traumatic stress disorder? It is the kind of show that generates more than 5,000 legal claims! Celebrities are lightning rods for allegations, conflict, and litigation, even when they are doing things aboveboard and by the book. In the realm of the music and entertainment industries, lawsuits occur frequently and for many reasons, thus a well-rounded entertainment attorney should be prepared to file a complaint on such occasions, and whenever necessary: whether the client has a dispute with a business client or a member of the band, believes her musical composition and/or sound recording has been infringed, or believes a contract to which she is a party has been breached. The first chapter described the general process of filing a complaint for copyright infringement in the court of first impression and the series of events that the process kicks off when the complaint is served. In this chapter, the focus will be on the finer points of putting together a complaint, as well as the claims and causes of actions available, explored in the context of an ongoing lawsuit filed in November 2021 as a result of the disastrous events that took place at Travis Scott's Astroworld Festival that occurred earlier that same month.

The Astroworld Festival is a multiday music event created by American hip-hop, rapper artist Travis Scott. The event was co-organized and managed by Scott's agency, Live Nation. Apple Music licensed the rights to stream the performances live online in real time. Scott's performances are well-known for his antiestablishment incitements to violence, perhaps brought on by his childhood fascination with wrestling and his unfulfilled desire to become a Worldwide Wrestling Federation wrestler. One CNN writer

© hurricanehank/Shutterstock.com

described his raucous concerts as "teeter[ing] on the brink of chaos." Similar concerts in the years prior to Astroworld in Arkansas, Illinois, and elsewhere ended with Scott being charged and arrested with numerous misdemeanors such as disorderly conduct, inciting a riot, and endangering the welfare of minors. In most of those cases, Scott pushed the limits of negligence, urging concertgoers to ignore and even abuse security agents, rush the stage to crush each other, and jump from high balconies into the crowds below. Scott frequently describes his fans as "ragers" and can be heard shouting instructions to the crowd to "rage hard," "let me see some ragers," "f**k security," and "f**k him up" in reference to an unruly fan. The events are so out of control that Irving Azoff, powerful entertainment mogul, manager, and executive at Live Nation, described Scott as "unmanageable" and withdrew his representation in 2020.

© Bryan Regan/Shutterstock.com

On the day of November 5, 2021, the Astroworld Festival was set to occur at NRG Park in Houston, Texas. It was estimated that the sold-out festival would have approximately 50,000 people in attendance, enough that the Houston police chief expressed concern to Scott and his security chief in a pre-concert meeting to discuss public safety and Scott's sometimes outrageous exhortations to the crowds. Despite those cautionary meetings, overzealous fans began to line up at the festival's outer perimeter just before 5 am, some throwing objects at each other and crowd surfing, and before the venue gates opened at 10 am, there had already been several breaches of security at checkpoints and gates from Scott's fans, and attendees of the concert and calls had gone out to officials for riot gear and crowd control units. These violations were consistent throughout the whole day and leading up to the main event where the casualties and deaths occurred. By 8 pm, the medical workers were so overwhelmed with traumatic injuries and overdoses that they stopped documenting patients and began triage to isolate the most severe injuries.

By the time Scott took the stage just after 9 pm that evening, the density of the crowd surrounding the stage had already increased to the point of creating what is called a "human crush"—about five to six people per square foot—where the fluid-like pressures of the overcrowded situations began to literally crush people, people struggled to stay on their feet, became asphyxiated and, those who cannot escape quickly suffered physical injury and even death. On stage, Scott ignored the chaotic tragedy that was unfolding quickly literally right in front of his eyes, with fans passing out, getting trampled, and stepped on; he ignored the emergency sirens and lights that surrounded the event as medics and nurses attempted to rescue injured concertgoers; he ignored the fans in several quadrants of the arena that twice started to chant "stop the show"; he continuously offered encouragement to riotous crowd to continue giving "the finger" to the authorities who were trying to help the injured, and asking the crowd on several occasions if they were "a' ight" to raise their hands, even while pointing into the crowd at people who were trampled. Once security officer who fell unconscious reported the sensation of feeling a prick in his neck causing a puncture wound consistent with an injection. Incredibly, the deadly chaotic show continued for a full hour before Scott sang his last song—40 minutes after authorities had declared it a "mass casualty event"—but not before it had caused the untimely death of eleven individuals ranging from 9 to 27 years of age and including an unborn child. Following the incident, almost 5,000 legal claims were filed in addition to those for the deaths, 732 for physical injury with extensive medical treatment and 1,649 for physical injury with less extensive medical treatment. The medical examiner ultimately confirmed the cause of death for all victims was accidental compressive asphyxiation. Ultimately, the magistrate divided the defendants in the case into four categories: those who were killed, those who suffered traumatic brain injury, those with bodily injury, and those with post-traumatic stress disorder. The causes of actions included negligence, *respondeat superior*, wrongful death, and premises liability. Additional defendants, such as the streaming services, record labels, handlers, entourage, managers, agents, hangers-on, promoters, organizers, or sponsors,[1] are specifically included under the theory of *respondeat superior*, as here, these entities with control over certain aspects of what happened are directly responsible for the negligent acts of their employees and/or agents when acting as such within the *scope of their employment.*

© Melvin Parker/Shutterstock.com

Shortly following the event, the Houston Police Department announced it was cooperating with the FBI to investigate the incident for criminal liability and the governor a task force to investigate and report on concert safety. On December 22, 2021, the United States House of Representatives Committee on Oversight and Reform announced the launch of a bipartisan investigation into Live Nation's role in the incident. Many of the investigations are ongoing as of the time of this writing. When a tragedy like this one occurs, everyone wants to find out who is responsible. Is the city of Houston responsible for improper permitting and oversight? Are Live Nation and Apple responsible for not better coordinating security and police enforcement for an event where such violent

---

[1] They include Drake, Apple Music, Tri Star Sports & Entertainment Group, Cactus Jack Records, Grand Hustle Management, Epic Records, ASM Global, and Live Nation.

activity is arguably foreseeable? Is the festival management responsible for not stopping the show sooner? Is Scott responsible for encouraging further destructive activities even as he becomes aware of fans passing out and being trampled in the "VIP" section? In legal parlance, the answer to each of these questions hinges on the concept of *negligence,* and questions of negligence can only be answered as a result of a lawsuit on behalf of those injured and/or the estates of those who died.

Sorting and analyzing negligence claims can get complex, with such issues as foreseeability versus unforeseeability and gross versus simple negligence. The seminal case that every first-year tort student studies with regard to negligence issues is the New York case of *Palsgraf v. Long Island Railroad* decided by Chief Judge Benjamin Cardozo sitting on the New York Court of Appeals.[2] In August 1924, Helen Palsgraf planned a wonderful day for her and her daughters at Rockaway Beach. While waiting for the train at a Long Island Rail Road (LIRR) station, she stood next to a large, coin-operated scale. In order to board an earlier train that was departing, two men rushed by one of which was carrying a package. As the railroad employees attempted to help the two men board the train, one of the employees pushed the man with the package, causing him to drop it. The package exploded—there was speculation that it was fireworks for an Italian-American celebration—causing the very heavy, industrial, coin-operated scale to topple over and fall on Ms. Palsgraf, creating serious injuries, including shock and bruises. A few days after the incident, she developed a stammer. Palsgraf sued the LIRR for negligence.

© Scott Heaney/Shutterstock.com

After a two-day trial, the jury of twelve men ruled in favor of the plaintiff, Ms. Palsgraf, and awarded her $6,000, the equivalent of about $100,000 today, finding that the train workers did not exercise "prudent and careful" safety procedures and that it was reasonably foreseeable that, as a result of such failure, Ms. Palsgraf would be injured. After several appeals, the case ended up in the New York Court of Appeals, the state's highest court. Writing for a 4–3 majority, Justice Cardozo ruled in favor of the LIRR that there was no negligence. In helping the man board, Cardozo reasoned, the railroad employees did not have a duty of care to Palsgraf as injury to her as it was not foreseeable that she would incur harm from their aiding the man with the package. The original jury verdict was overturned, and the railroad won the case.

Applying the foreseeability requirement of *Palsgraf* to the facts of the Astroworld Music Festival, then, the plaintiffs would have to argue that the crowd surge was a *casually related* event connected to, and that could have been *reasonably foreseen* based upon, the prior conduct of Scott. In other words, *but for* Scott's incitement to riot, plaintiffs' injuries and/or death would not have been sustained. On the other hand,

---

[2] 248 N.Y. 339 (1928). Cardozo, of course, later became a Supreme Court justice.

like the LIRR, Scott and his co-defendants would have to base their defense on unforeseeability, that is, there was no *causal relationship* between the injuries caused by the riotous crowd and their actions.

Negligence occurs when there is a breach of a person's *duty of care.* To establish negligence in a legal situation, it is necessary to prove the existence of four elements: (1) duty of care, (2) the breach of that duty, (3) a causal connection between the breach of that duty and the injury caused, and (4) actual damage or loss. *Ordinary negligence* is caused by a careless mistake or act of inattention that results in an injury to another person, whereas *gross negligence* is caused by a reckless disregard or purposeful indifference for the reasonable safety of others. In a recent case against Scott filed by plaintiffs Emma Ruiz and Justin Trujillo from Colorado, they allege that their "injuries were [the] inevitable and predictable result of defendants' conscious disregard of the extreme risks of harm to concertgoers that had been escalating since hours earlier."[3] The lawsuits against Scott, like most lawsuits claiming negligence, are typically filed in civil court, but in circumstances involving gross negligence, *criminal liability* can occur when a person knowingly disregards obvious risks to human life and safety. Here, the FBI and Houston authorities are still investigating criminal charges against Scott and possibly other defendants.

It would be surprising if Scott does not ultimately face criminal charges for engaging in a sustained pattern of proudly promoting violent behavior that was perpetuated at the Astroworld Festival resulting in the catastrophe resulting harm and death. There is little doubt that he was indifferent to his duty to, and recklessly disregarded the safety of his fans, failing to, among other things: (1) plan a safely executed concert; (2) cooperate with local authorities and security personnel; (3) provide adequate security, medical services, and logistics; (4) warn concertgoers of dangers involved; (5) stop enraging the crowd and encouraging the destructive behavior of his fans; (6) immediately stop the performance once it was clear that injuries were occurring; and (7) secure concert grounds for unticketed entrants. In fact, Scott intentionally incited the crowd, specifically *encouraging* the dangerous atmosphere, and continued the concert for over an hour knowing that there were previous and ongoing security and safety issues, even while large swaths of the fans in the audience were chanting for him to stop the concert.

Many of the additional defendants, as noted earlier, maybe a liability on theories of respondeat superior or contributory negligence. Abbot's Task Force on Concert Safety reported that was confusion as to which agency, state or private, was responsible for logistics, which made it unclear as to which authority to be needed to take charge when things went awry. In addition, the process for obtaining a permit and establishing occupancy load requirements proved to be inconsistent and jurisdiction, normally ceded in the fire department, was unclear. Finally, the responsibility for responding to an emergency call for event incidents was split between the fire department and city 911 personnel, so consistency amongst the emergency crews was not present. These mitigating factors may distribute some of the damages among the various defendants but will not eliminate the responsibilities of Mr. Scott.

The complaint filed in this litigation is instructive for purposes of illustrating how a proper pleading should be drafted. The complaint, sometimes as here known as a "petition," is the first step necessary to file a lawsuit in any jurisdiction. Most jurisdictions have guidelines for the style that should be followed when drafting a petition or complaint. This case, as you can see from the style, was filed in a Texas state court, the District

---

[3] "Latest Astroworld Festival lawsuit claims disaster was 'months, if not years, in the making,'" ABC 13 Eyewitness News.

Court of Harris County, Texas, where the incidents took place. One of the first considerations that is examined when an attorney drafts a complaint is which court has *subject matter jurisdiction* over the matter, and subject matter jurisdiction is easy to ascertain when an act of negligence occurs in the court's sovereignty.[4]

Once subject matter jurisdiction is established, the style of the case can evolve, and the parties are identified in the left-hand column, whereas the court having jurisdiction is identified in the right-hand column of the style. You may also note that the right-hand column also obtains a case number. When the court clerk accepts the complaint for filing, a number is assigned to the litigation for the court and attorneys to track it. Finally, the style also contains a very important indicator as to whether the plaintiff wishes to have her case tried by a jury of her peers, as is her Sixth Amendment right, or tried by the bench. If a jury trial is desired, it is usually indicated here and, in most jurisdictions, is a requirement. In the federal courts, the "form" of the complaint is dictated by the Federal Rules of Civil Procedure (FRCP). With regard to the "caption," as it is called there, the Rule 10 states:

> **Caption; Names of Parties.** Every pleading must have a caption with the court's name, a title, a file number, and a Rule 7(a) designation. The title of the complaint must name all the parties; the title of other pleadings, after naming the first party on each side, may refer generally to other parties.

Following the caption or style of the complaint will be the title of the documents—in the reference Scott case it is titled "PLAINTIFFS' ORIGINAL PETITION" followed by an introduction, usually a paragraph or two, that describes the incidents that led up to the filing of the complaint. It is important to notice at this point that the Astroworld Petition was a state court action based on negligence, and as such the paragraphs are not numbered seriatim; if this were a federal court, each of the paragraphs is required to be numbered as required by Rule 10, cited earlier, so that the following pleadings, such as the defendants' answers, can reference the paragraphs in order.

The next relevant section in the Astroworld Petition, Section III, identifies the parties.[5] These are identified either individually or by description of a business entity. In federal complaints, they are numbered

[4] There are other ways to establish subject matter jurisdiction, which are not relevant to the discussion here.

[5] Section II of the Astroworld Petition contained a reference to the chosen "Discovery Control Plan" based on local rules. In almost every jurisdiction, whether state courts or federal, each circuit or district will likely have their own set of local rules to which a drafter must comply.

in sequence. Since the complaint is a product of the plaintiff, the descriptions of the plaintiffs will be somewhat more general than the descriptions of the defendants, which will almost certainly include statements designed to show to the court that it has *personal jurisdiction* over that defendant and, in some case, telling the court where service may be made. For example, in the Astroworld Petition, when describing Apple, Inc., the description is:

> Defendant Apple, Inc. is a foreign corporation formed under California law and based in Cupertino, California. Defendant has *systematic, continuous, and specific contacts conduct, and business activities, including, but not limited to, its conduct relating to the subject incident, within Texas* such that it is at home in the state. This Defendant may be served through its Texas based registered agent, C T Corp System, at 1999 Bryan St., Ste. 900, Dallas, TX 75201-3136 USA.

This description is telling the court that the contact that the Apple corporation has sufficient contact with both the state of Texas and the incident out of which the cause of action arises to warrant it being considered "at home in the state." Personal jurisdiction or *in personam* jurisdiction refers to a court's power over a person (or entity) who is a party to, or involved in, a case or controversy before the court, including its power to render judgments affecting that person's rights.[6] The concept of personal jurisdiction is based on the due process clause of the Fifth Amendment to the U.S. Constitution, ratified in 1791, which states that "[n]o person shall be. . . deprived of life, liberty, or property, without due process of law. . . ." In the early days of the United States, following the American Revolution, the interaction between state and federal laws was still very much in fluctuation. A resident of a different state who received an adverse judgment from another state's court could wait until the winning party sought to obtain enforcement of the judgment in their state. At that time, the nonresident could challenge the foreign court's order on the basis of personal jurisdiction, that is, that the court did not have the power to affect their personal rights or enforce any judgment against them.

In 1868, when the Fourteenth Amendment's equal protection under the law was ratified, the due process rights were extended to the states:

> No State shall make or enforce any law which shall abridge the privileges or immunities of citizens of the United States; nor shall any State deprive any person of life, liberty, or property, without due process of law; nor deny to any person within its jurisdiction the equal protection of the laws.

The Supreme Court's 1877 decision in *Pennoyer v. Neff*[7] addressed the enforceability of an adverse order issued by an Oregon resident against a nonresident where the nonresident had not been personally served but, rather, the "service" was by publication in a newspaper. The Supreme Court in *Pennoyer* clarified the issue of personal jurisdiction as a federal question based on the fairly new Fourteenth Amendment and thereby restricted the power of state courts to render final judgments

---

[6] *Personal Jurisdiction*, Black's Law Dictionary, 10th Ed. (2014).

[7] 95 U.S. 714 (1878).

affecting the personal rights of defendants who do not reside within the state's territory. Such a defendant may obtain a direct review of a state court's judgment in federal court on the grounds that the state court lacked personal jurisdiction.

Over the half-century or so following the ratification of the Fourteenth and the *Pennoyer* decision the Supreme Court refined *in personam* jurisdiction, most notably in *International Shoe,* in which they bifurcated personal jurisdiction in *general* and *specific* types.[8] A state court may constitutionally exercise specific jurisdiction when a nonresident defendant has sufficient contacts with the forum "giving rise" to, that is, related to, the plaintiff's cause of action, for example, an act or occurrence caused by the defendant that takes place in the forum or has an impact there. In the Astroworld Petition, it can be said that many of the corporate defendants exercised specific jurisdiction by interacting with the state and with Scott to host a performance there and sell tickets to residents of that state. By contrast, a state court may exercise general jurisdiction over a nonresident defendant for any claim in which the defendant's activities in the forum state are so *substantial* that it is "reasonable" to require it to defend a lawsuit that did not arise out of its specific activities in the forum state and is unrelated to those activities. In more recent years, the Supreme Court has narrowed the application of general jurisdiction, significantly limiting the types of activities or affiliations sufficient for application of general jurisdiction, holding that those contacts must be "so substantial" as to render the defendant *essentially at home* in the forum state.[9] The court clarified the phrase "essentially at home" to mean, absent exceptional circumstances, that a corporate defendant is "at home" when it is incorporated in the forum state or maintains its principal place of business there (e.g., the corporation is headquartered in the state).[10] Referring to the Astroworld Petition at Section IV, every complaint whether state or federal will include such a statement as to the subject matter and personal jurisdiction of the court in order to establish that the court has authority over both the issues in the complaint and over the defendants personally.

[8] *Int'l Shoe Co. v. Washington*, 326 U.S. 310, 319 (1945).

[9] *Goodyear Dunlop Tires Operations, S.A. v. Brown*, 564 U.S. 915, 919 (2011) (a court may assert general jurisdiction over foreign (sister-state or foreign-country) corporations to hear any and all claims against them when their affiliations with the state are so "continuous and systematic" as to render them essentially at home in the forum state.).

[10] *Goodyear*, 564 U.S. at 924 (noting an individual's domicile and a corporation's place of incorporation or principal place of business as paradigm bases for general jurisdiction) (citation omitted); *id.* at 930 n.6 ([E]ven regularly occurring sales of a product in a state do not justify the exercise of jurisdiction over a claim unrelated to those sales.).

Once the legalities of the complaint have been addressed in the preliminary sections of the complaint, the attorney will then turn to a more systematic and detailed statement of the facts. In state court complaints, the organizational structure of this section may vary. In the Astroworld Petition, the complaint is structured according to each defendant to describe the factual situation that supports their causes of action against each, first by grouping the defendants based on their responsibilities and then, in the following section, associating the defendants with the claims being made in similar order. In the Astroworld Petition, defendants are in groupings related to the performer as well as the record labels, security entities, medical services, and those responsible for the physical structures of the event.

As noted above, when the complaint is being filed in federal court, the individual paragraphs in this section would be numbered, each seriatim, so that the defendant(s) can respond to each in kind. This section is where the attorney drafting the complaint can tell a story, perhaps exercising a bit of style as to how the facts are laid out, in order to clearly present the incident such that a judge or jury will have no trouble following along. Make no mistake, this is an art form.

Notice a couple of legal style techniques used in the Astroworld Petition, for example, when a defendant is first defined, the attorney assigned a defined term to that defendant, thus "Darryl Lamonte Platt (Live Nation Entertainment, Inc.'s Director of Operations), Live Nation Worldwide, Inc., and Live Nation Entertainment, Inc." become collectively "Live Nation." In other words, the shorthand "Live Nation" services identified all subsequent references to this collective set of defendants. In addition, perusing the Astroworld Petition, you will notice that the attorneys used multiple diagrams and photographs in telling the story of November 5th at Astroworld. Since a complaint consists primarily of what is called "notice pleading" under many jurisdictions, these illustrations serve simply to help tell the story and therefore should not be considered as evidence. In fact, in the courtroom, if an attorney introduces any one of these items as evidence to present to the witness and/or the jury, the attorney must first "lay a foundation" and establish the admissibility of the evidence.[11] People outside the legal profession often confuse the allegations and contents in a complaint with fact, but there are merely the assertions of the plaintiff, and they must still be weighed on the scales of Lady Justice and the defendant must get her "day in court."

Once the facts have been organized to tell the plaintiff's story in the clearest fashion, the remainder of the complaint essentially details the lawyer's theories of the case, organized by means of "claims" or "causes of actions," each identifying a separate allegation, explaining how the facts outlined to meet the required standard of proof for that cause of action, and asking the court to apply appropriate remedies. For example, on page 51 of the Astroworld Petition, after describing in detail the failures of all of the defendants that resulted in negligence in the fulfillment of their duty, the attorney summarizes that as "a direct and proximate result of the Defendants'" actions, the plaintiffs' "suffered serious injuries and damages including physical injuries, severe emotional distress, pain and suffering, medical expenses, and other economic

[11] Wide latitude is generally given under the Federal Rules of Evidence–FRE 401 defines "Relevant evidence" as "evidence having any tendency to make the existence of any fact that is of consequence to the determination of the action more probable or less probable than it would be without the evidence"–it is still necessary to lay a foundation I order to verify the origin and credibility of each piece of evidence.

and non-economic damages in amounts in excess of the jurisdictional limits of this Court." In the next paragraph, the attorney alleges that their conduct was "indifferent" and "malicious," mitigating factors that allegedly increase the negligence to a level of "gross negligence," which should result in "punitive damages . . . not subject to capping." In the Astroworld Petition, since the attorneys are representing a collective group of plaintiffs, there is an additional section following the causes of actions that then summarizes the specific damages incurred by each plaintiff.

Judicial remedies, that is, remedies available to a court sitting in civil judgment, are generally divided into two types: *legal* and *equitable*. Both types of damages are present in the Astroworld Petition. The common type of *legal* remedy, and the one most familiar to people, is money damages, that is, damages that somehow compensate the plaintiff, most often referred to in legal parlance as "compensatory" damages. These types of legal remedies arise in what is known as "courts of law." Compensatory damages are paid directly to the plaintiff to compensate her for loss and injury when the defendant is proven to be liable for a breach of duty resulting in damages. In cases where the plaintiff has been injured, it is sometimes relatively easy to calculate an amount that compensates them for actual out-of-pocket expenses associated with the incident, such as resulting medical expenses. *Consequential* damages, also known as *special* damages, on the other hand, are not as easily calculated: they are intended to compensate for the *indirect consequences* incurred by the defendant, such as loss of wages resulting from their injuries, and are awarded on a case-by-case basis due to the specific application to *ad hoc* fact patterns. In some circumstances, however, such as in this case where *malicious* activity rises to the level of *gross negligence*, the court can also employ another somewhat vaguely defined remedy known as *punitive damages*. Punitive damages employ the social reform theory of judicial activism, where the goal is to punish the defendant, discouraging her from engaging in the behavior that caused the damages and deterring others from engaging in similar behavior in the future. For this reason, in some jurisdictions, punitive damages may be referred to, as in the Astroworld Petition, as *exemplary* damages, because they are intended to set an example. Whatever they may be called, punitive or exemplary damages are awarded at the discretion of the court. Most, but not all, legal remedies are structured through a combination of common law, and state and federal statutes, where damages, or ranges of damages, are clearly defined and sometimes enumerated.[12]

© Vitalii Vodolazskyi/Shutterstock.com

In contrast to these legal remedies, originally were the purview of the courts of law, the original "courts of equity" from our English ancestry would dispense remedies that were *equitable* in nature, that is, when there was no sufficient remedy at law, the court would dispense an equitable remedy based on their sense of justice.

[12] Many federal laws, such as the Copyright Act of 1976, prescribe "statutory" damages.

Thus, the image of the blind lady justice weighing the equity of the situation was personified. In the twelfth and thirteenth centuries, the "Court of King's Bench" followed the King of England around the country dispensing justice, usually on an equitable basis. The King's Bench was made up of the *curia regis*, Latin for "royal counsel," consisting of various advisers, administrators, barons, and other royal officers. The King's Bench, as the name implies, served under the authority of the King himself. As it evolved over the centuries, the concept of an *equitable* remedy, then, is one that is dispensed at the discretion of the court, as it was in the King's Bench. In its broadest sense, this "equity" is said to operate on the *conscience* of the defendant, so an *equitable remedy* is always directed at a specific person, and that person's *state of mind* and *motives* may be relevant as to whether the remedy should be granted or not. In other words, the question, in equity, is what constitutes justice in this factual scenario. This discretionary application distinguishes equitable remedies from legal remedies. The most commonly applied equitable remedies are injunctive relief, specific performance of a contract, an accounting of profits, rescission of a contract, and equitable estoppel, among others.

© Maxx-Studio/Shutterstock.com

Finally, every complaint will end with a "prayer" to the court for specific amounts of relief separately identified, as found in Section X of the Astroworld Petition. The fact that is called a "prayer" connects it back to the English ancestry of our court system, when King Henry VIII was given the title of the "Defender of the Faith and Supreme Governor of the Church of England." As a nominal sovereign and head of the Church, the King stood in the position of God, as it were, at least in certain matters, particularly when acting as the head of justice. Even now, the standard mantra of British citizens is a form of prayer: "God save the King." From this historical context, it is easy to understand how this evolved into the modern practice of "praying" to the judge, the person in the courtroom who stands in for Lady Justice. In the Astroworld Petition, the plaintiff *prays* for legal damages in the amount of Five Hundred Million Dollars and punitive damages in the amount of Two Hundred Fifty Million Dollars.

Once the complaint is filed with the clerk of the court, the clerk issues summons to the various defendants which the plaintiff must serve individually on each defendant. The service of process, a part of the due process requirement of the constitution, can sometimes take months to complete. Once served, a defendant has between 20 and 60 days to respond, either by responding to the complaint in what is called an "answer" to the allegations, or by filing a motion to either dismiss the case for failure to state a claim. A motion to dismiss is warranted where the factual allegations, even if all are assumed to be true, do not establish a legally sufficient claim at law or equity. Frequently, when the defendant chooses to file an answer to the complaint, the defendant will raise counterclaims and affirmative defenses as components of the answer.

Once the complaint is filed and the defendants respond with motions and answers, the pleadings phase of the litigation is in full swing. Most courts will then set a date for a case management conference to discuss deadlines for various aspects of the case, including discovery, disclosures, and a trial date. The next phase in the litigation is the discovery phase, in which the parties serve interrogatories, document requests, and party and witness depositions, including experts. Once that phase is complete, the motion phase begins, which includes both dispositive and any pretrial motions. At the dispositive motion phase, both parties will generally ask the court to rule on summary judgment motions based on the facts derived from the discovery phase that are undisputed. If the summary judgment motions fail, the trial is scheduled and the fun begins!

12 Litigating Copyright Infringement Actions

CASE NO. 11	CHAPTER CASE STUDY	Debate Question	
		Can a collection of otherwise non-protectable ideas, taken as a whole, constitute an enforceable copyright?	
	Williams et al. v. Frankie Christian Gaye, et al., No. 15-56880 (Slip Op.; Dkt. 93-1) (2018 9th Cir.) cert. denied.	**Affirmative**	**Negative**
		Yes, if it conveys a "stamp of fresh authorship."	No, an idea is never entitled to copyright protection.

The enforcement of copyrights is one of the primary responsibilities of an entertainment attorney and, as we have seen, can be a prototype for litigation in all areas of intellectual property litigation. It is the most critical means by which a copyright owner can enforce a copyright. It is, in fact, the way the government supports contracts of all types, including social contracts, by giving its citizens a means to protect their rights and exclusive monopolies. Yet, in today's culture, the enforcement of copyright through infringement litigation is often portrayed in the

© arvzdix/Shutterstock.com

blogosphere and social media as conglomerate greed. Some antagonists who would prefer that society eliminate the concept of intellectual property have dubbed people who enforce their properties as "copyright trolls," which Wikipedia defines as "a . . . [person or company] that enforces copyrights it owns for purposes of making money through litigation, in a manner considered unduly aggressive or opportunistic. . . ." That definition comes very close to describing the enforcement of any kind of right, not just copyright, so great caution and careful thought should be given before a person or company is demonized for utilizing the mechanisms established over the course of centuries for enforcing and sustaining the delicate balance between the rights of society and those of an individual property owner. That balance is necessary for the function of government and is inherent in the social contract.

This negative trend in the zeitgeist of modern society can be clearly seen in the manipulation of the social media and blogosphere messaging that surrounded the recent case of *Williams et al. v. Frankie Christian Gaye et al.*[1] ("Williams"), which involved the infringement of Marvin Gaye's classic soul recording, "Got to Give It Up" by the song written by Williams for Robin Thicke called "Blurred Lines." The plaintiffs in that case, Williams and Thicke, and their Hollywood attorney, Howard King, effectively utilized the Internet and their massive social media followers to distribute the message that "Blurred Lines" was merely paying homage to Marvin Gaye as well as the entire genre of Motown artists, and Williams's intent in writing the song was simply to imitate a style or genre. If that depiction of the facts were true, the "sky is falling" mentality that became viral on the web may have been justified, since that would be merely copying an idea, the very building blocks of creativity we discussed earlier. But as will be seen as we dissect the case, King's theory of the case ended up biting him and his clients in the proverbial keister.

© Christopher David Howells/Shutterstock.com

The Williams case will be used as a template to examine the elements of copyright infringement because it is actually an excellent example of how the legal system works flawlessly. Historically, copyright infringement has been described as piracy, a word ultimately derived from the Greek word πειρατής (pronounced pira 'tis), which literally means "one who steals from ships." The implication is that copyright infringement is a type of stealing or theft. The word piracy was inserted into common parlance in the sixteenth and seventeenth centuries, in particular reference to people who exercised exclusive rights that belonged to others (*i.e.,* specifically copyright infringement). Ben Franklin's printing press in Philadelphia was, at least in part, responsible for its being used in America. Franklin was the preeminent "pirate" of his day, republishing the works of numerous British authors without asking permission and certainly without payment of royalties. This led to the objection of British authors such as Charles Dickens and Daniel DeFoe, both of whom complained that their popular London publications were being "pirated again and again" in the new colonies. Within two weeks of the publication of *A Christmas Carol*, for example, illicit copies were reportedly being sold on the streets of Philadelphia and New York for pennies on the dollar in comparison to the original publication. Dickens's objections to America's disrespect for his ownership rights were persistent, frequent, and cacophonic. When he came to America in 1842 to the accolades of adoring fans and colleagues, he naturally used his notoriety as a platform to implicate the American publishers who oppress the creative class by stealing their work for their own gain. His accusations that the

[1] No. 15-56880 (Slip Op.; Dkt. 93-1) (Mar. 21, 2018, 9th Cir.).

American press were pirates and his persistence that America adopt stronger international copyright protections for foreign writers were not well received by the American public or, of course, the press. Nonetheless, his stump speeches increased awareness of the problems and started a dialogue that would ultimately, in fact, lead to tighter U.S. controls and statutes[2]

© Everett Collection/Shutterstock.com

According to our current Copyright Act of 1976 any legal or beneficial owner of an exclusive right can bring an action against anyone who infringes those rights.[3] That section defines "who" can bring a copyright infringement action under the current regime. Note that, contrary to those who would ridicule the copyright troll who does not actually exploit the works it chooses to enforce, the only requirement here is that the enforcer is the legal or beneficial owner of the work or works being enforced. The statute does not specify the additional moral requirements of the antagonists.

© Drop of Light/Shutterstock.com

With regard to what types of infringing activities can be controlled through an action to enforce ownership of a copyright, 17 U.S.C. §501(a) specifies that "anyone who violates any of the exclusive rights of the copyright owner as provided by §§106–118, or who imports copies or phonorecords into the United States . . . is an infringer of the copyright." The §106 bundle of rights referred to in this section of the Act includes the right to publish, reproduce, and distribute the work, as well as the rights to create derivative works and publicly perform and display the work. Within those defined rights are the included privileges of selling, transferring, and assigning the works as well. This means the beneficial owner of a copyrighted work can bring a copyright infringement action against any person or entity that uses, or interferes with, any of those rights without his or her permission.

© Tolikoff Photography/Shutterstock.com

As indicated above, copyright law is federal legislation, and therefore a copyright infringement complaint must be filed in a Federal Court, specifically, a United States District Court.

[2] Kathryn Goldman, "Charles Dickens and the American Copyright Problem," Creative Law Center, accessed March 19, 2020, https://creativelawcenter.com/dickens-american-copyright/.

[3] 17 U.S.C. §501(b).

The complaint should allege sufficient facts to establish the essential elements of copyright infringement. The first element that must be alleged and established is that of the requirement of §501(a) that the plaintiff owns a valid copyright. Second, the plaintiff has to allege and prove that the defendant actually copied the copyright he or she owns. Finally, the plaintiff must allege and establish that the elements copied by the defendant amount to an improper appropriation of the original copyrighted work and that those misappropriated elements are substantially similar to the original. So, to summarize, the plaintiff in a copyright infringement action must show that the defendant actually copied elements of a copyright owned by the plaintiff and that those elements were misappropriated.

In order to prove the allegations of an infringement complaint to a trier of fact, the plaintiff must present sufficient evidence—facts, witnesses, and documents—establishing its burdens of proof (*i.e.,* the amount of evidence that must be produced to tip the scales of justice in plaintiff's favor and convince the trier of fact that the allegations contained in the complaint are true). The Act is vague about what the plaintiff's burden of proof is when establishing liability in an infringement case. Some courts have, to varying degrees, allocated burdens of proof in copyright infringement actions, but there is no direct statute on point. With regard to intellectual property in general, the Supreme Court has recently affirmed that in regard to patents specifically, the burden of proof is the clear and convincing standard. By comparative analysis, then, the burden in a copyright infringement action is this same standard, clear, and convincing, which means that the plaintiff must show that it is more probable than not that the matter asserted is true. That is an exceedingly high standard, just shy of the beyond a reasonable doubt standard with which most viewers of the popular *Law & Order and CSI* dramas will be familiar.

To illustrate how difficult it can be to prove an element with clear and convincing evidence, imagine yourself sitting on a park bench next to a walking trail. You are reading a book underneath a large tree, behind which is a row of bushes and plants. Next to you, along the path about three feet to your left, is a garbage can. After a few minutes of reading your book, you hear something hit the trash can and out of the corner of your eye see something land between you and the garbage can. You look up and notice a rock lying there. In this scenario, it really cannot be maintained that you have any credible evidence of anything, even though this minimal burden of proof is not remarkably high. To achieve the standard of credibility, if you are sitting there another few minutes, and the next time out of the corner of your eye you see a red blur and then hear the rock hit the trash can and bounce into the same location as the first rock, that adds another piece of evidence to the scales of justice, tipping them ever so slightly. Now, there may be sufficient evidence (*i.e.,* your testimony about the two rocks hitting the trash can and the red blur) to assert that it is more likely than not that something is propelling the rock toward the trash can in order to make it ricochet onto the same spot on the ground. Even at this level of proof, the conclusion is not certain and verifiable, as it could still be serendipitous that the two rocks landed in the same location. The next level of proof, substantial evidence, requires a little bit more certainty, but not too much. Another instance or two of the rock periodically hitting the trash can and falling into the same location would likely eliminate the element of coincidence and uncertainty experienced under the base-level burden of proof. This leads to the next level of proof, which is a preponderance of the evidence. A preponderance is the general level of evidence necessary to prove allegations in matters of civil litigation. Either party asserting a claim must introduce evidence that supports the elements by a preponderance of the evidence, meaning it is more likely than not that the matter asserted is true and factual. What would be required in our park bench scenario, then, for the evidence to rise to this level of persuasion? If you are still sitting on the bench after the four rocks have hit the can, each landing in the same spot, you will be more attuned to your surroundings. On the fifth occasion, then, again out of the corner of your eye, you see a red blur moving in the bushes behind and then the rock strikes the can and lands in the same spot. You quickly turn and see the faint blur of a red checkered shirt scuttling off behind you, out of sight. Now you are able to allege a highly likely conclusion that there is a person who is wearing a red plaid shirt, throwing rocks at the can in order to attract your attention, or playing a prank. That constitutes a preponderance of evidence and tips the scale more in favor of justice.

© Lightspring/Shutterstock.com

While some researchers have argued that preponderance is the burden of proof required in copy-right infringement actions,[4] in many jurisdictions the required proof is one step beyond this, which brings us to the clear and convincing burden. Where the preponderance standard is based on likely possibilities, the clear and convincing standard, as noted earlier, is based on probabilities, such that the evidence presented to the trier of fact must convince them that it is more probable than not that your allegation is true. Stated differently, to meet the clear and convincing burden, the plaintiff must produce evidence that satisfies the trier of fact that there is a high degree of probability that what is alleged is actually what happened. For our scenario, the final piece of evidence that might tip the scale from the point of preponderance to clear and convincing might be this: suppose you ask the next passerby on the walking trail if they saw anyone in the bushes and they indicate that, in fact, they saw a man in a red lumberjack shirt throwing something in the direction of the trash cans just a few minutes before, at approximately the same time you witnessed the red blur and heard the sixth rock hit the trash can. The second witness says, "Why yes, of course, I saw a young man with blonde hair and a red plaid flannel shirt running away from this area." That is clear and convincing evidence for the assertion that there is a man throwing rocks at the trash can and making them ricochet in your direction. The final standard, beyond a reasonable doubt, simply eliminates any other probabilities: the assertion being argued is the only conclusion (probability) that can be drawn under the facts. This last standard is never used in civil cases, including copyright infringement actions.

© Juli Hansen/Shutterstock.com

[4] See, for example, Lydia Pallas Loren and R. Anthony Reese, "Proving Infringement: Burdens of Proof in Copyright Infringement Litigation," *Lewis & Clark Review* 23, no. 2: 624.

The types of evidence a party can use to establish these various burdens can be grouped into two categories: direct and indirect. Direct evidence can be satisfied either by a defendant confessing or admitting to the alleged activity or by the testimony of a credible witness as to the allegations. It may also take the form of documentary or physical evidence. In the 2000 elections, when Associated Press photographer Manny Garcia accused Shepherd Fairy of infringing his photograph of President Barack Obama, Fairy ultimately admitted that Garcia's photograph was among those that he used to create the famous "Hope Poster." While a confession is great and of considerable weight and credibility, those are rare, particularly in copyright infringement actions, as the Ninth Circuit noted in the Williams matter where Robin Thicke gave several interviews to the press in which he stated that he asked Williams to create a song that sounded like his idol Marvin Gaye, and specifically the song at issue, "Got to Give It Up." His later denial that these statements were true because he was high at the time the statements were made actually gives more credibility to their probative value. More often than not, however, direct evidence is third-party testimony or physical evidence. If, for example, Fairy used an apprentice to help create the Hope Poster, and that apprentice supplied copies of the photographs used and testified that she assembled the photographs for Fairy that would constitute direct evidence.

If you watch enough Hollywood legal dramas, you inevitably hear one of the attorneys in a courtroom raise the objection "that is circumstantial, your Honor." That objection alludes to a second category called indirect evidence. In copyright infringement actions, since infringers rarely admit to the act as did Thicke, circumstantial evidence tends to be the most common: evidence that the songs sound substantially similar or use similar melodic melodies, or have lyrics in common. This type of indirect evidence requires that the trier of fact infer the fact of copying from the evidence presented. An expert musicologist, for example, uses circumstantial evidence when they present comparisons between the original song and the infringing song that show similarities between the two works so substantial that it allows the trier of fact to draw the inference not only that the defendant had access to the original work, but also that protectable elements were intentionally copied. The following quote is how the Ninth Circuit summarized the indirect evidence presented by the experts' testimony on behalf of Marvin Gaye on appeal of the Williams matter:

> Finell[5] testified that "Blurred Lines" and "Got To Give It Up" share many similarities, including the bass lines, keyboard parts, signature phrases, hooks, "Theme X," bass melodies, word painting, and the placement of the rap and "parlando" sections in the two songs. She opined that nearly every bar of "Blurred Lines" contains an element similar to "Got To Give It Up." Although the district court had filtered out "Theme X," the descending bass line, and the keyboard rhythms as unprotectable at summary judgment, Finell testified that those elements were in the deposit copy. Dr. [Ingrid] Monson played three audio-engineered "mash-ups" she created to show the melodic and harmonic compatibility between "Blurred Lines" and "Got To Give It Up." She testified that the two songs shared structural similarities on a sectional and phrasing level.

---

[5] Dr. Judith Finell, Quincy Jones Professor of African American Music at Harvard University, and musicologist.

Here, Dr. Finell's testimony that Williams placed a rap section in "Blurred Lines" that started and ended on the same measures where Marvin Gaye created the parlando (a precursor to rap) was clear and convincing indirect evidence that Williams had copied protectable elements of Marvin's original "Got to Give It Up." This allowed the jury to draw the inference and conclude that Williams was copying more than just the genre or style of Motown, but rather copied something that was unique to Marvin Gaye (*i.e.,* the parlando), that no other act in Motown used. This was perhaps the death knell that eviscerated King's theory of the case and swung the balance of the scales in Gaye's favor.

All evidence presented at trial, whether direct or indirect, is judged by the trier of fact. In a copyright infringement litigation, the trier of fact is chosen by the plaintiff and can either be a bench trial, where the judge is the trier of fact, or a jury trial, where the jurors are the triers of fact and the judge issues opinions and rulings of law. Either way, the trier of fact evaluates the evidence presented by both parties as to its weight, credibility, and value. This is where the symbolic scales of justice are tipped in favor of the winning party by the weight of evidence.

Returning to the discussion about the burden of proving the individual elements of copyright through direct and indirect evidence, most jurisdictions require a higher level of clear and convincing, while some will allow the standard of a preponderance, so it is important to research and understand the specific requirements in the plaintiff's jurisdiction to ascertain the proper burden of proof to apply to a copyright infringement action.[6] Regardless of the burden of proof applied, that burden is clearly on the shoulders of the plaintiff to establish each element of copyright infringement. The following analysis will examine and outline each element individually using the Williams trial as the prototype:

[6] The Supreme Court recently upheld the clear and convincing standard when applied to a different type of intellectual property (*i.e.,* patents), in Microsoft Corp. v. i4i Limited Partnership, 564 US 91 (2011) (finding that Microsoft needed to offer "clear and convincing evidence" to overcome the traditional presumption that patents approved by the U.S. Patent and Trademark Office are valid). The higher standard would most likely be required for proving the validity of a copyright as well.

Valid Ownership

For a plaintiff to prove ownership of a copyright, it is necessary to recall the Act's definition in 17 U.S. Code § 102(a), examined in the discussion of Feist above, which indicates that the owner may protect "*original* works of *authorship fixed* in any *tangible medium of expression*." The next section, 102(b), must also be considered as much as it exempts *ideas* and *concepts* from ownership.

© Debby Wong/Shutterstock.com

In order to own a **valid** copyright, then, a plaintiff's work must be *original*, that is it must possess what the *Feist* court called a *modicum of creativity* or, in another instance, a *stamp of fresh authorship. Feist* teaches that originality is the "*sine qua non* of copyright." This requirement accommodates a creator's need to build on the works of others by requiring copyrightable expression to be "independently created by the author" and have "at least some minimal degree of creativity"[7] must tip the needle of originality enough toward the §102(a) expression end of the spectrum to negate the argument that it is a mere idea or a building block of creation. On the other hand, if the needle does not move because the elements too closely resemble §102(b) facts, methods, or processes, then infringement is not possible.

In *Williams*, the plaintiffs Pharrell Williams and Robin Thicke were banking on the needle remaining on the ideal side of the spectrum. They adopted the strategy of their attorney, Howard King, and mounted a social media "sky is falling" blitz to spread the word that if they lost their case, songwriters could no longer use style or genre as inspiration for creation if they were found to be infringing. In her dissenting opinion in *Williams*, Judge Jacqueline H. Nguyen was clearly influenced by King's strategy when she parrots:

> "Blurred Lines" clearly shares the same "groove" or musical genre as "Got to Give It Up," which everyone agrees is an unprotectable idea. See, e.g., 2 William F. Patry, Patry on Copy-right § 4:14 (2017) ("[T]here is no protection for a communal style . . . ."). But what the majority overlooks is that two works in the same genre must share at least some protectable expression in order to run afoul of copyright law.[8]

But Judge Nguyen's analysis of the evidence presented by the musicologists in Williams, as ostensibly "complete" as it is, glosses over the most salient testimony of Dr. Finell regarding the parlando section of

[7] *Feist*, 499 U.S. at 345, 348.

[8] *Williams*, p. 61.

"Got to Give It Up" referenced earlier and dismisses it out of hand by mistakenly saying in a footnote that a parlando is merely a literary technique used by many, concluding without much discussion that:

> To say these two songs are substantially similar because they employ devices common to songwriting would be like saying two songs are substantially similar because they both have guitar solos in the middle even though the solos themselves bear no resemblance.[9]

Not only does Nguyen's conclusion shamelessly echo the plaintiff's strategy of the case, but also her guitar solo simile is misplaced and misguided, indicating a lack of understanding of basic copyright principles. Her analysis of the testimony recklessly ignores the weight and value of Dr. Finell's conclusions as a pre-eminent researcher and professor of African American Music at Harvard that the use of the parlando technique by Marvin Gaye was original to him and that no one else had used it in this way. In the context of the case, that technique is an indicator of originality, and the fact that Williams inserted a substantially similar technique at exactly the same location in his song allows the trier of fact to confidently draw the conclusion that an original element had been copied. Nguyen's analysis almost intentionally fails to address the connection.

© Kraft74/Shutterstock.com

A creator can also use direct evidence to prove *authorship* by taking the witness stand and testifying that they are the creator and relating details about how they created the work. Of course, she would be subject to the weight of cross-examination, and it would be up to the trier of fact to evaluate the credibility of the testimony against the effectiveness of that cross-examination. Weight can be added to her testimony, of course, if she was involved with a collaborator or an assistant who could verify her account of its creation, or if she kept a contemporaneous diary of the creation which supports the testimony.

Another amazingly effective means of directly proving *ownership* is to present the copyright registration certificate as evidence, which gives the registrant a *presumption* of the ownership information contained therein. This presumption means that the burden shifts and the defendant must then present evidence to contradict the presumption. In addition to the presumptive effect, the submission of a registration certificate is a *prerequisite* to filing a federal lawsuit. There is another important consideration to discuss in reference to registration. When a person registers his or her copyright, the Copyright Act requires that the registration include a deposit copy of the work, which was traditionally housed in the Library of Congress as a direct effect of the Progress Clause. This *deposit copy* is the reference point for copyright infringement actions; in that, it is what the presumptive owner is entitled to protect. In other words, the person alleging infringement must show that the infringer copied protectable elements of the deposit copy.

---

[9] *Ibid.*, pp. 78–79.

This issue also arose in the *Williams* matter. In 1977 when Marvin Gaye recorded and released "Got to Give It Up," most songwriters would submit sheet music as deposit copies, not the recordings of the musical composition as most songwriters do today. King relied on this to make a preliminary motion asking the judge to restrict the proof submitted to elements contained in the deposit copy (*i.e.,* the sheet music). He argued that it would be unfair for the jury to be able to listen to the sound recording of "Got to Give It Up." The district court agreed and limited the scope of Gaye's compositional copyright to what was contained in the six pages of sheet music on deposit with the United States Copyright Office. The result of this ruling is that the triers of fact never got to hear the Marvin Gaye recording in court, only a live rendition of the sheet music, and the expert musicologists had to base their analysis on the sheet music of "Got to Give It Up" versus the sound recording of "Blurred Lines." Even with that handicap, the jury was able to conclude that substantial similarities existed. In fact, this ruling may have actually contributed to the discovery that Williams's rap section was placed in the same measures as Gaye's unique parlando, which would not have been made as obvious by comparing recordings.

Fixed in a Tangible Medium

The final portion of §102(a) that must be proved is that the original work of authorship allegedly infringed be *fixed in a tangible medium of expression.* There are actually two components of this part: that the work is to be *fixed* and that it constitutes an *expression.*

The Act defines fixation in §101 as a work that is embodied in a sufficiently permanent or stable form in order "to permit it to be perceived, reproduced, or otherwise communicated *for a period of more than transitory duration.*" In the early evolution of computer-generated music and entertainment, the fixation issue came up in the context of a computer's random-access memory (RAM). RAM to a computer is like a notepad to a person on the phone. When the phone user receives instructions or directions, he or she writes them down on the notepad and then discards the note once the instructions are no longer needed. The same can be said about RAM: an electronic device places programming into RAM when it is being used and offloads it to the device's cache when the user needs to reference some other program or instruction with which it gets replaced in RAM. This is why if you have too many programs open on your device (*i.e.,* in RAM), the computer or device may be slower or inoperable because all of its memory is being utilized. Through the 1990s and 2000s, computer technology was advancing according to Moore's Law at a phenomenal rate of doubling in capacity every 2 years. This exponential growth in RAM speed created a significant copyright issue: is a creative work, such as a song, sufficiently fixed when it is streamed through a computer RAM such that it creates a copy in RAM as it is being used by the computer program to audibly play the music? Of course, copyright owners took

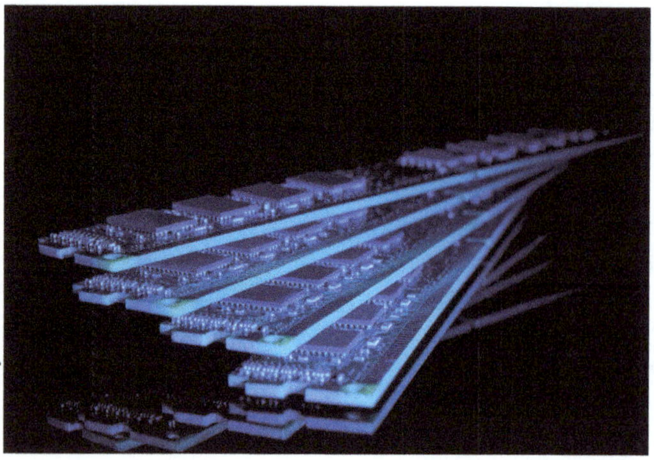

© Denis Dryashkin/Shutterstock.com

the position that a copy is a copy, but ultimately the courts arrived at a different conclusion. A copy made in computer RAM was not for "more than a transitory time" and was not therefore a *fixation* as defined in the Act, entitling its owner to copyright protection.[10] In the context of entertainment programs, the general consensus in the law now is that a creative work that is *streamed* over the Internet is not protected as a fixed copy, but rather as a public performance, whereas something that is *downloaded* to a device such as a file is sufficiently fixed to create a copy.

Expression

The last component of ownership as defined by §102 is that the work contains elements of expression as opposed to mere building blocks or ideas. This is the area of copyright law that the Supreme Court has referred to as *metaphysical* because copyright law protects things that are seemingly, at the time, intangible, while at the same time does not protect mere ideas (*i.e.,* the idea must be *expressed*). This concept supports the Progress Clause by offering protection for expressed ideas in order to encourage creators to share their thoughts and concepts with society to further progress. Refer back to the earlier section on *Feist* where this element was discussed in the context of the idea/expression dichotomy and its use in copyright infringement.

Actual Copying & Misappropriation

If it can be said from our analysis of the *ownership* element of copyright infringement that it is, perhaps, the most complex, then certainly it can be maintained that the most basic component of the copy "right" is the second element of *actual copying.* A detailed analysis of actual copying, however, also involves multiple levels of proof and dovetails nicely into the third element of *misappropriation.* First, it requires that the plaintiff proves that the defendant actually copied from the plaintiff's protected work rather than *independently* or *simultaneously* created a similar work based on a similar idea. Next, the proof must establish that the defendant's copy, or at least elements thereof, amounts to an *improper appropriation*, or misappropriation (*i.e.,* the defendant copied some elements from the plaintiff's copyrighted work that are protected by the idea/expression dichotomy). The plaintiff must show, in other words, that what was copied was an *expression* rather than an unprotected idea or building block.[11] Finally, the plaintiff must show that the defendant's actual copying of protected elements from the copyrighted work produced substantial similarity between the copied elements in the defendant's work and the protected expression in the plaintiff's work.

Logically, then copyright infringement begins with the defendant having *access* to the plaintiff's original expression. Simply put, in order to actually copy a person's work, the infringer would need *access* to that

[10] The two seminal cases on the issue were *MAI Systems Corp. v. Peak Computer, Inc.*, 991 F.2d 511, 518 (9th Cir. 1993), in which the 9th (2008), where the Second Circuit treated the RAM copy as a fixation and *Cartoon Network v. CSC Holdings,* 536 F.3d 1210 (2d Cir. Circuit disagreed and said that a buffered copy was transitory in nature and not fixed.).

[11] The idea/expression dichotomy permeates all elements of copyright infringement in order to balance the individual's right to own his or her creation against society's right to freely express ideas.

© Donna Vaughn/Shutterstock.com

work, just as a jewel thief needs to gain access to the jewel in order to pull off the heist. To prove access, the plaintiff would need to prove through the use of circumstantial evidence that it *is more likely than not* that the defendant had an opportunity to hear or view the copyrighted work. One means of indirectly proving that defendant had access to the work is to show that the work was distributed to the public over a widespread geographical area. For example, the photograph of Obama taken by Manny Garcia in the earlier example was distributed through the AP Newswire and was therefore printed in newspapers across the nation, giving rise to a significant probability that Shepherd would have had access to the photograph. Likewise, in the *Williams* case, Marvin Gaye's song "Got to Give It Up" peaked at No. 1 on the Billboard charts in 1977 and served as inspiration for not only Williams and Thicke but also over the generations, other artists such as Stevie Wonder and Michael Jackson. Like the Garcia photograph, as a number 1 hit, the Marvin Gaye recording had worldwide distribution and circulation as well as airplay on every major reporting station in the radio industry. Had Thicke and Williams not admitted to owning and listening to Gaye's work, which they did, access could have easily been shown by introducing indirect evidence of this widespread success.

Another way of proving access is for the plaintiff to prove that he or she distributed a copy of the work directly to the defendant through documentary evidence of delivery, testimony, or a combination of those two. Evidence of this type of widespread or direct access must show, by a clear and convincing standard, that the defendant had a *reasonable probability* of access, not just a *bare possibility*. Most publishers of books and music build their defense against this copyright infringement technique by *not accepting unsolicited material* sent randomly to their offices but rather establishing a standard operating procedure of documenting and destroying all such material received before opening the envelope. This way the publisher can credibly argue that even if the plaintiff submitted the work to them without their permission, it is most probable that it would have been deposited in the circular file.

© breakermaximus/Shutterstock.com

Even where the plaintiff establishes access by clear and convincing evidence, the connection between access to the work and actually copying is still somewhat tenuous, as there can exist a number of intervening causes. As we have seen, in fact, copying alone does not necessarily mean infringement. If a person copies a series of thematic references from a copyrighted book, they have certainly engaged in copying per se, but they most probably have not engaged in copyright infringement so long as the expression is not copied from the book. For copying to rise to the level of infringement, it must include a more than *de minimis* or trivial amount of copyrightable expression. The principle of copyright, called *scènes à faire*,[12] dictates that elements of a creative work *mandated by* or *customary to* a specific genre of works or by a scene are deemed to be not protected. If, for example, two separate authors write spy novels, each of which contains elements such as numbered Swiss bank accounts and safe deposit boxes filled with money and handguns, femme fatales, briefcases, exotic sports cars, and intriguing spy gadgets hidden in wristwatches, belts, shoes, and other personal effects, it can easily be concluded that, even if those elements seem to be in the same general order, the two separate authors independently created their separate expression based on the themes that are common in that genre of works.

Because of this tenuous connection between access and infringement, the plaintiff must also produce sufficient evidence for the trier of fact to conclude that there are *similarities* between the two works which are *substantial.* Furthermore, that evidence of similarity must tip the balance of probability in favor of *illicit* copying. In other words, the plaintiff must still show a *substantial similarity* between protectable elements of the copyrighted work and the alleged infringer's work that leads the trier of fact to the conclusion that it is more probable than not that the defendant had access. That will tip the scales of justice in favor of the plaintiff and a court will then presume that the defendant actually copied the plaintiff's work. Having established that necessary element, it must be pointed out that there are some rare cases where the similarities are so *striking* that a court may conclude that a defendant copied a work even if the plaintiff cannot prove that the defendant had access to the work, but a court would do so only when it believes that the similarities between the two works are so striking that there is *no reasonable possibility* that the defendant independently created the work and that the *similarities are coincidental.* Effectively in these civil cases, the court is saying that the evidence of striking similarity meets the criminal legal burden of *beyond a reasonable doubt.*

Even after the plaintiff has established access and substantial similarity, the Supreme Court still requires that the copyright be *improperly misappropriated.* The plaintiff must show that the defendant copied some of the *protected expressions* in the work (*i.e.,* those elements of the work entitled to copyright protection), which is the final element of copyright protection, *misappropriation.* In other words, the copyright must again be dissected and segregated into mere ideas and protectable

© Sunny Forest/Shutterstock.com

[12] French for "scene that must be done" or "derived from the scene." See, for example, *Walker v. Time Life Films, Inc.*, 615 F. Supp. 430 (S.D.N.Y. 1985).

expression using our idea/expression principle. In this regard, it may help to think of the copyright as a piece of Swiss cheese. I call this my *Swiss Cheese Theory* of copyright protection. While the Act indicates that the owner of the copyright owns an "undivided interest" in the whole piece of cheese, the ideas (*i.e.,* the holes), do not constitute part of what is owned. What is owned in substance must be separated from the empty holes and divots of ideas, concepts, themes, *scènes à faire*, and so on. These elements cannot be misappropriated, even though they can be, and are, essential components of the cheese.

In order to accomplish this centrifuge, the courts have developed several methodologies to determine whether unlawful appropriation has occurred. The first is often referred to as the subtractive method,[13] where elements that cannot be protected are subtracted from the whole before the fact finder determines whether substantial similarities exist between the protectable expression which remains and elements of the allegedly infringing work. A slight variation of this test is also known in some circuits as the *abstraction test.*[14] In contrast to the subtractive methodology, the *totality method* tries to examine the *total look and feel* of the creative works as a whole, including the ideas and the expression, when determining at first blush if substantial similarity exists.[15]

Using the totality methodology, the individual elements of the infringing work, when viewed in isolation, may be substantially different from their corresponding part in the original work but nevertheless *taken together,* that is, considered as a whole, be a clear misappropriation of copyrightable material. These two methodologies are polar opposites, and the result is that remarkably different results are produced throughout the various district and circuit courts with regard to cases that may be markedly similar on a factual basis. Because of that confusion, some courts have been known to combine the best of both methodologies in order to determine misappropriation, usually starting with the total look and feel to do a first blush, and then digging into the weeds by dissecting the works into their protectable components to see if the similarity holds up. This King Solomon "split the baby" approach can also result in various contradictory applications, as one method may find misappropriation where the other would not.[16]

Despite the problems, these methodologies can help refine the misappropriation element. Still, the application of this final prong of copyright infringement has raised contentious issues among both circuits and

[13] Adopted by the Sixth Circuit, for example, in *Kohus v. Mariol* (328 F.3d 848).

[14] The Ninth Circuit has its own terminology, referring to this as the "extrinsic" test because it requires a determination of what elements are protected. See, for example, *Sid & Marty Krofft Television Productions Inc. v. McDonald's Corp.,* 562 F.2d 1157 (9th Cir. 1977) (holding that a series of McDonald's commercials portraying "McDonaldland" had used as its basis the H.R. Pufnstuf television show. Corresponding characters to each, whereas displaying marked differences, taken altogether demonstrated that McDonald's commercials had captured the total concept and feel of the show and had thus infringed).

[15] In its ever-present vigilance to be different and novel, the Ninth Circuit calls this an "intrinsic" test because it asks whether the ordinary, reasonable observer would view the works as substantially similar.

[16] See, for example *Computer Associates International, Inc. v. Altai, Inc.,* 982 F.2d 693 (2nd Cir. 1992) (where court chose the subtraction method for two computer programs whose total concept were the same. Individual copied elements of the program were non-protectable material because they constituted a process or idea in the program, their utilitarian aspects barring copyright protection; no infringement found).

attorneys. When considering the proper analysis of misappropriation, recall the analysis of *Feist* where it was learned that although individual facts used to compose a compilation are not copyrightable in themselves, a compilation of facts is copyrightable if the selection and arrangement of the facts are sufficiently original. Applying this rationale to other works, it follows that although individual elements may not be copyrightable, the composite work would be protectable if the elements were assembled in a creative or original way. This is the Swiss Cheese approach. Substantial similarity and misappropriation in copyright infringement can be found in a combination of elements in a copyright, even if some of those elements would, taken individually, be unprotected.[17]

In *Williams*, both the court of first impression, a California district court, and the Ninth Circuit court of appeals, were obligated by precedence to use the abstraction or *extrinsic test* as California courts call it. When Williams filed for summary judgment prior to trial, Gaye's expert, Dr. Finell, offered her comparison of the two works *after removing the unprotected elements* per the extrinsic test, and opined that what remained was a "constellation" of eight similarities between "Got To Give It Up" and "Blurred Lines." These remaining similarities consisted of the signature phrase, hooks, hooks with backup vocals, "Theme X," backup hooks, bass melodies, keyboard parts, and unusual percussion choices. Williams's expert, Dr. Wilbur, disputed each area of similarity Finell identified and countered that there were *no substantial similarities* between the two compositions at issue if you focus solely on melodies, rhythms, harmonies, structures, and lyrics. Gaye's second expert, Dr. Monson, countered Wilbur's contradictory evidence by illustrating similarities between certain melodic and harmonic elements, as well as specific details such as the use of a cowbell, hand percussion, drum set parts, background vocals, and keyboard parts, as well as the parlando discussed before.

© James R. Martin/Shutterstock.com

The district court compared the various reports of the three musicologists and, pursuant to the extrinsic test, meticulously filtered out those elements it perceived were not in the deposit copy, including the backup vocals, the so-called Theme X, descending bass line, keyboard rhythms, and the percussion parts featuring the cowbell and drum sets. After performing this centrifuge, the court denied Williams's motion for summary judgment, identifying several of the remaining elements as *material issues of fact*, particularly the similarity of the songs' *signature phrases, hooks, bass lines, keyboard chords, harmonic structures, and vocal melodies*, all arguably *protectable elements* of Gaye's original expression.

[17] See, for example, *Satava v. Lowry*, 323 F.3d 805, 811 (9th Cir. 2003).

When the case went to trial, Gaye's lawyer, Nashville attorney Richard Busch, established through the testimony of his experts the important significance of the additional fact that the two songs had almost exactly the same number of measures as each other, and there was the *strikingly similar* occurrence of the rap section in "Blurred Lines" starting at exactly the same measure as the parlando section of "Got to Give It Up" and ending at the same measure as well. This critical piece of evidence proved to be a smoking gun, directly contradicting the King camp's theory of the case, as well as Judge Nguyen's reciting diatribe, that those elements that were appropriated by Williams in "Blurred Lines" were not just to "pay homage" to the *Motown genre* or some loosely defined "style," but rather were *protectable elements* that were the *unique expressions* of Marvin Gaye embedded in his original creation, "Got to Give It Up," his stamp of fresh authorship, in the words of *Feist.*

To summarize, Busch proved that "Blurred Lines" was an infringement of "Got to Give It Up" by building a preponderance of evidence to establish that Gaye owned the musical composition, that Williams and Thicke admitted that they had access to the work, and that substantially similar elements between the two works had been misappropriated. That is copyright infringement at its simplest.

13 Special Considerations in Music Infringement

CASE NO. 12			
	CHAPTER CASE STUDY	**Debate Question**	
		Can a songwriter subconsciously infringe on another musical composition?	
	Bright Tunes Music Corp. v. Harrisongs Music Ltd., 420 F. Supp. 177 (1976).	**Affirmative**	**Negative**
		Yes, if she is aware of the original song and subconsciously copies protectable elements.	No, copyright infringement requires awareness of copying, if not intent.

© PrinceOfLove/Shutterstock.com

The plaintiffs' misguided theory of the case in the *Williams*' matter—that is, that they were merely imitating a style—is nevertheless loosely based on the *correct* copyright principle that an individual cannot own any idea, including an entire genre of music, because of the prohibition of 17 U.S.C. §102(b). What made the plaintiffs' implementation of that section misguided was the fact that Williams had actually copied original elements of Gaye's creation. But the fact that there are a limited number of pleasing combinations of musical materials creates the inevitable possibility that there will be "overlaps" in notes, rhythms, chord progressions, stylistic choices, and so on, even though the permutations of musical compositions are unlimited. This occurs more frequently in the simplistic genres of today's music because of the frequent use of a limited set of chords and themes. With regard to comparing musical compositions for infringement purposes, however, it is crucial to keep the fact in mind that two works can be independently inspired by the same idea, and consequently similarities in musical works can coexist without the second work being a direct copy of the first work. In addition, similarities may be serendipitous or coincidental. One court summarized these principles as follows:

> It must be remembered that, while there are an enormous number of possible permutations of the musical notes of the scale, only a few are pleasing; and much fewer still suit the infantile demands of the popular ear. Recurrence is therefore not an inevitable badge of plagiarism.

There are, then, some special considerations involved in litigating copyright infringement actions involving musical compositions and/or sound recordings. The subtractive method of analyzing misappropriation discussed above is intended *precisely* to filter out any "elements that were not independently created" by the author and therefore do not possess the "minimal degree of creativity" to be original. This methodology, therefore, requires courts to identify which elements of the musical composition, if any, are *protected by copyright,* even before the works are compared analytically. Second, the courts must compare those protected elements of the original work to determine whether elements in the allegedly infringing work are "substantially similar" and therefore most likely copied. This second step requires the trier of fact to determine this similarity based on the judgment of the *ordinary lay observer.* This layman's approach simply asks the finder of fact to make a subjective determination as to whether the compared elements are similar.

Evidence of similarities between songs will usually focus on the melodic elements of the two musical compositions since the melody is the most memorable element of a song, particularly to the ordinary lay observer. Ironically, getting a layman to recognize the similarity often involves the use of expert witnesses. As was the case in *Williams,* similarities among other elements, such as lyrics, rhythm, and harmony, were compared, analyzed, and weighed by the experts. The plaintiff introduces expert evidence to prove that the defendant could not have independently created the infringing work because of the highly unique combination of elements both pieces share and *could not* exist without actual copying. In fact, some courts require a person with considerable musical training to analyze the two pieces of music in this manner and testify as to the substantial similarities between the two works.

Just like criminal defense attorneys, it is fairly common for the defense team in an infringement action to try to confuse the trier of fact in order to benefit their theory of the case and prove their client's "innocence." In the *Williams* matter, we noted that the defense team together with the defendants tried to influence the jury pool by forcing their theory of the case—that Williams was merely paying tribute to the Motown genre generally and Marvin Gaye specifically—to go viral in the social media world, a feat they achieved with great aplomb. An expert musicologist for the defendant will try to show that any similarities in the works are the result of either coincidence (simultaneous use of an idea or independent creation), using mere ideas that are not protected, fair use, prior art, or public domain materials.

As with all witnesses, the testimony of these expert musicologists is judged by the trier of fact as to its value, credibility, and weight of the evidence. It also must be remembered that experts are hired, and usually well-compensated, witnesses. That does not necessarily call into question their integrity, but they are most certainly incentivized, making it highly likely that they will testify in the manner that is most beneficial to their clients. This is a point that is often raised in their cross-examination.

Another consideration with regard to musical creation and copyright infringement is that it is based on *strict liability.* If you park your car on the corner of a city block without seeing or observing the "No Parking" sign hidden behind a tree branch, you will nonetheless most probably be issued a parking violation, as parking laws are also based on this concept of strict liability. Speed limit laws are similar in that it does not matter whether you *intend* to break the law, the fact that you are traveling 71 miles per hour in a 70-miles-per-hour speed zone means you broke the law and that makes you liable for the consequences under the strict liability theory. Applied to copyright infringement, this means that a person could infringe a previously created work based on what is in his or her *subconscious mind* at the time he or she created the musical composition, regardless of what his or her intention was at the time. This type of infringement hinges on something psychologists call *cryptomnesia,* which refers to the phenomenon of having an idea that *one believes to be original* to his or her, but which is *actually derived from some other, prior source.* These hidden memories lurk in our subconscious minds and sometimes march forth to masquerade as original thinking. The seminal case that dealt with the issue of subconscious infringement is *Bright Tunes Music Corp. v. Harrisongs Music, Ltd.*[1] in which the lead guitarist for The Beatles, George Harrison, is accused of infringing the Chiffon's top ten hit, "He's So Fine." In 1970, after the band broke up, George Harrison released his solo album, *All Things Must Pass,* from which the number one single "My Sweet Lord" was released in November of 1970. "My Sweet Lord" soared to the top of the Billboard charts in the U.S., reaching number one in record time, almost as if people were familiar with it already. That is because melodically, structurally, and rhythmically, the song was almost identical to "He's So Fine," written by Ronald Mack and recorded by the Chiffons in 1962. The original song also reached number one in America and charted at number twelve in England on June 1, 1963. That is significant because it is around the same time that the Beatles were touring Liverpool and paying their dues on their way to stardom. As a top twenty chart-topper, "He's So Fine" would have been playing in every club the Beatles played during their breaks.

© Angel DiBilio/Shutterstock.com

[1] 420 F. Supp. 177 (S.D.N.Y. 1976).

Mack's publisher, Bright Tunes, sued Harrison for copyright infringement in 1971. The musicologist for both sides agreed that "He's So Fine" incorporated three basic motifs. The first, G-E-D, or *sol-mi-re*, was repeated four times. The musicologists identified this as Motif A. The second, or Motif B, was *so-la-do-la-do* repeated four times. In the second occurrence of Motif B, a variation occurred in which a grace note was inserted, or Motif C, making the progression so-la-do-la-RE-do. Even though these progressions are building blocks from the public domain, both musicologists also agreed that this pattern of arrangement was "highly unusual."

The trier of fact was struck by the fact that "My Sweet Lord" uses the same patterns as "He's So Fine" and incorporates the *grace note* in exactly the same position. The court placed great significance on the positioning of the grace note as an indicator of actual copying. It is instructive to compare the identical placement of the grace note in this case to the facts of the *Williams* case where the exact positioning of the rap section in "Blurred Lines" occurred at the same measure as the parlando in "Got to Give it Up," a powerful similarity that mirrors the grace note in the *Harrison* case. In *Harrison*, the court also noted that the *harmonies* are identical, not an element that is normally part of consideration in copyright infringement since harmonies are generally said to be dictated by melodies. The *Harrison* case illustrates how the *selection of which harmonies* are included in a composition can be seen by the court as an element of protection. Comparing these two cases reveals that judges and juries understand that the common elements like rest notes, harmonies, and rhythmic features woven throughout a copyrighted work are actually part of its protected expression, just as the holes are a part of the Swiss cheese.

According to Harrison's testimony, he conceived the infringing song when he escaped the press following a performance in Copenhagen, Denmark. Slipping away into his dressing room, he began "scat singing" the phrases "Hallelujah" and "Hare Krishna" and playing some chords along with it. The melodic elements of "He's So Fine" ostensibly crept into the session and became part of his derivative work. The Court ruled that the songs were "virtually identical," with the exception of the lyrics, and concluded that Harrison had "subconsciously plagiarized" "He's So Fine." The court opined as to what happened:

> Seeking the wellsprings of musical composition [to discover] why a composer chooses the succession of notes and the harmonies he does whether it be George Harrison or Richard Wagner is a fascinating inquiry. It is apparent from the extensive colloquy between the Court and Harrison covering forty pages in the transcript that neither Harrison nor [his producer] were conscious of the fact that they were utilizing the "He's So Fine" theme. However, they in fact were, for it is perfectly obvious to the listener that in musical terms, the two songs are virtually identical . . . .
>
> What happened? I conclude that the [George Harrison] in seeking musical materials to clothe his thoughts, was working with various possibilities. As he tried this possibility and that, there came to the surface of his mind a particular combination that pleased him as being one he felt would be appealing to a prospective listener; in other words, that this combination of sounds would work. Why? Because his subconscious knew it already had worked in a song his conscious mind did not remember. Having arrived at this pleasing combination of sounds, the recording was made, the lead sheet prepared for copyright and

> the song became an enormous success. Did Harrison deliberately use the music of "He's So Fine"? I do not believe he did so deliberately. Nevertheless, it is clear that "My Sweet Lord" is the very same song as "He's So Fine" with different words, and Harrison had access to "He's So Fine." This is, under the law, infringement of copyright, and is no less so even though subconsciously accomplished.

In the last two sentences of the quoted section, note the court's implementation of the strict liability principles identified above. The Court ultimately determined that 75% of Harrison's song was attributable to the infringement of "He's So Fine," and awarded 75% of the profits, or $1,599,987, to Bright Tunes.

In early court decisions prior to the passage of the 1976 Copyright Act, courts were less supportive of the creative art of songwriting and music creation. One 1940 court proclaimed, "while there are an enormous number of possible permutations of the musical notes of the scale, only a few are pleasing; and much fewer still suit the infantile demands of the popular ear."[2] This opinion is not without modern support: some opponents of intellectual property ownership in today's society point to cases like *Williams* and *Bright Tunes* as anomalies, supportive of the position that one person should not be able to possess exclusive rights in a musical composition. As someone who has defended the rights of songwriters and publishers my entire career, I can easily say that such positions misunderstand not only the holdings in these two cases but the very nature of music itself. The Ancient Greeks, particularly Plato and Aristotle, were, perhaps more attuned to the mysterious and elusive qualities of music than our current society, believing that the very structure of our world was fundamentally musical and that, as such, music had the power to shape not only a person's mood but to change his or her character.[3] Aristotle believed that music "forms our minds."[4] Plato gives an example of how a mother can pacify a crying baby by singing it a lullaby. In fact, for Plato, the only kind of music a person should listen to is simple, regulated music which represents positive emotions or character traits. So, while modern iterations of simplistic music demanded by "infantile" ears, as the court above opined, may proliferate, they should not be used to discount the mysterious connections between nature and music that the Greeks long ago perceived. The Copyright Act recognizes the uniqueness of art with its requirement that it be a work of *original* authorship.[5] *Feist* describes what Plato and Aristotle are talking about as the author's "stamp of fresh authorship."[6]

Applying these considerations to writing a new country song based on the idea of a "truck driving down a dirt road," the songwriter will find that *a minimum amount of independent creativity* is required to create

---

[2] *Darrell v. Joe Morris Music Co.*, 133 F.2d 80 (2d. Cir. 1940).

[3] See, generally, Edward A. Lippman, *Musical Thought in Ancient Greece*, Columbia University Press (1964).

[4] Politics, Bk. 8, Pt. 5 ("Shall we argue that music conduces to virtue, on the ground that it can form our minds and habituate us to true pleasures as our bodies are made by gymnastics to be of a certain character?").

[5] *Feist,* at 1287 recognized that to qualify for copyright protection, a work must be original to the author (citing *Harper & Row, Publishers v. Nation Enter.*, 471 U.S. 539, 54749 (1985)).

[6] *Id.* at 1290 (*citing Harper*, at 547–48).

© Debby Wong/Shutterstock.com

a new work based on similar thematic ideas, even if the work very closely resembles or is identical to another prior musical composition about a truck and a dirt road, "so long as the resemblance is fortuitous, not the result of copying."[7] The Supreme Court has repeatedly taught us that the originality threshold is not very high, and the point at which the work becomes protected is "evanescent," that is, fades like a vapor. This is why the idea/expression dichotomy principle is so critical in copyright infringement cases involving modern, popular music. We know that the idea of a country boy driving his Ford pickup truck down a country dirt road is not original and therefore cannot be protected by copyright. We also know, however, that *Dirt Road Anthem*, written by Colt Ford and Brantley Gilbert, popularized by Jason Aldean on his 2010 album *My Kinda Party*, expresses that idea in a way that imparts a part of Gilbert and Ford's personality that advances it from a simple thematic idea into a protectable expression. Nuanced analysis such as this is required in the realm of infringement as applied to modern pop and country genres.

[7] *Feist*, 111 S. Ct. at 1287 (citing I NIMMER & NIMMER, supra note 18, §§ 2.01[A]-[B]).

14 Termination Rights

CASE NO. 13	CHAPTER CASE STUDY	Debate Question	
		Can a single cowriter exercise the rights of termination under the CopyrightA ct?	
		Affirmative	**Negative**
	Scorpio Music, S.A., et al. v Victor Willis Case No. 11cv1557 (Slip Op.) (2012 S.D. Cal)	Yes, §203 if one of the cowriters executed a grant of rights for his or her interests, he or she may terminate that grant without the other writers.	No, the statute clearly states that a majority of cowriters must agree to the termination.

The Copyright Act of 1976 allows the author of the copyrighted work to terminate agreements and grants regarding the work, during particular periods of time long after the original grant, and to recapture the rights granted under previous agreements, provided certain conditions exist and further provided that proper notice is served on the grantee. According to the Supreme Court, this right of termination is *inalienable*, that is, it cannot be waived or contracted away.[1] Different provisions of the Copyright Act apply to these termination rights, depending on when the work was created and/or assigned: 17 U.S.C. §304(c) applies to works created and/or grants executed before January 1, 1978, whereas 17 U.S.C. §203 applies to grants executed by the author on or after January 1, 1978.[2] Note that both of these provisions

---

[1] *Cf. Stewart v. Abend*, 495 U.S. 207, 230 (1990).

[2] It should also be noted that 17 U.S.C. §304(d) applies to copyrights for which the §304(c) termination was expired when the Sonny Bono Copyright Term Extension Act (CTEA) became effective in 1998, and for which a termination right was not previously exercised.

begin with a caveat that provides that termination rights *do not apply to works made for hire*, nor do they circumvent any grants made via estate planning. Congress intended these provisions to protect authors and their heirs against prior agreements by giving them an opportunity to share in the later economic success of their works.

For works with a grant date as of January 1, 1978, or after, §203 provides that either the *creator* or *statutory beneficiaries* may terminate a transfer during a 5-year window beginning at the earlier of either 35 years from the date of publication of the work or 40 years from the date the prior grant was executed. Under §304(c), applying to works protected under the 1909 Act, the termination notice must be given during the 5 years commencing as of the end of the 56 years after the *original copyright date.*[3] In promulgating these rules, the Copyright Office offers several definitions that guide in their interpretation: a *grant* of a copyright is a transfer or license of a copyright made with appropriate consideration; an *execution* of a grant is defined as the date an existing work is transferred (*i.e.*, one cannot execute a grant for a non-existent work); finally, a work's *date of publication* is when copies of the work are distributed to the public.

To illustrate how these defined terms can assist in the application of termination rights, assume, for example, that Don Henley of the Eagles signed an exclusive songwriting agreement with Asylum's publishing entity on January 1, 1975, with a term of 5 years. Like most exclusive songwriting agreements, the agreement would have contained a "Schedule A" identifying musical compositions that were written prior to the agreement, but it would also contain a delivery commitment requiring Henley to continue to deliver a certain number of songs each year during the 5-year term. Furthermore, assume that he wrote and delivered the hit single *Heartache Tonight* pursuant to the delivery commitment in July 1979. Does the musical composition transfer fall under §203 because it was written after 1978 or §304 because the exclusive songwriting agreement was executed in 1975? Recall that the execution of a grant was defined as the date *an existing work* is transferred.

[3] Under the 1909 Copyright Act, a work was protected for an initial period of 28 years and, if certain conditions were met, received an additional 28-year renewal term. The renewal term has been extended twice, once for 19 years and again under the CTEA for another 20, for a total of 67 years. The termination rights under §304 apply to grants made during the extension period only.

© Olga Steckel/Shutterstock.com

When Henley signed the exclusive songwriting agreement in 1975, *Heartache Tonight* did not exist and therefore could not have been transferred on that date, so that grant of rights did not apply to the musical compositions Henley wrote and delivered pursuant to the delivery commitment. Assuming that to be the case, we must turn to §203 to see if it applies to Henley's 1979 creation, however, that statute only applies to grants that were executed by the author either *on or after* January 1, 1978. Henley's "grant" of copyright under the 1975 songwriting agreement, therefore, is not terminable with regard to *Heartache Tonight* because it does not meet the statutory prerequisites of either. This scenario creates a potential "black hole" for works that fall under this scenario, for example, Charlie Daniel's *The Devil Went Down* to Georgia is a case in point, recorded in 1979 likely under a pre-1978 agreement. The Copyright Office refers to these as "gap grants" and concluded that such grants may be terminated under §203 because, as a matter of copyright law, a transfer that predates the existence of the copyrighted work cannot be effective until the work of authorship comes into existence. One saving grace in this situation is the contractual tendency of most music publishers requiring the songwriter to execute an assignment of copyright for every work delivered pursuant to the delivery commitment, and thus *generally* speaking Henley would have actually executed an assignment, that is, a grant, for *Heartache Tonight*, in 1979 which would be considered a separate grant and calculated under the provisions of §203. The Copyright Office will also record a notice of termination under §203 if the notice states that the date of execution for the grant is the date that the work was created.

Termination rights can be exercised by the author, if living when the rights vest; otherwise, the surviving widow and/or children and/or grandchildren may exercise the right, followed by the author's executors and/or the author's other next of kin if there are no surviving stirpes. The rights are effected by sending a notice of termination to the person or entity to whom the copyright was transferred. While there are slight variations between §203 and §304, in each instance a valid notice must be written and must include the following: (i) a statement as to which section of the code is being exercised (203, 304(c) or (d)); (ii) a description of the grant being terminated; (iii) a description of the specific work being recaptured, including, if possible, a registration number; (iv) the name of each person whose rights are being terminated (*i.e.,* the "grantee") or the grantee's successor in title; (v) each address at which service of the notice is being made; (vi) the effective date of the termination as calculated by the appropriate statute; and (vii) the signature of the person who signed the transfer or, if deceased, the surviving heir to the rights. The person seeking termination must conduct a "reasonable investigation" as to the appropriate address of the transferee and serve the notice by either first-class mail or some other form of personal service. To be valid, the notice must be served *at least* 2 years prior to the calculated date of termination, but in no event *more than* 10 years prior.

Several legal issues arise in relation to *who* can effectively terminate the transfer, particularly when the work was created through collaboration and some or all of the participants are deceased. If a grant was made by more than one author on or after January 1, 1978, it can be terminated by a *majority* of such authors. But if a grant by more than one author was made prior to that date, then *any one of those authors* can terminate the grant to the extent of his or her own share. The relevant section of the Copyright Act is 17 U.S.C. § 203(a)(1), which provides:

> (a) Conditions for Termination.–In the case of any work . . . the exclusive or nonexclusive grant of a transfer or license of copyright or of any right under a copyright, executed by the author on or after January 1, 1978 . . . is subject to termination under the following conditions:
>
> (1) . . .*In the case of a grant executed by two or more authors of a joint work*, termination of the grant may be effected by a *majority of the authors who executed it* . . . .

© s_bukley/Shutterstock.com

The United States District Court for the Southern District of California dealt squarely with this issue in *Scorpio Music, S.A., et al. v Victor Willis.*[4] This case involves the sole remaining member, Victor Willis, of the 1970s American disco group, Village People, known for its on-stage costumes and suggestive lyrics in their music. The group's founding members consisted of French producers Jacques Morali, Henri Belolo, and the lead singer Willis. Their most significant hit recording, *Y.M.C.A.*, was described by the Library of Congress described "an American phenomenon."[5] In March 2020, it was added to the National Recording Registry, which preserves audio recordings considered to be culturally significant. This lawsuit concerns the publisher's efforts to block Willis's attempt to terminate his post-1977 grants to 33 musical compositions, including *Y.M.C.A.* and all other significant musical compositions recorded by Village People.

The principal plaintiff, in this case, is Scorpio Music S.A., a French corporation engaged in the business of publishing and otherwise commercially exploiting musical compositions, which is joined by its American sub-publisher affiliates, Can't Stop Productions, Inc. and Can't Stop Music. When Village People transitioned from its French roots to American culture, between 1977 and 1979, they hired Willis to translate the lyrics of and/or create new lyrics for the original musical compositions, which were owned and published

[4] Case No. 11cv1557 (Slip Op.) (2012 S.D. Cal).

[5] *National Recording Registry Class Produces Ultimate 'Stay at Home' Playlist.* Library of Congress – National Recording Registry. March 25, 2020. Retrieved October 27, 2022.

in France by Scorpio. Willis is listed as one of the authors on the 33 U.S. copyright registration certificates at issue in this litigation. Willis served the proper notification of termination in March 2011, giving rise to this lawsuit, which was filed on July 14, 2011. The plaintiff sought to invalidate the termination on several grounds, including 17 U.S.C. § 203(a)(1) which requires, they say, that all authors and/or their estates join in the request for termination. In his defense, relying on the same section of 203, Willis argued that since he was the only one of the authors who executed the grants of his copyright interests in the compositions, he alone has the ability to terminate those grants. Willis filed a motion to dismiss in response to the complaint, which the court granted on the basis that the plaintiff failed to state a claim upon which relief could be granted.

Scorpio's primary argument was that the term "grant" as used in §203(a)(1) refers *collectively* to all transfers by joint authors, even if each transfer was a separate transaction, as it was with regard to Willis. The District Court was not persuaded by this argument, however, and pointed out that when Congress passed §203 was aware that a single joint author may grant his interest in a joint work separately from his or her other authors or may join in a grant with one or more of his or her co-authors. Therefore, when the provision says that "a majority of the authors who executed the grant is necessary for termination" of a transfer, it meant that *when* two or more authors of a joint work execute a joint grant, a majority of the authors *who executed the grant* is necessary to terminate the grant. The term "grant," the court said, is intended to refer to a single transfer document that may be signed by one of the authors or all of them. To rule otherwise would be contrary to the purpose of the termination rights, which was to "safeguard . . . authors against unremunerative transfers" and address "the unequal bargaining position of authors, resulting in part from the impossibility of determining a work's value until it has been exploited."[6]

Once a transferred copyright is effectively recaptured, the author terminating the transfer is entitled to an "undivided interest" in the *entire copyright*, together which his or her collaborators.[7] Thus, in *Scorpio*, the court ruled that "[up]on termination, Willis would get back what he transferred—his undivided interest in the whole,"[8] which meant that as one of three identified writers, he would be entitled to an undivided interest in the copyright and a full one-third of any royalties received therefrom, not the "20%" that plaintiff had argued should be his share.[9]

In a more recent case involving the work-for-hire component of §203,[10] Horror Inc. sued screenplay writer Victor Miller in the U.S.D.C. for the District of Connecticut, seeking a declaration that Miller wrote the screenplay as an *employee* and that the screenplay, therefore, was a work-for-hire, which would prevent Miller from terminating the companies' rights. In so doing, Horror relied primarily on labor law statutes.

---

[6] H.R. Rep. No. 94-1476, at 124 (1976), reprinted in 1976 U.S.C.C.A.N. 5659, 5740.

[7] *See,* §§101, 201; *cf.* Nimmer, David, *Nimmer on Copyright*, § 6.08 (Westlaw) and *Manual of Model Civil Jury Instructions*, Ninth Circuit, §17.9.

[8] Slip. Op., p 8.

[9] Willis' attorneys disputed at oral arguments whether one of the three listed writers, Henri Belolo, was, in fact, a joint author. If that were determined to be true, then Willis would be entitled to half of the royalties.

[10] *Horror Inc. v. Miller*, No. 18-3123-cv, 2021 WL 4468980 (2d Cir. Sept. 30, 2021).

In 1979, Miller, a professional screenplay writer and member of the Writers Guild of America (WGA), wrote the screenplay for a horror film, which would eventually be titled *Friday the* 13th, and created the film's iconic character, Jason Voorhees.[11] The movie debuted on May 9, 1980, and enjoyed "unprecedented box office success for a horror film," leading to eleven sequels to date and a host of other derivative products.[12] Miller assigned his rights to the screenplay to a film production and distribution company in an agreement in exchange for only $9,000.

The production companies argued that "Miller's membership in the WGA union created an 'inherent'" employer-employee relationship pursuant to the National Labor Relations Act (NLRA).[13] The NLRA permits screenwriters to unionize but classifies them as employees of the production company when they are on a "union" production. The district court rejected that argument, calling the plaintiff's efforts to "harmonize" the Copyright Act with labor laws "misguided."[14] Explaining that the Copyright Act and the NLRA serve different purposes, the former focusing on the benefit of arts to society and the second focusing on a different economic benefit derived from unionization, the court determined that each had "different conceptions of the employment relationship" which could not be reconciled.[15]

Instead, the Second Circuit held that it is guided by both the more restrictive[16] entry for "work made for hire" under §101 of the Copyright Act, which defines it as "a work prepared by an employee within the scope of his or her employment" and the so-called 13-factor "Reid Factors" created by the Supreme Court to determine whether a person is an employee-for-hire pursuant to the Copyright Act.[17] The Reid Factors generally include: the level of skill required for the task; who provides the tools; where the work is performed; who sets the work schedule; the duration of the relationship; whether the hiring

---

[11] *Ibid.,* at *1-2.

[12] *Id.*, at 3.

[13] See 29 U.S.C. §§ 151, *et seq.*

[14] *Miller, slip. op.*, p. 13.

[15] *Ibid.,* at 17.

[16] The Second Circuit contrasted §101's definition to the more "sweeping approach" of labor and employment laws where "the concept of employment is broader, adopting a more sweeping approach suitable to serve workers and their collective bargaining interests and establishing rights, their safety rights, and pay rights." *Ibid.,* p. 18, citations omitted.

[17] See, *Committee for Creative Non-Violence v. Reid*, 109 S. Ct 2166 (1989). The terms "employee," "employment," and "scope of employment" used in the relevant provisions of the Copyright Act are undefined; thus, Congress intended for the courts to define these in relation to the facts.

party can assign other tasks to the hired party; how the hired party is paid; whether employee benefits are provided; and how the arrangement is treated for tax purposes.

The plaintiffs argued, instead, that application of the Reid Factors was unnecessary and erroneous because as a member of the union, Miller was a "signatory" to the collective bargaining agreement between plaintiffs and the WGA, and as such his employment relationship with them was defined at its inception by the terms and conditions of the applicable WGA-multi-employer collective bargaining agreement. The Second Circuit rejected this analysis because it was in "direct conflict" with the Supreme Court's guidance in *Reid* as well as its own legal precedent, which requires an analysis of the common law concept of the agency relationship in determining whether a person is an employee or an independent contractor.[18]

In applying the Reid Factors, the Second Court noted that courts "adjudicating copyright cases involving professional creative artists have typically found the *skill factor* to weigh strongly in favor of independent contractor status."[19] Thus, the creative arts such as songwriters, screenwriters, architects, photographers, sculpture, and graphic artists are more probable than not to be treated as "highly skilled independent contractors" rather than employees for hire.[20]

After review, the Second Circuit found that the District Court had correctly set aside the NLRA-based doctrine in favor of the common law principles and the Reid Factors in analyzing whether Miller was plaintiffs' "employee" for purposes of this dispute. As such, it confirmed that Miller was *not*, in fact, an *employee-for-hire* of the production company and, as the author, his termination notices regarding the screenplay were valid and enforceable. Thus, the Second Circuit affirmed the district court's ruling, holding that for purposes of determining if a work is a work-for-hire, the Copyright Act—not labor law—determines whether the creator and a hiring party are in an employer-employee relationship.

---

[18] *Aymes v. Bonelli*, 980 F.2d 857, 860 (2d Cir. 1992) ("[T]he term 'employee' [under the Copyright Act] should be understood in light of the general common law of agency").

[19] *Miller, slip. op.*, at 29. *Cf.*, *Reid*, 490 U.S. at 752; *Aymes*, 980 F.2d at 862; *Carter v. Helmsley-Spear, Inc.*, 71 F.3d 77, 86–87 (2d Cir. 1995).

[20] *Citing*, *Aymes*, 980 F.2d at 862.

15 Rights of Publicity

CASE NO. 14	CHAPTER CASE STUDY	Debate Question	
		Does every individual have the right from preventing their name, image, and likeness from being used for commercial uses?	
	Roberson v. Rochester Folding Box Co., 171 N.Y. 538, 64 N.E. 442 (N.Y. 1902).	**Affirmative**	**Negative**
		Yes, the right of publicity can be found in the penumbras of the Bill of Rights.	No, the idea of a right of publicity is no more constitutional than the right of privacy.

One of the first cases in the evolution of the common law rights of publicity precedent in the United States was a New York case dating all the way back to 1902, *Roberson v. Rochester Folding Box Co.*[1] involving Abigail Roberson, a minor. Without her knowledge or consent, the Franklin Mills Co. obtained a photograph of Ms. Roberson and began using the image on bags of flour, marketing materials, lithographic prints, and photos, which they publicly displayed in stores and saloons that sold the product. All totaled, the defendant distributed over 25,000 copies of Abigail's image, all manufactured by the Rochester Folding Box Co. Roberson alleged that after the poster was "conspicuously posted and displayed in stores, warehouses, saloons and other public places" she was subjected to "scoffs and jeers" that were so humiliating she "suffered severe nervous shock" requiring the care of a doctor. When Franklin Mills refused to stop distributing the well-received

From the Collection of The Public Library of Cincinnati and Hamilton County. Reprinted by permission.

[1] 171 N.Y. 538, 64 N.E. 442 (N.Y. 1902).

advertisements, Ms. Roberson filed suit. Her complaint against Franklin Mills and Rochester Box Co. was based on the New York rights of privacy statute, still fairly novel at the time, as well as the more accepted count for emotional distress. She sought $15,000 in damages as well as an injunction prohibiting further distribution. When the lower court ruled in favor of Roberson, the defendant asked for a *demurrer* (*i.e.,* an objection that the plaintiff had not stated a valid claim), which the court granted. The case was then appealed to a higher court.

The appeals court ruled by a 4–3 majority that her claim was not valid under New York privacy law. Justice Alton B. Parker, writing for the majority, sympathized with the plaintiff's "embarrassment" and acknowledged the defendants' "impertinence" in using her photograph without her permission, whereas the majority made some effort to find legal support for her right to privacy claim in precedence and legal commentary. The court gave a nod to a *Harvard Review* article by Louis Brandeis and Samuel D. Warren III[2] while they were in law school, in which the future justices laid out the "penumbras" of the Bill of Rights that established a "right to be left alone." The court acknowledged the article "was presented with attractiveness and no inconsiderable ability," but in the end, the court was not persuaded and found "no precedent for such an action." The majority felt that the argument for the rights of privacy was a slippery slope that, when pushed too far, extended the right far beyond a person's reputation, which it viewed as a public phenomenon, to the world of purely personal and private feelings, which was ephemeral and evanescent. Thus, it held that the "so-called 'right of privacy'" was too much of a novelty to sustain the legal intervention. Justice John Clinton Gray disagreed and dissented with the majority opinion. In his minority opinion, Justice Gray maintained that the injury done to Roberson by the unauthorized use of her portrait was more than sufficient for the court to grant relief under a theory of right of privacy. The increasing scale of "modern" advertising made exploitation of personal portraits for commercial purposes "more formidable and more painful in its consequences than an actual bodily assault might be." Justice Gray revisited the court's nonchalant dismissal of Warren's & Brandeis's *The Right of Privacy* and its call for control over the circulation of photographs. Gray maintained that the court system would be derelict in its duty if they allowed commercial entities such as Rochester to use images of innocent young women such as Roberson and cause "mortifying notoriety" for the sole purpose of their own "selfish gain." With his dissent, Gray sowed the seeds of jurisprudence for the *right of publicity*, indirectly establishing its close relationship with the *right of privacy.* Roberson was ultimately awarded damages for her pain and suffering but received nothing for the violation of her right to privacy, which the New York courts were loath to recognize.

The most positive and lasting effect of the Rochester Folding Box case is that it led to the enactment of the New York Civil Rights Law by the state legislature in 1903, § 50 and §51 of which prohibit the use of the name, portrait, or picture of any living person without prior consent for "advertising purposes" or "for the purposes of trade." Violation of this statute is a criminal misdemeanor, and § 51 also extends the right to pursue civil action to an individual if their persona is exploited without their permission.[3]

---

[2] *The Right to Privacy* (4 Harvard L.R. 193 (Dec. 15, 1890).

[3] Victoria Prussen Spears, "The Case That Started it All: Roberson v. Rochester Folding Box Co.," *Privacy & Data Security Law Journal* (November 2008).

There are several important lessons to take from this case, and the resulting legislation is (1) the rights of publicity can be protected through both the exercise of common law principles, as in the litigation and statute, and (b) the rights of publicity are not the exclusive domain of the celebrity but rather can be applied by citizens who are not famous.[4]

Some states, such as Tennessee, California, Kentucky, Utah, and Wisconsin for example, do, in fact, recognize both a statutory and common law right of publicity. If the analysis is broadened to include actions based on all forms of torts, a total of more than forty states recognizes some form of right of publicity tort actions based on common law, statute, or both.[5] This confusing diversity of approaches under state laws leads to sometimes conflicting treatment of the right of publicity by both the lawyers drafting complaints and the judges deciding them.

As with statutory treatment, the elements of the common law tort for violation of a person's right of publicity vary from state to state, but in general, the most common components include that: (1) the use of a person's name, identity, or persona (some states include signature, photographs, voice, and other identifying characteristics as well); (2) the use of that right of publicity by the defendant for commercial gain (through advertisement and/or commercial activity); (3) without the consent or license of the person; and (4) causes some sort of injury to the plaintiff. These common law principles can be applied in federal courts too.

We see this bifurcated and disparate treatment between statute and common law in a case involving a 1980s Samsung advertisement entitled "The Longest Running Game Show 2012" that humorously featured the Wheel of Fortune tile turner, Vanna White, as a futuristic robot wearing a blonde wig. The Ninth Circuit refused to find in favor of White on the basis of that state's rights of publicity statute, but instead found that California's common law rights of publicity not only protected Ms. White's identity, but "anything that evokes [the celebrity's] personality" as well.[6]

All of this variation among the state laws leads to the conclusion that there is a definitive need for federal guidance in relation to personality rights, perhaps a law similar to other intellectual property statutes such

---

[4] It should be in the annals of the Supreme Court of the United States. In 1977, the Supreme Court decided the seminal case of Zacchini v. Scripps-Howard Broadcasting. Zacchini involved "The Great Hugo," a famous human can-nonball who sued Scripps-Howard for displaying his entire fifteen-second live performance on the local television news program. Zacchini argued that the intrinsic value of his act depended on the public's desire to witness the event, so displaying the entire event on television essentially eliminated the desire of the public to come out in person and pay to see it. In language reminiscent of the policies that support other intellectual property laws, Justice White supported Zacchini's "right of publicity" using language that could easily be the mission statement for copyright law, defending it in order to provide "an economic incentive for him to make the investment required to produce a performance of interest to the public." 32 be noted here that a few state statutes actually do limit the right of publicity to celebrities who made use of the right while they were alive.

[5] Kellie L. Sager and David Wright Tremaine, Summary of Rights of Publicity Issues.

[6] *Vanna White v. Samsung Electronics America, et al.*, 971 F.2d 1395 (Ninth Cir. 1992). In a similar action decided almost a decade earlier, the Sixth Circuit ruled that Johnny Carson's claim against a portable toilet manufacturer who advertised using his signature phrase "Here's Johnny" was liable for violating his rights of publicity. Carson v. Here's Johnny Portable Toilets, Inc., 698 F.2d. 831 (Sixth Cir. 1983).

© Everett Collection/Shutterstock.com

as the Copyright Act of 1976, the Lanham Act, or the Patent Act of 1946. There is a veritable drought when we look to the federal government for assistance and very little movement toward a consolidated treatment of the issue.

As for the highest court in our land, there is only one specific reference to a right of publicity in the annals of the Supreme Court of the United States. In 1977, the Supreme Court decided the seminal case of *Zacchini v. Scripps-Howard Broadcasting*. *Zacchini* involved "The Great Hugo," a famous human cannonball who sued Scripps-Howard for displaying his entire 15-second live performance on the local television news program. Zacchini argued that the intrinsic value of his act depended on the public's desire to witness the event, so displaying the entire event on television essentially eliminated the desire of the public to come out in person and pay to see it. In language reminiscent of the policies that support other intellectual property laws, Justice White supported Zacchini's "right of publicity" using language that could easily be the mission statement for copyright law, defending it in order to provide "an economic incentive for him to make the investment required to produce a performance of interest to the public."[7]

The *Zacchini* decision planted the right of publicity squarely in the realm of intellectual property law where it belongs. In particular, there are some noteworthy similarities between the right of publicity and trademark law. Specifically, the right of publicity is of the same genus as unfair competition and, more precisely, the *doctrine of misappropriation* and/or *false designation of origin*, which are hallmarks of trademark law as reflected in the Lanham Act.[8]

Similar to the way a company's trademark functions as an indicator as to the source of the goods or services, the celebrity's right of publicity functions as an assurance to a consumer of the quality of the celebrity's performance (*i.e.,* they know what to expect). A right of publicity also allows the celebrity to prevent others from reaping unjust rewards by misappropriating the celebrity's well-deserved fame. The Lanham Act makes a person liable in court if that person gives a false impression that the celebrity is somehow associated with his or her goods or services or otherwise uses a celebrity's name in connection with goods or services without permission.

This foundational trademark principle generally holds true even in those jurisdictions where the right of publicity is relegated solely to the common law; however, in those states, a person may have to rely on more traditional tort principles such as "passing off" or "pawning off" a trade name, risk of consumer confusion, or some form of unfair competition.

---

[7] 433 U.S. 562, 576 (1977).

[8] 15 U.S. Code §1125.

In *White v. Samsung Elecs. Am., Inc.*, for example, the Ninth Circuit held that Samsung's use of the robot likeness to call to mind the Wheel of Fortune letter-turner Vanna White created a *triable issue of fact* on whether Samsung's advertisements caused a *likelihood of confusion* as to Ms. White's endorsement of Samsung's products under the Lanham Act and violated Ms. White's right of publicity under state common law.[9]

While the use of these trademark principles to support a claim for rights of publicity is a powerful tool, the drawback is that it may limit the celebrity to the use of his or her name in association with goods and services and not more general infringements of the celebrity's rights. As a result, these techniques do not bestow the same level of protection offered by the broader rights of publicity statutes in those states that recognize them. In fact, courts that allow celebrity claims on the basis of the Lanham Act typically apply the same eight-factor analysis used in most trademark infringement actions requiring, among other things, evidence of actual consumer confusion,[10] which can sometimes be a very formidable task. In contrast, cases prosecuted under state rights of publicity statutes do not suffer from the same strict analysis as under the more stringent trademark analysis.

This close relationship between trademark and rights of publicity reflects the recent nomenclature of "branding" a personality, as we have explored throughout this chapter. Traditionally, the term "brand" was practically synonymous with a company's trademark. In today's media-driven world, a celebrity's fame is crafted and honed to the point where many celebrities also equate their personas as a type of brand as referenced in Daymond John's *The Brand Within: The Power of Branding from Birth to the Boardroom.*

As Locke's philosophy teaches us with regard to copyright, a celebrity's fame is ultimately the result of that celebrity's hard work, talent, and investment, and they should profit from the fruits of their labor. This brings us back into the realm of intellectual property, where the words of the great father of copyright, Melville Nimmer, written in 1954, are a particularly appropriate place to summarize:

> [E]very person is entitled to the fruit of his labors unless there are important countervailing public policy considerations. Yet, because of the inadequacy of traditional legal theories . . . persons who have long and laboriously nurtured the fruit of publicity values may be deprived of them, unless judicial recognition is given to what is here referred to as the right of publicity—that is, the right of each person to control and profit from the publicity values which he has created or purchased.[11]

Rather than "judicial recognition," as Nimmer suggests here, what this patchwork quilt of state law, common law, torts, and federal jurisprudence regarding personality rights actually illustrates more clearly is the dramatic need for a consistent application that can only come in the form of a federal law regarding rights of publicity. Until that time, the United States will continue to see the inconsistent application of this basic right. In the meantime, defending a celebrity's right to publicity involves the use of a combination of the Lanham Act, any applicable state statute, common law rights of publicity principles, and more traditional tort actions.

---

[9] *Op. cited, supra.*

[10] The factors were developed (pun intended) in *Polaroid Corp. v. Polarad Elect. Corp.*, 287 F.2d 492 (2d Cir. 1961), and are (a) the strength of his mark, (b) the degree of similarity between the two marks, (c) the proximity of the products and/or services, (d) the likelihood that the prior owner will bridge the gap, (e) actual confusion among consumers, (f) the defendant's good faith in adopting its own mark, (g) the quality of the defendant's product, and (h) the sophistication of the buyers.

[11] Melville B. Nimmer, "The Right of Publicity," 19 Law & Contemp. Probs. 203, 216 (1954).

16 Distinguishing Original Lyrics from Words, Titles, and Phrases

CASE NO. 15	CHAPTER CASE STUDY	**Debate Question**	
		Can a person obtain a copyright in a short lyrical phrase provided that the phrase is sufficiently original?	
	Sean Hall & Nathan Butler v. Taylor Swift, Slip. Op. No. 18-55426 (9th Cir. 2019)	**Affirmative**	**Negative**
		Yes, if the expression of the phrase is such that it exhibits a modicum of originality.	No, Copyright Law is clear that words, phrases, and titles cannot be the subject of protection.

One of the frequent issues that arises with regard to copyright infringement is when, if ever, a short phrase or title, or even a single word for that matter, is entitled to copyright protection. The Copyright Office has promulgated guidelines for registering a copyright, codified in Title 37 of the Code of Federal Regulation, and summarized, among other places, in Circular 33, *Works Not Protected by Copyright*. In that circular, the Copyright Office offers the following statement of their policy when it comes to names, titles, and slogans:

> Words and short phrases, such as names, titles, and slogans, are uncopyrightable because they contain an insufficient amount of authorship. The Office will not register individual words or brief combinations of words, even if the word or short phrase is novel, distinctive, or lends itself to a play on words.[1]

[1] Circular 33, p. 3. Codified at 37 CFR § 202.1(a). The authoritative source for U.S. copyright law is the Copyright Act, codified in Title 17 of the United States Code. Copyright Office regulations are codified in Title 37 of the Code of Federal Regulations. Copyright Office practices and procedures are summarized in the third edition of the Compendium of U.S. Copyright Office Practices, cited as the *Compendium*. The copyright law, regulations, and the *Compendium* are available on the Copyright Office website at www.copyright.gov.

© Ken Wolter/Shutterstock.com

In some instances, however, courts have found sufficient creativity in certain phrases to warrant protection, raising the question of when a lyric is simply a common phrase or title and thus not protectable and when it contains that "something more." This can be a difficult question to answer.

When Aaron Tippin ("Tippin") wrote and recorded *If you Don't Stand for Something, you'll Fall for Anything* in 1990, he was of the opinion that it contained sufficient originality to warranty protection, despite that being the title of the song. So, when Jostens, Inc. ("Jostens"), the company that produces and sells high school and college class rings, prominently featured that exact phrase in their advertising campaign in 1992—and used it as their theme "It's a Jostens thing. You got to stand for something"—Tippin's publishing company took offense. First, Acuff-Rose's attorney sent Jostens a *cease and desist* letter demanding that they stop using the phrase in their advertising and catalogs, to which they responded by referencing the Copyright Office Circular 33, cited earlier, that "titles and other short phrases or expressions are *noncopyrightable*." After several exchanges of communications between the parties, Jostens refused to stop using their slogan and Acuff-Rose filed a complaint in the United States District Court for the Southern District of New York.[2] The District Court dismissed the complaint pursuant to the defendant's motion, finding that when "[i]]solated from Tippin's vocal rendition of the words and melody, the lyric at issue lacks the requisite originality."[3] The court reviewed uses of the phrase that predates the creation of Tippin's song "far too numerous to be recounted. . ."[4] All of those prior uses, the Court opined, could not be dismissed as isolated references or mere derivatives of Tippin's song. In fact, the Court found that the phrase may have been circulating as early as New Testament times.[5] In addition, the exact phrase was used by many dignitaries and others, such as Martin Luther King, Jr., Malcolm X, former Chaplain of the United States Senate Peter

© carroteater/Shutterstock.com

[2] *Acuff-Rose Music, Inc. v. Jostens, Inc.,* 988 F. Supp. 289 (S.D.N.Y. 1997).

[3] *Ibid.,* at 294.

[4] *Id.,* at 294.

[5] 1 Corinthians 10:12: "Let him that thinketh he standeth take heed lest he fall."

Marshall, as well as several others cited. The District Court concluded that "[w]hile especially creative phrases may be protected, there is nothing unique about the use of standing/falling imagery to convey the importance of living a principled life."[6] Noting that Tippin "did not embellish the words in any way or otherwise infuse them with any 'creative spark,'"[7] the District Court held that the plaintiff had "shown only the copying of an unprotected cliché and 'mere generalized ideas or themes.'"[8] Thus, Jostens had not misappropriated any protected elements of Tippin's copyright.[9]

In stark contrast to the *Acuff-Rose* findings, compare the 2009 case involving simple lyrical words and phrases contained in George Clinton's musical composition, *Atomic Dawg*, owned by Bridgeport Music, Inc. ("Bridgeport"). In this case, Public Announcement's musical composition *D.O.G. in Me* featured similar uses of the word "dog" or "dawg" as well as the phrase "bow-wow-wow-yippie-yo-yippie yeah." Bridgeport filed suit in the Middle District of Tennessee against Universal Music Group (UMG) for infringement. UMG filed a motion for summary judgment, claiming that the allegedly infringing elements in "D.O.G. in Me"—the use of the word "dog" in a low voice as "musical punctuation," the rhythmic panting, and the Bow Wow refrain—were not copyrightable *as a matter of law*. The District Court denied the motion. After the subsequent 5-day trial, the jury rendered a verdict in Bridgeport's favor, finding UMG liable for $22,245 in actual damages and $88,980 in statutory damages. UMG appealed the case to the Sixth Circuit.[10]

On appeal, UMG claimed that the jury should not have been able to consider either the word "dog" used as musical punctuation or the rhythmic panting in "D.O.G. in Me" as infringement because those elements *are not original* and, thus, should have been filtered out. The District Court thus erred in allowing that issue to go to the jury. Referring to the trial transcript, the Sixth Circuit noted, however, that the co-creator of *Atomic Dog*, David Spradley, testified that Clinton exercised *some degree of creative control* over the panting by instructing the performers to create a certain rhythm.[11] The Sixth Circuit also found that:

> "[t]here was [additional] expert testimony that these elements were not just the 'mere abstract idea' of a dog or of the activity of panting because, in Clinton's composition, the word 'dog' constituted a 'stand-alone melody of one word' used as musical punctuation at intervals on the tonic note of the song and because the sound of panting followed the rhythm of the song."[12]

Based on their review of the transcript, the Sixth Circuit thus affirmed the lower court's decision.

---

[6] *Ibid.*

[7] *Ibid.*, at 295.

[8] *Ibid.*, at 296, *citing Warner Bros. Inc. v. American Broadcasting Companies,* 654 F.2d 204 (2d Cir.1981).

[9] It should be noted that if Tippin had desired to protect the phrase in the context of the services he provided as an entertainer, he could have registered the phrase as a trademark, where there are no such restrictions on what can be protected.

[10] *Bridgeport Music, Inc. v. Universal Music Group,* 585 F.3d 267 (6th Cir. 2009).

[11] *Bridgeport,* at 276.

[12] *Ibid.*

The principles in these two cases can help the copyright litigator distinguish between lyrics that can be protected and short, simple phrases or titles that cannot. Relying on the idea/expression dichotomy to weed out mere ideas or expressions that have merged with the idea being expressed, the attorney can ascertain whether what remains contains that "stamp of fresh authorship" that moves it along the spectrum and grants it protectable expression. In the case of *Acuff-Rose* involving Aaron Tippin's signature title, the court was dealing with a phrase that is, perhaps, as old as Abraham as it were, and certainly, one that has existed in the *zeitgeist* for decades. Tippin added none of his creativity to the phrase. In stark contrast, in the *Bridgeport* case, Clinton's use of the simple word "dog" to punctuate the downbeat and the phrase "bow-wow-wow-yippie-yo-yippie yeah" to break up the monotony was *imbued with his creativity* and originality. It was Clinton's very uniqueness that was directly copied by Public Announcement. Whether a word or short phrase contains sufficient originality to warrant protection is considered a *question of fact*; thus, cases involving such issues are often decided based on the intuition of the trier of fact as they parse these nuances.

© Brian Friedman/Shutterstock.com

A case that clearly will involve these nuances is a current Central District of California case involving a series of lyrics in Taylor Swift's 2014 musical composition, *Shake it Off*.[13] The lyrical phrases at issue in Swift's song are "cause the players gonna play, play, play, play, play" and "haters gonna hate, hate, hate, hate, hate," which bear a suspicious similarity to a musical composition written for 3LW titled *Playas Gon' Play* containing the lyrical phrases "playas, they gon' play" and "haters they gonna hate" written by Sean Hall and Nate Butler. The 3LW song was part of their self-titled debut album in 2000 and was released as a single in April 2001, reaching No. 81 on the United States charts and has been touted as one of the greatest girl group singles of all time by industry experts. Swift's subsequent recording of her song sold roughly 9 million copies after debuting atop the Billboard Hot 100 upon its initial release, making it one of her most successful songs to date.

It is important in cases such as this to consider *prior art* for references that may lead to the defense of simultaneous use of ideas, as learned from the *Tippin* title discussed earlier in the context of familiar idioms. For example, in 2013, a year prior to the Swift composition, Jesse Branham sought $42 million and writers' credit in a lawsuit alleging that *Shake it Off* absconded with the lyrics from his *Haters Gone Hate*, which included the following chorus using the refrains:

> Haters gon' hate, haters gon' hate
> Players gon' play, players gon' play
> Watch out for the fakers
> They'll fake you every day

[13] Swift cowrote the musical composition with Max Martin and Shellback.

Branham misguidedly filed the copyright infringement action against Swift *pro se*, which is Latin for "in one's on behalf," ignoring the adage that "he who serves as his own counsel has a fool for a lawyer and a jackass for a client."[14] That case was quickly dismissed and, regardless, Branham's 2013 composition follows the 2000 song written by Hall and Butler.

From an etymological viewpoint, the word "playa" is a Spanish word, translated to "beach," that itself ultimately derives from a much older proto-Indo-European word that later became the Latin word *plaga*, which meant a *tract or region of land*. It is uncertain, however, if the urban slang usage, which means someone who "plays the field sexually," is related to this early word, and certainly, there is no clear nor logical connection. Another slightly similar predecessor use in music, one closer in time to the Hall and Butler song, is Notorious B.I.G.'s 1997 composition *Playa Hater*, which includes the line "we have, the playas, and we have, the playa haters" as well as the choral refrain "Playa playa (hater), Playa playa (hater)" repeated four times. As a result of this creation, Marcus Reeves, author of *Somebody Scream! Rap Music's Rise to Prominence in the Aftershock of Black Power*, attributes the popularization of the term *player hater* to Notorious B.I.G, finding that it emerged in black culture in the late 1990s. However, *The Right Rhymes*, a hip-hop dictionary, traces the term back to an earlier date in the 1991 song *Psycobetabuckdown* by Cypress Hill.[15] From a more conceptual sense, Fleetwood Mac's 1977 classic *Dreams* contains the twice repeated line "players only love you when they're playing." None of these prior expressions of the idea of a "playa" being hated are as closely related in expression as the two phrases at issue in the *Swift* case.

So, Hall and Butler filed a complaint against Swift for copyright infringement on September 18, 2017,[16] to which the defendants responded with a motion to dismiss the case on January 3, 2018, arguing that "the . . . lyrics lacked [sufficient] originality to enjoy copyright protection." After hearing oral arguments from both sides, District Judge Michael W. Fitzgerald agreed with the defendant's argument that the lyrics lacked originality and therefore dismissed the case.[17] Justice Fitzgerald described the lyrics at issue as banal, concluding that "for such short phrases to be protected under the Copyright Act, *they must be more creative than the lyrics at issues here*."[18] The plaintiffs then appealed Fitzgerald's order of dismissal to the Ninth Circuit. On appeal, the Ninth Circuit reversed.

---

[14] In an article titled *A Man Who Is His Own Lawyer Has a Fool for a Client* on the online blog "Quote Investigator," the author attributes the original saying "he who will be his own Counselor, shall be sure to have a Fool for his Client" to the 1682 book *Humane Prudence, or, The Art by which a Man May Raise Himself and Fortune to Grandeur* by William De Britaine, although *The Cincinnati Enquirer* attributes the version cited here to Abraham Lincoln. The truth is that the saying is a common idiom, so feel free to use it in your next musical composition.

[15] A number of other songs by various artists including Too $hort, 2Pac, and Sir Mix-A-Lot use similar phraseology for the concept of a "player."

[16] In addition to the three songwriters, the complaint also identifies Sony/ATV Music Publishing and Big Machine Music Group, among others.

[17] *Citing Satava v. Lowry*, 323 F.3d 805, 810 (9th Cir. 2003) for the propositions that "[a]ny copyrighted expression must be 'original.' Although the amount of creative input . . . required to meet the originality standard is low, it is not negligible," which in turn, cited *Feist Publ'ns, Inc. v. Rural Tel. Serv. Co., Inc.*, 499 U.S. 340, 345, 362 (1991).

18 *Hall and Butler v Swift et al.*, Slip. Op. No.18-55426 (9th Cir. 2019), p. 3.

We can glean from the Ninth Circuit's review that equally critical in these types of cases involving lyrical phrases is consideration of the originality expressed by the songwriter in the context of the whole song, as we saw in the *Clinton* case illustrated above. The Ninth Circuit correctly reiterated that the issue of originality is a question of *fact* that must be presented to the *trier of fact*, a jury in this case, but chastised that Justice Fitzgerald had "constituted [him]self as the final judge of the worth of an expressive work."[19] The Circuit ruled that the "complaint still plausibly alleged *originality*"[20] and that nothing in the record established the *absence* of that originality.

On remand to the Central District Court, the defendants filed a motion for summary judgment, a procedurally different motion than its prior motion to dismiss; in that, it asks the court to rule as a matter of *law,* not fact, claiming that *Swift* was entitled to judgment as a matter of law since there were no genuine issues of triable fact. In ruling on the motion for summary judgment, Justice Fitzgerald noted that the defendants "[made] some persuasive arguments with regard to why various factors of the respective musical and literary work analyses do objectively distinguish 'Playas' and 'Shake,'" there were nonetheless issues of fact remaining such that he could not "eliminate the possibility that there is . . . potential substantial similarity between the lyrics and their sequential structure."

The cases discussed in this chapter serve to illustrate the concept that law, particularly the "metaphysical" copyright law, is not always black and white, but rather resides in the land of shades of gray, like the idea/expression dichotomy, where the slightest fact can push an idea into the realm of expression and grant it protection. A generally accepted prescription such as "words, phrases, and titles are not entitled to copyright protection," thus, is not a simple binary equation. A nuanced analysis of facts and law must be conducted to determine the validity of copyright protection in such cases.

---

19 *Ibid.*

20 *Id.*, at 1.

17 When is a Tattoo a Useful Article?

CASE NO. 16	CHAPTER CASE STUDY	**Debate Question**	
		Can a tattoo artist enforce her display rights in a tattoo when it is displayed on another person's body?	
		Affirmative	**Negative**
	Whitmill v. Warner Bros., Complaint, Civil Action No. 4:11-cv-752 (2011)	Yes, **if** there is a modicum of expression in the artwork *and* the tattoo is fixed on the second person's body, **then** that person is the *tangible format* required and the artist has the exclusive right of display.	No, a tattoo is arguably a useful article that does not afford its creator any more rights than she would otherwise possess, particularly when it interferes with the tattooed person's rights of privacy or publicity.

Most artists work in tangible mediums: the sculptor has his or her marble; the painter has his or her oils; the songwriter has his or her rhyme and rhythm; the dancer has his or her subtle and refined movements; and the author has his or her words. Such is the paradox of intellectual properties, that even though the monopoly is an intangible asset, it can only be protected in its tangible forms. The creative mind, however, is rarely bound by the physical and so, when an art form develops that mixes the metaphors and breaks the standard paradigms, it forces the rigid legal applications of copyright law to adjust and adapt, just as when Einstein taught us that our normal perspectives of the space/time continuum are relative to the constant speed of light. When one considers the art form of the tattoo, for instance, such paradigm-shifting issues can arise in copyright law.

In February 2003, Michael Gerard Tyson, better known as heavyweight boxing champion "Mike Tyson," walked into Paradox-Studio of Dermagraphics, a tattoo parlor in Los Vegas, Nevada. There he encountered S. Victor Whitmill, an award-winning visual artist whose work appears in various mediums.

© Kathy Hutchins/Shutterstock.com

In this instance, Tyson asked Whitmill to create, design, and apply a special tattoo on his temple, surrounding his left eye (the "Tyson Tattoo"). Whitmill agreed, and the two parties entered into a release form that included an acknowledgment "that all artwork, sketches and drawings related to [his] tattoo and any photographs of [his] tattoo" would belong to the studio. Whitmill applied the tattoo to Tyson and subsequently registered his copyright in the Tyson Tattoo with the United States Copyright Office. Prior to finding out about its usage, in this case, Whitmill had never applied the Tyson Tattoo to any other customer nor copied, distributed, or disseminated it in any other fashion.

In 2009, Warner Brothers Production Company began the development of a sequel to its highly successful 2009 movie, *The Hangover,* in which a group of four best friends travel to Las Vegas for a bachelor party. In the sequel, *The Hangover: Part II*, released in 2011, the roles of the same four cohorts are reprised, except this time—2 years later—they traveled to Thailand for another wedding, this time waking up to the sounds of a chain-smoking capuchin monkey in a dilapidated hotel room in Bangkok. One of the characters, Alan, finds that his head is shaved, and a second, Stu, discovers a face tattoo, which is a replica of the Tyson Tattoo. Tyson himself makes an appearance in the sequel performing a musical number at the wedding reception.

Just weeks prior to its Memorial Day release in 2011, and after learning about the appearance of his copyrighted Tyson Tattoo in the marketing materials for the movie, Whitmill filed a copyright infringement action against Warner Brothers in the United States District Court for the Eastern District of Missouri, where Whitmill was then a resident. In addition to damages for the infringement, Whitmill's action sought a preliminary injunction to prevent the release of the film.

© Hayk_Shalunts/Shutterstock.com

The defenses invoked in this litigation raise several interesting questions, one of which revolves around art as a "useful article," a phrase the 1976 Copyright Act defines as any "article having an *intrinsic utilitarian function* that is not merely to portray the appearance of the article or to convey information."[1] Examine the common door, for example. The door serves the intrinsic

[1] 17 U.S.C. §101.

utilitarian function of *egress* and *ingress*, in which an architect would not possess a copyright protection. By contrast, however, the definition of "useful article" in 17 U.S.C. §101 instructs us that the architect may very well have a copyright in the wrought iron sculptural features that may embellish the hinged utilitarian slab. To further illustrate, consider the typical adolescent birthday party clown, who creates balloon dogs to amuse the toddlers: the fact that he is "creating" the balloon animal dog *does not* give that clown the right to prevent the myriad of other birthday party clowns across the globe from creating dogs that are exact copies of the one she created. Consider, by contrast, that as part of his 1994 Celebration series, appropriation artist Jeff Koons did just that: by exhibiting an enormous, shiny, brightly colored balloon animal dog, appropriately titled *Balloon Dog*, afterward registering his "copyright" in the sculpture he created. In all other respects but for size, *Balloon Dog* is identical to the useful article that is the clown's inflatable version of the dog. Does that ownership prevent, say, the owner of a bodega, who saw Koon's Celebration exhibit, from traveling to China and having 1:64 scale balloon animal dogs created to sell in her store?

Almost a decade later, Koons' sculpture broke the record for the most expensive piece of art ever sold at 58.4 million dollars, raising the question of whether society's placement of value on such abstract utilitarian art affects the analysis of what Koon's can protect. Some see Koons as a pioneer while others simply see mass commercialism. As evaluators of copyright protection and defenders of the noble arts, a copyright attorney cannot look at the aesthetic qualities of the art, or at the value placed on individual art by society but must use the principles of copyright law to examine how far a work of art's protection can extend. In the case of Koons' *Balloon Dog*, just like Malevich's *Black Circle* examined earlier, the idea of the inflatable dog *has merged* into the massive expression of the same, and very little, if anything, garners any real protective force. The effect of this merger is that the owner of a tchotchke shop who sees Koons' sculpture of an inflatable dog and decides to have little figurines of balloon animals manufactured to sell in her store does not violate Koons' copyright in *Balloon Dog* because of the restrictions placed on owning useful articles by the Copyright Act.

Specifically, with reference to an artist's ability to protect the underlying useful article when he or she portrays a useful article as part of his or her expression, §113(b) states that the Copyright Act:

> does not afford the owner of copyright in a work that portrays a useful article *any greater or lesser rights* with respect to the making, distribution, or display of the useful article so portrayed *than those afforded to such works under the law.*

This section purports to apply solely to pictorial, graphic, and sculptural works. As one of the exceptions to the rights of a copyright owner specified in §106, §113(b) is a specific application of the idea/expression dichotomy, as well as the merger doctrine, designed to eliminate ownership of "staple articles"[2] and prevent the application of several of those rights, including adaptation, reproduction, and distribution.

---

[2] The Supreme Court applied the "staple article of commerce" doctrine in *Sony Corp. of America v. Universal City Studios, Inc.*, 464 U.S. 417 (1984), colloquially referred to as the "Betamax case." Section 271(c) of the Patent Act subjects the manufacturers of components of a patented inventions that are "*not a staple article or commodity of commerce suitable for substantial noninfringing use*" to liability as infringers. The Sony court famously adapted this standard to become the "Sony Test" for *contributory infringement* of copyrights by a machine: manufacturers would only be liable if their product was "capable of substantial noninfringing uses."

The useful article concept is more frequently applied in the context of artwork that is attached to buildings and other structures. If you have vacationed in "Music City," you may be familiar with another example of useful articles that are specifically addressed in another subsection of §113, that is, visual arts affixed to buildings, *i.e.,* murals. Nashville has more than its shares of these selfie-generating works of art thanks to Taylor Swift. In 2019, Swift confessed on social media that it was she who commissioned street artist Kelsey Montagu to create the colorful, building-tall set of wings, called the *Butterfly* mural, near Pine Street in the Gulch neighborhood of Nashville. Swift then dropped clues about the mural in some of her new music. This viral sensation led to the advent not only of Nashville becoming the Bridezilla capital of the world but also to dozens of murals painted on buildings all over the city. More broadly, in many major metropolises across the globe, *street art, aka* "public art" appears in the form of markings, photos, words, initials, or drawings that have been spray-painted, sketched, or even scratched onto walls, sidewalks, or any other publicly accessible areas, that is, *graffiti* that is created either a form of vandalism or a form of art or, perhaps, both simultaneously.[3]

Street art has its own special section of the Copyright Act, §113(d), which addresses works of visual art that are applied to buildings and other similar structures, that is, where a building or a sidewalk is the media in which the copyright is embodied. This applies not only to murals but also to other works of visual art such as sculpture and mosaics. This section comports with §202 of the Copyright Act, which provides that "ownership of a copyright, or of any of the exclusive rights under a copyright, is distinct from ownership of any material object in which the work is embodied." The provision of §113(d) specifically applies to visual art that has "been incorporated in or made part of a building in such a way that removing the work from the building will cause the destruction" to exclude the application of an artist's rights of *attribution* and *integrity,* provided through the *Visual Arts Rights Act of 1990* (VARA), codified at §106A.[4]

It is intriguing to consider how these varying sections of the Copyright Act weave together in the context of the Tyson Tattoo. While the tattoo is obviously a work of graphic arts, placing it squarely under the provisions of §113(a), does it also have some *intrinsic utilitarian function* such that it does not merely *portray the appearance of the article or convey information,* thereby landing it in the realm of the Sony Test, the staple article of commerce doctrine, that is,

[3] The term graffiti is actually a plural term, derived from the Italian word, *graffito,* which means an "incised inscription or design." *Graffito* is derivative of *graffiare* meaning "to scratch."

[4] These two rights of attribution and integrity are central features of the so-called *droit moral* rights that exist in every other country that is a member of the Berne Treaty, except for the United States. In the United States, an author only has moral rights with regard to visual works under VARA, that is, a songwriter, for example, does not have the right to be credited with writing a song (attribution) in the United States, whereas he would be in the other 180 signatories to the Berne Treaty.

a useful article? If so, §113(c) might apply to *exclude* any right to prevent the making, distribution, or display of pictures or photographs of such works. In that case, Whitmill would not have succeeded in his lawsuit to prevent Warner Brothers from displaying the Tyson Tattoo in the *Hangover Part II* movie, since §113(c) provides that "where such works have been lawfully used, copyright does not include any right to prevent the making, distribution, or display of photographs of such articles. . ."[5] In other words, Whitmill does not have the exclusive rights to display a depiction of the tattoo any more than Koons has exclusive rights to display a depiction of the balloon dog.

Consider also whether the Tyson Tattoo issue might be analogous to the murals and graffiti painted on the sides of buildings, such that §113(d) would apply. If so, there are two potential implications: (a) since the Tyson Tattoo was applied with Whitmill's consent, and since it is so integrated with Tyson that it cannot be removed without destroying the artwork, Whitmill would have *no rights* to prevent Tyson from *removing* the Tyson Tattoo should he so choose; and (b) if that were the case, then a good argument might be made that, should the champion decide to have the Tyson Tattoo removed, he might be required to give Whitmill 90-day notice of the impending destruction of his artwork in order for Whitmill to make a "copy" of the Tyson Tattoo for posterity.

As for Whitmill's specific request for a preliminary injunction to stop the release of the film, United States District Court Judge Catherine D. Perry denied the injunction after weighing the significant monetary loss it would have caused Warner Brothers if the film were enjoined. Notably, however, Judge Perry allowed the copyright infringement claim to move forward, indicating that there was a *strong likelihood* that the powerhouse production studio could be liable for copyright infringement in its recreation of Tyson's tattoo without first obtaining Whitmill's permission or consent. The judge's ruling left open the question of how far a copyright owner's rights extend in artwork that is literally embodied on another human being. Alas, Warner Brothers and Whitmill settled the copyright infringement lawsuit amicably during a mediation session, and of course, settlements are generally confidential, so the case is of no actual assistance for legal precedence for us to consider, except in theory.

© charnsitr/Shutterstock.com

Because of the *evanescent nature* of copyright in general, and because of the nature of the medium in which tattoo art is embodied—that is, a person's body—only a handful of copyright suits involve the infringement of tattoo artwork, and many settle before they reach the inside of a courtroom. In October 2022, a jury in the matter of *Catherine*

[5] 17 U.S.C. §113(c) only applies to photographs of the art used "in connection with *advertisements* or *commentaries* related to the distribution or display of such articles, or in connection with news reports," so it most likely would not be applicable to the use on the motion picture. Note that these arguments were not raised in the litigation, and the case regarding the motion picture was ultimately settled, so it is not certain which party would have prevailed on the issues.

Alexander v. Take-Two Interactive Software, Inc., et al. awarded the plaintiff, a tattoo artist, $3,750 in damages for infringing five original works—tribal designs, a Bible verse, a dove, a rose, and a skull—tattooed on World Wrestling Entertainment, Inc. (WWE) Champion Roy Orton, after Take-Two licensed Orton's persona, including the tattoo, from the WWE and reproduced the images in the video games "WWE 2K16," "WWE 2K17," and "WWE 2K18." In its short ruling, the Court stated that "as a matter of law, Alexander owns a valid copyright to the five tattoos at issue in this lawsuit." Given the obviousness of the copying in this matter, the court held that unless the defendants could raise an affirmative defense, they were guilty of copyright infringement. The defendants raised several, including the potential of an implied license, the fair use doctrine, and that the use of the tattoos was *de minimis*, but the United States District Court for the Southern District of Illinois found none of these defenses credible.[6]

© Jaguar PS/Shutterstock.com

In a new twist to this issue, famed tattoo artist and reality TV celebrity Katherine Von Drachenberg (aka Kat Von D) is actually being sued by a photographer who claims she copied his work as a tattoo, thus raising the unprecedented issue of whether a tattoo artist commits copyright infringement by using a copyrighted image as a reference when creating a client's tattoo? The plaintiff in this Central District of California case is famed photographer Jeffrey B. Sedlik, who took a very well-known photograph of jazz legend Miles Davis for the cover of JAZZIZ magazine in 1989 and owns the registered copyright. The portrait was featured by Life magazine in an annual "Pictures of the Year" issue and has since become an iconic representation of Davis. Sedlik has licensed it for use on posters, t-shirts, and art prints. Kat Von D's use of the photograph was admittedly not licensed and, to complicate the issue, she posted images of herself copying the image onto the arm of a lighting technician, Blake Farmer, on all of her social media feeds in 2017. When the parties filed cross-motions for summary judgment, they agreed as a matter of undisputed facts that Sedlik owned a *valid copyright* in his photo of Miles Davis, and that the defendants indeed used the image "as a reference" in creating Farmer's tattoo. The defendants instead made the argument that Von D *did not copy any protectable elements* from the copyrighted photograph.

In its ruling, the Court cited the Ninth Circuit's opinion in the well-known Michael Jordan "Jumpman" case, *Rentmeester v. Nike* for the proposition that the elements that make up a photo, pose, lighting, camera angle, etc., cannot be "abstracted" or divided into *protected* and *unprotected* elements to determine whether a defendant copied protected elements. Instead, a sufficiently original *selection and arrangement* of these elements are entitled to protection. In performing this analysis, the trier of fact must determine whether the copied photo and the derivative work are *substantially similar* with respect

[6] *Alexander v. Take-Two Interactive Software, Inc.*, 18-cv-966-SMY (S.D. Ill. Sep. 22, 2022), Slip. Op., p. 1.

© August_0802/Shutterstock.com

to this combination of selection and arrangement in order to find infringement.[7] There are subtle differences that can be noticed between the original photo and the tattoo including the lighting and shading, Davis's hairline, and the background. However, the District Court correctly found that the issue of substantial similarity was an issue for the jury to decide and thus denied the defendant's motion for summary judgment.

Just as the defendants did in *Take-Two*, Von D's lawyers also raised the issue of fair use, claiming that: (i) "its [fixation in a] human body" is done for personal reasons; (ii) the fact that Farmer is an avid Miles Davis fan; and (iii) Von D's hand-inked version created a "more melancholy aesthetic"; the tattoo thus *transformed* the photograph by creating an inherently different meaning. The court rejected all three defenses, holding that Farmer's motivation for obtaining the tattoo is irrelevant and not dispositive and finding that whether Von D's derivative work transformed the original is a triable issue of fact and cannot be decided on the basis of summary judgment. Furthermore, though she offered the red herring defense that the tattoo work was free of charge, the fact that Von D shared the tattoo on her social media platforms opens the argument that the purpose of the use was for commercial purposes, thus weighing against her fair use defense.

Of course, these tattoo-oriented copyright cases raise significant social and legal issues beyond the scope of copyright infringement. Could a court, for example, order the surgical removal of a tattoo as an equitable remedy? Does a court need to take the rights of a tattooed individual into account when deciding these types of cases? If a fan at a concert takes a photograph of a tattooed performance artist such as, for example, Adam Levine, is the photographer violating the tattoo artist's copyright?

[7] *Rentmeester v. Nike,* 883 F.3d 1111 at 1120 (2018).

18 Space/Time-Shifting and Contributory Negligence

CASE NO. 17		Debate Question	
	CHAPTER CASE STUDY	Is the manufacturer of a device intended to record copyright programming distributed over-the-air liable for contributory negligence when the purchaser records a movie to watch later?	
		Affirmative	**Negative**
	Sony Corp. of America v. Universal City Studios, Inc., 464 U.S. 417 (1984)	Yes, distribution of device that the manufacturer knows will be used for infringement is contributory.	No, if the allegedly infringing device is capable of substantial non-infringing uses and is socially beneficial, the manufacturer is not liable for infringement.

Most copyright infringement cases involve what is referred to as *direct infringement*, that is, the infringer actually copies the specific expression of the original artist. If a person is not directly involved in the infringement of a copyright, however, but instead *induces* or *authorizes* the direct infringer to violate the original copyright owner's rights, is the first person also guilty of copyright infringement? Furthermore, when a person somehow controls the means of infringement used by the direct infringer and thereby *facilitates* the infringement, is

© Feng Yu/Shutterstock.com

that person somehow liable as well? The two types of activity just described can create what is called *contributory* or *vicarious* liability, respectively.

Unlike direct infringement, the 1976 Copyright Act does not expressly address liability for these secondary types of contributory or vicarious infringement. Instead, like many U.S. laws, these doctrines are an extension of *general tort law*, that is the principle that, in addition to the tortfeasor, any person *contributing* to the tort should also be held liable for the tortfeasor's actions and the damages resulting therefrom.

The elements necessary to establish *contributory infringement* are that the defendant must have actual or constructive knowledge of the direct infringement and *materially contribute* to that infringement. Courts have found that either expressly promoting infringing activities and/or providing a website that is frequently used for infringing activities can constitute substantial or material contributions. In these cases, continued tolerance of the infringing activity contributes to the infringement, as does the promotion of the activity, and thus the contributing business may be just as liable for the infringement just as much as the direct infringer. *Vicarious infringement*, on the other hand, is established by showing that the secondary defendant had the right to *control* the infringing activity and somehow derives a *financial or commercial benefit* from the direct infringement. Unlike contributory infringement, vicarious liability can be imposed even in the absence of any so-called *mens rea*, that is, the intent or knowledge on part of the secondary defendant to allow the commission of infringement.[1] These two types of secondary liability can be critical in the process of litigating a copyright infringement action since damages are accessed on a *joint and several* bases, that is, when a copyright owner wins a copyright infringement lawsuit, he or she gets a judgment against all of the infringing parties and their liability for that judgment will be sought against all of them jointly, and/or severally, or individually, against each.

The Supreme Court dealt directly with the issues of secondary liability in its 1984 ruling regarding the infamous *Sony Betamax*[2] case. In the 1970s, television programming was distributed over-the-air (OTA) without any costs for the service. Users received the signal with an antenna. The programs were broadcast either for the hour or half hour, so if you wanted to watch a specific program, you had to be present

[1] In the famous *Napster* case, for example, the Court of Appeals for the Ninth Circuit observed that "[i]n the context of copyright law, vicarious liability extends beyond an employer/employee relationship to cases in which a defendant has the right and ability to supervise the infringing activity and also has a direct financial interest in such activities." *A&M Records, Inc. et al. v. Napster, Inc.*, 114 F.Supp.2d 896 at 920 (2000), *citations omitted.*

[2] 464 U.S. 417 (1984).

© LIAL/Shutterstock.com

at the scheduled hour. If you missed the program, you were unable to watch it unless the show was later rebroadcast as a "rerun." In order to remedy this timing issue, Sony began to develop a recording system, called the *Betamax* video tape recording machine together with a proprietary tape format to be used with their machine. Around the same timeframe, JVC also started working on the development of its competing VHS recording system with its "VCR" machine, both of which were universal and capable of being developed by other manufacturers. Both of these video recording systems provided the end users the ability to set up their home video recorders by attaching them to their OTA televisions receiving the broadcast signal and programming them to record their favorite television programs at the scheduled time, such that they could watch them later. As will be seen later, the Supreme Court described this process as *time-shifting.*

Several media production companies that were responsible for the broadcast programming, among them Universal Studios and the Walt Disney Company, were suspicious of this developing new technology, considering it a form of contributory, and possibly vicarious, infringement. Since the end-user was expected to "copy" the copyrighted programming onto a recording device, the effect would be a violation of the media companies' exclusive rights to distribution and reproduction, among other things. In 1976, at the time the lawsuit was initially filed, Congress was in the final stages of passing the 1976 Copyright Act, and so the media conglomerates felt that they would be unlikely to consider any additional privileges to film and movie makers. Thus, the media companies opted to bring an infringement action against Sony and its distributors in the United States District Court for the Central District of California in 1976, alleging that because they were manufacturing devices that could be used by endusers for copyright infringement, they were thereby liable for any infringement committed by purchasers of the device. The District Court ruled for Sony on the grounds that the noncommercial home recording should be considered a "fair use" and that access to free public information is a First Amendment public interest served by that use.[3] Significantly, the District Court based its arguments on the fact that the Sony technology was capable of significant "non-infringing" uses and, based on the analogous principle from patent law known as the *staple article of commerce* doctrine discussed earlier, dismissed the infringement claims.[4] The plaintiffs appealed this ruling to the Ninth Circuit.

---

[3] *Universal City Studios v. Sony Corp. of America*, 480 F. Supp. 429 (C.D. Cal. 1979).

[4] This traditional patent doctrine is now codified at 35 U.S.C. §271(c) which says that "the distribution of a component of a patented device will not violate the patent if it is suitable for use in other ways."

The Ninth Circuit was not persuaded by the District Court's novel staple use arguments, and thus reversed the lowers court's ruling, holding Sony liable for *contributory infringement* because the primary purpose of Betamax was *copying* the prerecorded broadcasts. The Circuit Court opined that the Betamax technology could not be a staple article because its main purpose was copying. The Ninth Circuit thus reversed the district's opinion and ordered the lower court to consider damages, injunctive relief, and compulsory licenses on remand.[5]

Sony filed a writ of certiorari to the Supreme Court, which was granted. After consideration of the oral arguments and the multitude of amicus briefs filed on behalf of both parties, the Supreme Court ruled 5-4 to reverse the Ninth Circuit in favor of Sony.[6] The Supreme Court's ruling resurrected the District Court's staple use doctrine, focusing on whether the video recording technology in question had significant *non-infringing* uses. The Supreme Court incorporated this principle when deciding to reverse the Ninth Circuit on the question of whether Sony could be described as "contributing" to copyright infringement by selling a machine capable of significant non-infringing uses. In the relevant kernel of its opinion, the Court stated:

> The question is thus whether the Betamax is capable of commercially significant non-infringing uses . . . one potential use of the Betamax plainly satisfies this standard, however it is understood: private, noncommercial time-shifting in the home. [. . .] [W]hen one considers the nature of a televised copyrighted audiovisual work. . . and that time-shifting merely enables a viewer to see such a work which he had been invited to witness in its entirety free of charge, the fact. . . that the entire work is reproduced. . . does not have its ordinary effect of militating against a finding of fair use.[7]

Essentially, the Betamax opinion creates a "safe harbor" for otherwise infringing technology provided it has "significant non-infringing usages." Since the Betamax machine was capable of noncommercial "time-shifting" in the home, it was deemed non-infringing. Immediately following their loss at the Supreme Court, the entertainment companies lobbied Congress to pass amendments to the 1976 Copyright Act that would protect them from the effects of these home copying technologies. However, due to the exponential sale of devices in the 8 years that had passed since the suit was initially filed, Congress was not prepared to take any action. Ironically, almost a decade later, the entertainment industry was successful in getting Congress to pass similar legislation with regard to the development of *digital audio recording* technology very similar to the Betamax and VCR technologies. In this instance, the Recording Industry Association of America (RIAA) and music publishers, concerned that consumers' ability to make perfect digital copies of music would destroy the market for audio recordings, were threatening to sue Sony and other manufacturing companies. They lobbied Congress to pass legislation imposing mandatory copy protection technology and royalties on devices and media, and Congress passed the Audio Home Recording Act of 1992 (AHRA), which assured that the RIAA and music

[5] *Universal City Studios v. Sony Corp. of America*, 659 F.2d 963 (9th Cir. 1982).

[6] 464 U.S. at 442 (1984).

[7] *Ibid.*, at 449–50.

publishers received royalties from the sale of Digital Audio Tapes (DATs) and, in exchange, allowed Sony and Philips to sale recordable digital formats such as DATs without fear of liability for lawsuits claiming contributory infringement. The AHRA contained a requirement that DATs contain an anti-circumvention provision, called the Serial Copy Management System (SCMS) requiring all digital audio recording devices that are sold, manufactured, or imported in the United States to include safeguards to avoid copyright infringement.[8]

© Hadrian/Shutterstock.com

Although it did not directly address the issue of contributory negligence, the first case decided under the AHRA's provisions was *Recording Indus. Ass'n of Am. v. Diamond Multimedia Sys., Inc.*,[9] involving that company's Diamond Rio—no, not the country band—MP3 player. The original Rio was a small device about 3 inches in diameter, with attachable headphones that required a user to download MP3 audio files, or rip them from the then-prevalent CDs to their computer and transfer them via cable to the Rio device and in order to listen to them anywhere. Before this technology, if a person wished to copy an original music recording, for example, create a cassette tape of a record or compact disc, that person was limited to analog technology to record their favorite song. When the end-user copied their original medium to an analog recording on a cassette tape, this "second-generation" copy suffered from a pronounced degradation in sound quality, that is, the highs and lows were truncated in the process. Each successive generation of recordings suffered a proportionally greater loss in quality. Unlike the analog process, the digital recordings were "lossless," meaning that each *copy* of the original sounded identical to the original. Since there is no degradation in sound quality regardless of how many generations of copies are made, thousands of perfect copies could be created from a single original recording. This technology opened the door to the world of music "pirates" who used the technology to create and distribute millions of perfect copies of commercially prepared recordings for which they have not licensed the copyrights. This devastated the music industry, causing a reduction in revenues of over 50% in less than 10 years and putting millions of people out of work, including the lowly songwriters whose royalties dried up and who became irrelevant.

The RIAA, an industry organization, fought hard against this new wave of infringement. In their complaint, they asserted that requiring the distribution of SCMS-embedded copies of copyrighted material, as required by the AHRA, would discourage illegal piracy and conversely encourage the purchase of legitimate recordings.

---

[8] 17 U.S.C. § 1002(a)(1), (2). This provision was later incorporated on a broader scale in the Digital Millennium Copyright Act of 1998.

[9] 180 F.3d 1072, 51 U.S.P.Q.2d (BNA) 1115 (9th Cir. 1999).

In reviewing the case, the Ninth Circuit looked at the Senate's congressional record of the passage of the AHRA to determine that "[t]he purpose of [the Act] is to ensure the right of consumers to make analog or digital audio recordings of copyrighted music for their private, noncommercial use."[10] But, even though this case did not involve claims of infringement or contributory liability, the Ninth Circuit draws from concepts in *Sony v. Universal* to suggest that noncommercial copying of recordings by an individual from a PC's hard disk to the Rio for personal use is a "fair." The ruling reads, in pertinent part:

> The Rio merely makes copies in order to render portable, or "space-shift," those files that already reside on a user's hard drive. *Cf. Sony Corp. of America v. Universal City Studios*, 464 U.S. 417, 455 (1984) (holding that "time-shifting" of copyrighted television shows with VCR's constitutes fair use under the Copyright Act, and thus is not an infringement). Such copying is paradigmatic non-commercial personal use entirely consistent with the purposes of the Act.[11]

In truth, the strategy of litigating the AHRA may have been the wrong approach by the RIAA, since that Act provides that copying to digital media is only allowed when the copying device or media is marketed specifically for *audio recording*, which triggers royalty requirements. The AHRA does not apply where copies are being made on computer hard drives and/or portable media players. Though this case was not appealed to the Supreme Court, its application of the Sony Test to a non-infringement issue is dubious. Nonetheless, this decision paved the pathway for the development of the portable digital player market and the copycat king, Apple, Inc., who began producing the first generation of iPods, copying both the Diamond Rio and Microsoft's Zune player. More importantly, Apple established iTunes, a music distribution platform, in order to sell more units of their fancy new MP3 player, the iPod!

---

[10] S. Rep. 102-294, at *86.

[11] *RIAA*, 180 F.3d at 1079.

19 Thought Experiments and Misappropriation

In prior chapters, I have explored the application of various contours of copyright, as defined by the Supreme Court, as well as other authorities' opinions, such as the Copyright Office itself, as to what constitutes a protectable expression. Beginning with *Feist* and the idea/expression dichotomy, we found that when a creative work moves along the spectrum between idea and expression, a spectrum that consists of increasing primordial originality, it begins to take on the stamp of an author's originality and takes on the form of expression, where copyright protection becomes available. As the court in *Feist* declared, originality is the *sine qua non*, or "essence," of protectability in copyright. As the essential ingredient in any copyright, then, originality must ultimately be the starting point of any inquiry into whether a work is protectable.

Underlying the *Feist* analysis is Justice Learned Hand's abstraction test, where we examined his metaphoric dividing line between the supporting skeleton and the substance of our body. We discover that his line is not a *fixed series of points* but rather is *mutable and fluid* depending on the facts of a particular case, just as it is difficult to ascertain where the bone ends and the flesh begins. Thus, to describe Justice Hand's analysis as an "abstraction test" is a misnomer in that it does not account for the mutability of the line between what is expression and the expression itself that Hand found so critical.

© art_of_galaxy/Shutterstock.com

Combining this mutability with what Justice O'Connor described as the *equitable rule of reason* we call "fair use," we incorporated that speech-protective contour, intended to avoid the rigid application of copyright protections where its application would otherwise stifle the very creativity Copyright Law is designed to foster. After applying these contours to everything from pop art to operating systems, we concluded, based on Justice Story's opinion in *Folsom*, that the fair use concept originated in common laws of the United States and England and was intended to secure the author's natural law property rights, even though it was abrogated, but not created, by the statutory monopoly allowed by the Progress Clause.

From these foundational principles, we have explored several of the more "evanescent" areas of copyright law in today's culture, specifically emotes, photographs, pop music, appropriation art, street art, graffiti, pantomime, dance, and tattoos. From what we found when we examined dance in particular, it is fair to conclude that judges who are steeped in the draconian laws and procedures of our legal system, and the regimented applications thereof, very frequently have difficulty deciphering the *nuanced contours* of protectable expression in a truly meaningful and consistent way. The subtleties of pantomimic expression are equally difficult to discern, as are the basic melodies and structures of pop music. Asking a judge to discern the nuanced and subtle rhythmic positions of a dancer's body, or the facial expression of a pantomime artist, conveyed in integrated movements through an expressive whole, may be somewhat akin to asking an auto mechanic to whip up a chocolate soufflé while he fixes the engine! These most subtle of copyrightable expressions illuminate the essence of copyright's evanescent quality, where the vapor can quickly fade when determining the requisite amount of *originality* required to move the spark of an idea along its way toward expression. It is important that we be able to perceive the evanescence when deciding on copyright infringement actions.

The justices arguably made the wrong decision in *Hanagami* when they compared a 480-step dance sequence to an "emote" in a video game, declaring that everything that was "copied" constituted a *lawful appropriation*. The court compared screenshots of the fluid art of dance to the compositional elements of a photograph evaluated by the Ninth Circuit in *Rentmeester*. The court found that "none of those elements is subject to copyright protection when viewed in isolation," referring in that instance to choices of the photographer related to the subject matter, pose, lighting, camera angle, depth of field, "*and the like*."[1] As we saw, the *Hanagami* court ruled that the "choreographic works [at issue in this case] are composed of *a number of individual poses* that, when 'viewed in isolation,' would not be protectable"[2] and that these "steps" copied from Hanagami's video were unprotectable when extracted from the context of the work. By conflating the individual "poses" in a fluid dance to

[1] 883 F.3d 1111, 1117 (9th Cir. 2018) (*emphasis added*).

[2] *Hanagami, slip. op.* at p. 15.

individual common dance "steps," as portrayed in screen captures, the court could not see the metaphoric "original" forest for the individual trees that were the focus of its abstraction test. Thus, the *Hanagami* court committed the logical fallacy of ambiguity. The *Hanagami* court should have taken a step backward, *no pun intended*, and considered the whole of the fluid dance creation as compared to the whole of the video sequence in order to discern the original contributions of Hanagami to the dance.

But contrast the *Hanagami* decision with the one in the *Bridgestone* case, where the court considered that George Clinton left his unique imprint on one word to *emphasize the downbeat*, and thereby created a *protectable* "one-note melody" worthy of protection. How can two courts come to such dramatically different conclusions relying on the same principles of analysis? Only in the context of intellectual property litigation is the application of black-letter principles so disparate and inconsistently applied and, as a result, multiple jurisdictions experience a proportionally higher share of difficulties as compared to other areas of law when they are trying to determine whether a copied element of nuanced art constitutes lawful or unlawful misappropriation. It is apparent that these art forms, which elude justices whose appreciation of the finer nuances may be observational at best, *demand a better tool for evaluation*. This is what Justice Learned Hand meant when he said that no one would ever be able to fix a line between the expression and what is expressed. It is apparent that he was envisioning a broader and more fluid system of analyzing a copyright infringement conflict that involved something more than a dichotomy.

When Justice Hand in *Nichols* made the statement that the line between idea and expression cannot be fixed, the metaphor he chose was the amalgamated relationship between the skeleton and the layers of organs, nerves, and blubber of the body. It was not so much an *immutable* "line" as it was a *mutable and amorphous* "glob" that oscillates depending on the facts, particularly the nature of the works being compared. In fact, he intended his abstraction test to be a more malleable process when he said that our concern in that test is with "the line between expression and what is expressed." Of particularly interesting note, Learned Hand *did not* use the word "idea" in his metaphor. In *Nichols*, Hand was comparing competing scripts involving instances of an Irish Catholic getting married to a Jewish spouse and the ensuing cultural entanglements and divisions that create. But Justice Hand evaluated the two works of art and determined that what was being copied were *universal concepts* and *stock characters*, not the expression of those ideas. What Justice Hand is referring to here should not be thought of as a binary dichotomy, but rather as an *evolution of originality*. Hand's solution in *Nichols* is more of a *mutable method* of analysis than a hard and fast test as it has since evolved. "Fixing" the correct *level of abstraction* must necessarily be *ad hoc*, based on the works of art as an issue. In his moment of despair, Hand himself was wont to find a better method as he declared that the line could not be fixed.

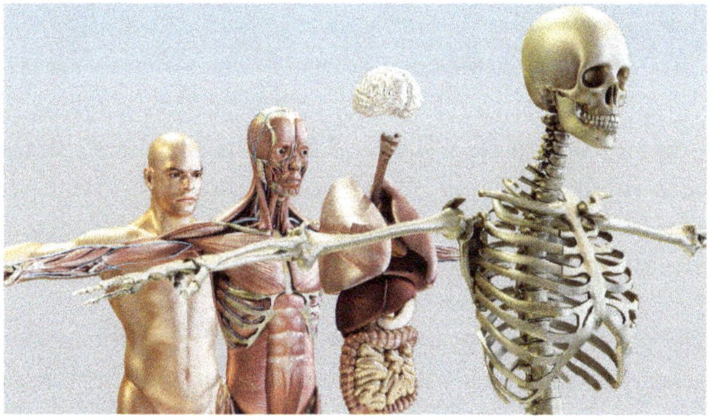

Hands' more fluid method of analyzing similarity, as well as misappropriation, is closer in form to the idea of copyright protection expressed in the English decision of *Donoghue*, where the court illustrated the concept by stating that "the person who has clothed the idea in form, whether by means of a picture, a play, or a book" owns the copyright. Extending this metaphor of clothing to a form to create expression, we might envision a couture with a seamstress dummy pinning various swaths of cloth here and there until suddenly it begins to take the shape of a sports jacket. To focus on each piece of cloth and declare that none of them are protectable is misguided. The couture infuses the creative work with sufficient originality that, at some point along the process of "clothing the form," she owns the expression.

Modern courts are engrained in the binary aspects of law, something is either *lawful* or it is *unlawful.* That is the way judges are programmed to think. Consequently, modern courts applying a misappropriation analysis to a copyright issue tend to gravitate toward the immutability of the idea/expression dichotomy. But when a fluid dance creation is reduced by the abstraction test to a few dozen photographs of extracted poses, then "viewed in isolation" by the judge, the process often is bastardized, bogged down in the binary weeds, and it becomes impossible to discern the *existence* of, much less the *emergence* of, an original thought.

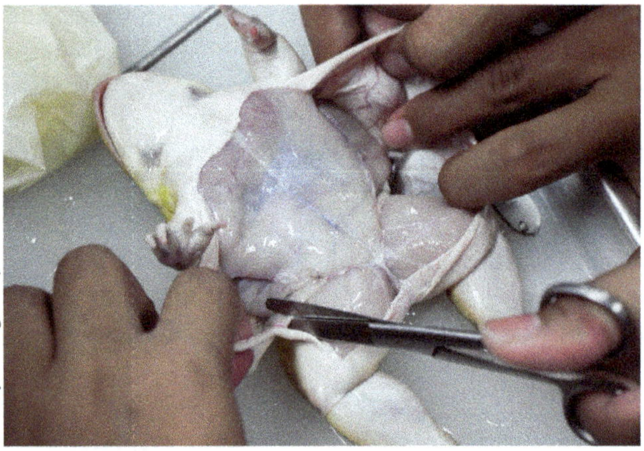

© Rattiya Thongdumhyu/Shutterstock.com

When I was a young boy around 5 years old, I received a biology kit containing a scalpel and a dead frog packaged in formaldehyde. After I completed the lackluster task of dissecting the dead frog, I had the brilliant adolescent idea to anesthetize a live one by dumping it in a vat of gasoline—which I thought would kill it—and dissecting it. Much to my horror, when I cut open its tiny chest, I discovered that the frog's heart was still beating. Unfortunately, in my effort to discover the *magic* that is the frog, I discovered that I had destroyed its *very essence.* I did not possess the means to restore the life in the frog and so it died. The modern abstraction test of ascertaining whether copyrightable elements have been misappropriated is analogous to my experiment with the frog. Once we reduce an original expression to the basic elements of what is expressed, dissected from their originality and in isolation from the overall expression, the *magic* is lost, and the very essence of the originality cannot be discerned.

The usual remedy for this conundrum is to use the modern "total look and feel" test for misappropriation, usually applied by a court *prior* to abstracting the non-protectable elements in our effort to "separate the wheat from the chaff," thus combining the two methodologies. This approach to ascertain misappropriation borrows more prevalently from the idea of the *Donoghue* court discussed above, in which the judge held that the copyright is owned by "the person who clothes an idea in form" where the emphasis is on the entire expression rather than its individual component parts. While this combined effort seems to achieve a better balance between the two approaches, in practical application it too can create inconsistent results. If we are watching two sets of professional dancers performing the same dance, such as, for example, the Spanish Pasodoble, it can be difficult from watching each version to draw any meaningful differences in the expressions simply by looking at the overall look and feel of the dance. The same might be said for a comparison of two pop compositions, which feature similar chord structure and 4/4 timing along with similar lyrics. In short, using the total look and feel approach makes it difficult to distinguish between a situation where one song is an infringement of the other, and a situation where two similarly sounding songs were the product of *simultaneous creation*, or where both songs borrowed ideas from a public domain work.

To resolve this perceived conundrum, I suggest that we apply the German concept of *Gedankenversuch*, or "thought experiments," to the evaluation of whether a work has been infringed, that is, protectable elements have been misappropriated from a protectable work. Many of Einstein's most influential theories, all of which he originated in his *anus mirabilis*, were derived from numerous thought experiments, a process he frequently used. Most of these experiments were likely "conducted" during the 7 years he worked at his mundane job at the Swiss patent office, shuffling through applications.

One of the more famous of Einstein's thought experiments was the elevator experiment, which led to what Einstein described as his "happiest thought," that gravity might be equivalent to acceleration. Einstein realized that when people consider gravity, they generally imagined it as a force that weighs objects down. If a person is sitting in a chair, for example, he or she might think that it is gravity that forces the body to remain in the chair and not float away. From that perspective of gravity, a person might think that this powerful force would cause a bowling ball, being heavier than a feather, to fall to the earth at a faster rate when dropped from a high precipice. Based on such a frame of reference, Aristotle drew the conclusion that objects fall proportional to their weight.[3] In fact, in our earthly constraint of space and time, it is indeed the perception that the objects weighing different amounts appear to fall at different rates, leading the experimenter to what has been proven to be the incorrect conclusion, as *Galileo* determined over a thousand years later in his famous *Leaning Tower of Pisa* experiment, which most actually consider a thought experiment as well. Aided by NASA's vacuum chamber at the Space Power Facility, using high-speed photographic technologies, Galileo's thought experiment was taken to a new level, and in a perfect vacuum, the bowling ball and feathers fall gracefully in unison as they descend more than 30 ft. These differences in perceptions of gravity are directly affected by a person's frame of reference.

© spauletail/Shutterstock.com

[3] In a text called *Physics* (Greek, φυσικὴ) that is attributed to the fourth-century BC philosopher.

Einstein realized that the typical examples of gravity people speak about were drawn from observations made from incorrect frames of reference. Why, he asked, do we need to talk about chairs, bowling balls, and feathers when we consider gravity? Gravity is a force of nature that exists separately from the objects it affects, so why not create an "experiment" that eliminates the connection? He determined that when conducting an experiment involving gravity in a physical elevator where an object is dropped, the observer cannot reasonably determine whether the movement of the object is caused by the *earth's gravitational pull* or by the *elevator's rapid upward motion.* This is due to the fact that the observer is enclosed in the elevator and unable to view the object in the elevator from an external all-encompassing perspective, that is, their frame of reference is tied to Earth.

© vchal/Shutterstock.com

To correct for these distorting frames of reference, Einstein "cut the cord" in order to create, in his mind, a zero-gravity space where all noticeable elements would fall at the same rate, that is, he performed a *Gedankenversuch* in which he envisions the observer trapped inside an imaginary elevator to which the cable had been severed, leaving the elevator floating, or more appropriately falling, but in the vacuum of space, just as the NASA experimenters did years later. In other words, Einstein eliminated the frame of reference by envisioning the experiment in his mind. By so doing, Einstein had the epiphany that what you are doing in a gravitational field when it is just you, alone in an elevator with just gravity, is free falling in the space–time continuum. So, Einstein's happiest thought was his leap from the observation that a *falling person feels no gravity* to the realization that *gravity might be equivalent to acceleration.*

Einstein realized that, if it is equivalent to acceleration, gravity *affects all bodies in the same way* because it is a *property* of the *curvature of spacetime.* Gravity is *not* a force propagating *through* spacetime like electromagnetic or nuclear forces, as we perceive in our daily existence, constrained to our earthly frame of reference. When Einstein conceived of gravity in this way, that it operates independently of an observer's choice of coordinates, this led to his discovery of the theory of general relativity.

Einstein extrapolated the conclusions of his elevator experiment to the motion of the Earth as it rotates on its axis and orbits the sun constrained by its massive gravitational pull, further regulated in spacetime by the pull of other larger planets in our solar system. In spacetime, everything enclosed within the Earth's atmosphere—everything we perceive—*is accelerating at precisely the same rate.* The Earth is therefore in a constant state of "falling" around the sun in its circular orbit. As such, the Earth is *weightless* in spacetime, just as a person parachuting from an airplane in free flight is "weightless" at the peak of their descent. One of the more interesting observations about Einstein's elevator experience is that a person or object can *fall in a circle.* From that observation, Einstein concluded that spacetime is *not linear* as we experience it, but rather is *curved*, and thus *all matter* is falling along the natural curves of spacetime.

That is what led Einstein to his paradigm-shifting theory of general relativity, that is, that *gravity* is not a force but is *curved spacetime.*

Just as Einstein eliminated the constraints of our daily experience of gravity in his mind, thought experimentation allows a person to eliminate all of the unnecessary considerations that confuse the analysis of an issue, and eliminate the extraneous interferences, allowing the person's thoughts to hone in on only the essential considerations. How, you might be wondering at this point, does this possibly relate to the analysis of *copyright* and the *elimination of non-protectable elements*? Drawing from Einstein's process, described above, the falling objects observed within the enclosed elevator might be analogous to the non-protectable elements in a creative work, whereas the vacuum of space could be analogized to the originality that permeates the idea-expression dichotomy. This approach to the analysis could serve to eliminate some of the inconsistent judicial applications arising from combining the intrinsic and extrinsic tests for misappropriation.

© Marta Design/Shutterstock.com

Currently, when a court uses the abstraction analysis as it has evolved in modern times, it will *reduce* or *abstract* a copyrighted work down to the point where all is remaining are §102(b) non-protectable ideas, the notes and chords in a musical composition, the steps in a dance movement, the words and phrases in a literary work, and the colors and shapes in a visual work. Describing §102 as the idea/expression dichotomy, the starting point of the abstraction test, is an unfortunate description of Hand's bone/body metaphor. By too strictly applying the distinctions found in §102, the court has eliminated any scraps of the author's originality, and all that remains is the essential building blocks of creativity. Case in point, when examining the copyrighted dance sequence in *Hanagami*, consisting of 480 steps, the court isolated the still images of only a handful of poses from the entire original sequence of Hanagami's dance, forcing itself to focus solely on the fact that those poses, *isolated from the creative wo*rk, were not protectable. The court also incorrectly focused on the fact that the dancer and the setting were physical, whereas the derivative creation was an animated character in a virtual setting. Therefore, based on its clinical, by the book abstraction analysis, the court ruled that there was no infringement. But those elements of the dance, the poses, when taken in isolation, in no way represent the originality of Hanagami's work of expression, that is, the fluid movement of the dance. In other words, the *Hanagami* court was quite literally constrained by its *frame of reference* from seeing the essence of originality in the dance sequence.

Thus, when courts rely solely on the modern abstraction test, they fail to observe the sometimes-subtle layers and subtext of a work and cannot perceive the originality, just as the typical person interprets gravity as a force. By so doing, they overemphasize the *observation* of gravity *in the earth's atmosphere*, overlooking the more *elemental nature of gravity* as it relates to the space–time continuum, which Einstein discovered.

Likewise, by breaking a copyrighted work down into elements independent of the work itself to determine its copyrightability, the court fails to incorporate the *transformative and inspirational use* of these elements, which is the essence of originality, the *sine qua non*. In other words, by dissecting the work, they kill the frog, just as I did when I was an aspiring Leonardo Da Vinci. When the court analyzes the basic elements of a work in isolation from the broader transformational view of the work as a whole, it can be blinded by its preconceived frame of reference when determining the originality of a copyrighted work.

Some courts will go the other extreme instead and focus on the work in its entirety without consideration of its isolated basic components. But by emphasizing the "dichotomy" aspect of §102 as a frame of reference, courts focus only on those two aspects of the creative work—the idea side and the expression side—thereby *eliminating the spectrum of originality* that exists between those two termini in almost every work, that is, the blob of organs and flesh that are inextricably linked to our skeletons, *à la* Justice Hand's apropos metaphor. Neither the intrinsic nor the extrinsic test, nor a combination thereof, serves the intended purpose thereof, that is, to determine whether the creative and original elements of a copyrighted work have been misappropriated, and therefore, infringed. Hand's abstraction test is not a way of distinguishing an idea from an expression, but rather a way of distinguishing protectable ideas from unprotectable ideas based on a criterion of generality—courts must routinely use the dichotomy as a means to weed out the unprotectable elements, but the modern abstraction test has eliminated this component of generality from Hand's analysis.

My proposal for a solution is to recast Einstein's thought experiment into a *legales Gedankenversuch*, a "legal thought experiment" wherein we eliminate all of the unnecessary considerations that confuse the analysis of misappropriation, extraneous interferences such as the still images of a dance sequence, and allow our thoughts to focus solely on the essential consideration of the "evanescent" qualities of a work, that is, the "magic," to determine whether the work's originality has been appropriated illegally, or whether the author of the derivative has simply applied general elements and ideas to a new form of expression.

In any consideration of whether an original work has been infringed by a derivative, it is quickly obvious what *ideas* or *building blocks* are shared by both works, that is, we can see that the notes, chords, and much if not all of the rhythm and harmonies are frequently substantially similar, and we know that none of these are protectable *in isolation from the original work*. This is the reason courts and litigators rely so heavily on the testimonies of expert musicologists and historians. So, the pertinent question is why, in the name of abstraction, do we perform *a dissection* of the original work into its elemental building blocks? Would it not be better to apply the legal thought experiment of experiencing the intended essence of both works of art, without consideration of the specific building blocks, whether that be visually, aurally or otherwise? This experiment might allow the trier of fact to experience the originality in the work.

The *Bridgeport* case involving George Clinton's *Atomic Dog* is a perfect example. Had the courts used the abstraction analysis to determine misappropriation, the outcome most likely would have been different. In fact, on appeal, the defense, in that case, insisted that "the jury should not have been able to consider either the word 'dog' used as musical punctuation or the rhythmic panting in 'D.O.G. in Me' as infringement because those elements are not original and, thus, should have been filtered out," that is, *they cannot be misappropriated*.[4] Having so allowed, they argued, the district court committed reversible error.

[4] *Bridgeport Music, Inc. v. UMG Recordings, Inc.*, No. 07-5596 (6th Cir. Nov. 4, 2009).

Abstracted and isolated from the entirety of the song and Clinton's unique style and personality, it is true that the word "dog" is merely a word, not entitled to copyright protection. But what is not clear is whether the alleged infringer was using the general word for canine to create a new expression, or did they steal Clinton's expression to convey it. Fortunately, the Sixth Circuit disagreed with the appellant and affirmed the expert testimony that allowed the trier of fact to determine that the word "dog," in the context of the song and Clinton's style, constituted a "*stand-alone melody of one word*" used as musical punctuation at intervals on the tonic note of the song and that the sound of panting followed the rhythm of the song.[5] Likewise, another expert in the case testified the "bow, wow, wow, yippee you ki yay" line in the song was one of its most recognizable and was frequently licensed as a stand-alone phrase. Though the Clinton case has been scrutinized and criticized for being one of the few, if not the only, case that has held that one word can constitute a "stand-alone" melody, if you listen to the two songs at issue in this case, it is clear that the court is correct, and that the derivative version copied original elements of Clinton's creation and did not simultaneously use a generic idea. But if the courts had relied on the abstraction test, these crucial elements, the *crux* of Clinton's song that evinced a stamp of his originality, would likely have been eliminated from consideration as non-protectable elements, and the case would arguably have been improperly adjudicated.

Likewise, in the *Williams* case considered in Chapter 12, sole reliance on the total look and feel, or *intrinsic* analysis would have produced an incorrect result. The plaintiffs in that case, Pharrell Williams and Robin Thicke, relied on a theory of the case that emphasized the overall *feel* of each musical composition, specifically claiming that Williams was simply paying "homage" to the Motown genre, or copying *a style*, rather than copying the original Marvin Gaye composition. In their complaint, they asked the court to enter an order declaring that their actions were not infringement on that basis. Had the court agreed, they would have been ignoring the evidence presented by the defendant's Estate that Williams actually inserted elemental copies of Gaye's composition into his own at the exact same measures in his song, usually corresponding in time measures. In the most pertinent of those instances, Williams copied a characteristic "stamp" of Gaye's originality, the *parlando*, with a section of rap that was the same number of measures. No other Motown artists used that characteristic Gaye technique. In other words, these basic elements, although standing alone, are not necessarily protectable, combined to illustrate Gaye's originality that was infused in *Got to Give It Up*. By copying Gaye's originality, Williams committed the infringement, even though some of them would not be entitled to protection under copyright outside the context of Gaye's creation. It took the masterful assembly of two experts by lead counsel Richard Busch of Nashville, one a musicologist and one an expert in African-American Music, to construct the spacetime curvature of the song and illustrate this uniqueness to the jury.

What the *Clinton* and *Williams* cases illustrate is that it is more important in the analysis of substantial similarity to focus on something beyond the total look and feel combined with the abstracted elements that are not entitled to copyright protection. The focus instead should be on the *kernels of originality* embedded in the fluidity of the copyright, that is, the "spacetime curvature" of the copyright. By de-emphasizing the elements that are not protectable (and obvious), as well as comparing the overall feel of the two works, and focusing instead on the *heart* or *crux* of the copyright, that is, the goal of the legal

---

[5] *Ibid.*

thought experiment would be to eliminate the distraction of the analyses and, at least in cases involving musical compositions, *listen to the music* in an effort to ascertain the soul of the creator. Thus, the copying of a *relatively small* but *qualitatively important* or *crucial element* can be an appropriate basis upon which to find substantial similarity and, therefore, misappropriation. One court noted that if a single copied line or a few copied words are an "integral part" of a protected work, and are "readily recognizable" as such—such as, for example, "E.T. phone home" in connection with the movie—copying such normally unprotectable elements constitutes an actionable infringement.[6] To do that, more information about the artist who created the original work and their inspiration for its creation will be needed. However, courts rarely arrive at the correct conclusions using the traditional test for misappropriation, that is, total look and feel versus abstraction, but rather must understand the creative impetus and originality that flows through the "curvature" of the work in its own space–time continuum. In that, the trier of fact must immerse themselves in order to understand the artist's creativity. That task requires a bit more than the clinical abstraction analysis. It requires a *legales Gedankenversuch* along the lines of Einstein's thought experiments.

[6] See *Murray Hill Publ'ns, Inc. v. ABC Comm., Inc.*, 264 F.3d 622, 633 (6th Cir. 2001).

Appendix[1]

FEIST PUBLICATIONS, INC. v. RURAL TELEPHONE SERVICE CO., INC.

No. 89–1909

SUPREME COURT OF THE UNITED STATES

499 U.S. 340 (1991)

January 9, 1991, Argued

March 27, 1991, Decided

O'Connor, J., delivered the opinion of the Court, in which Rehnquist, C. J., and White, Marshall, Stevens, Scalia, Kennedy, and Souter, JJ., joined. Blackmun, J., concurred in the judgment.

This case requires us to clarify the extent of copyright protection available to telephone directory white pages.

I.

Rural Telephone Service Company, Inc., is a certified public utility that provides telephone service to several communities in northwest Kansas. It is subject to a state regulation that requires all telephone companies operating in Kansas to issue annually an updated telephone directory. Accordingly, as a condition of its monopoly franchise, Rural publishes a typical telephone directory, consisting of white pages and yellow pages. The white pages list in alphabetical order the names of Rural's subscribers, together with their towns and telephone numbers. The yellow pages list Rural's business subscribers alphabetically by category and feature classified advertisements of various sizes. Rural distributes its directory free of charge to its subscribers, but earns revenue by selling yellow pages advertisements.

Feist Publications, Inc., is a publishing company that specializes in area-wide telephone directories. Unlike a typical directory, which covers only a particular calling area, Feist's area-wide directories cover a much larger geographical range, reducing the need to call directory assistance or consult multiple directories. The Feist directory that is the subject of this litigation covers 11 different telephone service areas in 15 counties and contains 46,878 white pages listings—compared to Rural's approximately 7,700 listings. Like Rural's directory, Feist's is distributed free of charge and includes both white pages and yellow pages. Feist and Rural compete vigorously for yellow pages advertising.

[1] "The cases in this Appendix have been condensed where indicated by the following marker "*****"

As the sole provider of telephone service in its service area, Rural obtains subscriber information quite easily. Persons desiring telephone service must apply to Rural and provide their names and addresses; Rural then assigns them a telephone number. Feist is not a telephone company, let alone one with monopoly status, and therefore lacks independent access to any subscriber information. To obtain white pages listings for its area-wide directory, Feist approached each of the 11 telephone companies operating in northwest Kansas and offered to pay for the right to use its white pages listings.

Of the 11 telephone companies, only Rural refused to license its listings to Feist. Rural's refusal created a problem for Feist, as omitting these listings would have left a gaping hole in its area-wide directory, rendering it less attractive to potential yellow pages advertisers. In a decision subsequent to that which we review here, the District Court determined that this was precisely the reason Rural refused to license its listings. The refusal was motivated by an unlawful purpose "to extend its monopoly in telephone service to a monopoly in yellow pages advertising." *Rural Telephone Service Co. v. Feist Publications, Inc.*, 737 F. Supp. 610, 622 (Kan. 1990).

Unable to license Rural's white pages listings, Feist used them without Rural's consent. Feist began by removing several thousand listings that fell outside the geographic range of its area-wide directory, then hired personnel to investigate the 4,935 that remained. These employees verified the data reported by Rural and sought to obtain additional information. As a result, a typical Feist listing includes the individual's street address; most of Rural's listings do not. Notwithstanding these additions, however, 1,309 of the 46,878 listings in Feist's 1983 directory were identical to listings in Rural's 1982–1983 white pages. App. 54 (P 15–16), 57. Four of these were fictitious listings that Rural had inserted into its directory to detect copying.

Rural sued for copyright infringement in the District Court for the District of Kansas taking the position that Feist, in compiling its own directory, could not use the information contained in Rural's white pages. Rural asserted that Feist's employees were obliged to travel door-to-door or conduct a telephone survey to discover the same information for themselves. Feist responded that such efforts were economically impractical and, in any event, unnecessary because the information copied was beyond the scope of copyright protection. The District Court granted summary judgment to Rural, explaining that "courts have consistently held that telephone directories are copyrightable" and citing a string of lower court decisions. 663 F. Supp. 214, 218 (1987). In an unpublished opinion, the Court of Appeals for the Tenth Circuit affirmed "for substantially the reasons given by the district court." App. to Pet. for Cert. 4a, judgt. order reported at 916 F. 2d 718 (1990). We granted certiorari, 498 U.S. 808 (1990), to determine whether the copyright in Rural's directory protects the names, towns, and telephone numbers copied by Feist.

II.

A

This case concerns the interaction of two well-established propositions. The first is that facts are not copyrightable; the other, that compilations of facts generally are. Each of these propositions possesses an impeccable pedigree. That there can be no valid copyright in facts is universally understood. The most fundamental axiom of copyright law is that "no author may copyright his ideas or the facts he narrates." *Harper & Row, Publishers, Inc. v. Nation Enterprises,* 471 U.S. 539, 556 (1985). Rural wisely concedes this point, noting in its brief that "facts and discoveries, of course, are not themselves subject to copyright protection." Brief for Respondent 24. At the same time, however, it is beyond dispute that compilations of facts are within the subject matter of copyright. Compilations were expressly mentioned in the Copyright Act of 1909, and again in the Copyright Act of 1976.

There is an undeniable tension between these two propositions. Many compilations consist of nothing but raw data—*i.e.*, wholly factual information not accompanied by any original written expression. On what basis may one claim a copyright in such a work?

*****

The key to resolving the tension lies in understanding why facts are not copyrightable. The sine qua non of copyright is originality. To qualify for copyright protection, a work must be original to the author. See Harper & Row, supra, at 547–549. Original, as the term is used in copyright, means only that the work was independently created by the author (as opposed to copied from other works), and that it possesses at least some minimal degree of creativity. M. Nimmer & D. Nimmer, Copyright §§2.01[A], [B] (1990) (hereinafter Nimmer). To be sure, the requisite level of creativity is extremely low; even a slight amount will suffice. The vast majority of works make the grade quite easily, as they possess some creative spark, "no matter how crude, humble or obvious" it might be. Id., §1.08[C][1]. Originality does not signify novelty; a work may be original even though it closely resembles other works so long as the similarity is fortuitous, not the result of copying.

*****

Originality is a constitutional requirement. The source of Congress' power to enact copyright laws is Article I, §8, cl. 8, of the Constitution, which authorizes Congress to "secure for limited Times to Authors . . . the exclusive Right to their respective Writings." In two decisions from the late 19th century—*The Trade-Mark Cases, 100 U.S. 82* (1879); and *Burrow-Giles Lithographic Co. v. Sarony,* 111 U.S. 53 (1884)—this Court defined the crucial terms "authors" and "writings." In so doing, the Court made it unmistakably clear that these terms presuppose a degree of originality.

In The Trade-Mark Cases, the Court addressed the constitutional scope of "writings." For a particular work to be classified "under the head of writings of authors," the Court determined, "originality is required." 100 U.S., at 94. The Court explained that originality requires independent creation plus a modicum of creativity: "While the word writings may be liberally construed, as it has been, to include original designs for engraving, prints, &c., it is only such as are original, and are founded in the creative powers of the mind. The writings which are to be protected are the fruits of intellectual labor, embodied in the form of books, prints, engravings, and the like." Ibid. (emphasis in original).

In Burrow-Giles, the Court distilled the same requirement from the Constitution's use of the word "authors." The Court defined "author," in a constitutional sense, to mean "he to whom anything owes its origin; originator; maker." 111 U.S., at 58 (internal quotation marks omitted). As in The Trade-Mark Cases, the Court emphasized the creative component of originality. It described copyright as being limited to "original intellectual conceptions of the author," 111 U.S., at 58, and stressed the importance of requiring an author who accuses another of infringement to prove "the existence of those facts of originality, of intellectual production, of thought, and conception." Id., at 59–60.

The originality requirement articulated in The Trade-Mark Cases and Burrow-Giles remains the touchstone of copyright protection today. See *Goldstein v. California,* 412 U.S. 546, 561–562 (1973). It is the very "premise of copyright law." *Miller v. Universal City Studios, Inc.,* 650 F. 2d 1365, 1368 (CA5 1981).

*****

It is this bedrock principle of copyright that mandates the law's seemingly disparate treatment of facts and factual compilations. "No one may claim originality as to facts." Id., §2.11[A], p. 2–157. This is because facts do not owe their origin to an act of authorship. The distinction is one between creation and discovery: The first person to find and report a particular fact has not created the fact; he or she has merely discovered its existence. To borrow from Burrow-Giles, one who discovers a fact is not its "maker" or "originator." 111 U.S., at 58. "The discoverer merely finds and records." Nimmer §2.03[E].

*****

Factual compilations, on the other hand, may possess the requisite originality. The compilation author typically chooses which facts to include, in what order to place them, and how to arrange the collected data so that they may be used effectively by readers. These choices as to selection and arrangement, so long as they are made independently by the compiler and entail a minimal degree of creativity, are sufficiently original that Congress may protect such compilations through the copyright laws. Nimmer §§2.11[D], 3.03; Denicola 523, n. 38. Thus, even a directory that contains absolutely no protectable written expression, only facts, meets the constitutional minimum for copyright protection if it features an original selection or arrangement. See Harper & Row, 471 U.S., at 547. Accord, Nimmer §3.03.

This protection is subject to an important limitation. The mere fact that a work is copyrighted does not mean that every element of the work may be protected. Originality remains the sine qua non of copyright; accordingly, copyright protection may extend only to those components of a work that are original to the author. Patterson & Joyce 800–802; Ginsburg, Creation and Commercial Value: Copyright Protection of Works of Information, 90 Colum. L. Rev. 1865, 1868, and n. 12 (1990) (hereinafter Ginsburg). Thus, if the compilation author clothes facts with an original collocation of words, he or she may be able to claim a copyright in this written expression. Others may copy the underlying facts from the publication, but not the precise words used to present them. In Harper & Row, for example, we explained that President Ford could not prevent others from copying bare historical facts from his autobiography, see 471 U.S., at 556–557, but that he could prevent others from copying his "subjective descriptions and portraits of public figures." Id., at 563. Where the compilation author adds no written expression but rather lets the facts speak for themselves, the expressive element is more elusive. The only conceivable expression is the manner in which the compiler has selected and arranged the facts. Thus, if the selection and arrangement are original, these elements of the work are eligible for copyright protection. See Patry, Copyright in Compilations of Facts (or Why the "White Pages" Are Not Copyrightable), 12 Com. & Law 37, 64 (Dec. 1990) (hereinafter Patry). No matter how original the format, however, the facts themselves do not become original through association. See Patterson & Joyce 776.

This inevitably means that the copyright in a factual compilation is thin. Notwithstanding a valid copyright, a subsequent compiler remains free to use the facts contained in another's publication to aid in preparing a competing work, so long as the competing work does not feature the same selection and arrangement. As one commentator explains it: "No matter how much original authorship the work displays, the facts and ideas it exposes are free for the taking. . . . The very same facts and ideas may be divorced from the context imposed by the author, and restated or reshuffled by second comers, even if the author was the first to discover the facts or to propose the ideas." Ginsburg 1868.

*****

Copyright treats facts and factual compilations in a wholly consistent manner. Facts, whether alone or as part of a compilation, are not original and therefore may not be copyrighted. A factual compilation is eligible for copyright if it features an original selection or arrangement of facts, but the copyright is limited to the particular selection or arrangement. In no event may copyright extend to the facts themselves.

B

As we have explained, originality is a constitutionally mandated prerequisite for copyright protection. The Court's decisions announcing this rule predate the Copyright Act of 1909, but ambiguous language in the 1909 Act caused some lower courts temporarily to lose sight of this requirement.

The 1909 Act embodied the originality requirement, but not as clearly as it might have. See Nimmer §2.01. The subject matter of copyright was set out in §§3 and 4 of the Act. Section 4 stated that copyright was available to "all the writings of an author." 35 Stat. 1076. By using the words "writings" and "author"—the same words used in Article I, §8, of the Constitution and defined by the Court in The Trade-Mark Cases and Burrow-Giles—the statute necessarily incorporated the originality requirement articulated in the Court's decisions. It did so implicitly, however, thereby leaving room for error.

Section 3 was similarly ambiguous. It stated that the copyright in a work protected only "the copyrightable component parts of the work." It thus stated an important copyright principle, but failed to identify the specific characteristic—originality—that determined which component parts of a work were copyrightable and which were not.

Most courts construed the 1909 Act correctly, notwithstanding the less-than-perfect statutory language. They understood from this Court's decisions that there could be no copyright without originality.

*****

But some courts misunderstood the statute. See, e. g., *Leon v. Pacific Telephone & Telegraph Co.*, 91 F. 2d 484 (CA9 1937); *Jeweler's Circular Publishing Co. v. Keystone Publishing Co.*, 281 F. 83 (CA2 1922). These courts ignored §§3 and 4, focusing their attention instead on §5 of the Act. Section 5, however, was purely technical in nature: It provided that a person seeking to register a work should indicate on the application the type of work, and it listed 14 categories under which the work might fall. One of these categories was "books, including composite and cyclopaedic works, directories, gazetteers, and other compilations." §5(a). Section 5 did not purport to say that all compilations were automatically copyrightable. Indeed, it expressly disclaimed any such function, pointing out that "the subject-matter of copyright is defined in section four." Nevertheless, the fact that factual compilations were mentioned specifically in §5 led some courts to infer erroneously that directories and the like were copyrightable per se, "without any further or precise showing of original—personal—authorship." Ginsburg 1895.

Making matters worse, these courts developed a new theory to justify the protection of factual compilations. Known alternatively as "sweat of the brow" or "industrious collection," the underlying notion was that copyright was a reward for the hard work that went into compiling facts. The classic formulation of the doctrine appeared in Jeweler's Circular Publishing Co., 281 F., at 88:

"The right to copyright a book upon which one has expended labor in its preparation does not depend upon whether the materials which he has collected consist or not of matters which are publici juris, or whether such materials show literary skill or originality, either in thought or in language, or anything more than industrious collection. The man who goes through the streets of a town and puts down the names of each of the inhabitants, with their occupations and their street number, acquires material of which he is the author" (emphasis added).

The "sweat of the brow" doctrine had numerous flaws, the most glaring being that it extended copyright protection in a compilation beyond selection and arrangement—the compiler's original contributions—to the facts themselves. Under the doctrine, the only defense to infringement was independent creation. A subsequent compiler was "not entitled to take one word of information previously published," but rather had to "independently work out the matter for himself, so as to arrive at the same result from the same common sources of information." Id., at 88–89 (internal quotations omitted). "Sweat of the brow" courts thereby eschewed the most fundamental axiom of copyright law—that no one may copyright facts or ideas. See *Miller v. Universal City Studios, Inc.*, 650 F. 2d, at 1372 (criticizing "sweat of the brow" courts because "ensuring that later writers obtain the facts independently . . . is precisely the scope of protection given . . . copyrighted matter, and the law is clear that facts are not entitled to such protection").

Decisions of this Court applying the 1909 Act make clear that the statute did not permit the "sweat of the brow" approach.

*****

Recognizing that §5 of the Act specifically mentioned "'periodicals, including newspapers,'" §5(b), the Court acknowledged that news articles were copyrightable. Id., at 234. It flatly rejected, however, the notion that the copyright in an article extended to the factual information it contained: "The news element—the information respecting current events contained in the literary production—is not the creation of the writer, but is a report of matters that ordinarily are publici juris; it is the history of the day." Ibid.*

*****

C

"Sweat of the brow" decisions did not escape the attention of the Copyright Office. When Congress decided to overhaul the copyright statute and asked the Copyright Office to study existing problems, see *Mills Music, Inc. v. Snyder*, 469 U.S. 153, 159 (1985), the Copyright Office promptly recommended that Congress clear up the confusion in the lower courts as to the basic standards of copyrightability. The Register of Copyrights explained in his first report to Congress that "originality" was a "basic requisite" of copyright under the 1909 Act, but that "the absence of any reference to [originality] in the statute seems to have led to misconceptions as to what is copyrightable matter." Report of the Register of

Copyrights on the General Revision of the U.S. Copyright Law, 87th Cong., 1st Sess., p. 9 (H. Judiciary Comm. Print 1961). The Register suggested making the originality requirement explicit. Ibid.

Congress took the Register's advice. In enacting the Copyright Act of 1976, Congress dropped the reference to "all the writings of an author" and replaced it with the phrase "original works of authorship." 17 U. S. C. §102(a). In making explicit the originality requirement, Congress announced that it was merely clarifying existing law: "The two fundamental criteria of copyright protection [are] originality and fixation in tangible form. . . . The phrase 'original works of authorship,' which is purposely left undefined, is intended to incorporate without change the standard of originality established by the courts under the present [1909] copyright statute." H. R. Rep. No. 94-1476, p. 51 (1976) (emphasis added) (hereinafter H. R. Rep.); S. Rep. No. 94-473, p. 50 (1975) (emphasis added) (hereinafter S. Rep.). This sentiment was echoed by the Copyright Office: "Our intention here is to maintain the established standards of originality. . . ." Supplementary Report of the Register of Copyrights on the General Revision of U.S. Copyright Law, 89th Cong., 1st Sess., pt. 6, p. 3 (H. Judiciary Comm. Print 1965) (emphasis added).

To ensure that the mistakes of the "sweat of the brow" courts would not be repeated, Congress took additional measures. For example, §3 of the 1909 Act had stated that copyright protected only the "copyrightable component parts" of a work, but had not identified originality as the basis for distinguishing those component parts that were copyrightable from those that were not. The 1976 Act deleted this section and replaced it with §102(b), which identifies specifically those elements of a work for which copyright is not available: "In no case does copyright protection for an original work of authorship extend to any idea, procedure, process, system, method of operation, concept, principle, or discovery, regardless of the form in which it is described, explained, illustrated, or embodied in such work." Section 102(b) is universally understood to prohibit any copyright in facts. Harper & Row, supra, at 547, 556. Accord, Nimmer §2.03[E] (equating facts with "discoveries"). As with §102(a), Congress emphasized that §102(b) did not change the law, but merely clarified it: "Section 102(b) in no way enlarges or contracts the scope of copyright protection under the present law. Its purpose is to restate . . . that the basic dichotomy between expression and idea remains unchanged." H. R. Rep., at 57; S. Rep., at 54.

Congress took another step to minimize confusion by deleting the specific mention of "directories . . . and other compilations" in §5 of the 1909 Act. As mentioned, this section had led some courts to conclude that directories were copyrightable per se and that every element of a directory was protected. In its place, Congress enacted two new provisions. First, to make clear that compilations were not copyrightable per se, Congress provided a definition of the term "compilation." Second, to make clear that the copyright in a compilation did not extend to the facts themselves, Congress enacted §103.

The definition of "compilation" is found in §101 of the 1976 Act. It defines a "compilation" in the copyright sense as "a work formed by the collection and assembling of preexisting materials or of data that are selected, coordinated, or arranged in such a way that the resulting work as a whole constitutes an original work of authorship" (emphasis added).

The purpose of the statutory definition is to emphasize that collections of facts are not copyrightable per se. It conveys this message through its tripartite structure, as emphasized above by the italics. The statute identifies three distinct elements and requires each to be met for a work to qualify as a copyrightable compilation: (1) the collection and assembly of pre-existing material, facts, or data; (2) the selection, coordination, or arrangement of those materials; and (3) the creation, by virtue of the particular selection, coordination, or arrangement, of an "original" work of authorship. "This tripartite conjunctive structure is self-evident, and should be assumed to 'accurately express the legislative purpose.'" Patry 51, quoting Mills Music, 469 U.S., at 164.

At first glance, the first requirement does not seem to tell us much. It merely describes what one normally thinks of as a compilation—a collection of pre-existing material, facts, or data. What makes it significant is that it is not the sole requirement. It is not enough for copyright purposes that an author collects and assembles facts. To satisfy the statutory definition, the work must get over two additional hurdles. In this way, the plain language indicates that not every collection of facts receives copyright protection. Otherwise, there would be a period after "data."

The third requirement is also illuminating. It emphasizes that a compilation, like any other work, is copyrightable only if it satisfies the originality requirement ("an original work of authorship"). Although §102 states plainly that the originality requirement applies to all works, the point was emphasized with regard to compilations to ensure that courts would not repeat the mistake of the "sweat of the brow" courts by concluding that fact-based works are treated differently and measured by some other standard. As Congress explained it, the goal was to "make plain that the criteria of copyrightable subject matter stated in section 102 apply with full force to works . . . containing preexisting material." H. R. Rep., at 57; S. Rep., at 55.

The key to the statutory definition is the second requirement. It instructs courts that, in determining whether a fact-based work is an original work of authorship, they should focus on the manner in which the collected facts have been selected, coordinated, and arranged. This is a straightforward application of the originality requirement. Facts are never original, so the compilation author can claim originality, if at all, only in the way the facts are presented. To that end, the statute dictates that the principal focus should be on whether the selection, coordination, and arrangement are sufficiently original to merit protection.

Not every selection, coordination, or arrangement will pass muster. This is plain from the statute. It states that, to merit protection, the facts must be selected, coordinated, or arranged "in such a way" as to render the work as a whole original. This implies that some "ways" will trigger copyright, but that others will not. See Patry 57, and n. 76. Otherwise, the phrase "in such a way" is meaningless and Congress should have defined "compilation" simply as "a work formed by the collection and assembly of preexisting materials or data that are selected, coordinated, or arranged." That Congress did not do so is dispositive. In accordance with "the established principle that a court should give effect, if possible, to every clause and word of a statute," *Moskal v. United States,* 498 U.S. 103, 109–110 (1990) (internal quotation marks omitted), we conclude that the statute envisions that there will be some fact-based works in which the selection, coordination, and arrangement are not sufficiently original to trigger copyright protection.

*****

Even if a work qualifies as a copyrightable compilation, it receives only limited protection. This is the point of §103 of the Act. Section 103 explains that "the subject matter of copyright . . . includes compilations," §103(a), but that copyright protects only the author's original contributions—not the facts or information conveyed:

"The copyright in a compilation . . . extends only to the material contributed by the author of such work, as distinguished from the preexisting material employed in the work, and does not imply any exclusive right in the preexisting material." §103(b).

As §103 makes clear, copyright is not a tool by which a compilation author may keep others from using the facts or data he or she has collected. "The most important point here is one that is commonly misunderstood today: copyright . . . has no effect one way or the other on the copyright or public domain status of the preexisting material." H. R. Rep., at 57; S. Rep., at 55. The 1909 Act did not require, as "sweat of the brow" courts mistakenly assumed, that each subsequent compiler must start from scratch and is precluded from relying on research undertaken by another. See, e.g., Jeweler's Circular Publishing Co., 281 F., at 88–89. Rather, the facts contained in existing works may be freely copied because copyright protects only the elements that owe their origin to the compiler—the selection, coordination, and arrangement of facts.

In summary, the 1976 revisions to the Copyright Act leave no doubt that originality, not "sweat of the brow," is the touchstone of copyright protection in directories and other fact-based works. Nor is there any doubt that the same was true under the 1909 Act. The 1976 revisions were a direct response to the Copyright Office's concern that many lower courts had misconstrued this basic principle, and Congress emphasized repeatedly that the purpose of the revisions was to clarify, not change, existing law. The revisions explain with painstaking clarity that copyright requires originality, §102(a); that facts are never original, §102(b); that the copyright in a compilation does not extend to the facts it contains, §103(b); and that a compilation is copyrightable only to the extent that it features an original selection, coordination, or arrangement, §101.

*****

III.

There is no doubt that Feist took from the white pages of Rural's directory a substantial amount of factual information. At a minimum, Feist copied the names, towns, and telephone numbers of 1,309 of Rural's subscribers. Not all copying, however, is copyright infringement. To establish infringement, two elements must be proven: (1) ownership of a valid copyright, and (2) copying of constituent elements of the work that are original. See Harper & Row, 471 U.S., at 548. The first element is not at issue here; Feist appears to concede that Rural's directory, considered as a whole, is subject to a valid copyright because it contains some foreword text, as well as original material in its yellow pages advertisements. See Brief for Petitioner 18; Pet. for Cert. 9.

The question is whether Rural has proved the second element. In other words, did Feist, by taking 1,309 names, towns, and telephone numbers from Rural's white pages, copy anything that was "original" to Rural? Certainly, the raw data does not satisfy the originality requirement. Rural may have been the first to discover and report the names, towns, and telephone numbers of its subscribers, but this data does not "'owe its origin'" to Rural. Burrow-Giles, 111 U.S., at 58. Rather, these bits of information are uncopyrightable facts; they existed before Rural reported them and would have continued to exist if Rural had never published a telephone directory. The originality requirement "rules out protecting . . . names, addresses, and telephone numbers of which the plaintiff by no stretch of the imagination could be called the author." Patterson & Joyce 776.

Rural essentially concedes the point by referring to the names, towns, and telephone numbers as "preexisting material." Brief for Respondent 17. Section 103(b) states explicitly that the copyright in a compilation does not extend to "the preexisting material employed in the work."

The question that remains is whether Rural selected, coordinated, or arranged these uncopyrightable facts in an original way.

*****

The selection, coordination, and arrangement of Rural's white pages do not satisfy the minimum constitutional standards for copyright protection. As mentioned at the outset, Rural's white pages are entirely typical. Persons desiring telephone service in Rural's service area fill out an application and Rural issues them a telephone number. In preparing its white pages, Rural simply takes the data provided by its subscribers and lists it alphabetically by surname. The end product is a gardenvariety white pages directory, devoid of even the slightest trace of creativity.

Rural's selection of listings could not be more obvious: It publishes the most basic information—name, town, and telephone number—about each person who applies to it for telephone service. This is "selection" of a sort, but it lacks the modicum of creativity necessary to transform mere selection into copyrightable expression. Rural expended sufficient effort to make the white pages directory useful, but insufficient creativity to make it original.

We note in passing that the selection featured in Rural's white pages may also fail the originality requirement for another reason. Feist points out that Rural did not truly "select" to publish the names and telephone numbers of its subscribers; rather, it was required to do so by the Kansas Corporation Commission as part of its monopoly franchise. See 737 F. Supp., at 612. Accordingly, one could plausibly conclude that this selection was dictated by state law, not by Rural.

Nor can Rural claim originality in its coordination and arrangement of facts. The white pages do nothing more than list Rural's subscribers in alphabetical order. This arrangement may, technically speaking, owe its origin to Rural; no one disputes that Rural undertook the task of alphabetizing the names itself. But there is nothing remotely creative about arranging names alphabetically in a white pages directory. It is an age-old practice, firmly rooted in tradition and so commonplace that it has come to be expected as a matter of course. See Brief for Information Industry Association et al. as Amici Curiae 10 (alphabetical arrangement "is universally observed in directories published by local exchange telephone companies"). It is not only unoriginal, it is practically inevitable. This time-honored tradition does not possess the minimal creative spark required by the Copyright Act and the Constitution.

We conclude that the names, towns, and telephone numbers copied by Feist were not original to Rural and therefore were not protected by the copyright in Rural's combined white and yellow pages directory. As a constitutional matter, copyright protects only those constituent elements of a work that possess more than a de minimis quantum of creativity. Rural's white pages, limited to basic subscriber information and arranged alphabetically, fall short of the mark. As a statutory matter, 17 U. S. C. §101 does not afford protection from copying to a collection of facts that are selected, coordinated, and arranged in a way that utterly lacks originality. Given that some works must fail, we cannot imagine a more likely candidate.

Indeed, were we to hold that Rural's white pages pass muster, it is hard to believe that any collection of facts could fail.

Because Rural's white pages lack the requisite originality, Feist's use of the listings cannot constitute infringement. This decision should not be construed as demeaning Rural's efforts in compiling its directory, but rather as making clear that copyright rewards originality, not effort. As this Court noted more than a century ago, "'great praise may be due to the plaintiffs for their industry and enterprise in publishing this paper, yet the law does not contemplate their being rewarded in this way.'" *Baker v. Selden,* 101 U.S., at 105.

The judgment of the Court of Appeals is Reversed.

Justice Blackmun concurs in the judgment.

ELDRED ET AL. *v.* ASHCROFT, ATTORNEY GENERAL

CERTIORARI TO THE UNITED STATES COURT OF APPEALS FOR THE DISTRICT OF COLUMBIA CIRCUIT

No. 01-618. Argued October 9, 2002-Decided January 15, 2003

The Copyright and Patent Clause, U. S. Const., Art. I, § 8, cl. 8, provides as to copyrights: "Congress shall have Power . . . [t]o promote the Progress of Science . . . by securing [to Authors] for limited Times . . . the exclusive Right to their . . . Writings." In the 1998 Copyright Term Extension Act (CTEA), Congress enlarged the duration of copyrights by 20 years: Under the 1976 Copyright Act (1976 Act), copyright protection generally lasted from a work's creation until 50 years after the author's death; under the CTEA, most copyrights now run from creation until 70 years after the author's death, 17 U. S. C. § 302(a). As in the case of prior copyright extensions, principally in 1831, 1909, and 1976, Congress provided for application of the enlarged terms to existing and future copyrights alike.

Petitioners, whose products or services build on copyrighted works that have gone into the public domain, brought this suit seeking a determination that the CTEA fails constitutional review under both the Copyright Clause's "limited Times" prescription and the First Amendment's free speech guarantee. Petitioners do not challenge the CTEA's "life-plus-70-years" timespan itself. They maintain that Congress went awry not with respect to newly created works, but in enlarging the term for published works with existing copyrights. The "limited Tim[e]" in effect when a copyright is secured, petitioners urge, becomes the constitutional boundary, a clear line beyond the power of Congress to extend. As to the First Amendment, petitioners contend that the CTEA is a content-neutral regulation of speech that fails inspection under the heightened judicial scrutiny appropriate for such regulations. The District Court entered judgment on the pleadings for the Attorney General (respondent here), holding that the CTEA does not violate the Copyright Clause's "limited Times" restriction because the CTEA's terms, though longer than the 1976 Act's terms, are still limited, not perpetual, and therefore fit within Congress' discretion. The court also held that there are no First Amendment rights to use the copyrighted works of others. The District of Columbia Circuit affirmed. In that court's unanimous view, *Harper & Row, Publishers, Inc. v. Nation Enterprises,* 471 U. S. 539, foreclosed petitioners' First Amendment challenge to the CTEA. The appeals court reasoned that copyright does not impermissibly restrict free speech, for it grants the author an exclusive right only to the specific form of expression; it does not shield any idea or fact contained in the copyrighted work, and it allows for "fair use" even of the expression itself. A majority of the court also rejected petitioners' Copyright Clause claim. The court ruled that Circuit precedent precluded petitioners' plea for interpretation of the "limited Times" prescription with a view to the Clause's preambular statement of purpose: "To promote the Progress of Science." The court found nothing in the constitutional text or history to suggest that a term of years for a copyright is not a "limited Tim[e]" if it may later be extended for another "limited Tim[e]." Recounting that the First Congress made the 1790 Copyright Act applicable to existing copyrights arising under state copyright laws, the court held that that construction by contemporaries of the Constitution's formation merited almost conclusive weight under *Burrow-Giles Lithographic Co.* v. *Sarony,* 111 U. S. 53, 57. As early as *McClurg* v. *Kingsland,* 1 How. 202, the Court of Appeals recognized, this Court made it plain that the Copyright Clause permits Congress to amplify an existing patent's terms. The court added that this Court has been similarly deferential to Congress' judgment regarding copyright. *E.g., Sony Corp. of America* v. *Universal City Studios, Inc.*, 464 U. S. 417. Concerning petitioners' assertion that Congress could evade the limitation on its authority by stringing together an unlimited number of "limited Times," the court stated that such legislative misbehavior clearly was not before it. Rather, the court emphasized, the CTEA matched the baseline term for United States copyrights with the European Union term in order to meet contemporary circumstances.

Held: In placing existing and future copyrights in parity in the CTEA, Congress acted within its authority and did not transgress constitutional limitations. Pp. 199–222.

1. The CTEA's extension of existing copyrights does not exceed Congress' power under the Copyright Clause. Pp. 199–218.

   (a) Guided by text, history, and precedent, this Court cannot agree with petitioners that extending the duration of existing copyrights is categorically beyond Congress' Copyright Clause authority. Although conceding that the CTEA's baseline term of life plus 70 years qualifies as a "limited Tim[e]" as applied to future copyrights, petitioners contend that existing copyrights extended to endure for that same term are not "limited." In petitioners' view, a time prescription, once set, becomes forever "fixed" or "inalterable." The word "limited," however, does not convey a meaning so constricted. At the time of the Framing, "limited" meant what it means today: confined within certain bounds, restrained, or circumscribed. Thus understood, a timespan appropriately "limited" as applied to future copyrights does not automatically cease to be "limited" when applied to existing copyrights . . . Congress' consistent historical practice reflects a judgment that an author who sold his work a week before should not be placed in a worse situation than the author who sold his work the day after enactment of a copyright extension. The CTEA follows this historical practice by keeping the 1976 Act's duration provisions largely in place and simply adding 20 years to each of them.

   The CTEA is a rational exercise of the legislative authority conferred by the Copyright Clause. On this point, the Court defers substantially to Congress. *Sony,* 464 U. S., at 429. The CTEA reflects judgments of a kind Congress typically makes, judgments the Court cannot dismiss as outside the Legislature's domain. A key factor in the CTEA's passage was a 1993 European Union (EU) directive instructing EU members to establish a baseline copyright term of life plus 70 years and to deny this longer term to the works of any non-EU country whose laws did not secure the same extended term. By extending the baseline United States copyright term, Congress sought to ensure that American authors would receive the same copyright protection in Europe as their European counterparts. The CTEA may also provide greater incentive for American and other authors to create and disseminate their work in the United States. Additionally, Congress passed the CTEA in light of demographic, economic, and technological changes, and rationally credited projections that longer terms would encourage copyright holders to invest in the restoration and public distribution of their works. Pp. 199–208.

(b) Petitioners' Copyright Clause arguments, which rely on several novel readings of the Clause, are unpersuasive. Pp. 208–218.

(1) Nothing before this Court warrants construction of the CTEA's 20-year term extension as a congressional attempt to evade or override the "limited Times" constraint. Critically, petitioners fail to show how the CTEA crosses a constitutionally significant threshold with respect to "limited Times" that the 1831, 1909, and 1976 Acts did not. Those earlier Acts did not create perpetual copyrights, and neither does the CTEA. Pp. 208–210.

(2) Petitioners' dominant series of arguments, premised on the proposition that Congress may not extend an existing copyright absent new consideration from the author, are unavailing. The first such contention, that the CTEA's extension of existing copyrights overlooks the requirement of "originality," incorrectly relies on *Feist Publications, Inc.* v. *Rural Telephone Service Co.,* 499 U. S. 340, 345, 359. That case did not touch on the duration of copyright protection. Rather, it addressed only the core question of copyright ability. Explaining the originality requirement, *Feist* trained on the Copyright Clause words "Authors" and "Writings," id., at 346–347, and did not construe the "limited Times" prescription, as to which the originality requirement has no bearing. Also unavailing is petitioners' second argument, that the CTEA's extension of existing copyrights fails to "promote the Progress of Science" because it does not stimulate the creation of new works, but merely adds value to works already created. The justifications that motivated Congress to enact the CTEA, set forth *supra,* provide a rational basis for concluding that the CTEA "promote[s] the Progress of Science." Moreover, Congress' unbroken practice since the founding generation of applying new definitions or adjustments of the copyright term to both future works and existing works overwhelms petitioners' argument. Also rejected is petitioners' third contention, that the CTEA's extension of existing copyrights without demanding additional consideration ignores copyright's *quid pro quo,* whereby Congress grants the author of an original work an "exclusive Right" for a "limited Tim[e]" in exchange for a dedication to the public thereafter. Given Congress' consistent placement of existing copyright holders in parity with future holders, the author of a work created in the last 170 years would reasonably comprehend, as the protection offered her, a copyright not only for the time in place when protection is gained, but also for any renewal or extension legislated during that time. . . . (3) The "congruence and proportionality" standard of review described in cases evaluating exercises of Congress' power under § 5 of the Fourteenth Amendment has never been applied outside the § 5 context. It does not hold sway for judicial review of legislation enacted, as copyright laws are, pursuant to Article I authorization. Section 5 authorizes Congress to "enforce" commands contained in and incorporated into the Fourteenth Amendment. The Copyright Clause, in contrast, empowers Congress to *define* the scope of the substantive right.

See *Sony,* 464 U. S., at 429. Judicial deference to such congressional definition is "but a corollary to the grant to Congress of any Article I power." *Graham* v. *John Deere Co. of Kansas City,* 383 U. S. 1, 6. It would be no more appropriate for this Court to subject the CTEA to "congruence and proportionality" review than it would be to hold the Act unconstitutional *per se.* Pp. 217–218.

2. The CTEA's extension of existing and future copyrights does not violate the First Amendment. That Amendment and the Copyright Clause were adopted close in time. This proximity indicates the Framers' view that copyright's limited monopolies are compatible with free speech principles. In addition, copyright law contains built-in First Amendment accommodations. See *Harper & Row,* 471 U. S., at 560. First, 17 U. S. C. § 102(b), which makes only expression, not ideas, eligible for copyright protection, strikes a definitional balance between the First Amendment and copyright law by permitting free communication of facts while still protecting an author's expression. *Harper & Row,* 471 U. S., at 556. Second, the "fair use" defense codified at § 107 allows the public to use not only facts and ideas contained in a copyrighted work, but also expression itself for limited purposes. "Fair use" thereby affords considerable latitude for scholarship and comment, id., at 560, and even for parody, see *Campbell* v. *Acuff-Rose Music, Inc., 510* U. S. 569. The CTEA itself supplements these traditional First Amendment safeguards in two prescriptions: The first allows libraries and similar institutions to reproduce and distribute copies of certain published works for scholarly purposes during the last 20 years of any copyright term, if the work is not already being exploited commercially and further copies are unavailable at a reasonable price, § 108(h); the second exempts small businesses from having to pay performance royalties on music played from licensed radio, television, and similar facilities, § 110(5)(B). Finally, petitioners' reliance on *Turner Broadcasting System, Inc. v. FCC,* 512 U. S. 622, 641, is misplaced. *Turner Broadcasting* involved a statute requiring cable television operators to carry and transmit broadcast stations through their proprietary cable systems. The CTEA, in contrast, does not oblige anyone to reproduce another's speech against the carrier's will. Instead, it protects authors' original expression from unrestricted exploitation. The First Amendment securely protects the freedom to make—or decline to make—one's own speech; it bears less heavily when speakers assert the right to make other people's speeches. When, as in this case, Congress has not altered the traditional contours of copyright protection, further First Amendment scrutiny is unnecessary. See, *e.g., Harper & Row, 471* U. S., at 560. Pp. 218–222.

239 F. 3d 372, affirmed.

GINSBURG, J., delivered the opinion of the Court, in which REHNQUIST, C. J., and O'CONNOR, SCALIA, KENNEDY, SOUTER, and THOMAS, JJ., joined. STEVENS, J., *post,* p. 222, and BREYER, J., *post,* p. 242, filed dissenting opinions.

Lawrence Lessig argued the cause for petitioners. With him on the briefs were Kathleen M. Sullivan, Alan B. Morrison, Edward Lee, Charles Fried, Geoffrey S. Stewart, Donald B. Ayer, Robert P. Ducatman, Daniel H. Bromberg, Charles R. Nesson, and Jonathan L. Zittrain.

Solicitor General Olson argued the cause for respondent.

With him on the brief were Assistant Attorney General McCallum, Deputy Solicitor General Wallace, Jeffrey A. Lamken, William Kanter, and John S. Koppel.*

JUSTICE GINSBURG delivered the opinion of the Court. This case concerns the authority the Constitution assigns to Congress to prescribe the duration of copyrights. The Copyright and Patent Clause of the Constitution, Art. I, § 8, cl. 8, provides as to copyrights: "Congress shall have Power . . . [t]o promote the Progress of Science . . . by securing [to Authors] for limited Times . . . the exclusive Right to their . . . Writings." In 1998, in the measure here under inspection, Congress enlarged the duration of copyrights by 20 years. Copyright Term Extension Act (CTEA), Pub. L. 105–298, §§ 102(b) and (d), 112 Stat. 2827–2828 (amending 17 U. S. C. §§ 302, 304). As in the case of prior extensions, principally in 1831, 1909, and 1976, Congress provided for application of the enlarged terms to existing and future copyrights alike.

Petitioners are individuals and businesses whose products or services build on copyrighted works that have gone into the public domain. They seek a determination that the CTEA fails constitutional review under both the Copyright Clause's "limited Times" prescription and the First Amendment's free speech guarantee. Under the 1976 Copyright Act, copyright protection generally lasted from the work's creation until 50 years after the author's death. Pub. L. 94553, § 302(a), 90 Stat. 2572 (1976 Act). Under the CTEA, most copyrights now run from creation until 70 years after the author's death. 17 U. S. C. § 302(a). Petitioners do not challenge the "life-plus-70-years" timespan itself. "Whether 50 years is enough, or 70 years too much," they acknowledge, "is not a judgment meet for this Court." Brief for Petitioners 14.1 Congress went awry, petitioners maintain, not with respect to newly created works, but in enlarging the term for published works with existing copyrights. The "limited Tim[e]" in effect when a copyright is secured, petitioners urge, becomes the constitutional boundary, a clear line beyond the power of Congress to extend. See ibid. As to the First Amendment, petitioners contend that the CTEA is a content-neutral regulation of speech that fails inspection under the heightened judicial scrutiny appropriate for such regulations.

In accord with the District Court and the Court of Appeals, we reject petitioners' challenges to the CTEA. In that 1998 legislation, as in all previous copyright term extensions, Congress placed existing and future copyrights in parity. In prescribing that alignment, we hold, Congress acted within its authority and did not transgress constitutional limitations.

I.

A

We evaluate petitioners' challenge to the constitutionality of the CTEA against the backdrop of Congress' previous exercises of its authority under the Copyright Clause. The Nation's first copyright statute, enacted in 1790, provided a federal copyright term of 14 years from the date of publication, renewable for an additional 14 years if the author survived the first term. . . . The 1790 Act's renewable 14-year term applied to existing works (i.*e.*, works already published and works created but not yet published) and future works alike. *Ibid.* Congress expanded the federal copyright term to 42 years in 1831 (28 years from publication, renewable for an additional 14 years), and to 56 years in 1909 (28 years from publication, renewable for an additional 28 years). Both times, Congress applied the new copyright term to existing and future works, 1831 Act §§ 1, 16; 1909 Act §§ 23–24; to qualify for the 1831 extension, an existing work had to be in its initial copyright term at the time the Act became effective, 1831 Act §§ 1, 16.

. . . The 1976 Act aligned United States copyright terms with the then-dominant international standard adopted under the Berne Convention for the Protection of Literary and Artistic Works. See H. R. Rep. No. 94-1476, p. 135 (1976). For anonymous works, pseudonymous works, and works made for hire, the 1976 Act provided a term of 75 years from publication or 100 years from creation, whichever expired first. § 302(c).

. . .

The measure at issue here, the CTEA, installed the fourth major duration extension of federal copyrights. Retaining the general structure of the 1976 Act, the CTEA enlarges the terms of all existing and future copyrights by 20 years. For works created by identified natural persons, the term death. 17 U. S. C. § 302(a). This standard harmonizes the baseline United States copyright term with the term adopted by the European Union in 1993. See Council Directive 93/98/EEC of 29 October 1993 Harmonizing the Term of Protection of Copyright and Certain Related Rights, 1993 Official J. Eur. Corns. (L 290), p. 9 (EU Council Directive 93/ 98). For anonymous works, pseudonymous works, and works made for hire, the term is 95 years from publication or 120 years from creation, whichever expires first. 17 U. S. C. § 302(c).

Paralleling the 1976 Act, the CTEA applies these new terms to all works not published by January 1, 1978. §§ 302(a), 303(a). For works published before 1978 with existing copyrights as of the CTEA's effective date, the CTEA extends the term to 95 years from publication. §§ 304(a) and (b). Thus, in common with the 1831, 1909, and 1976 Acts, the CTEA's new terms apply to both future and existing copyrights.

B

Petitioners' suit challenges the CTEA's constitutionality under both the Copyright Clause and the First Amendment. On cross-motions for judgment on the pleadings, the District Court entered judgment for the Attorney General (respondent here). 74 F. Supp. 2d 1 (DC 1999). The court held that the CTEA does not violate the "limited Times" restriction of the Copyright Clause because the CTEA's terms, though longer than the 1976 Act's terms, are still limited, not perpetual, and therefore fit within Congress' discretion. *Id.,* at 3. The court also held that "there are no First Amendment rights to use the copyrighted works of others." *Ibid.*

The Court of Appeals for the District of Columbia Circuit affirmed. 239 F.3d 372 (2001). In that court's unanimous view, *Harper & Row, Publishers, Inc. v. Nation Enterprises,* 471 U. S. 539 (1985), foreclosed petitioners' First Amendment challenge to the CTEA. 239 F. 3d, at 375. Copyright, the court reasoned, does not impermissibly restrict free speech, for it grants the author an exclusive right only to the specific form of expression; it does not shield any idea or fact contained in the copyrighted work, and it allows for "fair use" even of the expression itself. *Id.,* at 375–376.

A majority of the Court of Appeals also upheld the CTEA against petitioners' contention that the measure exceeds Congress' power under the Copyright Clause. Specifically, the court rejected petitioners' plea for interpretation of the "limited Times" prescription not discretely but with a view to the "preambular statement of purpose" contained in the Copyright Clause: "To promote the Progress of Science." *Id.,* at 377–378. Circuit precedent, *Schnapper* v. *Foley, 667* F. 2d 102 (CADC 1981), the court determined, precluded that plea. In this regard, the court took into account petitioners' acknowledgment that the preamble itself places no substantive limit on Congress' legislative power. 239 F. 3d, at 378.

The appeals court found nothing in the constitutional text or its history to suggest that "a term of years for a copyright is not a 'limited Time' if it may later be extended for another 'limited Time.'" *Id.,* at 379. The court recounted that "the First Congress made the Copyright Act of 1790 applicable to subsisting copyrights arising under the copyright laws of the several states." *Ibid.* That construction of Congress' authority under the Copyright Clause "by [those] contemporary with [the Constitution's] formation," the court said, merited "very great" and in this case "almost conclusive" weight. *Ibid.* (quoting *Burrow-Giles Lithographic Co. v. Sarony,* 111 U. S. 53, 57 (1884)). . . .

Concerning petitioners' assertion that Congress might evade the limitation on its authority by stringing together "an unlimited number of 'limited Times,'" the Court of Appeals stated that such legislative misbehavior "clearly is not the situation before us." 239 F. 3d, at 379. Rather, the court noted, the CTEA "matches" the baseline term for "United States copyrights [with] the terms of copyrights granted by the European Union." *Ibid.* "[I]n an era of multinational publishers and instantaneous electronic transmission," the court said, "harmonization in this regard has obvious practical benefits" and is "a 'necessary and proper' measure to meet contemporary circumstances rather than a step on the way to making copyrights perpetual." *Ibid.*

. . . We granted certiorari to address two questions: whether the CTEA's extension of existing copyrights exceeds Congress' power under the Copyright Clause; and whether the CTEA's extension of existing and future copyrights violates the First Amendment. 534 U. S. 1126 and 1160 (2002). We now answer those two questions in the negative and affirm.

II.

A

We address first the determination of the courts below that Congress has authority under the Copyright Clause to extend the terms of existing copyrights. Text, history, and precedent, we conclude, confirm that the Copyright Clause empowers Congress to prescribe "limited Times" for copyright protection and to secure the same level and duration of protection for all copyright holders, present and future.

The CTEA's baseline term of life plus 70 years, petitioners concede, qualifies as a "limited Tim[e]" as applied to future copyrights.4 Petitioners contend, however, that existing copyrights extended to endure for that same term are not "limited." Petitioners' argument essentially reads into the text of the Copyright Clause the command that a time prescription, once set, becomes forever "fixed" or "inalterable." The word "limited," however, does not convey a meaning so constricted. At the time of the Framing, that word meant what it means today: "confine[d] within certain bounds," "restrain[ed]," or "circumscribe[d]." S. Johnson, A Dictionary of the English Language (7th ed. 1785); see T. Sheridan, A Complete Dictionary of the English Language (6th ed. 1796) ("confine[d] within certain bounds"); Webster's Third New International Dictionary 1312 (1976) ("confined within limits"; "restricted in extent, number, or duration"). Thus understood, a timespan appropriately "limited" as applied to future copyrights does not automatically cease to be "limited" when applied to existing copyrights. And as we observe, *infra,* at 209-210, there is no cause to suspect that a purpose to evade the "limited Times" prescription prompted Congress to adopt the CTEA.

To comprehend the scope of Congress' power under the Copyright Clause, "a page of history is worth a volume of logic." *New York Trust Co. v. Eisner,* 256 U. S. 345, 349 (1921) (Holmes, J.). History reveals an unbroken congressional practice of granting to authors of works with existing copyrights the benefit of term extensions so that all under copyright protection will be governed evenhandedly under the same regime. As earlier recounted, see *supra,* at 194, the First Congress accorded the protections of the Nation's first federal copyright statute to existing and future works alike. 1790 Act § 1.5 Since then, Congress has regularly applied duration extensions to both existing and future copyrights. 1831 Act §§ 1, 16; 1909 Act §§ 23–24; 1976 Act §§ 302–303; 17 U. S. C. § § 302–304.

. . . Congress' consistent historical practice of applying newly enacted copyright terms to future and existing copyrights reflects a judgment stated concisely by Representative Huntington at the time of the 1831 Act: "[J]ustice, policy, and equity alike forb[id]" that an "author who had sold his [work] a week ago, be placed in a worse situation than the author who should sell his work the day after the passing of [the] act." 7 Congo Deb. 424 (1831); accord, Symposium, The Constitutionality of Copyright Term Extension, 18 Cardozo Arts & Ent. L. J. 651, 694 (2000) (Prof. Miller) ("[S]ince 1790, it has indeed been Congress's policy that the author of yesterday's work should not get a lesser reward than the author of tomorrow's work just because Congress passed a statute lengthening the term today."). The CTEA follows this historical practice by keeping the duration provisions of the 1976 Act largely in place and simply adding 20 years to each of them. Guided by text, history, and precedent, we cannot agree with petitioners' submission that extending the duration of existing copyrights is categorically beyond Congress' authority under the Copyright Clause.

Satisfied that the CTEA complies with the "limited Times" prescription, we turn now to whether it is a rational exercise of the legislative authority conferred by the Copyright Clause. On that point, we defer substantially to Congress. *Sony,* 464 U. S., at 429 ("[I]t is Congress that has been assigned the task of defining the scope of the limited monopoly that should be granted to authors . . . in order to give the public appropriate access to their work product.").

The CTEA reflects judgments of a kind Congress typically makes, judgments we cannot dismiss as outside the Legislature's domain. As respondent describes . . . , a key factor in the CTEA's passage was a 1993 European Union (EU) directive instructing EU members to establish a copyright term of life plus 70 years. EU Council Directive 93/98, Art. 1(1), p. 11; see 144 Congo Rec. S12377-S12378 (daily ed. Oct. 12, 1998) (statement of Sen. Hatch). Consistent with the Berne Convention, the EU directed its members to deny this longer term to the works of any non-EU country whose laws did not secure the same extended term. See Berne Conv. Art. 7(8); P. Goldstein, International Copyright § 5.3, p. 239 (2001). By extending the baseline United States copyright term to life plus 70 years, Congress sought to ensure that American authors would receive the same copyright protection in Europe as their European counterparts. The CTEA may also provide greater incentive for American and other authors to create and disseminate their work in the United States. See Perlmutter, Participation in the International Copyright System as a Means to Promote the Progress of Science and Useful Arts, 36 Loyola (LA) L. Rev. 323, 330 (2002) ("[M]atching thee] level of [copyright] protection in the United States [to that in the EU] can ensure stronger protection for U. S. works abroad and avoid competitive disadvantages vis-a-vis foreign rightholders."); see also id., at 332 (the United States could not "playa leadership role" in the give-and-take evolution of the international copyright system, indeed it would "lose all flexibility," "if the only way to promote the progress of science were to provide incentives to create new works")

In addition to international concerns, 13 Congress passed the CTEA in light of demographic, economic, and technological changes, Brief for Respondent 25–26, 33, and nn. 23 and 24, 14 and rationally credited projections that longer terms would encourage copyright holders to invest in the restoration and public distribution of their works, id., at 34–37; see H. R. Rep. No. 105–452, p. 4 (1998) (term extension "provide[s] copyright owners generally with the incentive to restore older works and further disseminate them to the public").

In sum, we find that the CTEA is a rational enactment; we are not at liberty to second-guess congressional determinations and policy judgments of this order, however debatable or arguably unwise they may be. Accordingly, we cannot conclude that the CTEA-which continues the unbroken congressional practice of treating future and existing copyrights in parity for term extension purposes-is an impermissible exercise of Congress' power under the Copyright Clause.

B

Petitioners' Copyright Clause arguments rely on several novel readings of the Clause. We next address these arguments and explain why we find them unpersuasive.

1

Petitioners contend that even if the CTEA's 20-year term extension is literally a "limited Tim[e]," permitting Congress to extend existing copyrights allows it to evade the "limited Times" constraint by creating effectively perpetual copyrights through repeated extensions. We disagree.

As the Court of Appeals observed, a regime of perpetual copyrights "clearly is not the situation before us." 239 F. 3d, at 379. Nothing before this Court warrants construction of the CTEA's 20-year term extension as a congressional attempt to evade or override the "limited Times" constraint. Critically, we again emphasize, petitioners fail to show how the CTEA crosses a constitutionally significant threshold with respect to "limited Times" that the 1831, 1909, and 1976 Acts did not. See *supra,* at 194–196; Austin, *supra* n. 13, at 56 ("If extending copyright protection to works already in existence is constitutionally suspect," so is "extending the protections of U. S. copyright law to works by foreign authors that had already been created and even first published when the federal rights attached."). Those earlier Acts did not create perpetual copyrights, and neither does the CTEA.

2

Petitioners dominantly advance a series of arguments all premised on the proposition that Congress may not extend an existing copyright absent new consideration from the author. They pursue this main theme under three headings. Petitioners contend that the CTEA's extension of existing copyrights (1) overlooks the requirement of "originality," (2) fails to "promote the Progress of Science," and (3) ignores copyright's *quid pro quo.*

Petitioners' "originality" argument draws on *Feist Publications, Inc.* v. *Rural Telephone Service Co.,* 499 U. S. 340 (1991). In *Feist,* we observed that "[t]he *sine qua non* of copyright is originality," id., at 345, and held that copyright protection is unavailable to "a narrow category of works in which the creative spark is utterly lacking or so trivial as to be virtually nonexistent," *id.,* at 359. Relying on *Feist,* petitioners urge that even if a work is sufficiently "original" to qualify for copyright protection in the first instance, any extension of the copyright's duration is impermissible because, once published, a work is no longer original.

Feist, however, did not touch on the duration of copyright protection. Rather, the decision addressed the core question of copyrightability, i.*e.,* the "creative spark" a work must have to be eligible for copyright protection at all. Explaining the originality requirement, *Feist* trained on the Copyright Clause words "Authors" and "Writings." *Id.,* at 346–347. The decision did not construe the "limited Times" for which a work may be protected, and the originality requirement has no bearing on that prescription.

More forcibly, petitioners contend that the CTEA's extension of existing copyrights does not "promote the Progress of Science" as contemplated by the preambular language of the Copyright Clause. Art. I, § 8, cl. 8. To sustain this objection, petitioners do not argue that the Clause's preamble is an independently enforceable limit on Congress' power. See 239 F. 3d, at 378 (Petitioners acknowledge that "the preamble of the Copyright Clause is not a substantive limit on Congress' legislative power." (internal quotation marks omitted)). Rather, they maintain that the preambular language identifies the sole end to which Congress may legislate; accordingly, they conclude, the meaning of "limited Times" must be "determined in light of that specified end." Brief for Petitioners 19. The CTEA's extension of existing copyrights categorically fails to "promote the Progress of Science," petitioners argue, because it does not stimulate the creation of new works but merely adds value to works already created.

As petitioners point out, we have described the Copyright Clause as "both a grant of power and a limitation," *Graham* v. *John Deere Co. of Kansas City,* 383 U. S. 1, 5 (1966), and have said that "[t]he primary objective of copyright" is "[t]o promote the Progress of Science," *Feist,* 499 U. S., at 349. The "constitutional command," we have recognized, is that Congress, to the extent it enacts copyright laws at all, create a "system" that "promote[s] the Progress of Science." *Graham,* 383 U. S., at 6.

. . . On the issue of copyright duration, Congress, from the start, has routinely applied new definitions or adjustments of the copyright term to both future works and existing works not yet in the public domain. Such consistent congressional practice is entitled to "very great weight, and when it is remembered that the rights thus established have not been disputed during a period of [over two] centur[ies], it is almost conclusive." *Burrow-Giles Lithographic Co.* v. *Sarony,* 111 U. S., at 57. Indeed, "[t]his Court has repeatedly laid down the principle that a contemporaneous legislative exposition of the Constitution when the founders of our Government and framers of our Constitution were actively participating in public affairs, acquiesced in for a long term of years, fixes the construction to be given [the Constitution's] provisions." *Myers* v. *United States,* 272 U. S. 52, 175 (1926). Congress' unbroken practice since the founding generation thus overwhelms petitioners' argument that the CTEA's extension of existing copyrights fails *per se* to "promote the Progress of Science."

Closely related to petitioners' preambular argument, or a variant of it, is their assertion that the Copyright Clause "imbeds a quid pro quo." Brief for Petitioners 23. They contend, in this regard, that Congress may grant to an "Autho[r]" an "exclusive Right" for a "limited Tim[e]," but only in exchange for a "Writin[g]." Congress' power to confer copyright protection, petitioners argue, is thus contingent upon an exchange: The author of an original work receives an "exclusive Right" for a "limited Tim[e]" in exchange for a dedication to the public thereafter. Extending an existing copyright without demanding additional consideration, petitioners maintain, bestows an unpaid-for benefit on copyright holders and their heirs, in violation of the *quid pro quo* requirement.

We can demur to petitioners' description of the Copyright Clause as a grant of legislative authority empowering Congress "to secure a bargain-this for that." *Id.,* at 16; see *Mazer* v. *Stein,* 347 U. S. 201, 219 (1954) ("The economic philosophy behind the clause empowering Congress to grant patents and copyrights is the conviction that encouragement of individual effort by personal gain is the best way to advance public welfare through the talents of authors and inventors in 'Science and useful Arts.'"). But the legislative evolution earlier recalled demonstrates what the bargain entails. Given the consistent placement of existing copyright holders in parity with future holders, the author of a work created in the last 170 years would reasonably comprehend, as the "this" offered her, a copyright not only for the time in place when protection is gained, but also for any renewal or extension legislated during that time. Congress could rationally seek to "promote . . . Progress" by including in every copyright statute an express guarantee that authors would receive the benefit of any later legislative extension of the copyright term. Nothing in the Copyright Clause bars Congress from creating the same incentive by adopting the same position as a matter of unbroken practice. . . .

As an alternative to their various arguments that extending existing copyrights violates the Copyright Clause *per se,* petitioners urge heightened judicial review of such extensions to ensure that they appropriately pursue the purposes of the Clause. . . . Specifically, petitioners ask us to apply the "congruence and proportionality" standard described in cases evaluating exercises of Congress' power under § 5 of the Fourteenth Amendment. See, *e.g.,* City *of Boerne* v. *Flores,* 521 U. S. 507 (1997). But we have never applied that standard outside the § 5 context; it does not hold sway for judicial review of legislation enacted, as copyright laws are, pursuant to Article I authorization.

Section 5 authorizes Congress to *enforce* commands contained in and incorporated into the Fourteenth Amendment. Arndt. 14, § 5 ("The Congress shall have power to *enforce,* by appropriate legislation, the provisions of this article." (emphasis added)). The Copyright Clause, in contrast, empowers Congress to *define* the scope of the substantive right. See *Sony,* 464 U. S., at 429. Judicial deference to such congressional definition is "but a corollary to the grant to Congress of any Article I power." *Graham,* 383 U. S., at 6. It would be no more appropriate for us to subject the CTEA to "congruence and proportionality" review under the Copyright Clause than it would be for us to hold the Act unconstitutional *per se.*

For the several reasons stated, we find no Copyright Clause impediment to the CTEA's extension of existing copyrights.

III.

Petitioners separately argue that the CTEA is a content neutral regulation of speech that fails heightened judicial review under the First Amendment. We reject petitioners' plea for imposition of uncommonly strict scrutiny on a copyright scheme that incorporates its own speech-protective purposes and safeguards. The Copyright Clause and First Amendment were adopted close in time. This proximity indicates that, in the Framers' view, copyright's limited monopolies are compatible with free speech principles. Indeed, copyright's purpose is to *promote* the creation and publication of free expression. As *Harper & Row* observed: "[T]he Framers intended copyright itself to be the engine of free expression. By establishing a marketable right to the use of one's expression, copyright supplies the economic incentive to create and disseminate ideas." 471 U. S., at 558.

In addition to spurring the creation and publication of new expression, copyright law contains built-in First Amendment accommodations. See id., at 560. First, it distinguishes between ideas and expression and makes only the latter eligible for copyright protection. Specifically, 17 U. S. C. § 102(b) provides: "In no case does copyright protection for an original work of authorship extend to any idea, procedure, process, system, method of operation, concept, principle, or discovery, regardless of the form in which it is described, explained, illustrated, or embodied in such work." As we said in *Harper & Row,* this "idea/expression dichotomy strike[s] a definitional balance between the First Amendment and the Copyright Act by permitting free communication of facts while still protecting an author's expression." 471 U. S., at 556 (internal quotation marks omitted). Due to this distinction, every idea, theory, and fact in a copyrighted work becomes instantly available for public exploitation at the moment of publication. See *Feist,* 499 U. S., at 349–350.

Second, the "fair use" defense allows the public to use not only facts and ideas contained in a copyrighted work, but also expression itself in certain circumstances. Codified at 17 U. S. C. § 107, the defense provides: "[T]he fair use of a copyrighted work, including such use by reproduction in copies . . . , for purposes such as criticism, comment, news reporting, teaching (including multiple copies for classroom use), scholarship, or research, is not an infringement of copyright." The fair use defense affords considerable "latitude for scholarship and comment," *Harper & Row,* 471 U. S., at 560, and even for parody, see *Campbell* v. *Acuff-Rose Music, Inc.,* 510 U. S. 569 (1994) (rap group's musical parody of Roy Orbison's "Oh, Pretty Woman" may be fair use).

The CTEA itself supplements these traditional First Amendment safeguards. First, it allows libraries, archives, and similar institutions to "reproduce" and "distribute, display, or perform in facsimile or digital form" copies of certain published works "during the last 20 years of any term of copyright . . . for purposes of preservation, scholarship, or research" if the work is not already being exploited commercially and further copies are unavailable at a reasonable price. 17 U. S. C. § 108(h). . . . Second, Title II of the CTEA, known as the Fairness in Music Licensing Act of 1998, exempts small businesses, restaurants, and like entities from having to pay performance royalties on music played from licensed radio, television, and similar facilities. 17 U. S. C. § 110(5)(B). . . . James Sensenbrenner, Jr., et al. as *Amici Curiae* 5–6, n. 3.

Finally, the case petitioners principally rely upon for their First Amendment argument, *Turner Broadcasting System, Inc. v. FCC,* 512 U. S. 622 (1994), bears little on copyright. The statute at issue in *Turner* required cable operators to carry and transmit broadcast stations through their proprietary cable systems. Those "must-carry" provisions, we explained, implicated "the heart of the First Amendment," namely, "the principle that each person should decide for himself or herself the ideas and beliefs deserving of expression, consideration, and adherence." *Id.,* at 641.

The CTEA, in contrast, does not oblige anyone to reproduce another's speech against the carrier's will. Instead, it protects authors' original expression from unrestricted exploitation. Protection of that order does not raise the free speech concerns present when the government compels or burdens the communication of particular facts or ideas. The First Amendment securely protects the freedom to make or decline to make-one's own speech; it bears less heavily when speakers assert the right to make other people's speeches. To the extent such assertions raise First Amendment concerns, copyright's built-in free speech safeguards are generally adequate to address them. . .

IV.

If petitioners' vision of the Copyright Clause held sway, it would do more than render the CTEA's duration extensions unconstitutional as to existing works. Indeed, petitioners' assertion that the provisions of the CTEA are not severable would make the CTEA's enlarged terms invalid even as to tomorrow's work. The 1976 Act's time extensions, which set the pattern that the CTEA followed, would be vulnerable as well.

As we read the Framers' instruction, the Copyright Clause empowers Congress to determine the intellectual property regimes that, overall, in that body's judgment, will serve the ends of the Clause. . . . Beneath the facade of their inventive constitutional interpretation, petitioners forcefully urge that Congress pursued very bad policy in prescribing the CTEA's long terms. The wisdom of Congress' action, however, is not within our province to second-guess. Satisfied that the legislation before us remains inside the domain the Constitution assigns to the First Branch, we affirm the judgment of the Court of Appeals.

It is so ordered.

GOLAN ET AL. v. HOLDER, ATTORNEY GENERAL, ET AL.

CERTIORARI TO THE UNITED STATES COURT OF APPEALS FOR THE TENTH CIRCUIT

No. 10–545. Argued October 5, 2011—Decided January 18, 2012

The Berne Convention for the Protection of Literary and Artistic Works (Berne), which took effect in 1886, is the principal accord governing international copyright relations. Berne's 164 member states agree to provide a minimum level of copyright protection and to treat authors from other member countries as well as they treat their own. Of central importance in this case, Article 18 of Berne requires countries to protect the works of other member states unless the works' copyright term has expired in either the country where protection is claimed or the country of origin. A different system of transnational copyright protection long prevailed in this country. Throughout most of the 20th century, the only foreign authors eligible for Copyright Act protection were those whose countries granted reciprocal rights to American authors and whose works were printed in the United States. Despite Article 18, when the United States joined Berne in 1989, it did not protect any foreign works lodged in the U. S. public domain, many of them works never protected here. In 1994, however, the Agreement on Trade-Related Aspects of Intellectual Property Rights mandated implementation of Berne's first 21 articles, on pain of enforcement by the World Trade Organization.

In response, Congress applied the term of protection available to U. S. works to preexisting works from Berne member countries. Section 514 of the Uruguay Round Agreements Act (URAA) grants copyright protection to works protected in their country of origin, but lacking protection in the United States for any of three reasons: The United States did not protect works from the country of origin at the time of publication; the United States did not protect sound recordings fixed before 1972; or the author had not complied with certain U. S. statutory formalities. Works encompassed by §514 are granted the protection they would have enjoyed had the United States maintained copyright relations with the author's country or removed formalities incompatible with Berne. As a consequence of the barriers to U. S. copyright protection prior to §514's enactment, foreign works "restored" to protection by the measure had entered the public domain in this country. To cushion the impact of their placement in protected status, §514 provides ameliorating accommodations for parties who had exploited affected works before the URAA was enacted.

Petitioners are orchestra conductors, musicians, publishers, and others who formerly enjoyed free access to works §514 removed from the public domain. They maintain that Congress, in passing §514, exceeded its authority under the Copyright Clause and transgressed First Amendment limitations. The District Court granted the Attorney General's motion for summary judgment. Affirming in part, the Tenth Circuit agreed that Congress had not offended the Copyright Clause, but concluded that §514 required further First Amendment inspection in light of *Eldred v. Ashcroft,* 537 U. S. 186. On remand, the District Court granted summary judgment to petitioners on the First Amendment claim, holding that §514's constriction of the public domain was not justified by any of the asserted federal interests. The Tenth Circuit reversed, ruling that §514 was narrowly tailored to fit the important government aim of protecting U. S. copyright holders' interests abroad.

Held:

1. Section 514 does not exceed Congress' authority under the Copyright Clause. Pp. 13–23.

(a) The text of the Copyright Clause does not exclude application of copyright protection to works in the public domain. Eldred is largely dispositive of petitioners' claim that the Clause's confinement of a copyright's lifespan to a "limited Tim[e]" prevents the removal of works from the public domain. In Eldred, the Court upheld the Copyright Term Extension Act (CTEA), which extended, by 20 years, the terms of existing copyrights. The text of the Copyright Clause, the Court observed, contains no "command that a time prescription, once set, becomes forever 'fixed' or 'inalterable,'" and the Court declined to infer any such command. 537 U. S., at 199. The construction petitioners tender here is similarly infirm. The terms afforded works restored by §514 are no less "limited" than those the CTEA lengthened. Nor had the "limited Tim[e]" already passed for the works at issue here—many of them works formerly denied any U. S. copyright protection—for a period of exclusivity must begin before it may end. Petitioners also urge that the Government's position would allow Congress to legislate perpetual copyright terms by instituting successive "limited" terms as prior terms expire. But as in Eldred, such hypothetical misbehavior is far afield from this case. In aligning the United States with other nations bound by Berne, Congress can hardly be charged with a design to move stealthily toward a perpetual copyright regime. Pp. 13–15.

(b) Historical practice corroborates the Court's reading of the Copyright Clause to permit the protection of previously unprotected works. In the Copyright Act of 1790, the First Congress protected works that had been freely reproducible under State copyright laws. Subsequent actions confirm that Congress has not understood the Copyright Clause to preclude protection for existing works. Several private bills restored the copyrights and patents of works and inventions previously in the public domain. Congress has also passed generally applicable legislation granting copyrights and patents to works and inventions that had lost protection. Pp. 15–19.

(c) Petitioners also argue that §514 fails to "promote the Progress of Science" as contemplated by the initial words of the Copyright Clause. Specifically, they claim that because §514 affects only works already created, it cannot meet the Clause's objective. The creation of new works, however, is not the sole way Congress may promote "Science," i.e., knowledge and learning. In Eldred, this Court rejected a nearly identical argument, concluding that the Clause does not demand that each copyright provision, examined discretely, operate to induce new works. Rather the Clause "empowers Congress to determine the intellectual property regimes that, overall, in that body's judgment, will serve the ends of the Clause." 537 U. S., at 222. Nothing in the text or history of the Copyright Clause, moreover, confines the "Progress of Science" exclusively to "incentives for creation." Historical evidence, congressional practice, and this Court's decisions, in fact, suggest that inducing the dissemination of existing works is an appropriate means to promote science. Pp. 20–22.

(d) Considered against this backdrop, §514 falls comfortably within Congress' Copyright Clause authority. Congress had reason to believe that a well-functioning international copyright system would encourage the dissemination of existing and future works. And testimony informed Congress that full compliance with Berne would expand the foreign markets available to U. S. authors and invigorate protection against piracy of U. S. works abroad, thus benefitting copyright-intensive industries stateside and inducing greater investment in the creative process. This Court has no warrant to reject Congress' rational judgment that exemplary adherence to Berne would serve the objectives of the Copyright Clause. Pp. 22–23.

2. The First Amendment does not inhibit the restoration authorized by §514. Pp. 23–32.

(a) The pathmarking Eldred decision is again instructive. There, the Court held that the CTEA's enlargement of a copyright's duration did not offend the First Amendment's freedom of expression guarantee. Recognizing that some restriction on expression is the inherent and intended effect of every grant of copyright, the Court observed that the Framers regarded copyright protection not simply as a limit on the manner in which expressive works may be used, but also as an "engine of free expression." 537 U. S., at 219. The "traditional contours" of copyright protection, i.e., the "idea/expression dichotomy" and the "fair use" defense, moreover, serve as "built-in First Amendment accommodations." Ibid. Given the speech-protective purposes and safeguards embraced by copyright law, there was no call for the heightened review sought in Eldred. The Court reaches the same conclusion here. Section 514 leaves undisturbed the idea/expression distinction and the fair use defense. Moreover, Congress adopted measures to ease the transition from a national scheme to an international copyright regime. Pp. 23–26.

(b) Petitioners claim that First Amendment interests of a higher order are at stake because they—unlike their Eldred counterparts—enjoyed "vested rights" in works that had already entered the public domain. Their contentions depend on an argument already considered and rejected, namely, that the Constitution renders the public domain largely untouchable by Congress. Nothing in the historical record, subsequent congressional practice, or this Court's jurisprudence warrants exceptional First Amendment solicitude for copyrighted works that were once in the public domain. Congress has several times adjusted copyright law to protect new categories of works as well as works previously in the public domain. Section 514, moreover, does not impose a blanket prohibition on public access. The question is whether would-be users of certain foreign works must pay for their desired use of the author's expression, or else limit their exploitation to "fair use" of those works. By fully implementing Berne, Congress ensured that these works, like domestic and most other foreign works, would be governed by the same legal regime. Section 514 simply placed foreign works in the position they would have occupied if the current copyright regime had been in effect when those works were created and first published. Pp. 26–30.

609 F. 3d 1076, affirmed.

GINSBURG, J., delivered the opinion of the Court, in which ROBERTS, C. J., and SCALIA, KENNEDY, THOMAS, and SOTOMAYOR, JJ., joined. BREYER, J., filed a dissenting opinion, in which ALITO, J., joined. KAGAN, J., took no part in the consideration or decision of the case.

LAWRENCE GOLAN, ET AL., PETITIONERS v. ERIC H. HOLDER, JR., ATTORNEY GENERAL, ET AL.

I.

A

Members of the Berne Union agree to treat authors from other member countries as well as they treat their own. Berne Convention, Sept. 9, 1886, as revised at Stockholm on July 14, 1967, Art. 1, 5(1), 828 U. N. T.S. 221, 225, 231–233. Nationals of a member country, as well as any author who publishes in one of Berne's 164 member states, thus enjoy copyright protection in nations across the globe. Art. 2(6), 3. Each country, moreover, must afford at least the minimum level of protection specified by Berne. The copyright term must span the author's lifetime, plus at least 50 additional years, whether or not the author has complied with a member state's legal formalities. Art. 5(2), 7(1). And, as relevant here, a work must be protected abroad unless its copyright term has expired in either the country where protection is claimed or the country of origin. Art. 18(1)–(2).

. . .

The United States became party to Berne's multilateral, formality-free copyright regime in 1989. Initially, Congress adopted a "minimalist approach" to compliance with the Convention. H. R. Rep. No. 100–609, p. 7 (1988) (hereinafter BCIA House Report). The Berne Convention Implementation Act of 1988 (BCIA), 102 Stat. 2853, made "only those changes to American copyright law that [were] clearly required under the treaty's provisions," BCIA House Report, at 7. Despite Berne's instruction that member countries—including "new accessions to the Union"—protect foreign works under copyright in the country of origin, Art. 18(1) and (4), 828 U. N. T.S., at 251, the BCIA accorded no protection for "any work that is in the public domain in the United States," §12, 102 Stat. 2860. Protection of future foreign works, the BCIA indicated, satisfied Article 18. See §2(3), 102 Stat. 2853 ("The amendments made by this Act, together with the law as it exists on the date of the enactment of this Act, satisfy the obligations of the United States in adhering to the Berne Convention . . . ."). Congress indicated, however, that it had not definitively rejected "retroactive" protection for preexisting foreign works; instead it had punted on this issue of Berne's implementation, deferring consideration until "a more thorough examination of Constitutional, commercial, and consumer considerations is possible." BCIA House Report, at 51, 52.

. . . Berne, however, did not provide a potent enforcement mechanism. The Convention contemplates dispute resolution before the International Court of Justice. Art. 33(1). But it specifies no sanctions for noncompliance and allows parties, at any time, to declare themselves "not . . . bound" by the Convention's dispute resolution provision. Art. 33(2)–(3) 828 U. N. T. S., at 277. Unsurprisingly, no enforcement actions were launched before 1994. D. Gervais, The TRIPS Agreement 213, and n. 134 (3d ed. 2008). Although "several Berne Union Members disagreed with [our] interpretation of Article 18," the

USTR told Congress, the Berne Convention did "not provide a meaningful dispute resolution process." URAA Joint Hearing 137 (statement of Shapiro). This shortcoming left Congress "free to adopt a minimalist approach and evade Article 18." Karp, Final Report, Berne Article 18 Study on Retroactive United States Copyright Protection for Berne and other Works, 20 Colum.-VLA J. L. & Arts 157, 172 (1996).

The landscape changed in 1994. The Uruguay round of multilateral trade negotiations produced the World Trade Organization (WTO) and the Agreement on Trade-Related Aspects of Intellectual Property Rights (TRIPS). The United States joined both. TRIPS mandates, on pain of WTO enforcement, implementation of Berne's first 21 articles. TRIPS, Art. 9.1, 33 I. L. M. 1197, 1201 (requiring adherence to all but the "moral rights" provisions of Article 6bis). The WTO gave teeth to the Convention's requirements: Noncompliance with a WTO ruling could subject member countries to tariffs or cross-sector retaliation. See Gervais, supra, at 213; 7 W. Patry, Copyright §24:1, pp. 24–8 to 24–9 (2011). The specter of WTO enforcement proceedings bolstered the credibility of our trading partners' threats to challenge the United States for inadequate compliance with Article 18. See URAA Joint Hearing 137 (statement of Shapiro, USTR) ("It is likely that other WTO members would challenge the current U. S. implementation of Berne Article 18 under [WTO] procedures.").

Congress' response to the Uruguay agreements put to rest any questions concerning U. S. compliance with Article 18. Section 514 of the URAA, 108 Stat. 4976 (codified at 17 U. S. C. §104A, 109(a)), extended copyright to works that garnered protection in their countries of origin, but had no right to exclusivity in the United States for any of three reasons: lack of copyright relations between the country of origin and the United States at the time of publication; lack of subject-matter protection for sound recordings fixed before 1972; and failure to comply with U. S. statutory formalities (e.g., failure to provide notice of copyright status, or to register and renew a copyright). See §104A(h)(6)(B)–(C).

Works that have fallen into the public domain after the expiration of a full copyright term—either in the United States or the country of origin—receive no further protection under §514. Ibid. Copyrights "restored" under URAA §514 "subsist for the remainder of the term of copyright that the work would have otherwise been granted . . . if the work never entered the public domain." §104A(a)(1)(B). Prospectively, restoration places foreign works on an equal footing with their U. S. counterparts; assuming a foreign and domestic author died the same day, their works will enter the public domain simultaneously. See §302(a) (copyrights generally expire 70 years after the author's death). Restored works, however, receive no compensatory time for the period of exclusivity they would have enjoyed before §514's enactment, had they been protected at the outset in the United States. Their total term, therefore, falls short of that available to similarly situated U. S. works.

The URAA's disturbance of the public domain hardly escaped Congress' attention. Section 514 imposed no liability for any use of foreign works occurring before restoration. In addition, anyone remained free to copy and use restored works for one year following §514's enactment. See 17 U. S. C. §104A(h)(2)(A). Concerns about §514's compatibility with the Fifth Amendment's Takings Clause led Congress to include additional protections for "reliance parties"—those who had, before the URAA's enactment, used or acquired a foreign work then in the public domain. See §104A(h)(3)–(4). Reliance parties may continue to exploit a restored work until the owner of the restored copyright gives notice of intent to enforce—either by filing with the U. S. Copyright Office within two years of restoration, or by actually notifying the reliance party. §104A(c), (d)(2)(A)(i), and (B)(i). After that, reliance parties may continue to exploit existing copies for a grace period of one year. §104A(d)(2)(A)(ii), and (B)(ii). Finally, anyone who, before the URAA's enactment, created a "derivative work" based on a restored work may indefinitely exploit the derivation upon payment to the copyright holder of "reasonable compensation," to be set by a district judge if the parties cannot agree. §104A(d)(3).

B

In 2001, petitioners filed this lawsuit challenging §514. They maintain that Congress, when it passed the URAA, exceeded its authority under the Copyright Clause and transgressed First Amendment limitations. The District Court granted the Attorney General's motion for summary judgment. *Golan v. Gonzales,* No. Civ. 01–B–1854, 2005 WL 914754 (D. Colo., Apr. 20, 2005). In rejecting petitioners' Copyright Clause argument, the court stated that Congress "has historically demonstrated little compunction about removing copyrightable materials from the public domain." Id., at *14. The court next declined to part from "the settled rule that private censorship via copyright enforcement does not implicate First Amendment concerns." Id., at *17.

The Court of Appeals for the Tenth Circuit affirmed in part. *Golan v. Gonzales,* 501 F. 3d 1179 (2007). The public domain, it agreed, was not a "threshold that Congress" was powerless to "traverse in both directions." Id., at 1187 (internal quotations marks omitted). But §514, as the Court of Appeals read our decision in *Eldred v. Ashcroft,* 537 U. S. 186 (2003), required further First Amendment inspection, 501 F. 3d, at 1187. The measure "'altered the traditional contours of copyright protection,'" the court said—specifically, the "bedrock principle" that once works enter the public domain, they do not leave. Ibid. (quoting Eldred, 537 U. S., at 221). The case was remanded with an instruction to the District Court to address the First Amendment claim in light of the Tenth Circuit's opinion.

On remand, the District Court's starting premise was uncontested: Section 514 does not regulate speech on the basis of its content; therefore the law would be upheld if "narrowly tailored to serve a significant government interest." 611 F. Supp. 2d 1165, 1170–1171 (Colo. 2009) (quoting *Ward v. Rock Against Racism,* 491 U. S. 781, 791 (1989)). Summary judgment was due petitioners, the court concluded, because §514's constriction of the public domain was not justified by any of the asserted federal interests: compliance with Berne, securing greater protection for U. S. authors abroad, or remediation of the inequitable treatment suffered by foreign authors whose works lacked protection in the United States. 611 F. Supp. 2d, at 1172–1177.

The Tenth Circuit reversed. Deferring to Congress' predictive judgments in matters relating to foreign affairs, the appellate court held that §514 survived First Amendment scrutiny. Specifically, the court determined that the law was narrowly tailored to fit the important government aim of protecting U. S. copyright holders' interests abroad. 609 F. 3d 1076 (2010).

We granted certiorari to consider petitioners' challenge to §514 under both the Copyright Clause and the First Amendment, 562 U. S.____(2011), and now affirm.

II.

We first address petitioners' argument that Congress lacked authority, under the Copyright Clause, to enact §514. The Constitution states that "Congress shall have Power . . . [t]o promote the Progress of Science . . . by securing for limited Times to Authors . . . the exclusive Right to their . . . Writings." Art. I, §8, cl. 8. Petitioners find in this grant of authority an impenetrable barrier to the extension of copyright protection to authors whose writings, for whatever reason, are in the public domain. We see no such barrier in the text of the Copyright Clause, historical practice, or our precedents.

A

The text of the Copyright Clause does not exclude application of copyright protection to works in the public domain. Symposium, Congressional Power and Limitations Inherent in the Copyright Clause, 30 Colum. J. L. & Arts 259, 266 (2007). Petitioners' contrary argument relies primarily on the Constitution's confinement of a copyright's lifespan to a "limited Tim[e]." "Removing works from the public domain," they contend, "violates the 'limited [t]imes' restriction by turning a fixed and predictable period into one that can be reset or resurrected at any time, even after it expires." Brief for Petitioners 22.

Our decision in Eldred is largely dispositive of petitioners' limited-time argument. There we addressed the question whether Congress violated the Copyright Clause when it extended, by 20 years, the terms of existing copyrights. 537 U. S., at 192–193 (upholding Copyright Term Extension Act (CTEA)). Ruling that Congress acted within constitutional bounds, we declined to infer from the text of the Copyright Clause "the command that a time prescription, once set, becomes forever 'fixed' or 'inalterable.'" Id., at 199. "The word 'limited,'" we observed, "does not convey a meaning so constricted." Ibid. Rather, the term is best understood to mean "confine[d] within certain bounds," "restrain[ed]," or "circumscribed." Ibid. (internal quotation marks omitted). The construction petitioners tender closely resembles the definition rejected in Eldred and is similarly infirm.

. . .

Carried to its logical conclusion, petitioners persist, the Government's position would allow Congress to institute a second "limited" term after the first expires, a third after that, and so on. Thus, as long as Congress legislated in installments, perpetual copyright terms would be achievable. As in Eldred, the hypothetical legislative misbehavior petitioners posit is far afield from the case before us. See 537 U. S., at 198–200, 209–210. In aligning the United States with other nations bound by the Berne Convention, and thereby according equitable treatment to once disfavored foreign authors, Congress can hardly be charged with a design to move stealthily toward a regime of perpetual copyrights.

B

Historical practice corroborates our reading of the Copyright Clause to permit full U. S. compliance with Berne. Undoubtedly, federal copyright legislation generally has not affected works in the public domain. Section 514's disturbance of that domain, petitioners argue, distinguishes their suit from Eldred's. In adopting the CTEA, petitioners note, Congress acted in accord with "an unbroken congressional practice" of granting pre-expiration term extensions, 537 U. S., at 200. No comparable practice, they maintain, supports §514.

On occasion, however, Congress has seen fit to protect works once freely available. Notably, the Copyright Act of 1790 granted protection to many works previously in the public domain. Act of May 31, 1790 (1790 Act), §1, 1 Stat. 124 (covering "any map, chart, book, or books already printed within these United States"). Before the Act launched a uniform national system, three States provided no statutory copyright protection at all. Of those that did afford some protection, seven failed to protect maps; eight did not cover previously published books; and all ten denied protection to works that failed to comply with formalities. The First Congress, it thus appears, did not view the public domain as inviolate. As we have recognized, the "construction placed upon the Constitution by [the drafters of] the first [copyright] act of 1790 and the act of 1802 . . . men who were contemporary with [the Constitution's] formation, many of whom were members of the convention which framed it, is of itself entitled to very great weight." *Burrow-Giles Lithographic Co.* v. *Sarony,* 111 U. S. 53, 57 (1884).

Subsequent actions confirm that Congress has not understood the Copyright Clause to preclude protection for existing works. Several private bills restored the copyrights of works that previously had been in the public domain. See Act of Feb. 19, 1849 (Corson Act), ch. 57, 9 Stat. 763; Act of June 23, 1874 (Helmuth Act), ch. 534, 18 Stat. 618; Act of Feb. 17, 1898 (Jones Act), ch. 29, 30 Stat. 1396. These bills were unchallenged in court.

Analogous patent statutes, however, were upheld in litigation. In 1808, Congress passed a private bill restoring patent protection to Oliver Evans' flour mill. When Evans sued for infringement, first Chief Justice Marshall in the Circuit Court, *Evans v. Jordan,* 8 F. Cas. 872 (No. 4,564) (Va. 1813), and then Justice Bushrod Washington for this Court, *Evans v. Jordan,* 9 Cranch 199 (1815), upheld the restored patent's validity. After the patent's expiration, the Court said, "a general right to use [Evans'] discovery was not so vested in the public" as to allow the defendant to continue using the machinery, which he had constructed between the patent's expiration and the bill's passage. Id., at 202. See also *Blanchard v. Sprague,* 3 F. Cas. 648, 650 (No. 1,518) (CC Mass. 1839) (Story, J.) ("I never have entertained any doubt of the constitutional authority of congress" to "give a patent for an invention, which . . . was in public use and enjoyed by the community at the time of the passage of the act.").

This Court again upheld Congress' restoration of an invention to protected status in *McClurg* v. *Kingsland,* 1 How. 202 (1843). There we enforced an 1839 amendment that recognized a patent on an invention despite its prior use by the inventor's employer. Absent such dispensation, the employer's use would have rendered the invention unpatentable, and therefore open to exploitation without the inventor's leave. Id., at 206–209.

. . . Pointing to dictum in *Graham v. John Deere Co. of Kansas City,* 383 U. S. 1 (1966), petitioners would have us look past this history. In Graham, we stated that "Congress may not authorize the issuance of patents whose effects are to remove existent knowledge from the public domain, or to restrict free access to materials already available." Id., at 6; post, at 15. But as we explained in Eldred, this passage did not speak to the constitutional limits on Congress' copyright and patent authority. Rather, it "addressed an invention's very eligibility for patent protection." 537 U. S., at 202, n. 7. Installing a federal copyright system and ameliorating the interruptions of global war, it is true, presented Congress with extraordinary situations. Yet the TRIPS accord, leading the United States to comply in full measure with Berne, was also a signal event. See supra, at 7–8; cf. Eldred, 537 U. S., at 259, 264–265 (BREYER, J., dissenting) (acknowledging importance of international uniformity advanced by U. S. efforts to conform to the Berne Convention). Given the authority we hold Congress has, we will not second-guess the political choice Congress made between leaving the public domain untouched and embracing Berne unstintingly. Cf. id., at 212–213.

C

Petitioners' ultimate argument as to the Copyright and Patent Clause concerns its initial words. Congress is empowered to "promote the Progress of Science and useful Arts" by enacting systems of copyright and patent protection. U. S. Const., Art. I, §8, cl. 8. Perhaps counterintuitively for the contemporary reader, Congress' copyright authority is tied to the progress of science; its patent authority, to the progress of the useful arts. See Graham, 383 U.S., at 5, and n.1; Evans, 8 F.Cas., at 873 (Marshall, J.).

The "Progress of Science," petitioners acknowledge, refers broadly to "the creation and spread of knowledge and learning." Brief for Petitioners 21; accord post, at 1. They nevertheless argue that federal legislation cannot serve the Clause's aim unless the legislation "spur[s] the creation of . . . new works." Brief for Petitioners 24; accord post, at 1–2, 8, 17. Because §514 deals solely with works already created, petitioners urge, it "provides no plausible incentive to create new works" and is therefore invalid. Reply Brief 4.

The creation of at least one new work, however, is not the sole way Congress may promote knowledge and learning. In Eldred, we rejected an argument nearly identical to the one petitioners rehearse. The Eldred petitioners urged that the "CTEA's extension of existing copyrights categorically fails to 'promote the Progress of Science,' . . . because it does not stimulate the creation of new works." 537 U. S., at 211–212. In response to this argument, we held that the Copyright Clause does not demand that each copyright provision, examined discretely, operate to induce new works. Rather, we explained, the Clause "empowers Congress to determine the intellectual property regimes that, overall, in that body's judgment, will serve the ends of the Clause." Id., at 222. And those permissible ends, we held, extended beyond the creation of new works. See id., at 205–206 (rejecting the notion that "'the only way to promote the progress of science [is] to provide incentives to create new works'" (quoting Perlmutter, Participation in the International Copyright System as a Means to Promote the Progress of Science and Useful Arts, 36 Loyola (LA) L. Rev. 323, 332 (2002))).

. . .

Considered against this backdrop, §514 falls comfortably within Congress' authority under the Copyright Clause. Congress rationally could have concluded that adherence to Berne "promotes the diffusion of knowledge," Brief for Petitioners 4. A well-functioning international copyright system would likely encourage the dissemination of existing and future works. See URAA Joint Hearing 189 (statement of Professor Perlmutter). Full compliance with Berne, Congress had reason to believe, would expand the foreign markets available to U. S. authors and invigorate protection against piracy of U. S. works abroad, S. Rep. No. 103–412, pp. 224, 225 (1994); URAA Joint Hearing 291 (statement of Berman, RIAA); id., at 244, 247 (statement of Smith, IIPA), thereby benefitting copyright-intensive industries stateside and inducing greater investment in the creative process.

The provision of incentives for the creation of new works is surely an essential means to advance the spread of knowledge and learning. We hold, however, that it is not the sole means Congress may use "[t] o promote the Progress of Science." See Perlmutter, supra, at 332 (United States would "lose all flexibility" were the provision of incentives to create the exclusive way to promote the progress of science).

Congress determined that exemplary adherence to Berne would serve the objectives of the Copyright Clause. We have no warrant to reject the rational judgment Congress made.

III.

A

We next explain why the First Amendment does not inhibit the restoration authorized by §514. To do so, we first recapitulate the relevant part of our pathmarking decision in Eldred. The petitioners in Eldred, like those here, argued that Congress had violated not only the "limited Times" prescription of the Copyright Clause. In addition, and independently, the Eldred petitioners charged, Congress had offended the First Amendment's freedom of expression guarantee. The CTEA's 20-year enlargement of a copyright's duration, we held in Eldred, offended neither provision.

Concerning the First Amendment, we recognized that some restriction on expression is the inherent and intended effect of every grant of copyright. Noting that the "Copyright Clause and the First Amendment were adopted close in time," 537 U. S., at 219, we observed that the Framers regarded copyright protection not simply as a limit on the manner in which expressive works may be used. They also saw copyright as an "engine of free expression[:] By establishing a marketable right to the use of one's expression, copyright supplies the economic incentive to create and disseminate ideas." Ibid. (quoting Harper & Row, 471 U. S., at 558 (internal quotation marks omitted)); see id., at 546 ("rights conferred by copyright are designed to assure contributors to the store of knowledge a fair return for their labors").

We then described the "traditional contours" of copyright protection, i.e., the "idea/expression dichotomy" and the "fair use" defense. Both are recognized in our jurisprudence as "built-in First Amendment accommodations." Eldred, 537 U. S., at 219; see Harper & Row, 471 U. S., at 560 (First Amendment protections are "embodied in the Copyright Act's distinction between copyrightable expression and uncopyrightable facts and ideas," and in the "latitude for scholarship and comment" safeguarded by the fair use defense).

The idea/expression dichotomy is codified at 17 U. S. C. §102(b): "In no case does copyright protec[t] . . . any idea, procedure, process, system, method of operation, concept, principle, or discovery . . . described, explained, illustrated, or embodied in [the copyrighted] work." "Due to this [idea/expression] distinction, every idea, theory, and fact in a copyrighted work becomes instantly available for public exploitation at the moment of publication"; the author's expression alone gains copyright protection. Eldred, 537 U. S., at 219; see Harper & Row, 471 U. S., at 556 ("idea/expression dichotomy strike[s] a definitional balance between the First Amendment and the Copyright Act by permitting free communication of facts while still protecting an author's expression" (internal quotation marks omitted)).

The second "traditional contour," the fair use defense, is codified at 17 U. S. C. §107: "[T]he fair use of a copyrighted work, including such use by reproduction in copies . . . , for purposes such as criticism, comment, news reporting, teaching (including multiple copies for classroom use), scholarship, or research, is not an infringement of copyright." This limitation on exclusivity "allows the public to use not only facts and ideas contained in a copyrighted work, but also [the author's] expression itself in certain circumstances." Eldred, 537 U. S., at 219; see id., at 220 ("fair use defense affords considerable latitude for scholarship and comment, . . . even for parody" (internal quotation marks omitted)).

Given the "speech-protective purposes and safeguards" embraced by copyright law, see id., at 219, we concluded in Eldred that there was no call for the heightened review petitioners sought in that case. We reach the same conclusion here. Section 514 leaves undisturbed the "idea/expression" distinction and the "fair use" defense. Moreover, Congress adopted measures to ease the transition from a national scheme to an international copyright regime: It deferred the date from which enforcement runs, and it cushioned the impact of restoration on "reliance parties" who exploited foreign works denied protection before §514 took effect. See supra, at 10–11 (describing 17 U. S. C. §104A(c), (d), and (h)). See also Eldred, 537 U. S., at 220 (describing supplemental allowances and exemptions available to certain users to mitigate the CTEA's impact).

B

Petitioners attempt to distinguish their challenge from the one turned away in Eldred. First Amendment interests of a higher order are at stake here, petitioners say, because they—unlike their counterparts in Eldred—enjoyed "vested rights" in works that had already entered the public domain. The limited rights they retain under copyright law's "built-in safeguards" are, in their view, no substitute for the unlimited use they enjoyed before §514's enactment. Nor, petitioners urge, does §514's "unprecedented" foray into the public domain possess the historical pedigree that supported the term extension at issue in Eldred. Brief for Petitioners 42–43.

However spun, these contentions depend on an argument we considered and rejected above, namely, that the Constitution renders the public domain largely untouchable by Congress. Petitioners here attempt to achieve under the banner of the First Amendment what they could not win under the Copyright Clause: On their view of the Copyright Clause, the public domain is inviolable; as they read the First Amendment, the public domain is policed through heightened judicial scrutiny of Congress' means and ends. As we have already shown, see supra, at 13–19, the text of the Copyright Clause and the historical record scarcely establish that "once a work enters the public domain," Congress cannot permit anyone—"not even the creator—[to] copyright it," 501 F. 3d, at 1184. And nothing in the historical record, congressional practice, or our own jurisprudence warrants exceptional First Amendment solicitude for copyrighted works that were once in the public domain. Neither this challenge nor that raised in Eldred, we stress, allege Congress transgressed a generally applicable First Amendment prohibition; we are not faced, for example, with copyright protection that hinges on the author's viewpoint.

The Tenth Circuit's initial opinion determined that petitioners marshaled a stronger First Amendment challenge than did their predecessors in Eldred, who never "possessed unfettered access to any of the works at issue." 501 F. 3d, at 1193. See also id., at 1194 ("[O]nce the works at issue became free for anyone to copy, [petitioners] had vested First Amendment interests in the expressions, [thus] §514's interference with [petitioners'] rights is subject to First Amendment scrutiny."). As petitioners put it in this Court, Congress impermissibly revoked their right to exploit foreign works that "belonged to them" once the works were in the public domain. Brief for Petitioners 44–45.

To copyright lawyers, the "vested rights" formulation might sound exactly backwards: Rights typically vest at the outset of copyright protection, in an author or rightholder. See, e.g., 17 U. S. C. §201(a) ("Copyright in a work protected . . . vests initially in the author . . . ."). Once the term of protection ends, the works do not revest in any rightholder. Instead, the works simply lapse into the public domain. See, e.g., Berne, Art. 18(1), 828 U. N. T.S., at 251 ("This Convention shall apply to all works which . . . have not yet fallen into the public domain . . . ."). Anyone has free access to the public domain, but no one, after the copyright term has expired, acquires ownership rights in the once-protected works.

. . .

Section 514, we add, does not impose a blanket prohibition on public access. Petitioners protest that fair use and the idea/expression dichotomy "are plainly inadequate to protect the speech and expression rights that Section 514 took from petitioners, or . . . the public"—that is, "the unrestricted right to perform, copy, teach and distribute the entire work, for any reason." Brief for Petitioners 46–47. "Playing a few bars of a Shostakovich symphony," petitioners observe, "is no substitute for performing the entire work." Id., at 47.

But Congress has not put petitioners in this bind. The question here, as in Eldred, is whether would-be users must pay for their desired use of the author's expression, or else limit their exploitation to "fair use" of that work. Prokofiev's Peter and the Wolf could once be performed free of charge; after §514 the right to perform it must be obtained in the marketplace. This is the same marketplace, of course, that exists for the music of Prokofiev's U. S. contemporaries: works of Copland and Bernstein, for example, that enjoy copyright protection, but nevertheless appear regularly in the programs of U. S. concertgoers.

Before we joined Berne, domestic works and some foreign works were protected under U. S. statutes and bilateral international agreements, while other foreign works were available at an artificially low (because royalty-free) cost. By fully implementing Berne, Congress ensured that most works, whether foreign or domestic, would be governed by the same legal regime. The phenomenon to which Congress responded is not new: Distortions of the same order occurred with greater frequency—and to the detriment of both foreign and domestic authors—when, before 1891, foreign works were excluded entirely from U. S. copyright protection. See Kampelman, The United States and International Copyright, 41 Am. J. Int'l L. 406, 413 (1947) ("American readers were less inclined to read the novels of Cooper or Hawthorne for a dollar when they could buy a novel of Scott or Dickens for a quarter."). Section 514 continued the trend toward a harmonized copyright regime by placing foreign works in the position they would have occupied if the current regime had been in effect when those works were created and first published. Authors once deprived of protection are spared the continuing effects of that initial deprivation; §514 gives them nothing more than the benefit of their labors during whatever time remains before the normal copyright term expires.

Unlike petitioners, the dissent makes much of the so-called "orphan works" problem. See post, at 11–14, 23–24. We readily acknowledge the difficulties would-be users of copyrightable materials may face in identifying or locating copyright owners. See generally U. S. Copyright Office, Report on Orphan Works 21–40 (2006). But as the dissent concedes, see post, at 13, this difficulty is hardly peculiar to works restored under §514. It similarly afflicts, for instance, U. S. libraries that attempt to catalogue U. S. books. See post, at 12. See also Brief for American Library Association et al. as Amici Curiae 22 (Section 514 "exacerbated," but did not create, the problem of orphan works); U. S. Copyright Office, supra, at 41–44 (tracing orphan-works problem to Congress' elimination of formalities, commencing with the 1976 Copyright Act).

. . . [N]o one has suggested that the orphan-works issue should be addressed through our implementation of Berne, rather than through overarching legislation of the sort proposed in Congress and cited by the dissent. See post, at 23–24; U. S. Copyright Office, Legal Issues in Mass Digitization 25–29 (2011) (discussing recent legislative efforts). Our unstinting adherence to Berne may add impetus to calls for the enactment of such legislation. But resistance to Berne's prescriptions surely is not a necessary or proper response to the pervasive question, what should Congress do about orphan works.

IV.

Congress determined that U.S. interests were best served by our full participation in the dominant system of international copyright protection. Those interests include ensuring exemplary compliance with our international obligations, securing greater protection for U. S. authors abroad, and remedying unequal treatment of foreign authors. The judgment §514 expresses lies well within the ken of the political branches. It is our obligation, of course, to determine whether the action Congress took, wise or not, encounters any constitutional shoal. For the reasons stated, we are satisfied it does not. The judgment of the Court of Appeals for the Tenth Circuit is therefore Affirmed.

. . .

JUSTICE BREYER, with whom JUSTICE ALITO joins, dissenting.

In order "[t]o promote the Progress of Science" (by which term the Founders meant "learning" or "knowledge"), the Constitution's Copyright Clause grants Congress the power to "secur[e] for limited Times to Authors . . . the exclusive Right to their . . . Writings." Art. I, §8, cl. 8. This "exclusive Right" allows its holder to charge a fee to those who wish to use a copyrighted work, and the ability to charge that fee encourages the production of new material. In this sense, a copyright is, in Macaulay's words, a "tax on readers for the purpose of giving a bounty to writers"—a bounty designed to encourage new production. As the Court said in Eldred, "'[t]he economic philosophy behind the [Copyright] [C]lause . . . is the conviction that encouragement of individual effort by personal gain is the best way to advance public welfare through the talents of authors and inventors.'" *Eldred v. Ashcroft*, 537U.S.186, 212, n. 18 (2003) (quoting *Mazer v. Stein*, 347 U. S. 201, 219 (1954)). See T. Macaulay, Speeches on Copyright 25 (E. Miller ed. 1913); E. Walterscheid, The Nature of the Intellectual Property Clause: A Study in Historical Perspective 125–126 (2002) (hereinafter Walterscheid).

The statute before us, however, does not encourage anyone to produce a single new work. By definition, it bestows monetary rewards only on owners of old works—works that have already been created and already are in the American public domain. At the same time, the statute inhibits the dissemination of those works, foreign works published abroad after 1923, of which there are many millions, including films, works of art, innumerable photographs, and, of course, books—books that (in the absence of the statute) would assume their rightful places in computer-accessible databases, spreading knowledge throughout the world. See infra, at 10–13. In my view, the Copyright Clause does not authorize Congress to enact this statute. And I consequently dissent.

. . .

SUPREME COURT OF THE UNITED STATES

No. 92–1292

LUTHER R. CAMPBELL AKA LUKE SKYYWALKER, ET AL.,

PETITIONERS *v.* ACUFF-ROSE MUSIC, INC.

ON WRIT OF CERTIORARI TO THE UNITED STATES COURT OF APPEALS FOR THE SIXTH CIRCUIT

[March 7, 1994]

JUSTICE SOUTER delivered the opinion of the Court.

We are called upon to decide whether 2 Live Crew's commercial parody of Roy Orbison's song, "Oh, Pretty Woman," may be a fair use within the meaning of the Copyright Act of 1976, 17 U. S. C. § 107 (1988 ed. and Supp. IV). Although the District Court granted summary judgment for 2 Live Crew, the Court of Appeals reversed, holding the defense of fair use barred by the song's commercial character and excessive borrowing. Because we hold that a parody's commercial character is only one element to be weighed in a fair use enquiry, and that insufficient consideration was given to the nature of parody in weighing the degree of copying, we reverse and remand.

I.

In 1964, Roy Orbison and William Dees wrote a rock ballad called "Oh, Pretty Woman" and assigned their rights in it to respondent Acuff-Rose Music, Inc. See Appendix A, *infra*, at 26. Acuff-Rose registered the song for copyright protection.

Petitioners Luther R. Campbell, Christopher Wongwon, Mark Ross, and David Hobbs, are collectively known as 2 Live Crew, a popular rap music group.[1] In 1989, Campbell wrote a song entitled "Pretty Woman," which he later described in an affidavit as intended, "through comical lyrics, to satirize the original work. . . ." App. to Pet. for Cert. 80a. On July 5, 1989, 2 Live Crew's manager informed Acuff-Rose that 2 Live Crew had written a parody of "Oh, Pretty Woman," that they would afford all credit for ownership and authorship of the original song to Acuff-Rose, Dees, and Orbison, and that they were willing to pay a fee for the use they wished to make of it. Enclosed with the letter were a copy of the

[1] Rap has been defined as a "style of black American popular music consisting of improvised rhymes performed to a rhythmic accompaniment." The Norton/Grove Concise Encyclopedia of Music 613 (1988). 2 Live Crew plays "[b]ass music," a regional, hip-hop style of rap from the Liberty City area of Miami, Florida. Brief for Petitioners 34.

NOTICE: This opinion is subject to formal revision before publication in the preliminary print of the United States Reports. Readers are requested to notify the Reporter of Decisions, Supreme Court of the United States, Washington, D.C. 20543, of any typographical or other formal errors, in order that corrections may be made before the preliminary print goes to press.

lyrics and a recording of 2 Live Crew's song. See Appendix B, *infra*, at 27. Acuff-Rose's agent refused permission, stating that "I am aware of the success enjoyed by 'The 2 Live Crews', but I must inform you that we cannot permit the use of a parody of 'Oh, Pretty Woman.'" App. to Pet. for Cert. 85a. Nonetheless, in June or July 1989,[2] 2 Live Crew released records, cassette tapes, and compact discs of "Pretty Woman" in a collection of songs entitled "As Clean As They Wanna Be." The albums and compact discs identify the authors of "Pretty Woman" as Orbison and Dees and its publisher as Acuff-Rose.

Almost a year later, after nearly a quarter of a million copies of the recording had been sold, Acuff-Rose sued 2 Live Crew and its record company, Luke Skyywalker Records, for copyright infringement. The District Court granted summary judgment for 2 Live Crew,[3] reasoning that the commercial purpose of 2 Live Crew's song was no bar to fair use; that 2 Live Crew's version was a parody, which "quickly degenerates into a play on words, substituting predictable lyrics with shocking ones" to show "how bland and banal the Orbison song" is; that 2 Live Crew had taken no more than was necessary to "conjure up" the original in order to parody it; and that it was "extremely unlikely that 2 Live Crew's song could adversely affect the market for the original." 754 F. Supp. 1150, 1154–1155, 1157–1158 (MD Tenn. 1991). The District Court weighed these factors and held that 2 Live Crew's song made fair use of Orbison's original. *Id.*, at 1158–1159.

The Court of Appeals for the Sixth Circuit reversed and remanded. 972 F. 2d 1429, 1439 (1992). Although it assumed for the purpose of its opinion that 2 Live Crew's song was a parody of the Orbison original, the Court of Appeals thought the District Court had put too little emphasis on the fact that "every commercial use . . . is presumptively . . . unfair," *Sony Corp. of America* v. *Universal City Studios, Inc.*, 464 U. S. 417, 451 (1984), and it held that "the admittedly commercial nature" of the parody "requires the conclusion" that the first of four factors relevant under the statute weighs against a finding of fair use. 972 F. 2d, at 1435, 1437. Next, the Court of Appeals determined that, by "taking the heart of the original and making it the heart of a new work," 2 Live Crew had, qualitatively, taken too much. *Id.*, at 1438. Finally, after noting that the effect on the potential market for the original (and the market for derivative works) is "undoubtedly the single most important element of fair use," *Harper & Row, Publishers, Inc.* v. *Nation Enterprises*, 471 U. S. 539, 566 (1985), the Court of Appeals faulted the District Court for "refus[ing] to indulge the presumption" that "harm for purposes of the fair use analysis has been established by the presumption attaching to commercial uses." 972 F. 2d, at 1438–1439. In sum, the court concluded that its "blatantly commercial purpose . . . prevents this parody from being a fair use." *Id.*, at 1439.

We granted certiorari, 507 U. S.____(1993), to determine whether 2 Live Crew's commercial parody could be a fair use.

---

[2] The parties argue about the timing. 2 Live Crew contends that the album was released on July 15, and the District Court so held. 754 F. Supp. 1150, 1152 (MD Tenn. 1991). The Court of Appeals states that Campbell's affidavit puts the release date in June, and chooses that date. 972 F. 2d 1429, 1432 (CA6 1992). We find the timing of the request irrelevant for purposes of this enquiry. See n. 18, *infra*, discussing good faith.

[3] 2 Live Crew's motion to dismiss was converted to a motion for summary judgment. Acuff-Rose defended against the motion, but filed no cross-motion.

II.

It is uncontested here that 2 Live Crew's song would be an infringement of Acuff-Rose's rights in "Oh, Pretty Woman," under the Copyright Act of 1976, 17 U. S. C. § 106 (1988 ed. and Supp. IV), but for a finding of fair use through parody.[4] From the infancy of copyright protection, some opportunity for fair use of copyrighted materials has been thought necessary to fulfill copyright's very purpose, "[t]o promote the Progress of Science and useful Arts . . . ." U. S. Const., Art. I, § 8, cl. 8.[5] For as Justice Story explained, "[i]n truth, in literature, in science and in art, there are, and can be, few, if any, things, which in an abstract sense, are strictly new and original throughout. Every book in literature, science and art, borrows, and must necessarily borrow, and use much which was well known and used before." *Emerson* v. *Davies*, 8 F. Cas. 615, 619 (No. 4,436) (CCD Mass. 1845). Similarly, Lord Ellenborough expressed the inherent tension in the need simultaneously to protect copyrighted material and to allow others to build upon it when he wrote, "while I shall think myself bound to secure every man in the enjoyment of his copyright, one must not put manacles upon science." *Carey* v. *Kearsley*, 4 Esp. 168, 170, 170 Eng. Rep. 679, 681 (K.B. 1803). In copyright cases brought under the Statute of Anne of 1710[6], English courts held that in some instances "fair abridgements" would not infringe an author's rights, see W. Patry, The Fair Use Privilege in Copyright Law 6–17 (1985) (hereinafter Patry); Leval, Toward a Fair Use Standard, 103 Harv. L. Rev. 1105, 1105 (1990) (hereinafter Leval), and although the First Congress enacted our initial copyright statute, Act of May 31, 1790, 1 Stat. 124, without any explicit reference to "fair use," as it later came to be known[7], the doctrine was recognized by the American courts nonetheless.

In *Folsom* v. *Marsh*, Justice Story distilled the essence of law and methodology from the earlier cases: "look to the nature and objects of the selections made, the quantity and value of the materials used, and the

---

[4] Section 106 provides in part:

> "Subject to sections 107 through 120, the owner of copyright under this title has the exclusive rights to do and to authorize any of the following:
>
> "(1) to reproduce the copyrighted work in copies or phonorecords;
>
> "(2) to prepare derivative works based upon the copyrighted work;
>
> "(3) to distribute copies or phonorecords of the copyrighted work to the public by sale or other transfer of ownership, or by rental, lease, or lending . . . ."

A derivative work is defined as one "based upon one or more preexisting works, such as a translation, musical arrangement, dramatization, fictionalization, motion picture version, sound recording, art reproduction, abridgment, condensation, or any other form in which a work may be recast, transformed, or adapted. A work consisting of editorial revisions, annotations, elaborations, or other modifications which, as a whole, represent an original work of authorship, is a 'derivative work.'" 17 U. S. C. § 101.

2 Live Crew concedes that it is not entitled to a compulsory license under § 115 because its arrangement changes "the basic melody or fundamental character" of the original. § 115(a)(2).

[5] The exclusion of facts and ideas from copyright protection serves that goal as well. See § 102(b) ("In no case does copyright protection for an original work of authorship extend to any idea, procedure, process, system, method of operation, concept, principle, or discovery . . . "); *Feist Publications* v. *Rural Telephone Service Co.*, 499 U. S. 340, 359 (1991) ("[F]acts contained in existing works may be freely copied"); *Harper & Row, Publishers, Inc.* v. *Nation Enterprises*, 471 U. S. 539, 547 (1985) (copyright owner's rights exclude facts and ideas, and fair use).

[6] An Act for the Encouragement of Learning, 8 Anne, ch. 19.

[7] Patry 27, citing *Lawrence* v. *Dana*, 15 F. Cas. 26, 60 (No. 8,136) (CCD Mass. 1869).

degree in which the use may prejudice the sale, or diminish the profits, or supersede the objects, of the original work." 9 F. Cas. 342, 348 (No. 4,901) (CCD Mass. 1841). Thus expressed, fair use remained exclusively judge-made doctrine until the passage of the 1976 Copyright Act, in which Story's summary is discernible:[8]

*****

Congress meant §107 "to restate the present judicial doctrine of fair use, not to change, narrow, or enlarge it in any way" and intended that courts continue the common law tradition of fair use adjudication. H. R. Rep. No. 94–1476, p. 66 (1976) (hereinafter House Report); S. Rep. No. 94–473, p. 62 (1975) (hereinafter Senate Report). The fair use doctrine thus "permits [and requires] courts to avoid rigid application of the copyright statute when, on occasion, it would stifle the very creativity which that law is designed to foster." *Stewart* v. *Abend*, 495 U. S. 207, 236 (1990) (internal quotation marks and citation omitted).

The task is not to be simplified with bright-line rules, for the statute, like the doctrine it recognizes, calls for case-by-case analysis. *Harper & Row*, 471 U. S., at 560; *Sony*, 464 U. S., at 448, and n. 31; House Report, pp. 65–66; Senate Report, p. 62. The text employs the terms "including" and "such as" in the preamble paragraph to indicate the "illustrative and not limitative" function of the examples given, § 101; see *Harper & Row, supra*, at 561, which thus provide only general guidance about the sorts of copying that courts and Congress most commonly had found to be fair uses.[9] Nor may the four statutory factors be treated in isolation, one from another. All are to be explored, and the results weighed together, in light of the purposes of copyright. See Leval 1110–1111; Patry & Perlmutter, Fair Use Misconstrued: Profit, Presumptions, and Parody, 11 Cardozo Arts & Ent. L. J. 667, 685–687 (1993) (hereinafter Patry & Perlmutter).[10]

A

The first factor in a fair use enquiry is "the purpose and character of the use, including whether such use is of a commercial nature or is for nonprofit educational purposes." § 107(1). This factor draws on Justice Story's formulation, "the nature and objects of the selections made." *Folsom* v. *Marsh*, 9 F. Cas., at 348. The enquiry here may be guided by the examples given in the preamble to § 107, looking to whether the use is for criticism, or comment, or news reporting, and the like, see § 107. The central purpose of this investigation is to see, in Justice Story's words, whether the new work merely "supersede[s] the objects"

[8] Leval 1105. For a historical account of the development of the fair use doctrine, see Patry 1–64.

[9] See Senate Report, p. 62 ("[W]hether a use referred to in the first sentence of section 107 is a fair use in a particular case will depend upon the application of the determinative factors").

[10] Because the fair use enquiry often requires close questions of judgment as to the extent of permissible borrowing in cases involving parodies (or other critical works), courts may also wish to bear in mind that the goals of the copyright law, "to stimulate the creation and publication of edifying matter," Leval 1134, are not always best served by automatically granting injunctive relief when parodists are found to have gone beyond the bounds of fair use. See 17 U. S. C. § 502(a) (court "*may* . . . grant . . . injunctions on such terms as it may deem reasonable to prevent or restrain infringement") (emphasis added); Leval 1132 (while in the "vast majority of cases, [an injunctive] remedy is justified because most infringements are simple piracy," such cases are "worlds apart from many of those raising reasonable contentions of fair use" where "there may be a strong public interest in the publication of the secondary work [and] the copyright owner's interest may be adequately protected by an award of damages for whatever infringement is found"); *Abend* v. *MCA, Inc.*, 863 F. 2d 1465, 1479 (CA9 1988) (finding "special circumstances" that would cause "great injustice" to defendants and "public injury" were injunction to issue), aff'd *sub nom. Stewart* v. *Abend*, 495 U. S. 207 (1990).

of the original creation, *Folsom* v. *Marsh*, *supra*, at 348; accord, *Harper & Row*, *supra*, at 562 ("supplanting" the original), or instead adds something new, with a further purpose or different character, altering the first with new expression, meaning, or message; it asks, in other words, whether and to what extent the new work is "transformative." Leval 1111. Although such transformative use is not absolutely necessary for a finding of fair use, *Sony*, *supra*, at 455, n. 40,[11] the goal of copyright, to promote science and the arts, is generally furthered by the creation of transformative works. Such works thus lie at the heart of the fair use doctrine's guarantee of breathing space within the confines of copyright, see, *e.g.*, *Sony*, *supra*, at 478–480 (Blackmun, J., dissenting), and the more transformative the new work, the less will be the significance of other factors, like commercialism, that may weigh against a finding of fair use.

*****

The germ of parody lies in the definition of the Greek *parodeia*, quoted in Judge Nelson's Court of Appeals dissent, as "a song sung alongside another." 972 F. 2d, at 1440, quoting 7 Encyclopedia Britannica 768 (15th ed. 1975). Modern dictionaries accordingly describe a parody as a "literary or artistic work that imitates the characteristic style of an author or a work for comic effect or ridicule,"[12] or as a "composition in prose or verse in which the characteristic turns of thought and phrase in an author or class of authors are imitated in such a way as to make them appear ridiculous."[13] For the purposes of copyright law, the nub of the definitions, and the heart of any parodist's claim to quote from existing material, is the use of some elements of a prior author's composition to create a new one that, at least in part, comments on that author's works. See, *e.g.*, *Fisher* v. *Dees*, *supra*, at 437; *MCA, Inc.* v. *Wilson*, 677 F. 2d 180, 185 (CA2 1981). If, on the contrary, the commentary has no critical bearing on the substance or style of the original composition, which the alleged infringer merely uses to get attention or to avoid the drudgery in working up something fresh, the claim to fairness in borrowing from another's work diminishes accordingly (if it does not vanish), and other factors, like the extent of its commerciality, loom larger.[14] Parody needs to mimic an original to make its point, and so has some claim to use the creation of its victim's (or collective victims') imagination, whereas satire can stand on its own two feet and so requires justification for the very act of borrowing.[15] See *Ibid.*; Bisceglia, Parody and Copyright Protection: Turning the Balancing Act Into a Juggling Act, in ASCAP, Copyright Law Symposium, No. 34, p. 25 (1987).

---

[11] The obvious statutory exception to this focus on transformative uses is the straight reproduction of multiple copies for classroom distribution.

[12] The American Heritage Dictionary 1317 (3d ed. 1992).

[13] 11 The Oxford English Dictionary 247 (2d ed. 1989).

[14] A parody that more loosely targets an original than the parody presented here may still be sufficiently aimed at an original work to come within our analysis of parody. If a parody whose wide dissemination in the market runs the risk of serving as a substitute for the original or licensed derivatives (see *infra*, discussing factor four), it is more incumbent on one claiming fair use to establish the extent of transformation and the parody's critical relationship to the original. By contrast, when there is little or no risk of market substitution, whether because of the large extent of transformation of the earlier work, the new work's minimal distribution in the market, the small extent to which it borrows from an original, or other factors, taking parodic aim at an original is a less critical factor in the analysis, and looser forms of parody may be found to be fair use, as may satire with lesser justification for the borrowing than would otherwise be required.

[15] Satire has been defined as a work "in which prevalent follies or vices are assailed with ridicule," 14 The Oxford English Dictionary 500 (2d ed. 1989), or are "attacked through irony, derision, or wit," The American Heritage Dictionary 1604 (3d ed. 1992).

The fact that parody can claim legitimacy for some appropriation does not, of course, tell either parodist or judge much about where to draw the line. Like a book review quoting the copyrighted material criticized, parody may or may not be fair use, and petitioner's suggestion that any parodic use is presumptively fair has no more justification in law or fact than the equally hopeful claim that any use for news reporting should be presumed fair, see *Harper & Row*, 471 U. S., at 561. The Act has no hint of an evidentiary preference for parodists over their victims, and no workable presumption for parody could take account of the fact that parody often shades into satire when society is lampooned through its creative artifacts, or that a work may contain both parodic and non-parodic elements. Accordingly, parody, like any other use, has to work its way through the relevant factors, and be judged case by case, in light of the ends of the copyright law.

Here, the District Court held, and the Court of Appeals assumed, that 2 Live Crew's "Pretty Woman" contains parody, commenting on and criticizing the original work, whatever it may have to say about society at large. As the District Court remarked, the words of 2 Live Crew's song copy the original's first line, but then "quickly degenerat[e] into a play on words, substituting predictable lyrics with shocking ones . . . [that] derisively demonstrat[e] how bland and banal the Orbison song seems to them." 754 F. Supp., at 1155 (footnote omitted). Judge Nelson, dissenting below, came to the same conclusion, that the 2 Live Crew song "was clearly intended to ridicule the white-bread original" and "reminds us that sexual congress with nameless streetwalkers is not necessarily the stuff of romance and is not necessarily without its consequences. The singers (there are several) have the same thing on their minds as did the lonely man with the nasal voice, but here there is no hint of wine and roses." 972 F. 2d, at 1442. Although the majority below had difficulty discerning any criticism of the original in 2 Live Crew's song, it assumed for purposes of its opinion that there was some. *Id.*, at 1435–1436, and n. 8.

We have less difficulty in finding that critical element in 2 Live Crew's song than the Court of Appeals did, although having found it we will not take the further step of evaluating its quality. The threshold question when fair use is raised in defense of parody is whether a parodic character may reasonably be perceived.[16] Whether, going beyond that, parody is in good taste or bad does not and should not matter to fair use. As Justice Holmes explained, "[i]t would be a dangerous undertaking for persons trained only to the law to constitute themselves final judges of the worth of [a work], outside of the narrowest and most obvious limits. At the one extreme some works of genius would be sure to miss appreciation. Their very novelty would make them repulsive until the public had learned the new language in which their author spoke." *Bleistein* v. *Donaldson Lithographing Co.*, 188 U. S. 239, 251 (1903) (circus posters have copyright protection); cf. *Yankee Publishing Inc.* v. *News America Publishing, Inc.*, 809 F. Supp. 267, 280 (SDNY 1992) (Leval, J.) ("First Amendment protections do not apply only to those who speak clearly, whose jokes are funny, and whose parodies succeed") (trademark case).

While we might not assign a high rank to the parodic element here, we think it fair to say that 2 Live Crew's song reasonably could be perceived as commenting on the original or criticizing it, to some degree. 2 Live Crew juxtaposes the romantic musings of a man whose fantasy comes true, with degrading taunts,

---

[16] The only further judgment, indeed, that a court may pass on a work goes to an assessment of whether the parodic element is slight or great, and the copying small or extensive in relation to the parodic element, for a work with slight parodic element and extensive copying will be more likely to merely "supersede the objects" of the original. See *infra*, at____, discussing factors three and four.

a bawdy demand for sex, and a sigh of relief from paternal responsibility. The later words can be taken as a comment on the naivete of the original of an earlier day, as a rejection of its sentiment that ignores the ugliness of street life and the debasement that it signifies. It is this joinder of reference and ridicule that marks off the author's choice of parody from the other types of comment and criticism that traditionally have had a claim to fair use protection as transformative works.[17]

The Court of Appeals, however, immediately cut short the enquiry into 2 Live Crew's fair use claim by confining its treatment of the first factor essentially to one relevant fact, the commercial nature of the use. The court then inflated the significance of this fact by applying a presumption ostensibly culled from *Sony*, that "every commercial use of copyrighted material is presumptively . . . unfair . . . ." *Sony*, 464 U. S., at 451. In giving virtually dispositive weight to the commercial nature of the parody, the Court of Appeals erred.

The language of the statute makes clear that the commercial or nonprofit educational purpose of a work is only one element of the first factor enquiry into its purpose and character. Section 107(1) uses the term "including" to begin the dependent clause referring to commercial use, and the main clause speaks of a broader investigation into "purpose and character." As we explained in *Harper & Row*, Congress resisted attempts to narrow the ambit of this traditional enquiry by adopting categories of presumptively fair use, and it urged courts to preserve the breadth of their traditionally ample view of the universe of relevant evidence. 471 U. S., at 561; House Report, p. 66. Accordingly, the mere fact that a use is educational and not for profit does not insulate it from a finding of infringement, any more than the commercial character of a use bars a finding of fairness. If, indeed, commerciality carried presumptive force against a finding of fairness, the presumption would swallow nearly all of the illustrative uses listed in the preamble paragraph of § 107, including news reporting, comment, criticism, teaching, scholarship, and research, since these activities "are generally conducted for profit in this country." *Harper & Row*, *supra*, at 592 (Brennan, J., dissenting). Congress could not have intended such a rule, which certainly is not inferable from the common-law cases, arising as they did from the world of letters in which Samuel Johnson could pronounce that "[n]o man but a blockhead ever wrote, except for money." 3 Boswell's Life of Johnson 19 (G. Hill ed. 1934).

Sony itself called for no hard evidentiary presumption. There, we emphasized the need for a "sensitive balancing of interests," 464 U. S., at 455, n. 40, noted that Congress had "eschewed a rigid, bright-line approach to fair use," *id.*, at 449, n. 31, and stated that the commercial or nonprofit educational character of a work is "not conclusive," *id.*, at 448–449, but rather a fact to be "weighed along with other[s] in fair use decisions." *Id.*, at 449, n. 32 (quoting House Report, p. 66). The Court of Appeals's elevation of one sentence from *Sony* to a *per se* rule thus runs as much counter to *Sony* itself as to the long common-law tradition of fair use adjudication. Rather, as we explained in *Harper & Row*, *Sony* stands for the proposition that the "fact that a publication was commercial as opposed to nonprofit is a separate factor that tends to weigh against a finding of fair use." 471 U. S., at 562. But that is all, and the fact that even the force of that tendency will vary with the context is a further reason against elevating commerciality to

---

[17] We note in passing that 2 Live Crew need not label its whole album, or even this song, a parody in order to claim fair use protection, nor should 2 Live Crew be penalized for this being its first parodic essay. Parody serves its goals whether labeled or not, and there is no reason to require parody to state the obvious, (or even the reasonably perceived). See Patry & Perlmutter 716–717.

hard presumptive significance. The use, for example, of a copyrighted work to advertise a product, even in a parody, will be entitled to less indulgence under the first factor of the fair use enquiry, than the sale of a parody for its own sake, let alone one performed a single time by students in school. See generally Patry & Perlmutter 679–680; *Fisher* v. *Dees*, 794 F. 2d, at 437; *Maxtone-Graham* v. *Burtchaell*, 803 F. 2d 1253, 1262 (CA2 1986); *Sega Enterprises Ltd.* v. *Accolade, Inc.*, 977 F. 2d 1510, 1522 (CA9 1992).[18]

B

The second statutory factor, "the nature of the copyrighted work," § 107(2), draws on Justice Story's expression, the "value of the materials used." *Folsom* v. *Marsh*, 9 F. Cas., at 348. This factor calls for recognition that some works are closer to the core of intended copyright protection than others, with the consequence that fair use is more difficult to establish when the former works are copied. See, *e.g.*, *Stewart* v. *Abend*, 495 U. S., at 237–238 (contrasting fictional short story with factual works); *Harper & Row*, 471 U. S., at 563–564 (contrasting soon-to-be-published memoir with published speech); *Sony*, 464 U. S., at 455, n. 40 (contrasting motion pictures with news broadcasts); *Feist*, 499 U. S., 348–351 (contrasting creative works with bare factual compilations); 3 M. Nimmer & D. Nimmer, Nimmer on Copyright § 13.05[A][2] (1993) (hereinafter Nimmer); Leval 1116. We agree with both the District Court and the Court of Appeals that the Orbison original's creative expression for public dissemination falls within the core of the copyright's protective purposes. 754 F. Supp., at 1155–1156; 972 F. 2d, at 1437. This fact, however, is not much help in this case, or ever likely to help much in separating the fair use sheep from the infringing goats in a parody case, since parodies almost invariably copy publicly known, expressive works.

C

The third factor asks whether "the amount and substantiality of the portion used in relation to the copyrighted work as a whole," § 107(3) (or, in Justice Story's words, "the quantity and value of the materials used," *Folsom* v. *Marsh*, *supra*, at 348) are reasonable in relation to the purpose of the copying. Here, attention turns to the persuasiveness of a parodist's justification for the particular copying done, and the enquiry will harken back to the first of the statutory factors, for, as in prior cases, we recognize that the extent of permissible copying varies with the purpose and character of the use. See *Sony*, 464 U. S., at 449–450 (reproduction of entire work "does not have its ordinary effect of militating against a finding of fair use" as to home videotaping of television programs); *Harper & Row*, 471 U. S., at 564 ("[E]ven substantial quotations might qualify as fair use in a review of a published work or a news account of a speech" but not in a scoop of a soon-to-be-published memoir). The facts bearing on this factor will also tend to address the fourth, by revealing the degree to which the parody may serve as a market substitute for the original or potentially licensed derivatives. See Leval 1123.

[18] Finally, regardless of the weight one might place on the alleged infringer's state of mind, compare *Harper & Row*, 471 U. S., at 562 (fair use presupposes good faith and fair dealing) (quotation marks omitted), with *Folsom* v. *Marsh*, 9 F. Cas. 342, 349 (No. 4,901) (CCD Mass. 1841) (good faith does not bar a finding of infringement); Leval 1126–1127 (good faith irrelevant to fair use analysis), we reject Acuff-Rose's argument that 2 Live Crew's request for permission to use the original should be weighed against a finding of fair use. Even if good faith were central to fair use, 2 Live Crew's actions do not necessarily suggest that they believed their version was not fair use; the offer may simply have been made in a good faith effort to avoid this litigation. If the use is otherwise fair, then no permission need be sought or granted. Thus, being denied permission to use a work does not weigh against a finding of fair use. See *Fisher* v. *Dees*, 794 F. 2d 432, 437 (CA9 1986).

The District Court considered the song's parodic purpose in finding that 2 Live Crew had not helped themselves overmuch. 754 F. Supp., at 1156–1157. The Court of Appeals disagreed, stating that "[w]hile it may not be inappropriate to find that no more was taken than necessary, the copying was qualitatively substantial. . . . We conclude that taking the heart of the original and making it the heart of a new work was to purloin a substantial portion of the essence of the original." 972 F. 2d, at 1438.

The Court of Appeals is of course correct that this factor calls for thought not only about the quantity of the materials used, but about their quality and importance, too. In *Harper & Row*, for example, the Nation had taken only some 300 words out of President Ford's memoirs, but we signalled the significance of the quotations in finding them to amount to "the heart of the book," the part most likely to be newsworthy and important in licensing serialization. 471 U. S., at 564–566, 568 (internal quotation marks omitted). We also agree with the Court of Appeals that whether "a substantial portion of the infringing work was copied verbatim" from the copyrighted work is a relevant question, see *id.*, at 565, for it may reveal a dearth of transformative character or purpose under the first factor, or a greater likelihood of market harm under the fourth; a work composed primarily of an original, particularly its heart, with little added or changed, is more likely to be a merely superseding use, fulfilling demand for the original.

Where we part company with the court below is in applying these guides to parody, and in particular to parody in the song before us. Parody presents a difficult case. Parody's humor, or in any event its comment, necessarily springs from recognizable allusion to its object through distorted imitation. Its art lies in the tension between a known original and its parodic twin. When parody takes aim at a particular original work, the parody must be able to "conjure up" at least enough of that original to make the object of its critical wit recognizable. See, *e.g.*, *Elsmere Music*, 623 F. 2d, at 253, n. 1; *Fisher* v. *Dees*, 794 F. 2d, at 438–439. What makes for this recognition is quotation of the original's most distinctive or memorable features, which the parodist can be sure the audience will know. Once enough has been taken to assure identification, how much more is reasonable will depend, say, on the extent to which the song's overriding purpose and character is to parody the original or, in contrast, the likelihood that the parody may serve as a market substitute for the original. But using some characteristic features cannot be avoided.

We think the Court of Appeals was insufficiently appreciative of parody's need for the recognizable sight or sound when it ruled 2 Live Crew's use unreasonable as a matter of law. It is true, of course, that 2 Live Crew copied the characteristic opening bass riff (or musical phrase) of the original, and true that the words of the first line copy the Orbison lyrics. But if quotation of the opening riff and the first line may be said to go to the "heart" of the original, the heart is also what most readily conjures up the song for parody, and it is the heart at which parody takes aim. Copying does not become excessive in relation to parodic purpose merely because the portion taken was the original's heart. If 2 Live Crew had copied a significantly less memorable part of the original, it is difficult to see how its parodic character would have come through. See *Fisher* v. *Dees*, 794 F. 2d, at 439.

This is not, of course, to say that anyone who calls himself a parodist can skim the cream and get away scot free. In parody, as in news reporting, see *Harper & Row*, *supra*, context is everything, and the question of fairness asks what else the parodist did besides go to the heart of the original. It is significant that 2 Live Crew not only copied the first line of the original, but thereafter departed markedly from the

Orbison lyrics for its own ends. 2 Live Crew not only copied the bass riff and repeated it,[19] but also produced otherwise distinctive sounds, interposing "scraper" noise, overlaying the music with solos in different keys, and altering the drum beat. See 754 F. Supp., at 1155. This is not a case, then, where "a substantial portion" of the parody itself is composed of a "verbatim" copying of the original. It is not, that is, a case where the parody is so insubstantial, as compared to the copying, that the third factor must be resolved as a matter of law against the parodists.

Suffice it to say here that, as to the lyrics, we think the Court of Appeals correctly suggested that "no more was taken than necessary," 972 F. 2d, at 1438, but just for that reason, we fail to see how the copying can be excessive in relation to its parodic purpose, even if the portion taken is the original's "heart." As to the music, we express no opinion whether repetition of the bass riff is excessive copying, and we remand to permit evaluation of the amount taken, in light of the song's parodic purpose and character, its transformative elements, and considerations of the potential for market substitution sketched more fully below.

D

The fourth fair use factor is "the effect of the use upon the potential market for or value of the copyrighted work." § 107(4). It requires courts to consider not only the extent of market harm caused by the particular actions of the alleged infringer, but also "whether unrestricted and widespread conduct of the sort engaged in by the defendant . . . would result in a substantially adverse impact on the potential market" for the original. Nimmer § 13.05[A][4], p. 13–102.61 (footnote omitted); accord *Harper & Row*, 471 U. S., at 569; Senate Report, p. 65; *Folsom* v. *Marsh*, 9 F. Cas., at 349. The enquiry "must take account not only of harm to the original but also of harm to the market for derivative works." *Harper & Row, supra*, at 568.

Since fair use is an affirmative defense,[20] its proponent would have difficulty carrying the burden of demonstrating fair use without favorable evidence about relevant markets.[21] In moving for summary judgment, 2 Live Crew left themselves at just such a disadvantage when they failed to address the effect on the market for rap derivatives, and confined themselves to uncontroverted submissions that there was no likely effect on the market for the original. They did not, however, thereby subject themselves to the evidentiary presumption applied by the Court of Appeals. In assessing the likelihood of significant market harm, the Court of Appeals quoted from language in *Sony* that "'[i]f the intended use is for commercial gain, that likelihood may be presumed. But if it is for a noncommercial purpose, the likelihood must be demonstrated.'" 972 F. 2d, at 1438, quoting *Sony*, 464 U. S., at 451. The court reasoned that because "the use of the copyrighted work is wholly commercial, . . . we presume a likelihood of future harm to

---

[19] This may serve to heighten the comic effect of the parody, as one witness stated, App. 32a, Affidavit of Oscar Brand; see also *Elsmere Music, Inc.* v. *National Broadcasting Co.*, 482 F. Supp. 741, 747 (SDNY 1980) (repetition of "I Love Sodom"), or serve to dazzle with the original's music, as Acuff-Rose now contends.

[20] *Harper & Row*, 471 U. S., at 561; H. R. Rep. No. 102–836, p. 3, n. 3 (1992).

[21] Even favorable evidence, without more, is no guarantee of fairness. Judge Leval gives the example of the film producer's appropriation of a composer's previously unknown song that turns the song into a commercial success; the boon to the song does not make the film's simple copying fair. Leval 1124, n. 84. This factor, no less than the other three, may be addressed only through a "sensitive balancing of interests." *Sony*, 464 U. S., at 455, n. 40. Market harm is a matter of degree, and the importance of this factor will vary, not only with the amount of harm, but also with the relative strength of the showing on the other factors.

Acuff-Rose exists." 972 F. 2d, at 1438. In so doing, the court resolved the fourth factor against 2 Live Crew, just as it had the first, by applying a presumption about the effect of commercial use, a presumption which as applied here we hold to be error.

No "presumption" or inference of market harm that might find support in *Sony* is applicable to a case involving something beyond mere duplication for commercial purposes. *Sony*'s discussion of a presumption contrasts a context of verbatim copying of the original in its entirety for commercial purposes, with the non-commercial context of *Sony* itself (home copying of television programming). In the former circumstances, what *Sony* said simply makes common sense: when a commercial use amounts to mere duplication of the entirety of an original, it clearly "supersede[s] the objects," *Folsom* v. *Marsh*, 9 F. Cas., at 348, of the original and serves as a market replacement for it, making it likely that cognizable market harm to the original will occur. *Sony*, 464 U. S., at 451. But when, on the contrary, the second use is transformative, market substitution is at least less certain, and market harm may not be so readily inferred. Indeed, as to parody pure and simple, it is more likely that the new work will not affect the market for the original in a way cognizable under this factor, that is, by acting as a substitute for it ("supersed[ing] [its] objects"). See Leval 1125; Patry & Perlmutter 692, 697–698. This is so because the parody and the original usually serve different market functions. Bisceglia, ASCAP, Copyright Law Symposium, No. 34, p. 23.

We do not, of course, suggest that a parody may not harm the market at all, but when a lethal parody, like a scathing theater review, kills demand for the original, it does not produce a harm cognizable under the Copyright Act. Because "parody may quite legitimately aim at garroting the original, destroying it commercially as well as artistically," B. Kaplan, An Unhurried View of Copyright 69 (1967), the role of the courts is to distinguish between "[b]iting criticism [that merely] suppresses demand [and] copyright infringement[, which] usurps it." *Fisher* v. *Dees*, 794 F. 2d, at 438.

This distinction between potentially remediable displacement and unremediable disparagement is reflected in the rule that there is no protectable derivative market for criticism. The market for potential derivative uses includes only those that creators of original works would in general develop or license others to develop. Yet the unlikelihood that creators of imaginative works will license critical reviews or lampoons of their own productions removes such uses from the very notion of a potential licensing market. "People ask . . . for criticism, but they only want praise." S. Maugham, Of Human Bondage 241 (Penguin ed. 1992). Thus, to the extent that the opinion below may be read to have considered harm to the market for parodies of "Oh, Pretty Woman," see 972 F. 2d, at 1439, the court erred. Accord, *Fisher* v. *Dees*, 794 F. 2d, at 437; Leval 1125; Patry & Perlmutter 688–691.[22]

In explaining why the law recognizes no derivative market for critical works, including parody, we have, of course, been speaking of the later work as if it had nothing but a critical aspect (*i.e.*, "parody pure and simple," *supra*, at 22). But the later work may have a more complex character, with effects not only in the arena of criticism but also in protectable markets for derivative works, too. In that sort of case, the law looks beyond the criticism to the other elements of the work, as it does here. 2 Live Crew's song comprises

[22] We express no opinion as to the derivative markets for works using elements of an original as vehicles for satire or amusement, making no comment on the original or criticism of it.

not only parody but also rap music, and the derivative market for rap music is a proper focus of enquiry, see *Harper & Row,* 471 U. S., at 568; Nimmer § 13.05[B]. Evidence of substantial harm to it would weigh against a finding of fair use,[23] because the licensing of derivatives is an important economic incentive to the creation of originals. See 17 U. S. C. § 106(2) (copyright owner has rights to derivative works). Of course, the only harm to derivatives that need concern us, as discussed above, is the harm of market substitution. The fact that a parody may impair the market for derivative uses by the very effectiveness of its critical commentary is no more relevant under copyright than the like threat to the original market.[24]

Although 2 Live Crew submitted uncontroverted affidavits on the question of market harm to the original, neither they, nor Acuff-Rose, introduced evidence or affidavits addressing the likely effect of 2 Live Crew's parodic rap song on the market for a non-parody, rap version of "Oh, Pretty Woman." And while Acuff-Rose would have us find evidence of a rap market in the very facts that 2 Live Crew recorded a rap parody of "Oh, Pretty Woman" and another rap group sought a license to record a rap derivative, there was no evidence that a potential rap market was harmed in any way by 2 Live Crew's parody, rap version. The fact that 2 Live Crew's parody sold as part of a collection of rap songs says very little about the parody's effect on a market for a rap version of the original, either of the music alone or of the music with its lyrics. The District Court essentially passed on this issue, observing that Acuff-Rose is free to record "whatever version of the original it desires," 754 F. Supp., at 1158; the Court of Appeals went the other way by erroneous presumption. Contrary to each treatment, it is impossible to deal with the fourth factor except by recognizing that a silent record on an important factor bearing on fair use disentitled the proponent of the defense, 2 Live Crew, to summary judgment. The evidentiary hole will doubtless be plugged on remand.

III.

It was error for the Court of Appeals to conclude that the commercial nature of 2 Live Crew's parody of "Oh, Pretty Woman" rendered it presumptively unfair. No such evidentiary presumption is available to address either the first factor, the character and purpose of the use, or the fourth, market harm, in determining whether a transformative use, such as parody, is a fair one. The court also erred in holding that 2 Live Crew had necessarily copied excessively from the Orbison original, considering the parodic purpose of the use. We therefore reverse the judgment of the Court of Appeals and remand for further proceedings consistent with this opinion.

It is so ordered.

---

[23] See Nimmer § 13.05[A][4], p. 13–102.61 ("a substantially adverse impact on the potential market"); Leval 1125 ("reasonably substantial" harm); Patry & Perlmutter 697–698 (same).

[24] In some cases it may be difficult to determine whence the harm flows. In such cases, the other fair use factors may provide some indicia of the likely source of the harm. A work whose overriding purpose and character is parodic and whose borrowing is slight in relation to its parody will be far less likely to cause cognizable harm than a work with little parodic content and much copying.

APPENDIX A

"Oh, Pretty Woman" by Roy Orbison and William Dees

Pretty Woman, walking down the street,
Pretty Woman, the kind I like to meet,
Pretty Woman, I don't believe you,
    you're not the truth,
No one could look as good as you
Mercy

Pretty Woman, won't you pardon me,
Pretty Woman, I couldn't help but see,
Pretty Woman, that you look lovely as can be
Are you lonely just like me?

Pretty Woman, stop a while,
Pretty Woman, talk a while,
Pretty Woman give your smile to me
Pretty woman, yeah, yeah, yeah
Pretty Woman, look my way,
Pretty Woman, say you'll stay with me
'Cause I need you, I'll treat you right
Come to me baby, Be mine tonight

Pretty Woman, don't walk on by,
Pretty Woman, don't make me cry,
Pretty Woman, don't walk away,
Hey, O. K.
If that's the way it must be, O. K.
I guess I'll go on home, it's late
There'll be tomorrow night, but wait!

What do I see
Is she walking back to me?
Yeah, she's walking back to me!
Oh, Pretty Woman.

APPENDIX B

"Pretty Woman" as Recorded by 2 Live Crew

Pretty woman walkin' down the street
Pretty woman girl you look so sweet
Pretty woman you bring me down to that knee
Pretty woman you make me wanna beg please
Oh, pretty woman

Big hairy woman you need to shave that stuff
Big hairy woman you know I bet it's tough
Big hairy woman all that hair it ain't legit
'Cause you look like 'Cousin It'
Big hairy woman

Bald headed woman girl your hair won't grow
Bald headed woman you got a teeny weeny afro
Bald headed woman you know your hair could look nice
Bald headed woman first you got to roll it with rice
Bald headed woman here, let me get this hunk of biz for ya
Ya know what I'm saying you look better than rice a roni
Oh bald headed woman

Big hairy woman come on in
And don't forget your bald headed friend
Hey pretty woman let the boys
Jump in

Two timin' woman girl you know you ain't right
Two timin' woman you's out with my boy last night
Two timin' woman that takes a load off my mind
Two timin' woman now I know the baby ain't mine
Oh, two timin' woman
Oh pretty woman

CASE 5

11-1197-cv

Patrick Cariou v. Richard Prince, et al.

UNITED STATES COURT OF APPEALS

FOR THE SECOND CIRCUIT

August Term, 2011

(Argued: May 21, 2012 Decided: April 25, 2013)

Docket No. 11-1197-cv

PATRICK CARIOU,

Plaintiff-Appellee,

v.

RICHARD PRINCE,

Defendant-Appellant,

GAGOSIAN GALLERY, INC., LAWRENCE GAGOSIAN,

Defendants-Cross-Defendants-Appellants.

Before: B.D. PARKER, HALL, and WALLACE, Circuit Judges.

Appeal from a judgment of the United States District Court for the Southern District of New York (Batts, J.), on Plaintiff-Appellee Patrick Cariou's claim that Defendant-Appellant Richard Prince's artworks infringe on Cariou's registered copyrights in certain photographs. We conclude that the district court applied the incorrect standard to determine whether Prince's artworks make fair use of Cariou's copyrighted photographs. We further conclude that all but five of Prince's works do make fair use of Cariou's copyrighted photographs. With regard to the remaining five Prince artworks, we remand to the district court to consider, in the first instance, whether Prince is entitled to a fair use defense.

REVERSED in part, VACATED in part, and REMANDED.

B.D. PARKER, J., delivered the opinion of the Court, in which HALL, J., joined.

WALLACE, J., filed an opinion concurring in part and dissenting in part.

JOSHUA I. SCHILLER (Jonathan D. Schiller, George F. Carpinello, on the brief), Boies, Schiller & Flexner 4 LLP, New York, NY, for Defendant-Appellant 5 Richard Prince.

HOLLIS ANNE GONERKA BART, CHAYA WEINBERG-7 BRODT, DARA G. HAMMERMAN, AZMINA N. JASANI, Withers Bergman LLP, New York, NY, for Defendants-Appellants Gagosian Gallery, Inc. And Lawrence Gagosian.

DANIEL J. BROOKS (Seth E. Spitzer, Eric A. Boden, on the brief), Schnader Harrison Segal & Lewis LLP, New York, NY, for Plaintiff-Appellee Patrick Cariou.

ANTHONY T. FALZONE, JULIE A. AHRENS, DANIEL K. NAZER, Stanford Law School Center for Internet and Society, Stanford, CA; VIRGINIA RUTLEDGE, New York, NY; ZACHARY J. ALINDER, JOHN A. POLITO, Bingham McCutchen LLP, San Francisco, CA, for Amicus The Andy Warhol Foundation for the Visual Arts.

JOSEPH C. GRATZ, Durie Tangri, LLP, San Francisco, CA; OLIVERMETZGER, Google Inc., Mountain View, CA, for Amicus Google Inc.

CLIFFORD M. SLOAN, BRADLEY A. KLEIN, Skadden, 26 Arps, Slate, Meagher & Flom LLP, Washington, DC, for Amici The Association of Art Museum Directors, The Art Institute of Chicago, The Indianapolis Museum of Art, The Metropolitan Museum of Art, The Museum of Modern Art, Museum Associates d.b.a. Los Angeles County Museum of Art, The New Museum, The Solomon R. Guggenheim Foundation, The Walker Art Center, and The Whitney Museum of American Art.

MICHAEL WILLIAMS, DALE M. CENDALI, CLAUDIA RAY, Kirkland & Ellis LLP, Washington, DC, for Amici American Society of Media Photographers, Inc., and Picture Archive Council of America.

BARRINGTON D. PARKER, Circuit Judge:

In 2000, Patrick Cariou published Yes Rasta, a book of classical portraits and landscape photographs that he took over the course of six years spent living among Rastafarians in Jamaica. Richard Prince altered and incorporated several of Cariou's Yes Rasta photographs into a series of paintings and collages, called Canal Zone, that he exhibited in 2007 and 2008, first at the Eden Rock hotel in Saint Barthélemy ("St. Barth's") and later at New York's Gagosian Gallery. In addition, Gagosian published and sold an exhibition catalog that contained reproductions of Prince's paintings and images from Prince's workshop. Cariou sued Prince and Gagosian, alleging that Prince's Canal Zone works and exhibition catalog infringed on Cariou's copyrights in the incorporated Yes Rasta photographs. The defendants raised a fair use defense. After the parties cross-moved for summary judgment, the United States District Court for the Southern District of New York (Batts, J.) granted Cariou's motion, denied the defendants', and entered a permanent injunction. It compelled the defendants to deliver to Cariou all infringing works that had not yet been sold, for him to destroy, sell, or otherwise dispose of. Prince and Gagosian principally contend on appeal that Prince's work is transformative and constitutes fair use of Cariou's copyrighted photographs, and that the district court imposed an incorrect legal standard when it concluded that, in order to qualify for a fair use defense, Prince's work must "comment on Cariou, on Cariou's Photos, or on aspects of popular culture closely associated with Cariou or the Photos." *Cariou v. Prince*, 784 F. Supp. 2d 337, 349 (S.D.N.Y. 2011). We agree with Appellants that the law does not require that a secondary use comment on the original artist or work, or popular culture, and we conclude that twenty-five of Prince's artworks do make fair use Cariou's copyrighted photographs. With regard to the remaining five artworks, we remand to the district court, applying the proper standard, to consider in the first instance whether Prince is entitled to a fair use defense.

BACKGROUND

The relevant facts, drawn primarily from the parties' submissions in connection with their cross-motions for summary judgment, are undisputed. Cariou is a professional photographer who, over the course of six years in the mid-1990s, lived and worked among Rastafarians in Jamaica. The relationships that Cariou developed with them allowed him to take a series of portraits and landscape photographs that Cariou published in 2000 in a book titled Yes Rasta. As Cariou testified, Yes Rasta is "extreme classical photography [and] portraiture," and he did not "want that book to look pop culture at all." Cariou Dep. 187:8-15, Jan. 12, 2010. Cariou's publisher, PowerHouse Books, Inc., printed 7,000 copies of Yes Rasta, in a single printing. Like many, if not most, such works, the book enjoyed limited commercial success. The book is currently out of print. As of January 2010, PowerHouse had sold 5,791 copies, over sixty percent of which sold below the suggested retail price of sixty dollars. PowerHouse has paid Cariou, who holds the copyrights to the Yes Rasta photographs, just over $8,000 from sales of the book. Except for a handful of private sales to personal acquaintances, he has never sold or licensed the individual photographs. Prince is a well-known appropriation artist. The Tate Gallery has defined appropriation art as "the more or less direct taking over into a work of art a real object or even an existing work of art." J.A. 446. Prince's work, going back to the mid-1970s, has involved taking photographs and other images that others have produced and incorporating them into paintings and collages that he then presents, in a different context, as his own. He is a leading exponent of this genre and his work has been displayed in museums around the world, including New York's Solomon R. Guggenheim Museum and Whitney Museum, San Francisco's Museum of Modern Art, Rotterdam's Museum Boijmans van Beuningen, and Basel's Museum fur Gegenwartskunst. As Prince has described his work, he "completely tr[ies] to change [another artist's work] into something that's completely different." Prince Dep. 338:4-8, Oct. 6, 2009.

Prince first came across a copy of Yes Rasta in a bookstore in St. Barth's in 2005. Between December 2007 and February 2008, Prince had a show at the Eden Rock hotel in St. Barth's that included a collage, titled Canal Zone (2007), comprising 35 photographs torn out of Yes Rasta and pinned to a piece of plywood. Prince altered those photographs significantly, by among other things painting "lozenges" over their subjects' facial features and using only portions of some of the images. In June 2008, Prince purchased three additional copies of Yes Rasta. He went on to create thirty additional artworks in the Canal Zone series, twenty-nine of which incorporated partial or whole images from Yes Rasta. The portions of Yes Rasta photographs used, and the amount of each artwork that they constitute, vary significantly from piece to piece. In certain works, such as James Brown Disco Ball, Prince affixed headshots from Yes Rasta onto other appropriated images, all of which Prince placed on a canvas that he had painted. In these, Cariou's work is almost entirely obscured. The Prince artworks also incorporate photographs that have been enlarged or tinted, and incorporate photographs appropriated from artists other than Cariou as well. Yes Rasta is a book of photographs measuring approximately 9.5" × 12". Prince's artworks, in contrast, comprise inkjet printing and acrylic paint, as well as pasted-on elements, and are several times that size. For instance, Graduation measures 72 3/4" × 52 1/2" and James Brown Disco Ball 100 1/2" × 104 1/2". The smallest of the Prince artworks measures 40" × 30", or approximately ten times as large as each page of Yes Rasta.

In other works, such as Graduation, Cariou's original work is readily apparent: Prince did little more than paint blue lozenges over the subject's eyes and mouth, and paste a picture of a guitar over the subject's body. Between November 8 and December 20, 2008, the Gallery put on a show featuring twenty-two of Prince's Canal Zone artworks, and also published and sold an exhibition catalog from the show. The catalog included all of the Canal Zone artworks (including those not in the Gagosian show) except for one, as well as, among other things, photographs showing Yes Rasta photographs in Prince's studio. Prince never sought or received permission from Cariou to use his photographs.

Prior to the Gagosian show, in late August, 2008, a gallery owner named Cristiane Celle contacted Cariou and asked if he would be interested in discussing the possibility of an exhibit in New York City. Celle did not mention Yes Rasta, but did express interest in photographs Cariou took of surfers, which he published in 1998 in the aptly titled Surfers. Cariou responded that Surfers would be republished in 2008, and inquired whether Celle might also be interested in a book Cariou had recently completed on gypsies. The two subsequently met and discussed Cariou's exhibiting work in Celle's gallery, including prints from Yes Rasta. They did not select a date or photographs to exhibit, nor did they finalize any other details about the possible future show.

At some point during the Canal Zone show at Gagosian, Celle learned that Cariou's photographs were "in the show with Richard Prince." Celle then phoned Cariou and, when he did not respond, Celle mistakenly concluded that he was "doing something with Richard Prince . . . . [Maybe] he's not pursuing me because he's doing something better, bigger with this person. . . . [H]e didn't want to tell the French girl I'm not doing it with you, you know, because we had started a relation and that would have been bad." Celle Dep. 88:15-89:7, Jan. 26, 2010. At that point, Celle decided that she would not put on a "Rasta show" because it had been "done already," and that any future Cariou exhibition she put on would be of photographs from Surfers. Celle remained interested in exhibiting prints from Surfers, but Cariou never followed through.

According to Cariou, he learned about the Gagosian Canal Zone show from Celle in December 2008. On December 30, 2008, he sued Prince, the Gagosian Gallery, and Lawrence Gagosian, raising claims of copyright infringement. See 17 U.S.C. §§ 106, 501. The defendants asserted a fair use defense, arguing that Prince's artworks are transformative of Cariou's photographs and, accordingly, do not violate Cariou's copyrights. See, e.g., *Campbell v. Acuff Rose Music, Inc.*, 510 U.S. 569, 578-79 (1994). Ruling on the parties' subsequently-filed cross16 motions for summary judgment, the district court (Batts, J.) "impose[d] a requirement that the new work in some way comment on, relate to the historical context of, or critically refer back to the original works" in order to be qualify as fair use, and stated that "Prince's Paintings are transformative only to the extent that they comment on the Photos." *Cariou v. Prince*, 784 F. Supp. 2d 337, 348-49 (S.D.N.Y. 2011). The court concluded that "Prince did not intend to comment on Cariou, on Cariou's Photos, or on aspects of popular culture closely associated with Cariou or the Photos when he appropriated the Photos," id. at 349, and for that reason rejected the defendants' fair use defense and granted summary judgment to Cariou. The district court also granted sweeping injunctive relief, ordering the defendants to "deliver up for impounding, destruction, or other disposition, as [Cariou] determines, all infringing copies of the Photographs, including the Paintings and unsold copies of the Canal Zone exhibition book, in their possession." id. at 355. This appeal followed.

DISCUSSION

I.

We review a grant of summary judgment de novo. See *Blanch v. Koons*, 467 F.3d 244, 249-50 (2d Cir. 2006). The well known standards for summary judgment set forth in Rule 56(c) apply. See Fed. R. Civ. P. 56. "Although fair use is a mixed question of law and fact, this court has on numerous occasions resolved fair use determinations at the summary judgment stage where . . . there are no genuine issues of material fact." Blanch, 467 F.3d at 250 (quotation marks and brackets omitted); see also *Harper & Row, Publishers, Inc. v. Nation Enters.*, 471 U.S. 539, 560 (1985); *Castle Rock Entm't, Inc. v. Carol Publ'g Grp., Inc.*, 150 F.3d 132, 137 (2d Cir. 1998). This case lends itself to that approach.

II.

The purpose of the copyright law is "[t]o promote the Progress of Science and useful Arts. . . ." U.S. Const., Art. I, § 8, cl. 8. As Judge Pierre Leval of this court has explained, "[t]he copyright is not an inevitable, divine, or natural right that confers on authors the absolute ownership of their creations. It is designed rather to stimulate activity and progress in the arts for the intellectual enrichment of the public." Pierre N. Leval, Toward a Fair Use Standard, 103 Harv. L. Rev. 1105, 1107 (1990) (hereinafter "Leval"). Fair use is "necessary to fulfill [that] very purpose." Campbell, 510 U.S. at 575. Because "'excessively broad protection would stifle, rather than advance, the law's objective,'" fair use doctrine "mediates between" "the property rights [copyright law] establishes in creative works, which must be protected up to a point, and the ability of authors, artists, and the rest of us to express themor ourselves by reference to the works of others, which must be protected up to a point." Blanch, 467 F.3d at 250 (brackets omitted) (quoting Leval at 1109). The doctrine was codified in the Copyright Act of 1976, which lists four non-exclusive factors that must be considered in determining fair use. Under the statute,

> [T]he fair use of a copyrighted work . . . for purposes such as criticism, comment, news reporting, teaching (including multiple copies for classroom use), scholarship, or research, is not an infringement of copyright. In determining whether the use made of a work in any particular case is a fair use the factors to be considered shall include—
>
> 1. the purpose and character of the use, including whether such use is of a commercial nature or is for nonprofit educational purposes;
> 2. the nature of the copyrighted work;
> 3. the amount and substantiality of the portion used in relation to the copyrighted work as a whole; and
> 4. the effect of the use upon the potential market for the value of the copyrighted work.

17 U.S.C. § 107. As the statute indicates, and as the Supreme Court and our court have recognized, the fair use determination is an open-ended and context-sensitive inquiry. Campbell, 510 U.S. at 577-78; Blanch, 467 F.3d at 251. The statute "employs the terms 'including' and 'such as' in the preamble paragraph to indicate the illustrative and not limitative function of the examples given, which thus provide only general guidance about the sorts of copying that courts and Congress most commonly had found to be fair uses." Campbell, 510 U.S. at 577-78 (quotation marks and citation omitted). The "ultimate test of fair use . . . is whether the copyright law's goal of 'promoting the Progress of Science and useful Arts' . . . would be better served by allowing the use than by preventing it." Castle Rock, 150 F.3d at 141 (brackets and citation omitted).

The first statutory factor to consider, which addresses the manner in which the copied work is used, is "[t]he heart of the fair use inquiry." Blanch, 467 F.3d at 251. We ask

> whether the new work merely 'supersedes the objects' of the original creation, or instead adds something new, with a further purpose or different character, altering the first with new expression, meaning, or message [,] . . . in other words, whether and to what extent the new work is transformative. . . . [T]ransformative works . . . lie at the heart of the fair use doctrine's guarantee of breathing space . . . .

Campbell, 510 U.S. at 579 (citations and some quotation marks omitted) (quoting *Folsom v. Marsh*, 9 F. Cas. 342, 348 *No. 4,901) (C.C.D. Mass. 1841) (Story, J.)). "If 'the secondary use adds value to the original—if [the original work] is used as raw material, transformed in the creation of new information, new aesthetics, new insights and understandings—this is the very type of activity that the fair use doctrine intends to protect for the enrichment of society.'" Castle Rock, 150 F.3d at 142 (quoting Leval 1111). For a use to be fair, it "must be productive and must employ the quoted matter in a different manner or for a different purpose from the original." Leval at 1111.

The district court imposed a requirement that, to qualify for a fair use defense, a secondary use must "comment on, relate to the historical context of, or critically refer back to the original works." Cariou, 784 F. Supp. 2d at 348. Certainly, many types of fair use, such as satire and parody, invariably comment on an original work and/or on popular culture. For example, the rap group 2 Live Crew's parody of Roy Orbison's "Oh, Pretty Woman" "was clearly intended to ridicule the white-bread original." Campbell, 510 U.S. at 582 (quotation marks omitted). Much of Andy Warhol's work, including work incorporating appropriated images of Campbell's soup cans or of Marilyn Monroe, comments on consumer culture and explores the relationship between celebrity culture and advertising. As even Cariou concedes, however, the district court's legal premise was not correct. The law imposes no requirement that a work comment on the original or its author in order to be considered transformative, and a secondary work may constitute a fair use even if it serves some purpose other than those (criticism, comment, news reporting, teaching, scholarship, and research) identified in the preamble to the statute. Id. at 577; Harper & Row, 471 U.S. at 561. Instead, as the Supreme Court as well as decisions from our court have emphasized, to qualify as a fair use, a new work generally must alter the original with "new expression, meaning, or message." Campbell, 510 U.S. at 579; see also Blanch, 467 F.3d at 253 (original must be employed "in the creation of new information, new aesthetics, new insights and understandings" (quotation marks omitted)); Castle Rock, 150 F.3d at 142.

Here, our observation of Prince's artworks themselves convinces us of the transformative nature of all but five, which we discuss separately below. These twenty-five of Prince's artworks manifest an entirely different aesthetic from Cariou's photographs. Where Cariou's serene and deliberately composed portraits and landscape photographs depict the natural beauty of Rastafarians and their surrounding environs, Prince's crude and jarring works, on the other hand, are hectic and provocative. Cariou's black-and-white photographs were printed in a 9 1/2" × 12" book. Prince has created collages on canvas that incorporate color, feature distorted human and other forms and settings, and measure between ten and nearly a hundred times the size of the photographs. Prince's composition, presentation, scale, color palette, and media are fundamentally different and new compared to the photographs, as is the expressive nature of Prince's work. See Campbell, 510 U.S. at 579.

Prince's deposition testimony further demonstrates his drastically different approach and aesthetic from Cariou's. Prince testified that he "[doesn't] have any really interest in what [another artist's] original intent is because . . . what I do is I completely try to change it into something that's completely different. . . . I'm trying to make a kind of fantastic, absolutely hip, up to date, contemporary take on the music scene." Prince Dep. 338:4-339:3, Oct. 6, 2009. As the district court determined, Prince's Canal Zone artworks relate to a "post-apocalyptic screenplay" Prince had planned, and "emphasize themes [of Prince's planned screenplay] of equality of the sexes; highlight 'the three relationships in the world, which are men and women, men and men, and women and women'; and portray a contemporary take on the music scene." Cariou, 784 F. Supp. 2d at 349; see Prince Dep. 339:3-7, Oct. 6, 2009.

The district court based its conclusion that Prince's work is not transformative in large part on Prince's deposition testimony that he "do[es]n't really have a message," that he was not "trying to create anything with a new meaning or a new message," and that he "do[es]n't have any . . . interest in [Cariou's] original intent." Cariou, 784 F. Supp. 2d at 349; see Prince Dep. 45:25-46:2, 338:5-6, 360:18-20, Oct. 6, 2009. On appeal, Cariou argues that we must hold Prince to his testimony and that we are not to consider how Prince's works may reasonably be perceived unless Prince claims that they were satire or parody. No such rule exists, and we do not analyze satire or parody differently from any other transformative use.

It is not surprising that, when transformative use is at issue, the alleged infringer would go to great lengths to explain and defend his use as transformative. Prince did not do so here. However, the fact that Prince did not provide those sorts of explanations in his deposition—which might have lent strong support to his defense—is not dispositive. What is critical is how the work in question appears to the reasonable observer, not simply what an artist might say about a particular piece or body of work. Prince's work could be transformative even without commenting on Cariou's work or on culture, and even without Prince's stated intention to do so. Rather than confining our inquiry to Prince's explanations of his artworks, we instead examine how the artworks may "reasonably be perceived" in order to assess their transformative nature. Campbell, 510 U.S. at 582; *Leibovitz v. Paramount Pictures Corp.*, 137 F. 3d 109, 113-14 (2d Cir. 1998) (evaluating parodic nature of advertisement in light of how it "may reasonably be perceived"). The focus of our infringement analysis is primarily on the Prince artworks themselves, and we see twenty-five of them as transformative as a matter of law.

. . .

Here, looking at the artworks and the photographs side-by-side, we conclude that Prince's images, except for those we discuss separately below, have a different character, give Cariou's photographs a new expression, and employ new aesthetics with creative and communicative results distinct from Cariou's. Our conclusion should not be taken to suggest, however, that any cosmetic changes to the photographs would necessarily constitute fair use. A secondary work may modify the original without being transformative. For instance, a derivative work that merely presents the same material but in a new form, such as a book of synopses of televisions shows, is not transformative. See Castle Rock, 150 F.3d at 143; *Twin Peaks Prods., Inc. v. Publ'ns Int'l, Ltd.*, 996 F.2d 1366, 1378 (2d Cir. 1993). In twenty-five of his artworks, Prince has not presented the same material as Cariou in a different manner, but instead has "add[ed] something new" and presented images with a fundamentally different aesthetic. Leibovitz, 137 F.3d at 114.

The first fair use factor—the purpose and character of the use—also requires that we consider whether the allegedly infringing work has a commercial or nonprofit educational purpose. See, e.g., Blanch, 467 F.3d at 253. That being said, "nearly all of the illustrative uses listed in the preamble paragraph of § 107, including news reporting, comment, criticism, teaching, scholarship, and research . . . are generally conducted for profit." Campbell, 510 U.S. at 584 (quotation marks omitted). "The commercial/nonprofit dichotomy concerns the unfairness that arises when a secondary user makes unauthorized use of copyrighted material to capture significant revenues as a direct consequence of copying the original work." Am. *Geophysical Union v. Texaco Inc.*, 60 F.3d 913, 922 (2d Cir. 1994). This factor must be applied with caution because, as the Supreme Court has recognized, Congress "could not have intended" a rule that commercial uses are presumptively unfair. Campbell, 510 U.S. at 584 Instead, "[t]he more transformative the new work, the less will be the significance of other factors, like commercialism, that may weigh against a finding of fair use." id. at 579. Although there is no question that Prince's artworks are commercial, we do not place much significance on that fact due to the transformative nature of the work.

We turn next to the fourth statutory factor, the effect of the secondary use upon the potential market for the value of the copyrighted work, because such discussion further demonstrates the significant differences between Prince's work, generally, and Cariou's. Much of the district court's conclusion that Prince and Gagosian infringed on Cariou's copyrights was apparently driven by the fact that Celle decided not to host a Yes Rasta show at her gallery once she learned of the Gagosian Canal Zone show. The district court determined that this factor weighs against Prince because he "has unfairly damaged both the actual and potential markets for Cariou's original work and the potential market for derivative use licenses for Cariou's original work." Cariou, 784 F. Supp. 2d at 353.

Contrary to the district court's conclusion, the application of this factor does not focus principally on the question of damage to Cariou's derivative market. We have made clear that "our concern is not whether the secondary use suppresses or even destroys the market for the original work or its potential derivatives, but whether the secondary use usurps the market of the original work." Blanch, 467 F.3d at 258 (quotation marks omitted) (emphasis added); *NXIVM Corp. v. Ross Inst.,* 364 F.3d 471, 481-82 (2d Cir. 2004). "The market for potential derivative uses includes only those that creators of original works would in general develop or license others to develop." Campbell, 510 U.S. at 592. Our court has concluded that an accused infringer has usurped the market for copyrighted works, including the derivative market, where the infringer's target audience and the nature of the infringing content is the same as the original. For instance, a book of trivia about the television show Seinfeld usurped the show's market because the trivia book "substitute[d] for a derivative market that a television program copyright owner . . . would in general develop or license others to develop." Castle Rock, 150 F.3d at 145 (quotation marks omitted). Conducting this analysis, we are mindful that "[t]he more transformative the secondary use, the less likelihood that the secondary use substitutes for the original," even though "the fair use, being transformative, might well harm, or even destroy, the market for the original." Id.

. . .

Prince's work appeals to an entirely different sort of collector than Cariou's. Certain of the Canal Zone artworks have sold for two million or more dollars. The invitation list for a dinner that Gagosian hosted in conjunction with the opening of the Canal Zone show included a number of the wealthy and famous such as the musicians Jay-Z and Beyonce Knowles, artists Damien Hirst and Jeff Koons, professional football player Tom Brady, model Gisele Bundchen, Vanity Fair editor Graydon Carter, Vogue editor Anna Wintour, authors Jonathan Franzen and Candace Bushnell, and actors Robert DeNiro, Angelina Jolie, and Brad Pitt. Prince sold eight artworks for a total of $10,480,000, and exchanged seven others for works by painter Larry Rivers and by sculptor Richard Serra. Cariou on the other hand has not actively marketed his work or sold work for significant sums, and nothing in the record suggests that anyone will not now purchase Cariou's work, or derivative non-transformative works (whether Cariou's own or licensed by him) as a result of the market space that Prince's work has taken up. This fair use factor therefore weighs in Prince's favor.

The next statutory factor that we consider, the nature of the copyrighted work, "calls for recognition that some works are closer to the core of intended copyright protection than others, with the consequence that fair use is more difficult to establish when the former works are copied." Campbell, 510 U.S. at 586. We consider "'(1) whether the work is expressive or creative, . . . with a greater leeway being allowed to a claim of fair use where the work is factual or informational, and (2) whether the work is published or unpublished, with the scope for fair use involving unpublished works being considerably narrower.'" Blanch, 467 F.3d at 256 (quoting 2 Howard B. Abrams, The Law of Copyright, § 15:52 (2006)).

Here, there is no dispute that Cariou's work is creative and published. Accordingly, this factor weighs against a fair use determination. However, just as with the commercial character of Prince's work, this factor "may be of limited usefulness where," as here, "the creative work of art is being used for a transformative purpose." *Bill Graham Archives v. Dorling Kindersley Ltd.*, 448 F.3d 605, 612 (2d Cir. 2006).

The final factor that we consider in our fair use inquiry is "the amount and substantiality of the portion used in relation to the copyrighted work as a whole." 17 U.S.C. § 107(3). We ask "whether the quantity and value of the materials used[] are reasonable in relation to the purpose of the copying." Blanch, 467 F.3d at 257 (quotation marks omitted). In other words, we consider the proportion of the original work used, and not how much of the secondary work comprises the original.

Many of Prince's works use Cariou's photographs, in particular the portrait of the dreadlocked Rastafarian at page 118 of Yes Rasta, the Rastafarian on a burro at pages 83 to 84, and the dreadlocked and bearded Rastafarian at page 108, in whole or substantial part. In some works, such as Charlie Company, Prince did not alter the source photograph very much at all. In others, such as Djuana Barnes, Natalie Barney, Renee Vivien and Romaine Brooks take over the Guanahani, the entire source photograph is used but is also heavily obscured and altered to the point that Cariou's original is barely recognizable. Although "[n]either our court nor any of our sister circuits has ever ruled that the copying of an entire work favors fair use[,] . . . . courts have concluded that such copying does not necessarily weigh against fair use because copying the entirety of a work is sometimes necessary to make a fair use of the image." Bill Graham, 448 F.3d at 613. "[T]he third-factor inquiry must take into account that the extent of permissible copying varies with the purpose and character of the use." Id. (internal quotation marks omitted).

The district court determined that Prince's "taking was substantially greater than necessary." Cariou, 784 F. Supp. 2d at 352. We are not clear as to how the district court could arrive at such a conclusion. In any event, the law does not require that the secondary artist may take no more than is necessary. See Campbell, 510 U.S. at 588; Leibovitz, 137 F.3d at 114. We consider not only the quantity of the materials taken but also "their quality and importance" to the original work. Campbell, 510 U.S. at 587. The secondary use "must be [permitted] to 'conjure up' at least enough of the original" to fulfill its transformative purpose. Id. at 588 (emphasis added); Leibovitz, 137 F.3d at 114. Prince used key portions of certain of Cariou's photographs. In doing that, however, we determine that in twenty-five of his artworks, Prince transformed those photographs into something new and different and, as a result, this factor weighs heavily in Prince's favor.

. . .

Certainly, there are key differences in those artworks compared to the photographs they incorporate. Graduation, for instance, is tinted blue, and the jungle background is in softer focus than in Cariou's original. Lozenges painted over the subject's eyes and mouth—an alteration that appears frequently throughout the Canal Zone artworks—make the subject appear anonymous, rather than as the strong individual who appears in the original. Along with the enlarged hands and electric guitar that Prince pasted onto his canvas, those alterations create the impression that the subject is not quite human. Cariou's photograph, on the other hand, presents a human being in his natural habitat, looking intently ahead. Where the photograph presents someone comfortably at home in nature, Graduation combines divergent elements to create a sense of discomfort. However, we cannot say for sure whether Graduation constitutes fair use or whether Prince has transformed Cariou's work enough to render it transformative.

. . .

We believe the district court is best situated to determine, in the first instance, whether such relatively minimal alterations render Graduation, Meditation, Canal Zone (2007), Canal Zone (2008), and Charlie Company fair uses (including whether the artworks are transformative) or whether any impermissibly infringes on Cariou's copyrights in his original photographs. We remand for that determination.

III.

In addition to its conclusion that Prince is liable for infringing on Cariou's copyrights, the district court determined that the Gagosian defendants are liable as vicarious and contributory infringers. Cariou, 784 F. Supp. 2d at 354. With regard to the twenty-five of Prince's artworks, which, as we have held, do not infringe on Cariou's copyrights, neither Lawrence Gagosian nor the Gallery may be liable as a vicarious or contributory infringer. See *Faulkner v. Nat'l Geographic Enters., Inc.*, 409 F.3d 26, 40 (2d Cir. 2005). If the district court concludes on remand that Prince is liable as a direct infringer with regard to any of the remaining five works, the district court should determine whether the Gagosian defendants should be held liable, directly or secondarily, as a consequence of their actions with regard to those works. See Copyright Act, 17 U.S.C. §§ 106(1), (2), (3), (5).

CONCLUSION

For the reasons discussed, we hold that all except five (Graduation, Meditation, Canal Zone (2007), Canal Zone (2008), and Charlie Company) of Prince's artworks make fair use of Cariou's photographs. We express no view as to whether the five are also entitled to a fair use defense. We REMAND with respect to those five so that the district court, applying the proper standard, can determine in the first instance whether any of them infringes on Cariou's copyrights or whether Prince is entitled to a fair use defense with regard to those artworks as well. The judgment of the district court is REVERSED in part and VACATED in part. The case is REMANDED for further proceedings consistent with this opinion.

. . .

19-2420-cv

The Andy Warhol Foundation for The Visual Arts, Inc. v. Lynn Goldsmith, et al.

UNITED STATES COURT OF APPEALS

FOR THE SECOND CIRCUIT

August Term, 2020

Argued: September 15, 2020 Decided: March 26, 2021

Docket No. 19-2420-cv

THE ANDY WARHOL FOUNDATION FOR THE VISUAL ARTS, INC.,

Plaintiff-Counter

Defendant-Appellee,

— v. —

LYNN GOLDSMITH, LYNN GOLDSMITH, LTD.,

Defendants-Counter

Plaintiffs-Appellants.

B e f o r e:
JACOBS, LYNCH, and SULLIVAN, Circuit Judges.

Defendants-Appellants Lynn Goldsmith and Lynn Goldsmith, Ltd., appeal from a judgment of the United States District Court for Southern District of New York (Koeltl, J.) granting summary judgment to Plaintiff-Appellee The Andy Warhol Foundation for the Visual Arts, Inc. on its complaint for a declaratory judgment of fair use and dismissing Defendants-Appellants' counterclaim for copyright infringement. We conclude that the district court erred in its assessment and application of the fair-use factors and that the works in question do not qualify as fair use as a matter of law. We likewise conclude that the Prince Series works are substantially similar to the Goldsmith Photograph as a matter of law. We therefore REVERSE the judgment of the district court and REMAND the case for further proceedings consistent with this opinion.

JUDGE SULLIVAN concurs in the Court's opinion, and files a concurring opinion in which JUDGE JACOBS joins.

JUDGE JACOBS concurs in the Court's opinion, and files a concurring opinion.

. . .

GERARD E. LYNCH, Circuit Judge:

This case concerns a series of silkscreen prints and pencil illustrations created by the visual artist Andy Warhol based on a 1981 photograph of the musical artist Prince that was taken by Defendant-Appellant Lynn Goldsmith in her studio, and in which she holds copyright. In 1984, Goldsmith's agency, Defendant-Appellant Lynn Goldsmith, Ltd. ("LGL"), then known as Lynn Goldsmith, Inc., licensed the photograph to Vanity Fair magazine for use as an artist reference. Unbeknownst to Goldsmith, that artist was Warhol. Also unbeknownst to Goldsmith (and remaining unknown to her until 2016), Warhol did not stop with the image that Vanity Fair had commissioned him to create, but created an additional fifteen works, which together became known as the Prince Series.

Goldsmith first became aware of the Prince Series after Prince's death in 2016. Soon thereafter, she notified Plaintiff-Appellee The Andy Warhol Foundation for the Visual Arts, Inc. ("AWF"), successor to Warhol's copyright in the Prince Series, of the perceived violation of her copyright in the photo. In 2017, AWF sued Goldsmith and LGL for a declaratory judgment that the Prince Series works were non-infringing or, in the alternative, that they made fair use of Goldsmith's photograph. Goldsmith and LGL countersued for infringement. The United States District Court for the Southern District of New York (John G. Koeltl, J.) granted summary judgment to AWF on its assertion of fair use and dismissed Goldsmith and LGL's counterclaim with prejudice.

Goldsmith and LGL contend that the district court erred in its assessment and application of the four fair-use factors. In particular, they argue that the district court's conclusion that the Prince Series works are transformative was grounded in a subjective evaluation of the underlying artistic message of the works rather than an objective assessment of their purpose and character. We agree. We further agree that the district court's error in analyzing the first factor was compounded in its analysis of the remaining three factors. We conclude upon our own assessment of the record that all four factors favor Goldsmith and that the Prince Series works are not fair use as a matter of law. We further conclude that the Prince Series works are substantially similar to the Goldsmith Photograph as a matter of law.

. . .

BACKGROUND

Goldsmith is a professional photographer primarily focusing on celebrity photography, including portrait and concert photography of rock-and-roll musicians. Goldsmith has been active since the 1960s, and her work has been featured widely, including on over 100 record album covers. Goldsmith also founded LGL, the first photo agency focused on celebrity portraiture. LGL represents the work of over two hundred photographers worldwide, including Goldsmith herself.

Andy Warhol, né Andrew Warhola, was an artist recognized for his significant contributions to contemporary art in a variety of media. Warhol is particularly known for his silkscreen portraits of contemporary celebrities. Much of his work is broadly understood as "comment[ing] on consumer culture and explor[ing] the relationship between celebrity culture and advertising." *Cariou v. Prince*, 714 F.3d 694, 706 (2d Cir. 2013). AWF is a New York not-for-profit corporation established in 1987 after

Warhol's death. AWF holds title to and copyright in much of Warhol's work, which it licenses to generate revenue to further its mission of advancing the visual arts, "particularly work that is experimental, under-recognized, or challenging in nature." J. App'x at 305.

On December 3, 1981, while on assignment from Newsweek magazine, Goldsmith took a series of portrait photographs of (then) up-and-coming musician Prince Rogers Nelson (known through most of his career simply as "Prince") in her studio. Goldsmith testified that, prior to Prince's arrival at her studio, she arranged the lighting in a way to showcase his "chiseled bone structure." Id. at 706. Goldsmith also applied additional makeup to Prince, including eyeshadow and lip gloss, which she testified was intended both to build a rapport with Prince and to accentuate his sensuality. Goldsmith further testified that she was trying to capture Prince's "willing[ness] to bust through what must be [his] immense fears to make the work that [he] wanted to [make]." Id. at 1557. Goldsmith took black-and-white and color photographs using a Nikon 35-mm camera and a mixture of 85 and 105-mm lenses, which she chose to best capture the shape of Prince's face.

Prince, who according to Goldsmith appeared nervous and uncomfortable, retired to the green room shortly after the session began and ultimately left without allowing Goldsmith to take any additional photographs. During the truncated session, Goldsmith took 23 photographs, 12 in black and white and 11 in color. Goldsmith retained copyright in each of the photographs that she took. Most relevant to this litigation is the following photograph, hereinafter referred to as the "Goldsmith Photograph".

In 1984, Goldsmith, through LGL, licensed the Goldsmith Photograph to Vanity Fair magazine for use as an artist reference. Esin Goknar, who was photo editor at Vanity Fair in 1984, testified that the term "artist reference" meant that an artist "would create a work of art based on [the] image reference." Id. at 783. The license permitted Vanity Fair to publish an illustration based on the Goldsmith Photograph in its November 1984 issue, once as a full page and once as a quarter page. The license further required that the illustration be accompanied by an attribution to Goldsmith. Goldsmith was unaware of the license at the time and played no role in selecting the Goldsmith Photograph for submission to Vanity Fair.

Vanity Fair, in turn, commissioned Warhol to create an image of Prince for its November 1984 issue. Warhol's illustration, together with an attribution to Goldsmith, was published accompanying an article about Prince by Tristan Vox. In addition to the credit that ran alongside the image, a separate attribution to Goldsmith was included elsewhere in the issue, crediting her with the "source photograph" for the Warhol illustration. Vanity Fair did not advise Goldsmith that Warhol was the artist for whom her work would serve as a reference, and she did not see the article when it was initially published.

Unbeknownst to Goldsmith and LGL, Warhol created 15 additional works based on the Goldsmith Photograph, known collectively, and together with the Vanity Fair image, as the "Prince Series." The Prince Series comprises fourteen silkscreen prints (twelve on canvas, two on paper) and two pencil illustrations. . .

. . .

At some point after Warhol's death, AWF acquired title to and copyright in the Prince Series. Between 1993 and 2004, AWF sold or otherwise transferred custody of 12 of the original Prince Series works to third parties, and, in 1998, transferred custody of the other four works to The Andy Warhol Museum.

AWF retains copyright in the Prince Series images and, through The Artist Rights Society (a third-party organization that serves as AWF's agent), continues to license the images for editorial, commercial, and museum usage.

On April 22, 2016, the day after Prince died, Condé Nast, Vanity Fair's parent company, contacted AWF. Its initial intent in doing so was to determine whether AWF still had the 1984 image, which Condé Nast hoped to use in connection with a planned magazine commemorating Prince's life. After learning that AWF had additional images from the Prince Series, Condé Nast ultimately obtained a commercial license, to be exclusive for three months, for a different Prince Series image for the cover of the planned tribute magazine. Condé Nast published the tribute magazine in May 2016 with a Prince Series image on the cover. Goldsmith was not given any credit or attribution for the image, which was instead attributed solely to AWF.

It was at this point that Goldsmith first became aware of the Prince Series. In late July 2016, Goldsmith contacted AWF to advise it of the perceived infringement of her copyright. That November, Goldsmith registered the Goldsmith Photograph with the U.S. Copyright Office as an unpublished work. On April 7, 2017, AWF sued Goldsmith and LGL for a declaratory judgment of non-infringement or, in the alternative, fair use. Goldsmith countersued for copyright infringement under 17 U.S.C. §§ 106, 501.

On July 1, 2019, the district court granted summary judgment for AWF on its fair-use claim. See Andy Warhol Found. for the *Visual Arts, Inc. v. Goldsmith*, 382 F. Supp. 3d 312, 316 (S.D.N.Y. 2019). Upon evaluating the four statutory fair-use factors set forth in 17 U.S.C. § 107, the court concluded that: (1) the Prince Series was "transformative" because, while the Goldsmith Photograph portrays Prince as "not a comfortable person" and a "vulnerable human being," the Prince Series portrays Prince as an "iconic, larger-than-life figure," id. at 326; (2) although the Goldsmith Photograph is both creative and unpublished, which would traditionally weigh in Goldsmith's favor, this was "of limited importance because the Prince Series works are transformative works," id. at 327; (3) in creating the Prince Series, Warhol "removed nearly all [of] the [Goldsmith] [P]hotograph's protectable elements," id. at 330; and (4) the Prince Series works "are not market substitutes that have harmed—or have the potential to harm—Goldsmith," id. At 331. This appeal followed.

DISCUSSION

I. Standard of Review

"We review a grant of summary judgment de novo," applying the standards set forth in Federal Rule of Civil Procedure 56(c). Cariou, 714 F.3d at 704. While fair use presents a mixed question of law and fact, it may be resolved on summary judgment where, as here, the material facts are not in dispute. See, e.g., *Harper & Row Publishers, Inc. v. Nation Enters.*, 471 U.S. 539, 560 (1985).

II. Copyright, Derivative Works, and Fair Use

The Constitution empowers Congress to enact copyright laws "[t]o promote the Progress of Science and useful Arts." U.S. Const. art. I, § 8, cl. 8. Congress has exercised this delegated authority continuously since the earliest days of the nation, beginning with the Copyright Act of 1790 and, more recently, through the Copyright Act of 1976. Under the 1976 Act, copyright protection extends both to the original creative work itself and to derivative works, which it defines as, in relevant part, "a work based upon one or more preexisting works, such as a[n] . . . art reproduction, abridgement, condensation, or any other form in which a work may be recast, transformed, or adapted." 17 U.S.C. § 101.

The doctrine of fair use has developed along with the law of copyright. "[A]s Justice Story explained, 'in truth, in literature, in science and in art, there are, and can be, few, if any, things, which in an abstract sense, are strictly new and original throughout. Every book in literature, science and art, borrows, and must necessarily borrow, and use much which was well known and used before.'" *Campbell v. Acuff-Rose Music, Inc.*, 510 U.S. 569, 575 (1994), quoting *Emerson v. Davies*, 8 F. Cas. 615, 619 (No. 4,436) (C.C.D. Mass. 1845) (alterations adopted). The fair use doctrine seeks to strike a balance between an artist's intellectual property rights to the fruits of her own creative labor, including the right to license and develop (or refrain from licensing or developing) derivative works based on that fruit, and "the ability of [other] authors, artists, and the rest of us to express them- or ourselves by reference to the works of others." *Blanch v. Koons*, 467 F.3d 244, 250 (2d Cir. 2006).

Though it developed as a creature of common law, the fair-use defense was formally codified with the passage of the 1976 Act. The statute provides a nonexclusive list of four factors that courts are to consider when evaluating whether the use of a copyrighted work is "fair." These factors are:

1. the purpose and character of the use, including whether such use is of a commercial nature or is for nonprofit educational purposes;
2. the nature of the copyrighted work;
3. the amount and substantiality of the portion used in relation to the copyrighted work as a whole; and
4. the effect of the use upon the potential market for or value of the copyrighted work.

17 U.S.C. § 107.

As the Supreme Court has held, fair use presents a holistic context sensitive inquiry "not to be simplified with bright-line rules[.] . . . All [four statutory factors] are to be explored, and the results weighed together, in light of the purposes of copyright." Campbell, 510 U.S. at 577-78; see also, e.g., Cariou, 714 F.3d at 705 ("[T]he fair use determination is an open-ended and context-sensitive inquiry."). We consider each factor in turn.

A. The Purpose and Character of the Use

This factor requires courts to consider the extent to which the secondary work is "transformative," as well as whether it is commercial. We address these considerations separately below.

1. Transformative Works and Derivative Works

Following the Supreme Court's decision in Campbell, our assessment of this first factor has focused chiefly on the degree to which the use is "transformative," i.e., "whether the new work merely supersedes the objects of the original creation, or instead adds something new, with a further purpose or different character, altering the first with new expression, meaning, or message." 510 U.S. at 579 (internal quotations marks and citations omitted) (alterations adopted). We evaluate whether a work is transformative by examining how it may "reasonably be perceived." Cariou, 714 F.3d at 707, quoting Campbell, 510 U.S. at 582; see also, e.g., *Leibovitz v. Paramount Pictures Corp.*, 137 F.3d 109, 113-15 (2d Cir. 1998). Paradigmatic examples of transformative uses are those Congress itself enumerated in the preamble to § 107: "criticism, comment, news reporting, teaching . . . , scholarship, or research." And, as the Supreme Court recognized in Campbell, parody, which "needs to mimic an original to make its point," 510 U.S. at 580-81, is routinely held transformative. See, e.g., *Brownmark Films, LLC v. Comedy Partners*, 682 F.3d 687, 693 (7th Cir. 2012). These examples are easily understood: the book review excerpting a passage of a novel in order to comment upon it serves a manifestly different purpose from the novel itself. See Authors *Guild v. Google, Inc.*, 804 F.3d 202, 215-16 (2d Cir. 2015) ("[C]opying from an original for the purpose of criticism or commentary on the original . . . tends most clearly to satisfy Campbell's notion of the 'transformative' purpose involved in the analysis of Factor One.").

Although the most straightforward cases of fair use thus involve a secondary work that comments on the original in some fashion, in *Cariou v. Prince*, we rejected the proposition that a secondary work must comment on the original in order to qualify as fair use. See 714 F.3d at 706. In that case, we considered works of appropriation artist Richard Prince that incorporated, among other materials, various black-and-white photographs of Rastafarians taken by Patrick Cariou. See id. at 699. After concluding that the district court had imposed a requirement unsupported by the Copyright Act, we conducted our own examination of Prince's works and concluded that twenty-five of the thirty at issue were transformative of Cariou's photographs as a matter of law. See id. At 706. In reaching this conclusion, we observed that Prince had incorporated Cariou's "serene and deliberately composed portraits and landscape photographs" into his own "crude and jarring works . . . [that] incorporate[d] color, feature[d] distorted human and other forms and settings, and measure[d] between ten and nearly a hundred times the size of the photographs." Id. Thus, we concluded that these works "used [Cariou's photographs] as raw material, transformed in the creation of new information, new aesthetics, new insights and understanding," and were transformative within the meaning of this first factor. Id., quoting *Castle Rock Ent. v. Carol Publ'g Grp.*, 150 F.2d 132, 142 (2d Cir. 1998).

In adjudging the Prince Series transformative, the district court relied chiefly on our decision in Cariou, which we have previously described as the "high-water mark of our court's recognition of transformative works." *TCA Television Corp. v. McCollum*, 839 F.3d 168, 181 (2d Cir. 2016). And, as we have previously observed, that decision has not been immune from criticism. See id. (collecting critical authorities). While we remain bound by Cariou, and have no occasion or desire to question its correctness on its own facts, our review of the decision below persuades us that some clarification is in order.

As discussed supra, both this Court and the Supreme Court have emphasized that fair use is a context-sensitive inquiry that does not lend itself to simple bright-line rules. E.g., Campbell, 510 U.S. at 577-78; Cariou, 714 F.3d at 705. Notwithstanding, the district court appears to have read Cariou as having announced such a rule, to wit, that any secondary work is necessarily transformative as a matter of law "[i]f looking at the works side-by-side, the secondary work has a different character, a new expression, and employs new aesthetics with [distinct] creative and communicative results." Warhol, 382 F. Supp. 3d at 325-26 (internal quotation marks omitted) (alterations adopted). Although a literal construction of certain passages of Cariou may support that proposition, such a reading stretches the decision too far.

Of course, the alteration of an original work "with 'new expression, meaning, or message,'" Cariou, 714 F.3d at 706, quoting Campbell, 510 U.S. at 579, whether by the use of "new aesthetics," id., quoting Blanch, 467 F.3d at 253, by placing the work "in a different context," *Perfect 10, Inc. v. Amazon.com, Inc.*, 508 F.3d 1146, 1165 (9th Cir. 2007), or by any other means is the sine qua non of transformativeness. It does not follow, however, that any secondary work that adds a new aesthetic or new expression to its source material is necessarily transformative.

. . .

We addressed derivative works in Cariou, characterizing them as secondary works that merely present "the same material but in a new form" without "add[ing] something new." 714 F.3d at 708 (citation omitted); see also Google, 804 F.3d at 215-16 ("[D]erivative works generally involve transformations in the nature of changes of form.") (emphasis in original). While that description may be a useful shorthand, it is likewise susceptible to misapplication if interpreted too broadly. Indeed, many derivative works "add something new" to their source material.

. . .

In evaluating the extent to which a work is transformative or derivative (or neither), we typically consider the purpose of the primary and secondary works. In *Bill Graham Archives v. Dorling Kindersley Ltd.*, for example, we held that the reproduction in a book about the Grateful Dead of images of posters originally created to advertise Grateful Dead concerts was transformative because that use was "plainly different from the original purpose for which they were created." 448 F.3d 605, 609-10 (2d Cir. 2006). Likewise, in HathiTrust we held that the defendants' creation of a searchable "digital corpus" comprising scanned copies of tens of millions of books that enabled researchers, scholars, and others to pinpoint the exact page of any book in the catalogue on which the searched term was used was a "quintessentially transformative use." 755 F.3d at 97. In Google, we reached the same conclusion when faced with a larger digital corpus complete with tools that enabled researchers to track how a specific word or phrase has been used throughout the development of the English language, despite the fact that, unlike the database in Hathitrust, Google's database also permitted the searcher to view a "snippet" from the original text showing the context in which the word or phrase had appeared. 804 F.3d at 216-17.

But purpose is perhaps a less useful metric where, as here, our task is to assess the transformative nature of works of visual art that, at least at a high level of generality, share the same overarching purpose (i.e., to serve as works of visual art). While this is not the first time we have had to conduct this inquiry, our cases on such works are considerably fewer in number, and a brief review of them yields conflicting guidance. In *Blanch v. Koons*, for example, we adjudged transformative a Jeff Koons painting that incorporated a copyrighted photograph drawn from a fashion magazine where Koons had testified that he intended to "us[e] Blanch's image as fodder for his commentary on the social and aesthetic consequences of mass media." 467 F.3d at 253. Some time earlier, however, in *Rogers v. Koons*, we denied Koons's fair-use defense as applied to a three dimensional sculpture recreating a photograph, notwithstanding his claim that he intended his sculpture to serve as a commentary on modern society. 960 F.2d 301, 309-11 (2d Cir. 1992).2 And, in Cariou, we held twenty-five of Richard Prince's works transformative as a matter of law even though Prince had testified that he "was not 'trying to create anything with a new meaning or a new message.'" 714 F.3d at 707.

. . .

A common thread running through these cases is that, where a secondary work does not obviously comment on or relate back to the original or use the original for a purpose other than that for which it was created, the bare assertion of a "higher or different artistic use," Rogers, 960 F.2d at 310, is insufficient to render a work transformative. Rather, the secondary work itself must reasonably be perceived as embodying an entirely distinct artistic purpose, one that conveys a "new meaning or message" entirely separate from its source material. While we cannot, nor do we attempt to, catalog all of the ways in which an artist may achieve that end, we note that the works that have done so thus far have themselves been distinct works of art that draw from numerous sources, rather than works that simply alter or recast a single work with a new aesthetic.

Which brings us back to the Prince Series. The district court held that the Prince Series works are transformative because they "can reasonably be perceived to have transformed Prince from a vulnerable, uncomfortable person to an iconic, larger-than-life figure." Warhol, 382 F. Supp. 3d at 326. That was error.

Though it may well have been Goldsmith's subjective intent to portray Prince as a "vulnerable human being" and Warhol's to strip Prince of that humanity and instead display him as a popular icon, whether a work is transformative cannot turn merely on the stated or perceived intent of the artist or the meaning or impression that a critic—or for that matter, a judge—draws from the work. Were it otherwise, the law may well "recogniz[e] any alteration as transformative." 4 Melville B. Nimmer & David Nimmer, Nimmer on Copyright § 13.05(B)(6); see also Google, 804 F.3d at 216 n.18 ("[T]he word 'transformative,' if interpreted too broadly, can also seem to authorize copying that should fall within the scope of an author's derivative rights."). Rather, as we have discussed, the court must examine how the works may reasonably be perceived.

In conducting this inquiry, however, the district judge should not assume the role of art critic and seek to ascertain the intent behind or meaning of the works at issue. That is so both because judges are typically unsuited to make aesthetic judgments and because such perceptions are inherently subjective. As Goldsmith argues, her own stated intent notwithstanding, "an audience viewing the [Goldsmith] [P]hotograph today, across the vista of the singer's long career, might well see him in a different light than Goldsmith saw him that day in 1981." Appellants' Br. at 40. We agree; it is easy to imagine that a whole generation of Prince's fans might have trouble seeing the Goldsmith Photograph as depicting anything other than the iconic songwriter and performer whose musical works they enjoy and admire.

Instead, the judge must examine whether the secondary work's use of its source material is in service of a "fundamentally different and new" artistic purpose and character, such that the secondary work stands apart from the "raw material" used to create it. Although we do not hold that the primary work must be "barely recognizable" within the secondary work, as was the case with the works held transformative in Cariou, the secondary work's transformative purpose and character must, at a bare minimum, comprise something more than the imposition of another artist's style on the primary work such that the secondary work remains both recognizably deriving from, and retaining the essential elements of, its source material.

With this clarification, viewing the works side-by-side, we conclude that the Prince Series is not "transformative" within the meaning of the first factor. That is not to deny that the Warhol works display the distinct aesthetic sensibility that many would immediately associate with Warhol's signature style—the elements of which are absent from the Goldsmith photo. But the same can be said, for example, of the Ken Russell film, from a screenplay by Larry Kramer, derived from D.H. Lawrence's novel, Women in Love: the film is as recognizable a "Ken Russell" as the Prince Series are recognizably "Warhols." But the film, for all the ways in which it transforms (that is, in the ordinary meaning of the word, which indeed is used in the very definition of derivative works, see 17 U.S.C § 101) its source material, is also plainly an adaptation of the Lawrence novel. . . .

Warhol created the series chiefly by removing certain elements from the Goldsmith Photograph, such as depth and contrast, and embellishing the flattened images with "loud, unnatural colors." Warhol, 382 F. Supp. 3d at 326. Nonetheless, although we do not conclude that the Prince Series works are necessarily derivative works as a matter of law, they are much closer to presenting the same work in a different form, that form being a high-contrast screenprint, than they are to being works that make a transformative use of the original. Crucially, the Prince Series retains the essential elements of the Goldsmith Photograph without significantly adding to or altering those elements.

Indeed, the differences between the Goldsmith Photograph and the Prince Series here are in many respects less substantial than those made to the five works that we could not find transformative as a matter of law in Cariou. Unlike the Prince Series, those works unmistakably deviated from Cariou's original portraiture in a manner that suggested an entirely distinct artistic end; rather than recasting those photographs in a new medium, Richard Prince added material that pulled them in new directions. See, e.g., Cariou, 714 F.3d at 711 ("Where [Cariou's] photograph presents someone comfortably at home in nature, [Prince's] Graduation combines divergent elements to present a sense of discomfort."). Nevertheless, we could not confidently determine whether those modest alterations "amount[ed] to a substantial transformation of the original work[s] of art such that the new work[s] were transformative," and remanded the case to the district court to make that determination in the first instance. Id.

In contrast, the Prince Series retains the essential elements of its source material, and Warhol's modifications serve chiefly to magnify some elements of that material and minimize others. While the cumulative effect of those alterations may change the Goldsmith Photograph in ways that give a different impression of its subject, the Goldsmith Photograph remains the recognizable foundation upon which the Prince Series is built.

Finally, we feel compelled to clarify that it is entirely irrelevant to this analysis that "each Prince Series work is immediately recognizable as a 'Warhol.'" Warhol, 382 F. Supp. 3d at 326. Entertaining that logic would inevitably create a celebrity-plagiarist privilege; the more established the artist and the more distinct that artist's style, the greater leeway that artist would have to pilfer the creative labors of others. But the law draws no such distinctions; whether the Prince Series images exhibit the style and characteristics typical of Warhol's work (which they do) does not bear on whether they qualify as fair use under the Copyright Act. As Goldsmith notes, the fact that Martin Scorsese's recent film The Irishman is recognizably "a Scorsese" "do[es] not absolve [him] of the obligation to license the original book" on which it is based. Appellants' Br. at 37.

In reaching this conclusion, we do not mean to discount the artistic value of the Prince Series itself. As used in copyright law, the words "transformative" and "derivative" are legal terms of art that do not express the simple ideas that they carry in ordinary usage. We do not disagree with AWF's contention that the cumulative effect of Warhol's changes to the Goldsmith Photograph is to produce a number of striking and memorable images. And our conclusion that those images are closer to what the law deems "derivative" than "transformative" does not imply that the Prince Series (or Warhol's art more broadly) is "derivative," in the pejorative artistic sense, of Goldsmith's work or of anyone else's. As Goldsmith succinctly puts it, "[t]here is little doubt . . . that the Prince Series reflects Andy Warhol's talent, creativity, and distinctive aesthetic." Appellants' Br. at 36. But the task before us is not to assess the artistic worth of the Prince Series nor its place within Warhol's oeuvre; that is the domain of art historians, critics, collectors, and the museum-going public. Rather, the question we must answer is simply whether the law permits Warhol to claim it as his own, and AWF to exploit it, without Goldsmith's permission. And, at least as far as this aspect of the first factor is concerned, we conclude that the answer to that question is "no."

2. Commercial Use

The statutory language of the first factor also specifically directs courts to consider "whether [the] use is of a commercial nature or is for nonprofit educational purposes." 17 U.S.C. § 107(1). Although finding that a secondary use is commercial "tends to weigh against" finding that it is fair, we apply the test with caution since "nearly all of the illustrative uses listed in the preamble paragraph of § 107 . . . are generally conducted for profit in this country." Campbell, 510 U.S. at 584-85 (citation and internal quotation marks omitted). And, since "[t]he crux of the profit/nonprofit distinction is . . . whether the user stands to profit from exploitation of the copyrighted material without paying the customary price," Harper & Row, 471 U.S. at 562, the commercial nature of a secondary use is of decreased importance when the use is sufficiently transformative such that the primary author should not reasonably expect to be compensated. See, e.g., Blanch, 467 F.3d at 254.

We agree with the district court that the Prince Series works are commercial in nature, but that they produce an artistic value that serves the greater public interest. See Warhol, 382 F. Supp. 3d at 325. We also agree that, although more relevant to the character of the user than of the use, the fact that AWF's mission is to advance the visual arts, a mission that is doubtless in the public interest, may militate against the simplistic assertion that AWF's sale and licensing of the Prince Series works necessarily derogates from a finding of fair use. Nevertheless, just as we cannot hold that the Prince Series is transformative as a matter of law, neither can we conclude that Warhol and AWF are entitled to monetize it without paying Goldsmith the "customary price" for the rights to her work, even if that monetization is used for the benefit of the public.

Of course, even where the secondary use is not transformative, the extent to which it serves the public interest, either in and of itself or by generating funds that enable the secondary user to further a public-facing mission, may be highly relevant when assessing equitable remedies, including whether to enjoin the distribution or order the destruction of infringing works. But just as the commercial nature of a transformative secondary use does not itself preclude a finding that the use is fair, the fact that a commercial non-transformative work may also serve the public interest or that the profits from its commercial use are turned to the promotion of non-commercial ends does not factor significantly in favor of finding fair use under the circumstances present here.

B. The Nature of the Copyrighted Work

The second factor directs courts to consider the nature of the copyrighted work, including (1) whether it is "expressive or creative . . . or more factual, with a greater leeway being allowed to a claim of fair use where the work is factual or informational, and (2) whether the work is published or unpublished, with the scope of fair use involving unpublished works being considerably narrower." Blanch, 467 F.3d at 256 (citation omitted). Although courts are required to consider and weigh this factor, it "has rarely played a significant role in the determination of a fair use dispute." Google, 804 F.3d at 220.

The district court correctly held that the Goldsmith Photograph is both unpublished and creative but nonetheless concluded that the second factor should favor neither party because LGL had licensed the Goldsmith Photograph to Vanity Fair and because the Prince Series was highly transformative. See Warhol, 382 F. Supp. 3d at 327. That was error. That Goldsmith, through LGL, made the Goldsmith Photograph available for a single use on limited terms does not change its status as an unpublished work nor diminish the law's protection of her choice of "when to make a work public and whether to withhold a work to shore up demand." Id., citing 4 Nimmer on Copyright § 13.05(A)(2)(b). Further, though we have previously held that this factor "may be of limited usefulness where the creative work is being used for a transformative purpose," Bill Graham Archives, 448 F.3d at 612, this relates only to the weight assigned to it, not whom it favors. See also Blanch, 467 F.3d at 257 ("[T]he second fair-use factor has limited weight in our analysis because Koons used Blanch's work in a transformative manner.").

Having recognized the Goldsmith Photograph as both creative and unpublished, the district court should have found this factor to favor Goldsmith irrespective of whether it adjudged the Prince Series works transformative within the meaning of the first factor. And, because we disagree that the Prince Series works are transformative, we would accord this factor correspondingly greater weight.

C. The Amount and Substantiality of the Use

The third factor considers "the amount and substantiality of the portion used in relation to the copyrighted work as a whole." 17 U.S.C. § 107(3). "In assessing this factor, we consider not only 'the quantity of the materials used' but also 'their quality and importance'" in relation to the original work. TCA Television, 839 F.3d at 185, quoting Campbell, 510 U.S. at 587. The ultimate question under this factor is whether "the quantity and value of the materials used are reasonable in relation to the purpose of the copying." Campbell, 510 U.S. at 586 (citation and internal quotation marks omitted). To that end, there is no bright line separating a permissible amount of borrowing from an impermissible one; indeed, we have rejected the proposition that this factor necessarily favors the copyright holder even where the secondary user has copied the primary work in toto in service of a legitimate secondary purpose. See *Swatch Grp. Mgmt. Servs. Ltd. v. Bloomberg L.P.*, 756 F.3d 73, 89-90 (2d Cir. 2014); see also Rogers, 960 F.2d at 310-11 ("Sometimes wholesale copying may be permitted, while in other cases taking even a small percentage of the original work has been held unfair use.").

In this case, AWF argues, and the district court concluded, that this factor weighs in its favor because, by cropping and flattening the Goldsmith Photograph, thereby removing or minimizing its use of light, contrast, shading, and other expressive qualities, Warhol removed nearly all of its copyrightable elements. We do not agree.

We begin with the uncontroversial proposition that copyright does not protect ideas, but only "the original or unique way that an author expresses those ideas, concepts, principles, or processes." Rogers, 960 F. 2d at 308. As applied to photographs, this protection encompasses the photographer's "posing the subjects, lighting, angle, selection of film and camera, evoking the desired expression, and almost any other variant involved." Id. at 307. The cumulative manifestation of these artistic choices—and what the law ultimately protects—is the image produced in the interval between the shutter opening and closing, i.e., the photograph itself. This is, as we have previously observed, the photographer's "particular expression" of the idea underlying her photograph. Leibovitz, 137 F. 3d at 115-16.

It is thus easy to understand why AWF's contention misses the mark. The premise of its argument is that Goldsmith cannot copyright Prince's face. True enough. Were it otherwise, nobody else could have taken the man's picture without either seeking Goldsmith's permission or risking a suit for infringement. But while Goldsmith has no monopoly on Prince's face, the law grants her a broad monopoly on its image as it appears in her photographs of him, including the Goldsmith Photograph. *Cf. Mattel, Inc. v. Goldberger Doll Mfg.* Co., 365 F.3d 133, 136-37 (2d Cir. 2004) (vacating summary judgment where district court had concluded that "defendant could freely copy the central facial features of the Barbie dolls" and holding that Mattel could not monopolize the idea of a doll with "upturned nose, bow lips, and wide eyes," but the law protected its specific rendition thereof). And where, as here, the secondary user has used the photograph itself, rather than, for example, a similar photograph, the photograph's specific depiction of its subject cannot be neatly reduced to discrete qualities such as contrast, shading, and depth of field that can be stripped away, taking the image's entitlement to copyright protection along with it.

With that in mind, we readily conclude that the Prince Series borrows significantly from the Goldsmith Photograph, both quantitatively and qualitatively. While Warhol did indeed crop and flatten the Goldsmith Photograph, the end product is not merely a screenprint identifiably based on a photograph of Prince. Rather it is a screenprint readily identifiable as deriving from a specific photograph of Prince, the Goldsmith Photograph. A comparison of the images in the Prince Series makes plain that Warhol did not use the Goldsmith Photograph simply as a reference or aide-mémoire in order to accurately document the physical features of its subject. Instead, the Warhol images are instantly recognizable as depictions or images of the Goldsmith Photograph itself.

. . .

The district court, reasoning that Warhol had taken only the unprotected elements of the Goldsmith Photograph in service of a transformative purpose, held that this factor strongly favored AWF. Because we disagree on both counts, we conclude that this factor strongly favors Goldsmith.

D. The Effect of the Use on the Market for the Original

The fourth factor asks "whether, if the challenged use becomes widespread, it will adversely affect the potential market for the copyrighted work." Bill Graham Archives, 448 F.3d at 613. "Analysis of this factor requires us to balance the benefit the public will derive if the use is permitted and the personal gain the copyright owner will receive if the use is denied." *Wright v. Warner Books, Inc.*, 953 F.2d 731, 739 (2d Cir. 1991) (internal quotation marks omitted). In assessing market harm, we ask not whether the second work would damage the market for the first (by, for example, devaluing it through parody or criticism), but whether it usurps the market for the first by offering a competing substitute. See, e.g., Bill Graham Archives, 448 F.3d at 614. This analysis embraces both the primary market for the work and any derivative markets that exist or that its author might reasonably license others to develop, regardless of whether the particular author claiming infringement has elected to develop such markets. See *Salinger v. Colting*, 607 F.3d 68, 74, 83 (2d Cir. 2010) (affirming that fourth factor favored J.D. Salinger in suit over unauthorized sequel to Catcher in the Rye despite the fact that Salinger had publicly disclaimed any intent to author or authorize a sequel, but vacating preliminary injunction on other grounds). As we have previously observed, the first and fourth factors are closely linked, as "the more the copying is done to achieve a purpose that differs from the purpose of the original, the less likely it is that the copy will serve as a satisfactory substitute for the original." Google, 804 F.3d at 223, citing Campbell, 510 U.S. at 591.

We agree with the district court that the primary market for the Warhol Prince Series (that is, the market for the original works) and the Goldsmith Photograph do not meaningfully overlap, and Goldsmith does not seriously challenge that determination on appeal. We cannot, however, endorse the district court's implicit rationale that the market for Warhol's works is the market for "Warhols," as doing so would permit this aspect of the fourth factor always to weigh in favor of the alleged infringer so long as he is sufficiently successful to have generated an active market for his own work. Notwithstanding, we see no reason to disturb the district court's overall conclusion that the two works occupy distinct markets, at least as far as direct sales are concerned.

We are unpersuaded, however, by the district court's conclusion that the Prince Series poses no threat to Goldsmith's licensing markets. While Goldsmith does not contend that she has sought to license the Goldsmith Photograph itself, the question under this factor is not solely whether the secondary work harms an existing market for the specific work alleged to have been infringed. *Cf.* Castle Rock, 150 F.3d at 145-46 ("Although Castle Rock has evidenced little if any interest in exploiting this market for derivative works . . . the copyright law must respect that creative and economic choice."). Rather, we must also consider whether "unrestricted and widespread conduct of the sort engaged in by [AWF] would result in a substantially adverse impact on the potential market" for the Goldsmith Photograph. Campbell, 510 U.S. at 590 (internal quotation marks omitted) (alterations adopted)); see also *Fox News Network, LLC v. TVEyes, Inc.*, 883 F.3d 169, 179 (2d Cir. 2018).

. . .

Finally, the district court entirely overlooked the potential harm to Goldsmith's derivative market, which is likewise substantial. Most directly, AWF's licensing of the Prince Series works to Condé Nast without crediting or paying Goldsmith deprived her of royalty payments to which she would have otherwise been entitled. Although we do not always consider lost royalties from the challenged use itself under the fourth factor (as any fair use necessarily involves the secondary user using the primary work without paying for the right to do so), we do consider them where the secondary use occurs within a traditional or reasonable market for the primary work. See Fox News, 883 F.3d at

180; On *Davis v. Gap, Inc.*, 246 F.3d 152, 176 (2d Cir. 2001). And here, that market is established both by Goldsmith's uncontroverted expert testimony that photographers generally license others to create stylized derivatives of their work in the vein of the Prince Series, see J. App'x 584-99, and by the genesis of the Prince Series: a licensing agreement between LGL and Vanity Fair to use the Goldsmith Photograph as an artist reference.

Further, we also must consider the impact on this market if the sort of copying in which Warhol engaged were to become a widespread practice. That harm is also self-evident. There currently exists a market to license photographs of musicians, such as the Goldsmith Photograph, to serve as the basis of a stylized derivative image; permitting this use would effectively destroy that broader market, as, if artists "could use such images for free, there would be little or no reason to pay for [them]." *Barcroft Media, Ltd. v. Coed Media Grp., LLC*, 297 F. Supp. 3d 339, 355 (S.D.N.Y. 2017); see also Seuss, 983 F.3d at 461 ("[T]he unrestricted and widespread conduct of the sort ComicMix is engaged in could result in anyone being able to produce" their own similar derivative works based on Oh, the Places You'll Go!). This, in turn, risks disincentivizing artists from producing new work by decreasing its value—the precise evil against which copyright law is designed to guard.

Thus, although the primary market for the Goldsmith Photograph and the Prince Series may differ, the Prince Series works pose cognizable harm to Goldsmith's market to license the Goldsmith Photograph to publications for editorial purposes and to other artists to create derivative works based on the Goldsmith Photograph and similar works. Accordingly, the fourth factor favors Goldsmith.

E. Weighing the Factors

"[T]his court has on numerous occasions resolved fair use determinations at the summary judgment stage where there are no genuine issues of material fact." Cariou, 714 F.3d at 704 (internal quotation marks omitted) (alteration adopted) (collecting cases). As no party contends that there exist any issues of material fact in this case, we believe it appropriate to exercise that discretion here.

Having considered each of the four factors, we find that each favors Goldsmith. Further, although the factors are not exclusive, AWF has not identified any additional relevant considerations unique to this case that we should take into account. Accordingly, we hold that AWF's defense of fair use fails as a matter of law.

III. Substantial Similarity

AWF asks this Court to affirm the district court's decision on the alternate grounds that the Prince Series works are not substantially similar to the Goldsmith Photograph. We decline that invitation, because we conclude that the works are substantially similar as a matter of law.

The district court did not analyze the issue of substantial similarity because, in its view, "it [was] plain that the Prince Series works are protected by fair use." Warhol, 382 F. Supp. 3d at 324. While "it is our distinctly preferred practice to remand such issues for consideration by the district court in the first instance," *Schonfeld v. Hilliard*, 218 F.3d 164, 184 (2d Cir. 2000), we are not required to do so. In this case, because the question of substantial similarity is logically antecedent to that of fair use—since there would be no need to invoke the fair use defense in the absence of actionable infringement—and because the factors we have already discussed with respect to fair use go a considerable way toward resolving the substantial similarity issue, we do not believe a remand to address that issue is necessary in this case.

. . .

Though substantial similarity often presents a jury question, it may be resolved as a matter of law where "access to the copyrighted work is conceded, and the accused work is so substantially similar to the copyrighted work that reasonable jurors could not differ on this issue." Rogers, 960 F.2d at 307 (citation omitted); see also Gaito, 602 F.3d at 63 ("The question of substantial similarity is by no means exclusively reserved for resolution by a jury.").

Here, AWF has conceded that the Goldsmith Photograph served as the "raw material" for the Prince Series works. See Appellee's Br. at 6-7. AWF nevertheless attempts to compare this case to several decisions from our sister circuits concluding that the secondary works in question were not substantially similar to the original photographs on which they were based. See, e.g., *Rentmeester v. Nike, Inc.,* 883 F.3d 1111, 1121-23 (9th Cir. 2018) (Nike's iconic "Jumpman" logo and the photograph used to create it were not substantially similar to a photograph of Michael Jordan dunking a basketball); *Harney v. Sony Pictures Television, Inc.*, 704 F.3d 173, 188 (1st Cir. 2013) (recreated image in madefor-TV movie was not substantially similar to the photograph that inspired it). But the secondary users in those cases did not merely copy the original photographs at issue; they instead replicated those photographs using their own subjects in similar poses. By contrast, Warhol did not create the Prince Series by taking his own photograph of Prince in a similar pose as in the Goldsmith Photograph. Nor did he attempt to copy merely the "idea" conveyed in the Goldsmith Photograph. Rather, he produced the Prince Series works by copying the Goldsmith Photograph itself—i.e., Goldsmith's particular expression of that idea. This case therefore stands in sharp contrast to the situation presented by Rentmeester, for example, in which the court explained that "[w]hat [the original] photo and the [allegedly infringing] photo share are similarities in general ideas or concepts: Michael Jordan attempting to dunk in a pose inspired by ballet's grand jeté; an outdoor setting stripped of most of the traditional trappings of basketball; a camera angle that captures the subject silhouetted against the sky." 883 F.3d at 1122-23.

This is not to say that every use of an exact reproduction constitutes a work that is substantially similar to the original. But here, given the degree to which Goldsmith's work remains recognizable within Warhol's, there can be no reasonable debate that the works are substantially similar. See Rogers, 960 F.3d 307-08. As we have noted above, Prince, like other celebrity performing and creative artists, was much photographed. But any reasonable viewer with access to a range of such photographs including the Goldsmith Photograph would have no difficulty identifying the latter as the source material for Warhol's Prince Series.

CONCLUSION

For the foregoing reasons, we REVERSE the grant of AWF's motion for summary judgment, VACATE the judgment entered below dismissing Lynn Goldsmith and LGL's amended counterclaim, and REMAND this case for further proceedings consistent with this opinion.

. . .

SUPREME COURT OF THE UNITED STATES

Syllabus

GOOGLE LLC v. ORACLE AMERICA, INC.

CERTIORARI TO THE UNITED STATES COURT OF APPEALS FOR THE FEDERAL CIRCUIT

No. 18–956. Argued October 7, 2020—Decided April 5, 2021

Oracle America, Inc., owns a copyright in Java SE, a computer platform that uses the popular Java computer programming language. In 2005, Google acquired Android and sought to build a new software platform for mobile devices. To allow the millions of programmers familiar with the Java programming language to work with its new Android platform, Google copied roughly 11,500 lines of code from the Java SE program. The copied lines are part of a tool called an Application Programming Interface (API). An API allows programmers to call upon prewritten computing tasks for use in their own programs. Over the course of protracted litigation, the lower courts have considered (1) whether Java SE's owner could copyright the copied lines from the API, and (2) if so, whether Google's copying constituted a permissible "fair use" of that material freeing Google from copyright liability. In the proceedings below, the Federal Circuit held that the copied lines are copyrightable. After a jury then found for Google on fair use, the Federal Circuit reversed, concluding that Google's copying was not a fair use as a matter of law. Prior to remand for a trial on damages, the Court agreed to review the Federal Circuit's determinations as to both copyrightability and fair use.

Held: Google's copying of the Java SE API, which included only those lines of code that were needed to allow programmers to put their accrued talents to work in a new and transformative program, was a fair use of that material as a matter of law. Pp. 11–36.

(a) Copyright and patents, the Constitution says, serve to "promote the Progress of Science and useful Arts, by securing for limited Times to Authors and Inventors the exclusive Right to their respective Writings and Discoveries." Art. I, §8, cl. 8. Copyright encourages the production of works that others might cheaply reproduce by granting the author an exclusive right to produce the work for a period of time. Because such exclusivity may trigger negative consequences, Congress and the courts have limited the scope of copyright protection to ensure that a copyright holder's monopoly does not harm the public interest.

This case implicates two of the limits in the current Copyright Act. First, the Act provides that copyright protection cannot extend to "any idea, procedure, process, system, method of operation, concept, principle, or discovery . . . ." 17 U. S. C. §102(b). Second, the Act provides that a copyright holder may not prevent another person from making a "fair use" of a copyrighted work. §107. Google's petition asks the Court to apply both provisions to the copying at issue here. To decide no more than is necessary to resolve this case, the Court assumes for argument's sake that the copied lines can be copyrighted, and focuses on whether Google's use of those lines was a "fair use." Pp. 11–15.

(b) The doctrine of "fair use" is flexible and takes account of changes in technology. Computer programs differ to some extent from many other copyrightable works because computer programs always serve a functional purpose. Because of these differences, fair use has an important role to play for computer programs by providing a contextbased check that keeps the copyright monopoly afforded to computer programs within its lawful bounds. Pp. 15–18.

(c) The fair use question is a mixed question of fact and law. Reviewing courts should appropriately defer to the jury's findings of underlying facts, but the ultimate question whether those facts amount to a fair use is a legal question for judges to decide de novo. This approach does not violate the Seventh Amendment's prohibition on courts reexamining facts tried by a jury, because the ultimate question here is one of law, not fact. The "right of trial by jury" does not include the right to have a jury resolve a fair use defense. Pp. 18–21.

(d) To determine whether Google's limited copying of the API here constitutes fair use, the Court examines the four guiding factors set forth in the Copyright Act's fair use provision: the purpose and character of the use; the nature of the copyrighted work; the amount and substantiality of the portion used in relation to the copyrighted work as a whole; and the effect of the use upon the potential market for or value of the copyrighted work. §107. The Court has recognized that some factors may prove more important in some contexts than in others. Campbell v. Acuff-Rose Music, Inc., 510 U. S. 569, 577. Pp. 21–35.

(1) The nature of the work at issue favors fair use. The copied lines of code are part of a "user interface" that provides a way for programmers to access prewritten computer code through the use of simple commands. As a result, this code is different from many other types of code, such as the code that actually instructs the computer to execute a task. As part of an interface, the copied lines are inherently bound together with uncopyrightable ideas (the overall organization of the API) and the creation of new creative expression (the code independently written by Google). Unlike many other computer programs, the value of the copied lines is in significant part derived from the investment of users (here computer programmers) who have learned the API's system. Given these differences, application of fair use here is unlikely to undermine the general copyright protection that Congress provided for computer programs. Pp. 21–24.

(2) The inquiry into the "the purpose and character" of the use turns in large measure on whether the copying at issue was "transformative," i.e., whether it "adds something new, with a further purpose or different character." Campbell, 510 U. S., at 579. Google's limited copying of the API is a transformative use. Google copied only what was needed to allow programmers to work in a different computing environment without discarding a portion of a familiar programming language. Google's purpose was to create a different task-related system for a different computing environment (smartphones) and to create a platform—the Android platform—that would help achieve and popularize that objective. The record demonstrates numerous ways in which reimplementing an interface can further the development of computer programs. Google's purpose was therefore consistent with that creative progress that is the basic constitutional objective of copyright itself. Pp. 24–28.

(3) Google copied approximately 11,500 lines of declaring code from the API, which amounts to virtually all the declaring code needed to call up hundreds of different tasks. Those 11,500 lines, however, are only 0.4 percent of the entire API at issue, which consists of 2.86 million total lines. In considering "the amount and substantiality of the portion used" in this case, the 11,500 lines of code should be viewed as one small part of the considerably greater whole. As part of an interface, the copied lines of code are inextricably bound to other lines of code that are accessed by programmers. Google copied these lines not because of their creativity or beauty but because they would allow programmers to bring their skills to a new smartphone computing environment. The "substantiality" factor will generally weigh in favor of fair use where, as here, the amount of copying was tethered to a valid, and transformative, purpose. Pp. 28–30.

(4) The fourth statutory factor focuses upon the "effect" of the copying in the "market for or value of the copyrighted work." §107(4). Here the record showed that Google's new smartphone platform is not a market substitute for Java SE. The record also showed that Java SE's copyright holder would benefit from the reimplementation of its interface into a different market. Finally, enforcing the copyright on these facts risks causing creativity-related harms to the public. When taken together, these considerations demonstrate that the fourth factor—market effects—also weighs in favor of fair use. Pp. 30–35.

(e) The fact that computer programs are primarily functional makes it difficult to apply traditional copyright concepts in that technological world. Applying the principles of the Court's precedents and Congress' codification of the fair use doctrine to the distinct copyrighted work here, the Court concludes that Google's copying of the API to reimplement a user interface, taking only what was needed to allow users to put their accrued talents to work in a new and transformative program, constituted a fair use of that material as a matter of law. In reaching this result, the Court does not overturn or modify its earlier cases involving fair use. Pp. 35–36.

886 F. 3d 1179, reversed and remanded.

BREYER, J., delivered the opinion of the Court, in which ROBERTS, C. J., and SOTOMAYOR, KAGAN, GORSUCH, and KAVANAUGH, JJ., joined. THOMAS, J., filed a dissenting opinion, in which ALITO, J., joined. BARRETT, J., took no part in the consideration or decision of the case.

SUPREME COURT OF THE UNITED STATES

No. 18–956

GOOGLE LLC, PETITIONER v.

ORACLE AMERICA, INC.

ON WRIT OF CERTIORARI TO THE UNITED STATES COURT OF APPEALS FOR THE FEDERAL CIRCUIT

[April 5, 2021]

JUSTICE BREYER delivered the opinion of the Court.

Oracle America, Inc., is the current owner of a copyright in Java SE, a computer program that uses the popular Java computer programming language. Google, without permission, has copied a portion of that program, a portion that enables a programmer to call up prewritten software that, together with the computer's hardware, will carry out a large number of specific tasks. The lower courts have considered (1) whether Java SE's owner could copyright the portion that Google copied, and (2) if so, whether Google's copying nonetheless constituted a "fair use" of that material, thereby freeing Google from copyright liability. The Federal Circuit held in Oracle's favor (i.e., that the portion is copyrightable and Google's copying did not constitute a "fair use"). In reviewing that decision, we assume, for argument's sake, that the material was copyrightable. But we hold that the copying here at issue nonetheless constituted a fair use. Hence, Google's copying did not violate the copyright law.

I.

In 2005, Google acquired Android, Inc., a startup firm that hoped to become involved in smartphone software. Google sought, through Android, to develop a software platform for mobile devices like smartphones. 886 F. 3d 1179, 1187 (CA Fed. 2018); App. 137–138, 242–243. A platform provides the necessary infrastructure for computer programmers to develop new programs and applications. One might think of a software platform as a kind of factory floor where computer programmers (analogous to autoworkers, designers, or manufacturers) might come, use sets of tools found there, and create new applications for use in, say, smartphones. (For visual explanations of "platforms" and other somewhat specialized computer-related terms, youmight want to look at the material in Appendix A, infra.)

Google envisioned an Android platform that was free and open, such that software developers could use the tools found there free of charge. Its idea was that more and more developers using its Android platform would develop ever more Android-based applications, all of which would make Google's Android-based smartphones more attractive to ultimate consumers. Consumers would then buy and use ever more of those phones. Oracle America, Inc. v. Google Inc., 872 F. Supp. 2d 974, 978 (ND Cal. 2012); App. 111, 464. That vision required attracting a sizeable number of skilled programmers.

At that time, many software developers understood and wrote programs using the Java programming language, a language invented by Sun Microsystems (Oracle's predecessor). 872 F. Supp. 2d, at 975, 977. About six million programmers had spent considerable time learning, and then using, the Java language. App. 228. Many of those programmers used Sun's own popular Java SE platform to develop new programs primarily for use in desktop and laptop computers. Id., at 151–152, 200. That platform allowed developers using the Java language to write programs that were able to run on any desktop or laptop computer, regardless of the underlying hardware (i.e., the programs were in large part "interoperable"). 872 F. Supp. 2d, at 977. Indeed, one of Sun's slogans was "'write once, run anywhere.'" 886 F. 3d, at 11 86.

Shortly after acquiring the Android firm, Google began talks with Sun about the possibility of licensing the entire Java platform for its new smartphone technology. Oracle, 872 F. Supp. 2d, at 978. But Google did not want to insist that all programs written on the Android platform be interoperable. 886 F. 3d, at 1187. As Android's founder explained, "[t]he whole idea about [an] open source [platform] is to have very, very few restrictions on what people can do with it," App. 659, and Sun's interoperability policy would have undermined that free and open business model. Apparently, for reasons related to this disagreement, Google's negotiations with Sun broke down. Google then built its own platform.

The record indicates that roughly 100 Google engineers worked for more than three years to create Google's Android platform software. Id., at 45, 117, 212. In doing so, Google tailored the Android platform to smartphone technology, which differs from desktop and laptop computers in important ways. A smartphone, for instance, may run on a more limited battery or take advantage of GPS technology. Id., at 197–198. The Android platform offered programmers the ability to program for that environment. To build the platform, Google wrote millions of lines of new code. Because Google wanted millions of programmers, familiar with Java, to be able easily to work with its new Android platform, it also copied roughly 11,500 lines of code from the Java SE program. 886 F. 3d, at 1187. The copied lines of code are part of a tool called an Application Programming Interface, or API.

What is an API? The Federal Circuit described an API as a tool that "allow[s] programmers to use . . . prewritten code to build certain functions into their own programs, rather than write their own code to perform those functions from scratch." Oracle America, Inc. v. Google, Inc., 750 F. 3d 1339, 1349 (2014). Through an API, a programmer can draw upon a vast library of prewritten code to carry out complex tasks. For lay persons, including judges, juries, and many others, some elaboration of this description may prove useful.

Consider in more detail just what an API does. A computer can perform thousands, perhaps millions, of different tasks that a programmer may wish to use. These tasks range from the most basic to the enormously complex. Ask the computer, for example, to tell you which of two numbers is the higher number or to sort one thousand numbers in ascending order, and it will instantly give you the right answer. An API divides and organizes the world of computing tasks in a particular way. Programmers can then use the API to select the particular task that they need for their programs. In Sun's API (which we refer to as the Sun Java API), each individual task is known as a "method." The API groups somewhat similar methods into larger "classes," and groups somewhat similar classes into larger "packages." This method-class-package organizational structure is referred to as the Sun Java API's "structure, sequence, and organization," or SSO.

For each task, there is computer code, known as "implementing code," that in effect tells the computer how to execute the particular task you have asked it to perform (such as telling you, of two numbers, which is the higher). See Oracle, 872 F. Supp. 2d, at 979–980. The implementing code (which Google independently wrote) is not at issue here. For a single task, the implementing code may be hundreds of lines long. It would be difficult, perhaps impossible, for a programmer to create complex software programs without drawing on prewritten task-implementing programs to execute discrete tasks. But how do you as the programmer tell the computer which of the implementing code programs it should choose, i.e., which task it should carry out? You do so by entering into your own program a command that corresponds to the specific task and calls it up. Those commands, known as "method calls," help you carry out the task by choosing those programs written in implementing code that will do the trick, i.e., that will instruct the computer so that your program will find the higher of two numbers. If a particular computer might perform, say, a million different tasks, different method calls will tell the computer which of those tasks to choose. Those familiar with the Java language already know countless method calls that allow them to invoke countless tasks.

And how does the method call (which a programmer types) actually locate and invoke the particular implementing code that it needs to instruct the computer how to carry out a particular task? It does so through another type of code, which the parties have labeled "declaring code." Declaring code is part of the API. For each task, the specific command entered by the programmer matches up with specific declaring code inside the API. That declaring code provides both the name for each task and the location of each task within the API's overall organizational system (i.e., the placement of a method within a particular class and the placement of a class within a particular package). In this sense, the declaring code and the method call form a link, allowing the programmer to draw upon the thousands of prewritten tasks, written in implementing code. See id., at 979–980. Without that declaring code, the method calls entered by the programmer would not call up the implementing code.

The declaring code therefore performs at least two important functions in the Sun Java API. The first, more obvious, function is that the declaring code enables a set of shortcuts for programmers. By connecting complex implementing code with method calls, it allows a programmer to pick out from the API's task library a particular task without having to learn anything more than a simple command. For example, a programmer building a new application for personal banking may wish to use various tasks to, say, calculate a user's balance or authenticate a password. To do so, she need only learn the method calls associated with those tasks. In this way, the declaring code's shortcut function is similar to a gas pedal in a car that tells the car to move faster or the QWERTY keyboard on a typewriter that calls up a certain letter when you press a particular key. As those analogies demonstrate, one can think of the declaring code as part of an interface between human beings and a machine.

The second, less obvious, function is to reflect the way in which Java's creators have divided the potential world of different tasks into an actual world, i.e., precisely which set of potentially millions of different tasks we want to have our Java-based computer systems perform and how we want those tasks arranged and grouped. In this sense, the declaring code performs an organizational function. It determines the structure of the task library that Java's creators have decided to build. To understand this organizational system, think of the Dewey Decimal System that categorizes books into an accessible system or a travel guide that arranges a city's attractions into different categories. Language itself provides a rough analogy to the declaring code's organizational feature, for language itself divides into sets of concepts a world that in certain respects other languages might have divided differently. The developers of Java, for example, decided to place a method called "draw image" inside of a class called "graphics."

Consider a comprehensive, albeit farfetched, analogy that illustrates how the API is actually used by a programmer. Imagine that you can, via certain keystrokes, instruct a robot to move to a particular file cabinet, to open a certain drawer, and to pick out a specific recipe. With the proper recipe in hand, the robot then moves to your kitchen and gives it to a cook to prepare the dish. This example mirrors the API's task-related organizational system. Through your simple command, the robot locates the right recipe and hands it off to the cook. In the same way, typing in a method call prompts the API to locate the correct implementing code and hand it off to your computer. And importantly, to select the dish that you want for your meal, you do not need to know the recipe's contents, just as a programmer using an API does not need to learn the implementing code. In both situations, learning the simple command is enough.

Now let us consider the example that the District Court used to explain the precise technology here. Id., at 980–981. A programmer wishes, as part of her program, to determine which of two integers is the larger. To do so in the Java language, she will first write java.lang. Those words (which we have put in bold type) refer to the "package" (or by analogy to the file cabinet). She will then write Math. That word refers to the "class" (or by analogy to the drawer). She will then write max. That word refers to the "method" (or by analogy to the recipe). She will then make two parentheses (). And, in between the parentheses she will put two integers, say 4 and 6, that she wishes to compare. The whole expression—the method call—will look like this: "java.lang.Math.max(4, 6)." The use of this expression will, by means of the API, call up a task-implementing program that will determine the higher number.

In writing this program, the programmer will use the very symbols we have placed in bold in the precise order we have placed them. But the symbols by themselves do nothing. She must also use software that connects the symbols to the equivalent of file cabinets, drawers, and files. The API is that software. It includes both the declaring code that links each part of the method call to the particular task-implementing program, and the implementing code that actually carries it out. (For an illustration of this technology, see Appendix B, infra.)

Now we can return to the copying at issue in this case. Google did not copy the task-implementing programs, or implementing code, from the Sun Java API. It wrote its own task-implementing programs, such as those that would determine which of two integers is the greater or carry out any other desired (normally far more complex) task. This implementing code constitutes the vast majority of both the Sun Java API and the API that Google created for Android. App. 212. For most of the packages in its new API, Google also wrote its own declaring code. For 37 packages, however, Google copied the declaring code from the Sun Java API. Id., at 106–107. As just explained, that means that, for those 37 packages, Google necessarily copied both the names given to particular tasks and the grouping of those tasks into classes and packages.

In doing so, Google copied that portion of the Sun Java API that allowed programmers expert in the Java programming language to use the "task calling" system that they had already learned. As Google saw it, the 37 packages at issue included those tasks that were likely to prove most useful to programmers working on applications for mobile devices. In fact, "three of these packages were . . . fundamental to being able to use the Java language at all." Oracle, 872 F. Supp. 2d, at 982. By using the same declaring code for those packages, programmers using the Android platform can rely on the method calls that they are already familiar with to call up particular tasks (e.g., determining which of two integers is the greater);

but Google's own implementing programs carry out those tasks. Without that copying, programmers would need to learn an entirely new system to call up the same tasks.

We add that the Android platform has been successful. Within five years of its release in 2007, Android-based devices claimed a large share of the United States market. Id., at 978. As of 2015, Android sales produced more than $42 billion in revenue. 886 F. 3d, at 1187. In 2010 Oracle Corporation bought Sun. Soon thereafter Oracle brought this lawsuit in the United States District Court for the Northern District of California.

II.

The case has a complex and lengthy history. At the outset Oracle complained that Google's use of the Sun Java API violated both copyright and patent laws. For its copyright claim, Oracle alleged that Google infringed its copyright by copying, for 37 packages, both the literal declaring code and the nonliteral organizational structure (or SSO) of the API, i.e., the grouping of certain methods into classes and certain classes into packages. For trial purposes the District Court organized three proceedings. The first would cover the copyright issues, the second would cover the patent issues, and the third would, if necessary, calculate damages. Oracle, 872 F. Supp. 2d, at 975. The court also determined that a judge should decide whether copyright law could protect an API and that the jury should decide whether Google's use of Oracle's API infringed its copyright and, if so, whether a fair use defense nonetheless applied.Ibid.

After six weeks of hearing evidence, the jury rejected Oracle's patent claims (which have since dropped out of the case). It also found a limited copyright infringement. It deadlocked as to whether Google could successfully assert a fair use defense. Id., at 976. The judge then decided that, regardless, the API's declaring code was not the kind of creation to which copyright law extended its protection. The court noted that Google had written its own implementing code, which constituted the vast majority of its API. It wrote that "anyone is free under the Copyright Act to write his or her own code to carry out exactly the same" tasks that the Sun Java API picks out or specifies. Ibid. Google copied only the declaring code and organizational structure that was necessary for Java-trained programmers to activate familiar tasks (while, as we said, writing its own implementing code). Hence the copied material, in the judge's view, was a "system or method of operation," which copyright law specifically states cannot be copyrighted. Id., at 977 (citing 17 U. S. C. §102(b)).

On appeal, the Federal Circuit reversed. That court held that both the API's declaring code and its organizational structure could be copyrighted. Oracle, 750 F. 3d, at 1354. It pointed out that Google could have written its own declaring code just as it wrote its own implementing code. And because in principle Google might have created a whole new system of dividing and labeling tasks that could be called up by programmers, the declaring code (and the system) that made up the Sun Java API was copyrightable. Id., at 1361.

The Federal Circuit also rejected Oracle's plea that it decide whether Google had the right to use the Sun Java API because doing so was a "fair use," immune from copyright liability. The Circuit wrote that fair use "both permits and requires 'courts to avoid rigid application of the copyright statute when, on occasion, it would stifle the very creativity which that law is designed to foster.'" Id., at 1372–1373. But, it added, this "is not a case in which the record contains sufficient factual findings upon which we could base a de novo assessment of Google's affirmative defense of fair use." Id., at 1377. And it remanded the case for another trial on that question. Google petitioned this Court for a writ of certiorari, seeking review of the Federal Circuit's copyrightability determination. We denied the petition. Google, Inc. v. Oracle America, Inc., 576 U. S. 1071 (2015).

On remand the District Court, sitting with a jury, heard evidence for a week. The court instructed the jury to answer one question: Has Google "shown by a preponderance of the evidence that its use in Android" of the declaring code and organizational structure contained in the 37 Sun Java API packages that it copied "constitutes a 'fair use' under the Copyright Act?" App. 294. After three days of deliberation the jury answered the question in the affirmative. Id., at 295. Google had shown fair use.

Oracle again appealed to the Federal Circuit. And the Circuit again reversed the District Court. The Federal Circuit assumed all factual questions in Google's favor. But, it said, the question whether those facts constitute a "fair use" is a question of law. 886 F. 3d, at 1193. Deciding that question of law, the court held that Google's use of the Sun Java API was not a fair use. It wrote that "[t]here is nothing fair about taking a copyrighted work verbatim and using it for the same purpose and function as the original in a competing platform." Id., at 1210. It remanded the case again, this time for a trial on damages.

Google then filed a petition for certiorari in this Court. It asked us to review the Federal Circuit's determinations as to both copyrightability and fair use. We granted its petition.

III.

A

Copyright and patents, the Constitution says, are to "promote the Progress of Science and useful Arts, by securing for limited Times to Authors and Inventors the exclusive Right to their respective Writings and Discoveries." Art. I, §8, cl. 8. Copyright statutes and case law have made clear that copyright has practical objectives. It grants an author an exclusive right to produce his work (sometimes for a hundred years or more), not as a special reward, but in order to encourage the production of works that others might reproduce more cheaply. At the same time, copyright has negative features. Protection can raise prices to consumers. It can impose special costs, such as the cost of contacting owners to obtain reproduction permission. And the exclusive rights it awards can sometimes stand in the way of others exercising their own creative powers. See generally Twentieth Century Music Corp. v. Aiken, 422 U. S. 151, 156 (1975); Mazer v. Stein, 347 U. S. 201, 219 (1954).

Macaulay once said that the principle of copyright is a "tax on readers for the purpose of giving a bounty to writers." T. Macaulay, Speeches on Copyright 25 (E. Miller ed. 1913). Congress, weighing advantages and disadvantages, will determine the more specific nature of the tax, its boundaries and conditions, the existence of exceptions and exemptions, all by exercising its own constitutional power to write a copyright statute.

Four provisions of the current Copyright Act are of particular relevance in this case. First, a definitional provision sets forth three basic conditions for obtaining a copyright. There must be a "wor[k] of authorship," that work must be "original," and the work must be "fixed in any tangible medium of expression." 17 U. S. C. §102(a); see also Feist Publications, Inc. v. Rural Telephone Service Co., 499 U. S. 340, 345 (1991) (explaining that copyright requires some original "creative spark" and therefore does not reach the facts that a particular expression describes).

Second, the statute lists certain kinds of works that copyright can protect. They include "literary," "musical," "dramatic," "motion pictur[e]," "architectural," and certain other works. §102(a). In 1980, Congress expanded the reach of the Copyright Act to include computer programs. And it defined "computer program" as "'a set of statements or instructions to be used directly or indirectly in a computer in order to bring about a certain result.'" §10, 94 Stat. 3028 (codified at 17 U. S. C. §101).

Third, the statute sets forth limitations on the works that can be copyrighted, including works that the definitional provisions might otherwise include. It says, for example, that copyright protection cannot be extended to "any idea, procedure, process, system, method of operation, concept, principle, or discovery . . . ." §102(b). These limitations, along with the need to "fix" a work in a "tangible medium of expression," have often led courts to say, in shorthand form, that, unlike patents, which protect novel and useful ideas, copyrights protect "expression" but not the "ideas" that lie behind it. See Sheldon v. Metro-Goldwyn Pictures Corp., 81 F. 2d 49, 54 (CA2 1936) (Hand, J.); B. Kaplan, An Unhurried View of Copyright 46–52 (1967).

Fourth, Congress, together with the courts, has imposed limitations upon the scope of copyright protection even in respect to works that are entitled to a copyright. For example, the Copyright Act limits an author's exclusive rights in performances and displays, §110, or to performances of sound recordings, §114. And directly relevant here, a copyright holder cannot prevent another person from making a "fair use" of copyrighted material. §107.

We have described the "fair use" doctrine, originating in the courts, as an "equitable rule of reason" that "permits courts to avoid rigid application of the copyright statute when, on occasion, it would stifle the very creativity which that law is designed to foster." Stewart v. Abend, 495 U. S. 207, 236 (1990) (internal quotation marks omitted). The statutory provision that embodies the doctrine indicates, rather than dictates, how courts should apply it. The provision says:

> "[T]he fair use of a copyrighted work, . . . for purposes such as criticism, comment, news reporting, teaching . . . scholarship, or research, is not an infringement of copyright. In determining whether the use made of a work in any particular case is a fair use the factors to be considered shall include—
>
> 1. the purpose and character of the use, including whether such use is of a commercial nature or is for nonprofit educational purposes;
> 2. the nature of the copyrighted work;
> 3. the amount and substantiality of the portion used in relation to the copyrighted work as a whole; and "(4) the effect of the use upon the potential market for or value of the copyrighted work." §107.

In applying this provision, we, like other courts, have understood that the provision's list of factors is not exhaustive (note the words "include" and "including"), that the examples it sets forth do not exclude other examples (note the words "such as"), and that some factors may prove more important in some contexts than in others. See Campbell v. Acuff-Rose Music, Inc., 510 U. S. 569, 577 (1994); Harper & Row, Publishers, Inc. v. Nation Enterprises, 471 U. S. 539, 560 (1985); see also Leval, Toward a Fair Use Standard, 103 Harv. L. Rev 1105, 1110 (1990) (Leval) ("The factors do not represent a score card that promises victory to the winner of the majority"). In a word, we have understood the provision to set forth general principles, the application of which requires judicial balancing, depending upon relevant circumstances, including "significant changes in technology." Sony Corp. of America v. Universal City Studios, Inc., 464 U. S. 417, 430 (1984); see also Aiken, 422 U. S., at 156 ("When technological change has rendered its literal terms ambiguous, the Copyright Act must be construed in light of its basic purpose").

B

Google's petition for certiorari poses two questions. The first asks whether Java's API is copyrightable. It asks us to examine two of the statutory provisions just mentioned, one that permits copyrighting computer programs and the other that forbids copyrighting, e.g., "process[es]," "system[s]," and "method[s] of operation." Pet. for Cert. 12. Google believes that the API's declaring code and organization fall into these latter categories and are expressly excluded from copyright protection. The second question asks us to determine whether Google's use of the API was a "fair use." Google believes that it was.

A holding for Google on either question presented would dispense with Oracle's copyright claims. Given the rapidly changing technological, economic, and business-related circumstances, we believe we should not answer more than is necessary to resolve the parties' dispute. We shall assume, but purely for argument's sake, that the entire Sun Java API falls within the definition of that which can be copyrighted. We shall ask instead whether Google's use of part of that API was a "fair use." Unlike the Federal Circuit, we conclude that it was.

IV.

The language of §107, the "fair use" provision, reflects its judge-made origins. It is similar to that used by Justice Story in Folsom v. Marsh, 9 F. Cas. 342, 348 (No. 4,901) (CC Mass. 1841). See Campbell, 510 U. S., at 576 (noting how "Justice Story's summary [of fair use considerations] is discernable" in §107). That background, as well as modern courts' use of the doctrine, makes clear that the concept is flexible, that courts must apply it in light of the sometimes conflicting aims of copyright law, and that its application may well vary depending upon context. Thus, copyright's protection may be stronger where the copyrighted material is fiction, not fact, where it consists of a motion picture rather than a news broadcast, or where it serves an artistic rather than a utilitarian function. See, e.g., Stewart, 495 U. S., at 237–238; Harper & Row, 471 U. S., at 563; see also 4 M. Nimmer & D. Nimmer, Copyright §13.05[A][2][a] (2019) (hereinafter Nimmer on Copyright) ("[C]opyright protection is narrower, and the corresponding application of the fair use defense greater, in the case of factual works than in the case of works of fiction or fantasy"). Similarly, courts have held that in some circumstances, say, where copyrightable material is bound up with uncopyrightable material, copyright protection is "thin." See Feist, 499 U. S., at 349 (noting that "the copyright in a factual compilation is thin"); see also Experian Information Solutions, Inc. v. Nationwide Marketing Servs. Inc., 893 F. 3d 1176, 1186 (CA9 2018) ("In the context of factual compilations, . . . there can be no infringement unless the works are virtually identical" (internal quotation marks omitted)).

Generically speaking, computer programs differ from books, films, and many other "literary works" in that such programs almost always serve functional purposes. These and other differences have led at least some judges to complain that "applying copyright law to computer programs is like assembling a jigsaw puzzle whose pieces do not quite fit." Lotus Development Corp. v. Borland Int'l, Inc., 49 F. 3d 807, 820 (CA1 1995) (Boudin, J., concurring).

These differences also led Congress to think long and hard about whether to grant computer programs copyright protection. In 1974, Congress established a National Commission on New Technological Uses of Copyrighted Works (CONTU) to look into the matter. §§201–208, 88 Stat. 1873–1875. After several years of research, CONTU concluded that the "availability of copyright protection for computer programs is desirable." Final Report 11 (July 31, 1978). At the same time, it recognized that computer programs had unique features. Mindful of not "unduly burdening users of programs and the general public," it wrote that copyright "should not grant anyone more economic power than is necessary to achieve the incentive to create." Id., at 12. And it believed that copyright's existing doctrines (e.g., fair use), applied by courts on a case-by-case basis, could prevent holders from using copyright to stifle innovation. Ibid. ("Relatively few changes in the Copyright Act of 1976 are required to attain these objectives"). Congress then wrote computer program protection into the law. See §10, 94 Stat. 3028.

The upshot, in our view, is that fair use can play an important role in determining the lawful scope of a computer program copyright, such as the copyright at issue here. It can help to distinguish among technologies. It can distinguish between expressive and functional features of computer code where those features are mixed. It can focus on the legitimate need to provide incentives to produce copyrighted material while examining the extent to which yet further protection creates unrelated or illegitimate harms in other markets or to the development of other products. In a word, it can carry out its basic purpose of providing a context-based check that can help to keep a copyright monopoly within its lawful bounds. See H. R. Rep. No. 94– 1476, pp. 65–66 (1976) (explaining that courts are to "adapt the doctrine [of fair use] to particular situations on a caseby-case basis" and in light of "rapid technological change"); see, e.g., Lexmark Int'l, Inc. v. Static Control Components, Inc., 387 F. 3d 522, 543–545 (CA6 2004) (discussing fair use in the context of copying to preserve compatibility); Sony Computer Entertainment, Inc. v. Connectix Corp., 203 F. 3d 596, 603–608 (CA9 2000) (applying fair use to intermediate copying necessary to reverse engineer access to unprotected functional elements within a program); Sega Enterprises Ltd. v. Accolade, Inc., 977 F. 2d 1510, 1521–1527 (CA9 1992) (holding that wholesale copying of copyrighted code as a preliminary step to develop a competing product was a fair use).

JUSTICE THOMAS' thoughtful dissent offers a very different view of how (and perhaps whether) fair use has any role to play for computer programs. We are told that no attempt to distinguish among computer code is tenable when considering "the nature of the work," see post, at 10, even though there are important distinctions in the ways that programs are used and designed, post, at 18 ("The declaring code is what attracted programmers"). We are told that no reuse of code in a new program will ever have a valid "purpose and character," post, at 16, even though the reasons for copying computer code may vary greatly and differ from those applicable to other sorts of works, ibid. (accepting that copying as part of "reverse engineer[ing] a system to ensure compatibility" could be a valid purpose). And we are told that our fair use analysis must prioritize certain factors over others, post, at 9, n. 5, even though our case law instructs that fair use depends on the context, see Campbell, 510 U. S., at 577–578.

We do not understand Congress, however, to have shielded computer programs from the ordinary application of copyright's limiting doctrines in this way. By defining computer programs in §101, Congress chose to place this subject matter within the copyright regime. Like other protected works, that means that the owners of computer programs enjoy the exclusive rights set forth in the Act, including the right to "reproduce [a] copyrighted work" or to "prepare derivative works." 17 U. S. C. §106. But that also means that exclusive rights in computer programs are limited like any other works. Just as fair use distinguishes among books and films, which are indisputably subjects of copyright, so too must it draw lines among computer programs. And just as fair use takes account of the market in which scripts and paintings are bought and sold, so too must it consider the realities of how technological works are created and disseminated. We do not believe that an approach close to "all or nothing" would be faithful to the Copyright Act's overall design.

V.

At the outset, Google argues that "fair use" is a question for a jury to decide; here the jury decided the question in Google's favor; and we should limit our review to determining whether "substantial evidence" justified the jury's decision. The Federal Circuit disagreed. It thought that the "fair use" question was a mixed question of fact and law; that reviewing courts should appropriately defer to the jury's findings of underlying facts; but that the ultimate question whether those facts showed a "fair use" is a legal question for judges to decide de novo.

We agree with the Federal Circuit's answer to this question. We have said, "[f]air use is a mixed question of law and fact." Harper & Row, 471 U. S., at 560. We have explained that a reviewing court should try to break such a question into its separate factual and legal parts, reviewing each according to the appropriate legal standard. But when a question can be reduced no further, we have added that "the standard of review for a mixed question all depends—on whether answering it entails primarily legal or factual work." U. S. Bank N. A. v. Village at Lakeridge, LLC, 583 U. S. ____, ____(2018) (slip op., at 9).

In this case, the ultimate "fair use" question primarily involves legal work. "Fair use" was originally a concept fashioned by judges. Folsom, 9 F. Cas., at 348. Our cases still provide legal interpretations of the fair use provision. And those interpretations provide general guidance for future cases. See, e.g., Campbell, 510 U. S., at 592–593 (describing kinds of market harms that are not the concern of copyright); Harper & Row, 471 U. S., at 564 ("scope of fair use is narrower with respect to unpublished works"); Sony, 464 U. S., at 451 (wholesale copying aimed at creating a market substitute is presumptively unfair). This type of work is legal work. U. S. Bank, 583 U. S., at ____ (slip op., at 8) ("When applying the law involves developing auxiliary legal principles for use in other cases[,] appellate courts should typically review a decision de novo").

Applying a legal "fair use" conclusion may, of course, involve determination of subsidiary factual questions, such as "whether there was harm to the actual or potential markets for the copyrighted work" or "how much of the copyrighted work was copied." 886 F. 3d, at 1196; see, e.g., Peter F. Gaito Architecture, LLC v. Simone Development Corp., 602 F. 3d 57, 63 (CA2 2010) (noting that in an infringement suit "the question of substantial similarity typically presents an extremely close question of fact"). In this case the Federal Circuit carefully applied the fact/law principles we set forth in U. S. Bank, leaving factual determinations to the jury and reviewing the ultimate question, a legal question, de novo.

Next, Google argues that the Federal Circuit's approach violates the Seventh Amendment. The Amendment both requires that "the right of trial by jury . . . be preserved" and forbids courts to "re-examin[e]" any "fact tried by a jury." U. S. Const., Amdt. 7; see also Gasperini v. Center for Humanities, Inc., 518 U. S. 415, 432–433 (1996). The Reexamination Clause is no bar here, however, for, as we have said, the ultimate question here is one of law, not fact. It does not violate the Reexamination Clause for a court to determine the controlling law in resolving a challenge to a jury verdict, as happens any time a court resolves a motion for judgment as a matter of law. See, e.g., Neely v. Martin K. Eby Constr. Co., 386 U. S. 317, 322 (1967).

Nor is Google correct that "the right of trial by jury" includes the right to have a jury resolve a fair use defense. That Clause is concerned with "the particular trial decision" at issue. Markman v. Westview Instruments, Inc., 517 U. S. 370, 376 (1996). Even though it is possible to find pre-Revolutionary English cases in which a judge sent related questions like fair abridgment to a jury, those questions were significantly different from the "fair use" doctrine as courts apply it today. See, e.g., Gyles v. Wilcox, 2 Atk. 141, 142–144, 26 Eng. Rep. 489, 490–491 (Ch. 1740) (asking theCourt to resolve the narrow question whether a shortened work could be considered a new work); Sayre v. Moore, 1 East 361, n., 102 Eng. Rep. 138, 139, n. (K. B. 1785) (discussing the jury's role in resolving whether copying constituted infringement). As far as contemporary fair use is concerned, we have described the doctrine as an "equitable,"not a "legal," doctrine. We have found no case suggesting that application of U. S. Bank here would fail "to preserve the substance of the common-law [jury trial] right as it existed in 1791." Markman, 517 U. S., at 376.

VI.

We turn now to the basic legal question before us: Was Google's copying of the Sun Java API, specifically its use of the declaring code and organizational structure for 37 packages of that API, a "fair use." In answering this question, we shall consider the four factors set forth in the fair use statute as we find them applicable to the kind of computer programs before us. We have reproduced those four statutory factors supra, at 13–14. For expository purposes, we begin with the second.

A. "The Nature of the Copyrighted Work"

The Sun Java API is a "user interface." It provides a way through which users (here the programmers) can "manipulate and control" task-performing computer programs "via a series of menu commands." Lotus Development Corp., 49 F. 3d, at 809. The API reflects Sun's division of possible tasks that a computer might perform into a set of actual tasks that certain kinds of computers actually will perform. Sun decided, for example, that its API would call up a task that compares one integer with another to see which is the larger. Sun's API (to our knowledge) will not call up the task of determining which great Arabic scholar decided to use Arabic numerals (rather than Roman numerals) to perform that "larger integer" task. No one claims that the decisions about what counts as a task are themselves copyrightable—although one might argue about decisions as to how to label and organize such tasks (e.g., the decision to name a certain task "max" or to place it in a class called "Math." Cf. Baker v. Selden, 101 U. S. 99 (1880)).

As discussed above, supra, at 3–5, and in Appendix B, infra, we can think of the technology as having three essential parts. First, the API includes "implementing code," which actually instructs the computer on the steps to follow to carry out each task. Google wrote its own programs (implementing programs) that would perform each one of the tasks that its API calls up.

Second, the Sun Java API associates a particular command, called a "method call," with the calling up of each task. The symbols java.lang., for example, are part of the command that will call up the program (whether written by Sun or, as here, by Google) that instructs the computer to carry out the "larger number" operation. Oracle does not here argue that the use of these commands by programmers itself violates its copyrights.

Third, the Sun Java API contains computer code that will associate the writing of a method call with particular "places" in the computer that contain the needed implementing code. This is the declaring code. The declaring code both labels the particular tasks in the API and organizes those tasks, or "methods," into "packages" and "classes." We have referred to this organization, by way of rough analogy, as file cabinets, drawers, and files. Oracle does claim that Google's use of the Sun Java API's declaring code violates its copyrights.

The declaring code at issue here resembles other copyrighted works in that it is part of a computer program. Congress has specified that computer programs are subjects of copyright. It differs, however, from many other kinds of copyrightable computer code. It is inextricably bound together with a general system, the division of computing tasks, that no one claims is a proper subject of copyright. It is inextricably bound up with the idea of organizing tasks into what we have called cabinets, drawers, and files, an idea that is also not copyrightable. It is inextricably bound up with the use of specific commands known to programmers, known here as method calls (such as java.lang.Math.max, etc.), that Oracle does not here contest. And it is inextricably bound up with implementing code, which is copyrightable but was not copied.

Moreover, the copied declaring code and the uncopied implementing programs call for, and reflect, different kinds of capabilities. A single implementation may walk a computer through dozens of different steps. To write implementing programs, witnesses told the jury, requires balancing such considerations as how quickly a computer can execute a task or the likely size of the computer's memory. One witness described that creativity as "magic" practiced by an API developer when he or she worries "about things like power management" for devices that "run on a battery." App. 143; see also id., at 147, 204. This is the very creativity that was needed to develop the Android software for use not in laptops or desktops but in the very different context of smartphones.

The declaring code (inseparable from the programmer's method calls) embodies a different kind of creativity. Sun Java's creators, for example, tried to find declaring code names that would prove intuitively easy to remember. Id., at 211. They wanted to attract programmers who would learn the system, help to develop it further, and prove reluctant to use another. See post, at 10 ("Declaring code . . . is user facing. It must be designed and organized in a way that is intuitive and understandable to developers so that they can invoke it"). Sun's business strategy originally emphasized the importance of using the API to attract programmers. It sought to make the API "open" and "then . . . compete on implementations." App. 124–125. The testimony at trial was replete with examples of witnesses drawing this critical line between the user-centered declaratory code and the innovative implementing code. Id., at 126–127, 159–160, 163–164, 187, 190–191.

These features mean that, as part of a user interface, the declaring code differs to some degree from the mine run of computer programs. Like other computer programs, it is functional in nature. But unlike many other programs, its use is inherently bound together with uncopyrightable ideas (general task division and organization) and new creative expression (Android's implementing code). Unlike many other programs, its value in significant part derives from the value that those who do not hold copyrights, namely, computer programmers, invest of their own time and effort to learn the API's system. And unlike many other programs, its value lies in its efforts to encourage programmers to learn and to use that system so that they will use (and continue to use) Sun-related implementing programs that Google did not copy.

Although copyrights protect many different kinds of writing, Leval 1116, we have emphasized the need to "recogni[ze] that some works are closer to the core of [copyright] than others," Campbell, 510 U. S., at 586. In our view, for the reasons just described, the declaring code is, if copyrightable at all, further than are most computer programs (such as the implementing code) from the core of copyright. That fact diminishes the fear, expressed by both the dissent and the Federal Circuit, that application of "fair use" here would seriously undermine the general copyright protection that Congress provided for computer programs. And it means that this factor, "the nature of the copyrighted work," points in the direction of fair use.

B. "The Purpose and Character of the Use"

In the context of fair use, we have considered whether the copier's use "adds something new, with a further purpose or different character, altering" the copyrighted work "with new expression, meaning or message." Id., at 579. Commentators have put the matter more broadly, asking whether the copier's use "fulfill[s] the objective of copyright law to stimulate creativity for public illumination." Leval 1111. In answering this question, we have used the word "transformative" to describe a copying use that adds something new and important. Campbell, 510 U. S., at 579. An "'artistic painting'" might, for example, fall within the scope of fair use even though it precisely replicates a copyrighted "'advertising logo to make a comment about consumerism.'" 4 Nimmer on Copyright §13.05[A][1][b] (quoting Netanel, Making Sense of Fair Use, 15 Lewis & Clark L. Rev. 715, 746 (2011)). Or, as we held in Campbell, a parody can be transformative because it comments on the original or criticizes it, for "[p]arody needs to mimic an original to make its point." 510 U. S., at 580–581.

Google copied portions of the Sun Java API precisely, and it did so in part for the same reason that Sun created those portions, namely, to enable programmers to call up implementing programs that would accomplish particular tasks. But since virtually any unauthorized use of a copyrighted computer program (say, for teaching or research) would do the same, to stop here would severely limit the scope of fair use in the functional context of computer programs. Rather, in determining whether a use is "transformative," we must go further and examine the copying's more specifically described "purpose[s]" and "character." 17 U. S. C. §107(1).

Here Google's use of the Sun Java API seeks to create new products. It seeks to expand the use and usefulness of Android-based smartphones. Its new product offers programmers a highly creative and innovative tool for a smartphone environment. To the extent that Google used parts of the Sun Java API to create a new platform that could be readily used by programmers, its use was consistent with that creative "progress" that is the basic constitutional objective of copyright itself. Cf. Feist, 499 U. S., at 349–350 ("The primary objective of copyright is not to reward the labor of authors, but '[t]o promote the Progress of Science and useful Arts'" (quoting U. S. Const., Art. I, §8,cl. 8)).

The jury heard that Google limited its use of the Sun Java API to tasks and specific programming demands related to Android. It copied the API (which Sun created for use in desktop and laptop computers) only insofar as needed to include tasks that would be useful in smartphone programs. App. 169–170. And it did so only insofar as needed to allow programmers to call upon those tasks without discarding a portion of a familiar programming language and learning a new one. Id., at 139–140. To repeat, Google, through

Android, provided a new collection of tasks operating in a distinct and different computing environment. Those tasks were carried out through the use of new implementing code (that Google wrote) designed to operate within that new environment. Some of the amici refer to what Google did as "reimplementation," defined as the "building of a system . . . that repurposes the same words and syntaxes" of an existing system—in this case so that programmers who had learned an existing system could put their basic skills to use in a new one. Brief for R Street Institute et al. As Amici Curiae 2.

The record here demonstrates the numerous ways in which reimplementing an interface can further the development of computer programs. The jury heard that shared interfaces are necessary for different programs to speak to each other. App. 125 ("We have to agree on the APIs so that the application I write to show a movie runs on your device"). It heard that the reimplementation of interfaces is necessary if programmers are to be able to use their acquired skills. Id., at 191 ("If the API labels change, then either the software wouldn't continue to work anymore or the developer . . . would have to learn a whole new language to be able to use these API labels"). It heard that the reuse of APIs is common in the industry. Id., at 115, 155, 663. It heard that Sun itself had used pre-existing interfaces in creating Java. Id., at 664. And it heard that Sun executives thought that widespread use of the Java programming language, including use on a smartphone platform, would benefit the company. Id., at 130–133.

Amici supporting Google have summarized these same points—points that witnesses explained to the jury. See, e.g., Brief for Copyright Scholars as Amici Curiae 25 ("[T]he portions of Java SE that Google reimplemented may have helped preserve consistency of use within the larger Java developer community"); Brief for Microsoft Corporation as Amicus Curiae 22 ("[A]llowing reasonable fair use of functional code enables innovation that creates new opportunities for the whole market to grow"); Brief for 83 Computer Scientists as Amici Curiae 20 ("Reimplementing interfaces fueled widespread adoption of popular programming languages" (emphasis deleted)); Brief for R Street Institute et al. as Amici Curiae 15–20 (describing Oracle's reimplementation of other APIs); see also Brief for American Antitrust Institute as Amicus Curiae 7 ("Copyright on largely functional elements of software that [have] become an industry standard gives a copyright holder anti-competitive power").

These and related facts convince us that the "purpose and character" of Google's copying was transformative—to the point where this factor too weighs in favor of fair use.

There are two other considerations that are often taken up under the first factor: commerciality and good faith. The text of §107 includes various noncommercial uses, such as teaching and scholarship, as paradigmatic examples of privileged copying. There is no doubt that a finding that copying was not commercial in nature tips the scales in favor of fair use. But the inverse is not necessarily true, as many common fair uses are indisputably commercial. For instance, the text of §107 includes examples like "news reporting," which is often done for commercial profit. So even though Google's use was a commercial endeavor—a fact noparty disputed, see 886 F. 3d, at 1197—that is not dispositive of the first factor, particularly in light of the inherently transformative role that the reimplementation played in the new Android system.

As for bad faith, our decision in Campbell expressed some skepticism about whether bad faith has any role in a fair use analysis. 510 U. S., at 585, n. 18. We find this skepticism justifiable, as "[c]opyright is not a privilege reserved for the well-behaved." Leval 1126. We have no occasion here to say whether good faith is as a general matter a helpful inquiry. We simply note that given the strength of the other factors pointing toward fair use and the jury finding in Google's favor on hotly contested evidence, that fact bound consideration is not determinative in this context.

C. "The Amount and Substantiality of the Portion Used"

If one considers the declaring code in isolation, the quantitative amount of what Google copied was large. Google copied the declaring code for 37 packages of the Sun Java API, totaling approximately 11,500 lines of code. Those lines of code amount to virtually all the declaring code needed to call up hundreds of different tasks. On the other hand, if one considers the entire set of software material in the Sun Java API, the quantitative amount copied was small. The total set of Sun Java API computer code, including implementing code, amounted to 2.86 million lines, of which the copied 11,500 lines were only 0.4 percent. App. 212.

The question here is whether those 11,500 lines of code should be viewed in isolation or as one part of the considerably greater whole. We have said that even a small amount of copying may fall outside of the scope of fair use where the excerpt copied consists of the "'heart'" of the original work's creative expression. Harper & Row, 471 U. S., at 564–565. On the other hand, copying a larger amount of material can fall within the scope of fair use where the material copied captures little of the material's creative expression or is central to a copier's valid purpose. See, e.g., Campbell, 510 U. S., at 588; New Era Publications Int'l, ApS v. Carol Publishing Group, 904 F. 2d 152, 158 (CA2 1990). If a defendant had copied one sentence in a novel, that copying may well be insubstantial. But if that single sentence set forth one of the world's shortest short stories—"When he awoke, the dinosaur was still there."—the question looks much different, as the copied material constitutes a small part of the novel but the entire short story. See A. Monterroso, El Dinosaurio, in Complete Works & Other Stories 42 (E. Grossman transl. 1995). (In the original Spanish, the story reads: "Cuando despertó, el dinosaurio todavía estaba allí.")

Several features of Google's copying suggest that the better way to look at the numbers is to take into account the several million lines that Google did not copy. For one thing, the Sun Java API is inseparably bound to those task implementing lines. Its purpose is to call them up. For another, Google copied those lines not because of their creativity, their beauty, or even (in a sense) because of their purpose. It copied them because programmers had already learned to work with the Sun Java API's system, and it would have been difficult, perhaps prohibitively so, to attract programmers to build its Android smartphone system without them. Further, Google's basic purpose was to create a different task-related system for a different computing environment (smartphones) and to create a platform—the Android platform—that would help achieve and popularize that objective. The "substantiality" factor will generally weigh in favor of fair use where, as here, the amount of copying was tethered to a valid, and transformative, purpose. Supra, at 25–26; see Campbell, 510 U. S., at 586–587 (explaining that the factor three "enquiry will harken back to the first of the statutory factors, for . . . the extent of permissible copying varies with the purpose and character of the use").

We do not agree with the Federal Circuit's conclusion that Google could have achieved its Java-compatibility objective by copying only the 170 lines of code that are "necessary to write in the Java language." 886 F. 3d, at 1206. In our view, that conclusion views Google's legitimate objectives too narrowly. Google's basic objective was not simply to make the Java programming language usable on its Android systems. It was to permit programmers to make use of their knowledge and experience using the Sun Java

API when they wrote new programs for smartphones with the Android platform. In principle, Google might have created its own, different system of declaring code. But the jury could have found that its doing so would not have achieved that basic objective. In a sense, the declaring code was the key that it needed to unlock the programmers' creative energies. And it needed those energies to create and to improve its own innovative Android systems. We consequently believe that this "substantiality" factor weighs in favor of fair use.

D. Market Effects

The fourth statutory factor focuses upon the "effect" of the copying in the "market for or value of the copyrighted work." 17 U. S. C. §107(4). Consideration of this factor, at least where computer programs are at issue, can prove more complex than at first it may seem. It can require a court to consider the amount of money that the copyright owner might lose. As we pointed out in Campbell, "verbatim copying of the original in its entirety for commercial purposes" may well produce a market substitute for an author's work. 510 U. S., at 591. Making a film of an author's book may similarly mean potential or presumed losses to the copyright owner. Those losses normally conflict with copyright's basic objective: providing authors with exclusive rights that will spur creative expression.

But a potential loss of revenue is not the whole story. We here must consider not just the amount but also the source of the loss. As we pointed out in Campbell, a "lethal parody, like a scathing theatre review," may "kil[l] demand for the original." Id., at 591–592. Yet this kind of harm, even if directly translated into foregone dollars, is not "cognizable under the Copyright Act." Id., at 592.

Further, we must take into account the public benefits the copying will likely produce. Are those benefits, for example, related to copyright's concern for the creative production of new expression? Are they comparatively important, or unimportant, when compared with dollar amounts likely lost (taking into account as well the nature of the source of the loss)? Cf. MCA, Inc. v. Wilson, 677 F. 2d 180, 183 (CA2 1981) (calling for a balancing of public benefits and losses to copyright owner under this factor).

We do not say that these questions are always relevant to the application of fair use, not even in the world of computer programs. Nor do we say that these questions are the only questions a court might ask. But we do find them relevant here in helping to determine the likely market effects of Google's reimplementation.

As to the likely amount of loss, the jury could have found that Android did not harm the actual or potential markets for Java SE. And it could have found that Sun itself (now Oracle) would not have been able to enter those markets successfully whether Google did, or did not, copy a part of its API. First, evidence at trial demonstrated that, regardless of Android's smartphone technology, Sun was poorly positioned to succeed in the mobile phone market. The jury heard ample evidence that Java SE's primary market was laptops and desktops. App. 99, 200. It also heard that Sun's many efforts to move into the mobile phone market had proved unsuccessful. Id., at 135, 235, 671. As far back as 2006, prior to Android's release, Sun's executives projected declining revenue for mobile phones because of emerging smartphone technology. Id., at 240. When Sun's former CEO was asked directly whether Sun's failure to build a smartphone was attributable to Google's development of Android, he answered that it was not. Id., at 650. Given the evidence showing that Sun was beset by business challenges in developing a mobile phone product, the jury was entitled to agree with that assessment.

Second, the jury was repeatedly told that devices using Google's Android platform were different in kind from those that licensed Sun's technology. For instance, witnesses explained that the broader industry distinguished between smartphones and simpler "feature phones." Id., at 237. As to the specific devices that used Sun-created software, the jury heard that one of these phones lacked a touchscreen, id., at 359–360, while another did not have a QWERTY keyboard, id., at 672. For other mobile devices, the evidence showed that simpler products, like the Kindle, used Java software, id., at 396, while more advanced technology, like the Kindle Fire, were built on the Android operating system, id., at 206. This record evidence demonstrates that, rather than just "repurposing [Sun's] code from larger computers to smaller computers," post, at 16, Google's Android platform was part of a distinct (and more advanced) market than Java software.

Looking to these important differences, Google's economic expert told the jury that Android was not a market substitute for Java's software. As he explained, "the two products are on very different devices," and the Android platform, which offers "an entire mobile operating stack," is a "very different typ[e] of produc[t]" than Java SE, which is "just an applications programming framework." App. 256; see also id., at 172–174. Taken together, the evidence showed that Sun's mobile phone business was declining, while the market increasingly demanded a new form of smartphone technology that Sun was never able to offer. Finally, the jury also heard evidence that Sun foresaw a benefit from the broader use of the Java programming language in a new platform like Android, as it would further expand the network of Java-trained programmers. Id., at 131–133; see also id., at 153 ("Once an API starts getting reimplemented, you know it has succeeded"). In other words, the jury could have understood Android and Java SE as operating in two distinct markets. And because there are two markets at issue, programmers learning the Java language to work in one market (smartphones) are then able to bring those talents to the other market (laptops). See 4 Nimmer on Copyright §13.05[A][4] (explaining that factor four asks what the impact of "widespread conduct of the sort engaged in by the defendant" would be on the market for the present work).

Sun presented evidence to the contrary. Indeed, the Federal Circuit held that the "market effects" factor militated against fair use in part because Sun had tried to enter the Android market. 886 F. 3d, at 1209 (Sun sought licensing agreement with Google). But those licensing negotiations concerned much more than 37 packages of declaring code, covering topics like "the implementation of [Java's] code" and "branding and cooperation" between the firms. App. 245; see also 4 Nimmer on Copyright §13.05[A][4] (cautioning against the "danger of circularity posed" by considering unrealized licensing opportunities because "it is a given in every fair use case that plaintiff suffers a loss of a potential market if that potential is defined as the theoretical market for licensing the very use at bar"). In any event, the jury's fair use determination means that neither Sun's effort to obtain a license nor Oracle's conflicting evidence can overcome evidence indicating that, at a minimum, it would have been difficult for Sun to enter the smartphone market, even had Google not used portions of the Sun Java API.

On the other hand, Google's copying helped Google make a vast amount of money from its Android platform. And enforcement of the Sun Java API copyright might give Oracle a significant share of these funds. It is important, however, to consider why and how Oracle might have become entitled to this money. When a new interface, like an API or a spreadsheet program, first comes on the market, it may attract new users because of its expressive qualities, such as a better visual screen or because of its superior functionality. As time passes, however, it may be valuable for a different reason, namely, because users, including programmers, are just used to it. They have already learned how to work with it. See Lotus Development Corp., 49 F. 3d, at 821(Boudin, J., concurring).

The record here is filled with evidence that this factor accounts for Google's desire to use the Sun Java API. See, e.g., App. 169–170, 213–214. This source of Android's profitability has much to do with third parties' (say, programmers') investment in Sun Java programs. It has correspondingly less to do with Sun's investment in creating the Sun Java API. We have no reason to believe that the Copyright Act seeks to protect third parties' investment in learning how to operate a created work. Cf. Campbell, 510 U. S., at 591–592 (discussing the need to identify those harms that are "cognizable under the Copyright Act").

Finally, given programmers' investment in learning the Sun Java API, to allow enforcement of Oracle's copyright here would risk harm to the public. Given the costs and difficulties of producing alternative APIs with similar appeal to programmers, allowing enforcement here would make of the Sun Java API's declaring code a lock limiting the future creativity of new programs. Oracle alone would hold the key. The result could well prove highly profitable to Oracle (or other firms holding a copyright in computer interfaces). But those profits could well flow from creative improvements, new applications, and new uses developed by users who have learned to work with that interface. To that extent, the lock would interfere with, not further, copyright's basic creativity objectives. See Connectix Corp., 203 F. 3d, at 607; see also Sega Enterprises, 977 F. 2d, at 1523–1524 ("An attempt to monopolize the market by making it impossible for others to compete runs counter to the statutory purpose of promoting creative expression"); Lexmark Int'l, 387 F. 3d, at 544 (noting that where a subsequent user copied a computer program to foster functionality, it was not exploiting the programs "commercial value as a copyrighted work" (emphasis in original)). After all, "copyright supplies the economic incentive to [both] create and disseminate ideas," Harper & Row, 471 U. S., at 558, and the reimplementation of a user interface allows creative new computer code to more easily enter the market.

The uncertain nature of Sun's ability to compete in Android's market place, the sources of its lost revenue, and the risk of creativity-related harms to the public, when taken together, convince that this fourth factor—market effects—also weighs in favor of fair use.

***

The fact that computer programs are primarily functional makes it difficult to apply traditional copyright concepts in that technological world. See Lotus Development Corp., 49 F. 3d, at 820 (Boudin, J., concurring). In doing so here, we have not changed the nature of those concepts. We do not overturn or modify our earlier cases involving fair use—cases, for example, that involve "knockoff " products, journalistic writings, and parodies. Rather, we here recognize that application of a copyright doctrine such as fair use has long proved a cooperative effort of Legislatures and courts, and that Congress, in our view, intended that it so continue. As such, we have looked to the principles set forth in the fair use statute, §107, and set forth in our earlier cases, and applied them to this different kind of copyrighted Work.

We reach the conclusion that in this case, where Google reimplemented a user interface, taking only what was needed to allow users to put their accrued talents to work in a new and transformative program, Google's copying of the Sun Java API was a fair use of that material as a matter of law. The Federal Circuit's contrary judgment is reversed, and the case is remanded for further proceedings in conformity with this opinion.

It is so ordered.

JUSTICE BARRETT took no part in the consideration or decision of this case.

. . .

6 Hunt Mer. Mag. 175, 2 Story 100, 9 F.Cas. 342, No. 4901

(Cite as: 6 Hunt Mer. Mag. 175, 9 F.Cas. 342)

C

Case No. 4,901, 2 Story, 100;[1] 6 Hunt, Mer. Mag. 175

FOLSOM et al.

v.

MARSH et al.

Oct. Term, 1841.

Bill in equity for piracy of the copyright of the writings of Washington. The bill in substance stated, that Jared Sparks was the author of a work entitled, 'The Writings of George Washington, being his correspondence, addresses, messages, and other papers, official and private, selected and published from the original manuscripts, with a life of the author, notes, and illustrations, by Jared Sparks,' consisting of 12 volumes, of all of which the copyright was duly taken out, the term of which copyright has still more than eight years to run. That the plaintiffs, Charles Folsom, Thomas G. Wells and Lyman Thurston, printers and publishers, under the style of Folsom, Wells and Thurston, had assumed a part of the risk and responsibility of publishing the said work, and that being in the receipt of large sums, the proceeds of the sale of the said work, Bela Marsh, Nahum Capen, Thomas B. Wabb, and Gardner P. Lyon, booksellers, under the firm of Marsh, Capen and Lyon, and Charles W. Upham, all well knowing that the said Sparks held such copyright, and that the said Fulsom, Wells and Thurston, were interested as aforesaid, and deliberately, after due notice, intending to infringe upon the said copyright, at Boston, on August 5th, 1840, and at divers times before and since, without the allowance or consent of the orators, or either of them, published, and exposed to sale, and sold, a book in two volumes, entitled 'The Life of Washington in the Form of an Autobiography, the narrative being to a great extent conducted by himself, in extracts and selections from his own writings, with portraits and other engravings,' consisting of 866 pages, which they still continue to expose to sale, having had due notice, and well knowing, that the same is a copy from, and an infringement and piracy of, the said Life and Writings of George Washington so published by the plaintiffs. That 388 pages of the said piratical book are copied verbatim et literatim from the said work compiled by the said Sparks, consisting of matter published originally by the said Sparks, under his copyright, and which had never before been published or printed, and which the said Sparks had the exclusive right and privilege to print, publish, and sell. And that many other parts of the piratical work are infringements of the said Sparks's said copyright, whereby the plaintiffs have sustained great damage, and that the said Marsh, Capen and Lyon still threaten to continue to print, publish and sell, copies of the said piratical work. In consideration whereof, the plaintiffs pray that the defendants be decreed to render an account of the copies of the said piratical work, which they have sold, and to pay over the profits thereof to the plaintiffs; to surrender and deliver up all the copies on hand, and the stereotype plates of the said work, to an officer of the court, to be cancelled and destroyed; to pay the plaintiffs their costs, and that they be restrained by injunction from

[1] Reported by William W. Story, Esq. Circuit Court, D. Massachusetts.

selling or exposing to sale, or causing to be exposed to sale or sold, or otherwise of disposing of any copies of the said piratical work, and for such other relief as shall seem meet, or as equity shall require.

The answer stated as follows: That the defendants, not confessing or acknowledging any of the matters and things alleged in the bill, are informed and believe that the said complainants are the publishers of the said Life and Writings of Washington, as alleged by the complainants, and that the said Sparks is author thereof. But that they totally deny that the said Sparks has, or has heretofore had, any copyright, whereby he is entitled to any exclusive publication of the said writings, correspondence, addresses, messages, and other papers. That the defendants did, on August the 5th, 1840, publish and sell, and before and since have, without the allowance and consent of the plaintiffs, published and sold copies of the said work, in two volumes, entitled a 'Life of Washington, in the Form of an Autobiography,' but that the said work is not a copy from, nor a piracy of the said work, by the said Sparks. The defendants deny that any part of the said work, published by the defendants, is copied verbatim et literatim from any portion of the said work by the said Sparks, to which he has any exclusive right and privilege to print, or publish, or sell. But they aver, that they have, in the work published by them, made such use as they might lawfully do, of the writings, correspondence, messages, addresses, and other papers, by George Washington, printed in the work compiled by the said Sparks, and that they have copied many pages of the said writings, from the original manuscript thereof, and from printed works, printed and published before the publication of the said work by the said Sparks, and that they have made such use thereof, as they might do in a work entirely distinct from and independent of the said work by the said Sparks, and they allege, that the said work published by them, is entirely a distinct and independent work from the work by the said Sparks.

The general replication being filed, the cause was referred to George Hillard, Esq., master in chancery, to ascertain and report the facts to the court. His report in substance stated as follows: The work, of which the plaintiffs are the proprietors, is comprised in twelve octavo volumes, varying in length from five hundred and forty to five hundred and ninety-two pages, and containing in the whole six thousand seven hundred and sixty-three pages, including one hundred and fifty-eight pages of index in the twelfth volume. The first volume consists of an original life of Washington by Mr. Sparks, one of the plaintiffs, and the remaining eleven, of the writings and correspondence of Washington, with editorial notes and illustrations by Mr. Sparks. The work, of which the defendants are the proprietors, is in two volumes, duodecimo. The first volume consists of four hundred and forty-three pages, including forty-one pages of glossary and index. The second volume consists of four hundred and twenty-three pages, including thirty-five pages of glossary and index. The whole amount of pages of the two volumes, is, therefore, eight hundred and sixty-six, including seventy-six pages of glossary and index. I find the whole number of pages in the two volumes of the defendants' work, which correspond with the passages in the plaintiffs' work, and are identical with them, to be (discarding fractions) three hundred and fifty-three. Of these pages, three hundred and nineteen have never appeared in print before the publication of the plaintiffs' work, and I accordingly report them to have been copied by the defendants from the work of the plaintiffs. The remaining thirty-four pages have appeared before, in various other publications, with the variations here-inbefore stated. In view of these variations, and also in consideration of the fact, that these passages in the defendants' work, generally speaking, differ in punctuation and other typographical peculiarities from the same passages as contained in works, other than that of the plaintiffs, I find that these thirty-nine pages were taken by the defendants from the plaintiffs' work, and none other. The whole of these three hundred and fifty-three pages, in the two volumes of the defendants' work, are taken from the last eleven volumes of the work of the plaintiffs. Of the three hundred and nineteen pages, above mentioned, which are in the work of the defendants, and which have not been published in any other work than that of the plaintiffs, I report sixty-four pages to be official letters and documents, and two hundred and fifty-five pages to be private. Of the remaining thirty-four pages, I report fifteen pages to be private, and nineteen pages to be official. Under the head of 'official' letters and papers, I class the following: Letters addressed by Washington, as commander-in-chief, to the president of congress. Official letters to governors of states and speakers of legislative bodies. Circular letters. General orders. Communications (official) addressed as president to his cabinet. Letter accepting the command of the army, on our expected war with France. All others I class as 'private.'

The cause was argued upon the master's report, (no exception having been filed thereto,) by Mr. Robbins and Willard Phillips for the plaintiffs, and by R. Rantoul for the defendants.

The points made by the defendants were as follows:

I. The papers of George Washington are not subjects of copyright. 1. They are manuscripts of a deceased person, not injured by publication of them. 2. They are not literary, and, therefore, are not literary property. 3. They are public in their nature, and, therefore, are not private property. 4. They were meant by the author for public use.

II. Mr. Sparks is not the owner of these papers, but they belong to the United States, and may be published by any one.

III. An author has a right to quote, select, extract or abridge from another, in the composition of a work essentially new.

STORY, Circuit Justice.

This is one of those intricate and embarrassing questions, arising in the administration of civil justice, in which it is not, from the peculiar nature and character of the controversy, easy to arrive at any satisfactory conclusion, or to lay down any general principles applicable to all cases. Patents and copyrights approach, nearer than any other class of cases belonging to forensic discussions, to what may be called the metaphysics of the law, where the distinctions are, or at least may be, very subtile and refined, and, sometimes, almost evanescent. In many cases, indeed, what constitutes an infringement of a patented invention, is sufficiently clear and obvious, and stands upon broad and general agreements and differences; but, in other cases, the lines approach very near to each other, and, sometimes, become almost evanescent, or melt into each other. So, in cases of copyright, it is often exceedingly obvious, that the whole substance of one work has been copied from another, with slight omissions and formal differences only, which can be treated in no other way than as studied evasions; whereas, in other cases, the identity of the two works in substance, and the question of piracy, often depend upon a nice balance of the comparative use made in one of the materials of the other; the nature, extent, and value of the materials thus used; the objects of each work; and the degree to which each writer may be fairly presumed to have resorted to the same common sources of information, or to have exercised the same common diligence in the selection and arrangement of the materials. Thus, for example, no one can doubt that a reviewer may fairly cite largely from the original work, if his design be really and truly to use the passages for the purposes of fair and reasonable criticism. On the other hand, it is as clear, that if he thus cites the ***345** most important parts of the work, with a view, not to criticise, but to supersede the use of the original work, and substitute the review for it, such a use will be deemed in law a piracy. A wide interval might, of course, exist between these two extremes, calling for great caution and involving great difficulty, where the court is approaching the dividing middle line which separates the one from the other. So, it has been decided that a fair and bonb ona fide abridgment of an original work, is not a piracy of the copyright of the author. See Dodsley v. Kinnersley, 1 Amb. 403; Whittingham v. Wooler, 2 Swanst. 428, 430, 431, note; Tonson v. Walker, 3 Swanst. 672-679, 681. But, then, what constitutes a fair and bonb ona fide abridgment, in the sense of the law, is one of the most difficult points, under particular circumstances, which can well arise for judicial discussion. It is clear, that a mere selection, or different arrangement of parts of the original work, so as to bring the work into a smaller compass, will not be held to be such an abridgment. There must be real, substantial condensation of the materials, and intellectual labor and judgment bestowed thereon; and not merely the facile use of the scissors; or extracts of the essential parts, constituting the chief value of the original work. See Gyles v. Wilcox, 2 Atk. 141.

In the present case, the work alleged to be pirated, is the Writings of President Washington, in twelve volumes, royal octavo, containing nearly seven thousand pages, of which the first volume contains a life of Washington, by the learned editor, Mr. Sparks, in respect to which no piracy is asserted or proved. The other eleven volumes consist of the letters of Washington, private and official, and his messages and other public acts, with explanatory notes and occasional illustrations by the editor. That the original work is of very great, and, I may almost say, of inestimable value, as the repository of the thoughts and opinions of that great man, no one pretends to doubt. The work of the defendants is in two volumes, duodecimo, containing eight hundred and sixty-six pages. It consists of a Life of Washington, written by the learned defendant, (the Rev. Charles W. Upham), which is formed upon a plan different from that of Mr. Sparks, and in which Washington is made mainly to tell the story of his own life, by inserting therein his letters and his messages, and other written documents, with such connecting lines in the narrative, as may illustrate and explain the times and circumstances, and occasions of writing them. Now, as I have already said, there is no complaint, that Mr. Upham has taken his narrative part, substantially, from the Life by Mr. Sparks. The gravamen is, that he has used the letters of Washington, and inserted, verbatim, copies thereof from the collection of Mr. Sparks. The master finds, by his report, that the whole number of pages in Mr. Upham's work, corresponding and identical with the passages in Mr. Sparks's work, are three hundred and fifty-three pages out of eight hundred and sixty-six, a fraction more than one third of the two volumes of the defendants. Of these three hundred and fifty-three pages, the report finds that three hundred and nineteen pages consist of letters of Washington, which have been taken from Mr. Sparks's work, and have never been published before; namely, sixty-four pages are official letters and documents, and two hundred and fifty-five pages are private letters of Washington. The question, therefore, upon this admitted state of the facts, resolves itself into the point, whether such a use, in the defendants' work, of the letters of Washington, constitutes a piracy of the work of Mr. Sparks.

It is objected, in the first place, on behalf of the defendants, that the letters of Washington are not, in the sense of the law, proper subjects of copyright, for several reasons: (1) Because they are the manuscripts of a deceased person, not injured by the publication thereof; (2) because they are not literary compositions, and, therefore, not susceptible of being literary property, nor esteemed of value by the author; (3) because they are, in their nature and character, either public or official letters, or private letters of business; and (4) because they were designed by the author for public use, and not for copyright, or private property. Now, in relation to the last objection, it is most manifest, that President Washington deemed them his own private property, and bequeathed them to his nephew, the late Mr. Justice Washington, through whom the late Mr. Chief Justice Marshall and Mr. Sparks acquired an interest therein; and, as appears from the contract between these gentlemen, annexed to the report, the publication of these writings was undertaken by Mr. Sparks, as editor, for their joint benefit; and the work itself has been accomplished at great expense and labor, and after great intellectual efforts, and very patient and comprehensive researches, both at home and abroad. The publication of the defendants, therefore, to some extent, must be injurious to the rights of property of the representatives and assignees of President Washington. Indeed, as we shall presently see, congress have actually purchased these very letters and manuscripts, at a great price, for the benefit of the nation, from their owner and possessor under the will of Mr. Justice Washington, as private and most valuable property. That President Washington, therefore, intended them exclusively for public use, as a donation to the public, or did not esteem them of value as his own private property, appears to me to be a proposition, completely disproved by the evidence. Unless, indeed, there be a most unequivocal dedication of private letters and papers by the ***346** author, either to the public, or to some private person, I hold, that the author has a property therein, and that the copyright thereof exclusively belongs to him. Then as to the supposed distinction between letters of business, or of a mere private or domestic character, and letters, which, from their character and contents, are to be treated as literary compositions, I am not prepared to admit its soundness or propriety. It is extremely difficult to say, what letters are or are not literary compositions. In one sense, all letters are literary, for they consist of the thoughts and language of the writer reduced to written characters, and show his style and his mode of constructing sentences, and his habits of composition. Many letters of business also embrace critical remarks and expressions of opinion on various subjects, moral, religious, political and literary. What is to be done in such cases? Even in compositions confessedly literary, the author may not intend, nay, often does not intend them for publication; and yet, no one on that account doubts his right of property therein, as a subject of value to himself and to his posterity. If subsequently published by his representatives, would they not have a copyright therein? It is highly probable, that neither Lord Chesterfield, nor Lord Orford, nor the poet Gray, nor Cowper, nor Lady Russell, nor Lady Montague, ever intended their letters for publication as literary compositions, although they abound with striking remarks, and elegant sketches, and sometimes with the most profound, as well as affecting, exhibitions of close reflection, and various knowledge and experience, mixed up with matters of business, personal anecdote, and family gossip.

There is no small confusion in the books, in reference to the question of copyright in letters. Some of the dicta seem to suppose that no copyright can exist, except in letters which are professedly literary; while others again recognize a much more enlarged and liberal doctrine. See Gods. Pat. (Ed. 1840, London) pp. 327-"332; Gee v. Pritchard, 2 Swanst. 403, 405, 426, 427; Perceval v. Phipps, 2 Ves. & B. 19, 24, 25, 28. Without attempting to reconcile, or even to comment upon the language of the authorities on this head, I wish to state what I conceive to be the true doctrine upon the whole subject. In the first place, I hold, that the author of any letter or letters, (and his representatives,) whether they are literary compositions, or familiar letters, or letters of business, possess the sole and exclusive copyright therein; and that no persons, neither those to whom they are addressed, nor other persons, have any right or authority to publish the same upon their own account, or for their own benefit. But, consistently with this right, the persons to whom they are addressed, may have, nay, must, by implication, possess, the right to publish any letter or letters addressed to them, upon such occasions, as require, or justify, the publication or public use of them; but this right is strictly limited to such occasions. Gee v. Pritchard, 2 Swanst. 415, 419. Thus, a person may justifiably use and publish, in a suit at law or in equity, such letter or letters as are necessary and proper, to establish his right to maintain the suit, or defend the same. So, if he be aspersed or misrepresented by the writer, or accused of improper conduct, in a public manner, he may publish such parts of such letter or letters, but no more, as may be necessary to vindicate his character and reputation, or free him from unjust obloquy and reproach.

If he attempt to publish such letter or letters on other occasions, not justifiable, a court of equity will prevent the publication by an injunction, as a breach of private confidence or contract, or of the rights of the author; and a fortiori, if he attempt to publish them for profit; for then it is not a mere breach of confidence or contract, but it is a violation of the exclusive copyright of the writer. In short, the person, to whom letters are addressed, has but a limited right, or special property, (if I may so call it), in such letters, as a trustee, or bailee, for particular purposes, either of information or of protection, or of support of his own rights and character. The general property, and the general rights incident to property, belong to the writer, whether the letters are literary compositions, or familiar letters, or details of facts, or letters of business. The general property in the manuscripts remains in the writer and his representatives, as well as the general copyright. A fortiori, third persons, standing in no privity with either party, are not entitled to publish them, to subserve their own private purposes of interest, or curiosity, or passion. If the case of Perceval v. Phipps, 2 Ves. & B. 21,28, before the then vice chancellor (Sir Thomas Plumer), contains a different doctrine, all I can say is, that I do not accede to its authority; and I fall back upon the more intelligible and reasonable doctrine of Lord Hardwicke, in Pope v. Curl, 2 Atk. 342, and Lord Apsley, in the case of Thompson v. Stanhope, Amb. 737, and of Lord Keeper Henley, in the case of Duke of Queensberry v. Sheffeare, 2 Eden, 329 (cited 4 Burrows, 2329), which Lord Eldon has not scrupled to hold to be binding authorities upon the point in Gee v. Pritchard, 2 Swanst. 403, 414, 415, 419, 426, 427. But I do not understand that Sir Thomas Plumer did, in Perceval v. Phipps, deny the right of property of the writer in his own letters; and so he was understood by Lord Eldon in Gee v. Pritchard; who, however, said, that that case admitted of much remark. Indeed, if the doctrine were otherwise, that no person, or his representatives, could have a copyright in his own private or familiar letters, written to friends, upon interesting political and other occasions, ***347** or containing details of facts and occurrences, passing before the writer, it would operate as a great discouragement upon the collection and preservation thereof; and the materials of history would become far more scanty, than they otherwise would be. What descendant, or representative of the deceased author, would undertake to publish, at his own risk and expense, any such papers; and what editor would be willing to employ his own learning, and judgment, and researches, in illustrating such works, if, the moment they were successful, and possessed the substantial patronage of the public, a rival bookseller might republish them, either in the same, or in a cheaper form, and thus either share with him, or take from him the whole profits? It is the supposed exclusive copyright in such writings, which now encourages their publication thereof, from time to time, after the author has passed to the grave. To this we owe, not merely, the publication of the writings of Washington, but of Franklin, and Jay, and Jefferson and Madison, and other distinguished statesmen of our own country. It appears to me, that the copyright act of 1831, c. 16, § 9, [4 Stat. 436], fully recognizes the doctrine for which I contend. It gives by implication to the author, or legal proprietor of any manuscript whatever, the sole right to print and publish the same, and expressly authorizes the courts of equity of the United States to grant injunctions to restrain the publication thereof, by any person or persons, without his consent.

In respect to official letters, addressed to the government, or any of its departments, by public officers, so far as the right of the government extends, from principles of public policy, to withhold them from publication, or to give them publicity, there may be a just ground of distinction. It may be doubtful, whether any public officer is at liberty to publish them, at least, in the same age, when secrecy may be required by the public exigencies, without the sanction of the government. On the other hand, from the nature of the public service, or the character of the documents, embracing historical, military, or diplomatic information, it may be the right, and even the duty, of the government, to give them publicity, even against the will of the writers. But this is an exception in favor of the government, and stands upon principles allied to, or nearly similar to, the rights of private individuals, to whom letters are addressed by their agents, to use them, and publish them, upon fit and justifiable occasions. But assuming the right of the government to publish such official letters and papers, under its own sanction, and for public purposes, I am not prepared to admit, that any private persons have a right to publish the same letters and papers, without the sanction of the government, for their own private profit and advantage. Recently the Duke of Wellington's despatches have (I believe) been published, by an able editor, with the consent of the noble duke, and under the sanction of the government. It would be a strange thing to say, that a compilation involving so much expense, and so much labor to the editor, in collecting and arranging the materials, might be pirated and republished by another bookseller, perhaps to the ruin of the original publisher and editor. Before my mind arrives at such a conclusion, I must have clear and positive lights to guide my judgment, or to bind me in point of authority. However, it is not necessary, in this case, to dispose of this point, because, of the letters and documents published by the defendants, not more than one fifth part are of an official character.

Another and distinct objection urged on behalf of the defendants, is, that congress have purchased the manuscripts of these letters and documents, and they have become public property, and may be published by any one. An answer, in part, has been already given to this objection. Congress have, indeed, authorized the purchase of these manuscripts from the owner and possessor thereof, and paid the liberal price of 25,000 dollars therefor; and they have thus become national property. But it is an entirely inadmissible conclusion that, therefore, every private person has a right to use them, and publish them. It might be contended, with as much force and correctness, that every private person had an equal right to use any other national property at his pleasure, such as the arms, the ammunition, the ships, or the custom houses, belonging to the government. But a reason, which is entirely conclusive upon this point, is, that the government purchased the manuscripts, subject to the copyright already acquired by the plaintiffs in the publication thereof. The vendor took them subject to that copyright, and could convey no title which he did not himself possess, or beyond what he possessed. Nor is there any pretence to say that he either did convey, or intended to convey, to the government, the property in these manuscripts, except subject to the copyright already acquired.

The next and leading objection is, that the defendants had a right to abridge and select, and use the materials which they have taken for their work, which, though it embraces the number of letters above stated, is an original and new work, and that it constitutes, in no just sense, a piracy of the work of the plaintiffs. This, in truth, is the real hinge of the whole controversy, and involves the entire merits of the suit. It is certainly true, that the defendants' work cannot properly be treated as an abridgment of that of the plaintiffs; neither is it strictly and wholly a mere compilation from the latter. So far as the narrative goes, it is either original, or derived (at least as far as the matter has been brought before the court) from common sources of information, open to all authors. ***348** It is not even of the nature of a collection of beauties of an author; for it does not profess to give fugitive extracts, or brilliant passages from particular letters. It is a selection of the entire contents of particular letters, from the whole collection or mass of letters of the work of the plaintiffs. From the known taste and ability of Mr. Upham, it cannot be doubted, that these letters are the most instructive, useful and interesting to be found in that large collection.

The question, then, is, whether this is a justifiable use of the original materials, such as the law recognizes as no infringement of the copyright of the plaintiffs. It is said, that the defendant has selected only such materials, as suited his own limited purpose as a biographer. That is, doubtless, true; and he has produced an exceedingly valuable book. But that is no answer to the difficulty. It is certainly not necessary, to constitute an invasion of copyright, that the whole of a work should be copied, or even a large portion of it, in form or in substance. If so much is taken, that the value of the original is sensibly diminished, or the labors of the original author are substantially to an injurious extent appropriated by another, that is sufficient, in point of law, to constitute a piracy pro tanto. The entirety of the copyright is the property of the author; and it is no defence, that another person has appropriated a part, and not the whole, of any property. Neither does it necessarily depend upon the quantity taken, whether it is an infringement of the copyright or not. It is often affected by other considerations, the value of the materials taken, and the importance of it to the sale of the original work. Lord Cottenham, in the recent cases of Bramwell v. Halcomb, 3 Mylne & C. 737, 738, and Saunders v. Smith, Id. 711, 736, 737, adverting to this point, said: 'When it comes to a question of quantity, it must be very vague. One writer might take all the vital part of another's book, though it might be but a small proportion of the book in quantity. It is not only quantity, but value, that is always looked to. It is useless to refer to any particular cases, as to quantity.' In short, we must often, in deciding questions of this sort, look to the nature and objects of the selections made, the quantity and value of the materials used, and the degree in which the use may prejudice the sale, or diminish the profits, or supersede the objects, of the original work. Many mixed ingredients enter into the discussion of such questions. In some cases, a considerable portion of the materials of the original work may be fused, if I may use such an expression, into another work, so as to be undistinguishable in the mass of the latter, which has other professed and obvious objects, and cannot fairly be treated as a piracy; or they may be inserted as a sort of distinct and mosaic work, into the general texture of the second work, and constitute the peculiar excellence thereof, and then it may be a clear piracy. If a person should, under color of publishing 'Elegant Extracts' of poetry, include all the best pieces at large of a favorite poet, whose volume was secured by a copyright, it would be difficult to say why it was not an invasion of that right, since it might constitute the entire value of the volume. The case of Mawman v. Tegg, 2 Russ. 385, is to this purpose. There was no pretence in that case, that all the articles of the encyclopedia of the plaintiffs had been copied into that of the defendants; but large portions of the materials of the plaintiffs' work had been copied. Lord Eldon, upon that occasion, held, that there might be a piracy of part of a work, which would entitle the plaintiffs to a full remedy and relief in equity. In prior cases, he had affirmed the like doctrine. In Wilkins v. Aikin, 17 Ves. 422, 424, he said: 'There is no doubt, that a man cannot, under the pretence of quotation, publish either the whole or a part of another's book, though he may use, what in all cases it is difficult to define, fair quotation.' In Roworth v. Wilkes, 1 Camp. 94, Lord Ellenborough said: 'A review will not, in general, serve as a substitute for the book reviewed; and even there, if so much is extracted, that it communicates the same knowledge with the original work, it is an actionable violation of literary property. The intention to pirate is not necessary in an action of this sort; it is enough, that the publication complained of is in substance a copy, whereby a work vested in another is prejudiced. A compilation of this kind (an encyclopedia) may differ from a treatise published by itself; but there must be certain limits fixed to its transcripts; it must not be allowed to sweep up all modern works, or an encyclopedia would be a recipe for completely breaking down literary property.' The vice chancellor (Sir L. Shadwell), in Sweet v. Shaw, 1 Jur. (London) 212 [3 Jur. 217], referring to the remarks of Lord Ellenborough, cited by counsel, said: 'That does not mean a substitute for the whole work. From what you state, suppose a book to contain one hundred articles, and ninety-nine were taken, still it would not be a substitute.' And in this very case he granted an injunction, being of opinion, that there was primp rima facie, at law, an invasion of the plaintiffs' right; not only an injury, but also a damage to the plaintiffs, in copying from several volumes of Reports, published by the plaintiffs, although eleven only had been copied verbatim, but a considerable number of what were called 'abridged cases,' were, in truth, copies of the plaintiffs' volumes, with little, or trifling, alterations. It is manifest, also, from what fell from Lord Chancellor Cottenham, in Saunders v. Smith, 3

Mylne & C. 711, that he entertained no doubt, (although he did not decide the point,) that there might be a violation of the copyright of volumes of Reports, by copying verbatim a part only of the cases reported. Much must, in such cases, depend upon the nature of the new work, the value and extent of the copies, and the degree in which the original authors may be injured thereby. In Lewis v. Fullarton, 2 Jur. (London) 127 [3 Jur. 669], 2 Beav. 6, Lord Langdale, in the case of a topographical dictionary, held, that largely copying from the work in another book having a similar object, was a violation of that copyright, although the same information might have been (but, in fact, was not) obtained from common sources, open to all persons. On that occasion, he said: 'None are entitled to save themselves trouble and expense, by availing themselves, for their own profit, of other men's works, still entitled to the protection of copyright;' and, accordingly, in that case, he granted an injunction as to the parts pirated, although it was admitted, on all hands, that there was much which was original in the new work.

In the present case, I have no doubt whatever, that there is an invasion of the plaintiffs' copyright; I do not say designedly, or from bad intentions; on the contrary, I entertain no doubt, that it was deemed a perfectly lawful and justifiable use of the plaintiffs' work. But if the defendants may take three hundred and nineteen letters, included in the plaintiffs' copyright, and exclusively belonging to them, there is no reason why another bookseller may not take other five hundred letters, and a third, one thousand letters, and so on, and thereby the plaintiffs' copyright be totally destroyed. Besides; every one must see, that the work of the defendants is mainly founded upon these letters, constituting more than one third of their work, and imparting to it its greatest, nay, its essential value. Without those letters, in its present form the work must fall to the ground. It is not a case, where abbreviated or select passages are taken from particular letters; but the entire letters are taken, and those of most interest and value to the public, as illustrating the life, the acts, and the character of Washington. It seems to me, therefore, that it is a clear invasion of the right of property of the plaintiffs, if the copying of parts of a work, not constituting a major part, can ever be a violation thereof; as upon principle and authority, I have no doubt it may be. If it had been the case of a fair and bona fide abridgment of the work of the plaintiffs, it might have admitted of a very different consideration.

I have come to this conclusion, not without some regret, that it may interfere, in some measure, with the very meritorious labors of the defendants, in their great undertaking of a series of works adapted to school libraries. But a judge is entitled in this case, as in others, only to know and to act upon his duty. I hope, however, that some means may be found, to produce an amicable settlement of this unhappy controversy. The report of the master must stand confirmed, and a perpetual injunction be awarded, restraining the defendants, their agents, servants and salesmen, from farther printing, publishing, selling, or disposing of any copy or copies of the work complained of; the 'Life of Washington,' by the Rev. Charles W. Upham, containing any of the three hundred and nineteen letters of Washington, stated in the report of the master, and never before published; and that it be referred to a master, to take an account of the profits made by the defendants, in the premises; with leave for either party to apply to the court for farther directions.

C.C.Mass.,1841.
Folsom v. Marsh
6 Hunt Mer. Mag. 175, 2 Story 100, 9 F.Cas. 342,
No. 4901

END OF DOCUMENT

UNITED STATES DISTRICT COURT
CENTRAL DISTRICT OF CALIFORNIA

Kyle Hanagami, *plaintiff* v. Epic Games, Inc., *defendant*

Case No. 2:22-cv-02063-SVW-MRW

STEPHEN V. WILSON, U.S. DISTRICT JUDGE

ORDER GRANTING MOTION TO DISMISS [38]

I. INTRODUCTION

Before the Court is a motion to dismiss filed by Defendant Epic Games against Plaintiff Hanagami. Bringing suit under the Copyright Act and California's Unfair Competition Law, Plaintiff alleges that Defendant copied Plaintiff's Registered Choreography by creating an animated dance for Defendant's *Fortnite* game.

For the below reasons, Defendant's motion to dismiss is GRANTED.

II. BACKGROUND

Plaintiff Kyle Hanagami is a professional choreographer and dance instructor in Los Angeles, California. Compl. ¶ 11, ECF No. 1. On November 11, 2017, Plaintiff published a YouTube video of himself and others dancing to the song "How Long," by Charlie Puth. *Id.* ¶ 16. The approximately five-minute long video[1] includes five different groups of two or three dancers performing the same choreography. *Id.*; *see* Declaration of Dale M. Cendali ("Cendali Decl."), Ex. A.[2]

Plaintiff's video is registered with the United States Copyright Office on February 20, 2021, at Copyright Registration Number PA 2-277-839, which "covers the 'How Long' Choreography," but excludes "music" from the registration (the "Registered Choreography"). *Id.* ¶ 1, *see* Ex. A.

Defendant Epic Games, Inc., is a video game company that develops and distributes various video games. Compl. ¶¶ 18–19. One of its games is *Fortnite*, a free-to-play multiplayer shooting game where players can explore a virtual world, build and destroy structures, and compete to be the last player alive. *Id.* ¶¶ 4, 20–22.

Though *Fortnite* is free to play, it has an in-game marketplace (the "Item Shop") where players can purchase virtual currency to, in turn, purchase virtual customizations for their in-game characters. *Id.* ¶ 22. These customizations include new clothes, weapons, or, as relevant here, "emotes." *Id.* Emotes are animated movements or dances, which players can perform in *Fortnite*. *Id.*

The emote at the heart of this case is called "It's Complicated." *Id.* ¶ 38. Players can purchase the "It's Complicated" emote in the Item Shop to perform while playing *Fortnite*. *Id.* ¶ 39; *see* Cendali Decl., Ex. B.

---

[1] As of July 27, 2022, the video is available at the following URL: https://www.youtube.com/watch?v=iW2yUrXXRTI.

[2] In deciding the motion to dismiss, the Court may consider the pleadings, exhibits attached to the Complaint, and other materials integral to the Complaint. *Tellabs, Inc. v. Makor Issues & Rights, Ltd.*, 551 U.S. 308, 322–23.

Plaintiff alleges that the "It's Complicated" emote contains "the most recognizable portion of Plaintiff's Registered Choreography, the portion for the hook at the beginning of the chorus of the song[.]" *Id.* ¶ 40.

The portion of the work at issue is set to four counts of music; the dancers repeat the movements twice in the song's chorus (the "Steps"). Having reviewed Plaintiff's video and Defendant's emote, the Court compared side-by-side still images of the dances, which are included at the end of this order in an appendix. *See* Appendix. Ten of the poses in the video and the emote are the same. *See Id.*[3]

Plaintiff brings claims of direct and contributory copyright infringement and a claim for unfair competition. Compl. ¶¶ 53–88. Defendant moves to dismiss each of Plaintiff's claims.

III. LEGAL STANDARD

A motion to dismiss under Rule 12(b)(6) challenges the legal sufficiency of the claims stated in the complaint. *See* Fed. R. Civ. P. 12(b)(6). To survive a motion to dismiss, the plaintiff's complaint "must contain sufficient factual matter, accepted as true, to 'state a claim to relief that is plausible on its face.'" *Ashcroft v. Iqbal*, 556 U.S. 662, 678 (2009) (quoting *Bell Atlantic Corp. v. Twombly*, 550 U.S. 544, 570 (2007)). A claim is facially plausible "when the plaintiff pleads factual content that allows the court to draw the reasonable inference that the defendant is liable for the misconduct alleged." *Iqbal*, 556 U.S. at 678. A complaint that offers mere "labels and conclusions" or "a formulaic recitation of the elements of a cause of action will not do." *Id.*; *see also Moss v. U.S. Secret Serv.*, 572 F.3d 962, 969 (9th Cir. 2009) (citing *Iqbal*, 556 U.S. at 678).

In reviewing a Rule 12(b)(6) motion, a court "must accept as true all factual allegations in the complaint and draw all reasonable inferences in favor of the nonmoving party." *Retail Prop. Trust v. United Bhd. of Carpenters & Joiners of Am.*, 768 F.3d 938, 945 (9th Cir. 2014). Thus, "[w]hile legal conclusions can provide the complaint's framework, they must be supported by factual allegations. When there are well-pleaded factual allegations, a court should assume their veracity and then determine whether they plausibly give rise to an entitlement to relief." *Iqbal*, 556 U.S. at 679

IV. DISCUSSION

A. Copyright Infringement

A plaintiff bringing a claim for copyright infringement must sufficiently allege: (1) ownership of a valid copyright, and (2) copying of constituent elements of the work that are original. *Feist Pubs., Inc. v. Rural Tel. Serv. Co.*, 499 U.S. 340, 361 (1991). The "second element has two distinct components: 'copying' and

[3] The parties reference the works by discussing the number of counts or beats each work contains, but arrive at different numbers. First is Plaintiff's Registered Choreography, which he refers to as a 96-count choreography, repeated five times. *See* Opp'n at 16. Defendant refers to the work as including 104 counts of music, repeated five times. *See* Mot. at 4. Second are Plaintiff's steps, which are set to four beats of music and performed twice (but non-consecutively) in the sixteen-beat chorus. Third is the "It's Complicated" emote, which includes sixteen beats of music. Plaintiff's Steps are performed over the first four beats of Defendant's sixteen-beat emote.

'unlawful appropriation.'" *Rentmeester v. Nike, Inc.*, 883 F.3d 1111, 1117 (9th Cir. 2018). Here, Plaintiff alleges ownership of the Registered Choreography and copying. *See* Compl. ¶ 1. The question before this Court is whether the Plaintiff has sufficiently stated a claim of "unlawful appropriation." *Rentmeester*, 883 F.3d at 1117.

To evaluate "unlawful appropriation," courts look to whether the works are "substantially similar." *Rentmeester v. Nike, Inc.*, 883 F.3d 1111, 1118 (9th Cir. 2018). The test for substantial similarity in the Ninth Circuit contains both an "extrinsic" and an "intrinsic" component. The extrinsic component compares "specific criteria which can be listed and analyzed" to determine whether the works are substantially similar. *Funky Films, Inc. v. Time Warner Entm't Co.*, L.P., 462 F.3d 1072, 1077 (9th Cir. 2006). The intrinsic component examines an ordinary person's subjective impressions of the similarities between the two works. *Id.*

"Only the extrinsic test's application may be decided by the court as a matter of law." *Rentmeester*, 883 F.3d at 1118 (citations omitted). Before comparing the works under the extrinsic test, the Court "must 'filter out' the unprotectable elements of the plaintiff's work—primarily ideas and concepts, material in the public domain, and *scènes à faire* (stock or standard features that are commonly associated with the treatment of a given subject)." *Id.* (citations omitted). "The protectable elements that remain are then compared to corresponding elements of the defendant's work to assess similarities in the objective details of the works." *Id.* (citations omitted).

1. Filtering

Defendant argues that Plaintiff's Steps are unprotectable and must therefore be "filtered out" in assessing the similarity between the two works. The Court begins with *Rentmeester*, which both parties rely on. The plaintiff alleged that the defendant, Nike, copied a photograph of Michael Jordan leaping toward basketball hoop with a basketball above his head in a "*grand jeté*" pose. *Rentmeester*, 883 F.3d at 1115. Alone, this pose was unprotectable. *Id.* at 1119.

However, the Ninth Circuit grappled with the difficulty of "filtering out" a work's protected and unprotected elements. *See Rentmeester*, 883 F.3d at 1117–23. The court explained, "[c]ertain types of works can be dissected into protected and unprotected elements more readily than others." *Id.* at 1118. For example, with "novels, plays, and motion pictures," many "protectable elements of expression" like "plot, themes, dialogue, mood, setting, pace, characters, and sequence of events" can be objectively compared. *Id.* at 1118–19.

In terms of "filtering," however, the court explained that, though "photos can be broken down into objective elements that reflect the various creative choices the photographer made in composing the image—choices related to subject matter, pose, lighting, camera angle, depth of field, and the like[,] [citation], none of those elements is subject to copyright protection when viewed in isolation." *Id.* at 1119.

> The Ninth Circuit explained:
>
> For example, a photographer who produces a photo using a highly original lighting technique or a novel camera angle cannot prevent other photographers from using those same techniques to produce new images of their own, provided the new images are not substantially similar to the earlier, copyrighted photo. With respect to a photograph's subject matter, no photographer can claim a monopoly on the right to photograph a particular subject just

> because he was the first to capture it on film. A subsequent photographer is free to take her own photo of the same subject, again so long as the resulting image is not substantially similar to the earlier photograph.

Id. Though one of the photo's "highly original elements" was Jordan's pose, the pose alone was not copyrightable. Rather, the photographer was "entitled to protection only for the way the pose is expressed in his photograph, a product of not just the pose but also the camera angle, timing, and shutter speed [the photographer] chose." *Id.* Nevertheless, the court did not "filter out" the pose or any of the elements that, when "viewed in isolation," would not be subject to protection. *See Id.*

Choreography is similar. Defined as "the composition and arrangement of a related series of dance movements and patterns organized into a coherent whole," choreographic works are composed of a number of individual poses that, when "viewed in isolation," would not be protectable.

Here, Defendant contends that not only are the individual poses unprotectable, but the Steps as a whole—the two-second combination of eight bodily movements, set to four beats of music—are unprotectable. Defendant argues that the Steps are similar to the pose in *Rentmeester*, an idea or "building blocks for a choreographer's expression."[4]

In large part, Defendant relies on guidance from the U.S. Copyright Office, which recognizes the continuum between copyrightable choreography and uncopyrightable dance. *See* U.S. Copyright Office, Compendium of U.S. Copyright Office Practices § 805.1 (3d ed. 2017) ("Compendium (Third)"); *see also Horgan v. Macmillan, Inc.*, 789 F.2d 157, 161 (2d Cir. 1986) ("Social dance steps and simple routines are not copyrightable. . . . Thus, for example, the basic waltz step, the hustle step, and the second position of classical ballet are not copyrightable.").[1] Courts defer to the Copyright Office's views expressed in such materials "only to the extent that those interpretations have the 'power to persuade.'" *Inhale, Inc. v. Starbuzz Tobacco, Inc.*, 755 F.3d 1038, 1042 (9th Cir. 2014), *as amended* (July 9, 2014).

Guidance from the Copyright Office suggests that the Steps are unprotectable. For example, the Copyright Office rejected a claim to steps called the "Floss," but when those steps were incorporated into a longer work, the Copyright Office registered the work. *See* Cendali Decl., Ex. D, Ex. E. The Copyright Office rejected a claim to the "Carlton" because it was merely a "simple routine," *see Id.*, Ex. F at 6, and a claim to a dance called the "Five-Petal Flower" routine, *Id.*, Ex. H. And the Copyright Office explained in its Compendium, that even if the "Made in the USA" dance might be registered as a whole when "[d]uring the chorus, the dancers form the letters 'U, S, A' with their arms. . .the Office would reject a claim limited to the 'U, S, A' gesture." Compendium (Third) § 805.5(A).

---

[4] Conceptually, this is similar to *Newton v. Diamond*, where the district court considered whether three notes sampled from a song were protectable, and decided they were not. *See Newton v. Diamond*, 204 F. Supp. 2d 1244, 1254 (C.D. Cal. 2002). On appeal, the Ninth Circuit "assum[ed] that the sampled segment of the composition was sufficiently original to merit copyright protection, [but] nevertheless affirm[ed] on the ground that [the defendants'] use was *de minimis* and therefore not actionable." *Newton v. Diamond*, 388 F.3d 1189, 1192 (9th Cir. 2004). Plaintiff reads this line to suggest that the Ninth Circuit disagreed with the district court's decision; however, the Ninth Circuit did not reach the question. The parties do not cite any other authorities that would enable the Court to compare music sampling and Defendant's "sampling" of Plaintiff's choreography. Facially, Defendant's conduct here could be analogized to a defendant copying a brief phrase from an underlying musical composition and incorporating that into its own work. However, because the issue is not before the Court, the Court thinks it inappropriate to resolve at this stage.

To a degree, Plaintiff's Steps here involve more creativity than "the basic waltz step, the hustle step, and the second position of classical ballet." *Horgan*, 789 F.2d at 161. But Plaintiff's Steps resemble the Floss, the Carlton, or other examples in the Copyright Compendium:

> José Eduardo da Silva created the choreography for a complex dance production titled, Tango de Janeiro. One of the dances in the production incorporates an extensive number of steps and routines from a social dance. While the overall production could be registered as a choreographic work, the U.S. Copyright Office would reject a claim limited to the adapted social dance.
>
> Butler Beauchamp is a wide receiver for a college football team. Whenever he scores a touchdown, Butler performs a celebratory dance in the endzone. The dance merely consists of a few movements of the legs, shoulders, and arms. The Office would refuse to register this dance as a choreographic work.

See Compendium (Third), §§ 805.4(D), 805.5(A).

Moreover, the Copyright Act's legislative history specifically states that "choreographic works do not include social dance steps and simple routines." H.R. Rep. No. 94-1476, at 54 (1976), reprinted in 1976 U.S.C.C.A.N. at 5667; S. Rep. No. 94-473, at 52 (1975); *see Brantley v. Epic Games, Inc.*, 463 F. Supp. 3d 616, 623 (D. Md. 2020) (discussing, but not deciding, whether the Running Man dance could be subject to copyright protection). And the Compendium recognizes that "social dances, simple routines, and other uncopyrightable movements cannot be registered as separate and distinct works of authorship, *even if they contain a substantial amount of creative expression*." *See* Compendium (Third), § 805.4(D) (emphasis added).

Plaintiff does nothing to distinguish this guidance, simply arguing it is not persuasive without explaining why. Rather, Plaintiff references his originality and creativity in composing the Steps, something to which the Court is sympathetic. *See Rentmeester*, 883 F.3d at 1115; *compare Folkens*, 882 F.3d at 774 ("[A] depiction of two dolphins crossing under sea, one in a vertical posture and the other in a horizontal posture, is an idea first expressed in nature and as such is within the common heritage of humankind."). But whichever way the Court evaluates Plaintiff's Steps—two seconds, four beats of music, or eight body positions, repeated ten times throughout the Registered Choreography—Defendant has the better of the argument. There is no authority to suggest that Plaintiff's Steps are protectable when viewed out of the context of the whole of Plaintiff's work; indeed, the weight of authority suggests otherwise.

On the continuum of choreography, the Steps are closer to a short routine like the "Floss" dance or to the "U, S, A" movements, neither of which would not be protectable. Numerically, the Steps make up as small component of Plaintiff's work, suggesting that the Copyright Office would not register the two-second Steps as a discrete work.[5] "The fact that a dance or movement may contain more than a trivial amount of original authorship is irrelevant to th[e] determination." Compendium (Third), § 805.5(B).

[5] By Plaintiff's count, there are 480 counts of choreography in Plaintiff's total work (96 counts of choreography, repeated five times). The Steps are performed for a total of 40 counts (eight counts in each chorus). This amounts to 8% of Plaintiff's work. The Court references this figure not to suggest that Defendant's copying was *de minimis*, but because it illustrates that Plaintiff's Steps are only a small component of Plaintiff's work. This too weighs against a finding that the Steps are protectable in isolation.

Accordingly, the Court concludes that, like in *Rentmeester*, Plaintiff is "entitled to protection only for the way the [Steps] [are] expressed in his [Registered Choreography]," a product of the various creative choices Plaintiff made in composing the Registered Choreography—i.e., in the entire five-minute work. *See Rentmeester*, 883 F.3d at 1119; *see also Feist*, 499 U.S. at 347–48 (finding that an author's selection and arrangement of factual material are entitled to protection if sufficiently original, even though the author cannot claim copyright protection for the underlying factual material).

2. Substantial Similarity

With the above discussion in mind, the Court evaluates the "similarities in the objective details of the works." *Rentermeester*, 883 F.3d at 1118. (citations omitted). In conducting an extrinsic analysis, the Ninth Circuit requires the works to be "considered as a whole." *Apple Comput., Inc. v. Microsoft Corp.*, 35 F.3d 1435, 1443 (9th Cir. 1994).[6]

Choreographic works are based on a myriad of creative elements, including rhythmic movement in a defined space, compositional arrangement, musical or textual accompaniment,[7] dramatic content, presentation before an audience, and execution by skilled performance. *See* Compendium (Third), § 805.2(A)–(F). Here, the two works are not substantially similar, because other than the four identical counts of poses—which are unprotected alone—Plaintiff and Defendant's works do not share any creative elements. *See Pasillas v. McDonald's Corp.*, 927 F.2d 440, 443 (9th Cir. 1991) (no infringement where unprotectable elements copied). The two works contain a series of different poses performed in different settings and by different types of performers: Plaintiff's dance is performed by humans in the physical world, and Defendant's Emote by animated characters in a virtual world. The works are performed for different audiences, as Plaintiff's video was performed at Plaintiff's dance studio and published for a YouTube audience. Defendant's Emote is performed by *Fortnite* players in-game for an in-game audience. Beyond the Steps, Plaintiff identifies no other similar creative elements in Plaintiff and Defendant's choreographic works.

Therefore, dismissal of Plaintiff's copyright claims is appropriate.

B. Unfair Competition Law

Next, Defendant moves to dismiss Plaintiff's Unfair Competition Claim, which Defendant asserts is preempted by the Copyright Act.[8] The Ninth Circuit applies a two-part test to evaluate preemption in this context. *See Laws v. Sony Music Ent. Inc.*, 448 F.3d 1134, 1137 (9th Cir. 2006).

---

[6] Though Defendant argues that the Steps make up only a small portion of the entirety of the *Fortnite* ecosystem, this invites an incorrect analysis: in *Newton*, the Ninth Circuit recognized that the substantiality of the copying "is measured by considering the qualitative and quantitative significance of the copied portion in relation to the *plaintiff's* work as a whole." *Newton*, 388 F.3d at 1192 (emphasis added).

[7] Here, Plaintiff's copyright registration excludes music. *See* Compl., Ex. A.\

[8] Defendant also makes a motion to strike based on anti-SLAPP grounds. Because Plaintiff's unfair competition claim is preempted, the Court need not address this motion.

There is no dispute that the first element of the test, whether the "subject matter" of the state law claim falls within the "subject matter" of copyright, is satisfied. Thus, the Court turns to the second element—whether the rights asserted under state law are equivalent to the "exclusive rights" of copyright holders. *Id.* at 1137–38; *see also Maloney v. T3Media, Inc.*, 853 F.3d 1004, 1019 (9th Cir. 2017).

1. Equivalent Rights Requirement

Section 106 affords copyright owners the "exclusive rights" to display, perform, reproduce, or distribute copies of a copyrighted work, to authorize others to do those things, and to prepare derivative works based upon the copyrighted work. *Maloney*, 853 F.3d at 1019 (citing 17 U.S.C. § 106). "To survive preemption, the state cause of action must protect the rights which are qualitatively different from the copyright rights. The state claim must have an extra element which changes the nature of the action." *Id.* (citation omitted).

Plaintiff argues that Defendant's use of the Registered Choreography created a "false impression" that Plaintiff endorsed *Fortnite*. Opp'n at 22–23 (citing Compl. at ¶¶ 48–49, 83–84). However, the cited portions of the complaint make clear that Plaintiff's claim is based on the copying of Plaintiff's registered choreography.[9] Without more, this is insufficient to avoid preemption. *See Brantley*, 463 F. Supp. 3d at 623; *see also Pellegrino v. Epic Games, Inc.*, 451 F. Supp. 3d 373, 390 n. 9 (E.D. Pa. 2020)

Laws, which held that the Copyright Act preempted the plaintiff's right to publicity claim, is illustrative. *Laws v. Sony Music Ent. Inc.*, 448 F.3d 1134, 1137 (9th Cir. 2006). There, the plaintiff brought a right of publicity claim against a defendant who reproduced a sample of the plaintiff's voice in a song. *Id.* at 1136. The court held that even though the right to publicity claim included an additional element—"commercial use"—plaintiff's claim was still, in essence, a copyright claim. *Id.*; *see also Del Madera Props. v. Rhodes & Gardner*, 820 F.2d 973, 977 (9th Cir. 1987), *overruled on other grounds, Fogerty v. Fantasy, Inc.*, 510 U.S. 517 (1994) (finding unfair competition claim preempted where plaintiff alleged unlawful misappropriation that was "part and parcel of the copyright claim").

Here, too, Plaintiff's argument that Epic's use of the choreography involves the additional element of "false endorsement" does not transform the nature of the action. *See* Compl. ¶ 84 ("By misappropriating Hanagami's dance and through the improper copying and use of the Registered Choreography, Defendants have engaged in business acts or practices that constitute unfair competition [.]"). To the contrary, the unfair competition claim is based exclusively on the misappropriation of the original work, which is "part and parcel of the copyright claim." *See Del Madera*, 920 F.2d at 977.

Therefore, Plaintiff's Unfair Competition claim is preempted by the Copyright Act.

V. CONCLUSION

For the foregoing reasons, Defendant's motion to dismiss is GRANTED.

IT IS SO ORDERED.

---

[9] Paragraphs 48 and 49 assert in a conclusory manner that Defendant created a "false impression that Hanagami endorsed Fortnite." Without additional facts, these conclusions are insufficient to state a claim or "transform the nature of the action." *Laws*, 448 F.3d at 1144.

APPENDIX

Plaintiff's Choreography | **Defendant's Emote**

1.

2.

3.

4.

5.

6.

7.

8.

9.

10.

11.

11/16/2021 4:20 PM
Marilyn Burgess—District Clerk Harris County
Envelope No. 59200503
By: Lisa Thomas
Filed: 11/16/2021 4:20 PM

CAUSE NO. ____________

EDGAR RAUL ACOSTA, INDIVIDUALLY, AND AS REPRESENTATIVE OF THE ESTATE OF AXEL ACOSTA, DECEASED, GLEYSY SIMEONI, ON BEHALF OF MINOR CHILD G.S., ADRIAN GALVAN, JR., ADYAMI GIL DE LAMADRID, ALEXIA PENA, ALEXIA TORRES, ALEXIS SAMANTHA GRAY, ALYSSA CURIEL, ADAM EKLEBERRY, ANGELINA FLORES ON BEHALF OF MINOR CHILDREN O.J.R. and F.C.R., ANNE-MARIE COWART FAVORITI, INDIVIDUALLY, AND ON BEHALF OF MINOR CHILD, C.M.F., ARIANNA MEDLIN, ARIONA CISNEROS, AYXA LARA, CHRISTOPHER GONZALEZ, BRIANNA SANCHEZ, BRITTANY CASTANEDA, BRITTANY GARZA, CHARLES ALFORD, CHASE PERALES, CRUZ V. RAMIREZ-CERON ON BEHALF OF MINOR CHILD B.S., DARIAN ALEXANDRIA ECHEVARRIA-JUARBE, DEJUAN ADAMS, DENISE STALCUP ON BEHALF OF MINOR CHILD A.S., DERRICK DAY, DEVIN PROPES, DOMINIQUE CHRISTOPHER, EMALAY WOZNIAK, EMILY CARBAJAL, ERIK SIFUENTES, GABRIELA ALEJANDRA RODRIGUEZ, GERLEENA CALHOUN ON BEHALF OF MINOR CHILD B.W., HEIDI ORTIZ, IRENA PEREZ, IZAK	§ §	IN THE DISTRICT COURT OF

ISMAEL CARBAJAL, JASMINE	§	
RANGEL, JODI VELLA	§	
INDIVIDUALLY, AND ON BEHALF	§	
OF MINOR CHILD A.G., JOSEPH	§	
VILLARREAL, KASSANDRA	§	
TORRES, KATRINA MCCUEN,	§	
KIMBERLY SANCHEZ, LEANN	§	
GERMAN, LETHANIEL ORDELL,	§	
LORAN SALINAS, MALCOM AVERY	§	
JOHNSON, OMAR LUNA, PATRICK	§	
EDWARD TAPAYAN, PEGGY	§	
VARGAS ON BEHALF OF MINOR	§	
CHILD J.F.E., PENNIE JACKSON,	§	
SAMANTHA CERDA, TYLER	§	
VARGAS, VICTOR HERNANDEZ,	§	
JR., INDIVIDUALLY, AND	§	
ON BEHALF OF MINOR	§	
CHILD V.J.H., VICTORIA	§	
STOCKMAN, YASMIN	§	
GONZALEZ, YOLANDA	§	
ALMENDAREZ, LARISSA	§	
TORRES, ON BEHALF	§	
OF MINOR CHILD R.T., ANDREW	§	
SOSA, JIMMY LEAL, KEITH	§	
SCHEFFIELD, LANA BLACKMAN	§	
ON BEHALF OF MINOR CHILD	§	
W.B., JAMES COSTELLO, JORGE	§	
OLVERA, ANGEL JAVIER SILVA,	§	
JR., EVONNE CARDENAS,	§	
INDIVIDUALLY AND ON BEHALF	§	HARRIS COUNTY, TEXAS
OF MINOR CHILD C.D., ROSA	§	
SERENO ON BEHALF OF MINOR	§	
CHILD I.S., JESUS ULYSES MEJIA,	§	
JAVIER VERA, MARIA SHIPLEY,	§	
INDIVIDUALLY AND ON BEHALF	§	
OF MINOR CHILDREN N.S. AND J.S.,	§	
SALMA RUIZ SANDOVAL,	§	
SHIRLINA MOHAMED ON BEHALF	§	
OF MINOR CHILD F.P., LETICIA	§	
LONG, JORGE LOPEZ ON BEHALF	§	
OF MINOR CHILD G.L., TIMOTHY	§	
CORNETT, JUAN TENIENTE,	§	
DESHAWN JONES, LUIS	§	
RODRIGUEZ, JR., ALAIHN	§	
VASQUEZ, DANIEL VASQUEZ,	§	

IGNACIO LARA, JR., ERIK	§	
GIRALDEZ, JUAN GARZA,	§	
GILBERT VASQUEZ, III, JASON	§	
RODRIGUEZ, IZABELLA RAMIREZ,	§	
EMMANUEL VARGAS, LINDSAY	§	
ELAINE AYALA, KAELYN AYALA,	§	
RASHAWNDA BROOKS ON BEHALF	§	
OF MINOR CHILD S.B., STEPHAN	§	
JAMES HESTER, JOSE RODRIGUEZ,	§	
CHRISTIAN HINOJOSA, BRYAN	§	
RODRIGUEZ, NICOLAS ALVAREZ,	§	
ALEX LONGORIA, XENN FRIETZE,	§	
JESIKAH RICHMOND, ON BEHALF	§	
OF MINOR CHILD C.G., ETHAN	§	
GREEN, TIM SHARKEY, GREGORIO	§	
VILLANUEVA, GERARDO A.	§	
VILLANUEVA, NICOLAS	§	
MELENDEZ, ERICA SUTTON, JUAN	§	
GUERRERO, MARKEYONNA	§	
BENTON, HORTENCIA FRAUSTO,	§	
BRENDA STRAYTON, MICHAEL	§	
CARPENTER, JUAN GARCIA,	§	
DAMETRICE POTTS, MARIAH	§	
OCHA, ANDRE BOOKER, DESIREE	§	
GRACIA, ADELA ALVAREZ,	§	
PHILLIP CONN ON BEHALF OF	§	
MINOR CHILD A.C., MADISON	§	
DIES, MICHAEL RASSI ON BEHALF	§	
OF MINOR CHILD A.R., JACOB	§	
HERNANDEZ, JEREMY CORTINAS,	§	
and SELENA ELIZONDO,	§	
Plaintiffs,	§	JUDICIAL DISTRICT
	§	
v.	§	
	§	
APPLE, INC., JACQUES BERMAN	§	
WEBSTER, II aka TRAVIS SCOTT,	§	
ABREY GRAHAM aka DRAKE,	§	
TRISTAR SPORTS &	§	
ENTERTAINMENT GROUP,	§	
CACTUS JACK RECORDS, LLC,	§	
GRAND HUSTLE MANAGEMENT,	§	
INC. d/b/a GRAND HUSTLE	§	
RECORDS, EPIC RECORDS, INC.	§	
d/b/a EPIC RECORDS, ASM	§	
GLOBAL, LLC, ASM GLOBAL	§	
PARENT, INC., SCOREMORE	§	
HOLDINGS, LLC, SCOREMORE	§	

<table>
<tr><td>LLC, SCOREMORE, MGMT, LLC,
SASCHA STONE
GUTTFREUND, LIVE NATION
WORLDWIDE, INC., LIVE NATION
ENTERTAINMENT, INC., DARRYL
LAMONTE PLATT,
CONTEMPORARY SERVICES
CORPORATION, APEX SECURITY,
MARK MILLER, KEITH DREW
BUTLER, FUSE TECHNICAL
GROUP, LLC, PARADOCS
WORLDWIDE, Inc. d/b/a PARADOCS
EVENT MEDICAL SERVICES,
SOUTH TEXAS EMS, LLC,
RE:SOURCE EVENT GROUP, LLC,
STATE PATROL SERVICES, LLC
d/b/a SPS SECURITY, VALLE
SECURITY TEXAS, LLC, TREY
HICKS, and Harris County Sports &
Convention Corporation,
Defendants.</td><td>§
§
§
§
§
§
§
§
§
§
§
§
§
§
§
§
§
§
§
§
§</td><td>

JURY TRIAL DEMANDED</td></tr>
</table>

PLAINTIFFS' ORIGINAL PETITION

I.
INTRODUCTION

On November 5, 2021, well over 50,000 mostly young people attended a two-day concert put on by Travis Scott and the other Defendants, and live streamed by Apple Music. Before the first night of the concert was through, eight of the concertgoers were dead, two others died days later, and scores of others were severely injured. One of the deceased is twenty-one-year-old Axel Acosta. Axel was crushed by the incited, unruly and out-of-control crowd with such force that he could no longer breath; with such force that the air in his lungs was literally slowly squeezed out of him, sending his heart into cardiac arrest. When Axel collapsed, he was trampled by those fighting to prevent themselves from being crushed. As he lay there under a mass of humanity, dying, the music played and streamed on—for almost forty minutes. When Axel was finally removed from the thick of human bodies by a few good Samaritans, he lay lifeless on the wet, littered grass at the edge of the chaos, while frantic and understaffed medical professionals worked to restart his heart—to no avail. Axel died that night on the muddy ground at a concert he attended for fun. Axel Acosta loved and adored Travis Scott and the other performers at Astroworld—the feeling was not mutual; certainly, neither Travis Scott nor his exclusive partners, streaming service, record labels, handlers, entourage, managers, agents, hangers on, promoters, organizers,[1] or sponsors cared enough about Axel Acosta and the other concertgoers to make an even minimal effort to keep them safe.

The victims on that night went to Astroworld for fun. Neither they nor their families were ever warned that they were walking into an extremely dangerous situation. The deaths and injuries that occurred were needless[2] and senseless, and the suffering caused the families and all others involved will be endless. This case is brought by more than 125 victims of the Defendants' senseless gross negligence. The damages sought are those for the loss of mental and physical health, and human life. **The Plaintiffs bring this case, in this Honorable Court, seeking more than $750,000,000**. No amount of money will ever make these Plaintiffs whole; no amount of money can restore human life. But, the damages sought in this case attempts to fix, help, or make up for the harms and losses suffered by these Plaintiffs—nothing more and nothing less. The quantum sought includes sufficient punitive damages to punish and make an example

---

[1] The Plaintiffs have been offered a full refund for the cost of the concert. Such offer is a transparent and grotesque effort of the Defendants to limit their liability, after the fact, to the families of those killed or injured. These Defendants will no doubt argue that their exposure is limited to the price of the ticket, and, failing that, will attempt to force all concertgoers—regardless of their age or adequate notice—into binding arbitration, so a jury trial can be avoided. Attempts in this regard are based on a hidden legal language that is difficult to find for an attorney, and is rarely if ever seen by the concert goer.

[2] The concertgoers were placed in needless endangerment. Needless endangerment is always negligent—in this case grossly negligent. No one exercising ordinary care ever needlessly endangers anyone; prudent promoters and organizers of concerts simply do not needlessly endanger anyone. It is axiomatic that, when there are two available ways to accomplish the same benefit and the second safest choice contains some danger and the first safest choice does not, then failing to choose the safer choice is unreasonable, and negligent. Safer is always better. Second safest is never good enough. "Safe enough" does not count, especially when the activities involve children. The bottom line is this: nothing is safe enough when it allows danger when a safer choice can achieve the identical benefit.

of all involved in the streaming, promotion, organization and failed execution of the concert, and also to encourage those who engage in such activity in the future to do so with safety at the forefront, not just as an afterthought.[3]

II.
DISCOVERY CONTROL PLAN

This case is intended to be governed by Discovery Level 3.

III. PARTIES

Plaintiff **Edgar Raul Acosta**, as next friend of Axel Acosta, deceased, resides in Washington state.

Plaintiff **Gleysy Simeoni**, is an individual, residing in Harris County, Texas. She is the guardian of minor child G.S.

Plaintiff **Adrian Galvan, Jr.** is an individual, residing in Harris County, Texas.

Plaintiff **Adyami Gil De Lamadrid** is an individual, residing in Harris County, Texas.

Plaintiff **Alexia Pena** is an individual, residing in Harris County, Texas.

Plaintiff **Alexia Torres** is an individual, residing in Harris County, Texas.

Plaintiff **Alexis Samantha Gray** is an individual, residing in Harris County, Texas.

Plaintiff **Alyssa Curiel** is an individual, residing in Harris County, Texas.

Plaintiff **Adam Ekleberry** is an individual, residing in Denton County, Texas.

Plaintiff **Angelina Flores**, filing on behalf of two minor children O.J.R and F.C.R, is an individual, residing in Hidalgo County, Texas.

Plaintiff **Anne-Marie Cowart Favoriti**, filing on behalf of herself and the minor child C.M.F. is an individual, residing in Harris County, Texas.

Plaintiff **Arianna Medlin** is an individual, residing in Harris County, Texas.

Plaintiff **Ariona Cisneros** is an individual, residing in Harris County, Texas.

Plaintiff **Ayxa Lara** is an individual, residing in Harris County, Texas.

Plaintiff **Christopher Gonzalez** is an individual, residing in Hidalgo County, Texas.

Plaintiff **Brianna Sanchez** is an individual, residing in Harris County, Texas.

Plaintiff **Brittany Castaneda** is an individual, residing in Galveston County, Texas.

---

[3] Webster has indicated that he intends to pay for the funeral expenses of the deceased. He has made sure that his intentions in this regard were publicly reported. The Acosta family would rather Webster have privately spent money on proper planning, adequate security and medical staff before the concert, instead of publicly stating that he would pay for the funerals of those that were crushed and killed. Webster's efforts, regardless of their insincerity, are far too little, and far too late.

Plaintiff **Brittany Garza** is an individual, residing in Texas.

Plaintiff **Charles Alford** is an individual, residing in Kings County, New York.

Plaintiff **Chase Perales** is an individual, residing in Texas.

Plaintiff **Cruz V. Ramirez-Ceron**, filing on behalf of minor child B.S., is an individual, residing in Harris County, Texas.

Plaintiff **Darian Alexandria Echevarria-Juarbe** is an individual, residing in Harris County, Texas.

Plaintiff **Dejuan Adams** is an individual, residing in Fort Bend County, Texas.

Plaintiff **Denise Stalcup**, filing on behalf of minor child A.S., is an individual, residing in Montgomery County, Texas.

Plaintiff **Derrick Day** is an individual, residing in Harris County, Texas.

Plaintiff **Devin Propes** is an individual, residing in Texas.

Plaintiff **Dominique Christopher** is an individual, residing in Harris County, Texas.

Plaintiff **Emalay Wozniak** is an individual, residing in Montgomery County, Texas.

Plaintiff **Emily Carbajal** is an individual, residing in Texas.

Plaintiff **Erik Sifuentes** is an individual, residing in Harris County, Texas.

Plaintiff **Gabriela Alejandra Rodriguez** is an individual, residing in Hidalgo County, Texas.

Plaintiff **Gerleena Calhoun**, filing on behalf of minor child B.W., is an individual, residing in Cuyohoga County, Ohio.

Plaintiff **Heidi Ortiz** is an individual, residing in Harris County, Texas.

Plaintiff **Irena Perez** is an individual, residing in Harris County, Texas.

Plaintiff **Izak Ismael Carbajal** is an individual, residing in Harris County, Texas.

Plaintiff **Jasmine Rangel** is an individual, residing in Texas.

Plaintiff **Jodi Vella**, filing on behalf of minor child A.G., is an individual, residing in Galveston County, Texas.

Plaintiff **Joseph Villarreal** is an individual, residing in Harris County, Texas.

Plaintiff **Kassandra Torres** is an individual, residing in Brazoria County, Texas.

Plaintiff **Katrina McCuen** is an individual, residing in Galveston County, Texas.

Plaintiff **Kimberly Sanchez** is an individual, residing in Harris County, Texas.

Plaintiff **Leann German** is an individual, residing in Texas.

Plaintiff **Lethaniel Ordell** is an individual, residing in Willoughby County, Ohio.

Plaintiff **Loran Salinas** is an individual, residing in Harris County, Texas.

Plaintiff **Malcom Avery Johnson** is an individual, residing in Baltimore County, Maryland.

Plaintiff **Omar Luna** is an individual, residing in Los Angeles County, California.

Plaintiff **Patrick Edward Tapayan** is an individual, residing in Travis County, Texas.

Plaintiff **Peggy Vargas**, filing on behalf of minor child J.F.E., is an individual, residing in Harris County, Texas.

Plaintiff **Pennie Jackson** is an individual, residing in Harris County, Texas.

Plaintiff **Samantha Cerda** is an individual, residing in Harris County, Texas.

Plaintiff **Tyler Vargas** is an individual, residing in Harris County, Texas.

Plaintiff **Victor Hernandez, Jr.**, filing on behalf of himself and the minor child V.J.H. is an individual, residing in Harris County, Texas.

Plaintiff **Victoria Stockman** is an individual, residing in Travis County, Texas.

Plaintiff **Yasmin Gonzalez** is an individual, residing in Texas.

Plaintiff **Yolanda Almendarez** is an individual, residing in Harris County, Texas.

Plaintiff **Larissa Torres**, filing on behalf of minor child R.T., is an individual, residing in Harris County, Texas.

Plaintiff **Andrew Sosa** is an individual, residing in Hidalgo County, Texas.

Plaintiff **Jimmy Leal** is an individual, residing in Harris County, Texas.

Plaintiff **Keith Scheffield** is an individual, residing in Harris County, Texas.

Plaintiff **Lana Blackman**, filing on behalf of minor child W.B., is an individual, residing in Bell County, Texas.

Plaintiff **James Costello** is an individual, residing in Harris County, Texas.

Plaintiff **Jorge Olvera** is an individual, residing in Harris County, Texas.

Plaintiff **Angel Javier Silva, Jr.** is an individual, residing in Harris County, Texas.

Plaintiff **Evonne Cardenas**, filing on behalf of herself and the minor child C.D., is an individual, residing in Harris County, Texas.

Plaintiff **Rosa Sereno**, filing on behalf of minor child L.S., is an individual, residing in Harris County, Texas.

Plaintiff **Jesus Ulyses Mejia** is an individual, residing in Harris County, Texas.

Plaintiff **Javier Vera** is an individual, residing in Harris County, Texas.

Plaintiff **Maria Shipley**, filing on behalf of herself and the minor children N.S. and J.S., is an individual, residing in Harris County, Texas.

Plaintiff **Salma Ruiz Sandoval** is an individual, residing in Hidalgo County, Texas.

Plaintiff **Shirlina Mohamed**, filing on behalf of minor child F.P., is an individual, residing in Harris County, Texas.

Plaintiff **Leticia Long** is an individual, residing in Harris County, Texas.

Plaintiff **Jorge Lopez**, filing on behalf of minor child G.L., is an individual, residing in Texas.

Plaintiff **Timothy Cornett** is an individual, residing in Galveston County, Texas.

Plaintiff **Juan Teniente** is an individual, residing in Dallas County, Texas.

Plaintiff **Deshawn Jones** is an individual, residing in Harris County, Texas.

Plaintiff **Luis Rodriguez, Jr.** is an individual, residing in Harris County, Texas.

Plaintiff **Aliahn Vasquez** is an individual, residing in Hidalgo County, Texas.

Plaintiff **Daniel Vasquez** is an individual, residing in Texas.

Plaintiff **Ignacio Lara, Jr.** is an individual, residing in Harris County, Texas.

Plaintiff **Erik Giraldez** is an individual, residing in Texas.

Plaintiff **Juan Garza** is an individual, residing in Harris County, Texas.

Plaintiff **Gilbert Vasquez, III** is an individual, residing in Harris County, Texas.

Plaintiff **Jason Rodriguez** is an individual, residing in Harris County, Texas.

Plaintiff **Izabella Ramirez** is an individual, residing in Galveston County, Texas.

Plaintiff **Emmanuel Vargas** is an individual, residing in Harris County, Texas.

Plaintiff **Lindsay Elaine Ayala** is an individual, residing in Harris County, Texas.

Plaintiff **Kaelyn Ayala** is an individual, residing in Harris County, Texas.

Plaintiff **Rashawnda Brooks**, filing on behalf of minor child S.B., is an individual, residing in Harris County, Texas.

Plaintiff **Stephan James Hester** is an individual, residing in Harris County, Texas.

Plaintiff **Jose Rodriguez** is an individual, residing in Dallas County, Texas.

Plaintiff **Christian Hinojosa** is an individual, residing in Harris County, Texas.

Plaintiff **Bryan Rodriguez** is an individual, residing in Harris County, Texas.

Plaintiff **Nicolas Alvarez** is an individual, residing in Texas.

Plaintiff **Alex Longoria** is an individual, residing in Texas.

Plaintiff **Xenn Frietze** is an individual, residing in Texas.

Plaintiff **Jesikah Richmond**, filing on behalf of minor child C.G., is an individual, residing in Harris County, Texas.

Plaintiff **Ethan Green** is an individual, residing in Harris County, Texas.

Plaintiff **Tim Sharkey** is an individual, residing in Webb County, Texas.

Plaintiff **Gregorio Villanueva** is an individual, residing in Harris County, Texas.

Plaintiff **Gerardo A. Villanueva** is an individual, residing in Harris County, Texas.

Plaintiff **Nicolas Melendez** is an individual, residing in Texas.

Plaintiff **Erica Sutton** is an individual, residing in Texas.

Plaintiff **Juan Guerrero** is an individual, residing in Texas.

Plaintiff **Markeyonna Benton** is an individual, residing in Texas.

Plaintiff **Hortencia Frausto** is an individual, residing in Harris County, Texas.

Plaintiff **Brenda Strayton** is an individual, residing in Wharton County, Texas.

Plaintiff **Michael Carpenter** is an individual, residing in Harris County, Texas.

Plaintiff **Juan Garcia** is an individual, residing in San Bernardino County, California

Plaintiff **Dametrice Potts** is an individual, residing in Texas.

Plaintiff **Mariah Ocha** is an individual, residing in Texas.

Plaintiff **Andre Booker** is an individual, residing in Wharton County, Texas.

Plaintiff **Desiree Gracia** is an individual, residing in Fort Bend County, Texas.

Plaintiff **Adela Alvarez** is an individual, residing in Fort Bend County, Texas.

Plaintiff **Phillip Conn**, filing on behalf of minor child A.C., is an individual, residing in Harris County, Texas.

Plaintiff **Madison Dies** is an individual, residing in West Baton Rouge Parish, Louisiana.

Plaintiff **Michael Rassi**, filing on behalf of minor child A.R., is an individual, residing in Harris County, Texas.

Plaintiff **Jacob Hernandez** is an individual, residing in Galveston County, Texas.

Plaintiff **Jeremy Cortinas** is an individual, residing in San Bernadino County, California.

Plaintiff **Selena Elizondo** is an individual, residing in Hidalgo County, Texas.

Defendant **Apple, Inc.** is a foreign corporation formed under California law and based in Cupertino, California. Defendant has systematic, continuous, and specific contacts conduct, and business activities, including, but not limited to, its conduct relating to the subject incident, within Texas such that it is at home in the state. This Defendant may be served through its Texas based registered agent, C T Corp System, at 1999 Bryan St., Ste. 900, Dallas, TX 75201-3136 USA.

Defendant **Jacques Berman Webster, II aka "Travis Scott"** is an individual domiciled in the state of California. Defendant Webster has systematic, continuous, and specific contacts, conduct, and business activities, including, but not limited to, maintaining a home in Texas at 5750 Main Street Houston, Texas 77005, as well as his conduct relating to the subject incident, within Texas such that he is at home in the state. Defendant Webster may be served via the Texas Secretary of State at P.O. Box 12079 Austin, Texas 78711-2079, to be forwarded to Defendant at his home address of 12255 Sky Lane, Los Angeles, California 90049.

Defendant **Aubrey Drake Graham aka "Drake"** is an individual domiciled in the state of California. Defendant Graham has systematic, continuous, and specific contacts, conduct, and business activities, including, but not limited to, his conduct relating to the subject incident, within Texas such that he is at home in the state. Defendant Webster may be served via the Texas Secretary of State at P.O. Box 12079 Austin, Texas 78711-2079, to be forwarded to Defendant at his home address of 5841 Round Meadow Road, Hidden Hills, California 91302.

Defendant **Tristar Sports & Entertainment Group, Inc.** is a foreign corporation formed under Delaware law and based in Nashville, Tennessee. Defendant has systematic, continuous, and specific contacts conduct, and business activities, including, but not limited to, its conduct relating to the subject incident, within Texas such that it is at home in the state. This Defendant may be served through the Secretary of State of Texas at P.O. Box 12079 Austin, Texas 78711-2079, to be forwarded to its Tennessee based registered agent, Louise M. Taylor, at 11 Music Cir S, Nashville, Tennessee 37203-4335.

Defendant **Cactus Jack Records, LLC** is a Limited Liability Company formed under Texas law and is based in Houston, Texas. It may be served with process through its registered agent Resident Agent, Inc. at 823 Congress Avenue, Suite P-4, Austin, TX 78701.

Defendant **Grand Hustle Management, Inc. d/b/a Grand Hustle Records** is a foreign corporation formed under Georgia law and based in Atlanta, Georgia. Defendant has systematic, continuous, and specific contacts conduct, and business activities, including, but not limited to, its conduct relating to the subject incident, within Texas such that it is at home in the state. This Defendant may be served through the Secretary of State of Texas at P.O. Box 12079 Austin, Texas 78711-2079, to be forwarded to its Georgia based registered agent, Tai Greene, at 2221 Peachtree Rd., STE D-325, Atlanta, GA, 30309.

Defendant **Epic Records, Inc. d/b/a Epic Records** is a foreign corporation formed under New York law and based in New York, New York. Defendant has systematic, continuous, and specific contacts conduct, and business activities, including, but not limited to, its conduct relating to the subject incident, within Texas such that it is at home in the state. This Defendant may be served through the Secretary of State of Texas at P.O. Box 12079 Austin, Texas 78711-2079, to be forwarded to its New York based registered agent, Corporation Service Company, at 80 State Street, Albany, New York 12207-2543.

Defendant **ASM Global, LLC** is a limited liability company formed under Delaware law and based in West Conshohocken, Pennsylvania. This Defendant may be served through its Texas based registered agent, Corporation Service Company dba CSC—Lawyers Incorporating Service Company, at 211 E. 7th Street, Suite 620 Austin, Texas.

Defendant **ASM Global Parent, Inc.** is a corporation formed under Delaware law and based in West Conshohocken, Pennsylvania. This Defendant may be served through its Texas based registered agent, Corporation Service Company dba CSC—Lawyers Incorporating Service Company, at 211 E. 7th Street, Suite 620 Austin, Texas.

Defendant **Mark Miller** is an individual domiciled in the State of Texas. He may be served with citation through personal service at his domicile in Fort Bend County, Texas located at 10060 Plantation Mill PL, APT P, Missouri City, Texas 77459-6530 or wherever he may be found.

Defendant **Keith Drew Butler** is an individual domiciled in the State of Texas. He may be served with citation through personal service at his place of business in Harris County, Texas located at NRG Stadium, South Lobby, Houston, Texas 77054 or wherever he may be found.

Defendant **Scoremore Holdings, LLC** is a limited liability company formed under Texas law and based in Houston, Texas. It may be served with process by serving its registered agent Corporate Creations Network Inc. at 4265 San Felipe 1100, Houston, Texas 77027.

Defendant **Scoremore, LLC** is a limited liability company formed under Texas law and based in Austin, Travis County, Texas. It may be served with process by serving its registered agent Sascha Stone Guttfreund at 5704 West Hwy 290, Austin, Texas 78735.

Defendant **Scoremore Mgmt, LLC** is a limited liability company formed under Texas law and based in Austin, Travis County, Texas. It may be served with process by serving its registered agent Sascha Stone Guttfreund at 5704 West Hwy 290, Austin, Texas 78735.

Defendant **Sascha Stone Guttfreund** is an individual domiciled in the state of Texas. Defendant Gutt freund may be served at her domicile located at 5704 West Hwy 290, Austin, Texas 78735, or wherever she may be found.

Defendant **Trey Hicks** is an individual domiciled in the State of Texas. He may be served with citation through personal service at his domicile in Williamson County, Texas located at 4133 Sequoia Trail W, Georgetown, Texas 78628-1430 or wherever he may be found.

Defendant **Live Nation Worldwide, Inc.** is a corporation formed under Delaware law and based in Austin, Texas. Defendant has systematic, continuous, and specific contacts conduct, and business activities, including, but not limited to, its conduct relating to the subject incident, within Texas such that it is at home in the state. This Defendant may be served through its registered agent, Corporate Creations Network Inc., at 5444 Westheimer #1000 Houston, TX 77056.

Defendant **Live Nation Entertainment, Inc.** is a foreign corporation formed under Delaware law and based in Beverly Hills, California. Defendant has systematic, continuous, and specific contacts conduct, and business activities, including, but not limited to, its conduct relating to the subject incident, within Texas such that it is at home in the state. This Defendant may be served through its local registered agent, Corporate Creations Network Inc., at 5444 Westheimer #1000 Houston, TX 77056.

Defendant **Darryl Lamonte Platt** is an individual domiciled in the State of Texas. He may be served with citation through personal service at his domicile in Brazoria County, Texas located at 2614 Sunshade Ct, Pearland, Texas 77584-4076 or wherever he may be found.

Defendant **Contemporary Services Corporation** is a foreign corporation formed under California law and based in Northridge, California. Defendant has systematic, continuous, and specific contacts conduct, and business activities, including, but not limited to, its conduct relating to the subject incident, within Texas such that it is at home in the state. This Defendant may be served through its Texas based registered agent, Corporation Service Company dba CSC—Lawyers Incorporating Service Company, at 211 E. 7th Street, Suite 620 Austin, Texas.

Defendant **Apex Security** is an unincorporated sole proprietorship formed under the laws of Texas and based in Humble, Texas. It is owned by Wilfredo P. Ordonez, who may be served at 16819 Vandergrift Drive, Humble, Texas or wherever he may be found.

Defendant **Paradocs Worldwide, Inc.** is a foreign corporation formed under New York law and based in New York City, New York. Defendant has systematic, continuous, and specific contacts conduct, and business activities, including, but not limited to, its conduct relating to the subject incident, within Texas such that it is at home in the state. This Defendant may be served through the Secretary of State of Texas at P.O. Box 12079 Austin, Texas 78711-2079, to be forwarded to its New York based registered agent, The Corporation, at 550 Vanderbilt Avenue, Suite #722, Brooklyn, New York, United States, 11238.

Defendant **South Texas EMS, LLC** is a limited liability company formed under Texas law and based in Houston, Texas. This Defendant may be served at its principal place of business at 9898 Bissonnet Street, Houston, Texas, 77036.

Defendant **Valle Security Texas, LLC** is a limited liability company formed under Texas law and based in Grand Prairie, Texas. This Defendant may be served through its registered agent Johnathan Elliot at 1313 Burleson St. Grand Prairie, TX 75050.

Defendant **State Patrol Services, LLC d/b/a SPS Security** is a limited liability company formed under Texas law and based in Houston, Texas. This Defendant may be served through its registered agent Sirwan Hasan Muhammed, at 1600 Eldridge Pkwy #1004 Houston, Texas 77077USA.

Defendant **Re:source Event Group, LLC** is a foreign limited liability company formed under Florida law and based in Miramar, Florida. Defendant has systematic, continuous, and specific contacts conduct, and business activities, including, but not limited to, its conduct relating to the subject incident, within Texas such that it is at home in the state. This Defendant may be served through the Secretary of State of Texas at P.O. Box 12079 Austin, Texas 78711-2079, to be forwarded to its Florida based registered agent, Eric R. Rodriguez, at 1520 SW 190 Avenue, Pembroke Pines, Florida 33029.

Defendant **Fuse Technical Group, LLC** is a foreign corporation formed under Illinois law and based in Schiller Park, Illinois. Defendant has systematic, continuous, and specific contacts conduct, and business activities, including, but not limited to, its conduct relating to the subject incident, within Texas such that it is at home in the state. This Defendant may be served through its Texas based registered agent, Business Filings Incorporated, at 701 Brazos Street, Ste. 720, Austin, TX 78701.

Defendant **Harris County Sports & Convention Corporation** is a corporation formed under Texas law and based in Houston, Texas. This Defendant may be served through its registered agent Kevin H. Hoffman, at One NRG Park, Houston, Texas 77054.

IV.
JURISDICTION AND VENUE

This Court has subject matter jurisdiction over this cause of action because it involves an amount in excess of the minimum jurisdictional limits of this Court.

This case is not removable because no federal question is raised, and, although more than $75,000 is sought, exclusive of interest and costs, there is not complete diversity amongst the parties. Specifically, there are Plaintiffs from California, New York, and Texas suing Defendants from California, New York, and Texas. Further, despite bringing claims on behalf of more than 100 persons, this action is not removable as a "mass action" under 28 U.S.C. § 1332(d)(11)(B)(i) because (ii)(I) of the same section, excepts civil actions where "all of the claims in the action arise from an event or occurrence in the State in which the action was filed."

This Court has personal jurisdiction over Defendants because of Defendants' systematic and continuous contacts with the state of Texas, and, importantly, the causes of action arise from Defendants' specific contacts with Texas; Defendants' conduct occurred in Texas, and the Plaintiffs were killed or injured here. The exercise of personal jurisdiction over all Defendants comports with traditional notions of fair play and substantial justice.

Venue is proper in Harris County, Texas because the events that give rise to liability occurred here.

V.
FACTUAL BACKGROUND

A. Introduction to the Parties.

1. Apple, Inc.

Apple, Inc. ("Apple") is a multinational technology company with hundreds of subsidiaries providing a multitude of music services. One of its services, Apple Music, partnered with Live Nation and ASM in order to promote and live stream the events of Astroworld 2021. Apple actively promoted and advertised the partnership and the Astroworld concert, and intended to profit handsomely from it. Apple was well aware of Webster's violent lyrics ("*And it ain't a mosh pit if ain't no injuries*"), and his encouragement of conduct that would cause injury at the event. Apple was well aware of Webster's repeated violent rhetoric, both at concerts and on social media. Apple knew he had encouraged his fans to attempt to attend his concerts without a ticket. Apple knew that Webster had been arrested for inciting crowds. Apple knew that Webster in the past had repeatedly encouraged the concert crowd to disregard security. Apple knew that Webster had encouraged concertgoers to jump from the balcony, causing at least one to fall and be paralyzed. Apple knew that Webster had, in the past, encouraged concertgoers to attack and beat individuals that Webster pointed out in the crowd. Further, Apple was well aware of Live Nation's long and tortured history of reckless disregard to concertgoers. Apple's involvement in the concert placed a stamp of credibility to the concert and created even more excitement about it, exacerbating the wild and out of control atmosphere. Apple made no efforts to ensure that the concert and performance that it promoted, and that it had exclusive rights to, was executed safely. Apple made no efforts to warn participants of the danger involved.

Apple's decision to partner with Live Nation, Webster, Graham, and Scoremore makes it complicit and jointly and severally responsible for the deaths and injuries that foreseeably occurred. Apple cannot reap the benefits of an exclusive partnership and streaming video from the concert without sharing in the blame for how horribly it was managed. As a large corporation with considerable influence, Apple could have and should have made demands regarding the safety of the event. And Apple's extensive experience with concerts as the largest music streaming platform in the world should have certainly identified issues with the execution of the event had it bothered to perform even a cursory review of the operation plans. That did not happen. What did happen was Apple choosing to live stream some of the chaos on their platform before ultimately cutting away. In the clip on the left side, the lights on top of a police vehicle are seen from the stage as it attempts to render aid while Defendant Webster continues to perform. Shortly after the camera cuts away, rowdy concertgoers incited by Webster climbed on top of the vehicle and impeded its ability to help those in need. Further, everyone who watched the Apple live stream saw a concert goer on the stage, pleading for the performance to stop. Apple along with its partners, however, chose to turn a blind eye.

2. Jacques Berman Webster II aka "Travis Scott"

Jacques Berman Webster II is a native Houstonian who currently resides in Los Angeles, California. Using the stage name "Travis Scott," Webster has amassed a global following as a rapper and performer. His particular style of music often glorifies violence and other dangerous behaviors, while insinuating that these actions are consequence free by associating them with his lavish lifestyle. Despite full awareness of his largely adolescent fanbase's impressionable nature, Webster has made a prolific career out of these ideas and practices. For instance, Webster refers to his most die-hard fans as "sickos," and commands their anti-social conduct with an almost militaristic discipline; such was demonstrated during the events that give rise to this suit.

Examples of Webster's reckless stewardship of his stardom number in the dozens, with just as many victims. One particular instance of note resulted in Webster being placed on court supervision for a year after pleading guilty to a 2015 charge for reckless conduct. That charge resulted from a performance during Chicago's Lollapalooza at which Webster encouraged his "sickos" to put their "middle finger(s) up to security right now" and chant "we want rage!" In response to both Webster's and the crowd's behavior, the police on scene were forced to stop Webster's performance after only five minutes. They also detained Webster for questioning and then charged him after he attempted to flee. Unlike the officials at Astroworld

2021, the police providing security at Lollapalooza were prepared for the worst and in fact warned Webster and his staff that the performance would be halted if he acted dangerously. Their prior warning was in response to a concert tour littered with dangerous events earlier that year. Webster himself encouraged and celebrated these dangerous events from his "Travis Scott" Instagram account. Some of this foolishness is shown below:

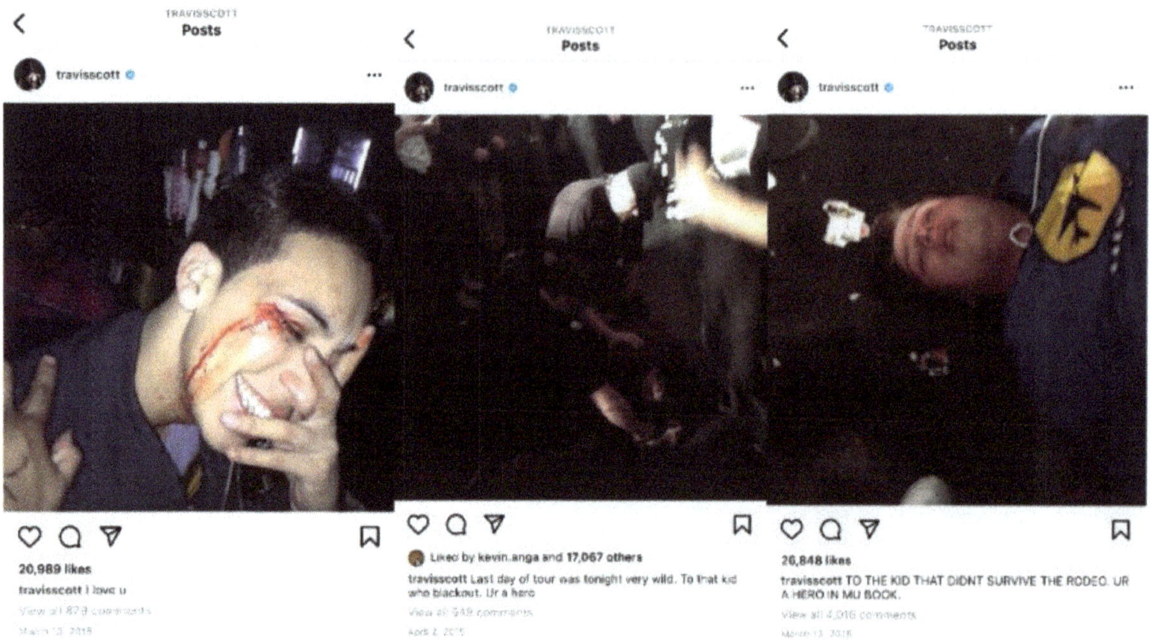

The photos above show Webster glorifying events where young fans suffered bodily injury, lost consciousness, and received life-saving medical treatment at a Webster concert; these injuries occurred as a result of the environment Webster intentionally fostered and profited from. Webster then published these photos with captions of encouragement, indicating that he relished these outcomes essentially asking for more. The thousands of "likes" on Webster's Instagram posts paint a grim picture of the fan base he has amassed with his antics.

Webster was interviewed by GQ magazine where he was asked about the atmosphere of his shows and why it seemed he encouraged his crowds in attendance to become violent with one another, Webster responded that "I always want to make it feel like it's the WWF or some shit." The matches put on by the WWF (World Wrestling Federation,) are, of course, staged—with fake emotion, fake rhetoric, fake violence, fake injuries and fake blood. The emotion, violence, and rhetoric at Webster's concerts are all too real, and have resulted in real injuries and real death.

In 2015, Webster was accused of inciting a crowd against his own security personnel at one of his performances. He even began fighting with security personnel himself when they intervened to try and restrain an unruly fan. The entire interaction was videotaped. It paints a disturbing picture.

Throughout the video Webster shouts into his microphone "Fuck those lime green shirt wearing motherfuckers! Fuck them up!" He goes on to chant, repeatedly: "We want rage!" to an already very violent and extremely unruly crowd.

In April of 2017, at a performance in New York City, Webster encouraged fans to jump from an upper deck balcony in order to "crowd surf," a dangerous practice where concertgoers take what could be potentially lethal leaps from great heights into crowds of other fans, in the hopes that they will be caught before they hit the ground. As with many of his antics, Webster can be seen on video taunting young fans saying things like "They gonna catch you. Don't be scared. Don't be scared!" and "I see you, but are you gonna do it?" One young concert goer, who attended this particular show, sued Webster for serious injuries, claiming that he never intended to jump, but was pushed by other fans incited by Mr. Webster. That young man is now paralyzed.

Later in 2017, Webster was arrested and charged with inciting a riot, disorderly conduct, and endangering the welfare of a minor. The charges stemmed from his encouragement of concertgoers to bypass security

and rush the stage, during his performance at the Walmart Arkansas Music Pavilion. Several people, including staff members at the concert, were injured in the ensuing chaos. Webster pleaded guilty to disorderly conduct and paid restitution to injured concertgoers.

During the 2019 Astroworld music festival, Webster encouraged his fans to storm the entry barricades. Webster's use of the phrase "be safe" couched in the middle of a comment clearly intended to appeal to the violent tendencies of the crowd; Webster's attempt to encourage but also incite in the same message would be laughable if it was not so tragic. Three people were hospitalized as a result of the violent turmoil at the 2019 Astroworld music festival.

Webster's affinity for the storming of barricades and ignoring security measures appears to border on an obsession at times. Reports from

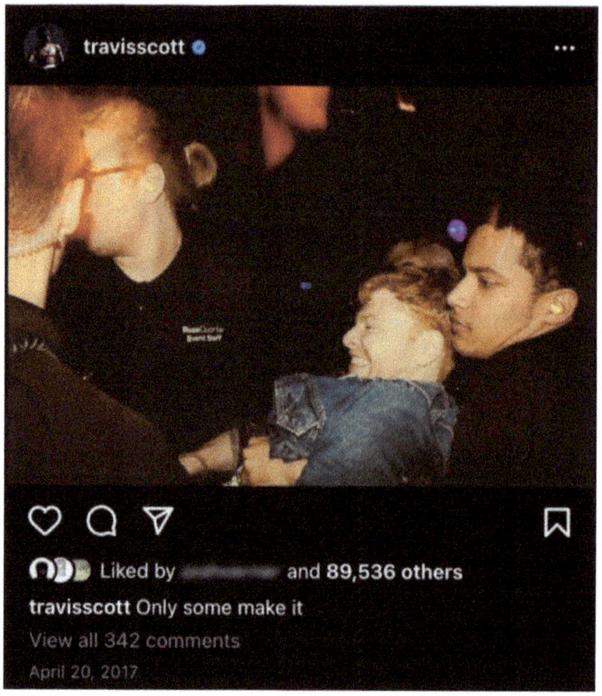

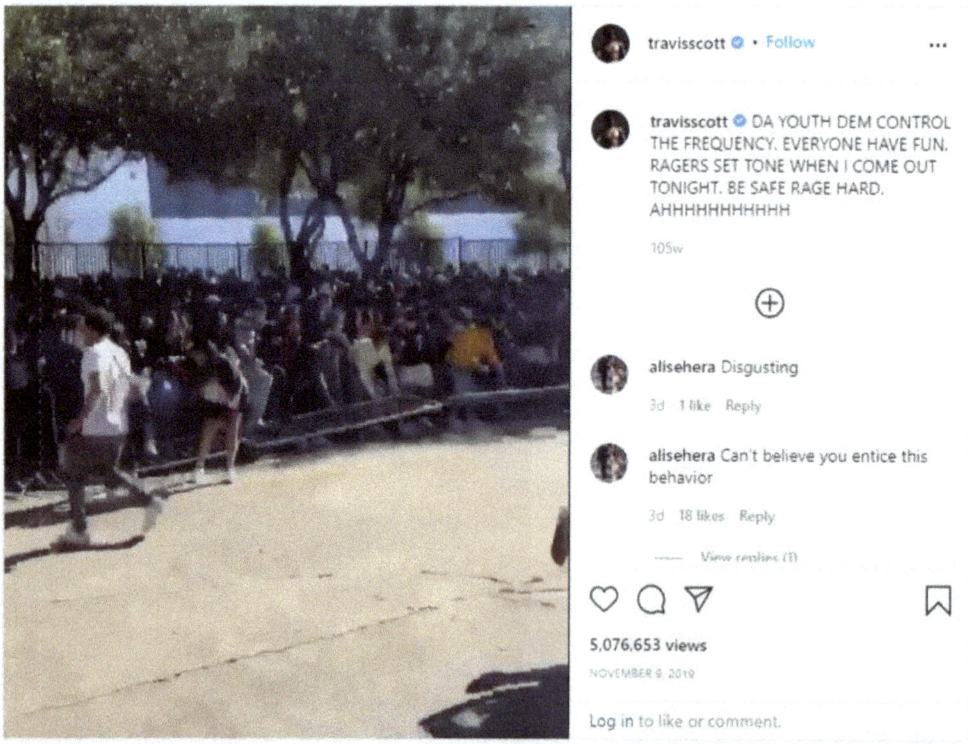

multiple shows, including Astroworld 2021, describe ticketless fans waiting outside the venues for the "signal" from Webster. These fans are either to sneak into the show by climbing over or around whatever fencing may be in place or are to use mob force to knock down barriers.

A Webster tweet from May of 2021 (shown on the left side), which was sent after the event had quickly sold out, indicates similar intent for Astroworld 2021. Webster, of course, has since deleted this tweet.

In addition to posts he makes via twitter, Instagram and other social media before his concerts, and in addition to the way he conducts himself at the concerts, Webster's lyrics themselves perfectly describe his attitude about concerts and how concertgoers should behave there. As an example, the following lyrics appear in a main verse of "Stargazing," one of the more popular songs Webster has released:

Packin' out Toyota like I'm in the league
And it ain't a mosh pit if ain't no injuries
I got 'em stage divin' out the nosebleeds

It is difficult to take these words at anything other than face value. Words have an impact onimpressionable young fans.

3. Aubrey Drake Graham aka "Drake"

Defendant Graham, like Defendant Webster, is a popular musician who performed at the 2021 Astroworld. While Graham does not have as prolific of a history inciting violence as does Webster, Graham has greatly benefitted from Webster's "sicko" legacy. Graham has performed with Webster on multiple occasions, making millions of dollars, despite the numerous incidents described above. When Graham accepted Webster's invitation to perform at Astroworld 2021, Graham was well aware of the damage Webster had caused at his shows in the past. Graham was also well aware of the anticipated size and volatility of the crowd, and the likelihood of incitement. Graham of course could have insisted on more and stricter security, and more and better trained medical staff, prior to having his name and brand associated with the event. Graham failed to do so. Instead, Graham did exactly the opposite, he bolstered Webster's credibility and crowd size by performing alongside him with no stipulations. Graham also refused to end the concert as the deadly chaos ensued, just a few feet in front of the performers' faces. Indeed, rather than end the concert, Graham continued, and then after went for a party at Dave & Buster's, and then to a strip club where he spent more than $1 million.

4. Tristar Sports & Entertainment Group

Tri Star Sports & Entertainment Group ("Tri Star") handles business management for Defendant Webster. Upon information and belief, this corporation has represented Webster throughout all the incidents described herein. This Defendant was well aware of Webster's repeated violent rhetoric, both at concerts and on social media. This Defendant knew he had encouraged his fans to attempt to attend his concerts without a ticket. This Defendant knew that Webster had been arrested for inciting crowds. This Defendant knew that he had been known to encourage the concert crowd to disregard security. This Defendant knew that Webster had encouraged concertgoers to jump from the balcony, causing at least one to fall and be paralyzed. This Defendant knew that Webster had, in the past, encouraged concertgoers to attack and beat individuals that Webster pointed out in the crowd. Tri Star is well aware of, and has participated in, each incident where fans have been attacked, mangled, injured, and trampled upon.

MonaLisaney81

Of course Travis Scott wouldn't stop the show. His business manager is Lou M. Taylor. All they care about is money, no matter who gets hurt. I hope they sue the shit out of Travis Scott & Lou's company Tri Star Sports & Entertainment Group.

5. Cactus Jack Records, LLC, Grand Hustle Records, and Epic Records

Cactus Jack Records, LLC ("Cactus Jack") is a record label founded in 2017 by Defendant Webster. Webster started Cactus Jack not only to gain greater financial control over his music, but also to profit from other talent he signed to the label. Cactus Jack has branded itself as a label that promotes and encourages violence and recklessness. Cactus Jack is now known for such behavior.

Grand Hustle Management, Inc. ("Grand Hustle") is an Atlanta based record label founded by rapper Clifford Joseph Harris, Jr. ("T.I."), and his business partner Jason Geter.

Epic Records, Inc. ("Epic") is a New York based Record label owned by Sony Music Entertainment and a subsidiary of Sony Corporation of America.

Cactus Jack, Grand Hustle, and Epic (collectively "Record Labels") are credited with producing the Astroworld 2021 event, and upon information and belief, provided the "Travis Scott" merchandise available for sale at the event, as this is typically a role of an artist's record label at their concert. These Defendants were well aware of Webster's repeated violent rhetoric, both at concerts and on social media. These Defendants knew he had encouraged his fans to attempt to attend his concerts without a ticket. These Defendants knew that Webster had been arrested for inciting crowds. These Defendants knew that he had been known to encourage the concert crowd to disregard security. These Defendants knew that Webster had encouraged concertgoers to jump from the balcony, causing at least one to fall and be paralyzed. These Defendants knew that Webster had, in the past, encouraged concertgoers to attack and beat individuals that Webster pointed out in the crowd. The Record Labels participated in Astroworld 2021 despite the glaring safety concerns and this knowledge, and did so for the sole purpose of profiting from it.

6. The ASM Defendants

ASM Global Parent, Inc., through its subsidiary ASM Global, LLC (collectively "ASM"), managed all events and activities held at NRG Park in Houston, Texas. ASM's General manager Mark Miller, and its Sales Manager Keith Butler, were both supposed to have direct oversight of the Astroworld 2021 concert headlined by Defendant Webster. These Defendants were directly responsible for the safety of all attendees at the concert. They were well aware of his repeated violent rhetoric, both at concerts and on social media. They knew he had encouraged his fans to attempt to attend his concerts without a ticket. They knew that Webster had been arrested for inciting crowds. They knew that he had been known to encourage the concert crowd to disregard security. They knew that Webster had encouraged concertgoers to jump from the balcony, causing at least one to fall and be paralyzed. They knew that Webster had, in the past, encouraged concertgoers to attack and beat individuals that Webster pointed out in the crowd.

7. The Scoremore Defendants

Scoremore Holdings, LLC, Scoremore LLC, Scoremore, Mgmt, LLC, and Sascha Stone Guttfreund, Scoremore Managing Member/Co-founder, and Trey Hicks (collectively the "Scoremore Defendants"), served as promoters, public relations managers, and operators for the Astroworld 2021 Festival. These Defendants were in a unique position to manage the rhetoric around the event, and the attitude regarding safety for the event. These Defendants were well aware of Defendant Webster's repeated antics, at prior Astroworld concerts and others. They were well aware of his repeated violent rhetoric, both at concerts and on social media. They knew he had encouraged his fans to attempt to attend his concerts without a ticket. They knew that Webster had been arrested for inciting crowds. They knew that he had been known to encourage the concert crowd to disregard security. They knew that Webster had encouraged concertgoers to jump from the balcony, causing at least one to fall and be paralyzed. They knew that Webster had, in the past, encouraged concertgoers to attack and beat individuals that Webster pointed out in the crowd. the Scoremore Defendants could have chosen to temper Webster's rhetoric with public messages and statements regarding safety and compliance with security measures. These Defendants also could have encouraged stricter security at the event itself. There exists no evidence of any attempt on the part of the Scoremore Defendants to counteract Webster's violent and ultimately deadly rhetoric.

According to former employees of Scoremore, it is surprising that it took this long for something tragic to happen at an event they were associated with. Former Scoremore employees paint a picture of a company with a history of disorganization, cost-cutting, and unprofessionalism. These former employees make clear there was no real structure to the business. Vital roles remained unfilled for long periods of time, and bottom-line driven decisions that put profits over people.

8. The Live Nation Defendants

Astroworld 2021 was originally the brain child of Darryl Lamonte Platt (Live Nation Entertainment, Inc.'s Director of Operations), Live Nation Worldwide, Inc., and Live Nation Entertainment, Inc. (Collectively "Live Nation"). Live Nation approached ASM about holding the Astroworld festival on the grounds of NRG Park. Live Nation ostensibly wanted a space large enough to accommodate tens of thousands of fans. Live Nation insisted on an event using standing room only seating, rather than providing rows of assigned seats. Standing room only seating allows the promotor and organizer the ability to put more people into one space, and thus earning more revenue for the same amount of space. Live Nation sought to extract maximum profits from the Astroworld music festival. In an effort to generate more revenue, Live Nation also arranged for live streaming and merchandising sales at the event. Practically everything Live Nation did in relation to this event was designed to generate more revenue. This Defendant was well aware of Webster's repeated violent rhetoric, both at concerts and on social media. This Defendant knew he had encouraged his fans to attempt to attend his concerts without a ticket. This Defendant knew that Webster had been arrested for inciting crowds. This Defendant knew that he had been known to encourage the concert crowd to disregard security. This Defendant knew that Webster had encouraged concertgoers to jump from the balcony, causing at least one to fall and be paralyzed. This Defendant knew that Webster had, in the past, encouraged concertgoers to attack and beat individuals that Webster pointed out in the crowd. Despite possessing this knowledge, Defendant Live Nation took no special precautions, and allowed the concert to proceed, unfettered.

Live Nation also contracted for security and medical care at the event. However, Live Nation did not seek to ensure these services had adequate training and staff for an event expecting more than 50,000 attendees. Live Nation sought to only "check off the box" for providing security and medical care, and instead focused on the revenue generating aspects of the venture. This is evidenced by the total lack of control starting in the early morning hours and continuing throughout the course of the day on November 5, 2021.

This is not the first time Live Nation has been negligently discharged its duty to maintain a safe environment for its patrons and staff. According to a review of court records, official complaints and news reports, since 2006, Live Nation has been linked to at least 750 injuries and approximately 200 deaths at its events in seven countries. Live Nation has also come under federal scrutiny for work safety and antitrust violations.[4] In 2017, Live Nation was forced to reach informal settlements, in lieu of steep penalties, regarding numerous worker related violations. Among some its more notable failures to protect its patrons are:

- A lawsuit in 2016 which named Live Nation as being negligent in allowing a crowd surge that resulted in the trampling and broken leg of a woman attending the concert;
- An explosion set off by a suicide bomber that killed 22 people at an Ariana Grande concert in Manchester, England in 2017;
- A mass shooting at a country music festival in Las Vegas in 2017 that killed 60;
- A terrorist attack at a concert hall in Paris where 89 people were slain;
- A stage collapse at the Indiana State Fair in 2011 that killed 61 people, a tragedy for which Live Nation settled for $50 Million; and
- A 2018 stampede caused by poor crowd control at a concert in Central Park in New York City. Patrons at the show sued and stated in court documents that they were trampled, pummeled, and assaulted.

The sad truth is that many have tried to hold Live Nation accountable for its reckless and intentionally harmful practices in the past, but as evidenced by its repeated issues and the tragic events of Astroworld 2021, those efforts have been largely unsuccessful.

---

[4] Astroworld promoters oversaw other events where concertgoers trampled fellow fans, broke barricades (houstonchronicle.com)

9. Contemporary Services Corporation, Apex Security, SPS Security, and Valle Security, LLC

Contemporary Services Corporation, Apex Security, SPS Security, and Valle Security, LLC (collectively "Security Defendants") are security entities contracted by ASM and Live Nation to provide security and safety to concertgoers and staff at Astroworld 2021. According to personal accounts from concertgoers, security personnel were few and far between. And, finding anyone with authority to help alleviate some of the anguish was next to impossible. Not only that, many report the security at the event appeared ambivalent to the suffering of those there, recording surging crowds and people begging for help with their cell phones instead of rendering the aid they were hired to perform. In some more disturbing accounts, security guards were actually assaulting concertgoers who attempted to come to them for help. A video posted to twitter shows a security guard from the event body slamming a patron seemingly just for being in his way. In the screenshot below, NRG stadium can be seen in the background and a purple Astroworld banner can be seen just above the unnamed security guard, who is in the process of throwing a patron over a barricade and slamming his head onto the concrete. Shortly after the events in this portion of the clip, another security guard steps up and attacks the person filming, knocking his phone from his hand. The security companies at Astroworld were ill equipped to deal with 50,000 concertgoers, much less the many more that attended. Moreover, the security personnel were not adequately trained, for the most part had never worked together, and had never worked a mass event such as Astroworld. Further, and importantly, the security companies had never worked together before, and there was no overall coordination amongst them. The lack of security, from even before the opening of the gates at 10am on the morning of the concert, was evident, and was reason enough to stop the concert even before any performer ever took the stage.

10. Re:Source Event Group, LLC and Fuse Technical Group, LLC

Re:source Event Group, LLC and Fuse Technical Group, LCC (Collectively "Design Defendants") are event design companies based out of Florida and Illinois, respectively. They contracted with ASM and Live Nation in order to design the stages and sets used at Astroworld 2021. According to many news reports and experts, a lack of foresight and poor stage design contributed to the tragedy that occurred at Astroworld 2021. Operators of the event had full knowledge that more than 50,000 concertgoers could potentially be in attendance, and that these concertgoers would attempt to gather in front of the stage where Defendant Webster would be performing. Yet the stage designed by Re:source was far too small, and was ill equipped, to handle that many people. This inadequacy resulted in people being tightly crammed into the small pits near the stage, where many eventually fell and were trampled. Many of the victims were injured or died as a result of the surge from the rear as bodies became propelled forward and crushed against one another.

11. Paradocs Worldwide/South Texas EMS

Paradocs Worldwide and South Texas EMS were two of the medical service providers that were charged with providing medical services to concert attendees. Despite being well aware of Webster's previous antics, and despite knowing that more than 50,000 individuals would attend, these Defendants were severely understaffed and limited in resources. Many of the individuals who were charged with providing medical service had never worked an event such as Astroworld before. Further, inadequate efforts were made to coordinate amongst the medical service providers, the organizers, and security. Further, because NRG Park is a county property, city resources, such as the 151 surrounding fire stations with ample EMS staff, had no jurisdiction. The organizers and promoters of Astroworld failed to include the ample resources of the Houston Fire Department in to the plan, but rather chose to save money contract with private services with limited resources. Both Paradocs and South Texas EMS both boast extensive experience with providing medical services to events and concerts. It defies logic that companies claiming such experience could bring such limited resources to a concert expected to attract 50,000 attendees. The gross negligence of the medical service providers contributed to the tragedy of Astroworld 2021.

12. Harris County Sports & Convention Corporation

Harris County Sports & Convention Corporation ("HCSCC") owns the physical structures at NRG park, including the stadium, other buildings, the parking lot, and everything else—except for the ground itself, which is officially owned by Harris County. HCSCC had a duty to all individuals who came onto its property. HCSCC sought to delegate this duty to festival organizers such as ASM and Live Nation. HCSCC cannot, however, delegate the blame for the horrible mismanagement and negligence that occurred. HCSCC was well aware of Webster's repeated violent rhetoric, both at concerts and on social media. HCSCC knew he had encouraged his fans to attempt to attend his concerts without a ticket. HCSCC knew that Webster had been arrested for inciting crowds. HCSCC knew that he had been known to encourage the concert crowd to disregard security. HCSCC knew that Webster had encouraged concertgoers to jump from the balcony, causing at least one to fall and be paralyzed. HCSCC knew that Webster had, in the past, encouraged concertgoers to attack and beat individuals that Webster pointed out in the crowd. Further, A HCSCC was well aware of Live Nation's long and tortured history of reckless disregard to concertgoers. HCSCC turned control—not all control, but certainly some—of its park over to Live Nation. This act, without putting precautions in place, was negligence and gross negligence.

B. Astroworld 2021 Was Destined for Failure from the Moment before it Ever Began

The narrative regarding Astroworld 2021 to date is that deaths and injuries occurred because a sea of out-of-control individuals rushed the stage around 9:00 pm. According to reports, immediately prior and then during the time that Webster and Graham were on the stage, a crowd surge towards the stage occurred, causing injury and death. This widely reported narrative paints an incomplete picture. The truth is that the tragedy of Astroworld 2021 was in the making weeks before the event.

1. The Week Leading Up to the Deadly Concert

NRG Park is located on property owned by Harris County. Harris county officials have authority and oversight for all events held in the park. However, within the city's power is the authority to regulate what are designated as "special events," to include events occurring at NRG Park. Emails, permit applications, and plans related to Astroworld 2021 reveal a pattern of late filings, rubber stamp approvals, and half-hearted efforts to ensure safe execution of the event. These documents reveal that the failures of Astroworld began well before the first concert goer crashed the security barricades the morning of November 5, 2021.

Despite Defendant Webster announcing the event on April 30, 2021, the first communication regarding Astroworld 2021 from Webster with the Mayor's Office of Special Events did not occur until October 25, 2021, little more than a week before the event was scheduled to take place. On October 31, 2021, in response to concerns raised at a public meeting, Webster submitted revised plans. Although the Mayor's Office approved those revised plans the next day, debate between officials regarding them continued. On November 2, 2021, a project manager in the Mayor's Office notified a state transportation official of several NRG Park requests and complained that they had arrived "extremely late to run through the typical steps." The plan, however, had already been approved by the Mayor's Office and the concert was set to go on in just three days. The one-page security plan included in the approved package only assigned twenty-six officers to crowd control and sixty to traffic control. After the death and injuries occurred, the city of Houston claimed that 528 Houston Police Officers were ultimately on the scene, but did not specify how they were approved to work the festival or when they got there. According to a statement released by Houston Police Chief Finner, he met with Defendant Webster just prior to the event taking place to express his public safety concerns associated with the event. The truth is, despite his long history, and despite the lack of planning or promptness in providing required documentation, Webster knew that City officials would not cancel his event—he knew that he could be tardy in his submissions; he knew that he could provide incomplete and shoddy planning documents; he knew that he could flout the rules and, yet, the show would go on. And it did.

The Astroworld event operations plan turned out to be a cut-and-paste document, shoddily thrown together with little forethought, evidencing a complete disregard to previous like events and the reckless conduct of the star performer. The plan included details on how to respond to threats such as lost individuals, missing children, traumatic injuries, deaths, active shooters and unruly fans, but it did not address unauthorized concertgoers, unruly crowds, mass casualties, or crowd surges. Given Webster's previous conduct, the operations plan ignored the most deadly and foreseeable threats that would be encountered that day.

2. Astroworld 2021

Harris County owns NRG Park. The City of Houston permits "special events." To ensure that there are no gaps in safety or confusion in execution, proper prior planning of an event at NRG is essential. Failure to properly plan can create gaps in safety and blind spots in security and medical care for those that attend events at NRG. One such gap at Astroworld 2021 was the insistence on using private medical providers service to provide care for any sick or injured. The capabilities of the Houston Fire Department (HFD) dwarf most of like services in the United States. For cost purposes, however, the professionals at HFD were not employed. Even had a few HFD first responders been allowed inside NRG's gates—which they were not—such individuals would have had the resources of the entire HFD available to them in the event a mass casualty event occurred, or even if it appeared one would likely occur. Despite not being engaged,

HFD did in fact station one team outside NRG's gates. Those individuals logged the activity in the park. The log's timeline paints a dark picture of an event that was well out of hand from the moment it began.

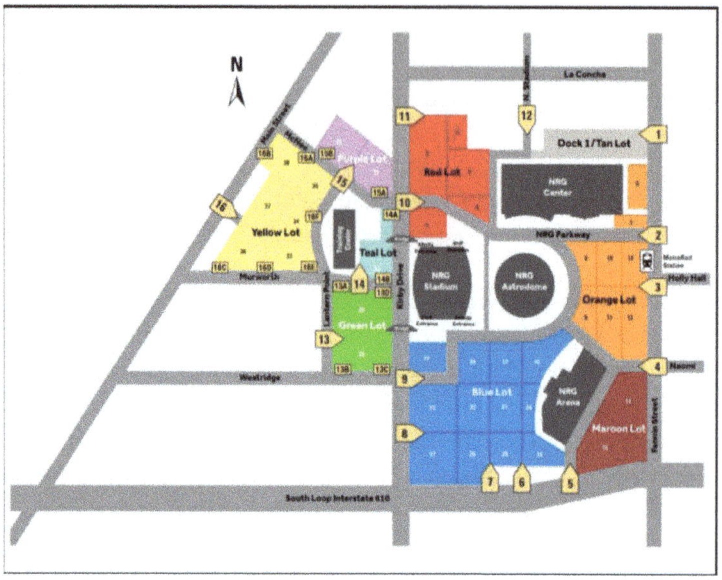

- 8:15 A.M. Lt. Barrow requests riot equipment.
- 9:15 A.M. HPD preparing to open gates to participants.
- 9:20 A.M. Participants have breached secondary checkpoint.
- 9:23 A.M. Participants have breached main gate and bypassed covid testing checkpoint.
- 9:25 A.M. HPD request medical for 4 individuals.

It is clear to see that things are already beginning to get out of control even before the gateswere officially opened.

- 9:35 A.M. Apex Security requests assistance at venue gates.
- 10:00 A.M. Venue gates opened.
- 10:02 A.M. Venue fences damaged, no control of participants.
- 10:05 A.M. Breached Merchandising lines (no control over Merchandise).
- 10:19 A.M. Crowd trying to push down final barrier—merchandising.
- 10:30 A.M. More police requested behind merchandising.
- 10:54 A.M. Approximately 100 participants jumping the fence into purple lot.
- 11:10 A.M. Request for Medic at Merch shop @ green lot.
- 11:18 A.M. Group of 200 approaching McNee/Kirby near gate 10. Group of 200 rushing gate 10. Participants are now dismantling barricades.
- 11:21 A.M. HPD—Attempt to shut down Bridge to Green Lot if needed.

Less than two hours later, large groups presumably comprised of "sickos" outnumber the requested number of police and are already rushing the gates and dismantling barricades. Police begin discussing the possibility of shutting down lots and entrances to try and control access to the event.

The above diagram shows the layout of NRG Park for demonstrative purposes. The extensive number of access points, both those authorized and those forcibly opened, show just how difficult it must have been for the meager forces to maintain security and control.

- 11:32 A.M.—Two participants jump fence into Texans practice field.
- 11:33 A.M. Need medical to blue lot for female patient having seizure.
- 11:36 A.M. Participants storming venue entrance
- 11:39 A.M. Multiple people without wristbands arriving @ green lot.
- 11:49 A.M. HPD to shut down merchandising.
- 12:07 P.M. Participants going under fence @ 1313 Green lot.
- 12:13 P.M. Adult detainees to purple lot. Juveniles to reunification.
- 12:17 P.M. Participants have broken gate 13 in Green lot.
- 12:38 P.M. S.W.A.T. drone reported in Teal Lot.
- 12:56 P.M. Field Force Five assigned to Green Lot.
- 12:59 P.M. Participants attempting to get under fence.

- 1:21 P.M. All 5 Harris County transports in service. Possible issue with Apex transporting HPD officers.
- 1:26 P.M. Participants using bolt cutters to enter into green lot.
- 1:58 P.M. Large Crowd Rushing VIP entrance.
- 2:44 P.M. Report of breached fence 2686 Murworth, Wilshire
- 2:59 P.M. Report of group of individuals causing damage to property @ Murworth/Lanternpoint.
- 3:21 P.M. HPD requests assistance to yellow lot for large group trying to go over fence at Main/Murworth corner. HPD also requests medical to yellow lot.
- 3:54 P.M. Paradocs reports 54 patients treated since beginning of event.
- 4:20 Large group charged Main gate unsuccessfully.
- 4:41 P.M. Approximately 150 rushing gates at Kirby and Westridge.

The images on the pages 297–298 show mobs pushing through ten-foot fences by sheer force and rushing into the venue.

- 4:45 P.M. HPD requesting assistance to yellow lot for imminent fence breach, SW corner.
- 4:51 P.M. HPD reports that crowd is pushing down fence around stage 2.
- 4:54 P.M. HPD reports of dangerous crowd conditions at stage 2. 2686 Murworth report of individuals with guns, 15-20 people witnessed.
- 5:05 Paradoc reporting 2/3 full—26,021 security scanned, 3-5K not scanned, per NRG Command.
- 6:42 P.M. Main & Murworth group of people wanting to rush fence.
- 6:48 P.M. [Paradocs] state 174+4 transported by HCEC (Harris County Emergency Crew)
- 6:48 P.M. Main & Murworth HPD states the crowd is growing and discussing rushing the gate.

- 6:54 P.M. Large crowd runs into hotel.
- 6:55 P.M. Large crowd rushes VIP Area, 100+
- 7:15 P.M Mob by Main Street
- 7:24 P.M. 250 Participants rushing pedestrian bridge.
- 7:30 P.M. Participants have knocked down fence at stage 1.
- 7:46 P.M. Multiple individuals on Texans practice field.
- 7:50 P.M. [HPD requests buses to transports detainees]

By the 8:00 pm, HPD is requesting buses to move the detainees, due to the sheer number of unruly individuals. Keeping them detained on site requires resources to be pulled away from other crowd control measures. It is clear that the security personnel and police presence were grossly overwhelmed.

- 9:02 P.M. HPD indicated approximately 55,000 participants at the event.
- 9:06 P.M. Group reported to be scaling fence in purple lot at McNee.
- 9:08 P.M. 200 breaching fence from Main Street into yellow lot.
- 9:11 P.M. Barricade around stage 2 compromised
- 9:18 P.M. reports of individuals with crush injury/breathing difficulty, Paradocs en route.
- 9:28 P.M. "This is when it all got real"

The quote from 9:28 P.M. confirms the outcome that the events of the day have been leading up to. Sheer chaos had erupted as breach after breach, crowd rush after crowd rush had overtaken the festival. Barricades had been destroyed or pushed aside, and Defendant Webster's "sickos" had entered the premises unauthorized and rushed the stages causing panic, trampling, and deadly crowd surges.

- 9:30 P.M. HPD reports multiple people trampled, passed out in front of stage, security is remaining to rear of stage.
- 9:32 P.M. HPD report of unconscious female in the middle of crowd.
- 9:33 P.M. report of multiple people down in the crowd.
- 9:35 P.M. HFD radio operator advised we have at least five 9-1-1 calls related to unconscious persons in crowd. Report of possible CPR.

HFD personnel outside NRG gates declared a mass casualty event at 9:38 pm. Despite this declaration, Defendant Webster continued the show for another forty minutes, even introducing and preforming with Defendant Graham. These Defendants continued to perform, despite accounts that lifeless bodies being passed through the crowd in full view of the stage. Emergency vehicles that attempted to render aid in the crowd were attacked and jumped on (shown below). As people fell and were stepped on, and as multiple episodes of cardiac arrest were occurring throughout the crowd, the show raged on, and the "sickos" loved it. At one point (shown below), Defendant Webster can even be seen looking in the direction of a lifeless body being dragged away as he performs only a few feet away. Defendant Webster did not even acknowledge the scene in front of him.

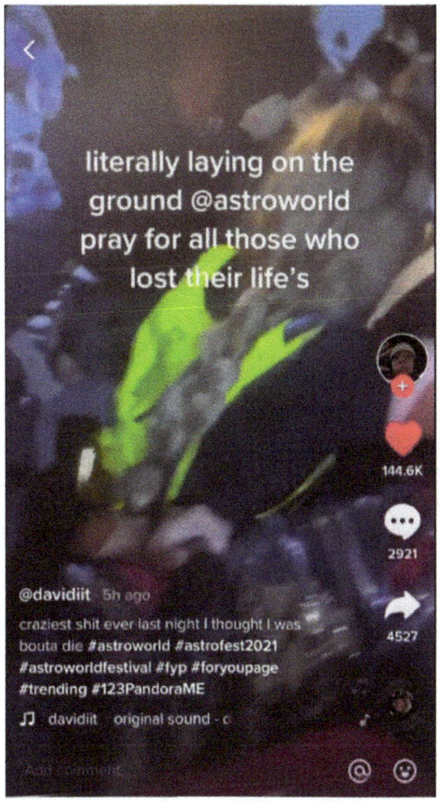

The above images demonstrate the extent of the chaos occurring within the crowd while Defendants Webster and Graham continued to perform. In one of the widely circulated images above, a woman climbs through what she described as a "sinkhole of bodies" to reach a camera operator on top of the stage. She attempts to inform the camera operator of the death just below him and he does not seem to respond in anyway other than telling her that she is not allowed to be on the stage with him.

- 9:52 P.M. IC requests level 1 MCI
- 10:01 P.M. Reported Cardiac in progress
- 11:16 P.M. Cardiac Arrrests: 2x Herman TMC, 2x Ben Taub, 1x Methodist, 1x Park Plaza, 5x Unknown transports.
- 12:08 A.M. 11 CPR—9 total fatalities, 1 critical, 2 admissions.

The last log entry reveals the carnage from the night's activities: preventable deaths and hundreds of preventable injuries. As victims were being transported either to the morgue or the hospital, Webster and Graham were enroute to their after party. They both now claim they had no idea that individuals had been killed and severely injured. Their claims of ignorance are belied by the fact that they were mere feet from bodies being carried from the crowd.

The real-time logs of HFD reveal that the organizers, promoters, security, medical provider companies, performers, and every other entity and individual involved had ample opportunity to stop the event long before anyone was injured—and they should have. All are jointly and severally responsible for failing to do so.

VI.
CAUSES OF ACTION

A. Negligence/Gross Negligence (All Defendants; Only the minor Plaintiffs bring suit against Live Nation at this time)

Plaintiffs incorporate the above paragraphs as if set forth in full below.

At all relevant times, Defendants had a duty of reasonable to those that attended Astroworld 2021. Defendants breached that duty of reasonable care in the following ways, including but not limited to:

- Failing to properly plan the concert so that it could be executed safely;
- Failing to properly train security personnel;
- Failing to have an adequate security plan;
- Failing to have an adequate medical services plan;
- Failing to have an adequate operations plan in place;
- Failing to learn from past mistakes;
- Engaging in or allowing incitation of the crowd;
- Engaging in or allowing encouragement of the entry of nonticketed individuals;
- Failing to responsibly deal with City and County officials;
- Failing to engage adequate security;
- Failing to properly train employees and contractors or ensure they were trained;
- Failing to engage adequate medical personnel;
- Failing to provide adequate water and other essentials;
- Failing to properly secure the concert grounds from un-ticketed entrants;
- Failing to monitor the premises before and during the concert;
- Failing to have adequate equipment on site;
- Failing to timely respond or otherwise act upon patrons' need for immediate medical attention;
- Failing to notice or take precautions against crowd surge;
- Failing to adequately staff employees and security to maintain control of the crowd;
- Failing to adequately train and supervise employees on the reporting and discovery of injured individuals and/or person and/or injurious activity;
- Failing to adequately provide safe entrance and exit plans in general and in emergency situations;
- Failing to employ adequate safety measures;
- Proceeding with concert despite knowing that it was not properly planned;
- Continuing to promote the concert knowing that there were past security and safety issues;
- Continuing to promote and participate in the concert knowing that there were serious security and safety issues even before it began;
- Continuing to participate in the concert knowing that there were ongoing security and safety issues;
- Failing to warn concert goers of the dangers involved;

- Encouraging the performers to engage in dangerous conduct for the purposes of profit;
- Encouraging a dangerous, out of control atmosphere at the concert;
- Failing to prevent unsafe conditions; and
- Failing to stop the festival when it became dangerous and life-threatening for its attendees.

At all relevant times, Defendants knew or should have known that it was reasonably foreseeable that breach of their duties could foreseeably result in catastrophic injury and harm to others, including staff, guests, first responders, and concertgoers, such as Plaintiffs, and the community at large.

As a direct and proximate result of Defendants' negligence, Plaintiffs sustained serious injuries and damages, including physical injuries, severe emotional distress, pain and suffering, medical expenses, and other economic and non-economic damages in amounts in excess of the jurisdictional limits of this Court.

Defendants' conduct indicates that Defendants knew of the risk of harm, but proceeded with indifference to the welfare of the Plaintiffs. As such, Defendants' conduct was malicious and grossly negligent. Because Defendants' conduct was felonious, the punitive damages sought are not subject to capping.

B. Respondeat Superior/Agency (All Defendants)

Plaintiffs incorporate the above paragraphs as if set forth in full below.

At all times, Defendants' employees were agents and/or servants on behalf of Defendants. These Defendants exercised control over their employees, and at all relevant times, Defendants' employees were operating within the scope of their employment for them.

As such, these Defendants are responsible for the conduct and damages caused by any conduct of their employees that contributed to the damages sought in this suit.

C. Wrongful Death—Axel Acosta

Plaintiff Edgar Raul Acosta brings suit for the wrongful death of his son, Axel Acosta against all Defendants. The Estate of Axel Acosta also seeks survival damages, to include the conscious predeath pain and suffering and mental anguish of Axel Acosta.

D. Premises Liability—All Defendants Who Had Some Control of Site

Plaintiffs reallege and incorporate by reference, every allegation contained in this Petition, as though set forth fully herein.

At all relevant times, Defendants had a duty of reasonable care in the protection and safeguarding of persons on the NRG Park premises where the third annual Astroworld Festival 2021 was held on November 5, 2021.

Defendants breached their duty of reasonable care in conducting the Astroworld Festival on the NRG Park premises, including but not limited to: (1) failing to design, build, provide, and mark adequate exits in case of emergency; (2) failing to provide an adequate space to accommodate the size of the expected crowd of 50,000 people, (3) failing to provide a standing surface where participants were not prone to falling; (4) failing to properly train and supervise employees in an appropriate plan of action in case of a foreseeable event, such as a crowd surge and other emergencies; and (5) failing to ensure individuals responsible for safety, security, and the provision of medical services were adequately staffed and trained.

VII.
DAMAGES

A. Edgar Raul Acosta

This action is partly brought pursuant to §§ 71.001-71.012 of the Texas Civil Practice and Remedies Code. Plaintiff Edgar Raul Acosta brings an action for the wrongful death of Axel Acosta. Plaintiff, under the wrongful death statute, is entitled to recover damages for:

1. Pecuniary Loss: Pecuniary loss resulting from the death of Axel Acosta, including, but not limited to, the loss of advice and counsel, care, maintenance, support, services, and earning capacity, as well as the reasonable contributions of pecuniary value that Plaintiff or any heirs would in reasonable probability have received from him had he lived.
2. Mental Anguish: Mental anguish suffered as a result of the death of Axel Acosta, including, but not limited to, the emotional pain, torment, and suffering that Plaintiff's or Decedent's heirs would in reasonably probability, experience from the death of a family member.
3. Loss of Companionship and Society: Loss resulting from Axel Acosta's death, including, but not limited to, love, companionship, comfort, and society that Plaintiffs and Decedent's heirs would in reasonable probability had experienced if David Loree had lived;
4. Loss of Inheritance: The earnings, if any, of Axel Acosta, in excess of the amount he would have used for the support of himself and his family, and in which reasonable probability would have been added to his estate and left to Plaintiffs or Decedent's heirs at his natural death had he lived.
5. Medical and Death Expenses: Actual damages, including, but not limited to, medical expenses, death expenses, and funeral expenses caused by Defendants' conduct.

Additionally, on behalf of the Estate of Axel Acosta, Plaintiff Edgar Raul Acosta also seeks survival damages, to include damages for the conscious pain and suffering and mental anguish that his son, Axel Acosta, experienced prior to his death.

B. Remaining Plaintiffs

As a direct and proximate result of the foregoing events, the remaining Plaintiffs suffered damages in the past and, in reasonable probability, will continue to suffer damages in the future, including physical pain and mental anguish, loss of wages and loss of earning capacity, disfigurement, physical impairment, and medical care, all for which Plaintiffs seek recovery herein. Plaintiffs seek all allowable damages for their injuries allowed by Texas law, to include damages for past, present and futuremental anguish, pain and suffering, and medical expenses.

C. All Plaintiffs

The damages sought herein are the direct and/or proximate result of the foregoing events, and Plaintiffs or Decedent's heirs have suffered damages in the past and, in reasonable probability, will continue to suffer damages in the future, all for which Plaintiffs seek recovery herein. Because the conduct of the Defendants is the type that involve egregiousness, malice, and proceeding in the face of a known risk without regard for Plaintiffs' well-being, Plaintiffs also seek punitive damages, costs, pre-judgment and post-judgement interest. Because the conduct of one or more of the Defendants was felonious, such punitive damages are not subject to capping.

VIII.
JURY TRIAL DEMAND

Plaintiffs demand a jury trial and tender the appropriate fee with this Petition.

IX.
CONDITIONS PRECEDENT

All conditions precedent to Plaintiffs' right to recover have been fully performed, or have been waived by Defendants.

X.
PRAYER

Plaintiffs pray for judgment against Defendants in the amount of five hundred million dollars ($500,000,000) for actual damages for pecuniary losses, mental anguish, loss of companionship and society, loss of inheritance, pain and mental anguish, medical expenses, and funeral expenses; two hundred and fifty million dollars ($250,000,000) in exemplary damages; pre- and post-judgment interest as allowed by law; all costs of Court; and all such other and further relief, at law and in equity, to which Plaintiffs may be justly entitled.

Respectfully submitted,

THE BUZBEE LAW FIRM

By: /s/ *Anthony G. Buzbee*
Anthony G. Buzbee
State Bar No. 24001820
tbuzbee@txattorneys.com
Chris J. Leavitt
State Bar No. 24053318
cleavitt@txattorneys.com
Ryan S. Pigg
State Bar No. 24088227
rpigg@txattorneys.com
Lionel Sims III
State Bar No. 24107465
lsims@txattorneys.com
J.P. Morgan Chase Tower
600 Travis, Suite 7300
Houston, Texas 77002
Telephone: (713) 223-5393
Facsimile: (713) 223-5909
www.txattorneys.com

Attorneys For Plaintiffs

BRIGHT TUNES MUSIC CORP., Plaintiff,

v.

HARRISONGS MUSIC, LTD., et al., Defendants.

No. 71 Civ. 602.

420 F. Supp. 177 (1976)

United States District Court, S. D. New York.

August 31, 1976.

As Amended September 1, 1976.

Pryor, Cashman & Sherman, by Gideon Cashman, James A. Janowitz, New York City, for plaintiff.

Hardee, Barovick, Konecky & Braun, by Joseph J. Santora, Robert B. McKay, Michael Perlstein, New York City, for defendants Harrisongs Music, Ltd., George Harrison, Apple Records, Inc. and Apple Records, Ltd.

Leibman & Schreier, by Leonard S. Leibman, New York City, for defendant Broadcast Music, Inc.

Netter, Dowd, Ness, Alfieri & Stern, by Edward Berman, New York City, for defendant Hansen Publications, Inc.

OPINION AND ORDER

OWEN, District Judge

This is an action in which it is claimed that a successful song, My Sweet Lord, listing George Harrison as the composer, is plagiarized from an earlier successful song, He's So Fine, composed by Ronald Mack, recorded by a singing group called the "Chiffons," the copyright of which is owned by plaintiff, Bright Tunes Music Corp.

He's So Fine, recorded in 1962, is a catchy tune consisting essentially of four repetitions of a very short basic musical phrase, "sol-mi-re," (hereinafter motif A),[1] altered as necessary to fit the words, followed by four repetitions of another short basic musical phrase, "sol-la-do-la-do," (hereinafter motif B).[2] While neither motif is novel, the four repetitions of A, followed by four repetitions of B, is a highly

---

1 

2 

unique pattern.[3] In addition, in the second use of the motif B series, there is a grace note inserted making the phrase go "sol-la-do-la-*re*-do."[4]

My Sweet Lord, recorded first in 1970, also uses the same motif A (modified to suit the words) four times, followed by motif B, repeated three times, not four. In place of He's So Fine's fourth repetition of motif B, My Sweet Lord has a transitional passage of musical attractiveness of the same approximate length, with the identical grace note in the identical second repetition.[5] The harmonies of both songs are identical.[6]

George Harrison, a former member of The Beatles, was aware of He's So Fine. In the United States, it was No. 1 on the billboard charts for five weeks; in England, Harrison's home country, it was No. 12 on the charts on June 1, 1963, a date upon which one of the Beatle songs was, in fact, in first position. For seven weeks in 1963, He's So Fine was one of the top hits in England.

According to Harrison, the circumstances of the composition of My Sweet Lord were as follows. Harrison and his group, which include an American black gospel singer named Billy Preston,[7] were in Copenhagen, Denmark, on a singing engagement. There was a press conference involving the group going on backstage. Harrison slipped away from the press conference and went to a room upstairs and began "vamping" some guitar chords, fitting on to the chords he was playing the words, "Hallelujah" and "Hare Krishna" in various ways.[8] During the course of this vamping, he was alternating between what musicians call a Minor II chord and a Major V chord.

At some point, germinating started and he went down to meet with others of the group, asking them to listen, which they did, and everyone began to join in, taking first "Hallelujah" and then "Hare Krishna" and putting them into four part harmony. Harrison obviously started using the "Hallelujah," etc., as repeated sounds, and from there developed the lyrics, to wit, "My Sweet Lord," "Dear, Dear Lord," etc. In any event, from this very free-flowing exchange of ideas, with Harrison playing his two chords and everybody singing "Hallelujah" and "Hare Krishna," there began to emerge the My Sweet Lord text idea, which Harrison sought to develop a little bit further during the following week as he was playing it on his guitar. Thus developed motif A and its words interspersed with "Hallelujah" and "Hare Krishna."

Approximately one week after the idea first began to germinate, the entire group flew back to London because they had earlier booked time to go to a recording studio with Billy Preston to make an album. In the studio, Preston was the principal musician. Harrison did not play in the session. He had given

[3] All the experts agreed on this.

[4] 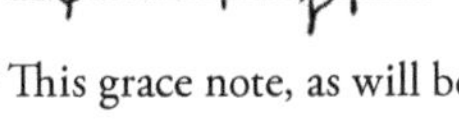

[5] This grace note, as will be seen *infra,* has a substantial significance in assessing the claims of the parties hereto.

[6] Expert witnesses for the defendants asserted crucial differences in the two songs. These claimed differences essentially stem, however, from the fact that different words and number of syllables were involved. This necessitated modest alterations in the repetitions or the places of beginning of a phrase, which, however, has nothing to do whatsoever with the essential musical kernel that is involved.

[7] Preston recorded the first Harrison copyrighted recording of My Sweet Lord, of which more *infra,* and from his musical background was necessarily equally aware of He's So Fine.

[8] These words ended up being a "responsive" interjection between the eventually copyrighted words of My Sweet Lord. In He's So Fine the Chiffons used the sound "dulang" in the same places to fill in and give rhythmic impetus to what would otherwise be somewhat dead spots in the music.

Preston his basic motif A with the idea that it be turned into a song, and was back and forth from the studio to the engineer's recording booth, supervising the recording "takes." Under circumstances that Harrison was utterly unable to recall, while everybody was working toward a finished song, in the recording studio, somehow or other the essential three notes of motif A reached polished form.

"Q. [By the Court]: . . . you feel that those three notes . . . the motif A in the record, those three notes developed somewhere in that recording session?

"Mr. Harrison: I'd say those three there were finalized as beginning there."

*****

"Q. [By the Court]: Is it possible that Billy Preston hit on those [notes comprising motif A]?

"Mr. Harrison: Yes, but it's possible also that I hit on that, too, as far back as the dressing room, just scat singing."

Similarly, it appears that motif B emerged in some fashion at the recording session as did motif A. This is also true of the unique grace note in the second repetition of motif B.

"Q. [By the Court]: All I am trying to get at, Mr. Harrison, is if you have a recollection when that [grace] note popped into existence as it ends up in the Billy Preston recording.

*****

"Mr. Harrison: . . . [Billy Preston] might have put that there on every take, but it just might have been on one take, or he might have varied it on different takes at different places."

The Billy Preston recording, listing George Harrison as the composer, was thereafter issued by Apple Records. The music was then reduced to paper by someone who prepared a "lead sheet" containing the melody, the words and the harmony for the United States copyright application.[9]

Seeking the wellsprings of musical composition why a composer chooses the succession of notes and the harmonies he does whether it be George Harrison or Richard Wagner is a fascinating inquiry. It is apparent from the extensive colloquy between the Court and Harrison covering forty pages in the transcript that neither Harrison nor Preston were conscious of the fact that they were utilizing the He's So Fine theme.[10]

---

[9] It is of interest, but not of legal significance, in my opinion, that when Harrison later recorded the song himself, he chose to omit the little grace note, not only in his musical recording but in the printed sheet music that was issued following that particular recording. The genesis of the song remains the same, however modestly Harrison may have later altered it. Harrison, it should be noted, regards his song as that which he sings at the particular moment he is singing it and not something that is written on a piece of paper.

[10] Preston may well have been the "composer" of motif B and the telltale grace note appearing in the second use of the motif during the recording session, for Harrison testified:

"The Court: To be as careful as I can now in summing this up, you can't really say that you or Billy Preston or somebody else didn't somewhere along the line suggest these; all you know is that when Billy Preston sang them that way at the recording session, you felt they were a successful way to sing this, and you kept it?

"The Witness: Yes, I mean at that time we chose what is a good performance.

"The Court: And you felt it was a worthy piece of music?

"The Witness: Yes . . . ."

However, they in fact were, for it is perfectly obvious to the listener that in musical terms, the two songs are virtually identical except for one phrase. There is motif A used four times, followed by motif B, four times in one case, and three times in the other, with the same grace note in the second repetition of motif B. Even Harrison's own expert witness, Harold Barlow, long in the field, acknowledged that although the two motifs were in the public domain, their use here was so unusual that he, in all his experience, had never come across this unique sequential use of these materials. He testified:

"The Court: And I think you agree with me in this, that we are talking about a basic three-note structure that composers can vary in modest ways, but we are still talking about the same heart, the same essence?

"The Witness: Yes.

"The Court: So you say that you have not seen anywhere four A's followed by three B's or four?

"The Witness: Or four A's followed by four B's."

The uniqueness is even greater when one considers the identical grace note in the identical place in each song.

What happened? I conclude that the composer,[11] in seeking musical materials to clothe his thoughts, was working with various possibilities. As he tried this possibility and that, there came to the surface of his mind a particular combination that pleased him as being one he felt would be appealing to a prospective listener; in other words, that this combination of sounds would work. Why? Because his subconscious knew it already had worked in a song his conscious mind did not remember. Having arrived at this pleasing combination of sounds, the recording was made, the lead sheet prepared for copyright and the song became an enormous success. Did Harrison deliberately use the music of He's So Fine? I do not believe he did so deliberately. Nevertheless, it is clear that My Sweet Lord is the very same song as He's So Fine with different words,[12] and Harrison had access to He's So Fine. This is, under the law, infringement of copyright, and is no less so even though subconsciously accomplished. *Sheldon v. Metro-Goldwyn Pictures Corp.,* 81 F.2d 49, 54 (2d Cir. 1936); *Northern Music Corp. v. Pacemaker Music Co., Inc.,* 147 U.S.P.Q. 358, 359 (S.D.N.Y. 1965).

Given the foregoing, I find for the plaintiff on the issue of plagiarism, and set the action down for trial on November 8, 1976 on the issue of damages and other relief as to which the plaintiff may be entitled. The foregoing constitutes the Court's findings of fact and conclusions of law.

So Ordered.

[11] I treat Harrison as the composer, although it appears that Billy Preston may have been the composer as to part. (See fn. 10 *supra*). Even were Preston the composer as to part, this is immaterial. *Peter Pan Fabrics, Inc. v. Dan River Mills, Inc.,* 295 F. Supp. 1366, 1369 (S.D. N.Y.), *aff'd,* 415 F.2d 1007 (2d Cir. 1969).

[12] Harrison himself acknowledged on the stand that the two songs were substantially similar. This same conclusion was obviously reached by a recording group called the "Belmonts" who recorded My Sweet Lord at a later time. With "tongue in cheek" they used the words from *both* He's So Fine and My Sweet Lord interchangeably at certain points.

UNITED STATES DISTRICT COURT

SOUTHERN DISTRICT OF CALIFORNIA

SCORPIO MUSIC S.A., et al.,

Plaintiffs,

v.

VICTOR WILLIS,

Defendant.

Case No. 11cv1557 BTM(RBB)

ORDER GRANTING MOTION TO DISMISS

Defendant Victor Willis ("Willis" or "Defendant") has filed a motion to dismiss Plaintiffs' Complaint. On March 20, 2012, the Court held oral argument on the motion. For the reasons discussed below, Defendant's motion is **GRANTED**.

I. FACTUAL BACKGROUND

Defendant Victor Willis is the original lead singer of the Village People. This lawsuit concerns Willis's attempt to terminate his post-1977 grants to Can't Stop Music of his copyright interests in 33 musical compositions ("Compositions"), including the hit songs, "YMCA," "In the Navy," and "Go West."

Plaintiff Scorpio Music S.A. ("Scorpio") is a French corporation engaged in the business of publishing and otherwise commercially exploiting musical compositions. (Compl. ¶ 1.) Plaintiff Can't Stop Productions, Inc., ("CSP") is the exclusive sub-publisher and administrator in the United States of musical compositions published and owned by Scorpio Music. (Compl. ¶ 2.) Can't Stop Music ("CSM") is a division of Plaintiff Can't Stop Productions, Inc.

Plaintiffs allege that between 1977 and 1979, they hired Willis to translate the lyrics of and/or create new lyrics for certain musical compositions which were owned and published in France by Scorpio. Copyright registrations for the 33 Compositions at issue credit Willis as being one of several writers. (Compl. ¶ 12.) By way of Adaptation Agreements, Willis transferred his copyright interests in the subject Compositions to CSM, and CSM thereupon assigned to Scorpio its rights in the lyrics. (Compl. ¶ 11.) The Adaptation Agreements provided that Willis would receive a set percentage (12%-20%, depending on the composition) of CSM's gross receipts from exploitation of the Compositions.

In January 2011, Willis served on Plaintiffs a "Notice of Termination of Post-1977 Grants of Copyright on Certain Works of Victor Willis" with respect to his interests in the 33 Compositions. (Ex. A to Complaint.)

On July 14, 2011, Plaintiffs commenced this lawsuit. Plaintiffs challenge the validity of the termination and seek a declaratory judgment that Willis has no right, title, or interest in the copyrights to the

Compositions, requiring Willis to withdraw the notice of termination, and enjoining Willis from making any claims to the copyrights in the Compositions. In the event that Willis is found to have a right to terminate, Plaintiffs seek a declaration that (1) Willis's reversion of rights be limited to "the same percentage ownership as he receives as compensation relating to the Compositions and as set forth in the Adaptation Agreements"; and (2) Willis be enjoined from terminating any licenses issued or derivative works authorized, by Plaintiffs, which existed prior to the termination of the copyright assignment.

II. DISCUSSION

A. Valdiity of the Notice of Termination

Plaintiffs' main argument is that Willis's notice of termination is not valid because Willis is the only author who served a notice of termination. According to Plaintiffs, under 17 U.S.C. § 203(a)(1), a majority of all of the authors who transferred their copyright interests in a joint work, whether their transfers were part of the same transaction or separate transactions, must join in a termination for it to be valid. Willis and Amicus Songwriters' Guild of America ("SGA"), on the other hand, contend that since Willis was the only person who executed the grants of his copyright interests in the Compositions, he alone has the ability to terminate those grants. The Court agrees with Willis and SGA.

Because the transfers of copyright at issue in this case occurred after January 1, 1978, the Copyright Act of 1976 ("Act") governs. The Act provides authors and their statutory successors with the ability to terminate a transfer of copyright or license by serving advance notice under specified time limits and conditions.

> 17 U.S.C. § 203 provides:
>
> (a) Conditions for Termination—In the case of any work other than a work made for hire, the exclusive or nonexclusive grant of a transfer or license of copyright or of any right under a copyright, executed by the author on or after January 1, 1978, otherwise than by will, is subject to termination under the following conditions:
>
>> *(1) In the case of a grant executed by one author, termination of the grant may be effected by that author* or, if the author is dead, by the person or persons who, under clause (2) of this subsection, own and are entitled to exercise a total of more than one-half of that author's termination interest. *In the case of a grant executed by two or more authors of a joint work, termination of the grant may be effected by a majority of the authors who executed it*; if any of such authors is dead, the termination interest of any such author may be exercised as a unit by the person or persons who, under clause (2) of this subsection, own and are entitled to exercise a total of more than one-half of that author's interest.

Termination of the grant may be effected at any time during a period of five years beginning at the end of thirty-five years from the date of execution of the grant. 17 U.S.C. § 203(a)(3). To terminate a grant, a termination notice must be served on the grantee or grantee's successor not less than two nor more than ten years before the date of termination specified in the notice. 17 U.S.C. § 203(a)(4)(A).

The issue before the Court is whether, in a case where joint authors of a work transfer their respective copyright interests through separate agreements, a single author may alone terminate his separate grant of his copyright interest in the joint work or whether a majority of all the authors is necessary to terminate that grant. Upon consideration of the language and purpose of 17 U.S.C. § 203 in conjunction with the law governing the rights of joint authors, the Court concludes that a joint author who separately transfers his copyright interest may unilaterally terminate that grant.

When interpreting a statute, we start with the "plain meaning" of the statue's text. In re Roman Catholic Archbishop of Portland in Oregon, 661 F.3d 417, 433 (9th Cir. 2011). As explained by the Supreme Court, "courts must presume that a legislature says in a statute what it means and means in a statute what it says there." Conn. Nat'l Bank v. Germain, 503 U.S. 249, 253-54 (1992). However, "we do more than view word or sub-sections in isolation. We derive meaning from context, and this requires reading the relevant statutory provisions as a whole." Hanford Downwinders Coal., Inc. v. Dowdle, 71 F.3d 1469, 1475 (9th Cir. 1995).

Section 203(a)(1) provides, "In the case of a grant executed by one author, termination of the grant may be effected by that author." Section 203(a)(1) goes on to provide, "In the case of a grant executed by two or more authors of a joint work, termination of the grant may be effected by a majority of the authors who executed it." When referring to a grant executed by two or more authors of a joint work, section 203(a)(1) refers to a "grant" in the singular, not "grants." Thus, under the plain meaning of the statute, if two or more joint authors join in a grant of their copyright interests, a majority of the authors is necessary to terminate the grant. If, however, a single joint author enters into a grant of his copyright interest, that author alone can terminate his grant.

The Court's reading of section 203(a)(1) harmonizes with the law governing the rights of joint authors, both as it existed at the time of the passage of the Act and as it exists today. As recognized in the House Report accompanying the passage of the Copyright Act of 1976, "Under the bill, as under the present law, coowners of a copyright would be treated generally as tenants in common, with each coowner having an independent right to use of [sic] license the use of a work, subject to a duty of accounting to the other coowners for any profit." H.R.Rep. No. 94-1476, at 121 (1976), reprinted in 1976 U.S.C.C.A.N. 5659, 5736.[1] Then, as now, each co-owner of a joint work becomes a holder of an undivided interest in the whole. Pye v. Mitchell, 574 F.2d 476, 480 (9th Cir. 1978) (citing to 1 Nimmer on Copyright § 69 (1976)). Thus, "[i]n the absence of an agreement to the contrary, one joint owner may always transfer his interest in the joint work to a third party, subject only to the general requirements of a valid transfer of copyright." Nimmer on Copyright § 6.11 (2011) ("Nimmer").

Congress was aware that a single joint author may grant his interest in the joint work separately from his co-authors or may join in a grant with one or more of his co-authors. Knowing this, Congress legislated that "*[i]n the case* of a grant executed by two or more authors of a joint work," a majority of the authors who executed the grant is necessary for termination. 18 U.S.C. § 203(a)(1) (Emphasis added.) In other words, *when* two or more authors of a joint work execute a joint grant, a majority of the authors who executed the grant is necessary to terminate the grant. Section 203(a)(1) certainly does not *require* that a joint author enter into a joint grant with one or more of his co-authors. Nor does the statute provide that

[1] The Act added section 201(a), which states, "The authors of a joint work are coowners of copyright in the work."

where two or more joint authors enter into separate *grants*, a majority of those authors is needed to terminate any one of those *grants*.

Plaintiffs argue that the term "grant" as used in section 203(a)(1) refers collectively to all transfers by joint authors, even if the transfers were separate transactions. This argument is not persuasive. Nowhere does the statute indicate that the term "grant" has a special meaning and encompasses all transfers of interest by joint authors, regardless of whether the joint authors individually transferred their interests through different instruments at different times.[2]

Furthermore, it makes sense to interpret the term "grant" to refer to a *single* transaction whereby the rights of one or more joint authors was transferred, because the time for terminating a grant is calculated from the date of execution of the grant. Under Plaintiffs' interpretation, in the case of separate transfers by joint authors, there would be uncertainty regarding the date of execution, which could become a moving target. For example, if joint authors A, B, C, and D each separately transferred their interests, with an interval of several years between each transfer, would the "date of execution" keep changing as each author transfers his/her interest? If so, it could be many years after A's transfer that the "grant" is considered "executed."

Finally, it would be contrary to the purpose of the Act to require a majority of all joint authors who had, at various times, transferred their copyright interests in a joint work to terminate the legally permissible *separate* grant by one joint author of his undivided copyright interest in the work. The purpose of the Act was to "safeguard[ ] authors against unremunerative transfers" and address "the unequal bargaining position of authors, resulting in part from the impossibility of determining a work's value until it has been exploited." H.R. Rep. No. 94-1476, at 124 (1976), reprinted in 1976 U.S.C.C.A.N. 5659, 5740. Under Plaintiffs' interpretation, it would be more difficult to terminate an individual grant than it would be to make it in the first place.

Plaintiffs attempt to support their position by pointing to the law governing pre-1978 grants. Grants executed prior to January 1, 1978 are terminable by each executing joint author (to the extent of the particular author's interest), even if a majority of the executing joint authors do not join in the termination. 17 U.S.C. § 304(c)(1). As discussed in Nimmer, § 11.03, it appears that Congress treated pre-1978 grants differently because if a grantor of renewal rights failed to survive until such rights vested, the renewal rights would pass to the grantor's successors and the original grantee would take nothing. Accordingly, "[b]ecause joint-author grants of renewal rights thus terminate individually by operation of law upon an author's death, it was thought 'inappropriate' to require anything more than individual termination via the termination provisions." Id. The stricter requirement for termination of post-1977 grants begs the question of whether a "grant" may encompass separate transfers of interest by joint authors and does not shed any light on the matter before the Court.

Plaintiffs attempt to support their position by relying on language in Sweet Music, Inc v. Melrose Music Corp., 189 F. Supp. 655 (S.D. Cal. 1960), where the court explained that it did not make a difference to the outcome of the case that plaintiff joined in the same assignment agreement as the deceased co-author as opposed to having executed a separate assignment. However, Sweet Music concerned the enforceability

[2] In this case, it also appears that at least some of the joint authors granted their copyright interests to Scorpio, not CSM, as Willis did. Thus, Plaintiffs would include under the umbrella of a "grant," separate transactions where copyright interests were transferred to related but different entities.

of an assignment of renewal interests by one author where a co-author, who also assigned his renewal interests, died prior to renewal. Sweet Music did not concern the termination of grants under the Copyright Act of 1976 and does not shed light on the issue before the Court.

The Court concludes that because Willis granted his copyright interests in the Compositions separately from the other co-authors, Willis may, under 17 U.S.C. § 203, unilaterally terminate his grants. Thus, Plaintiffs' declaratory relief claim fails to the extent it is based on the inability of Willis to terminate his grants of copyright. To be clear, Willis's termination affects only the copyright interests that he previously transferred (his undivided interest in the joint work). The copyright interests transferred by the other co-authors will not be affected by Willis's termination.

B. Writer for Hire

In their Complaint, Plaintiffs allege that Willis has no rights in the copyrights at issue because he was a "writer for hire" who rendered his services as an employee of CSM. At oral argument, counsel for Plaintiffs represented that they were withdrawing this claim.

C. Percentage of Copyright Interest

In the event Willis is found to have a right to terminate his grants of copyright interest in the Compositions, Plaintiffs seek a declaration that Willis "be limited to the same percentage ownership as he receives as compensation relating to the Compositions and as set forth in the Agreements." (Compl. at 9.) However, Plaintiffs' claim is not supported by the law.

Upon termination, Willis would get back what he transferred—his undivided interest in the whole. See 17 U.S.C. § 203(b) (explaining that upon the effective date of termination, "all rights under this title that were covered by the terminated grants revert to the author . . . .") Absent a different agreement among the joint authors (of which there is no evidence in this case), the joint authors shared equally in the ownership of the joint work, even if their respective contributions to the joint work were not equal. Nimmer, § 6.08. Thus, if Willis was one of three joint authors of a musical composition, Willis would have a 1/3 undivided copyright interest in the composition. If Willis granted his copyright interest in the composition to CSM and then later terminated that grant, Willis would get back his 1/3 undivided copyright interest, regardless of what percentage royalty he was paid during CSM's ownership of the copyright interest.

Plaintiffs do not claim that the royalty percentages, which ranged from 12 to 20%, were based on the percentage of Willis's copyright interests, and it does not appear that this was the case. For example, Willis is one of three authors listed on the copyright registration for "YMCA." (Def. Ex. C.) Assuming the three authors were actually joint authors, Willis has a 1/3 undivided interest in the copyright. However, the Adaptation Agreement pertaining to YMCA provides for a 20% royalty. (Def. Ex. B.)

Plaintiffs do not cite any legal authority supporting the proposition that upon termination of his grants, Willis does not get back the percentage of copyright interest he granted, but, rather, is limited to a percentage of ownership equal to the royalty percentage. The Court concludes that Plaintiffs' position lacks merit and dismisses Plaintiffs' declaratory relief claim on this issue.

It appears that there is a dispute between Plaintiffs and Willis, with respect to some or all of the Compositions, regarding the percentage of copyright interest Willis originally held, granted, and wants back. At oral argument, counsel for Willis indicated that Willis contends that Henri Belolo, one of the individuals listed as an author on the copyright registrations for some or all of the Compositions, was not actually a joint author. If Willis is correct, his undivided interest in the Compositions is larger than it appears. For example, Willis would have a 1/2 undivided interest in YMCA instead of a 1/3 undivided interest.

The Complaint makes a passing reference to the dispute regarding authorship. The Complaint states that upon information and belief, Willis claims the right to recapture at least half of the copyrights in each of the Compositions. (Compl. ¶ 34.) The Complaint also states that Willis "ignores the existence of other people listed as writers of the Compositions to claim that he, alone, wrote all of their lyrics." (Compl. ¶ 35.) However, the Complaint does not seek a declaration regarding the determination of the issue of authorship and the percentage of copyright interest Willis granted and is entitled to receive back.

It is necessary for Plaintiffs to know what percentage of the copyright interest Willis is entitled to receive back, because, among other things, it will affect Plaintiffs' duty to account to Willis and the other joint author(s). Therefore, the Court will allow Plaintiffs to amend their Complaint to seek declaratory relief on this issue.

D. Statute of Limitations

In the Complaint, Plaintiffs allege that Willis's claim to the copyright in the Compositions is somehow time-barred.

To the extent Plaintiffs argue that Willis is time-barred from arguing that a "co-author" listed on a copyright registration is not actually a joint author, this argument is premature. As already discussed, Plaintiffs have not yet sought a declaration regarding the percentage of Willis's copyright interest in each of the Compositions. To the extent Plaintiff's argue that Willis is time-barred from claiming that the percentage of his copyright interests exceeds the royalty percentages set forth in the Adaptation Agreements, the Court rejects Plaintiff's argument. For the reasons discussed above, Plaintiffs' claim that the percentage of copyright interest recoverable by Willis is capped by the royalty percentage has no legal basis, and Plaintiffs have not explained why Willis should be time-barred from asserting his rights under the law.

E. Termination of Existing Licenses and Derivative Works

Plaintiffs also seek a declaration that Willis is precluded from terminating any licenses issued or derivative works authorized by Plaintiffs prior to the termination of the copyright assignment. Willis does not dispute that existing derivative works may continue to be exploited under existing licenses under the terms of the grants and the existing licenses. See 17 U.S.C. § 203(b)(1). Therefore, it does not appear that there is a controversy in this regard. If Plaintiffs can point to facts showing that there is a controversy regarding utilization of derivative works prepared prior to the termination of the grants, Plaintiffs may amend their Complaint to include these facts.

III. CONCLUSION

For the reasons discussed above, Willis's motion to dismiss is **GRANTED**. Plaintiffs' Complaint is **DISMISSED** for failure to state a claim. The Court grants Plaintiffs leave to file an amended complaint within 30 days of the entry of this Order. If Plaintiffs do not file an amended complaint, this case shall be closed.

IT IS SO ORDERED

DATED: May 7, 2012

BARRY TED MOSKOWITZ, Chief Judge
United States District Court

Court of Appeals of the State of New York

Roberson v. Rochester Folding Box Co.

171 N.Y. 538 (N.Y. 1902) • 64 N.E. 442

Decided Jun 27, 1902

Argued February 13, 1902

Decided June 27, 1902

Elbridge L. Adams for appellants. *Milton E. Gibbs* for respondent.

PARKER, Ch. J.

The Appellate Division has certified that the following questions of law have arisen in this case, and ought to be reviewed by this court: 1. Does the complaint herein state a cause of action at law against the defendants or either of them? 2. Does the complaint herein state a cause of action in equity against the defendants or either of them? These questions are presented by a demurrer to the complaint, which is put upon the ground that the complaint does not state facts sufficient to constitute a cause of action.

As a demurrer admits not only those facts which are expressly alleged in the complaint, but everything which can be implied by fair and reasonable intendment from its allegations (*Marie* v. *Garrison*, 83 N.Y. 14, 23) we are to inquire whether the complaint, regarded from the standpoint of this rule, can be said to show any right to relief either in law or in equity.

The complaint alleges that the Franklin Mills Co., one of the defendants, was engaged in a general milling business and in the manufacture and sale of flour; that before the commencement of the action, without the knowledge or consent of plaintiff, defendants, knowing that they had no right or authority so to do, had obtained, made, printed, sold and circulated about 25,000 lithographic prints, photographs and likenesses of plaintiff, made in a manner particularly set up in the complaint; that upon the paper upon which the likenesses were printed and above the portrait there were printed, in large, plain letters, the words, "Flour of the Family," and below the portrait in large capital letters, "Franklin Mills Flour," and in the lower right-hand corner in smaller capital letters, "Rochester Folding Box Co., Rochester, N.Y.;" that upon the same sheet were other advertisements of the flour of the Franklin Mills Co.; that those 25,000 likenesses of the plaintiff thus ornamented have been conspicuously posted and displayed in stores, warehouses, saloons and other public places; that they have been recognized by friends of the plaintiff and other people with the result that plaintiff has been greatly humiliated by the scoffs and jeers of persons who have recognized her face and picture on this advertisement and her good name has been attacked, causing her great distress and suffering both in body and mind; that she was made sick and suffered a severe nervous shock, was confined to her bed and compelled to employ a physician, because of these facts; that defendants had continued to print, make, use, sell and circulate the said lithographs, and that by reason of the foregoing facts plaintiff had suffered damages in the sum of $15,000. The complaint prays that defendants be enjoined from making, printing, publishing, circulating or using in any manner any likenesses of plaintiff in any form whatever, for further relief (which it is not necessary to consider here) and for damages.

It will be observed that there is no complaint made that plaintiff was libeled by this publication of her portrait. The likeness is said to be a very good one, and one that her friends and acquaintances were able to recognize; indeed, her grievance is that a good portrait of her, and, therefore, one easily recognized, has been used to attract attention toward the paper upon which defendant mill company's advertisements appear. Such publicity, which some find agreeable, is to plaintiff very distasteful, and thus, because of defendants' impertinence in using her picture without her consent for their own business purposes, she has been caused to suffer mental distress where others would have appreciated the compliment to their beauty implied in the selection of the picture for such purposes; but as it is distasteful to her, she seeks the aid of the courts to enjoin a further circulation of the lithographic prints containing her portrait made as alleged in the complaint, and as an incident thereto, to reimburse her for the damages to her feelings, which the complaint fixes at the sum of $15,000.

There is no precedent for such an action to be found in the decisions of this court; indeed the learned judge who wrote the very able and interesting opinion in the Appellate Division said, while upon the threshold of the discussion of the question: "It may be said in the first place that the theory upon which this action is predicated is new, at least in instance if not in principle, and that few precedents can be found to sustain the claim made by the plaintiff, if indeed it can be said that there are any authoritative cases establishing her right to recover in this action." Nevertheless, that court reached the conclusion that plaintiff had a good cause of action against defendants, in that defendants had invaded what is called a "right of privacy"—in other words, the right to be let alone. Mention of such a right is not to be found in Blackstone, Kent or any other of the great commentators upon the law, nor so far as the learning of counsel or the courts in this case have been able to discover, does its existence seem to have been asserted prior to about the year 1890, when it was presented with attractiveness and no inconsiderable ability in the Harvard Law Review (Vol. IV, page 193) in an article entitled, "The Right of Privacy."

The so-called right of privacy is, as the phrase suggests, founded upon the claim that a man has the right to pass through this world, if he wills, without having his picture published, his business enterprises discussed, his successful experiments written up for the benefit of others, or his eccentricities commented upon either in handbills, circulars, catalogues, periodicals or newspapers, and, necessarily, that the things which may not be written and published of him must not be spoken of him by his neighbors, whether the comment be favorable or otherwise. While most persons would much prefer to have a good likeness of themselves appear in a responsible periodical or leading newspaper rather than upon an advertising card or sheet, the doctrine which the courts are asked to create for this case would apply as well to the one publication as to the other, for the principle which a court of equity is asked to assert in support of a recovery in this action is that the right of privacy exists and is enforceable in equity, and that the publication of that which purports to be a portrait of another person, even if obtained upon the street by an impertinent individual with a camera, will be restrained in equity on the ground that an individual has the right to prevent his features from becoming known to those outside of his circle of friends and acquaintances.

If such a principle be incorporated into the body of the law through the instrumentality of a court of equity, the attempts to logically apply the principle will necessarily result, not only in a vast amount of litigation, but in litigation bordering upon the absurd, for the right of privacy, once established as a legal doctrine, cannot be confined to the restraint of the publication of a likeness but must necessarily embrace as well the publication of a word-picture, a comment upon one's looks, conduct, domestic relations or habits. And were the right of privacy once legally asserted it would necessarily be held to include the same things if spoken instead of printed, for one, as well as the other, invades the right to be absolutely let alone. An insult would certainly be in violation of such a right and with many persons would more seriously wound the feelings than would the publication of their picture. And so we might add to the list of things that are spoken and done day by day which seriously offend the sensibilities of good people to which the principle which the plaintiff seeks to have imbedded in the doctrine of the law would seem to apply. I have gone only far enough to barely suggest the vast field of litigation which would necessarily be opened up should this court hold that privacy exists as a legal right enforceable in equity by injunction, and by damages where they seem necessary to give complete relief.

The legislative body could very well interfere and arbitrarily provide that no one should be permitted for his own selfish purpose to use the picture or the name of another for advertising purposes without his consent. In such, event no embarrassment would result to the general body of the law, for the rule would be applicable only to cases provided for by the statute. The courts, however, being without authority to legislate, are required to decide cases upon principle, and so are necessarily embarrassed by precedents created by an extreme, and, therefore, unjustifiable application of an old principle.

The court below properly said that "while it may be true that the fact that no precedent can be found to sustain an action in any given case, is cogent evidence that a principle does not exist upon which the right may be based, it is not the rule that the want of a precedent is a sufficient reason for turning the plaintiff out of court," provided—I think should be added—there can be found a clear and unequivocal principle of the common law which either directly or mediately governs it or which by analogy or parity of reasoning ought to govern it.

It is undoubtedly true that in the early days of chancery jurisdiction in England the chancellors were accustomed to deliver their judgments without regard to principles or precedents and in that way the process of building up the system of equity went on, the chancellor disregarding absolutely many established principles of the common law. "In no other way," says Pomeroy, "could the system of equity jurisprudence have been commenced and continued so as to arrive at its present proportions." (Pomeroy's Eq. Jur. § 48.) In their work the chancellors were guided not only by what they regarded as the eternal principles of absolute right, but also by their individual consciences, but after a time when "the period of infancy was passed and an orderly system of equitable principles, doctrines and rules began to be developed out of the increasing mass of precedents, this theory of a personal conscience was abandoned; and 'the conscience,' which is an element of the equitable jurisdiction, came to be regarded, and has so continued to the present day, as a metaphorical term, designating the common standard of civil right and expediency combined, based upon general principles and limited by established doctrines to which the court appeals, and by which it tests the conduct and rights of suitors—a juridical and not a personal conscience." (Pomeroy's Eq. Jur. § 57.)

The importance of observing the spirit of this rule cannot be overestimated, for, while justice in a given case may be worked out by a decision of the court according to the notions of right which govern the individual judge or body of judges comprising the court, the mischief which will finally result may be almost incalculable under our system which makes a decision in one case a precedent for decisions in all future cases which are akin to it in the essential facts.

So in a case like the one before us, which is concededly new to this court, it is important that the court should have in mind the effect upon future litigation and upon the development of the law which would necessarily result from a step so far outside of the beaten paths of both common law and equity, assuming—what I shall attempt to show in a moment—that the right of privacy as a legal doctrine enforceable in equity has not, down to this time, been established by decisions.

The history of the phrase "right of privacy" in this country seems to have begun in 1890 in a clever article in the Harvard Law Review—already referred to—in which a number of English cases were analyzed, and, reasoning by analogy, the conclusion was reached that—notwithstanding the unanimity of the courts in resting their decisions upon property rights in cases where publication is prevented by injunction—in reality such prevention was due to the necessity of affording protection to thoughts and sentiments expressed through the medium of writing, printing and the arts, which is like the right not to be assaulted or beaten; in other words, that the principle, actually involved though not always appreciated, was that of an inviolate personality, not that of private property.

This article brought forth a reply from the Northwestern Review (Vol. III, page 1) urging that equity has no concern with the feelings of an individual or with considerations of moral fitness, except as the inconvenience or discomfort which the person may suffer is connected with the possession or enjoyment of property, and that the English authorities cited are consistent with such view. Those authorities are now to be examined in order that we may see whether they were intended to and did mark a departure from the established rule which had been enforced for generations; or, on the other hand, are entirely consistent with it.

The first case is *Prince Albert* v. *Strange* (1 Macn. G. 25; 2 De G. S. 652). The queen and the prince, having made etchings and drawings for their own amusement, decided to have copies struck off from the etched plates for presentation to friends and for their own use. The workman employed, however, printed some copies on his own account, which afterwards came into the hands of Strange, who purposed exhibiting them, and published a descriptive catalogue. Prince Albert applied for an injunction as to both exhibition and catalogue, and the vice-chancellor granted it, restraining defendant from publishing "at least by printing or writing, *though not by copy or resemblance*," a description of the etchings. An examination of the opinion of the vice-chancellor discloses that he found two reasons for granting the injunction, namely, that the property rights of Prince Albert had been infringed, and that there was a breach of trust by the workman in retaining some impressions for himself. The opinion contained no hint whatever of a right of privacy separate and distinct from the right of property.

Pollard v. *Photographic Co.* (L.R. 40 Ch. Div. 345) is certainly not an authority for granting an injunction on the ground of threatened injury to the feelings, although it is true, as stated in the opinion of the Appellate Division, that the court did say in the course of the discussion that the right to grant an injunction does not depend upon the existence of property; but the decision was, in fact, placed upon the ground that there was a breach of an implied contract. The facts, briefly stated, were that a photographer had been applied to by a woman to take her photograph, she ordering a certain number of copies, as is usual in such cases. The photographer made copies for himself and undertook to exhibit them, and also sold copies to a stationer, who used them as Christmas cards. Their action was restrained by the court on the ground that there was an implied contract not to use the negative for any other purpose than to supply the sitter with copies of it for a price. During the argument of plaintiff's counsel, the court asked this question: "Do you dispute that if the negative likeness were taken on the sly, the person who took it might exhibit copies?" Counsel replied: "In that case there would be no consideration to support a contract."

In *Gee* v. *Pritchard* (2 Swanst. 402) B attempted to print a private letter written him by A, and he was restrained on the ground that the property of that private letter remained in A, B having it only for the qualified purpose for which it was sent to him, the basis of the decision, therefore, being the idea of plaintiff's property in the thing published, as being the product of his mind, written by him and put into the hands of B for a limited purpose only.

The same judge, Lord ELDON, also granted the injunction in *Abernathy* v. *Hutchinson* (3 L.J. Ch. 209) restraining the publication in the "Lancet" of lectures delivered at a hospital by the plaintiff. The court expressed a doubt in that case whether there could be property in lectures which had not been reduced to writing, but granted the injunction on the ground that it was a breach of confidence on the part of a pupil who was admitted to hear the lectures to publish them, inasmuch as they were delivered for the information of the pupils and not for sale and profit by them.

Mayhall v. *Higbey* (1 I I. C. 188) was also a case where an injunction was granted and nominal damages awarded on the ground that plaintiff had a property right in certain photographic negatives which he had loaned to a person who, subsequently, became insolvent and whose assignee, without right, sold them to defendant who printed copies from them which he published and sold.

In *Duke of Queensberry* v. *Shebbeare* (2 Eden, 329) the Earl of Clarendon delivered to one Gwynne an original manuscript of his father's, "Lord Clarendon's History." Gwynne's administrator afterwards sold it to Shebbeare, and the court, upon the application of the personal representatives of Lord Clarendon, restrained its publication on the ground that they had a property right in the manuscript which it was not intended that Gwynne should have the benefit of by multiplying the number of copies in print for profit.

In not one of these cases, therefore, was it the basis of the decision that the defendant could be restrained from performing the act he was doing or threatening to do on the ground that the feelings of the plaintiff would be thereby injured; but, on the contrary, each decision was rested either upon the ground of breach of trust or that plaintiff had a property right in the subject of litigation which the court could protect.

A more recent English case, decided in 1898, is more nearly in point and negatives the contention that plaintiff may restrain an unauthorized publication which is offensive to him—namely, *Dockrell* v. *Dougall* (78 L.T.R. 840). In that case defendant, the owner of a medicine called "Sallyco," published the following substantially true but unauthorized statement about plaintiff: "Dr. Morgan Dockrell, physician to St. John's Hospital, London, is prescribing Sallyco as an habitual drink. Dr. Dockrell says nothing has done his gout so much good." In the course of the opinion the court said, in effect, that plaintiff claimed to be entitled to an injunction restraining defendant from using plaintiff's name in his advertisements on the ground that an injunction should be granted in every such case where it can be shown that the use of the plaintiff's name is unauthorized and is calculated to injure him in his profession, and after saying that he did not think that this was right, he stated the proper rule to be that "In order that an injunction may issue to restrain a defendant from using a plaintiff's name the use of it must be such as to injure the plaintiff's reputation or property."

None of the other English cases brought to our attention are claimed to have a direct bearing upon this question, and it seems to us very clear that they do not in anywise support the position of plaintiff.

The case that seems to have been more relied upon than any other by the learned Appellate Division in reaching the conclusion that the complaint in this case states a cause of action, is *Schuyler* v. *Curtis* (147 N.Y. 434). In that case certain persons attempted to erect a statue or bust of a woman no longer living, and one of her relatives commenced an action in equity to restrain such erection, alleging that his feelings and the feelings of other relatives of deceased would be injured thereby. At Special Term an injunction was granted on that ground. (19 N.Y. Supp. 264.) The General Term affirmed the decision. (64 Hun, 594.) This court reversed the judgment, Judge PECKHAM writing, and so far as the decision is concerned, therefore, it is not authority for the existence of a right of privacy which entitles a party to restrain another from doing an act which, though not actionable at common law, occasions plaintiff mental distress. In the course of the argument, however, expressions were used which it is now claimed indicate that the court recognized the existence of such a right. A sufficient answer to that contention is to be found in the opinion written on the motion for reargument in *Colonial City Tr. Co.* v. *Kingston City R.R. Co.* (154 N.Y. 493) in which it was said: "It was not our intention to decide any case but the one before us. * * * If, as sometimes happens, broader statements were made by way of argument or otherwise than were essential to the decision of the questions presented, they are the dicta of the writer of the opinion and not the decision of the court. A judicial opinion, like evidence, is only binding so far as it is relevant, and when it wanders from the point at issue it no longer has force as an official utterance." The question up for decision in the *Schuyler* case was whether the relatives could restrain the threatened action of defendants, and not whether Mrs. Schuyler could have restrained it had she been living. The latter question not being before the court it was not called upon to decide it, and, as we read the opinion, there is no expression in it which indicates an intention either to decide it or to seriously consider it, but rather, it proceeds upon the assumption that if such a right did exist in Mrs. Schuyler, her relatives did not succeed to it upon her death; all of which will sufficiently appear from the following extracts from the opinion:

"This action is of a nature somewhat unusual and dependent for its support upon the application of certain principles which are themselves not very clearly defined or their boundaries very well recognized or plainly laid down. Briefly described, the action is founded upon the alleged violation of *what is termed the right of privacy.*"

"It is not necessary, however, to the view which we take of this case, to lay down precise and accurate rules which shall apply to all cases touching upon this *alleged right.*"

"*For the purposes we have in view, it is unnecessary to wholly deny the existence of the right of privacy* to which the plaintiff appeals as the foundation of his cause of action."

"*While not assuming to decide what this right of privacy is in all cases,* we are quite clear that such a right would not be violated by the proposed action of the defendants."

"There are two other cases in this state bearing upon this question: *Marks* v. *Jaffa* (26 N.Y. Supp. 908), decided at Special Term, and *Murray* v. *Gast Lithographic Engraving Co.* (8 Misc. Rep. 36) decided at an Equity Term of the Court of Common Pleas at New York. In the first case the relief prayed for was granted upon the authority of the decision of the General Term in the *Schuyler* case, which was subsequently reversed in this court. In the *Murray* case, in a well-reasoned opinion by Judge BISCHOFF, it is held that a parent cannot maintain an action to enjoin an unauthorized publication of the portrait of an infant child, and for damages for injuries to his sensibilities caused by the invasion of his child's privacy, because "the law takes no cognizance of a sentimental injury, independent of a wrong to person or property." In the course of his opinion he quotes from the opinion of LUMPKIN, J., in *Chapman* v. *West. U.T. Co.* (88 Ga. 763) as follows: "The law protects the person and the purse. The person includes the reputation. The body, reputation and property of the citizen are not to be invaded without responsibility in damages to the sufferer. But, outside these protected spheres, the law does not yet attempt to guard the peace of mind, the feelings or the happiness of everyone by giving recovery of damages for mental anguish produced by mere negligence. There is no right, capable of enforcement by process of law, to possess or maintain, without disturbance, any particular condition of feeling. The law leaves feeling to be helped and vindicated by the tremendous force of sympathy. The temperaments of individuals are various and variable, and the imagination exerts a powerful and incalculable influence in injuries of this kind. There are many moral obligations too delicate and subtle to be enforced in the rude way of giving money compensation for their violation. Perhaps the feelings find as full protection as it is possible to give in moral law and a responsive public opinion. The civil law is a practical business system, dealing with what is tangible, and does not undertake to redress psychological injuries."

Outside of this jurisdiction the question seems to have been presented in two other cases in this country: *Corliss* v. *E.W. Walker* Co. (57 Fed. Rep. 434; 64 Fed. Rep. 280) and *Atkinson* v. *Doherty* (121 Mich. 372). The *Corliss* case was an action in equity to restrain the publication of the biography and picture of Mr. Corliss. It was based upon an alleged invasion of the right of privacy. The court denied the injunction as to the publication of the biography but granted it as to the use of certain plates from which the defendant was to make a picture of Mr. Corliss, upon the ground that they had been obtained upon conditions which defendant had not complied with. In the course of the opinion the court said: "Under our laws one can speak and publish what he desires, provided he commit no offense against public morals or private reputation. * * * There is another objection which meets us at the threshold of this case. The subject-matter of the jurisdiction of a court of equity is civil property, and injury to property, whether actual or prospective is the foundation on which its jurisdiction rests. (*Re Sawyer,* 124 U.S. 200, 210; Kerr. Inj. [2d ed.] p. 1.) It follows from this principle that a court of equity has no power to restrain a libelous publication." Both the opinion and the decision necessarily negative the existence of an actionable right of privacy; but subsequently upon a motion to dissolve the injunction, which was granted upon the ground that Mr. Corliss was a public character, and hence the publishers were entitled to use his picture, the learned court expressed the opinion that a private individual has the right to be protected from the publication of his portrait in any form. Now, while this suggestion was *obiter,* it merits discussion, and an examination of that which it promulgates as doctrine discloses what we deem a fatal objection to the establishment of a rule of privacy. The learned judge says: "I believe the law to be that a private individual has a right to be protected in the representation of his portrait in any form; that this is a property as well as a personal right, and that it belongs to the same class of rights which forbids the reproduction of a private manuscript or painting, or the publication of private letters, or of oral lectures delivered by a teacher to his class, or the revelation of the contents of a merchant's book by a clerk. * * * But, while the right of a private individual to prohibit the reproduction of his picture or photograph should be recognized and enforced, this right may be surrendered or dedicated to the public by the act of the individual, just the same as a private manuscript, book or painting becomes (when not protected by copyright) public property by the act of publication. The distinction in the case of a picture or photograph lies, it seems to me, between public and private characters. A private individual should be protected against the publication of any portrait of himself, but where an individual becomes a public character the case is different. A statesman, author, artist or inventor, who asks for and desires public recognition, may be said to have surrendered his right to the public." This distinction between public and private characters cannot possibly be drawn. On what principle does an author or artist forfeit his right of privacy and a great orator, a great preacher, or a great advocate retain his? Who can draw a line of demarcation between public characters and private characters, let that line be as wavering and irregular as you please? In the very case then before the judge, what had Mr. Corliss done by which he surrendered his right of privacy? In what respect did he by his inventions "ask for and desire public recognition" any more than a banker or merchant who prosecutes his calling? Or is the right of privacy the possession of mediocrity alone, which a person forfeits by giving rein to his ability, spurs to his industry or grandeur to his character? A lady may pass her life in domestic privacy when, by some act of heroism or self-sacrifice, her name and fame fill the public ear. Is she to forfeit by her good deed the right of privacy she previously possessed? These considerations suggest the answer we would make to the position of the learned judge and at the same time serve to make more clear what we have elsewhere attempted to point out, namely, the absolute impossibility of dealing with this subject save by legislative enactment, by which may be drawn arbitrary distinctions which no court should promulgate as a part of general jurisprudence.

Atkinson v. *Doherty* was a suit in equity brought by the widow of Colonel John Atkinson, a well-known lawyer in Detroit, to enjoin the defendant, a cigar manufacturer, from using the name and portrait of Colonel Atkinson upon boxes of cigars manufactured by defendant. The suit was dismissed by the Circuit Court, and its decree was unanimously affirmed by the Supreme Court. The case quite closely resembles the *Schuyler* case, which was brought to the attention of that court, and in the course of the opinion the contention that the Schuyler case intimated the existence of a right of privacy was met as follows: "We think it should not be considered as containing a *dictum* even in support of the doctrine contended for." The method adopted by the court in the *Atkinson* case in treating the question was different from that employed by this court in the *Schuyler* case, however, for the opinion proceeds to a review of the authorities upon which the right of privacy is said to rest, reaching the conclusion that all of the authorities which are entitled to respect are based upon property or contract rights, and hence "that Colonel Atkinson would himself be remediless were he alive, and the same is true of his friends who survive." The opinion concludes as follows: "This law of privacy seems to have gained a foothold at one time in the history of our jurisprudence—not by that name, it is true—but in effect. It is evidenced by the old maxim, 'the greater the truth the greater the libel,' and the result has been the emphatic expression of public disapproval, by the emancipation of the press and the establishment of freedom of speech, and the abolition in most of the states of the maxim quoted by constitutional provisions. The limitations upon the exercise of these rights being the law of slander and libel, whereby the publication of an untruth that can be presumed or shown to the satisfaction, not of the plaintiff, but of others (*i.e.,* an impartial jury), to be injurious, not alone to the feelings, but to the reputation, is actionable. Should it be thought that it is a hard rule that is applied in this case, it is only necessary to call attention to the fact that a ready remedy is to be found in legislation. We are not satisfied, however, that the rule is a hard one, and think that the concensus of opinion must be that the complainants contend for a much harder one. The law does not remedy all evils. It cannot, in the nature of things; and deliberation may well be used in considering the propriety of an innovation such as this case suggests. We do not wish to be understood as belittling the complaint. We have no reason to doubt the feeling of annoyance alleged. Indeed, we sympathize with it, and marvel at the impertinence which does not respect it. We can only say that it is one of the ills that under the law cannot be redressed."

An examination of the authorities leads us to the conclusion that the so-called "right of privacy" has not as yet found an abiding place in our jurisprudence, and, as we view it, the doctrine cannot now be incorporated without doing violence to settled principles of law by which the profession and the public have long been guided.

I do not say that, even under the existing law, in every case of the character of the one before us, or indeed in this case, a party whose likeness is circulated against his will is without remedy. By section 245 of the Penal Code any malicious publication by picture, effigy or sign which exposes a person to contempt, ridicule or obloquy is a libel, and it would constitute such at common law. Malicious in this definition means simply intentional and willful. There are many articles, especially of medicine, whose character is such that using the picture of a person, particularly that of a woman, in connection with the advertisement of those articles might justly be found by a jury to cast ridicule or obloquy on the person whose picture was thus published. The manner or posture in which the person is portrayed might readily have a like effect. In such cases both a civil action and a criminal prosecution could be maintained. But there is no allegation in the complaint before us that this was the tendency of the publication complained of, and the absence of such an allegation is fatal to the maintenance of the action, treating it as one of libel. This case differs from an action brought for libelous words. In such case the alleged libel is stated in the complaint, and if the words are libelous *per se* it is unnecessary to charge that their effect exposes the plaintiff to disgrace, ridicule or obloquy. The law attributes to them that result. But where the libel is a picture which does not appear in the record, to make it libelous there must be a proper allegation as to its character.

The judgment of the Appellate Division and of the Special Term should be reversed and questions certified answered in the negative, without costs, and with leave to the plaintiff to serve an amended complaint within twenty days, also without costs.

GRAY, J. (dissenting).

The question arises on the defendants' demurrer to the sufficiency of the complaint to state a cause of action. The complaint alleges that, without the knowledge of the plaintiff, the defendants, "knowing that they had no right or authority so to do, had obtained, made, printed, sold and circulated about 25,000 lithographic prints, photographs or likenesses of plaintiff, for the purpose of profit and gain to themselves;" that upon the paper upon which the likeness was printed, are the words above the portrait, in large, plain letters, "Flour of the Family," and below, in large capital letters, "Franklin Mills Flour," and in the lower right hand corner, in small capital letters, are the words "Rochester Folding Box Company;" that upon the same paper are the advertisements of the flour of the Franklin Mills Company; that these 25,000 likenesses of the plaintiff thus ornamented have been "conspicuously posted and displayed in stores, warehouses and saloons, throughout the United States and other countries, and particularly in the vicinity where the plaintiff resides;" that the result has been to greatly humiliate her, by the scoffs and jeers of persons who have recognized her face upon these advertisements, and her good name has been attacked and that, because of these facts, "she was made sick and suffered a severe nervous shock, was confined to her bed and was compelled to employ a physician." The plaintiff, further, alleges that the defendants "are now wrongfully printing, making, using, selling and circulating these lithographs," and that, by reason of these facts, she has suffered damages in the sum of $15,000. The relief demanded is that the defendants be enjoined from making, printing, publishing, obtaining, or using, in any manner, any likeness of the plaintiff in any form whatever. The facts contained within these allegations must be regarded as admitted, under the defendant's demurrer; as must all other facts which can be implied, by reasonable and fair intendment. (*Marie* v. *Garrison*, 83 N.Y. 14.) These defendants stand before the court, admitting that they have made, published and circulated, without the knowledge or the authority of the plaintiff, 25,000 lithographic portraits of her, for the purpose of profit and gain to themselves; that these portraits have been conspicuously posted in stores, warehouses and saloons, in the vicinity of the plaintiff's residence and throughout the United States, as advertisements of their goods; that the effect has been to humiliate her and to render her ill and, yet, claiming that she makes out no cause of action. They say that no law on the statute books gives her a right of action and that her right to privacy is not an actionable right, at law or in equity.

Our consideration of the question thus presented has not been foreclosed by the decision in *Schuyler* v. *Curtis*, (147 N.Y. 434). In that case, it appeared that the defendants were intending to make, and to exhibit, at the Columbian Exposition of 1893, a statue of Mrs. Schuyler, formerly Miss Mary M. Hamilton and conspicuous in her lifetime for her philanthropic work, to typify "Woman as the Philanthropist" and, as a companion piece, a statue of Miss Susan B. Anthony, to typify the "Representative Reformer." The plaintiff, in behalf of himself, as the nephew of Mrs. Schuyler, and of other immediate relatives, sought by the action to restrain them from carrying out their intentions as to the statue of Mrs. Schuyler; upon the grounds, in substance, that they were proceeding without his consent, (whose relationship was conceded to be such as to warrant such an action, if it were maintainable at all), or that of the other immediate members of the family; that their proceeding was disagreeable to him, because it would have been disagreeable and obnoxious to his aunt, if living, and that it was annoying to have Mrs. Schuyler's memory associated with principles, which Miss Susan B. Anthony typified and of which Mrs. Schuyler did not approve. His right to maintain the action was denied and the denial was expressly placed upon the ground that he, as a relative, did not represent any right of privacy which Mrs. Schuyler possessed in her lifetime and that, whatever her right had been, in that respect, it died with her. The existence of the individual's right to be protected against the invasion of his privacy, if not actually affirmed in the opinion, was, very certainly, far from being denied. "It may be admitted," Judge PECKHAM observed, when delivering the opinion of the court, "that courts have power, in some cases, to enjoin the doing of an act, where the nature, or character, of the act itself is well calculated to wound the sensibilities of an individual, and where the doing of the act is wholly unjustifiable, and is, in legal contemplation, a wrong, *even though the existence of no property*, as that term is usually used, *is involved in the subject.*"

That the individual has a right to privacy, which he can enforce and which equity will protect against the invasion of, is a proposition which is not opposed by any decision in this court and which, in my opinion, is within the field of accepted legal principles. It is within the very case supposed by Judge PECKHAM in *Schuyler* v. *Curtis*. In the present case, we may not say that the plaintiff's complaint is fanciful, or that her alleged injury is, purely, a sentimental one. Her objection to the defendants' acts is not one born of caprice; nor is it based upon the defendants' act being merely "distasteful" to her. We are bound to assume, and I find no difficulty in doing so, that the conspicuous display of her likeness, in various public places, has so humiliated her by the notoriety and by the public comments it has provoked, as to cause her distress and suffering, in body and in mind, and to confine her to her bed with illness.

If it were necessary, to be entitled to equitable relief, that the plaintiff's sufferings, by reason of the defendants' acts, should be serious, and appreciable by a pecuniary standard, clearly, we might well say, under the allegations of the complaint, that they were of such degree of gravity. However, I am not of the opinion that the gravity of the injury need be such as to be capable of being estimated by such a standard. If the right of privacy exists and this complaint makes out a case of its substantial violation, I think that the award of equitable relief, by way of an injunction, preventing the continuance of its invasion by the defendants, will not depend upon the complainant's ability to prove substantial pecuniary damages and, if the court finds the defendants' act to be without justification and for selfish gain and purposes, and to be of such a character, as is reasonably calculated to wound the feelings and to subject the plaintiff to the ridicule, or to the contempt of others, that her right to the preventive relief of equity will follow; without considering how far her sufferings may be measurable by a pecuniary standard.

The right of privacy, or the right of the individual to be let alone, is a personal right, which is not without judicial recognition. It is the complement of the right to the immunity of one's person. The individual has always been entitled to be protected in the exclusive use and enjoyment of that which is his own. The common law regarded his person and property as inviolate, and he has the absolute right to be let alone. (Cooley on Torts, p. 29.) The principle is fundamental and essential in organized society that every one, in exercising a personal right and in the use of his property, shall respect the rights and properties of others. He must so conduct himself, in the enjoyment of the rights and privileges which belong to him as a member of society, as that he shall prejudice no one in the possession and enjoyment of those which are exclusively his. When, as here, there is an alleged invasion of some personal right, or privilege, the absence of exact precedent and the fact that early commentators upon the common law have no discussion upon the subject are of no material importance in awarding equitable relief. That the exercise of the preventive power of a court of equity is demanded in a novel case, is not a fatal objection. (*Niagara Falls Int. Bridge Co.* v. *Great Western Ry. Co.*, 39 Barb. 212; *Sherman* v. *Skuse*, 166 N.Y. 352; *Hamilton* v. *Whitridge*, 11 Md. 145.) In the social evolution, with the march of the arts and sciences and in the resultant effects upon organized society, it is quite intelligible that new conditions must arise in personal relations, which the rules of the common law, cast in the rigid mould of an earlier social status, were not designed to meet. It would be a reproach to equitable jurisprudence, if equity were powerless to extend the application of the principles of common law, or of natural justice, in remedying a wrong, which, in the progress of civilization, has been made possible as the result of new social, or commercial conditions. Sir Henry Maine, in his work on Ancient Law, has observed of equity, that it is an agency "by which law is brought into harmony with society," and that it is one of the factors, which operate in judicial evolution. It succeeds legal fictions, or those judicial assumptions, through which a rule of law is modified in its operation, and it precedes legislation. (See Maine's Ancient Law, pp. 22 to 28.) Equity has neither fixed boundaries, nor logical subdivisions and its origin, both in Rome and in England, was that there was a wrong for which there was no remedy at law. (See 1st Story Eq. Juris. secs. 49 and 50.) It supplements the deficiencies of the common law, by applying, where otherwise there would result a wrong, those principles of natural justice, which are analogous to settled principles of the common law. (See Story's Eq. Jur. sec. 671, note.) Lord Chancellor COTTENHAM observed, in *Wallworth* v. *Holt*, (4 Myl. C. 619), "I think it is the duty of this court, (meaning equity), to adopt its practice and course of proceeding to the existing state of society and not, by a strict adherence to forms and rules, under different circumstances, to decline to administer justice and enforce rights for which there is no other remedy. * * * If it were necessary to go much further than it is, in opposition to some sanctioned opinions, in order to open the doors of this court to those who could not obtain it elsewhere, I should not shrink from the responsibility of doing so." As I have suggested, that the exercise of this peculiar preventive power of a court of equity is not found in some precisely analogous case, furnishes no valid objection, at all, to the assumption of jurisdiction, if the particular circumstances of the case show the performance, or the threatened performance, of an act by a defendant, which is wrongful, because constituting an invasion, in some novel form, of a right to something, which is, or should be conceded to be, the plaintiff's and as to which the law provides no adequate remedy. It would be a justifiable exercise of power, whether the principle of interference be rested upon analogy to some established common-law principle, or whether it is one of natural justice. In an article in the Harvard Law Review, of December 15th, 1890, which contains an impressive argument upon the subject of the "right of privacy," it was well said by the authors "that the individual shall have full protection in person and in property is a principle as old as the common law; but it has been found necessary from time to time to define anew the exact nature and extent of such protection. * * The right to life has come to mean the right to enjoy life—the right to be let alone; the right to liberty secures the exercise of extensive civil privileges; and the term 'property' has grown to comprise every form of possession—intangible, as well as tangible.

"Instantaneous photography is a modern invention and affords the means of securing a portraiture of an individual's face and form, *in invitum* their owner. While, so far forth as it merely does that, although a species of aggression, I concede it to be an irremediable and irrepressible feature of the social evolution. But, if it is to be permitted that the portraiture may be put to commercial, or other, uses for gain, by the publication of prints therefrom, then an act of invasion of the individual's privacy results, possibly more formidable and more painful in its consequences, than an actual bodily assault might be. Security of person is as necessary as the security of property; and for that complete personal security, which will result in the peaceful and wholesome enjoyment of one's privileges as a member of society, there should be afforded protection, not only against the scandalous portraiture and display of one's features and person, but against the display and use thereof for another's commercial purposes or gain. The proposition is, to me, an inconceivable one that these defendants may, unauthorizedly, use the likeness of this young woman upon their advertisement, as a method of attracting widespread public attention to their wares, and that she must submit to the mortifying notoriety, without right to invoke the exercise of the preventive power of a court of equity.

Such a view, as it seems to me, must have been unduly influenced by a failure to find precedents in analogous cases, or some declaration by the great commentators upon the law of a common-law principle which would, precisely, apply to and govern the action; without taking into consideration that, in the existing state of society, new conditions affecting the relations of persons demand the broader extension of those legal principles, which underlie the immunity of one's person from attack. I think that such a view is unduly restricted, too, by a search for some property, which has been invaded by the defendants' acts. Property is not, necessarily, the thing itself, which is owned; it is the right of the owner in relation to it. The right to be protected in one's possession of a thing, or in one's privileges, belonging to him as an individual, or secured to him as a member of the commonwealth, is property, and as such entitled to the protection of the law. The protective power of equity is not exercised upon the tangible thing, but upon the right to enjoy it; and, so, it is called forth for the protection of the right to that which is one's exclusive possession, as a property right. It seems to me that the principle, which is applicable, is analogous to that upon which courts of equity have interfered to protect the right of privacy, in cases of private writings, or of other unpublished products of the mind. The writer, or the lecturer, has been protected in his right to a literary property in a letter, or a lecture, against its unauthorized publication; because it is property, to which the right of privacy attaches. (*Woolsey* v. *Judd*, 4 Duer, 399; *Gee* v. *Pritchard*, 2 Swanst. 402; *Abernathy* v. *Hutchinson*, 3 L.J. Ch. 209; *Folsom* v. *Marsh*, 2 Story, 100.) I think that this plaintiff has the same property in the right to be protected against the use of her face for defendant's commercial purposes, as she would have, if they were publishing her literary compositions. The right would be conceded, if she had sat for her photograph; but if her face, or her portraiture, has a value, the value is hers exclusively; until the use be granted away to the public. Any other principle of decision, in my opinion, is as repugnant to equity; as it is shocking to reason. Judge COLT, of the United States Court, in *Corliss* v. *Walker Co.*, (64 Fed. Rep. 280-5), a case involving the same question of an invasion of the right of privacy, with respect to the publication of a printed likeness of Mr. Corliss, expressed the opinion that "independently of the question of contract, I believe the law to be that a private individual has a right to be protected in the representation of his portrait in any form; that this is a property as well as a personal right, and that it belongs to the same class of rights which forbids the reproduction of a private manuscript or painting, or the publication of private letters, or of oral lectures delivered by a teacher to his class, or the revelation of the contents of a merchant's books by a clerk." The case itself is not in point in its facts; because the complainant was the widow of Mr. Corliss and thus it came within the limitations of *Schuyler* v. *Curtis*.

The right to grant the injunction does not depend upon the existence of property, which one has in some contractual form. It depends upon the existence of property in any right which belongs to a person. In *Pollard* v. *Photographic Co.*, (40 Ch. Div. 345), it was held that the right to grant an injunction against selling copies of plaintiff's photographs did not depend upon the existence of property and that "it is quite clear that independently of any question as to the right at law, the Court of Chancery always had an original and independent jurisdiction to prevent what that court considered and treated as a wrong, whether arising from a violation of an unquestionable right, or from breach of confidence, or contract, as was pointed out by Lord COTTENHAM in *Prince Albert* v. *Strange*, (1 Macn. G. 25)." In *Prince Albert* v. *Strange*, Lord Chancellor COTTENHAM sustained the issuance of an injunction, upon the ground that the right of privacy had been invaded by the publication and sale of etchings, made by Prince Albert and Queen Victoria. Upon the original hearing, Vice-Chancellor KNIGHT-BRUCE, in granting the injunction, observed that, "upon the principle of protecting property, it is that the common law, in cases not aided or prejudiced by statute, shelters the privacy and seclusion of thoughts and sentiments committed to writing, and desired by the author to remain not generally known."

It would be, in my opinion, an extraordinary view which, while conceding the right of a person to be protected against the unauthorized circulation of an unpublished lecture, letter, drawing, or other ideal property, yet, would deny the same protection to a person, whose portrait was unauthorizedly obtained, and made use of, for commercial purposes. The injury to the plaintiff is irreparable; because she cannot be wholly compensated in damages for the various consequences entailed by defendants' acts. The only complete relief is an injunction restraining their continuance. Whether, as incidental to that equitable relief, she should be able to recover only nominal damages is not material; for the issuance of the injunction does not, in such a case, depend upon the amount of the damages in dollars and cents.

A careful consideration of the question presented upon this appeal leads me to the conclusion that the judgment appealed from should be affirmed.

O'BRIEN, CULLEN and WERNER, JJ., concur with PARKER, Ch. J.; BARTLETT and HAIGHT, JJ., concur with GRAY, J.

Judgment reversed, etc.

NOT FOR PUBLICATION

UNITED STATES COURT OF APPEALS

FOR THE NINTH CIRCUIT

FILED

OCT 28 2019

MOLLY C. DWYER, CLERK

U.S. COURT OF APPEALS

SEAN HALL, doing business as Gimme Some Hot Sauce Music, an individual; NATHAN BUTLER, doing business as Faith Force Music, an individual,	No. 18-55426
Plaintiffs-Appellants,	D.C. No.
	2:17-cv-06882-MWF-AS
v.	
TAYLOR SWIFT, an individual; et al.,	MEMORANDUM*
Defendants-Appellees.	

Appeal from the United States District Court
for the Central District of California
Michael W. Fitzgerald, District Judge, Presiding

Argued and Submitted October 15, 2019
San Diego, California

Before: HURWITZ, OWENS, and LEE, Circuit Judges.

Sean Hall and Nathan Butler (together, Hall) appeal from the district court's dismissal under Federal Rule of Civil Procedure 12(b)(6) of their complaint against Taylor Swift, Martin Sandberg, and Karl Schuster (together, Swift) alleging copyright infringement. The complaint alleged that Swift's hit song *Shake It Off* (2014) illegally copied a six-word phrase and a four-part lyrical sequence from Hall's *Playas Gon' Play* (2001). We have jurisdiction under 28 U.S.C. § 1291, and we review de novo the district court's dismissal under Rule 12(b)(6). *See Dougherty v. City of Covina*, 654 F.3d 892, 897 (9th Cir. 2011). As the parties are familiar with the facts, we do not recount them here. We reverse and remand.

---

* This disposition is not appropriate for publication and is not precedent except as provided by Ninth Circuit Rule 36-3.

The district court dismissed the complaint based on a lack of originality in the pertinent portions of Hall's work. *See Satava v. Lowry*, 323 F.3d 805, 810 (9th Cir. 2003) ("Any copyrighted expression must be 'original.' Although the amount of creative input . . . required to meet the originality standard is low, it is not negligible." (citing *Feist Publ'ns, Inc. v. Rural Tel. Serv. Co., Inc.*, 499 U.S. 340, 345, 362 (1991))); *see also* 1 Nimmer on Copyright § 2.05[B] (2017) (noting that originality is established when "the work originates in the author" and "has a spark that goes beyond the banal or trivial"). Even taking into account the matters of which the district court took judicial notice, *see United States v. Ritchie*, 342 F.3d 903, 907-08 (9th Cir. 2003), Hall's complaint still plausibly alleged originality. *See Ashcroft* v. *Iqbal*, 556 U.S. 662, 678 (2009).

Originality, as we have long recognized, is normally a question of fact. *See Dezendorf v. Twentieth Century-Fox Film Corp.*, 99 F.2d 850, 851 (9th Cir. 1938) (stating that the "question of originality . . . is one of fact, not of law" (internal quotation marks omitted)). Indeed, as Justice Holmes long ago cautioned:

> It would be a dangerous undertaking for persons trained only to the law to constitute themselves final judges of the worth of pictorial illustrations, outside of the narrowest and most obvious limits. At the one extreme, some works of genius would be sure to miss appreciation. Their very novelty would make them repulsive until the public had learned the new language in which their author spoke. . . . At the other end, copyright would be denied to pictures which appealed to a public less educated than the judge. . . . [A]nd the taste of any public is not to be treated with contempt.

Bleistein v. Donaldson Lithographing Co., 188 U.S. 239, 251–52 (1903).

Justice Holmes' century-old warning remains valid. By concluding that," for such short phrases to be protected under the Copyright Act, they must be more creative than the lyrics at issues here," the district court constituted itself as the final judge of the worth of an expressive work. Because the absence of originality is not established either on the face of the complaint or through the judicially noticed matters, we reverse the district court's dismissal under Rule 12(b)(6).[1]

REVERSED and REMANDED.

[1] Swift argues that this Court should affirm the district court's decision on other grounds. However, we decline to do so. The district court may consider Swift's alternative arguments on remand.

IN THE UNITED STATES DISTRICT COURT
FOR THE EASTERN DISTRICT OF MISSOURI
EASTERN DIVISION

S. VICTOR WHITMILL,	)	
	)	
Plaintiff,	)	
	)	
v.	)	Civil Action No. 4:11-cv-752
	)	
WARNER BROS. ENTERTAINMENT INC.,	)	**Jury Trial Demanded**
	)	
Defendant.	)	

VERIFIED COMPLAINT FOR INJUNCTIVE AND OTHER RELIEF

Plaintiff S. Victor Whitmill alleges the following against defendant Warner Bros. Entertainment Inc.

INTRODUCTION

Mr. Whitmill is a visual artist living in rural Missouri. Among his creations is one of the most distinctive tattoos in the nation, an original design he created on the upper left side of former world heavyweight champion boxer Mike Tyson's face (the "Original Tattoo") (*see* image on page 338, below). When Mr. Whitmill created the Original Tattoo, Mr. Tyson agreed that Mr. Whitmill would own the artwork and thus, the copyright in the Original Tattoo. Warner Bros. Entertainment, Inc.—without attempting to contact Mr. Whitmill, obtain his permission, or credit his creation—has copied Mr. Whitmill's Original Tattoo and placed it on the face of another actor in its upcoming motion picture, THE HANGOVER 2. For Mr. Whitmill, this case is not about Mike Tyson, Mike Tyson's likeness, or Mike Tyson's right to use or control his identity. This case is about Warner Bros. appropriation of Mr. Whitmill's art and Warner Bros. unauthorized use of that art, separate and apart from Mr. Tyson. Not only is this infringing copy (the "Pirated Tattoo) used throughout the movie, but Warner Bros. also uses the Pirated Tattoo extensively in advertisements and promotions without Mr. Tyson. (*See* image on page 339, below.) This unauthorized exploitation of the Original Tattoo constitutes copyright infringement.

Jurisdiction and Venue

This is an action for copyright infringement arising under the Copyright Act of 1976, as amended, 17 U.S.C. § 101 *et seq.* (the "Copyright Act"). The Court has subject matter jurisdiction under 17 U.S.C. § 501 and 28 U.S.C. §§ 1331 and 1338(a).

Venue is proper in this District under 28 U.S.C. §§ 1391(b) and 1400 because defendant does business, may be found, and is subject to personal jurisdiction here.

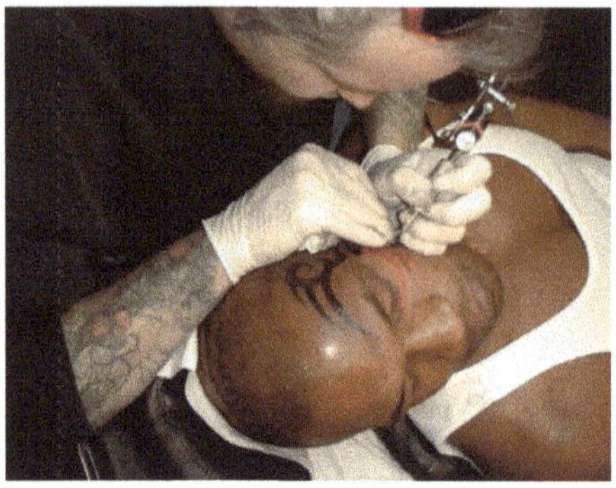

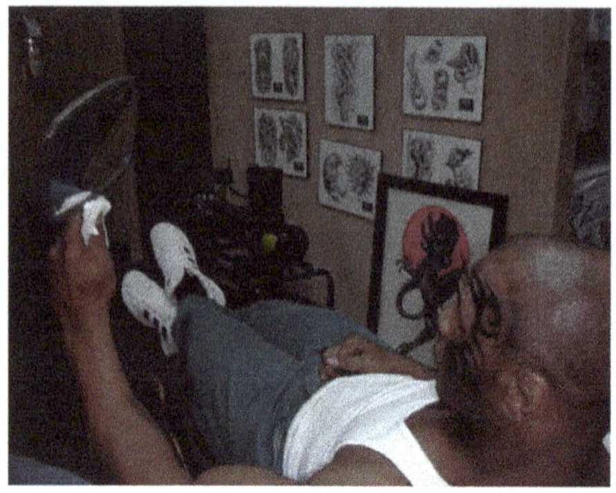

Plaintiff, His Art, and the Original Tattoo

Plaintiff S. Victor Whitmill is an award-winning visual artist who works in various mediums, including the creation, design, and application of tattoo art to bodies. He is a citizen of the State of Missouri and lives in a small town in the south-central portion of the state.

On February 10, 2003, while living in Las Vegas, Nevada, Mr. Whitmill created and applied an original and distinctive tattoo to the upper left side of the face of the former, world heavyweight champion boxer Michael Gerard "Mike" Tyson (the "Original Tattoo"). True and accurate photographs of Mr. Whitmill in the process of tattooing the Original Tattoo onto Mr. Tyson and of Mr. Tyson viewing the tattoo immediately after it was completed by Mr. Whitmill are displayed above and attached to this Complaint as Exhibits 1 and 2.

Mr. Whitmill, doing business at the time as Paradox-Studio of Dermagraphics, is the sole creator, author, and owner of all rights, including copyright, in the Original Tattoo, which is original and fixed in a tangible medium of expression.

On the day Mr. Whitmill created the Original Tattoo, Mr. Tyson signed a release form acknowledging "that all artwork, sketches and drawings related to [his] tattoo and any photographs of [his] tattoo are property of Paradox-Studio of Dermagraphics." (A true and accurate copy of the Feb. 10, 2003 Tattoo Release, redacted in accordance with the Court's rules is attached as Exhibit 3.)

A true and accurate photograph of Original Tattoo is shown to the right and attached as Exhibit 4.

Plaintiff has registered the copyright in Original Tattoo. A true and correct copy of the Certificate of Registration for the Original Tattoo, No. VA 1-767-704, is attached as Exhibit 5.

Plaintiff has never copied the Original Tattoo onto anyone else and has never licensed or otherwise authorized anyone else to copy, distribute, or publicly disseminate the Original Tattoo or make derivative works based upon it.

Defendants' Infringement

On information and belief, Defendant Warner Bros. Entertainment Inc. ("Warner Bros.") is a Delaware corporation with its principal place of business at 4000 Warner Boulevard, Burbank, California. Warner Bros. is engaged in the production, acquisition and distribution of motion pictures for theatrical exhibition, home entertainment and other forms of distribution.

Mr. Whitmill recently learned that Warner Bros. is planning to release a motion picture later this Spring entitled THE HANGOVER 2 (the "Movie").

On information and belief, the Movie features a virtually exact reproduction of the Original Tattoo, which appears on the upper left side of the Stu Price character's face, played by actor Ed Helms. As used in this Complaint, the term "Pirated Tattoo" shall refer to any version of the Original Tattoo that appears anywhere but where Mr. Whitmill originally created it, namely, on the upper left side of Mr. Tyson's face.

A close-up of the Pirated Tattoo from the advertising poster (attached as Exhibit 6), and the Original Tattoo from a photograph of Mr. Tyson are displayed side-by-side below.

On information and belief, the Pirated Tattoo is a recurring device and plays an important role in the plot of the Movie. The Pirated Tattoo is prominently featured in the marketing and promotional materials for the Movie as demonstrated by a current movie poster (the "Movie Poster") that defendants are using to advertise the Movie. A true and correct copy of the Movie Poster is attached as Exhibit 6 and reproduced on the next page.

At all relevant times, Warner Bros. has had access to the Original Tattoo.

There is substantial similarity between the copyrightable expression in the Original Tattoo and the Pirated Tattoo.

Mr. Whitmill has never been asked for permission for, and has never consented to, the use, reproduction, or creation of a derivative work based on his Original Tattoo, including the Pirated Tattoo. Nor

has he ever been asked or agreed to the public display and distribution of a motion picture containing the Pirated Tattoo, or to the use of any of his other exclusive rights in the Original Tattoo under the Copyright Act.

Warner Bros. has already infringed Mr. Whitmill's copyright through its unauthorized copying, distribution and public display of the Pirated Tattoo in advertising and promotion for the Movie and by making an unauthorized derivative work—namely, the Pirated Tattoo—that is based upon and copies virtually all of the copyrightable subject matter of the Original Tattoo.

If not enjoined, Warner Bros. will continue to infringe Mr. Whitmill's copyright by using the Pirated Tattoo to advertise, market, and promote the Movie; by releasing the Movie and otherwise distributing or licensing others to distribute the Movie in various formats and distribution channels; and, by distributing or licensing derivative works that include the Pirated Tattoo.

Defendant's conduct constitutes, at the very least, reckless copyright infringement in disregard of the rights of Mr. Whitmill.

These wrongful acts of defendant have caused irreparable injury to Mr. Whitmill, and unless this Court restrains defendant from further use of the Pirated Tattoo, Mr. Whitmill will continue to suffer irreparable injury for which he has no adequate remedy at law.

As a direct and proximate result of defendant's wrongful acts, defendant has been and will continue to be unjustly enriched, and Mr. Whitmill has suffered and will continue to suffer damages in an amount not yet fully determined.

WHEREFORE, Plaintiff prays that this Court enter judgment in its favor and against defendant as follows:

A. A preliminary injunction during the pendency of this action and a permanent injunction thereafter enjoining and restraining defendant, its agents, servants, employees, attorneys, partners, licensees, divisions, affiliates, parent corporation(s), and all others in active concert or participation with any of them from copying, distributing, publicly displaying, or otherwise making any use of the Pirated Tattoo, both in the Movie and otherwise.

B. An award of monetary damages sufficient to compensate Plaintiff for the injuries suffered as a result of Defendant's wrongful conduct;

C. An award of Defendant's profits and unjust enrichment realized from its infringement;

D. An award to Plaintiff of his costs and reasonable attorney's fees expended in this action; and

E. An award of such other and further relief as the Court deems just and proper.

Jury Demand

Plaintiff demands trial by jury of all issues so triable.

Respectfully submitted,

/s/ *Joseph A. Barrister.*
Dewey, Cheatum &
Howe Law Group
49 Music Square West
Nashville, Tennessee 37203

Attorneys for Plaintiff

SONY CORPORATION OF AMERICA ET AL. v. UNIVERSAL CITY STUDIOS, INC., ET AL. 464 U.S. 417 (1984)

JUSTICE STEVENS delivered the opinion of the Court.

Petitioners manufacture and sell home video tape recorders. Respondents own the copyrights on some of the television programs that are broadcast on the public airwaves. Some members of the general public use video tape recorders sold by petitioners to record some of these broadcasts, as well as a large number of other broadcasts. The question presented is whether the sale of petitioners' copying equipment to the general public violates any of the rights conferred upon respondents by the Copyright Act.

Respondents commenced this copyright infringement action against petitioners in the United States District Court for the Central District of California in 1976. Respondents alleged that some individuals had used Betamax video tape recorders (VTR's) to record some of respondents' copyrighted works which had been exhibited on commercially sponsored television and contended that these individuals had thereby infringed respondents' copyrights. Respondents further maintained that petitioners were liable for the copyright infringement allegedly committed by Betamax consumers because of petitioners' marketing of the Betamax VTR's. Respondents sought no relief against any Betamax consumer. Instead, they sought money damages and an equitable accounting of profits from petitioners, as well as an injunction against the manufacture and marketing of Betamax VTR's.

After a lengthy trial, the District Court denied respondents all the relief they sought and entered judgment for petitioners. 480 F.Supp. 429 (1979). The United States Court of Appeals for the Ninth Circuit reversed the District Court's judgment on respondents' copyright claim, holding petitioners liable for contributory infringement and ordering the District Court to fashion appropriate relief. 659 F.2d 963 (1981). We granted certiorari, 457 U.S. 1116 (1982); since we had not completed our study of the case last Term, we ordered reargument, 463 U.S. 1226 (1983). We now reverse.

An explanation of our rejection of respondents' unprecedented attempt to impose copyright liability upon the distributors of copying equipment requires a quite detailed recitation of the findings of the District Court. In summary, those findings reveal that the average member of the public uses a VTR principally to record a program he cannot view as it is being televised and then to watch it once at a later time. This practice, known as "time-shifting," enlarges the television viewing audience. For that reason, a significant amount of television programming may be used in this manner without objection from the owners of the copyrights on the programs. For the same reason, even the two respondents in this case, who do assert objections to time-shifting in this litigation, were unable to prove that the practice has impaired the commercial value of their copyrights or has created any likelihood of future harm. Given these findings, there is no basis in the Copyright Act upon which respondents can hold petitioners liable for distributing VTR's to the general public. The Court of Appeals' holding that respondents are entitled to enjoin the distribution of VTR's, to collect royalties on the sale of such equipment, or to obtain other relief, if affirmed, would enlarge the scope of respondents' statutory monopolies to encompass control over an article of commerce that is not the subject of copyright protection. Such an expansion of the copyright privilege is beyond the limits of the grants authorized by Congress.

I.

The two respondents in this action, Universal City Studios, Inc., and Walt Disney Productions, produce and hold the copyrights on a substantial number of motion pictures and other audiovisual works. In the current marketplace, they can exploit their rights in these works in a number of ways: by authorizing theatrical exhibitions, by licensing limited showings on cable and network television, by selling syndication rights for repeated airings on local television stations, and by marketing programs on prerecorded videotapes or videodiscs. Some works are suitable for exploitation through all of these avenues, while the market for other works is more limited.

Petitioner Sony manufactures millions of Betamax video tape recorders and markets these devices through numerous retail establishments, some of which are also petitioners in this action. Sony's Betamax VTR is a mechanism consisting of three basic components: (1) a tuner, which receives electromagnetic signals transmitted over the television band of the public airwaves and separates them into audio and visual signals; (2) a recorder, which records such signals on a magnetic tape; and (3) an adapter, which converts the audio and visual signals on the tape into a composite signal that can be received by a television set.

Several capabilities of the machine are noteworthy. The separate tuner in the Betamax enables it to record a broadcast off one station while the television set is tuned to another channel, permitting the viewer, for example, to watch two simultaneous news broadcasts by watching one "live" and recording the other for later viewing. Tapes may be reused, and programs that have been recorded may be erased either before or after viewing. A timer in the Betamax can be used to activate and deactivate the equipment at predetermined times, enabling an intended viewer to record programs that are transmitted when he or she is not at home. Thus a person may watch a program at home in the evening even though it was broadcast while the viewer was at work during the afternoon. The Betamax is also equipped with a pause button and a fast-forward control. The pause button, when depressed, deactivates the recorder until it is released, thus enabling a viewer to omit a commercial advertisement from the recording, provided, of course, that the viewer is present when the program is recorded. The fast-forward control enables the viewer of a previously recorded program to run the tape rapidly when a segment he or she does not desire to see is being played back on the television screen.

The respondents and Sony both conducted surveys of the way the Betamax machine was used by several hundred owners during a sample period in 1978. Although there were some differences in the surveys, they both showed that the primary use of the machine for most owners was "time-shifting"—the practice of recording a program to view it once at a later time, and thereafter erasing it. Time-shifting enables viewers to see programs they otherwise would miss because they are not at home, are occupied with other tasks, or are viewing a program on another station at the time of a broadcast that they desire to watch.

Both surveys also showed, however, that a substantial number of interviewees had accumulated libraries of tapes. Sony's survey indicated that over 80% of the interviewees watched at least as much regular television as they had before owning a Betamax. Respondents offered no evidence of decreased television viewing by Betamax owners.

Sony introduced considerable evidence describing television programs that could be copied without objection from any copyright holder, with special emphasis on sports, religious, and educational programming. For example, their survey indicated that 7.3% of all Betamax use is to record sports events, and representatives of professional baseball, football, basketball, and hockey testified that they had no objection to the recording of their televised events for home use.

Respondents offered opinion evidence concerning the future impact of the unrestricted sale of VTR's on the commercial value of their copyrights. The District Court found, however, that they had failed to prove any likelihood of future harm from the use of VTR's for time-shifting. . . .

II.

Article I, § 8, of the Constitution provides:

> "The Congress shall have Power . . . To Promote the Progress of Science and useful Arts, by securing for limited Times to Authors and Inventors the exclusive Right to their respective Writings and Discoveries."

The monopoly privileges that Congress may authorize are neither unlimited nor primarily designed to provide a special private benefit. Rather, the limited grant is a means by which an important public purpose may be achieved. It is intended to motivate the creative activity of authors and inventors by the provision of a special reward, and to allow the public access to the products of their genius after the limited period of exclusive control has expired.

"The copyright law, like the patent statutes, makes reward to the owner a secondary consideration. In *Fox Film Corp.* v. *Doyal*, 286 U.S. 123, 127, Chief Justice Hughes spoke as follows respecting the copyright monopoly granted by Congress, 'The sole interest of the United States and the primary object in conferring the monopoly lie in the general benefits derived by the public from the labors of authors.' It is said that reward to the author or artist serves to induce release to the public of the products of his creative genius." *United States* v. *Paramount Pictures, Inc.*, 334 U.S. 131, 158 (1948).

As the text of the Constitution makes plain, it is Congress that has been assigned the task of defining the scope of the limited monopoly that should be granted to authors or to inventors in order to give the public appropriate access to their work product. Because this task involves a difficult balance between the interests of authors and inventors in the control and exploitation of their writings and discoveries on the one hand, and society's competing interest in the free flow of ideas, information, and commerce on the other hand, our patent and copyright statutes have been amended repeatedly.

From its beginning, the law of copyright has developed in response to significant changes in technology. Indeed, it was the invention of a new form of copying equipment—the printing press—that gave rise to the original need for copyright protection. Repeatedly, as new developments have occurred in this country, it has been the Congress that has fashioned the new rules that new technology made necessary. Thus, long before the enactment of the Copyright Act of 1909, 35 Stat. 1075, it was settled that the protection given to copyrights is wholly statutory. *Wheaton* v. *Peters*, 8 Pet. 591, 661-662 (1834). The remedies for infringement "are only those prescribed by Congress." *Thompson* v. *Hubbard*, 131 U.S. 123, 151 (1889).

The judiciary's reluctance to expand the protections afforded by the copyright without explicit legislative guidance is a recurring theme. See, *e. g., Teleprompter Corp.* v. *Columbia Broadcasting System, Inc.*, 415 U.S. 394 (1974); *Fortnightly Corp.* v. *United Artists Television, Inc.*, 392 U.S. 390 (1968); *White-Smith Music Publishing Co.* v. *Apollo Co.*, 209 U.S. 1 (1908); *Williams & Wilkins Co.* v. *United States*, 203 Ct. Cl. 74, 487 F.2d 1345 (1973), aff'd by an equally divided Court, 420 U.S. 376 (1975). Sound policy, as well as history, supports our consistent deference to Congress when major technological innovations alter the market for copyrighted materials. Congress has the constitutional authority and the institutional ability to accommodate fully the varied permutations of competing interests that are inevitably implicated by such new technology.

In a case like this, in which Congress has not plainly marked our course, we must be circumspect in construing the scope of rights created by a legislative enactment which never contemplated such a calculus of interests. In doing so, we are guided by Justice Stewart's exposition of the correct approach to ambiguities in the law of copyright:

> "The limited scope of the copyright holder's statutory monopoly, like the limited copyright duration required by the Constitution, reflects a balance of competing claims upon the public interest: Creative work is to be encouraged and rewarded, but private motivation must ultimately serve the cause of promoting broad public availability of literature, music, and the other arts. The immediate effect of our copyright law is to secure a fair return for an 'author's' creative labor. But the ultimate aim is, by this incentive, to stimulate artistic creativity for the general public good. 'The sole interest of the United States and the primary object in conferring the monopoly,' this Court has said, 'lie in the general benefits derived by the public from the labors of authors.' *Fox Film Corp.* v. *Doyal*, 286 U.S. 123, 127. See *Kendall* v. *Winsor*, 21 How. 322, 327-328; *Grant* v. *Raymond*, 6 Pet. 218, 241-242. When technological change has rendered its literal terms ambiguous, the Copyright Act must be construed in light of this basic purpose." *Twentieth Century Music Corp.* v. *Aiken*, 422 U.S. 151, 156 (1975) (footnotes omitted).

Copyright protection "subsists . . . in original works of authorship fixed in any tangible medium of expression." 17 U. S. C. § 102(a) (1982 ed.). This protection has never accorded the copyright owner complete control over all possible uses of his work. Rather, the Copyright Act grants the copyright holder "exclusive" rights to use and to authorize the use of his work in five qualified ways, including reproduction of the copyrighted work in copies. § 106. All reproductions of the work, however, are not within the exclusive domain of the copyright owner; some are in the public domain. Any individual may reproduce a copyrighted work for a "fair use"; the copyright owner does not possess the exclusive right to such a use. Compare § 106 with § 107.

"Anyone who violates any of the exclusive rights of the copyright owner," that is, anyone who trespasses into his exclusive domain by using or authorizing the use of the copyrighted work in one of the five ways set forth in the statute, "is an infringer of the copyright." § 501(a). Conversely, anyone who is authorized by the copyright owner to use the copyrighted work in a way specified in the statute or who makes a fair use of the work is not an infringer of the copyright with respect to such use.

The Copyright Act provides the owner of a copyright with a potent arsenal of remedies against an infringer of his work, including an injunction to restrain the infringer from violating his rights, the impoundment and destruction of all reproductions of his work made in violation of his rights, a recovery of his actual damages and any additional profits realized by the infringer or a recovery of statutory damages, and attorney's fees. §§ 502-505.

The two respondents in this case do not seek relief against the Betamax users who have allegedly infringed their copyrights. Moreover, this is not a class action on behalf of all copyright owners who license their works for television broadcast, and respondents have no right to invoke whatever rights other copyright holders may have to bring infringement actions based on Betamax copying of their works. As was made clear by their own evidence, the copying of the respondents' programs represents a small portion of the total use of VTR's. It is, however, the taping of respondents' own copyrighted programs that provides them with standing to charge Sony with contributory infringement. To prevail, they have the burden of proving that users of the Betamax have infringed their copyrights and that Sony should be held responsible for that infringement.

III.

The Copyright Act does not expressly render anyone liable for infringement committed by another. In contrast, the Patent Act expressly brands anyone who "actively induces infringement of a patent" as an infringer, 35 U. S. C. § 271(b), and further imposes liability on certain individuals labeled "contributory" infringers, § 271(c). The absence of such express language in the copyright statute does not preclude the imposition of liability for copyright infringements on certain parties who have not themselves engaged in the infringing activity. For vicarious liability is imposed in virtually all areas of the law, and the concept of contributory infringement is merely a species of the broader problem of identifying the circumstances in which it is just to hold one individual accountable for the actions of another.

Such circumstances were plainly present in *Kalem Co.* v. *Harper Brothers*, 222 U.S. 55 (1911), the copyright decision of this Court on which respondents place their principal reliance. In *Kalem*, the Court held that the producer of an unauthorized film dramatization of the copyrighted book Ben Hur was liable for his sale of the motion picture to jobbers, who in turn arranged for the commercial exhibition of the film. Justice Holmes, writing for the Court, explained:

> "The defendant not only expected but invoked by advertisement the use of its films for dramatic reproduction of the story. That was the most conspicuous purpose for which they could be used, and the one for which especially they were made. If the defendant did not contribute to the infringement it is impossible to do so except by taking part in the final act. It is liable on principles recognized in every part of the law." *Id.*, at 62-63.

The use for which the item sold in *Kalem* had been "especially" made was, of course, to display the performance that had already been recorded upon it. The producer had personally appropriated the copyright owner's protected work and, as the owner of the tangible medium of expression upon which the protected work was recorded, authorized that use by his sale of the film to jobbers. But that use of the film was not his to authorize: the copyright owner possessed the exclusive right to authorize public performances of his work. Further, the producer personally advertised the unauthorized public performances, dispelling any possible doubt as to the use of the film which he had authorized.

Respondents argue that *Kalem* stands for the proposition that supplying the "means" to accomplish an infringing activity and encouraging that activity through advertisement are sufficient to establish liability for copyright infringement. This argument rests on a gross generalization that cannot withstand scrutiny. The producer in *Kalem* did not merely provide the "means" to accomplish an infringing activity; the producer supplied the work itself, albeit in a new medium of expression. Sony in the instant case does not supply Betamax consumers with respondents' works; respondents do. Sony supplies a piece of equipment that is generally capable of copying the entire range of programs that may be televised: those that are uncopyrighted, those that are copyrighted but may be copied without objection from the copyright holder, and those that the copyright holder would prefer not to have copied. The Betamax can be used to [*437] make authorized or unauthorized uses of copyrighted works, but the range of its potential use is much broader than the particular infringing use of the film Ben Hur involved in *Kalem*. *Kalem* does not support respondents' novel theory of liability.

Justice Holmes stated that the producer had "contributed" to the infringement of the copyright, and the label "contributory infringement" has been applied in a number of lower court copyright cases involving an ongoing relationship between the direct infringer and the contributory infringer at the time the infringing conduct occurred. In such cases, as in other situations in which the imposition of vicarious liability is manifestly just, the "contributory" infringer was in a position to control the use of copyrighted works by others and had authorized the use without permission from the copy-right owner.[1] This case, however, plainly does not fall in that category. The only contact between Sony and the users of the Betamax that is disclosed by this record occurred at the moment of sale. The District Court expressly found that "no employee of Sony, Sonam or DDBI had either direct involvement with the allegedly infringing activity or direct contact with purchasers of Betamax who recorded copyrighted works off-the-air." 480 F.Supp., at 460. And it further found that "there was no evidence that any of the copies made by Griffiths or the other individual witnesses in this suit were influenced or encouraged by [Sony's] advertisements." *Ibid.*

If vicarious liability is to be imposed on Sony in this case, it must rest on the fact that tit has sold equipment with constructive knowledge of the fact that its customers may use that equipment to

[1] The so-called "dance hall cases," *Famous Music Corp.* v. *Bay State Harness Horse Racing & Breeding Assn., Inc.*, 554 F.2d 1213 (CA1 1977) (racetrack retained infringer to supply music to paying customers); *KECA Music, Inc.* v. *Dingus McGee's Co.*, 432 F.Supp. 72 (WD Mo. 1977) (cocktail lounge hired musicians to supply music to paying customers); *Dreamland Ball Room, Inc.* v. *Shapiro, Bernstein & Co.*, 36 F.2d 354 (CA7 1929) (dance hall hired orchestra to supply music to paying customers), are often contrasted with the so-called landlord-tenant cases, in which landlords who leased premises to a direct infringer for a fixed rental and did not participate directly in any infringing activity were found not to be liable for contributory infringement. *E. g., Deutsch* v. *Arnold*, 98 F.2d 686 (CA2 1938).

make unauthorized copies of copyrighted material. There is no precedent in the law of copyright for the imposition of vicarious liability on such a theory. The closest analogy is provided by the patent law cases to which it is appropriate to refer because of the historic kinship between patent law and copyright law.[2]

In *Shapiro, Bernstein & Co.* v. *H. L. Green Co.*, 316 F.2d 304 (CA2 1963), the owner of 23 chainstores retained the direct infringer to run its record departments. The relationship was structured as a licensing arrangement, so that the defendant bore none of the business risk of running the department. Instead, it received 10% or 12% of the direct infringer's gross receipts. The Court of Appeals concluded:

"[The dance-hall cases] and this one lie closer on the spectrum to the employer-employee model, than to the landlord-tenant model. . . . [On] the particular facts before us, . . . Green's relationship to its infringing licensee, as well as its strong concern for the financial success of the phonograph record concession, renders it liable for the unauthorized sales of the 'bootleg' records.

. . . .

". . . [The] imposition of *vicarious* liability in the case before us cannot be deemed unduly harsh or unfair. Green has the power to police carefully the conduct of its concessionaire . . .; our judgment will simply encourage it to do so, thus placing responsibility where it can and should be effectively exercised." *Id.*, at 308 (emphasis in original).

In *Gershwin Publishing Corp.* v. *Columbia Artists Management, Inc.*, 443 F.2d 1159 (CA2 1971), the direct infringers retained the contributory infringer to manage their performances. The contributory infringer would contact each direct infringer, obtain the titles of the musical compositions to be performed, print the programs, and then sell the programs to its own local organizations for distribution at the time of the direct infringement. *Id.*, at 1161. The Court of Appeals emphasized that the contributory infringer had actual knowledge that the artists it was managing were performing copyrighted works, was in a position to police the infringing conduct of the artists, and derived substantial benefit from the actions of the primary infringers. *Id.*, at 1163.

In *Screen Gems-Columbia Music, Inc.* v. *Mark-Fi Records, Inc.*, 256 F.Supp. 399 (SDNY 1966), the direct infringer manufactured and sold bootleg records. In denying a motion for summary judgment, the District Court held that the infringer's advertising agency, the radio stations that advertised the infringer's works, and the service agency that boxed and mailed the infringing goods could all be held liable, if at trial it could be demonstrated that they knew or should have known that they were dealing in illegal goods.

[2] *E. g., United States* v. *Paramount Pictures, Inc.*, 334 U.S., at 158; *Fox Film Corp.* v. *Doyal*, 286 U.S., at 131; *Wheaton* v. *Peters*, 8 Pet. 591, 657-658 (1834). The two areas of the law, naturally, are not identical twins, and we exercise the caution which we have expressed in the past in applying doctrine formulated in one area to the other. See generally *Mazer* v. *Stein*, 347 U.S. 201, 217-218 (1954); *Bobbs-Merrill Co.* v. *Straus*, 210 U.S., at 345.

We have consistently rejected the proposition that a similar kinship exists between copyright law and trademark law, and in the process of doing so have recognized the basic similarities between copyrights and patents. *The Trade-Mark Cases*, 100 U.S. 82, 91-92 (1879); see also *United Drug Co.* v. *Theodore Rectanus Co.*, 248 U.S. 90, 97 (1918) (trademark right "has little or no analogy" to copyright or patent); *McLean* v. *Fleming*, 96 U.S. 245, 254 (1878); *Canal Co.* v. *Clark*, 13 Wall. 311, 322 (1872). Given the fundamental differences between copyright law and trademark law, in this copyright case we do not look to the standard for contributory infringement set forth in *Inwood Laboratories, Inc.* v. *Ives Laboratories, Inc.*, 456 U.S. 844, 854-855 (1982), which was crafted for application in trademark cases. There we observed that a manufacturer or distributor could be held liable to the owner of a trademark if it intentionally induced a merchant down the chain of distribution to pass off its product as that of the trademark owner's or if it continued to supply a product which could readily be passed off to a particular merchant whom it knew was mislabeling the product with the trademark owner's mark. If *Inwood*'s narrow standard for contributory trademark infringement governed here, respondents' claim of contributory infringement would merit little discussion. Sony certainly does not "intentionally [induce]" its customers to make infringing uses of respondents' copyrights, nor does it supply its products to identified individuals known by it to be engaging in continuing infringement of respondents' copyrights, see *id.*, at 855.

In the Patent Act both the concept of infringement and the concept of contributory infringement are expressly defined by statute. The prohibition against contributory infringement is confined to the knowing sale of a component especially made for use in connection with a particular patent. There is no suggestion in the statute that one patentee may object to the sale of a product that might be used in connection with other patents. Moreover, the Act expressly provides that the sale of a "staple article or commodity of commerce suitable for substantial noninfringing use" is not contributory infringement. 35 U. S. C. § 271(c).

When a charge of contributory infringement is predicated entirely on the sale of an article of commerce that is used by the purchaser to infringe a patent, the public interest in access to that article of commerce is necessarily implicated. A finding of contributory infringement does not, of course, remove the article from the market altogether; it does, however, give the patentee effective control over the sale of that item. Indeed, a finding of contributory infringement is normally the functional equivalent of holding that the disputed article is within the monopoly granted to the patentee.

For that reason, in contributory infringement cases arising under the patent laws the Court has always recognized the critical importance of not allowing the patentee to extend his monopoly beyond the limits of his specific grant. These cases deny the patentee any right to control the distribution of unpatented articles unless they are "unsuited for any commercial noninfringing use." *Dawson Chemical Co.* v. *Rohm & Hass Co.*, 448 U.S. 176, 198 (1980). Unless a commodity "has no use except through practice of the patented method," *id.*, at 199, the patentee has no right to claim that its distribution constitutes contributory infringement. "To form the basis for contributory infringement the item must almost be uniquely suited as a component of the patented invention." P. Rosenberg, Patent Law Fundamentals § 17.02[2] (2d ed. 1982). "[A] sale of an article which though adapted to an infringing use is also adapted to other and lawful uses, is not enough to make the seller a contributory infringer. Such a rule would block the wheels of commerce." *Henry* v. *A. B. Dick Co.*, 224 U.S. 1, 48 (1912), overruled on other grounds, *Motion Picture Patents Co.* v. *Universal Film Mfg. Co.*, 243 U.S. 502, 517 (1917).

We recognize there are substantial differences between the patent and copyright laws. But in both areas the contributory infringement doctrine is grounded on the recognition that adequate protection of a monopoly may require the courts to look beyond actual duplication of a device or publication to the products or activities that make such duplication possible. The staple article of commerce doctrine must strike a balance between a copyright holder's legitimate demand for effective—not merely symbolic—protection of the statutory monopoly, and the rights of others freely to engage in substantially unrelated areas of commerce. Accordingly, the sale of copying equipment, like the sale of other articles of commerce, does not constitute contributory infringement if the product is widely used for legitimate, unobjectionable purposes. Indeed, it need merely be capable of substantial noninfringing uses.

IV.

The question is thus whether the Betamax is capable of commercially significant noninfringing uses. In order to resolve that question, we need not explore *all* the different potential uses of the machine and determine whether or not they would constitute infringement. Rather, we need only consider whether on the basis of the facts as found by the District Court a significant number of them would be noninfringing. Moreover, in order to resolve this case we need not give precise content to the question of how much use is commercially significant. For one potential use of the Betamax plainly satisfies this standard, however it is understood: private, noncommercial time-shifting in the home. It does so both (A) because respondents have no right to prevent other copyright holders from authorizing it for their programs, and (B) because the District Court's factual findings reveal that even the unauthorized home time-shifting of respondents' programs is legitimate fair use.

A. Authorized Time-Shifting

Each of the respondents owns a large inventory of valuable copyrights, but in the total spectrum of television programming their combined market share is small. The exact percentage is not specified, but it is well below 10%. If they were to prevail, the outcome of this litigation would have a significant impact on both the producers and the viewers of the remaining 90% of the programming in the Nation. No doubt, many other producers share respondents' concern about the possible consequences of unrestricted copying. Nevertheless the findings of the District Court make it clear that time-shifting may enlarge the total viewing audience and that many producers are willing to allow private time-shifting to continue, at least for an experimental time period.

The District Court found:

> "Even if it were deemed that home-use recording of copyrighted material constituted infringement, the Betamax could still legally be used to record noncopyrighted material or material whose owners consented to the copying. An injunction would deprive the public of the ability to use the Betamax for this noninfringing off-the-air recording.
>
> "Defendants introduced considerable testimony at trial about the potential for such copying of sports, religious, educational and other programming. This included testimony from representatives of the Offices of the Commissioners of the National Football, Basketball, Baseball and Hockey Leagues and Associations, the Executive Director of National Religious Broadcasters and various educational communications agencies. Plaintiffs attack the weight of the testimony offered and also contend that an injunction is warranted because infringing uses outweigh noninfringing uses.
>
> "Whatever the future percentage of legal versus illegal home-use recording might be, an injunction which seeks to deprive the public of the very tool or article of commerce capable of some noninfringing use would be an extremely harsh remedy, as well as one unprecedented in copyright law." 480 F.Supp., at 468.

Although the District Court made these statements in the context of considering the propriety of injunctive relief, the statements constitute a finding that the evidence concerning "sports, religious, educational and other programming" was sufficient to establish a significant quantity of broadcasting whose copying is now authorized, and a significant potential for future authorized copying. That finding is amply supported by the record . . . .

If there are millions of owners of VTR's who make copies of televised sports events, religious broadcasts, and educational programs such as Mister Rogers' Neighborhood, and if the proprietors of those programs welcome the practice, the business of supplying the equipment that makes such copying feasible should not be stifled simply because the equipment is used by some individuals to make unauthorized reproductions of respondents' works. The respondents do not represent a class composed of all copyright holders. Yet a finding of contributory infringement would inevitably frustrate the interests of broadcasters in reaching the portion of their audience that is available only through timeshifting.

Of course, the fact that other copyright holders may welcome the practice of time-shifting does not mean that respondents should be deemed to have granted a license to copy their programs. Third-party conduct would be wholly irrelevant in an action for direct infringement of respondents' copyrights. But in an action for *contributory* infringement against the seller of copying equipment, the copyright holder may not prevail unless the relief that he seeks affects only his programs, or unless he speaks for virtually all copyright holders with an interest in the outcome. In this case, the record makes it perfectly clear that there are many important producers of national and local television programs who find nothing objectionable about the enlargement in the size of the television audience that results from the practice of time-shifting for private home use. The seller of the equipment that expands those producers' audiences cannot be a contributory infringer if, as is true in this case, it has had no direct involvement with any infringing activity.

B. Unauthorized Time-Shifting

Even unauthorized uses of a copyrighted work are not necessarily infringing. An unlicensed use of the copyright is not an infringement unless it conflicts with one of the specific exclusive rights conferred by the copyright statute. *Twentieth Century Music Corp.* v. *Aiken*, 422 U.S., at 154-155. Moreover, the definition of exclusive rights in § 106 of the present Act is prefaced by the words "subject to sections 107 through 118." Those sections describe a variety of uses of copyrighted material that "are not infringements of copyright" "notwithstanding the provisions of section 106." The most pertinent in this case is § 107, the legislative endorsement of the doctrine of "fair use."[3]

That section identifies various factors that enable a court to apply an "equitable rule of reason" analysis to particular claims of infringement. Although not conclusive, the first factor requires that "the commercial or nonprofit character of an activity" be weighed in any fair use decision. If the Betamax were used to make copies for a commercial or profitmaking purpose, such use would presumptively be unfair. The contrary presumption is appropriate here, however, because the District Court's findings plainly establish that time-shifting for private home use must be characterized as a noncommercial, nonprofit activity. Moreover, when one considers the nature of a televised copyrighted audiovisual work, see 17 U. S. C. § 107(2) (1982 ed.), and that time-shifting merely enables a viewer to see such a work which he had been invited to witness in its entirety free of charge, the fact that the entire work is reproduced, see § 107(3), does not have its ordinary effect of militating against a finding of fair use.

This is not, however, the end of the inquiry because Congress has also directed us to consider "the effect of the use upon the potential market for or value of the copyrighted work." § 107(4). The purpose of copyright is to create incentives for creative effort. Even copying for noncommercial purposes may impair

[3] The Copyright Act of 1909, 35 Stat. 1075, did not have a "fair use" provision. Although that Act's compendium of exclusive rights "to print, reprint, publish, copy, and vend the copyrighted work" was broad enough to encompass virtually all potential interactions with a copyrighted work, the statute was never so construed. The courts simply refused to read the statute literally in every situation. When Congress amended the statute in 1976, it indicated that it "intended to restate the present judicial doctrine of fair use, not to change, narrow, or enlarge it in any way." H. R. Rep. No. 94-1476, p. 66 (1976).

the copyright holder's ability to obtain the rewards that Congress intended him to have. But a use that has no demonstrable effect upon the potential market for, or the value of, the copyrighted work need not be prohibited in order to protect the author's incentive to create. The prohibition of such noncommercial uses would merely inhibit access to ideas without any countervailing benefit.

Thus, although every commercial use of copyrighted material is presumptively an unfair exploitation of the monopoly privilege that belongs to the owner of the copyright, noncommercial uses are a different matter. A challenge to a noncommercial use of a copyrighted work requires proof either that the particular use is harmful, or that if it should become widespread, it would adversely affect the potential market for the copyrighted work. Actual present harm need not be shown; such a requirement would leave the copyright holder with no defense against predictable damage. Nor is it necessary to show with certainty that future harm will result. What is necessary is a showing by a preponderance of the evidence that *some* meaningful likelihood of future harm exists. If the intended use is for commercial gain, that likelihood may be presumed. But if it is for a noncommercial purpose, the likelihood must be demonstrated.

In this case, respondents failed to carry their burden with regard to home time-shifting. The District Court described respondents' evidence as follows:

> "Plaintiffs' experts admitted at several points in the trial that the time-shifting without librarying would result in 'not a great deal of harm.' Plaintiffs' greatest concern about time-shifting is with 'a point of important philosophy that transcends even commercial judgment.' They fear that with any Betamax usage, 'invisible boundaries' are passed: 'the copyright owner has lost control over his program.'" 480 F.Supp., at 467.

Later in its opinion, the District Court observed:

> "Most of plaintiffs' predictions of harm hinge on speculation about audience viewing patterns and ratings, a measurement system which Sidney Sheinberg, MCA's president, calls a 'black art' because of the significant level of imprecision involved in the calculations." *Id.*, at 469.

There was no need for the District Court to say much about past harm. "Plaintiffs have admitted that no actual harm to their copyrights has occurred to date." *Id.*, at 451.

On the question of potential future harm from time-shifting, the District Court offered a more detailed analysis of the evidence. It rejected respondents' "fear that persons 'watching' the original telecast of a program will not be measured in the live audience and the ratings and revenues will decrease," by observing that current measurement technology allows the Betamax audience to be reflected. *Id.*, at 466. It rejected respondents' prediction "that live television or movie audiences will decrease as more people watch Betamax tapes as an alternative," with the observation that "[there] is no factual basis for [the underlying] assumption." *Ibid.* It rejected respondents' "fear that time-shifting will reduce audiences for telecast reruns," and concluded instead that "given current market practices, this should aid plaintiffs rather than harm them." *Ibid.* And it declared that respondents' suggestion that "theater or film rental exhibition of a program will suffer because of time-shift recording of that program" "lacks merit." *Id.*, at 467. . . .

The District Court's conclusions are buttressed by the fact that to the extent time-shifting expands public access to freely broadcast television programs, it yields societal benefits. In *Community Television of Southern*

California v. *Gottfried*, 459 U.S. 498, 508, n. 12 (1983), we acknowledged the public interest in making television broadcasting more available. Concededly, that interest is not unlimited. But it supports an interpretation of the concept of "fair use" that requires the copyright holder to demonstrate some likelihood of harm before he may condemn a private act of time-shifting as a violation of federal law.

When these factors are all weighed in the "equitable rule of reason" balance, we must conclude that this record amply supports the District Court's conclusion that home time-shifting is fair use. In light of the findings of the District Court regarding the state of the empirical data, it is clear that the Court of Appeals erred in holding that the statute as presently written bars such conduct.

In summary, the record and findings of the District Court lead us to two conclusions. First, Sony demonstrated a significant likelihood that substantial numbers of copyright holders who license their works for broadcast on free television would not object to having their broadcasts time-shifted by private viewers. And second, respondents failed to demonstrate that time-shifting would cause any likelihood of nonminimal harm to the potential market for, or the value of, their copyrighted works. The Betamax is, therefore, capable of substantial noninfringing uses. Sony's sale of such equipment to the general public does not constitute contributory infringement of respondents' copyrights.

V.

"The direction of Art. I is that *Congress* shall have the power to promote the progress of science and the useful arts. When, as here, the Constitution is permissive, the sign of how far Congress has chosen to go can come only from Congress." *Deepsouth Packing Co.* v. *Laitram Corp.*, 406 U.S. 518, 530 (1972).

One may search the Copyright Act in vain for any sign that the elected representatives of the millions of people who watch television every day have made it unlawful to copy a program for later viewing at home, or have enacted a flat prohibition against the sale of machines that make such copying possible.

It may well be that Congress will take a fresh look at this new technology, just as it so often has examined other innovations in the past. But it is not our job to apply laws that have not yet been written. Applying the copyright statute, as it now reads, to the facts as they have been developed in this case, the judgment of the Court of Appeals must be reversed.

It is so ordered.

JUSTICE BLACKMUN, with whom JUSTICE MARSHALL, JUSTICE POWELL, and JUSTICE REHNQUIST join, dissenting....

IV.

Fair Use

The doctrine of fair use has been called, with some justification, "the most troublesome in the whole law of copyright." *Dellar* v. *Samuel Goldwyn, Inc.*, 104 F.2d 661, 662 (CA2 1939); see *Triangle Publications, Inc.* v. *Knight-Ridder Newspapers, Inc.*, 626 F.2d 1171, 1174 (CA5 1980); *Meeropol* v. *Nizer*, 560 F.2d 1061, 1068 (CA2 1977), cert. denied, 434 U.S. 1013 (1978). Although courts have constructed lists of factors to be considered in determining whether a particular use is fair,[4] no fixed criteria have emerged by which that determination can be made. This Court thus far has provided no guidance; although fair use issues have come here twice, on each occasion the Court was equally divided and no opinion was forthcoming. *Williams & Wilkins Co.* v. *United States*, 203 Ct. Cl. 74, 487 F.2d 1345 (1973), aff'd, 420 U.S. 376 (1975); *Benny* v. *Loew's Inc.*, 239 F.2d 532 (CA9 1956), aff'd *sub nom. Columbia Broadcasting System, Inc.* v. *Loew's Inc.*, 356 U.S. 43 (1958).

Nor did Congress provide definitive rules when it codified the fair use doctrine in the 1976 Act; it simply incorporated a list of factors "to be considered": the "purpose and character of the use," the "nature of the copyrighted work," the "amount and substantiality of the portion used," and, perhaps the most important, the "effect of the use upon the *potential* market for or value of the copyrighted work" (emphasis supplied). § 107. No particular weight, however, was assigned to any of these, and the list was not intended to be exclusive. The House and Senate Reports explain that § 107 does no more than give "statutory recognition" to the fair use doctrine; it was intended "to restate the present judicial doctrine of fair use, not to change, narrow, or enlarge it in any way." 1976 House Report 66. See 1975 Senate Report 62; S. Rep. No. 93-983, p. 116 (1974); H. R. Rep. No. 83, 90th Cong., 1st Sess., 32 (1967); H. R. Rep. No. 2237, 89th Cong., 2d Sess., 61 (1966).

A

Despite this absence of clear standards, the fair use doctrine plays a crucial role in the law of copyright. The purpose of copyright protection, in the words of the Constitution, is to "promote the Progress of Science and useful Arts." Copyright is based on the belief that by granting authors the exclusive rights to reproduce their works, they are given an incentive to create, and that "encouragement of individual effort by personal gain is the best way to advance public welfare through the talents of authors and inventors in 'Science and the useful Arts.'" *Mazer* v. *Stein*, 347 U.S. 201, 219 (1954). The monopoly created by copyright thus rewards the individual author in order to benefit the public. *Twentieth Century Music Corp.* v. *Aiken*, 422 U.S., at 156; *Fox Film Corp.* v. *Doyal*, 286 U.S. 123, 127-128 (1932); see H. R. Rep. No. 2222, 60th Cong., 2d Sess., 7 (1909).

There are situations, nevertheless, in which strict enforcement of this monopoly would inhibit the very "Progress of Science and useful Arts" that copyright is intended to promote. An obvious example is the researcher or scholar whose own work depends on the ability to refer to and to quote the work of prior

---

[4] The precise phrase "fair use" apparently did not enter the case law until 1869, see *Lawrence* v. *Dana*, 15 F. Cas. 26, 60 (No. 8,136) (CC Mass.), but the doctrine itself found early expression in *Folsom* v. *Marsh*, 9 F. Cas. 342 (No. 4,901) (CC Mass. 1841). Justice Story was faced there with the "intricate and embarrassing [question]" whether a biography containing copyrighted letters was "a justifiable use of the original materials, such as the law recognizes as no infringement of the copyright of the plaintiffs." *Id.*, at 344, 348. In determining whether the use was permitted, it was necessary, said Justice Story, to consider "the nature and objects of the selections made, the quantity and value of the materials used, and the degree in which the use may prejudice the sale, or diminish the profits, or supersede the objects, of the original work. . . . Much must, in such cases, depend upon the nature of the new work, the value and extent of the copies, and the degree in which the original authors may be injured thereby." *Id.*, at 348-349.

Similar lists were compiled by later courts. See, *e. g., Tennessee Fabricating Co.* v. *Moultrie Mfg. Co.*, 421 F.2d 279, 283 (CA5), cert. denied, 398 U.S. 928 (1970); *Mathews Conveyer Co.* v. *Palmer-Bee Co.*, 135 F.2d 73, 85 (CA6 1943); *Columbia Pictures Corp.* v. *National Broadcasting Co.*, 137 F.Supp. 348 (SD Cal. 1955); *Shapiro, Bernstein & Co.* v. *P. F. Collier & Son Co.*, 26 USPQ 40, 43 (SDNY 1934); *Hill* v. *Whalen & Martell, Inc.*, 220 F. 359, 360 (SDNY 1914).

scholars. Obviously, no author could create a new work if he were first required to repeat the research of every author who had gone before him. The scholar, like the ordinary user, of course could be left to bargain with each copyright owner for permission to quote from or refer to prior works. But there is a crucial difference between the scholar and the ordinary user. When the ordinary user decides that the owner's price is too high, and forgoes use of the work, only the individual is the loser. When the scholar forgoes the use of a prior work, not only does his own work suffer, but the public is deprived of his contribution to knowledge. The scholar's work, in other words, produces external benefits from which everyone profits. In such a case, the fair use doctrine acts as a form of subsidy—albeit at the first author's expense—to permit the second author to make limited use of the first author's work for the public good. See Latman Fair Use Study 31; Gordon, Fair Use as Market Failure: A Structural Analysis of the *Betamax* Case and its Predecessors, 82 Colum. L. Rev. 1600, 1630 (1982).

A similar subsidy may be appropriate in a range of areas other than pure scholarship. The situations in which fair use is most commonly recognized are listed in § 107 itself; fair use may be found when a work is used "for purposes such as criticism, comment, news reporting, teaching, . . . scholarship, or research." The House and Senate Reports expand on this list somewhat, and other examples may be found in the case law. Each of these uses, however, reflects a common theme: each is a *productive* use, resulting in some added benefit to the public beyond that produced by the first author's work. The fair use doctrine, in other words, permits works to be used for "socially laudable purposes." See Copyright Office, Briefing Papers on Current Issues, reprinted in 1975 House Hearings 2051, 2055. I am aware of no case in which the reproduction of a copyrighted work for the sole benefit of the user has been held to be fair use.[5]

I do not suggest, of course, that every productive use is a fair use. A finding of fair use still must depend on the facts of the individual case, and on whether, under the circumstances, it is reasonable to expect the user to bargain with the copyright owner for use of the work. The fair use doctrine must strike a balance between the dual risks created by the copyright system: on the one hand, that depriving authors of their monopoly will reduce their incentive to create, and, on the other, that granting authors a complete monopoly will reduce the creative ability of others. The inquiry is necessarily a flexible one, and the endless variety of situations that may arise precludes the formulation of exact rules. But when a user reproduces an entire work and uses it for its original purpose, with no added benefit to the public, the doctrine of fair use usually does not apply. There is then no need whatsoever to provide the ordinary user with a fair use subsidy at the author's expense.

The making of a videotape recording for home viewing is an ordinary rather than a productive use of the Studios' copyrighted works. The District Court found that "Betamax owners use the copy for the same purpose as the original. They add nothing of their own." 480 F.Supp., at 453. Although applying the fair use doctrine to home VTR recording, as Sony argues, may increase public access to material broadcast

[5] *Williams & Wilkins* Co. v. *United States*, 203 Ct. Cl. 74, 487 F.2d 1345 (1973), aff'd by an equally divided Court, 420 U.S. 376 (1975), involved the photocopying of scientific journal articles; the Court of Claims stressed that the libraries performing the copying were "devoted solely to the advancement and dissemination of medical knowledge," 203 Ct. Cl., at 91, 487 F.2d, at 1354, and that "medical science would be seriously hurt if such library photocopying were stopped." Id., at 95, 487 F.2d, at 1356.

The issue of library copying is now covered by § 108 of the 1976 Act. That section, which Congress regarded as "[authorizing] certain photocopying practices which may not qualify as a fair use," 1975 Senate Report 67; 1976 House Report 74, permits the making of copies only for "private study, scholarship, or research." §§ 108(d)(1) and (e)(1).

free over the public airwaves, I think Sony's argument misconceives the nature of copyright. Copyright gives the author a right to limit or even to cut off access to his work. *Fox Film Corp.* v. *Doyal*, 286 U.S., at 127. A VTR recording creates no public benefit sufficient to justify limiting this right. Nor is this right extinguished by the copyright owner's choice to make the work available over the airwaves. Section 106 of the 1976 Act grants the copyright owner the exclusive right to control the performance and the reproduction of his work, and the fact that he has licensed a single television performance is really irrelevant to the existence of his right to control its reproduction. Although a television broadcast may be free to the viewer, this fact is equally irrelevant; a book borrowed from the public library may not be copied any more freely than a book that is purchased.

It may be tempting, as, in my view, the Court today is tempted, to stretch the doctrine of fair use so as to permit unfettered use of this new technology in order to increase access to television programming. But such an extension risks eroding the very basis of copyright law, by depriving authors of control over their works and consequently of their incentive to create. Even in the context of highly productive educational uses, Congress has avoided this temptation; in passing the 1976 Act, Congress made it clear that off-the-air videotaping was to be permitted only in very limited situations. See 1976 House Report 71; 1975 Senate Report 64. And, the Senate Report adds, "[the] committee does not intend to suggest . . . that off-the-air recording for convenience would under any circumstances, be considered 'fair use.'" *Id.*, at 66. I cannot disregard these admonitions.

B

I recognize, nevertheless, that there are situations where permitting even an unproductive use would have no effect on the author's incentive to create, that is, where the use would not affect the value of, or the market for, the author's work. Photocopying an old newspaper clipping to send to a friend may be an example; pinning a quotation on one's bulletin board may be another. In each of these cases, the effect on the author is truly *de minimis*. Thus, even though these uses provide no benefit to the public at large, no purpose is served by preserving the author's monopoly, and the use may be regarded as fair.

Courts should move with caution, however, in depriving authors of protection from unproductive "ordinary" uses. As has been noted above, even in the case of a productive use, § 107(4) requires consideration of "the effect of the use upon the *potential* market for or value of the copyrighted work" (emphasis added). "[A] particular use which may seem to have little or no economic impact on the author's rights today can assume tremendous importance in times to come." Register's Supplementary Report 14. Although such a use may seem harmless when viewed in isolation, "[isolated] instances of minor infringements, when multiplied many times, become in the aggregate a major inroad on copyright that must be prevented." 1975 Senate Report 65.

I therefore conclude that, at least when the proposed use is an unproductive one, a copyright owner need prove only a *potential* for harm to the market for or the value of the copyrighted work. See 3 M. Nimmer, Copyright § 13.05[E][4][c], p. 13-84 (1983). Proof of actual harm, or even probable harm, may be impossible in an area where the effect of a new technology is speculative, and requiring such proof would present the "real danger . . . of confining the scope of an author's rights on the basis of the present technology so that, as the years go by, his copyright loses much of its value because of unforeseen technical advances." Register's Supplementary Report 14. Infringement thus would be found if the copyright owner demonstrates a reasonable possibility that harm will result from the proposed use. When the use is one that creates no benefit to the public at large, copyright protection should not be denied on the basis that a new technology that may result in harm has not yet done so.

The Studios have identified a number of ways in which VTR recording could damage their copyrights. VTR recording could reduce their ability to market their works in movie theaters and through the rental or sale of prerecorded videotapes or videodiscs; it also could reduce their rerun audience, and consequently the license fees available to them for repeated showings. Moreover, advertisers may be willing to pay for only "live" viewing audiences, if they believe VTR viewers will delete commercials or if rating services are unable to measure VTR use; if this is the case, VTR recording could reduce the license fees the Studios are able to charge even for first-run showings. Library-building may raise the potential for each of the types of harm identified by the Studios, and time-shifting may raise the potential forsubstantial harm as well.[6]

Although the District Court found no likelihood of harm from VTR use, 480 F.Supp., at 468, I conclude that it applied an incorrect substantive standard and misallocated the burden of proof. The District Court reasoned that the Studios had failed to prove that library-building would occur "to any significant extent," *id.*, at 467; that the Studios' prerecorded videodiscs could compete with VTR recordings and were "arguably . . . more desirable," *ibid.*; that it was "not clear that movie audiences will decrease," *id.*, at 468; and that the practice of deleting commercials "may be too tedious" for many viewers, *ibid.* To the extent any decrease in advertising revenues would occur, the court concluded that the Studios had "marketing alternatives at hand to recoup some of that predicted loss." *Id.*, at 452. Because the Studios' prediction of harm was "based on so many assumptions and on a system of marketing which is rapidly changing," the court was "hesitant to identify 'probable effects' of home-use copying." *Ibid.*

The District Court's reluctance to engage in prediction in this area is understandable, but, in my view, the court was mistaken in concluding that the Studios should bear the risk created by this uncertainty. The Studios have demonstrated a potential for harm, which has not been, and could not be, refuted at this early stage of technological development.

The District Court's analysis of harm, moreover, failed to consider the effect of VTR recording on "the *potential* market for or the value of the copyrighted work," as required by § 107(4). The requirement that a putatively infringing use of a copyrighted work, to be "fair," must not impair a "potential" market for the work has two implications. First, an infringer cannot prevail merely by demonstrating that the copyright holder suffered no net harm from the infringer's action. Indeed, even a showing that the infringement has resulted in a net benefit to the copyright holder will not suffice. Rather, the infringer must demonstrate that he had not impaired the copyright holder's ability to demand compensation from (or to deny access to) any group who would otherwise be willing to pay to see or hear the copyrighted work. Second, the fact that a given market for a copyrighted work would not be available to the copyright holder were it not for the infringer's activities does not permit the infringer to exploit that market without

[6] A VTR owner who has taped a favorite movie for repeated viewing will be less likely to rent or buy a tape containing the same movie, watch a televised rerun, or pay to see the movie at a theater. Although time-shifting may not replace theater or rerun viewing or the purchase of prerecorded tapes or discs, it may well replace rental usage; a VTR user who has recorded a first-run movie for later viewing will have no need to rent a copy when he wants to see it. Both library-builders and time-shifters may avoid commercials; the library-builder may use the pause control to record without them, and all users may fast-forward through commercials on playback.

compensating the copyright holder. See *Iowa State University Research Foundation, Inc.* v. *American Broadcasting Cos.*, 621 F.2d 57 (CA2 1980).

In this case, the Studios and their *amici* demonstrate that the advent of the VTR technology created a potential market for their copyrighted programs. That market consists of those persons who find it impossible or inconvenient to watch the programs at the time they are broadcast, and who wish to watch them at other times. These persons are willing to pay for the privilege of watching copyrighted work at their convenience, as is evidenced by the fact that they are willing to pay for VTR's and tapes; undoubtedly, most also would be willing to pay some kind of royalty to copyright holders. The Studios correctly argue that they have been deprived of the ability to exploit this sizable market.

It is thus apparent from the record and from the findings of the District Court that time-shifting does have a substantial adverse effect upon the "potential market for" the Studios' copyrighted works. Accordingly, even under the formulation of the fair use doctrine advanced by Sony, time-shifting cannot be deemed a fair use.

V.
Contributory Infringement

From the Studios' perspective, the consequences of home VTR recording are the same as if a business had taped the Studios' works off the air, duplicated the tapes, and sold or rented them to members of the public for home viewing. The distinction is that home VTR users do not record for commercial advantage; the commercial benefit accrues to the manufacturer and distributors of the Betamax. I thus must proceed to discuss whether the manufacturer and distributors can be held contributorily liable if the product they sell is used to infringe.

It is well established that liability for copyright infringement can be imposed on persons other than those who actually carry out the infringing activity. *Kalem Co.* v. *Harper Brothers*, 222 U.S. 55, 62-63 (1911); 3 M. Nimmer, Copyright § 12.04[A] (1983); see *Twentieth Century Music Corp.* v. *Aiken*, 422 U.S., at 160, n. 11; *Buck* v. *Jewell-LaSalle Realty Co.*, 283 U.S. 191, 198 (1931). Although the liability provision of the 1976 Act provides simply that "[anyone] who violates any of the exclusive rights of the copyright owner . . . is an infringer of the copyright," 17 U. S. C. § 501(a) (1982 ed.), the House and Senate Reports demonstrate that Congress intended to retain judicial doctrines of contributory infringement. 1975 Senate Report 57; 1976 House Report 61.

The doctrine of contributory copyright infringement, however, is not well defined. One of the few attempts at definition appears in *Gershwin Publishing Corp.* v. *Columbia Artists Management, Inc.*, 443 F.2d 1159 (CA2 1971). In that case the Second Circuit stated that "one who, with knowledge of the infringing activity, induces, causes or materially contributes to the infringing conduct of another, may be

---

The Studios introduced expert testimony that both time-shifting and librarying would tend to decrease their revenue from copyrighted works. See 480 F.Supp., at 440. The District Court's findings also show substantial library-building and avoidance of commercials. Both sides submitted surveys showing that the average Betamax user owns between 25 and 32 tapes. The Studios' survey showed that at least 40% of users had more than 10 tapes in a "library"; Sony's survey showed that more than 40% of users planned to view their tapes more than once; and both sides' surveys showed that commercials were avoided at least 25% of the time. *Id.*, at 438-439.

held liable as a 'contributory' infringer." *Id.*, at 1162 (footnote omitted). While I have no quarrel with this general statement, it does not easily resolve the present case; the District Court and the Court of Appeals, both purporting to apply it, reached diametrically opposite results.

A

In absolving Sony from liability, the District Court reasoned that Sony had no direct involvement with individual Betamax users, did not participate in any off-the-air copying, and did not know that such copying was an infringement of the Studios' copyright. 480 F.Supp., at 460. I agree with the *Gershwin* court that contributory liability may be imposed even when the defendant has no formal control over the infringer. The defendant in *Gershwin* was a concert promoter operating through local concert associations that it sponsored; it had no formal control over the infringing performers themselves. 443 F.2d, at 1162-1163. See also *Twentieth Century Music Corp.* v. *Aiken*, 422 U.S., at 160, n. 11. Moreover, a finding of contributory infringement has never depended on actual knowledge of particular instances of infringement; it is sufficient that the defendant have reason to know that infringement is taking place. 443 F.2d, at1162; see *Screen Gems-Columbia Music, Inc.* v. *Mark-Fi Records, Inc.*, 256 F.Supp. 399 (SDNY 1966). In the socalled "dance hall" cases, in which questions of contributory infringement arise with some frequency, proprietors of entertainment establishments routinely are held liable for unauthorized performances on their premises, even when they have no knowledge that copyrighted works are being performed. In effect, the proprietors in those cases are charged with constructive knowledge of the performances.

Nor is it necessary that the defendant be aware that the infringing activity violates the copyright laws. Section504(c)(2) of the 1976 Act provides for a reduction in statutory damages when an infringer proves he "was not aware and had no reason to believe that his or her acts constituted an infringement of copyright," but the statute establishes no general exemption for those who believe their infringing activities are legal. Moreover, such an exemption would be meaningless in a case such as this, in which prospective relief is sought; once a court has established that the copying at issue is infringement, the defendants are necessarily aware of that fact for the future. It is undisputed in this case that Sony had reason to know the Betamax would be used by some owners to tape copyrighted works off the air. See 480 F.Supp., at 459-460.

The District Court also concluded that Sony had not caused, induced, or contributed materially to any infringing activities of Betamax owners. *Id.*, at 460. In a case of this kind, however, causation can be shown indirectly; it does not depend on evidence that particular Betamax owners relied on particular advertisements. In an analogous case decided just two Terms ago, this Court approved a lower court's conclusion that liability for contributory trademark infringement could be imposed on a manufacturer who "suggested, even by implication" that a retailer use the manufacturer's goods to infringe the trademark of another. *Inwood Laboratories, Inc.* v. *Ives Laboratories, Inc.*, 456 U.S. 844, 851 (1982); see *id.*, at 860 (opinion concurring in result). I think this standard is equally appropriate in the copyright context.

The District Court found that Sony has advertised the Betamax as suitable for off-the-air recording of "favorite shows," "novels for television," and "classic movies," 480 F.Supp., at 436, with no visible warning that such recording could constitute copyright infringement. It is only with the aid of the Betamax or some other VTR, that it is possible today for home television viewers to infringe copyright by recording off-the-air. Off-the-air recording is not only a foreseeable use for the Betamax, but indeed is its intended use. Under the circumstances, I agree with the Court of Appeals that if off-the-air recording is an infringement of copyright, Sony has induced and materially contributed to the infringing conduct of Betamax owners.

B

Sony argues that the manufacturer or seller of a product used to infringe is absolved from liability whenever the product can be put to any substantial noninfringing use. Brief for Petitioners 41-42. The District Court so held, borrowing the "staple article of commerce" doctrine governing liability for contributory infringement of patents. See 35 U. S. C. § 271. This Court today is much less positive. See *ante*, at 440-442. I do not agree that this technical judge-made doctrine of patent law, based in part on considerations irrelevant to the field of copyright, see generally *Dawson Chemical Co.* v. *Rohm & Haas Co.*, 448 U.S. 176, 187-199 (1980), should be imported wholesale into copyright law. Despite their common constitutional source, see U.S. Const., Art. I, § 8, cl. 8, patent and copyright protections have not developed in a parallel fashion, and this Court in copyright cases in the past has borrowed patent concepts only sparingly. See *Bobbs-Merrill Co.* v. *Straus*, 210 U.S. 339, 345-346 (1908).

I recognize, however, that many of the concerns underlying the "staple article of commerce" doctrine are present in copyright law as well. As the District Court noted, if liability for contributory infringement were imposed on the manufacturer or seller of every product used to infringe—a typewriter, a camera, a photocopying machine—the "wheels of commerce" would be blocked. 480 F.Supp., at 461; see also *Kalem Co.* v. *Harper Brothers*, 222 U.S., at 62.

I therefore conclude that if a *significant* portion of the product's use is *noninfringing*, the manufacturers and sellers cannot be held contributorily liable for the product's infringing uses. See *ante*, at 440-441. If virtually all of the product's use, however, is to infringe, contributory liability may be imposed; if no one would buy the product for noninfringing purposes alone, it is clear that the manufacturer is purposely profiting from the infringement, and that liability is appropriately imposed. In such a case, the copyright owner's monopoly would not be extended beyond its proper bounds; the manufacturer of such a product contributes to the infringing activities of others and profits directly thereby, while providing no benefit to the public sufficient to justify the infringement.

The Court of Appeals concluded that Sony should be held liable for contributory infringement, reasoning that "[videotape] recorders are manufactured, advertised, and sold for the primary purpose of reproducing television programming," and "[virtually] all television programming is copyrighted material." 659 F.2d, at 975. While I agree with the first of these propositions, the second, for me, is problematic. The key question is not the amount of television programming that is copyrighted, but rather the amount of VTR usage that is infringing. Moreover, the parties and their *amici* have argued vigorously about both the amount of television programming that is covered by copyright and the amount for which permission to copy has been given. The proportion of VTR recording that is infringing is ultimately aquestion of fact, 44 and the District Court specifically declined to make findings on the "percentage of legal versus illegal home-use recording." 480 F.Supp., at 468. In light of my view of the law, resolution of this factual question is essential. I therefore would remand the case for further consideration of this by the District Court.

VI.

The Court has adopted an approach very different from the one I have outlined. It is my view that the Court's approach alters dramatically the doctrines of fair use and contributory infringement as they have been developed by Congress and the courts. Should Congress choose to respond to the Court's decision, the old doctrines can be resurrected. As it stands, however, the decision today erodes much of the coherence that these doctrines have struggled to achieve.

The Court's disposition of the case turns on its conclusion that time-shifting is a fair use. Because both parties agree that time-shifting is the primary use of VTR's, that conclusion, if correct, would settle the issue of Sony's liability under almost any definition of contributory infringement. The Court concludes that time-shifting is fair use for two reasons. Each is seriously flawed.

The Court's first reason for concluding that time-shifting is fair use is its claim that many copyright holders have no objection to time-shifting, and that "respondents have no right to prevent other copyright holders from authorizing it for their programs." *Ante*, at 442. The Court explains that a finding of contributory infringement would "inevitably frustrate the interests of broadcasters in reaching the portion of their audience that is available only through time-shifting." *Ante*, at 446. Such reasoning, however, simply confuses the question of liability with the difficulty of fashioning an appropriate remedy. It may be that an injunction prohibiting the sale of VTR's would harm the interests of copyright holders who have no objection to others making copies of their programs. But such concerns should and would be taken into account in fashioning an appropriate remedy once liability has been found. Remedies may well be available that would not interfere with authorized time-shifting at all. The Court of Appeals mentioned the possibility of a royalty payment that would allow VTR sales and time-shifting to continue unabated, and the parties may be able to devise other narrowly tailored remedies. Sony may be able, for example, to build a VTR that enables broadcasters to scramble the signal of individual programs and "jam" the unauthorized recording of them. Even were an appropriate remedy not available at this time, the Court should not misconstrue copyright holders' rights in a manner that prevents enforcement of them when, through development of better techniques, an appropriate remedy becomes available.

The Court's second stated reason for finding that Sony is not liable for contributory infringement is its conclusion that even unauthorized time-shifting is fair use. *Ante*, at 447 *et seq*. This conclusion is even more troubling. The Court begins by suggesting that the fair use doctrine operates as a general "equitable rule of reason." That interpretation mischaracterizes the doctrine, and simply ignores the language of the statute. Section 107 establishes the fair use doctrine "for purposes such as criticism, comment, news reporting, teaching, . . . scholarship, or research." These are all1 productive uses. It is true that the legislative history states repeatedly that the doctrine must be applied flexibly on a case-by-case basis, but those references were only in the context of productive uses. Such a limitation on fair use comports with its purpose, which is to facilitate the creation of new works. There is no indication that the fair use doctrine has any application for purely personal consumption on the scale involved in this case, and the Court's application of it here deprives fair use of the major cohesive force that has guided evolution of the doctrine in the past.

Having bypassed the initial hurdle for establishing that a use is fair, the Court then purports to apply to timeshifting the four factors explicitly stated in the statute. The first is "the purpose and character of the use, including whether such use is of a commercial nature or is for nonprofit educational purposes." § 107(1). The Court confidently describes time-shifting as a noncommercial, nonprofit activity. It is clear, however, that personal use of programs that have been copied without permission is not what § 107(1) protects. The intent of the section is to encourage users to engage in activities the primary benefit of which accrues to others. Time-shifting involves no such humanitarian impulse. It is likewise something of a mischaracterization of time-shifting to describe it as noncommercial in the sense that that term is used in the statute. As one commentator has observed, time-shifting is noncommercial in the same sense that stealing jewelry and wearing it—instead of reselling it—is noncommercial. Purely consumptive uses are certainly not what the fair use doctrine was designed to protect, and the awkwardness of applying the statutory language to time-shifting only makes clearer that fair use was designed to protect only uses that are productive.

The next two statutory factors are all but ignored by the Court—though certainly not because they have no applicability. The second factor—"the nature of the copyrighted work"—strongly supports the view that time-shifting is an infringing use. The rationale guiding application of this factor is that certain types of works, typically those involving "more of diligence than of originality or inventiveness," *New York Times Co.* v. *Roxbury Data Interface, Inc.*, 434 F.Supp. 217, 221 (NJ 1977), require less copyright protection than other original works. Thus, for example, informational works, such as news reports, that readily lend themselves to productive use by others, are less protected than creative works of entertainment. Sony's own surveys indicate that entertainment shows account for more than 80% of the programs recorded by Betamax owners.

The third statutory factor—"the amount and substantiality of the portion used"—is even more devastating to the Court's interpretation. It is undisputed that virtually all VTR owners record entire works, see 480 F.Supp., at 454, thereby creating an exact substitute for the copyrighted original. Fair use is intended to allow individuals engaged in productive uses to copy small portions of original works that will facilitate their own productive endeavors. Timeshifting bears no resemblance to such activity, and the complete duplication that it involves might alone be sufficient to preclude a finding of fair use. It is little wonder that the Court has chosen to ignore this statutory factor.

The fourth factor requires an evaluation of "the effect of the use upon the potential market for or value of the copyrighted work." This is the factor upon which the Court focuses, but once again, the Court has misread the statute. As mentioned above, the statute requires a court to consider the effect of the use on the *potential* market for the copyrighted work. The Court has struggled mightily to show that VTR use has not *reduced* the value of the Studios' copyrighted works in their *present* markets. Even if true, that showing only begins the proper inquiry. The development of the VTR has created a new market for the works produced by the Studios. That market consists of those persons who desire to view television programs at times other than when they are broadcast, and who therefore purchase VTR recorders to enable them to time-shift. Because time-shifting of the Studios' copyrighted works involves the copying of them, however, the Studios are entitled to share in the benefits of that new market. Those benefits currently go to Sony through Betamax sales. Respondents therefore can show harm from VTR use simply by showing that the value of their copyrights would *increase* if they were compensated for the copies that are used in the new market. The existence ofthis effect is self-evident.

Because of the Court's conclusion concerning the legality of time-shifting, it never addresses the amount of noninfringing use that a manufacturer must show to absolve itself from liability as a contributory infringer. Thus, it is difficult to discuss how the Court's test for contributory infringement would operate in practice under a proper analysis of timeshifting. One aspect of the test as it is formulated by the Court, however, particularly deserves comment. The Court explains that a manufacturer of a product is not liable for contributory infringement as long as the product is *"capable* of substantial noninfringing uses." *Ante*, at 442 (emphasis supplied). Such a definition essentially eviscerates the concept of contributory infringement. Only the most unimaginative manufacturer would be unable to demonstrate that a image-duplicating product is "capable" of substantial noninfringing uses. Surely Congress desired to prevent the sale of products that are used almost exclusively to infringe copyrights; [*499] the fact that noninfringing uses exist presumably would have little bearing on that desire.

More importantly, the rationale for the Court's narrow standard of contributory infringement reveals that, once again, the Court has confused the issue of liability with that of remedy. The Court finds that a narrow definition of contributory infringement is necessary in order to protect "the rights of others freely to engage in substantially unrelated areas of commerce." *Ante*, at 442. But application of the contributory infringement doctrine implicates such rights only if the remedy attendant upon a finding of liability were an injunction against the manufacture of the product in question. The issue of an appropriate remedy is not before the Court at this time, but it seems likely that a broad injunction is not the remedy that would be ordered. It is unfortunate that the Court has allowed its concern over a remedy to infect its analysis of liability.

VII.

The Court of Appeals, having found Sony liable, remanded for the District Court to consider the propriety of injunctive or other relief. Because of my conclusion as to the issue of liability, I, too, would not decide here what remedy would be appropriate if liability were found. I concur, however, in the Court of Appeals' suggestion that an award of damages, or continuing royalties, or even some form of limited injunction, may well be an appropriate means of balancing the equities in this case. Although I express no view on the merits of any particular proposal, I am certain that, if Sony were found liable in this case, the District Court would be able to fashion appropriate relief. The District Court might conclude, of course, that a continuing royalty or other equitable relief is not feasible. The Studios then would be relegated to statutory damages for proven instances of infringement. But the difficulty of fashioning relief, and the possibility that complete relief may be unavailable, should not affect our interpretation of the statute.

Like so many other problems created by the interaction of copyright law with a new technology, "[there] can be no really satisfactory solution to the problem presented here, until Congress acts." *Twentieth Century Music Corp.* v. *Aiken*,422 U.S., at 167 (dissenting opinion). But in the absence of a congressional solution, courts cannot avoid difficult problems by refusing to apply the law. We must "take the Copyright Act . . . as we find it," *Fortnightly Corp.* v. *United Artists Television, Inc.*, 392 U.S., at 401-402, and "do as little damage as possible to traditional copyright principles . . . until the Congress legislates." *Id.*, at 404 (dissenting opinion).

About the Author

Barry Neil Shrum, Esquire is an entertainment attorney who has been practicing law for almost 30 years, representing serial entrepreneurs and businesses as well as some of the most famous celebrities in the entertainment and creative industries, including everyone's favorite Shark from ABC's Shark Tank, Daymond John. Many of his clients are familiar household names at the forefront of the technology, entertainment, business, music, movie, and licensing industries. Mr. Shrum has extensive expertise in litigating intellectual property cases at both the state and federal level. Mr. Shrum is also a professor teaching copyright, entertainment law, licensing, music publishing, and cyberlaw at the prestigious Mike Curb College of Entertainment and Music Business at Nashville's Belmont University. He currently lives in Franklin where he enjoys spending time with his wife and son, cooking, playing tennis, writing, riding bicycles, and pontificating about life in general.

To have Barry Neil Shrum, Esquire speak at your organization about the principles found in *Guitars, Gavels & Gold: Contemporary Legal Issues in the Arts, Entertainment and Music Business*, email info@shrumlaw.com. You can also find Mr. Shrum's first three works, *Defending the Noble Arts, Origins of an Idea* and *Counting Stars* on Amazon or find out more about his law practice at www.barryshrum.com. Follow Mr. Shrum on all your favorite social media platforms.

www.ingramcontent.com/pod-product-compliance
Ingram Content Group UK Ltd.
Pitfield, Milton Keynes, MK11 3LW, UK
UKHW052007041026
15590UKWH00008B/2197

9 798765 748459